Encyclopedia of the

SOCIAL *and* CULTURAL FOUNDATIONS *of* EDUCATION

Editorial Board

Encyclopedia of the
SOCIAL *and*
CULTURAL
FOUNDATIONS
of EDUCATION

1

General Editor
Eugene F. Provenzo, Jr.
University of Miami

Associate Editor
John P. Renaud
University of Miami

Managing Editor
Asterie Baker Provenzo

Los Angeles • London • New Delhi • Singapore • Washington DC

A SAGE Reference Publication

For information:

SAGE Publications, Inc.
2455 Teller Road
Thousand Oaks, California 91320
E-mail: order@sagepub.com

SAGE Publications Ltd.
1 Oliver's Yard
55 City Road
London EC1Y 1SP
United Kingdom

SAGE Publications India Pvt. Ltd.
B 1/I 1 Mohan Cooperative Industrial Area
Mathura Road, New Delhi 110 044
India

SAGE Publications Asia-Pacific Pte. Ltd.
33 Pekin Street #02-01
Far East Square
Singapore 048763

Printed in the United States of America.

Library of Congress Cataloging-in-Publication Data

Encyclopedia of the social and cultural foundations of education / editor, Eugene F. Provenzo, Jr.
    p. cm.
"A SAGE Reference Publication."
Includes bibliographical references and index.
ISBN 978-1-4129-0678-4 (cloth)
    1. Education—Encyclopedias. 2. Education—Sociological aspects. I. Provenzo, Eugene F., Jr.

LB17.E53 2009
370.3—dc22   2008022452

This book is printed on acid-free paper.

08 09 10 11 12   10 9 8 7 6 5 4 3 2 1

Publisher:	Rolf A. Janke
Acquisitions Editor:	Diane McDaniel
Assistant to the Publisher:	Michele Thompson
Developmental Editor:	Diana E. Axelsen
Reference Systems Manager:	Leticia Gutierrez
Production Editor:	Kate Schroeder
Copy Editors:	Liann Lech, Jamie Robinson
Typesetter:	C&M Digitals (P) Ltd.
Proofreader:	Penny Sippel
Indexer:	Julie Grayson
Cover Designer:	Michelle Lee Kenny
Marketing Manager:	Amberlyn Erzinger

Contents

List of Entries

Reader's Guide

Arts, Media, and Technology

Adaptive Technology
Aesthetics in Education
Arts Education Policy
Assistive Technology
Audiovisual Education, History of
Channel One
Computer-Assisted Instruction
Computing, Ethical Issues
Cultural Literacy
Digital Divide
Distance Learning
Folklore
Great Books of the Western World
Images of Teachers in Popular Culture
International Expositions
Internet, Social Impact of
Journalism and Education
Media Literacy
Multicultural Education
Popular Culture
Rap Music and Oral Literacy
Technoliteracy
Technologies in Education
Television, Public Educational
Video Games and Learning
Visual Instruction Movement

Biographies of Important Figures in Education

The entries in this section are placed together in a group in Volume 3 for the reader's convenience.

Addams, Jane
Allen, Elizabeth Almira

Apple, Michael Whitman
Aristotle
Armstrong, Samuel Chapman
Arnold, Matthew
Bagley, William Chandler
Banks, James A
Bell, Terrel Howard
Bernstein, Basil
Binet, Alfred
Bloom, Benjamin Samuel
Blow, Susan Elizabeth
Bond, Horace Mann
Bourdieu, Pierre
Bowers, C. A. (Chet)
Bruner, Jerome S.
Callahan, Raymond Eugene
Carson, Rachel
Childs, John L.
Chomsky, Avram Noam
Clapp, Elsie Ripley
Coleman, James S.
Comenius, John Amos (Komensky)
Comer, James P.
Cooper, Anna Julia Haywood
Counts, George Sylvester
Covello, Leonard
Cremin, Lawrence Arthur
Cubberley, Ellwood P.
Curry, Jabez Lamar Monroe
Davis, Jackson
de Hostos, Eugenio Maria
Dewey, John
Dewey, Melvil
Du Bois, William Edgar Burghardt
Durkheim, Émile
Eisner, Elliot

Woodson, Carter Godwin
Young, Ella Flagg

Curriculum

Abstinence-Only Sexual Education
Afrocentric Education
Alternative Schools
Antiracist Education
Arts Education Policy
Biography
Catechisms
Citizenship Education
Classical Curriculum
Comparative and International Education
Comprehensive High Schools
Confederate Textbooks
Cooperative Learning
Critical Geographies
    of Education
Critical Literacy
Critical Mathematics
Critical Psychology
Critical Thinking
Cultural Literacy
Cultural Pluralism
Cultural Studies
Culturally Responsive Teaching
Curriculum Challenges in Schools
Curriculum Theory
Delinquency Education
Democracy and Education
Discrimination and Prejudice
Drug Education
Ecojustice and Social Justice
Engineering Education, Origins
    and History of
Foreign Language Instruction
Hidden and Null Curriculum
HIV/AIDS
Holocaust Education
Immigrant Education: Contemporary Issues
Indigenous Knowledges
Life Adjustment Movement

Life Histories
Mainstreaming
Manual and Industrial Training
Medical Education
Migrant Education
Miseducation
Moral Education
Multicultural Education
New England Primer, The
Normal Schools, History of
Nursing Education, History of
Oral History
Peace Education
Penmanship
Philosophy of Education
Phonics and Whole Language
Physical Education in
    American Schools
Place-Based Education
Postcolonialism
Postmodernism
Progressive Education
Psychoanalysis and Education
Queer Theory
Reading, History of
Religion in the Public School Curriculum
Rural Education
Science, Impact on Twentieth-Century
    Education
Science, Technology, and Education:
    Historical Perspectives
Service Learning
Social Justice, Education for
Social Studies Education
Spirituality and Schooling
Sputnik
Standards
Technoliteracy
Textbooks, History of
Trivium and Quadrivium
Values Education
Visual Instruction Movement
Visual Literacy
Work-Based Learning

Economic Issues

Advertising in Schools
Boards of Education
Bureaucracy
Busing
Child Labor
Class Size
Commercialization of Schools
Company-Sponsored Schooling
Corporate Involvement in Education
Economic Inequality
Education and Economic Development
Family, School, and Community Partnerships
Federal and State Educational Jurisdiction
Fundraising in Schools
Great Depression
Hegemony
Homeless Children and Adolescents, Education of
Julius Rosenwald Fund
Lunch Programs
Migrant Education
Phelps Stokes Fund
Philanthropy, Educational
Privatization
School Funding
State Role in Education
United Negro College Fund
Vending Machines in Schools

Equality and Social Stratification

Achievement Gap
Affirmative Action
Antiracist Education
Bilingual Education, History of
Civil Rights Movement
Colorblindness
Culture-Fair Testing
Desegregation
Digital Divide
Disabilities and the Politics of Schooling
Disabilities, Physical Accommodations for People With
Discrimination and Prejudice
Ecojustice and Social Justice
Economic Inequality
Educational Equity: Gender

Educational Equity: Race/Ethnicity
English-Only Movement
Equal Access Act
Gifted Education, Diversity Issues and
Gifted Education, Policy Issues
Global Child Advocacy
Head Start
Human Rights Education
Individuals With Disabilities Education Act
Learning Disabilities and English Language Learners
Learning Disabilities and Higher Education Access
Least Restrictive Environment
Lesbian, Gay, Bisexual, and Transgendered Students
    and Teachers: Rights of
Marxism
Mexican Americans and Access to Equal Educational
    Opportunities
Migrant Education
Minority Disproportionality in Special Education
Minority Student Access to Higher Education
Native American Education, History of
Postcolonialism
Privilege
School Choice
School Funding
"Scientific" Racism
Slave Codes and Literacy
Social Justice, Education for
Special Education, Contemporary Issues
Special Education, History of
Tracking and Detracking
Vulnerability
White Privilege

Evaluation, Testing, and Research Methods

Accountability
Achievement Gap
Achievement Tests
Authentic Assessment
Culture-Fair Testing
Educational Indicators
Educational Reform
Gallup Polls
Hawthorne Effect

High-Stakes Testing
History Standards, National
Intelligence, Theories of
Intelligence Testing
Mixed Methods Research
Nation at Risk, A
No Child Left Behind Act
Observation Research
Plagiarism
Pygmalion Effect
Qualitative Research
Standardized Testing
Teachers as Researchers
Testing, History of Educational
U.S. Department of Education

History of Education

Activism and the Social Foundations of Education
Activist Teachers
After-School Education
American Education, Themes in the History of
American Sign Language
Biliteracy
Catholic Education, History of
Chautauqua Movement
Child Labor
Committee of Eight
Committee of Fifteen
Committee of Seven
Committee of Ten
Community of Practice
Compensatory Education
Desegregation Academies
Early Childhood Education
Education in the New American Republic
Education, Aims of
Education, History of
Educational Anthropology
Educational Research, History of
Eugenics
Family Literacy
Folklore
Free School Movement
Gifted Education, History of
Globalization and Education

Higher Education, History of
Immigrant Education: History
Libraries, History of
Literacy in the South
Lyceum Movement
Mentoring, Youth
Phrenology
Physical Education, History of
Playgrounds
Principalship, History of
Resistance, Student
School Architecture
Schools of Education
Social Action, Democratic Classrooms for
Social Frontier, The
Sociology of Education
Sports Mascots

Law and Public Policy

Academic Freedom
Affirmative Action
Alternative Accreditation for Teachers
Alternative Schools
Americanization Movement
Antiracist Education
Arts Education Policy
Athletics, Policy Issues
Bilingual Education, History of
Brown v. Board of Education
Bullying
Bureaucracy
Busing
Cardinal Principles of Secondary Education
Charter Schools
Child Abuse: Issues for Teachers
Child Labor
Church and State
Citizenship Education
Civil Rights Movement
Class Size
Clothing, Banning of Symbolic
Coeducation
Commercialization of Schools
Compulsory Educational Attendance Laws
Corporal Punishment

Literacy

Literacy in the South
Slave Codes and Literacy

Multiculturalism and Special Populations

Adult Education and Literacy
African American Education
African American Education: From Slave to Free
African American Private Academies
Asian American Education
Biracial Identity
Black English Vernacular
Blind, Education for the
Colorblindness
Cross-Cultural Learning in Adults
Deaf Culture
Deaf, Education for the
Disabilities, Physical Accommodations for People With
Drug-Exposed Children
Global Awareness Exchange
Globalization and Education
Hispanic Education
Homeless Children and Adolescents, Education of
Immigrant Education: Contemporary Issues
Learning Disabilities and English Language Learners
Learning Disabilities and Higher Education Access
Lesbian, Gay, Bisexual, and Transgendered Students: Advocacy Groups for
Lesbian, Gay, Bisexual, and Transgendered Students and Teachers: Rights of
Mental Retardation and Education
Mexican Americans and Access to Equal Educational Opportunities
Migrant Education
Minority Disproportionality in Special Education
Minority Student Access to Higher Education
Multicultural Education
Multiculturalism, Philosophical Implications
Muslim Students in U.S. Schools
Native American Higher Education
Prison Education
Rap Music and Oral Literacy
Rural and One-Room Schools
Rural Education

Special Education, Contemporary Issues
Tribal Colleges
Whiteness and Education
White Privilege

Organizations, Schools, and Institutions

African American Private Academies
Alternative Schools
American Federation of Teachers
American Labor Colleges
Anna T. Jeanes Foundation
Archives and Library Collections on Education
Boards of Education
Boston Latin School
Boy Scouts of America
Carlisle Barracks School
Charter Schools
Children's and Educational Museums, History of
Comprehensive High Schools
Correspondence Schools
Dalton School
Desegregation Academies
Education Commission of the States
Freedmen's Bureau
General Education Board (1901–1964)
Girl Scouts of America
Highlander Folk School
Historically Black Catholic Schools
Historically Black Colleges and Universities
History of Education Society
Holmes Group
Horace Mann School
John Dewey Society
Laboratory School, University of Chicago
Museums
National Education Association
New Harmony
Organizations for Teacher Educators
Parent Teacher Association (PTA)
Park Schools
Peabody Education Fund
Reserve Officer Training Corps (ROTC)
Rosenwald Schools
Rural and One-Room Schools

Gender and School Violence

HIV/AIDS

Homophobia and Schools

Lesbian, Gay, Bisexual and Transgendered Students: Advocacy Groups for

Lesbian, Gay, Bisexual, and Transgendered Students and Teachers: Rights of

Queer Theory

Sex Education

Sexual Orientation and Identity, Educational Policy on

Sexuality, Gender, and Education

Single-Sex Education

Social Foundations of Education: Feminist Perspectives

Stereotypes of Teachers

Women, Higher Education of

Teachers

Activist Teachers

Alternative Accreditation for Teachers

First-Person Accounts of Teaching

Images of Teachers in Popular Culture

Organizations for Teacher Educators

Parent Rights

Parent Teacher Association (PTA)

Schools of Education

Teacher Alienation and Burnout

Teacher Attitudes Toward the Teaching Profession

Teacher Beliefs About Students

Teacher Certification

Teacher Education in a Global Context

Teacher Preparation

Teacher Recruitment

Teachers as Researchers

Teacher Satisfaction

Teachers College, Columbia University

Teachers, Literary Portrayals of

Teachers, Professional Status of

Teachers, Religious Values of

Teaching Profession, History of

Theories, Models, and Philosophical Perspectives

Action Research in Education

Active Learning

Adult Education and Literacy

Authentic Assessment

Chaos Theory

Community of Practice

Comparative and International Education

Complexity Theory

Constructivism

Context in Education

Critical Geographies of Education

Critical Literacy

Critical Mathematics

Critical Psychology

Critical Race Theory

Critical Theory

Critical Thinking

Cultural Capital

Cultural Studies

Culture Epoch Theory

Curriculum Theory

Dalton Plan

Deskilling

Disability Studies

Discursive Practices

Education, Aims of

Educational Transfer

Educationese Hegemony

Feminist Theory in Education

Gary (Indiana) Model

Hampton Model

Hawthorne Effect

Head Start

Holistic Education

Ideology and Schooling

Intelligence, Theories of

Local Knowledge

Marxism

Mixed Methods Research

Models and Methods of Teaching

Multiculturalism, Philosophical Implications

New Harmony

Observation Research

Paideia

Performance Theory

Philosophy of Education

Place-Based Education

A Visual History of American Education

About the Editors

General Editor

Eugene F. Provenzo, Jr., is a professor in the Social and Cultural Foundations of Education in the Department of Teaching and Learning, School of Education at the University of Miami, where he has taught since 1976.

While continuing his duties as a professor, he served as the research coordinator and then as Associate Dean for Research for the School of Education, University of Miami, from May 1986 to June 1988.

He is the author, coauthor, or editor of over sixty books on schools, society, and technology, including *Critical Issues in Education: An Anthology of Readings* (2006); *Critical Literacy: What Every Educated American Ought to Know* (2005); *Du Bois on Education* (2002); *Schoolteachers and Schooling: Ethoses in Conflict* (1996); *Hurricane Andrew, the Public Schools and the Rebuilding of Community* (1995); *Schooling in the Light of Popular Culture* (1994); *Video Kids: Making Sense of Nintendo* (1991); *Religious Fundamentalism and American Education: The Battle for the Public Schools* (1990); *History of Education and Culture in America* (1983, 1989); *Beyond the Gutenberg Galaxy: Microcomputers and the Emergence of Post-Typographic Culture* (1986); and *The Complete Block Book* (1983). He is also the editor of Sage's four-volume collection *Foundations of Educational Thought* (2009).

Collaboration is integral to Provenzo's work. He sees himself as someone who learns through the process of research and writing. Undertaking various research projects with people in related fields of inquiry has played a critical role in his postgraduate education. For him to work effectively as a teacher, he feels that it is essential for him to combine his teaching with research, reflection, and writing. In October 1991, he won the university wide undergraduate teaching award at the University of Miami, and in 2008, the Provost's Award for Scholarly Activity.

Provenzo's research on computers and video games has been reviewed in the *New York Times, The Guardian, Mother Jones,* and *The London Economist.* He has been interviewed on National Public Radio, *ABC World News Tonight,* the *CBS Evening News, Good Morning America,* BBC radio, Britain's Central Television and Britain's Channels 2 and 4, as well as Australia's *LateLine.* In December 1993, he testified before the U.S. Senate joint hearing of the Judiciary Subcommittee on Juvenile Justice and the Government Affairs Subcommittee on Regulation and Government Information on the issue of violence in video games and television and in March 2000, before the Senate Transportation and Commerce Committee on issues of children and interactive technology. In December of 2003, he and his research were featured in *People* magazine.

In his spare time, Provenzo writes novels and is an assemblage and collage artist. He lives part of the year in central Virginia, where he is restoring a circa 1860 house with his wife and frequent coauthor, Asterie Baker Provenzo.

Associate Editor

John P. Renaud is Head of the Acquisitions Department for the University of Miami Libraries. He joined the libraries in 2002 as Education and Psychology Librarian and has also held the positions of Electronic Resources Librarian and Assistant Director of Collection Development. He has served on the Teaching Methods Committee of the Association of College and Research Libraries.

His areas of professional interest are the impact of journal and electronic resource price structures on library collections, the long-term costs of maintaining different types of library acquisitions, preservation of electronic acquisitions, and the development and support of alternative, sustainable modes of scholarly communication. He represents the libraries on the University of Miami Faculty Senate and has served as United Way Ambassador for the libraries and is part of the libraries' team in the annual Corporate Run to Benefit the Leukemia and Lymphoma Society.

Renaud has worked in the field of education since 1996. His career path includes working in alternative programs for at-risk middle and high school students and teaching English and history at college preparatory schools. He earned a BA in philosophy and political science from The American University and studied at St. Catherine's College, Oxford. He holds a master's degree in education from the University of Vermont and a master's degree in library and information studies from the University of Rhode Island.

Contributors

Natalie G. Adams
University of Alabama

Louise Adler
California State University, Fullerton

Enrique Alemán, Jr.
University of Utah

Louise Anderson Allen
South Carolina State University

Brent Allison
University of Georgia

Thomas L. Alsbury
North Carolina State University

Richard J. Altenbaugh
Slippery Rock University

Allison Daniel Anders
University of Tennessee at Knoxville

A. J. Angulo
Winthrop University

Peter Appelbaum
Arcadia University

David R. Arendale
University of Minnesota

Jan Armstrong
University of New Mexico

Diana E. Axelsen
Sage Publications, Inc.

Lucy E. Bailey
Oklahoma State University

Cerri Annette Banks
Hobart and William Smith Colleges

Patricia A. Bauch
University of Alabama

Jayne R. Beilke
Ball State University

John Beineke
Arkansas State University

Manuel Bello
University of Miami

Jo Bennett
University of Texas

Marvin J. Berlowitz
University of Cincinnati

Ilene R. Berson
University of South Florida

Michael J. Berson
University of South Florida

Pamela J. Bettis
Washington State University

Cheryl L. Beverly
James Madison University

Amy J. Binder
University of California, San Diego

Susan Birden
Buffalo State

William E. Blanton
University of Miami

Jackie M. Blount
Iowa State University

John-Michael Bodi
Bridgewater State College

Chara Haeussler Bohan
Georgia State University
George M. Boszilkov

Sue Books
State University of New York, New Paltz

Wm S Boozer
Georgia State University

George M. Boszilkov
University of Alabama

Chet Bowers
Portland State University

Deron R. Boyles
Georgia State University

Donna Adair Breault
Georgia State University

Rick A. Breault
Kennesaw State University

Felecia Briscoe
University of Texas at San Antonio

Jeffrey S. Brooks
Florida State University

Melanie C. Brooks
Florida State University

Richard A. Brosio
University of Wisconsin

Kathleen M. Brown
University of North Carolina at Chapel Hill

Gail Burnaford
Florida Atlantic University

Dan W. Butin
Cambridge College

Cory A. Buxton
Miami University

Jodi Hope Buyyounouski
University of Pennsylvania

David M. Callejo Perez
West Virginia University

Dick Michael Carpenter II
University of Colorado

Paul R. Carr
Youngstown State University

Cathryn A. Chappell
Ashland University

Ronald E. Chennault
DePaul University

Lina Lopez Chiappone
Nova Southeastern University

Rodney H. Clarken
Northern Michigan University

Mary K. Clingerman
Michigan State University

Ronald D. Cohen
Indiana University Northwest

John M. Collins
Pennsylvania State University

Brad Colwell
Southern Illinois University

Aaron Cooley
University of North Carolina at Chapel Hill

Bruce S. Cooper
Fordham University

J. José Cortez
Syracuse University

Jacqueline Cossentino
University of Maryland

Margaret Smith Crocco
Teachers College, Columbia University

Frances Putnam Crocker
Lenoir-Rhyne College

Nance Cunningham
University of Oklahoma

Erica R. Davila
Arcadia University

Melinda Moore Davis
University of Tennessee Knoxville

Matthew D. Davis
University of Missouri–St. Louis

O. L. Davis, Jr.
University of Texas at Austin

William Deese
University of Miami

Rocío Delgado
Trinity University

Kathleen deMarrais
University of Georgia

Cheryl Taylor Desmond
Millersville University

Carlos F. Diaz
Florida Atlantic University

Lilia DiBello
Barry University

Joshua Diem
University of Miami

William E. Doll, Jr.
Louisiana State University

Barbara J. Dray
Buffalo State College

Lee Dray
United States Air Force Academy

Bart Dredge
Austin College

Noah D. Drezner
University of Pennsylvania

Greg Dubrow
University of California, Berkeley

Charles Dukes
Florida Atlantic University

Nina L. Dulabaum
Judson University, Elgin Community College

James S. Dwight
Millersville University

William Edward Eaton
Southern Illinois University

Jeff Edmundson
Portland State University

Nirmala Erevelles
University of Alabama

Dorothy L. Espelage
University of Illinois, Urbana-Champaign

Jennifer Esposito
Georgia State University

Scot D. Evans
Wilfrid Laurier University

E. Thomas Ewing
Virginia Tech

Jill Beloff Farrell
Barry University

Meghann Fee
Villanova University

Abe Feuerstein
Bucknell University

Kara S. Finnigan
University of Rochester

David J. Flinders
Indiana University

Ronald D. Flowers
Eastern Michigan University

Haroldo Fontaine
Florida State University

Susan Douglas Franzosa
Fairfield University

Sheron Andrea Fraser-Burgess
Ball State University

Christopher J. Frey
Bowling Green State University

David Gabbard
East Carolina University

Vivian L. Gadsden
University of Pennsylvania

Jodie A. Galosy
Michigan State

Marybeth Gasman
University of Pennsylvania

Dianne Gereluk
Roehampton University

John Andrew Gillentine
University of Miami

Mark B. Ginsburg
Academy for Educational Development

Gerard Giordano
University of North Florida

Marietta Giovannelli
University of Illinois

Thomas L. Good
University of Arizona

Lester F. Goodchild
Santa Clara University

Mileidis Gort
University of Miami

Mary Bushnell Greiner
Queens College, City University of New York

Charles R. Green
Macalester College

Paul E. Green
University of California, Riverside

Satasha L. Green
Buffalo State College

Scott William Gust
Bowling Green State University

Horace R. Hall
DePaul University

Lynne Hamer
University of Toledo

Robert Hampel
University of Delaware

Rob Hardy
Carleton College

Elizabeth Harry
University of Miami

Juliet E. Hart
College of William & Mary

Mary E. Hauser
National-Louis University

Willis D. Hawley
American Association of School Administrators

William Hayes
Roberts Wesleyan College

Robert J. Helfenbein
Indiana University–Indianapolis

Elizabeth Hendrix
Missouri Western State University

John E. Henning
University of Northern Iowa

Sue Ellen Henry
Bucknell University

Kristen Ogilvie Holzer
University of Oklahoma

Charles L. Howell
Northern Illinois University

Nora L. Howley
Action for Healthy Kids

Pamela P. Hufnagel
Pennsylvania State University, DuBois

Roxanne Hughes
Florida State University

Thomas C. Hunt
University of Dayton

David Hutchison
Brock University

Kathy Hytten
Southern Illinois University

W. James Jacob
University of Pittsburgh

Michael E. Jennings
University of Texas at San Antonio

Michael C. Johanek
University of Pennsylvania

E. V. Johanningmeier
University of South Florida

Robert L. Johnson
University of South Carolina

Rachel Bailey Jones
University of North Carolina at Greensboro

Jeremy Jordan
University of Miami

Pamela Bolotin Joseph
University of Washington–Bothell

Richard Kahn
University of North Dakota

Douglas Kellner
University of California, Los Angeles

Kathleen Knight-Abowitz
Miami University

Victor N. Kobayashi
University of Hawai‘i at Manoa

Kelly Kolodny
Framingham State College

Philip Edward Kovacs
University of Alabama, Huntsville

E. Jennifer Monaghan
Brooklyn College, City University of New York

Charles Monaghan
Independent Scholar

Maribel Gloria Mora
University of Miami

Diana Moyer
University of Tennessee

James A. Muchmore
Western Michigan University

Donal E. Mulcahy
City University of New York

Susan P. Mullane
University of Miami

Moira Murphy
Tec de Monterrey

Mark Mussman
University of Cincinnati

Rodney Muth
University of Colorado Denver

Jason Eric Nelson
University of Washington

Joseph W. Newman
University of South Alabama

Roxanne Newton
Mitchell Community College

Tricia Niesz
Kent State University

George W. Noblit
University of North Carolina

Nel Noddings
Stanford University

Jana Noel
California State University, Sacramento

Rebecca R. Noel
Plymouth State University

J. Wesley Null
Baylor University

Ronald J Nuzzi
University of Notre Dame

Kristin Elizabeth Ogilvie
University of Oklahoma

Robert L Osgood
Indiana University Purdue

William A. Paquette
Tidewater Community College

João Menelau Paraskeva
University of Minho

Priya Parmar
Brooklyn College, City University of New York

Ana Maria Pazos-Rego
University of Miami

Kristeen L. Pemberton
San Jose State University

Shawn Pendley
University of Oklahoma

Yvonne Perry
University of Miami

Paola Pilonieta
University of North Carolina at Charlotte

Matthew Isaac Pinzur
Miami Herald

Peggy L. Placier
University of Missouri

Robert Pleasants
University of North Carolina

Brad J. Porfilio
Saint Louis University

Jeanne M. Powers
Arizona State University

Beth Powers-Costello
University of North Carolina at Chapel Hill

Sandra Spickard Prettyman
University of Akron

Alison Price-Rom
Academy for Educational Development

Isaac Prilleltensky
University of Miami

Ora Prilleltensky
University of Miami

Eugene F. Provenzo, Jr.
University of Miami

Asterie Baker Provenzo
Independent Scholar

John L. Puckett
University of Pennsylvania

Gabriel Quintana
University of Miami

Richard Race
Roehampton University

Al Ramirez
University of Colorado, Colorado Springs

John G. Ramsay
Carleton College

Todd C. Ream
Indiana Wesleyan University

John P. Renaud
University of Miami

Teresa Anne Rendon
University of Oklahoma

Kristen A. Renn
Michigan State University

Lisa L. Repaskey
University of Miami

W. Joshua Rew
Florida State University

Yvonne Cecelia Ribeiro de Souza-Campbell
University of Miami

David W. Robinson
Pioneer Pacific College

Bruce Romanish
Washington State University

Sabrina N. Ross
University of North Carolina, Greensboro

Steven E. Rowe
Chicago State University

Anthony G. Rud
Purdue University

John L. Rury
University of Kansas

Alan R. Sadovnik
Rutgers University

Elaine G. Sayre
Kalamazoo Public School District

Tracy Schandler
Chapman University

Carsten Schmidtke
Oklahoma State University–Okmulgee

Carri Anne Schneider
University of Cincinnati

Christina Schneider
CTB/McGraw-Hill

La Tefy G. Schoen
North Carolina State University

Dilys Schoorman
Florida Atlantic University

William H. Schubert
University of Illinois at Chicago

Brian D. Schultz
Northeastern Illinois University

Lisa J. Scott
City University of New York, Queens

Steven Selden
University of Maryland

Susan F. Semel
City University New York

Annis N. Shaver
Cedarville University

Melanie Shoffner
Purdue University

Lesley Shore
University of Toronto

Cathy J. Siebert
Ball State University

Harvey Siegel
University of Miami

Douglas J. Simpson
Texas Tech University

Michael W. Simpson
University of Wisconsin–Madison

Jean Theodora Slobodzian
College of New Jersey

Joan K. Smith
University of Oklahoma

Christopher M. Span
University of Illinois

Sam F. Stack, Jr.
West Virginia University

Gita Steiner-Khamsi
Teachers College, Columbia University

Barbara S. Stengel
Millersville University

Nancy Stern
City College of New York

Patrick Stevenson
Villanova University

Alan Stoskopf
Facing History and Ourselves

Gail L. Sunderman
University of California, Los Angeles

John V. Surr
OMEP-USNC

Kyle Sweitzer
Michigan State University

Zeena Tabbaa-Rida
Independent Scholar

Kenneth Teitelbaum
Kent State University

Martha May Tevis
University of Texas–Pan American

Barbara J. Thayer-Bacon
University of Tennessee

Timothy G. Thomas
James Madison University

Janet Y. Thomas
University of Pennsylvania

Connie Titone
Villanova University

Stephen Tomlinson
University of Alabama

Myriam N. Torres
New Mexico State University

Sandra Winn Tutwiler
Washburn University

James J. Van Patten
Florida Atlantic University

Terah Talei Venzant
Wellesley College

Ruth Vinz
Teachers College, Columbia University

Cally Waite
Teachers College, Columbia University

Stephanie J. Waterman
Syracuse University

William H. Watkins
University of Illinois at Chicago

Gregory Paul Wegner
University of Wisconsin–La Crosse

Burton Weltman
William Patterson University

Sally H. Wertheim
John Carroll University

Shannon White
Villanova University

Keith Whitescarver
College of William and Mary

Glenn Whitmann
St. Andrew's Episcopal School

Roy Wilson
Jury Simulation Research

Jeffrey William Wood
Laurentian University

Christine Woyshner
Temple University

Kai-Ju Yang
Indiana University

Michael Sean Young
Florida State University

Introduction

This is an encyclopedia of the Social and Cultural Foundations of Education. It is intended to provide a comprehensive background for those interested in issues involving schools and society. The Social and Cultural Foundations of Education is an interdisciplinary field, including disciplines (to name just a few) such as history and sociology, as well as topical areas such as globalization and technology.

More than any other field in education, the Social and Cultural Foundations of Education reflects many of the conflicts, tensions, and forces in American society. Perhaps this is inevitable, since the area's focus is on issues such as race, gender, socioeconomic class, the impact of technology on learning, what it means to be educated, and the role of teaching and learning in a societal context.

What constitutes the field has been open to considerable debate over the years. The Council of Learned Societies in Education defines the foundations of education as follows:

> Foundations of Education refers to a broadly-conceived field of educational study that derives its character and methods from a number of academic disciplines, combinations of disciplines, and area studies, including: history, philosophy, sociology, anthropology, religion, political science, economics, psychology, cultural studies, gender studies, comparative and international education, educational studies, and educational policy studies. . . . The purpose of foundations study is to bring these disciplinary resources to bear in developing interpretive, normative, and critical perspectives on education, both inside and outside of schools. (From Council of Learned Societies in Education, "Standards for Academic and Professional Instruction in Foundations of Education,

Educational Studies, and Educational Policy Studies," 2nd Edition [San Francisco: Caddo Gap Publishers, 1996]. Retrieved from http://members.aol.com/caddogap/standard.htm)

In a comprehensive essay, found in the third volume of this encyclopedia, titled "Toward a Renewed Definition of the Social Foundations of Education," the project's General Editor explores at length the evolution of the field and its current status. It is the philosophy and perspective outlined in this essay that has largely shaped the development of the overall work.

In creating the encyclopedia, eleven disciplinary and conceptual areas upon which the field is largely based were identified. Each of these areas has been assigned an anchor essay that has been written by an expert in that area. These include disciplinary areas such as comparative education, educational anthropology, educational sociology, the history of education, and the philosophy of education. Topical areas include cultural studies and education, ecojustice education and cultural studies, globalization and education, multiculturalism, policy studies, and technologies in education. Many of the topics overlap. Some represent emerging areas that are important to the field such as cultural studies, globalization and education, ecojustice, and technologies in education. Others are more traditional and have a longer history such as the history of education and the philosophy of education. Arguments could be made for including additional areas or for precluding some of the topics that have been included. Part of the editorial work has involved a careful examination of the field and a rationalization for the categories selected.

Content and Organization

This work consists of three volumes. The first two volumes include more than 400 A–Z entries. The third volume contains 130 biographical entries on important men and women in education, as well as a visual history of American education. This history is organized into 25 chapters and contains images from the colonial period through the 1950s. An overview of the encyclopedia's content is provided by a reader's guide that appears at the beginning of each volume. It lists all of the entries in the encyclopedia under one or more of the following topical areas:

- Arts, Media, and Technology
- Biographies of Important Figures in Education
- Curriculum
- Economic Issues
- Equality and Social Stratification
- Evaluation, Testing, and Research Methods
- History of Education
- Law and Public Policy
- Literacy
- Multiculturalism and Special Populations
- Organizations, Schools, and Institutions
- Religion and Social Values
- School Governance
- Sexuality and Gender
- Teachers
- Theories, Models, and Philosophical Perspectives

As mentioned earlier, a detailed essay by the encyclopedia's General Editor in Volume 3 outlines the history of the Social and Cultural Foundations of Education, its current status, and its possible future direction. In doing so, it seeks at a very general level to draw the connections between the various areas delineated in the first two volumes of the encyclopedia.

How This Work Was Created

The creation of the encyclopedia involved the following steps:

- The General Editor, Eugene F. Provenzo, Jr., was approached by the publisher to consider the possibility of putting together the work.
- A list of possible topics and headwords was developed.

- Leading specialists in different disciplinary and topical areas were contacted about joining the editorial board and were asked to review and contribute to the headword list.
- Potential contributors were identified by the editor-in-chief and members of the editorial board.
- Invitations to contribute to the project were sent. These invitations included basic guidelines and instructions regarding the articles.
- Electronic notices were sent through professional organizations and listservs asking for contributions to the project. As a result, many new headwords emerged—ones that reflected the interests and concerns of individuals in the field. Additional invitations were then sent for these new headwords.
- A group of special contributors emerged from the field. These were individuals who not only contributed significant articles, but also helped identify additional subjects, as well as potential contributors. As a result of their contributions, a final round of invitations to contribute to the project went out.
- The General Editor and the managing editor reviewed all of the articles and, in conjunction with developmental staff, asked for revisions of articles when appropriate.
- The content of the three volumes were compiled and finalized.

Acknowledgments

This project would not have been possible without the efforts of many people. First we would like to thank faculty and staff at the University of Miami for their encouragement and support of this project. In the School of Education, thanks go to the late Dean Sam Yarger and to Dean Isaac Prilleltensky. In the Department of Teaching and Learning, Jeanne Schumm and Walter Secada deserve special thanks. Thanks also go to William Walker, the director of the university's Otto G. Richter Library.

The publishing team at Sage has been exceptional. Diana Axelsen has provided careful editing and good advice throughout the project; Diane McDaniel took us on early in her tenure as an acquisitions editor. She has been a good friend, as well as a helpful advisor. Special thanks go to Arthur Pomponio, who first proposed the project.

We especially appreciate the contributions of our editorial board, as well as our board of special contributors. The editorial board members wrote the anchor essays for the project and provided extensive suggestions for topics and authors. The special contributors came onto the project as articles began to come in and be assigned. They helped identify topics, as well as potential authors, becoming a second less-formal editorial board. They and their contributions greatly enhanced the overall project. They include in alphabetical order A. J. Angulo, Susan Birden, Bruce Cooper, Barbara Dray, Juliet Hart, Tom Hunt, Jonathan Lightfoot, and Bill Schubert.

Eugene F. Provenzo, Jr., General Editor
University of Miami
John P. Renaud, Associate Editor
University of Miami
Asterie Baker Provenzo, Managing Editor
Independent Scholar

A

ABSTINENCE-ONLY SEXUAL EDUCATION

Abstinence-only sexual education (also "abstinence education" and "abstinence-until-marriage education") refers to a group of sexual education curricula intended to teach children that they should abstain from sexual intimacy with another individual until they become adults and usually until they are married. Many U.S. state and local boards of education have adopted these programs, which typically focus on sexual activity as inappropriate and/or impractical for adolescents and which avoid discussion of the specific details of sexual activity, contraception, and sexual disease prevention. These omissions have been protested by parents and civic organizations, who argue that adolescents must be informed with up-to-date and accurate information regarding sexuality so that they can make informed decisions about whether or not to engage in sexual activity.

While teaching about sexual abstinence has always been a salient part of sexuality education in the United States, only in the last decades of the 1900s did the idea of teaching sexual abstinence to the exclusion of other components of sexuality become the dominant discourse in sexuality education. For example, for fiscal year 2005, the U.S. federal government allotted $167 million for abstinence-only sexual education programs to be administered by state health departments, school districts, hospitals, religious organizations, and "pro-life" organizations. This amount was just over twice the amount allotted for such programs in 2001, but still over $100 million less than was proposed by the president.

Proponents of abstinence-only sexual education argue that teaching children about sex and contraception encourages them to engage in sexual behaviors and undermines the authority of their parents. They suggest that effective abstinence-only sexual education programs delay initiation of sexual activity, thus preventing teenage pregnancy and the transmission of sexual diseases.

Critics of abstinence-only sexuality education cite the lack of evidence of the effectiveness of abstinence-only programs, while arguing that some sexuality education programs that involve instruction in abstinence as well as contraception and disease prevention have been shown to have statistically significant results in delaying sexual initiation. Abstinence-only programs have also been criticized for confounding religion and science and for inaccurately presenting scientific evidence to exaggerate or misstate the effectiveness of contraception as a means of pregnancy and disease prevention. While some critics have allowed that particular abstinence-only programs have led to small delays in sexual initiation among young adolescent participants, they also cite evidence that suggests that many of these same individuals are less likely to use contraceptive devices when they do have sex and less likely to seek medical assistance if they contract a sex-related disease.

Wm S Boozer

1

See also Compulsory Heterosexuality; Moral Education; Sex Education; Sexuality, Gender, and Education

Further Readings

Kirby, D. (2001). *Emerging answers: Research findings on programs to reduce teen pregnancy.* Washington, DC: National Campaign to Reduce Teen Pregnancy.

ACADEMIC FREEDOM

Academic freedom refers to teachers having freedom to teach and students having freedom to learn without interference from within or from ideological conflicts outside the institution. Understanding the rights and responsibilities of teachers is essential in public discourse on academic freedom. This entry provides the historical background of the concept, its interpretation in the law, and current challenges.

Foundations of Academic Freedom

In the eleventh, twelfth, and thirteenth centuries, university faculties were representatives of the church and state. Peripatetic educators taught within the parameters of church doctrine. However, Peter Abelard, author of *Sic et Non,* was condemned for failure to adhere to church doctrine. Medieval universities were corporations or guilds of scholars. In 1200, the University of Paris received royal recognition from King Philip Augustus, placing masters and scholars under clerical rule rather than under harsh secular courts. In 1231, the university received further recognition from the pope, allowing the university to establish control over lectures and disputations. The resulting university autonomy has been, with exceptions, the model for colleges and universities since medieval times.

The modern concept of academic freedom originated in Germany, in Prussia, and with the founding of the University of Berlin in 1810. *Lehrfreiheit* was the freedom to teach, engage in research, and distribute results without interference, and the freedom of students to learn without interference. The changes of the Enlightenment influenced the universities of Germany more than those of other countries, and canonical text became a scholarly, systematic lecture focus.

In the United States, John Hopkins, a research university, was the first to adopt the German concept of academic freedom. Throughout American history, faculty and administrators have been terminated or criticized for expressing views that have offended some individual, business, or legislative body. Educational reformer John Dewey received many complaints about university faculty members being dismissed for statements made in class that offended powerful interests or were taken out of context. Arbitrary and capricious administrative action was common.

When noted economist Edward Ross lost his job at Stanford University in 1909 because Mrs. Leland Stanford did not like his views on the gold standard, professors across the nation were alarmed. In 1915, Arthur C. Lovejoy of John Hopkins University, E. R. A. Seligman and John Dewey of Columbia University, and others wrote *The General Report on Academic Freedom and Academic Tenure* for the American Association of University Professors (AAUP).

American universities have changed, but there was a cultural lag in the implementation of necessary academic freedoms. Dissident professors were often the victims; trustees and administrators were the culprits, the power of dismissal was the weapon, and loss of employment the wound. The 1915 report laid the foundation for job security, academic tenure, and due process. The report did not prohibit faculty from speaking out on issues foreign to their specialties, but the university could disown everything its members said, then let them publish whatever they pleased.

The threat to academic freedom is constant in higher education. Subtle infringements on academic freedom tend to occur, especially when faculty members speak publicly on controversial issues. McCarthyism occurs when donors, politicians, business, and religious leaders call for university investigation and dismissal of faculty who have controversial views. Criticism of faculty is particularly intense during periods of internal stress, social fragmentation, and global conflicts. University administrators feel a dual pressure to respond to external forces as well as to protect the freedom to learn and to teach on their campuses.

The American Association of University Professors developed a Statement of Principles on Academic Freedom and Tenure in 1940. The purpose of the statement was to ensure that higher education institutions are conducted for the common good, not to further the interest of the individual teacher or a particular institution. Academic freedom in teaching and research is fundamental to the advancement of truth and to the protection of the teacher's rights in teaching and the student's freedom in learning.

The governing bodies of the American Association of University Professors and the Association of American Colleges met in January 1990 to adopt several changes that removed gender-specific references from the original text. The AAUP statement on academic freedom includes the caution that teachers should be careful not to introduce controversial matters which have no relation to their subject. Limitations on academic freedom because of religious or other institutional aims should be clearly stated in writing at the time of the teacher's appointment. College and university teachers are citizens, and when they speak or write as citizens, their unique position in the community imposes special obligations. Faculty should be accurate, exercise appropriate restraint, show respect for the opinions of others, and indicate that they are not speaking for the institution. To meet emerging standards of academic protocol, the document continues to be updated. It provides a model and guide for universities as they strive to protect freedom of inquiry and teaching.

The Law and Academic Freedom

Federal court decisions indicate that academic freedom is used to denote both the freedom of the academy to pursue its ends without interference from the government and the freedom of individual teachers to pursue their ends without interference from the academy.

The Supreme Court underlined the importance of academic freedom in *Sweezy v. New Hampshire* (1957). The Court reversed a contempt judgment against a professor who in refusing to answer questions about a

lecture he had given at a university, articulated the rationale for academic freedom.

The essentiality of freedom in the community of American universities is almost self-evident. No one should underestimate the vital role in a democracy that is played by those who guide and train our youth. To impose any straitjacket upon the intellectual leaders in our colleges and universities would imperil the future of our nation. No field of education is so thoroughly comprehended by man that new discoveries cannot yet be made. Particularly is that true in the social sciences, where few, if any, principles are accepted as absolutes. Scholarship cannot flourish in an atmosphere of suspicion and distrust. Teachers and students must always remain free to inquire, to study, and to evaluate, to gain new maturity and understanding; otherwise, our civilization will stagnate and die. (354 U.S. 250)

The Supreme Court has consistently reinforced the vital necessity for freedom of speech in a democracy. It has used *Sweezy* as well as *Shelton v. Tucker* (1960) and *Keyishian v. Board of Regents* (1967) to reaffirm the special role of academic freedom in the academy. The Court notes that our nation is deeply committed to safeguarding academic freedom, which is of transcendent value to all of us and not merely to the teachers concerned. The classroom is peculiarly the "market place of ideas."

The Court found in *United States v. Associated Press* (1967) that the nation depends upon leaders trained through wide exposure to that robust exchange of ideas which discovers truth from a multitude of tongues, rather than through any kind of authoritarian selection.

Current Challenges

In the twenty-first century, there are a number of challenges to academic freedom. There is a growing trend of increased private financing and decreased public funding of higher education. The trend increases the risk of conflicts of interest with corporations and other sponsors of research. The new operating environment requires clear guidelines for transparency in such dealings and protections for the academic freedom of researchers to share their results within the scientific community. The market dictates that research results are to be treated as proprietary, to be sold not given away, for the public good.

The Internet

Thomas Jefferson's academic village has been supplanted with wired campuses and cyberspace information systems. In an Internet age individuals may use hate language against faculty and administration under the cloak of anonymity. Disinformation, misinformation, and groundless dogmatic authoritarian assertions made using a faculty member's identity can destroy careers. Identity theft in all its forms is part of our era. Explosive advances in technology are a challenge to providing standards for academic freedom.

The Internet culture is a moving target. In the cyberspace age, electronic and digital communications within our community of academic discourse have changed the way faculty, students, and administration engage in teaching and scholarship. The methods by which information is obtained and disseminated, the means of storing and retrieving such information, the speed at which wider audiences are reached, and the transition from familiar and tangible physical space to virtual space all make issues of academic freedom an open-ended challenge.

Curtailing offensive information might be detrimental to researchers. Protecting intellectual property rights becomes more difficult with the cyberspace age. The classroom is no longer limited to traditional classrooms, but is represented by Web sites, home pages, bulletin boards, and listservs. Requiring passwords and changing them periodically provides a safety network for computer networking. Controversial opining should include disclaimers that such views do not reflect those of the institution. Campus speech codes and verbal harassment rules can target digital or electronic hate messages as well as similarly spiteful print messages.

The AAUP revised text adapted by the association's council in November 2004, "Academic Freedom and Electronic Communications," stresses the importance of developing safeguards that will be applied to all areas of electronic communications within the campus community. This includes sensitivity to privacy needs in many situations where unauthorized disclosure of electronic messages and materials could jeopardize personal reputations and other vital interests, and ultimately deter free and open communications within the campus community. All these factors will require careful and extensive study by each institution and the tailoring of specific responses consistent with institutional needs and values, as well as with state and local laws. Academic freedom in an era of litigation, cultural wars, and social fragmentation, today as in the past, faces multiple challenges.

Tenure

Academic freedom requires protection from interference with the unfettered search for knowledge and truth in the academy. Tenure provides institutional commitment and support for teachers to be free to conduct their research, teaching, and service without fear of reprisal or dismissal for taking a controversial stand on issues and trends in their subject matter area. Tenure protection includes due process rights for tenure track probationary and tenured faculty.

Some new institutions do not have tenure. Also, there are a growing number of untenured adjunct and part-time faculty. Court decisions assure them First Amendment free speech protections. Academic freedom is essential in higher education and the strength of its protection depends on each college and university's faculty contracts as well as institutional custom and usage. Faculty have a responsibility for professional ethics and conduct in their institutional teaching, research, and service. Tenure, with exceptions, assures continued lifetime employment contracts.

James J. Van Patten

See also Democracy and Education

Further Readings

Academic freedom and electronic communications. (2005). *Academe, 91*(1), 55–59.
Butts, R. F. (1973). *The education of the West.* New York: McGraw-Hill.

Cross, T. (2006). Academic freedom and the hacker ethic. *Communications of the ACM, 49,* 37–40.

Gutek, G. L. (1997). *Historical and philosophical foundations of education.* Upper Saddle River, NJ: Prentice Hall.

Hook, S. (1970). *Academic freedom and academic anarchy.* New York: Cowles.

Kaplan, W. A., & Lee, B. A. (1995). *The law of higher education.* San Francisco: Jossey-Bass.

Keyishian v. Board of Regents, 385 U.S. 589 (1967).

Lyall, K., & Sell, K. R. (2006). The de facto privatization of American public higher education. *Change: The Magazine of Higher Learning, 38*(1), 6–13.

Metzner, W. P. (1981). Academic freedom in delocalized academic institutions. In P. G. Altbach, R. O. Berdahl, & P. J. Gumport (Eds.), *Higher education in American society* (pp. 37–54). New York: Prometheus Books.

The 1940 statement of principles on academic freedom and tenure with interpretive comments. (2006, July 4). American Association of University Professors. Retrieved July 4, 2006, from http://www.aaup.org.statements? redbook/1940stat.htm

Shelton v. Tucker, 364 U.S. 479 (1960).

Standler, R. B. (2000). *Academic freedom in the USA.* Retrieved from http://www.rbs2.com/afree.htm

Sweezy v. New Hampshire, 354 U.S. 234 (1957).

United States v. Associated Press, 385 U.S. 589 (1967).

ACCOUNTABILITY

The word *accountability* exploded onto the educational scene in the early 1980s following the publication of the National Commission on Excellence in Education's *A Nation at Risk* report. The language of accountability has been ubiquitous ever since. Almost all popular writers on education today use the term. They do so, however, without careful definition of what they mean when they use the language of accountability.

Accountability language may be used as a substitute for serious discussion of the purpose of American education. Early in the twentieth century, the language of "efficiency" and "social efficiency" sometimes served this same role. During the age of industrialization, efficiency became an end in and of itself rather than a means to a greater ideal for American education. This same phenomenon may be happening today, when accountability becomes an end in itself instead of a means to a higher end. This entry describes three main uses of *accountability* and then seeks to identify the common elements in these three popular uses of the term.

Economic Accountability

Economists use the term *accountability* in strictly financial terms. They apply the language and concepts of banking and the stock market to critiquing schools for not producing what they believe schools should produce. The purpose of education to economists, who by definition focus exclusively on the production and consumption of goods, is to produce skilled workers for businesses. In the eyes of economists, schools should be held accountable for producing the workers that businesspeople want.

The best "bottom line" that economists can determine for schools is test score production. To these thinkers, schools exist to produce test scores, which they have seized upon as a means to the production of skilled workers. Economic-minded thinkers then focus on producing elaborate accountability systems that they believe will determine who is to blame for not producing the workers that corporate executives want.

Political Accountability

Accountability in a more strictly political context is more difficult to define. The common theme in accountability language, however, is blame. To "hold someone accountable" is to blame that person for not fixing a problem when he or she has been labeled as the person responsible for fixing the problem. In this simplistic approach to teaching and learning, education is stripped of its moral dimension in the rush by public leaders to find someone to blame for the fact that all of our society's problems have not been fixed.

This view of politics stretches back to the beginning of the modern era in the West, to thinkers such as Niccolo Machiavelli (1469–1527), Thomas Hobbes (1588–1679), and John Locke (1632–1704). The current emphasis on accountability stems from the realization that the modern project that began in the seventeenth and eighteenth centuries has not produced the perfect society its adherents, such as Jean-Jacques Rousseau (1712–1788), Denis Diderot (1713–1784), and others, promised. In the wake of what some people believe is the failure of this modern project, someone must be blamed for the imperfect human nature that has been with us all along. The political game of blaming one group or another for what is a natural problem takes place under the guise of accountability driven political rhetoric.

Moral Accountability

Other people who use the language of accountability, however, focus almost exclusively on its moral element. People who use *accountability* in a moral sense are concerned about moral decline in American society. Accountability, to these individuals, takes on the urgency of a crusade to eradicate immoral behavior through education. The purpose of accountability to morally driven reformers is to root out what they believe are social problems, such as voter apathy, sexual immorality, and drug use. These reformers believe that bad education has given rise to a culture in which people are no longer accountable for their actions. Accountability and responsibility are closely related concepts to these reformers, but using accountability provides them with more leverage than using responsibility, because it allows them to identify and blame the people they wish to hold accountable for returning America to a perceived age when citizens were more responsible. They believe that accountability is the means by which principles such as respect for elders, love of country, and individual responsibility can be reinstilled in American youth.

In the language that surrounds modern discussions of education, these three meanings of accountability are intertwined. They are quite difficult to separate in the language of popular educational reformers. These three themes of economic, political, and moral accountability, however, always can be found in the public language of educational advocacy. The most popular accountability driven reformers manage to deliver speeches that integrate all three of these different conceptions of accountability, despite the fact that they are fundamentally at odds with one another. Public audiences are left with a vague sense that accountability is a good thing, but without any substantive meaning of what accountability is about.

Accountability driven reformers also tend to agree that "student achievement" is an idea that corresponds closely with accountability. Much like accountability, however, *student achievement* is a term that can be interpreted to correspond with economic, political, and moral purposes for schools. Questions such as "To what end should we hold people accountable?" and "To what end should we increase student achievement?" are rarely asked in the heated world of educational rhetoric. The unquestioned and too-often hollow rhetoric of accountability ultimately avoids the real question of purpose, which alone could give meaning to accountability as well as American education in general.

J. Wesley Null

See also Educational Reform; *Nation at Risk, A;* Politics of Education

Further Readings

Null, J. W. (2003). Education and knowledge, not "standards and accountability": A critique of popular reform rhetoric based on the work of Dewey, Bagley, and Schwab. *Educational Studies, 34,* 397–413.

Null, J. W. (2004). Social efficiency splintered: Multiple meanings instead of the hegemony of one. *Journal of Curriculum and Supervision, 19,* 99–124.

ACHIEVEMENT GAP

The *achievement gap* is defined as the disparity that exists between the test scores of White American students and African American and Hispanic or minority students. Test results indicate that White students score higher than minority students (except Asians) on measures of achievement. This gap is measured by test scores on a variety of instruments measuring intelligence, achievement, and aptitude. These include the National Assessment of Educational Progress, SAT, Iowa Tests of Basic Skills, and other instruments administered in the public schools of the United States.

The achievement gap is a major concern to policy makers and educators alike, and much research has been done to discover the cause of this test score difference. According to the National Assessment of Educational Progress (NAEP), the achievement gap between Whites and African Americans is between 0.80 and 1.14 standard deviations. Between Whites and Hispanics, it is between 0.40 and 1.00. According to NAEP data, this gap exists both in reading and in math. The educational, social, and economic implications for minority students are huge. The dropout rate for minority teens is higher than for White teens, the high school graduation rate lower, and as a result, opportunities in the job market are substantially limited. Education is purported to be the great equalizer, but this gap persists and points to a significant problem in the educational system in the United States. This entry looks at the question: What is the cause of this achievement gap, and can the gap be closed?

Possible Causes

In 1954, the Supreme Court decision reached in *Brown v. Board of Education* stated that the educational system in the United States was "separate and unequal." African American and other minority children attended class in dilapidated buildings, with limited funding and resources. These conditions and their inherent discriminatory practices contributed to the early gaps in test scores between White and minority students.

In more recent times, test bias has been alleged by theorists who claim that the contents of achievement tests are biased in favor of White students, and thus the tests discriminate against minorities. Others have said minority students are inherently inferior intellectually and the achievement gap is proof. There has been no clear-cut evidence to support this claim, however, though it has been made throughout the last few centuries by various pundits.

In addition to these assertions, the research has investigated many other factors that may contribute to this gap. These include race, socioeconomic status, culture, teacher expectations, instructional practices, parent level of education, parent involvement, cultural capital, and various societal elements, even rap music. Basically, there is no evidence suggesting a cause of the achievement gap in education.

While definitive causes may not be available, landmark research conducted by Betty Hart and Todd Risley offers insight into what may be the origins of the problem and as a result, likely solutions. These researchers studied children from ten months to three years old in families from three socioeconomic backgrounds: welfare, middle class, and professional (specifically college professors' families). Their study, which looked at the quantity of conversation in families as counted in words, suggests that for some children, the achievement gap begins before they enter the educational system.

They found that the average welfare child heard about 616 words per hour, compared to 1,251 words per hour for the average working-class child, and 2,153 words per hour for children in professional families. In four years of such experience, an average child in a professional family would have heard almost 45 million words, an average child in a working class family 26 million words, and an average child in a welfare family 13 million words. Thus, by the time the children enter school, their experiences are vastly different, with potential consequences. For example, a student who arrives at school having heard, let's say, the word *marvelous* 1,000 times will most likely know that word and its usage, as compared to a child who had only heard it ten times or not at all. Experience with language offers a decided advantage. These findings moved the government to fund and implement a comprehensive preschool system, Head Start, aimed at closing the gap for children born into poverty.

Possible Solutions

Since researchers can't come to a conclusion about why the achievement gap exists, they have sought solutions to decrease it. According to the National Assessment of Education Progress (NAEP), this goal was achieved for a period of thirteen years as indicated by data showing that the gap narrowed between 1975 and 1988. From 1990 to 1999, however, the gap remained the same or grew. In fact, according to the Education Trust, by the time African American and Hispanic students reach twelfth grade, their English, math, and science skills are similar to the skills of thirteen-year-old White students.

A Nation at Risk

What factors contributed to the narrowing of the achievement gap in the 1980s? Again there are many explanations espoused by the researchers. Title I supplied much needed government funding to economically depressed schools. Also, in 1983 the National Commission on Excellence in Education's report *A Nation at Risk* served notice on the entire educational system that the Unites States was lagging behind the nations of the world. The commission set forth the following recommendations:

- Graduation requirements should be strengthened in five *new* basics: English, mathematics, science, social studies, and computer science.
- Schools and colleges should adopt higher and measurable standards for academic performance.
- The amount of time students spend engaged in learning should be significantly increased.
- The teaching profession should be strengthened through higher standards for preparation and professional growth.

This prompted swift action as professional educational entities such as the National Council of Teachers of Mathematics, the National Council of Teachers of English, National Science Teachers Association, and the International Reading Association scrambled to raise the standards of academic achievement in our nation's schools through the establishment of national standards. These standards were meant to offer strong content-based curriculum practices intended to increase student achievement through content.

The report, which focused on the test scores of the general student population, and its subsequent reaction by the educational community, seems to have had the positive effect of narrowing the achievement gap, according to a 2006 article in the *American Journal of Education* by Douglas Harris and Carolyn Herrington. The authors also stated that during the 1980s, when *content* and *time* standards (what is taught, and the amount of time spent teaching and learning) were improved, the achievement gap narrowed. They added, however, that during the 1990s, the gap remained the same or grew at the onset of the accountability focus in the form of high-stakes tests, school takeovers, vouchers, charter schools, and other government- and market-based accountability programs.

Teacher Quality

Another factor said to narrow the achievement gap is teacher quality. Highly qualified teachers can narrow the achievement gap just as incompetent teachers can widen it. Research indicates that high quality teaching can have lasting effects on student achievement. Unfortunately, poor quality teachers are concentrated in low performing schools. According to research, this is no coincidence. Being taught by a poor quality teacher can seriously affect student achievement. Among other findings, Steven Rivkin, Eric Hanushek, and John Kain found that high quality instruction in primary school may offset disadvantages associated with low socioeconomic background.

Quality Reading Instruction

Additional measures have been employed to improve overall student performance and combat the widening achievement gap. In 2000, the National Reading Panel issued a meta-analysis detailing the "big five" of the instructional reading process: phonemic awareness, phonics, fluency, vocabulary and comprehension. The panel determined that systematic phonics instruction leads to significant positive benefits for students in kindergarten through sixth grade and for children with difficulty learning to read. They also found that professional development for teachers is necessary to improve the quality of reading instruction.

No Child Left Behind

No Child Left Behind (NCLB), the reauthorization of the Elementary and Secondary School Education Act, was signed into law on January 8, 2002. The U.S. Department of Education stated that the law helps schools improve by focusing on accountability for results, freedom for states and communities, proven education methods, and choices for parents. One of the primary objectives of the legislation is to close the achievement gap, as stated in Title I, Section 100-Statement of Purpose,

The purpose of this title is to ensure that all children have a fair, equal, and significant opportunity to obtain a high-quality education and reach, at a minimum, proficiency on challenging State academic achievement standards and state academic assessments. This purpose can be accomplished by . . . closing the achievement gap between high- and low-performing children, especially the achievement gaps between minority and nonminority students, and between disadvantaged children and their more advantaged peers. . . .

Various programs and projects, such as Reading First; Prevention and Intervention Programs for Children and Youth Who Are Neglected, Delinquent, or at Risk; Family Literacy; Drop-Out Prevention; Advanced Placement Programs; and Comprehensive School Reform are funded through NCLB.

With any new government initiative, however, comes debate. NCLB is no exception. Many believe the program has inordinately increased stress on teachers and students through the use of high stakes testing to measure goal compliance. In general, a great deal of spirited conversation surrounds the effectiveness of some of the NCLB's stipulations. Are the accountability measures improving teacher quality and academic achievement among all student groups? Is the achievement gap narrowing? Only time and data will be the judge.

Yvonne Perry

See also African American Education; No Child Left Behind Act

Further Readings

Baard, M. (2006). Scholars cite history's legacy, rap music for achievement gap. *Diverse Issues in Higher Education, 23,* 20.

Borman, G. D., & Kimball, S. M. (2005). Teacher quality and educational equality: Do teachers with higher standards-based evaluation ratings close student achievement gaps? *Elementary School Journal, 106,* 3–20.

Harris, D. N., & Herrington, C. D. (2006). Accountability, standards, and the growing achievement gap: Lessons from the past half-century. *American Journal of Education, 112,* 209–237.

Hart, B., & Risley, T. R. (1995). *Meaningful difference in the everyday experiences of young American children.* Baltimore: Paul H. Brookes.

Jencks, C., & Phillips, M. (Eds.). (1998). *The Black-White test score gap.* Washington, DC: Brookings Institution Press.

A nation at risk. Retrieved March 21, 2008, from http://www.ed.gov/pubs/NatAtRisk/index.html

Rivkin, S. G., Hanushek, E. A., & Kain, J. F. (2005). Teachers, schools, and academic achievement. *Econometrica, 73,* 417–458.

Stiefwl, L., Schwartz, A. E., & Ellen, I. G. (2006). Disentangling the racial test score gap: Probing the evidence in a large urban school district. *Journal of Policy Analysis and Management, 26,* 7–30.

Web Sites

National Reading Panel: http://www.nationalreadingpanel.org

No Child Left Behind, U.S. Department of Education: http://www.ed.gov/nclb/landing.jhtml

ACHIEVEMENT TESTS

Achievement tests are used to assess the current knowledge and skills of the person being examined. Achievement tests include those administered to students in elementary or secondary schools and those administered to candidates for certification or licensure in a professional field. In elementary and secondary schools, content areas assessed by achievement tests include reading, language arts, mathematics, science, and social studies. Licensure and certification examinations include test items that assess the knowledge, skills, and abilities that are required for professional practice. For example, a teacher licensure examination might include items on child development, curriculum, instructional methods, and assessment.

This entry describes achievement tests of various types and how they are developed, describes their uses, and provides some guidelines for selection of specific tests.

Test Formats

The most common item format used in achievement tests is multiple choice. Other item formats used in achievement tests are constructed-response items that require examinees to write a short response and extended-response items that require lengthier responses, such as essays. Also, the National Board of Professional Teaching Standards incorporates a portfolio as one component of its examination used to certify teachers as being "accomplished."

A majority of achievement tests are group administered. Some achievement tests, however, are individually administered. An example is the Woodcock Johnson-III Tests of Achievement, which assesses examinees' knowledge in language and mathematics skills. Also, some achievement tests are administered by computer. The Measures of Academic Progress produced by the Northwest Evaluation Association is a computer-adaptive test of reading, mathematics, and science that is used by school districts throughout the United States. An example of an Internet-based assessment is the South Carolina Arts Assessment Program in the visual and performing arts, which is administered to fourth-grade students.

Typically licensure and certification tests are national in focus, whereas, most achievement tests in primary and secondary schools are administered at the school district or state level. However, a nationwide achievement test administered in the United States is the National Assessment of Educational Progress (NAEP), which administers tests in such areas as reading, writing, mathematics, and science, to a national sample of students in Grades 4, 8, and 12. An example of an achievement test administered internationally is the Progress in International Reading Literacy Study, a literacy test administered in thrity-five countries or regions.

Types of Scores

Interpretations of scores from achievement tests are typically norm referenced or criterion referenced. Norm-referenced scores allow the comparison of a local examinee's performance to a group of peers from across the nation. To achieve this, during test development, a test company recruits a group of examinees from across the nation to take the newly developed achievement test. These examinees are referred to as a norm group. The achievement tests are administered

and scored, and the scores of the members of the norm group are converted to percentiles. A percentile rank indicates the percentage of the norm-group members scoring at or below a test score. The percentile scale ranges from 1 to 99, with the fiftieth percentile being considered average.

When a local examinee takes the test, his or her test score is compared to the scores of the norm group to determine the percentage of the norm group who scored at or below the local examinee's score. A local examinee scoring at, for example, the sixteenth percentile scored below average as compared to the norm group; whereas a local examinee scoring at the eighty-fifth percentile scored well above average. Given that a local examinee's performance is being compared to members of a norm group, if the percentile ranks are to be meaningful, then the norm group should be similar to local examinees in terms of demographics.

Criterion-referenced interpretations compare an examinee's score to some benchmark or performance level. In the case of high school exit examinations, licensure tests, and certification examinations, criterion-referenced scores typically indicate whether an examinee's score is pass/fail or mastery/nonmastery. At the elementary and middle school levels, states often use criterion-referenced scores that indicate a student's performance level (e.g., Advanced, Proficient, Basic, Below Basic).

Development of an Achievement Test

The process of developing an achievement test begins with an expert committee that identifies the important content in a field. In education, for state-level tests the committee reviews the subject-matter content standards developed by the state education department. For commercial, national, and international achievement tests, panels of experts review standards developed by national organizations (e.g., the International Reading Association) and the standards, curriculum documents, and texts used in a district, state, or region for which the test is being developed. In licensure and certification, the credentialing body completes a study to identify the knowledge, skills, and abilities critical to professionals in the conduct of their duties. Experts then determine what the test should include.

Based on the review, the test company or agency prepares a test blueprint that details the skills and content of the achievement test as well as the proportion of items devoted to each content area. Test personnel work with experts in the subject area or the professional field to draft test items. Subsequently, various expert committees review the items for appropriateness, clarity, and lack of bias. After the review, the developers field test the items by administering them to a sample of examinees. When the items are returned, protocols for scoring the items (e.g., multiple-choice and constructed-response) are established. After scoring, statistical analyses of field test items are completed in order to examine item quality.

The test blueprint is then used to assemble final test forms using the items that passed quality control. If the achievement test is a norm-referenced test, then the final forms of the test are administered to age- or grade-appropriate norm groups. If the test will provide criterion-referenced scores, then panels of experts review the test items to establish the scores required for passing or classification at a certain performance level. At the end of this process, the developers publish the test and a test manual that provides technical information.

Uses of Achievement Tests

A common use for achievement tests is for monitoring student progress across years. Achievement tests also are used to make high stakes decisions about examinees, such as testing for licensure or testing for placement into a gifted program or a special education program. Another purpose of achievement tests is to compare the performance of examinees within a school setting or in educational programs. As an example, achievement tests are used in some program evaluations to determine the effectiveness of an instructional technique.

Achievement tests are also used for accountability purposes to inform the public about how well examinees are performing. In education, state testing programs, as well as the federal testing program NAEP, classify students into performance levels based on the degree of achievement the student has demonstrated

in regard to either state or national standards. By reporting the percent of students who are classified into each performance level, achievement tests are used to inform policy makers and the public of the status of education. With the federal No Child Left Behind legislation (NCLB, Public Law 107-110), the use of criterion-referenced tests for policy-making purposes increased.

How to Select an Achievement Test

In education, school districts and states sometimes select a commercially produced test rather than develop a test. In selecting such an achievement test, decision makers should review the test to determine the degree to which the test content is appropriate for their curriculum. Selection of a standardized test should consider relevance of the test items; the recency and representativeness of the norms; the conorming of the achievement test with an aptitude test; the testing time required; the ease of administration; the articulation of the test across grade levels; and the costs of test materials, scoring, and score reports. In adopting an achievement test, users should also review potential test items to assure they do not promote racial or gender stereotypes.

The test user should also determine if the score of the examinee is reliable over time. Reliability is concerned with the question, "If the examinee were to retake the examination (or an examination with parallel content), would he or she be likely to receive the same score?" In determining if a test is reliable, the test user will also want to determine the error (i.e., unreliability) that is associated with a test score.

Finally, in selecting an achievement test, users should determine if the test has been validated for the intended use. To that end, test users should investigate what types of validity evidence are provided to support the interpretation of the test scores for a particular use. For example, information should be provided to the test user regarding the content that is being tested and how that content is related to the construct of interest.

Robert L. Johnson and Christina Schneider

See also High-Stakes Testing; Standardized Testing

Further Readings

Haladyna, T. (2002). *Essentials of standardized achievement testing: Validity and accountability.* Boston: Allyn & Bacon.

Hopkins, K. (1998). *Educational and psychological measurement and evaluation* (8th ed.). Needham Heights, MA: Allyn & Bacon.

South Carolina Arts Assessment Program. (2002). Sample tests. Retrieved from http://www.scaap.ed.sc.edu/ sampletest

Thorndike, R. (2005). *Measurement and evaluation in psychology and education* (7th ed.). Upper Saddle River, NJ: Pearson.

ACTION RESEARCH IN EDUCATION

Action research in education can be traced back to the 1940s and the work of Stephen Corey at Teachers College, Columbia University. Corey and his collaborators maintained that every teacher is a potential researcher and that participating in group research was necessary for good teaching. Action research fell out of popularity in the late 1950s, as policy makers began to depend on experts to create new educational knowledge and curriculums.

Interest in action research was renewed in the early 1980s when Donald Schön published his book *The Reflective Practitioner* (1983). In this work, Schön argued that professionals such as teachers must look beyond prescriptions and formulas to guide their instruction. According to him, in the real world of educational practice, problems that need to be addressed by teachers are not simply givens, but must be constructed from the reality that exists. This reality is often "puzzling, troubling and uncertain."

Schön's notion of the teacher as reflective practitioner set the stage for reconsidering Corey's earlier ideas concerning action research. Specifically, Schön called for teachers and other school personnel, including counselors and administrators, to do research about the settings in which they worked—to do research as participant observers. In doing so, it was assumed that they would, in turn, be able to reflect, further on their practice.

What are the basic elements of action research? According to education author G. E. Mills, action research involves four areas: (1) identifying a focus of research, (2) the collection of data, (3) the analysis and interpretation of what is found, and (4) the development of an action plan based on one's research. Action research can include both qualitative and quantitative data collection. It does require, however, that teachers become active observers of what they teach and how their students learn.

Action research as a model significantly complements the social and cultural foundations of education since it empowers teachers to better understand the classrooms in which they work. It also encourages them to use knowledge gained through observation and other data collection techniques to reflect upon their work and what they do in their work in schools. In particular, action research has the potential to help teachers contextualize what they actually do, and to better understand the reality that surrounds them in their day-to-day lives in the classroom.

Eugene F. Provenzo, Jr.

See also Teachers College, Columbia University

Further Readings

Mills, G. E. (2003). *Action research: A guide for the teacher researcher.* Upper Saddle River, NJ: Prentice Hall.

Schön, D. (1983). *The reflective practitioner: How professionals think in action.* New York: Basic Books.

Schön, D. (1988). *Educating the reflective practitioner: Toward a new design for teaching and learning in the professions.* San Francisco: Jossey-Bass.

ACTIVE LEARNING

Active learning is an educational approach in which teachers ask students to apply classroom content during instructional activities and to reflect on the actions they have taken. Teachers who employ active learning approaches can have students solve problems, work as part of a team, provide feedback to classmates, or peer-teach as ways to put new content to work. Active learning requires students to operate at high cognitive levels, to analyze, synthesize, and evaluate during instructional tasks. This entry looks at how active learning works and what research says about its outcomes, as well as some criticisms and challenges.

Method and Rationale

When students take notes quietly during a lecture, they are operating as passive learners. Lectures invite student passivity, and research shows that passive students learn less. Lectures are teacher-centered activities that require only the instructor to process the academic content. Active learning approaches, on the other hand, are student centered, requiring students to manipulate academic content during the lesson and placing the teacher in an advisory role. The bottom line in active learning is, in order to learn, students must do more than simply listen. With an active learning approach, teachers design instruction that invites students to take action and to reflect on the skills and/or the knowledge required to complete a task.

Active learning takes a variety of forms because no single application or set of strategies comprises an active learning approach. At a rudimentary level of instructional planning, instructors can ask students to discuss a question with a classmate or to compare notes with a partner during a break in a lecture. Of course, active learning applications can reflect more sophisticated planning as instructors ask students to perform a skit, respond to a case study, or otherwise apply classroom content.

With constructivism as a prevailing theoretical framework in schools, active learning is present in a variety of contexts, particularly in secondary and higher education settings. Biology, chemical engineering, and medical school classrooms are among the array of cross-disciplinary contexts where active learning is increasingly present. Technology affords new opportunities for active learning in classrooms. Wireless laptops hold the promise of increasing opportunities for student-centered lessons. A lecturer can invite students to problem solve independently or in small groups from their seats in the lecture hall, making a computer lab unnecessary.

A handful of well-known instructional approaches fall within the parameters of active learning. Cooperative learning, problem-based learning, and collaborative learning all require students to be the primary manipulators of content during a lesson. Active learning hinges on the consistent benefits of assigning students to small, collaborative groups for solving a problem.

Research Findings

Research on active learning has shown improved academic performance, or at least no evidence of diminished learning among students from active learning classrooms compared to students taught in traditional, teacher-centered contexts. Studies have also shown evidence of positive attitudes to active learning. Students who possess the attributes associated with active learning environments are very attractive to employers. These students exhibit improved team skills, as well as an ability to formulate questions and to devise unique solutions, traits that are not as prevalent in students from teacher-centered classrooms.

Teachers who have employed active learning approaches report better time management as well as increased opportunities to collaborate with others (teachers, administrators, and community members) in planning and delivering lessons. All in all, teachers who employ active learning approaches feel that the lessons they develop are more creative.

Critique and Challenges

Instructors are finding active learning approaches to be increasingly accepted and expected. Because active learning is student centered, it highlights the teacher's role as a planner. Teachers seeking to remake their teacher-centered lessons will require time to revise their lectures into active learning scenarios. These teachers must create a climate to cultivate active students willing to take risks. In addition, teachers must develop their own repertoire of active learning strategies with which they are comfortable and that are effective for teaching the content in their content area.

That said, when an instructor designs active learning lessons, he or she may face criticism from colleagues who are rooted in a more traditional teacher-centered philosophy. Or, some students may resist active learning approaches. Having grown accustomed to being passive receptors of information in teacher-centered classrooms, students may balk at teachers' requirements that require a greater responsibility from students for their own learning. Students may refuse to engage in higher order thinking or to function as members of a team.

In addition, even though the literature supports active learning as an effective way to increase student learning, teachers may not be receiving appropriate training to incorporate these methods. Active learning may not be the focus of sustained teacher professional development, or active learning approaches may not be being modeled during training sessions. Teachers who desire to create an active learning environment should spend additional energy devising the cooperative, risk-free climate in which students can work.

Students face concomitant adjustments in a classroom where active learning approaches are employed. Because the focus of active learning is less about transmitting a particular body of content and more about acquiring operational skills and cognitive abilities, students may feel unsure about whether they are receiving all the essential information about a subject that they believe they need.

Timothy G. Thomas

See also Constructivism; Cooperative Learning

Further Readings

Barak, M., Lipson, A., & Lerman, S. (2006). Wireless laptops as means for promoting active learning in large lecture halls. *Journal of Research on Technology in Education, 38*, 245–263.

Bonwell, C. C., & Eison, J. A. (1991). *Active learning: Creating excitement in the classroom.* Washington, DC: ERIC Clearinghouse on Higher Education/George Washington University.

Goodwin, L., Miller, J. E., & Cheetham, R. D. (1991). Teaching freshmen to think—does active learning work? *BioScience, 41*, 719–722.

The impact of active learning: 2002–03 evaluation findings (2004, January). *Focal Points, 26.* Available from http://eric.ed.gov/ERICDocs/data/ericdocs2/content_storage_01/0000000b/80/2c/71/d8.pdf

Prince, M. (2004). Does active learning work? A review of the research. *Journal of Engineering Education, 93*(3), 223–231.

Activism and the Social Foundations of Education

The people who established the social foundations of education during the 1920s and 1930s—William H. Kilpatrick, John Dewey, George S. Counts, and Harold Rugg—were all committed to social activism. This was particularly true during the 1930s and the Great Depression, when they developed a philosophy of "social reconstruction," whose goal was to overcome the failure of the capitalist economy system by establishing a more just and equitable economic and social system.

Perhaps nowhere is the concept of a social foundations scholar being engaged in social activism more clearly articulated than in the work of George S. Counts. In his 1932 book—*Dare the Schools Build a New Social Order?*—he called for teachers to act as conscious social agents. As educated and concerned citizens, he felt that they could point the students whom they taught and the communities in which they lived toward a more democratic and just model of society.

This theme was repeated again in various articles published by Counts and his followers in the journal *The Social Frontier,* as well as in courses such as the Education 200 F, the introductory social foundations course at Teachers College starting in the mid-1930s. In the 200 F course, Counts and Rugg argued that teachers and administrators in the schools had the obligation to act for the social betterment and improvement of their students and the communities in which they lived. In general, the social foundations professors at Teachers College saw their students as future activists and leaders, who needed to be prepared for "enlightened action" and "statesmanship."

Counts felt strongly that teachers needed to throw off what he saw as the slave psychology that had dominated the teaching profession since antiquity, and, through their actions, bridge the gap between school and society. The concept of teachers taking a more proactive role in social change has been a persistent theme in the social foundations of the education field.

During the late 1980s, for example, Henry Giroux argued in *Teachers as Intellectuals* that teachers need to function as "transformative intellectuals." According to him, they should combine reflection and action in the interest of empowering students with the skills and knowledge needed to address injustices and to be critical actors committed to developing a world free of oppression and exploitation. For Giroux, such intellectuals/educators should not just be concerned with raising the test scores of their students and promoting the individual achievement of their students, but they should also be concerned with empowering students so that they can critically read and change the world when needed.

Currently, the social activist tradition in the social foundations of education most clearly manifests itself in the tradition of social justice, which calls for the conscious creation of a more just and equitable society, in terms of race, gender, and socioeconomic class. While such efforts are certainly worthwhile, they are largely theoretical. If social activism is to play a truly meaningful role in the social foundations of education, new ways need to be found to create meaning through practice, ones that are consistent with the type of social action outlined by the founders of the field.

Eugene F. Provenzo, Jr.

See also Social Justice, Education for

Further Readings

Counts, G. S. (1932). *Dare the schools build a new social order.* New York: John Day.

Giroux, H. A. (1988). *Teachers as intellectuals: Toward a critical pedagogy of learning.* Granby, MA: Bergin & Garvey.

Rugg, H. (General Ed.). (1941). *Readings in the foundations of education* (Vol. 1). New York: Bureau of Publications, Teachers College.

ACTIVIST TEACHERS

While their causes may vary widely, activist teachers are generally understood as instructors who engage social justice issues and incorporate these ideas into their teaching practice. Democratic ideals are at the heart of an activist teacher's practice, in that the concept of social equality is paramount. Activist teachers' intentions lie on a spectrum between the needs of the individual and of society in general; their actions may involve collaboration and participation within and outside of schools. Activist teachers have historically been social reformers-suffragists, labor activists, and civil rights advocates, and their work with individuals seeks to create democratic change in society.

Activist teachers work toward creating places where individuals from various cultures meet and provide a space for these individuals to respectfully inform one another. The teachers are aware that schools can be sites of social reproduction but work against this dynamic. They facilitate and situate questioning of the status quo. They have a multifaceted relationship with their students. Activist teachers may use one or more of the following concepts in their teaching:

- Social justice
- Equity including race, class, and gender
- Facilitate and question the status quo
- Cultural sensitivity
- Interactive and creative methodology
- Democratic classrooms
- Critical pedagogy
- Feminist theory
- Politically progressive ideology
- Dialogic methodology
- Reflection

Women have been prominent in the development of educational activism as they have incorporated social reform issues, including suffrage, labor, women's rights, and civil rights into their practices as educators. Jane Addams (1860–1935) and Ida B. Wells (1862–1931) were two of the founders of the Settlement House Movement, the Women's Club Movement, and the NAACP (National Association for the Advancement of Colored People), educational endeavors that helped to establish community networks to support racial and gender equity. These endeavors challenged prevailing educational methods that were aimed at social efficiency and compartmentalization.

George S. Counts (1889–1974), an American educator and sociologist, was well known for his assertion that teachers should be agents for social change. In 1932, during the Great Depression, Counts combined three speeches into one volume titled *Dare the School Build a New Social Order.* In it he asserted that some form of democratic collectivism should replace traditional capitalism in American society. Further, he believed that teachers should be agents of social change in that they should shape their students to be receptive to the idea of collective control of the economy. Thus, schools would become the birthplace of cooperative endeavors and democratic ideals. While this approach was criticized as indoctrination, Counts believed that in essence all education is indoctrinating and therefore should be used to move toward a more fair and equitable society.

Activist teachers strive to be sensitive to the interconnectedness of race and gender in classrooms. This idea is highlighted by many current feminist activist educators, including bell hooks (1952–).

An activist teacher's classroom practice includes interactive methods and democratic ideals. It is aimed at balancing the needs of individuals and society as a whole. All members of the group must have shared activities and equal opportunity to give and take. These ideals are predicated on the work of John Dewey (1859–1952). Like Dewey, an activist educator would denounce rote learning for a more interactive and experiential approach to teaching and learning. Just as Dewey advocated, an activist teacher would also place emphasis on thinking, reflection, democratic ideals, and on the value of community.

In addition, action is linked with certain values. For activist teachers, education should be centered on lived experience and should have an emphasis on dialogue that enhances community in that it leads people to act in ways that would support justice and encourage human potential. Paulo Freire (1921–1997) is associated with this type of educational activist practice.

The Highlander School, founded by Myles Horton (1905–1990) and Don West (1906–1992), is an example of activist teaching in practice. Horton and West believed that education should lead to action. Their original mission was to educate rural workers to lead the way to a new social order. This mission was expanded to teach leadership skills to those who would challenge segregation and other oppressive aspects of society. In the 1950s Horton and his colleagues established the citizenship schools movement, an effective literacy campaign that emphasized the right to participate in a democratic society.

Currently in the United States, several organizations exist to support the endeavors of activist teachers. These include the Center for Anti-Oppressive Education, Teaching for Change, and Rethinking Schools.

Beth Powers-Costello

See also Activism and the Social Foundations of Education; Democracy and Education; Highlander Folk School; Social Justice, Education for

Further Readings

Casey, K. (1993). *I answer with my life: Life histories of women teachers working for social change.* New York: Routledge.

Counts, G. (1932). *Dare the school build a new social order?* New York: John Day.

Crocco, M. (1999). *Pedagogies of resistance: Women educator activists 1880–1960.* New York: Teachers College Press.

Sachs, J. (2003). *The activist teaching profession.* Buckingham, UK: Open University Press.

ADAPTIVE TECHNOLOGY

Adaptive technology, or assistive technology, is defined as the use of devices to increase, maintain, or improve the capabilities of a person with disabilities by providing physical and sensory access, for example, through the use of a wheelchair or Braille. When used with computers, adaptive technologies are also called adaptive hardware or software. The term *adaptive technology* has now broadened to include instructional technologies used to meet special teaching and learning needs in classrooms, including those of students identified as at risk of school failure and those identified as gifted and talented. This entry looks at how adaptive technology contributes in an educational setting.

Providing Help

Adaptive technology can potentially help individuals with disabilities achieve greater independence and self-confidence. The field of special education historically has had an interest in technology, specifically in assistive as well as instructional technologies that extend an individual's abilities in classroom environments and beyond.

Various assistive technology laws have been passed to provide guidance, funding, and standards for the development and distribution of these devices. Among these, the reauthorization of the Assistive Technology Act of 1998 (Public Law 108–364), a grant program, increases the availability of funding and access to assistive technology for states to continue implementing their technology-related assistance programs. Another important piece of legislation, The Rehabilitation Act of 1973, was amended in 1998 to include Section 508, which requires federal agencies to make electronic and information technology accessible to people with disabilities. Section 508 addresses the uses of special keyboards, touch screens, and closed captioning, for example, to facilitate access to electronic information.

Even with the efforts of the federal government and individual state programs to provide this type of assistance to the disabled, challenges remain. Standards for providing access, training, and support related to adaptive technologies can vary from state to state. Further, lack of resources, trained professionals, and timely acquisition and delivery of assistive devices can hamper successful implementation of these programs.

Despite these challenges, professionals working with the disabled can maximize individual success when using the devices by being knowledgeable about the needs and abilities of the disabled with whom they work, as well as by continuing to learn about adaptive technology and how to create a good fit between it and the user. Educational preparation programs and continued professional support are key to maintaining the best practices in the field.

Since the 1990s in public schools at the K–12 level, there has been a move toward inclusive classrooms in which special needs students receive instruction alongside children in the mainstream program. Because of this, teachers and other school professionals, for example, must be able to identify technologies that support all students and be able to adapt those technologies to meet the specific needs of students with disabilities who often encounter difficulties in meeting the demands of the school and classroom environment.

Adapting Computers

Working at a desk using a traditional QWERTY keyboard and a mouse is the most common way of interacting with a computer. However, this set-up is not useful for all. Adaptive input devices can help special needs students to send information to the computer. Standard keyboards can be adapted with Braille or raised character caps attached to the keys, or the auto repeat function can be disabled. Alternative keyboards are specifically designed for individuals with limited motor skills. These usually are larger in size than standard keyboards, have larger keys with increased spacing between them, and offer increased sensitivity. The letters and numbers are often arranged in sequential order and marked with pictures.

For individuals unable to use the traditional computer mouse, touch-sensitive screens, joysticks, and head-operated devices activate and control cursor movement with less demand on the user. A puff switch, for example, activates mouse functions as the individual puffs or sips through a tube. Other input devices include voice recognition software that can convert spoken words into text on the screen as well as replicate mouse functions. Students with limited mobility also can use an electronic pointing device operated by a headset that translates eye and head movement into cursor movements.

Similarly, output devices, such as computer screens and printers, can be adapted to produce large text and graphics, including Braille characters. Black type on white background screens can be reversed to show white characters on a black screen. Large print keyboards and oversized monitors are also helpful to the visually impaired. Speech output is possible with synthesized speech that can generate an unlimited amount of vocabulary and digitized speech that records and digitizes real voices but which is limited to words previously recorded.

Other Issues

In addition to computer hardware and software, other technologies assist a student with basic life activities such as standing and sitting straight, holding a utensil or pencil, or elevating his or her head. Seating and standing products such as therapeutic seats and active standers help persons with disabilities to sit or stand comfortably and safely, while maintaining or improving their health. Walking products such as canes and walkers, and wheeled mobility products such as wheelchairs and electric scooters, allow the physically challenged some freedom of movement.

Students with learning or language disabilities can use technology to help them experience success in classrooms. Students with learning disabilities, who often struggle to organize their thoughts and produce written documents, benefit from software features that help with outlining, spelling, and grammar. Word processors with speech output help students with writing tasks by reading out loud the students' writing. Software programs are also available to assist with hand-eye coordination, study skills, and cause and effect.

Presently, advocates for the disabled support the idea of universal accessibility, or universal design of devices and technologies to achieve excellent usability by all—persons with disabilities benefit from the design and the typical user can also benefit. For example, curb cuts in sidewalks, which allow a smooth and gradual transition from the sidewalk to the street level, help persons using wheelchairs and also those pushing baby strollers, carrying wheeled luggage, or skating. Recently, universal design concepts have been applied to computers in order to include disability accessibility software as part of the operating system so that access would be readily provided and not require specialists to make modifications to the computer before a disabled person can use it.

Universal design concepts are also being applied to learning—to support students with disabilities in gaining access to the general education curriculum. While modifications to instruction and materials occur regularly for these students, the changes are usually reactive, and students will tend to experience lag time in achieving access to the curriculum. Universal design seeks to change this by providing a proactive way of thinking about access.

Lina Lopez Chiappone

See also Blind, Education for the; Deaf, Education for the; Disabilities, Physical Accommodations for People With; Special Education, Contemporary Issues; Special Education, History of

Further Readings

Behrmann, M., & Schaff, J. (2001). Assisting educators with assistive technology: Enabling children to achieve independence in living and learning. *Children and Families, 42,* 24–28.

Skylar, A. A. (2006). Assistive technology online resources. *Journal of Special Education Technology, 21,* 45–47.

Starkman, N. (2007). Making the impossible possible. *T.H.E. Journal, 34,* 27–32.

ADULT EDUCATION AND LITERACY

Historically, adult education and literacy have evolved outside the formal system of education. Adult education and literacy programs have often been referred to as nonformal education. Typically, formal education stresses the development of academic skills, while informal education stresses the development of skills learned in the workplace, or the community at large.

Approaches

Several theories and philosophies guide adult education and literacy. This entry focuses on two well-known and distinctively opposed approaches: technicist-vocational and popular liberating education. The technicist-vocational approach targets mostly working class adults and stresses a utilitarian approach in which the learner gains essential knowledge and skills in reading, writing, and computation for effective functioning in society. The main concern is to help the participants fit into the existing socioeconomic structure, particularly jobs at the lower end of the economy.

The alternative approach to technical and functional adult education and literacy is adult popular education for social transformation. This approach, typified in the work of the Brazilian educator Paulo Freire, is aimed at enhancing human potential and dignity while working for a better world—that is, a more humane, just, equitable, and sustainable society. Adult education as popular education for social transformation is built upon a critique of the technicist functional approach, and looks toward expanding and enriching the narrow view of the latter.

The focus of this type of popular education is the poor, oppressed, and disenfranchised. Freire and Donaldo Macedo define *literacy* as "reading the word and the world." Accordingly, adult literacy takes place by adults reading and writing their own reality. From these theorists' perspective, no one is completely illiterate, and no one is completely literate. The popular knowledge coming from people's daily lives and experiences is valued and used, as well as challenged. Adults study not only what their reality is but also how this reality should and can be transformed. In doing so, they embrace education as a tool for their own empowerment.

Adult Education for Social Transformation

Education for social transformation involves a language of critique or denunciation, and a language of possibility or annunciation. Freire argues that all education is political and that participants in the educational process should be tactically inside and strategically outside the system. According to him, adult learners need to demystify the reality constructed for them through the mainstream media by those in power. The adult education curricula should be built with the participants by using their own experiences and realities to help them understand whose "reality" is constructed through the media, including textbooks. In addition to learning basic skills, they should be made aware of how public consent is manufactured. As citizens who contribute to the transformation of the world, adult learners should not merely learn basic skills but should focus on understanding the world so that they can contest hegemonic social practices and systems. In Freire's model of education, adult educators assist learners in unveiling the everyday taken-for-granted realities and prejudices that result in oppressive practices and inequity.

Goals of Adult Education for Social Transformation

According to Freire, embracing adult education for social transformation should lead to an understanding of how the dominant culture works and should thus provide a basis for joining forces toward transforming the oppressing conditions in which these adults and their families and communities live. Curricula should be developed by involving participants in dialogue in the context of democratic relationships between adult educators and adult participants. Participatory adult education should include theories of human and social sciences in addition to the enhancement of their job and life skills. Thus, participants learn both techniques, and the whys and the what for, from their own point of view and for their own benefit.

Denying the human and social aspects of adult education is detrimental to learners and their growth. Adult education for social transformation should go toward building counter-hegemonic power through collective action and solidarity. In brief, it is aimed at creating critical collective consciousness and action toward a better world from the point of view of the adult learners themselves.

Implementation

Engaging in adult education for social transformation implies two major goals: achieving critical consciousness and moving to work collectively toward improving life conditions, starting with those of participants themselves. Critical consciousness may be promoted, nourished, and supported through dialogue in culture circles, an idea introduced by Freire in adult literacy programs in Brazil in the early 1960s.

To promote participation and interaction, a culture circle has no more than fifteen participants. Dialogues among the participants are facilitated by tutors. The tutors are people from the community and/or very close to participants. They are prepared to understand the core notions of democratic liberating education, and to devise opportunities for the adult participants they are working with to understand more deeply and broadly their realities and to build an understanding of the whys of their situation and why the world is the way it is. Tutors also are prepared to carry out with the participants thematic research about the topics that are going to compose the curriculum. This way of developing a curriculum increases the possibility that it will be culturally relevant and socially responsive to participants and is essentially democratic.

Not all the topics that compose the curriculum come from adult participants; the adult educator also brings some that may help in the process. Freire always stressed the topic of culture. In the culture circle, adults are assisted to understand that culture is created by people, and that people like themselves are able to change those elements of culture that are harmful to themselves. Through dialogue, adult learners can discover what elements exist that need to be changed.

From the perspective of popular adult education for social transformation, genuine participatory democracy facilitates adult participants in bringing to the classroom the topics that really matter to them, and thus assures that adult learners have a purposeful and meaningful understanding of them. Dialogical participation means that the realities of the adult participants are part of the curriculum building and development, which is opposed to the top-down curricular decisions of the technical-functional model of adult education and literacy. An example of this is given by Colin Lankshear and Michele Knobel, who used the language/vocabulary of participants' fears, problems, hopes, and dreams as the basis for learning reading and writing in culture groups. In addition, the work of Erich Fromm in *The Revolution of Hope* helps us to clarify what should be the primary values and goals of society and consequently of education in general and adult education in particular. Indeed, the end should be human well-being and the enhancement of quality of life, not "efficiency" (to produce more and consume more) as an end in itself. Adult popular education and literacy thus should aim at human fulfillment and collective enhancement of life conditions as the primary goal, overshadowing the technical goal of preparation for entering the labor force. Adults as humans are not the means for meeting the needs of industry, which are driven by profit; on the contrary, labor is the means for human fulfillment and transformation of the world for the benefit of humankind and

the environment. From a sociohumanist view of life and education, human beings are always the ends in themselves, never the means; and the ends never justify the means—even when those ends are very noble and altruistic.

Myriam Noemy Torres

See also Social Justice, Education for

See Visual History Chapter 7, The Education of African Americans; Chapter 14, Immigration and Education; Chapter 17, Reading and Libraries

Further Readings

Brookfield, S. D. (2005). *The power of critical theory: Liberating adult learning and teaching.* San Francisco: Jossey-Bass.

Fals-Borda, O. (1985). *Knowledge and people's power: Lessons with peasants in Nicaragua, Mexico, and Colombia* (B. Maller, Trans.). New Delhi: Indian Social Institute.

Fals-Borda, O. (1991). Some basic ingredients. In O. Fals-Borda & M. A. Rahman (Eds.), *Action and knowledge: Breaking the monopoly with participatory action research* (pp. 3–12). New York: Apex Press.

Freire, P. (1992). *Pedagogy of the oppressed.* New York: Continuum.

Freire, P., & Macedo, D. (1987). *Literacy: Reading the word and the world.* Westport, CT: Bergin & Garvey.

Fromm, E. (1968). *The revolution of hope: Toward a humanized society.* New York: Harper & Row.

Hurst, J. (1995, Spring). Popular education: Education—A powerful tool. *Educator.* Retrieved from http://www-gse .berkeley.edu/Admin/ExtRel/educator/spring95.html

Lankshear, C., & Knobel, M. (2003). *New literacies: changing knowledge and classroom learning.* Buckingham, UK: Open University Press.

ADVERTISING IN SCHOOLS

Advertising has contributed to the fabric of education in America on many levels. Students willingly carry corporate logos on their bodies and learn in rooms with advertising on wall posters and from books with cartoon advertisements on the covers. Their teachers tell them to quietly watch Channel One, then go to their next class through a hallway lined by vending machines with exclusive rights. They leave school on a bus with advertising on the ceiling and come back to school for the football game on the billboard-lined stadium. They sell raffle tickets for a new car and coupon books for hundreds of local businesses.

Advertising in American schools gained legitimacy and rose to prominence during the twentieth century. Corporations desire partnerships with school systems in order to market directly to teachers, students, and community members. Schools favor partnerships with corporations because corporate sponsorship may increase the school's ability to fulfill certain needs.

There are other aspects of school advertising. Many private and charter schools, for example, use billboards, radio, and television to let the community know about their work and often send promotional material to other schools. In a time of accountability, public K–12s are also required, by No Child Left Behind (NCLB), to advertise school proficiency test scores. NCLB also has provided military recruiters with as much physical space as afforded colleges and universities. Military access to students has been challenged in high schools and colleges. Parents and students may attempt to "opt out" of military contact, but generally must do so on a yearly basis.

The greatest debate over school advertising, however, involves corporate advertising to teachers and students. The question is whether the benefits of revenue, technological equipment, or instructional assistance linked to corporate partnerships outweigh the potential detriment to students who may become more accepting, and less critical, of commercial messages.

The Education Market

The members of American schools are a large portion of the population and are seen by corporations as a likely partner. To corporations, eager to gain hold of a vast and powerful market, teachers represent the largest single-occupation market in America. School employees may be solicited by insurance agents, lending institutions, politicians, and unions within school walls. Beyond their large numbers, teachers also influence school boards in the selection of textbooks, which are the single largest portion of book sales in America. They make decisions on billions of dollars of classroom materials and fundraising options. Teachers often

receive "tie-in" curricular materials to supplement the viewing of current television shows and movies. Administrators and teachers are often expected to use marketing messages on students in order to increase the budget through partnership opportunities.

Students themselves influence billions of dollars of consumer purchases in America. Due to compulsory education, American students represent a "captive market" during school hours. Students may be discouraged from questioning advertising messages presented to them by their teachers or schools. Some teachers have discouraged students from obscuring advertisements on book covers because the advertisers who donated the book covers to the school expect the recognition.

American students are exposed to corporate logos, commercial icons, and other forms of subtle advertising on a daily basis. They are often encouraged to bring in cereal box "points" to raise money for their school. Some students are forced into selling promotional materials, such as pizza cards, magazines, theater tickets, or other consumer goods that promote partnerships between schools and corporations. Students may be perceived as undocumented representatives of the corporation, rather than representatives of the school. Many students see this as a necessary part of their school experience.

Opposing Views

Opponents of advertising in schools argue that students are encouraged to trust their teachers, and therefore, students may believe that all products advertised within their school are "good" and needed. Research suggests that advertisements in schools may also lead to an overall increase in consumeristic attitudes in students. A clear example of a powerful advertising-driven partnership can be found in Channel One, programming that reaches nearly one third of all students every school day. Channel One offers two minutes of commercial advertising per day. Each commercial spot is worth millions of dollars to corporations lining up to get their message to communities all across America. Proponents of Channel One, and much of the advertisement in schools in general, claim that students are already exposed to these commercial messages at home, and therefore, they should not significantly affect the student's learning experience.

Research has demonstrated that students in low-income communities are more likely to be exposed to advertising partnerships, such as Channel One, even though the students are often least able to purchase the advertised products. This may cause psychological damage, or an increase in frustration and consumerist attitudes. Proponents of Channel One claim that because low-income schools have such a great need, a partnership is the best way to help the schools get the latest technology and instructional equipment. Cash-strapped schools, which have only a small amount of money to spend on instructional materials, are often eager to find opportunities to supplement their budget.

Textbooks in America rarely contain methods of deciphering or evaluating the elaborate forms of advertiser messaging. Opponents of unregulated advertiser access to students claim that this omission may leave students incapable of making responsible purchasing decisions. Textbook publishers are likely to be part of a multinational media corporation and unlikely to want to enable students to question their advertising.

Mark Mussman

See also Channel One; Commercialization of Schools; No Child Left Behind Act; Technologies in Education

Further Readings

Barnouw, E. (1990). *Tube of plenty: The evolution of American television.* New York: Oxford University Press.
Boyles, D. (2005). Uncovering the coverings: The use of corporate-sponsored textbook covers in furthering uncritical consumerism. *Educational Studies, 37*(3), 255–266.
Klein, N. (1999). *No logo.* London: St. Martin's.
Spring, J. (2003). *Educating the consumer-citizen: A history of the marriage of schools, advertising, and media.* Mahwah, NJ: Lawrence Erlbaum.

AESTHETICS IN EDUCATION

Human knowledge is continually expanding and improving. Despite its growth and refinement, knowledge continues to be fragmentary and imperfect; areas of ambiguity and knowledge unattained remain. These are areas for which current scientific methods have not yielded satisfactory answers. The humanities have been a source for exploring such realms of knowing, with their continual reinterpretation and investigation of the self and its lived experiences. Some aspects of human experience are not universal; they are particular and situational. These are the realms of the arts and imagination, and what has been termed *aesthetics in education.*

Aesthetics refers not only to art, but also to particular types of interactions with learning and the environment. Aesthetics is a part of education in three veins relevant to social foundations of education: education that itself is aesthetic, aesthetic education, and aesthetics as a necessary component of a moral and thoughtful life.

Education as Aesthetic Experience

Education that is aesthetic utilizes multiple interpretations, unexpectedness, spontaneity, and ambiguity. Such education embraces students' and teachers' own interactions with the object of study as students and teachers move beyond assumptions that the body must be separate from the mind's engagement in learning. This approach makes use of Maurice Merleau-Ponty's exploration of subjective and bodily experience as establishing one's knowledge of the world. Merleau-Ponty's articulation of the phenomenological harkens to Alexander Gottlieb Baumgarten's project of "the cultivation of the body" with its ability to perceive the world through its senses, which is discussed below.

John Dewey explicitly addressed aesthetics in his persistent concern for experiences within education. Much of his work explored experiences, mapping their terrain and describing what makes them complete. For Dewey, an experience is a complete, bounded, unified event that is achieved through the aesthetic. It is not a repeatable event, as each experience depends upon its context, history, composite factors, and a particular satisfaction (which is by definition aesthetic) that must exist for an experience to be complete.

This conception of the aesthetics of experiences explains Dewey's concern that all educational experiences be aesthetic, that is, consciously constructed and perceived by the intellectual, emotional, and physical self. Educational experiences are aesthetic when students engage directly in the making, whether it is the production of an artwork, a historical investigation, or scientific exploration, rather then merely learning about what others have done. While students are involved in their learning, they are also actively aware of what they are doing, and reflect upon it.

An aesthetic experience occurs when the doing of something, and the perception of what is being created, are wholly in harmony. Students' engagement in real literature, active learning about the environment through a school garden, and solving real community problems exemplify potential aesthetic learning experiences. In contrast, the nonaesthetic experience is routine, mechanized, and conventional. Worksheets, standardized exams, and basal readers exemplify such routinization. According to Dewey, an aesthetic experience is intellectual, emotional, and physical; it connects to students' past and future activities in meaningful ways. These connections occur when the learner is aware of the real context of the experience. Aesthetic experiences occur in artistic creation, but can also exist in daily life when events are undertaken with consciousness and perception. Such everyday aesthetic experiences characterize a fulfilling life and should be the hallmark of educational practice.

Maxine Greene has expanded on Dewey's writings about aesthetic transactions with ordinary events in her repeated calls for "wide-awakeness" and attention to the darknesses and lights of our social lives. Like Dewey, Greene has argued for education and living that counteract tendencies toward the routine and unconscious. There is much in people's daily lives to which they pay little attention; schoolrooms are filled with actions taken without thoughtful intention or deliberateness. Schoolrooms instead could be locations of immediacy in which students and teachers engage in rich, meaningful activities and pay attention to their own unique responses to those activities. In so doing, the teaching and learning would be aesthetic, as aesthetic education embraces the particular meaning making those students and teachers create, meaning making which does not reflect an authoritarian assumption of knowledge. Aesthetic education, therefore, leads to the development of human freedom in democratic ideas and practice.

Aesthetic experiences often result from careful consideration of a work of art. Engaging with a work of art in the presence of others enables the viewer to be aware of how different people interact with an artwork. There is a strong correlation here between noticing how different learners make sense of an educational problem or topic and recognizing there are multiple paths to solving educational problems. Furthermore, because the arts are expressions of the range of human imagination, engagement with the arts enables a person to explore dimensions of human experience that may otherwise be inaccessible. The arts are expressions of the imagination and identify possibilities that may not exist in reality. What a person cannot directly experience may be explored through literature, music, dance, drama, and the visual arts.

Including aesthetics in education enables teaching and learning to be the development of active, independent thinking and questioning. Instead of taking another's statement as fixed fact, students of aesthetic education attend to their own experiences in addition to the diverse experiences of others. Hearing such diversity of opinion becomes part of the individual experience. Students' experiences may be informed by what others say, but the students remain free to challenge others' assumptions and stereotypes because their own unique experience remains valid. When expanded to society, these practices have profound implications—society's members freely think for themselves, rather than blindly follow authority.

It has been observed that much of education is notable for its lack of aesthetics when it involves a technocratic approach to teaching that does not accommodate the idiosyncrasies and individualities of teachers and students. Much of current society dulls the everyday aesthetic, and students and teachers must engage in aesthetic education to relearn how to fully engage in lived experience. Aesthetic education is about teaching and learning a way of living, of approaching the world. It is about fostering the imagination to the construction of all the possibilities therein. It involves teaching about how to experience art, and how to engage in any experience. The engagement with a work of art does not evolve naturally from the artwork itself, but from the ongoing interrelationship (what Dewey termed a "transaction") between the observer and the work of art.

Aesthetic education develops the ability to engage in aesthetic experiences. In contrast to the expansive stance described above, some art educators consider aesthetic education to involve learning a correct and agreed upon interpretation of a given work of art. This stance presumes that the uneducated eye will be unable to fully engage in a work of art because of its distance from common experience.

Aesthetic Education as a Discipline

Another approach to aesthetic education has been to consider it as its own field of study. Discipline-based art education (DBAE) exemplifies this approach, as it argues for teaching art through four topics: aesthetics, art history, art criticism, and the production of art. Promoted by the Getty Center for Education in the Arts in Los Angeles, DBAE presents aesthetic education as an intellectual subject of study necessary to fully understand the arts.

When aesthetics is a part of art education, it expands art students' participation beyond the production, critique, and history of art. As a philosophy of art, aesthetics provides a means for students to ask critical, reflective questions about their own engagements with the work of art. While students may do so naturally on their own, they are more likely to pursue that avenue with a teacher's guidance and thereby come to a greater understanding of the artwork's value and significance for themselves and others. The influence of DBAE in the development of art education, particularly through the *Journal of Aesthetic Education* founded in 1966, has been considerable.

Aesthetics as a Moral Compass

Education that is aesthetic, as well as DBAE, draws from historical ideals of education, notably articulated by Plato, the ancient Greeks, and some Continental philosophers. Study of fine arts such as painting, poetry, and music completes the education of a cultured person because it enables individuals to conduct their lives with grace and harmony. The study of art entails learning to discern beauty as it is demonstrated in art,

and thereby evaluate creative expressions for their embodiment of beauty. The ancient Greek ideal of *kalokagathia* brought together the beautiful (*kalos*) and the good (*agathos*) in a moral statement that beauty is inherently good, and that the nature of good is beauty. If one is educated to appreciate and create beauty, then the individual and by extension society will be morally just. According to this approach, aesthetic education involves learning to discern what makes an object beautiful and how that beauty could be applied to one's own life through contemplation of its higher values. Not only to ask, "What is art?" but also to identify the best qualities of art that exemplify beauty.

Alexander Gottlieb Baumgarten reframed the term *aesthetics* to refer to a cultivated appreciation of art and the "science of sensory cognition." He moved the study of art from one focused solely on the object to an inclusion of the perceiver's interaction with the art object. Aesthetic instruction is necessary, argued Baumgarten, to develop one's sensory perceptions in order to recognize beauty. Immanuel Kant advanced philosophical thinking about aesthetics by articulating the importance of the viewer's perception, rather than qualities inherent in the work of art. Kant notably cleaved aesthetic judgment from moral judgment, identifying the former to be subjective and the latter universal.

The Greek conflation of the beautiful with the good gained further examination in a series of letters to a Danish prince by Friedrich Schiller. In these letters, compiled under the title *On the Aesthetic Education of Man,* Schiller built on Immanuel Kant's argument concerning the relationship between perception and art. The beauty and goodness of art would be, for Schiller, people's liberation from the ignoble state humanity had suffered under since civilization's pinnacle, ancient Greece. If people were surrounded by great art, or "symbols of perfection," eventually the reality of their lives would come to resemble such noble beauty. Through an appreciation of art, Schiller argued, rationality and freedom would emerge. Without art, humanity would not be fully possible.

For the casual observer, "aesthetics" conflates with "beauty" and evokes ideals of harmony and grace in the arts. Classical ideals presume that students must be taught how to understand the magnificence of a masterwork beyond a rudimentary awareness of beauty. This approach to aesthetics in Western schools often has privileged Western classical art. As such, the study of aesthetics often has been positioned as a largely elitist activity which remains separate from daily life.

Despite this, aesthetics remains relevant to all arenas of education. Scholars such as John Dewey, Maxine Greene, Maurice Merleau-Ponty, Elliot Eisner, and Wolfgang Iser have persistently advocated a study and use of aesthetics that is available to all people and develops independent, critical thinkers. Aesthetics in education comprises the best of education both for the arts and for a society that values individuals capable of making their own judgments even while aware of the diversity of others' voices.

Mary Bushnell Greiner

See also Philosophy of Education; Social Justice, Education for

Further Readings

Baumgarten, A. G. (1961). *Aesthetica.* Hildesheim: G. Olms.

Dewey, J. (1980). *Art as experience.* New York: Perigee.

Eisner, E. W. (2002). *The arts and creation of mind.* New Haven, CT: Yale University Press.

Greene, M. (1995). *Releasing the imagination: Essays on education, the arts, and social change.* San Francisco: Jossey-Bass.

Iser, W. (2001). *The range of interpretation.* New York: Columbia University Press.

Kant, I. (1991). *Critique of pure reason.* London: J. M. Dent.

Kant, I. (2000). *Critique of judgment.* Amherst, NY: Prometheus.

Merleau-Ponty, M. (2002). *Phenomenology of perception.* New York: Routledge.

Schiller, F. von (1967). *On the aesthetic education of man* (E. M. Wilkinson & L. A. Willoughby, Trans.). Oxford, UK: Clarendon Press. (Original work published 1795)

Smith, R. A., & Simpson, A. (Eds.). (1991). *Aesthetics and arts education.* Chicago: University of Illinois Press.

AFFIRMATIVE ACTION

In the United States, *affirmative action* refers to policies designed to increase social, political, economic, and educational opportunities for groups that have

historically been excluded based on various ascriptive and descriptive characteristics including "race," ethnicity, national origin, gender, religion, skin color, disability, age, and sexual orientation. Typically, organizations that benefit from federal funding are admonished to review their recruitment programs for compliance with equal opportunity laws and constitutional rights. Affirmative action regulations do not endorse quota systems and instead encourage use of pragmatic diversity initiatives that minimize intergroup conflict and maximize diverse talent contribution.

Affirmative action policies are recognized as proactive attempts to remedy historical and contemporary discrimination against subordinate groups who have been denied access to public and private benefits normally available to dominant groups. Though the emphasis of these policies is on creating subordinate group access to opportunity, the hope is that subordinate group representation will increase to better reflect their proportionate demographic profile. The methods used to achieve parity and the language used to convey the message to institutional gatekeepers are subject to selective perception and interpretation, thus opening the door to heated debate and controversy. This entry looks at the historical roots of discrimination, describes the initiation of affirmative action, and summarizes the response and current debate.

Record of Discrimination

Immediately following the Civil War in 1865, the American government took drastic measures to reconstruct a nation that had been torn apart, largely over the issue of slavery. The Constitution was amended to emancipate enslaved people of African descent, grant them American citizenship, and enfranchise them. The federal government established the Freedmen's Bureau to oversee the monumental task of assisting freed former slaves to find housing, *paid* labor, and medical care and to help provide for their basic needs of food and clothing. The Bureau set up military courts to adjudicate complaints between former slaves and their masters, but perhaps its most critical duty was building schools to teach newly freed men and women how to read and write. Of all the needs the Bureau addressed in the aftermath of the war, education efforts produced the most successful results. Literacy rates among newly freed slaves catapulted from lows around 5 percent in 1865 to upward of 70 percent by 1900.

The Reconstruction era lasted from 1865 to 1877, during which time Congress passed the Civil Rights Act of 1866, foreshadowing the modern idea of affirmative action. Terrorist groups like the Ku Klux Klan, however, effectively dashed the hope of many people of African descent to fully realize their freedom to enjoy first-class American citizenship as granted by government decree. The Supreme Court decision *Plessy v. Ferguson* (1896), which established the separate but equal doctrine, ushered in the Jim Crow era and institutionalized legal segregation in American life.

Not until 1941 when President Roosevelt signed Executive Order 8802, which outlawed segregationist hiring policies by defense-related industries holding federal contracts, did things begin to change. Black trade union leader A. Philip Randolph is credited with helping to achieve this goal. President Truman established the President's Committee on Civil Rights, through which he desegregated the U.S. military with Executive Order 9981 in 1948. A year prior, in 1947, major league baseball signed Jackie Robinson, opening the door for other Black athletes to play for major league sports teams. In 1954, another Supreme Court decision under President Eisenhower, in *Brown v. Board of Education,* overturned *Plessy* and legally ended America's efforts to maintain the racially charged "separate but equal" contract.

President John F. Kennedy made the first reference to "affirmative action" in Executive Order 10925, which established the Committee on Equal Employment Opportunity and mandated that federally funded projects take affirmative action to eliminate hiring and employment practices that may be racially biased. The next president, Lyndon Johnson, signed the most comprehensive civil rights legislation since Reconstruction. The Civil Rights Act of 1964 prohibited any discrimination based on "race," color, religion, or national origin.

In a commencement speech given at Howard University the following year, Johnson used metaphor to frame the concept of affirmative action by asserting that civil rights laws alone were not enough to fight discrimination and produce equality. "You do not wipe away the scars of centuries by saying: 'Now you are free. . . . You do not take a man who for years has been hobbled by chains, liberate him, bring him to the starting line of the race, saying 'You are now free to compete with all the others.' . . ." A few months later, on September 24, 1965, President Johnson issued Executive Order 11246, enforcing affirmative action for the first time. It was amended a few weeks later to include discrimination based on gender. Public and private institutions and industries that used federal funding were now required to document their efforts to ensure equal employment opportunities along with the results or risk losing federal financial support and face other punitive consequences.

The Debate Begins

From its informal and formal beginnings, affirmative action has been highly controversial. Critics charge that such policies give preferential treatment to people based on their membership in a group and violate the principle that all citizens should be equal under the law. They argue the notion that contemporary Whites and men are made to suffer reverse discrimination at the hands of an overzealous government trying to remedy the effects of past discriminatory practices by their predecessors. Affirmative action advocates counter this rationale by noting that discrimination is, by definition, unfair treatment of people based on their membership in a certain group. Without effective strategies to systematically assist groups who suffer institutional discrimination, achieving an integrated society that affords equal opportunity regardless of group membership would be nearly impossible, they say. The language and the means used to implement affirmative action policies appear to inflame the critics, resulting in a plethora of lawsuits and legislative initiatives meant to define the scope and limitations.

Foremost among the challenges to affirmative action is the landmark Supreme Court ruling in *Regents of the University of California v. Bakke* (1978), which concluded that the work of remedying discrimination could continue—but not in a manner that results in what can be perceived as reverse discrimination. Strict quotas systems were effectively outlawed. Throughout the 1980s, 1990s, and 2000s the Supreme Court has been busy trying to balance the rights of the dominant fully represented groups with the rights of the subordinate underrepresented groups in business, education, and government arenas. *Fullilove v. Klutznick* (1980), *Wygant v. Jackson Board of Education* (1986), *United States v. Paradise* (1987), *City of Richmond v. J. A. Croson* (1989), *Adarand v. Pena* (1995), *Hopwood v. University of Texas Law School* (1996), and *Grutter v. Bollinger* (2002) were all argued at the federal level. In 2003 the Supreme Court (5–4) upheld affirmative action in university admissions on behalf of the University of Michigan Law School by ruling that "race" could be one of the many factors considered by colleges because it furthers "a compelling interest in obtaining the educational benefits that flow from a diverse student body."

The debate over affirmative action is in many ways a philosophic one centering on a number of key questions that challenge a people's collective sense of values, morals, ethics, and memory as a nation. Crucial questions must be answered: To what extent does systemic and episodic discrimination and bias still persist, and how does it affect the ability of historically oppressed groups to fully realize the benefits of first-class American citizenship? To what degree do Whites, particularly White men, lose privilege as a result of implementing affirmative action policies designed to create access for people of color, women, and other previously excluded groups?

Some civil rights advocates call America the "United States of Amnesia" because of what they see as the quick willingness to forget a painful past stained with blatant racism, classism, sexism, human exploitation, rape, lynching, theft, and other crimes against humanity. They believe that privileged critics of affirmative action, who are quick to disassociate themselves from the past, must reflect on the legacy of privilege they have inherited. Broadly speaking, Whites have enjoyed a normative system of "affirmative action" for nearly 400 years, whereas people of African descent, Native Americans, and women can count only about 40 tenuous years of affirmative action due to the ongoing court challenges that threaten its existence. The future of affirmative action looks a lot like its past, a continual struggle

to defend its necessity and society's ability to level the playing field and provide equal opportunity access to all Americans regardless of skin color, ethnicity, gender, sexual orientation, national origin, creed, or disability.

Jonathan Lightfoot

See also African American Education; *Brown v. Board of Education*; Civil Rights Movement; Desegregation; Educational Equity: Gender; Educational Equity: Race/Ethnicity; Individuals with Disabilities Education Act; Mexican Americans and Access to Equal Educational Opportunities; Minority Student Access to Higher Education; Privilege; Slave Codes and Literacy; State Role in Education; White Privilege; Women, Higher Education of

Further Readings

Bell, D. (2003). Diversity's distractions. *Columbia Law Review, 103,* 1622–1633.

Fullinwider, R. K., & Lichtenberg, J. (2004). *Leveling the playing field: Justice, politics, and college admissions.* Lanham, MD: Rowman & Littlefield.

Harris, L. C. (2003). Contesting the ambivalence and hostility to affirmative action within the Black community. In T. L. Lott (Ed.), *A companion to African-American philosophy* (pp. 324–332). Malden, MA: Blackwell.

Martinas, S. (1998). *Shinin' the lite on White privilege.* Retrieved on February 1, 2007, from http://www.prisonactivist.org/cws/sharon.html

Stroud, S. (1999). The aim of affirmative action. *Social Theory and Practice, 25,* 385–408.

African American Education

The long struggle of the African American community to secure the right to an education reflects the struggle of many other oppressed groups. The African American community, perhaps more than any other group, has worked diligently to obtain that highly regarded commodity only to encounter great opposition at almost every turn. Despite the vigilance with which their attempts were thwarted, the Black community has been able to make extraordinary strides and forever change the landscape of education in the United States. Characterized by oppression, resistance, and proactive effort, the complex history of African American education is not only the study of a marginalized group but is central to a holistic understanding of the social and cultural foundations of education.

This entry unfolds primarily chronologically, beginning with African American education in slavery and moving through Reconstruction, segregated schools, and the move for desegregation before reflecting upon contemporary issues related to African American education.

Education in Slavery

Although art and culture had been an integral part of their lives in Africa, the Africans forcibly brought to the United States from 1619 on found opportunities to expand their minds were actively limited. While their technical classification at this time was as indentured servants, their journey was not voluntary, and, unlike White indentured servants, their term of service had no time limit. The fear that an educated Black population would be a rebellious one led to the proliferation of laws against educating Blacks across the South beginning in 1680 in Virginia.

By the mid-1800s most Southern states had enacted laws prohibiting Black literacy, which often applied to free Blacks as well. While much focus is on the South's role at this time, Black children attempting to enter White schools in the North often met with hostility and even violence. The *Roberts v. Boston* (1949) decision upholding school segregation in Boston would later serve as precedent for the Supreme Court's sanction of segregated public schools nationwide in 1896.

The concern over Black literacy in the South may have had some merit since many successful escapees and leaders of slave rebellions were literate. The penalty for learning to read and write varied, but included having a thumb or forefinger removed, being whipped, and in some cases, even death. The vigilance with which these laws were enforced merely served to strengthen the resolve among many Black people to learn to read and write. Across the nation many Black people learned to read and write in any way they could—often teaching themselves, learning secretly at night or in clandestine schools, and even

taking informal lessons from the school-age children of White slave owners. Booker T. Washington taught himself to read while enslaved, remarking that the prohibited nature of learning to read only further fueled his curiosity and tenacity to do so.

The Postwar Years and Reconstruction

After their emancipation and the end of slavery in 1865, the thirst for an education among the newly freed people was acute; however, the Black community quickly found that obtaining an education would still be a difficult task. The value of an education was well known to the Black community, especially when it came time to negotiate labor contracts and settle prices for their crops after harvest. The ease with which illiterate Blacks could be taken advantage of was another motivation to push for an education.

Although their position in the new market was often precarious, many Blacks made the provision of a schoolhouse and teacher a condition of their employment contracts. One of the biggest problems was that very few school facilities existed in the South, even for White children, as the former planter class strongly opposed the concept of public education. The Black community used their newfound political power as well as their collective resources in the early years of Reconstruction to campaign for state-sponsored education. These efforts were largely successful, and in a few short years every Southern state had a provision for separate public schools for Blacks and Whites, albeit with limited funding for additional resources such as buildings, teachers, and supplies for poor White and Black children.

By 1870 nearly one quarter of Black school-age children were enrolled in school. The majority of the support came from within their own African American communities, but they also relied upon support from the Freedmen's Bureau, the Rosenwald Fund, benevolent Northern missionaries, and Southern Whites. Many Northern missionaries came south looking to assist with this enormous project and taught in freedman's schools, but also found an extensive existing network of stable and self-sufficient African American education collectives.

The tremendous progress made by the Black community toward the provision of education was abruptly ended in 1877. Reconstruction was effectively over when the botched presidential election of 1876 led to the famed Compromise of 1877, which elected Rutherford B. Hayes to the presidency in exchange for the removal of federal troops from the South. The former planter class had been campaigning to end Reconstruction efforts, particularly those directed toward education, because they threatened the hierarchical agrarian society integral to their continued rule. As they regained control of Southern governments, their efforts to thwart Black education became more entrenched.

By the latter half of the nineteenth century, the Black community's drive to provide education to its members could not be reversed. Blacks saw education as inextricably tied to their true exercise of freedom. This unyielding passion eventually forced the former planter class to become more moderate in their views of education, especially as it became clear that without intervention it was possible for a literate Black population to emerge in the face of a largely illiterate White population. However, as the system of public education became more widespread, the money collected from all taxpayers was systematically diverted toward the provision of education for White students.

The Black community continued to rely on itself to provide educational resources for its schools, often imposing a system of "double taxation" on itself whereby after their tax money was diverted to White schools they would tax themselves again to provide financial and tangible resources to their own schools. The support did not end there, as the Black community also contributed many tangible resources as well, including buses (transportation), desks, land, fuel and other essential resources. They continued to provide these resources even as these materials were freely provided to White schools.

The Black community was largely committed to a liberal education that would prepare Blacks for economic and political independence. Many Whites, however, including those providing critical (although meager) financial support, saw more merit in the provision of vocational education that would prepare Black people for lower agricultural and technical

positions and facilitate the continued control of the planter aristocracy. They saw the schoolhouse as an opportunity to educate Black children to accept their place in the Southern racial hierarchy. Educational materials furnished to Black schools, including materials received from Northern missionaries, were often designed to foster feelings of racial subordination.

This debate over the purpose and direction of Black education was captured by two central Black leaders of the time. Booker T. Washington, a former slave, advocated for the uplifting of the Black community through vocational education at institutions—such as Hampton, where he was educated, and Tuskegee, which he founded—to foster widespread economic and political independence. Harvard-educated W. E. B. Du Bois felt strongly about a classical liberal arts education, particularly for an elite "Talented Tenth" of the Black community.

Jim Crow Segregation

While segregation by race was the norm in the postwar years, it was formally codified into law in the 1896 *Plessy v. Ferguson* case where Homer Plessy, a man who was seven-eighths White, sued after being removed from the Whites-only car of a segregated train in Louisiana. He had intentionally sat in the car to challenge the constitutionality of the segregation law. To his surprise, the Supreme Court ruled that providing separate accommodations, as long as they were equal, was not a violation of the equal protection clause of the Fourteenth Amendment.

From here the Jim Crow era of segregation began and separate accommodations for Blacks and Whites were seen in every aspect of society, including education. However, while segregated facilities were common, they were seldom equal. For example, at the turn of the century, Mississippi's Black students comprised almost 60 percent of the school-age population yet received only 19 percent of the education expenditures. Alabama spent almost $23 for each of its White students, but less than $1 for each Black student. This trend continued throughout the era. In 1930 Alabama spent $37 per White student versus only $7 per Black student, Georgia spent $32 versus $7, Mississippi $31 versus $6, and South Carolina $53 per White student versus $5 per Black student. Despite the glaring disparities in Black-White school expenditures, historians such as Vanessa Siddle Walker have documented the success some of these Black schools had in educating their students.

Brown v. Board of Education and School Desegregation

In the late 1920s the fight against segregated schools began at Howard Law School under Charles Hamilton Houston. His vision was to train a cadre of Black lawyers who would go on, through what became the NAACP Legal Defense Fund, to fight Jim Crow segregation in schools. After a successful attack on racial segregation in higher education, the team, now led by Thurgood Marshall, turned its attention to segregation in elementary and secondary schools.

The case argued before the Supreme Court was actually comprised of five separate cases from across the nation. These were *Briggs v. Elliot* in South Carolina, *Davis v. Prince Edward County* in Virginia, *Bolling v. Sharpe* in Washington, D.C., *Beulah v. Gebhart* and *Belton v. Gebhart* in Delaware, and the infamous *Brown v. Board of Education of Topeka*, which originated in Kansas and became the banner under which all five cases would be brought to court. The Supreme Court issued its ruling, after some delay, on May 17, 1954, marking a historic moment in U.S. education.

Chief Justice Earl Warren read the unanimous opinion of the Court, which held that separating students for instruction solely on the basis of race, even if facilities were equal, was a denial of equal protection rights guaranteed under the Fourteenth Amendment. The doctrine of equal educational opportunity was created with this ruling. The Court offered a second ruling the following year as to the implementation of its decision. In this decision, referred to as *Brown II,* the Court held that these changes should occur "with all deliberate speed," a ruling for which the Court has been criticized for inciting massive delays and resistance to its prior ruling.

Reaction to the decision from Whites across the South was swift and overwhelmingly negative. There was little support from President Eisenhower or Congress either. Delays using the courts were a popular tactic in avoiding desegregation and at this time nearly 500 laws and resolutions to thwart desegregation efforts were undertaken across the South. Some schools opted to shut their public schools down entirely rather than submit to desegregation. In Little Rock, Arkansas, nine Black high school students, known as the "Little Rock Nine" faced opposition from the governor when trying to integrate Central High School and could only attend when President Eisenhower reluctantly sent in the National Guard.

Desegregation occurred very slowly, if at all, into the 1960s until the civil rights movement and a more favorable president and Congress enacted legislation containing the enforcement power to mandate desegregation without further delay. The 1964 Civil Rights Act, 1965 Voting Rights Act, 1965 Elementary and Secondary Education Act (ESEA), 1971 *Swann v. Charlotte-Mecklenberg Board of Education* Supreme Court decision, and the 1972 Emergency School Aid Act (ESAA) all served to forward the cause of school desegregation. Further legislative and judiciary action in the next several years continued the forward progress and rates of desegregation began to rise significantly.

The *Brown* decision could address desegregation only in the places where it was codified by law, known as *de jure* (by law) segregation. In other places racial segregation was known as *de facto,* or due to circumstances not mandated by law, such as residential segregation. Therefore, some schools, particularly in the North, were not held to the *Brown* decision even though Northern schools were often just as segregated. The 1974 *Milliken v. Bradley* case addressed desegregation in the North, where it was common for predominantly minority urban centers to be surrounded by White suburban districts. In this case, a plan to integrate Detroit through an interdistrict, city-suburban desegregation plan was implemented. It was blocked by the Supreme Court, which ruled that unless it could be proven that the suburban districts were liable for causing the segregation in the city, they could not be held to the remedy. The inability to include suburban districts in desegregation plans proved to be a significant roadblock to achieving meaningful desegregation in the North.

The *Milliken* case marked the beginning of the federal retreat from school desegregation efforts. School desegregation rates continued to climb, but the federal government increasingly backed away from these efforts. The tide of forward progress shifted drastically in the 1990s with three important Supreme Court cases, *Board of Education of Oklahoma City v. Dowell* (1991), *Freeman v. Pitts* (1992), and *Missouri v. Jenkins* (1995). Collectively, these cases served to remove federal mandates for further desegregation, effectively allowing schools to return to segregated schooling options, and preventing many school districts from continuing desegregation plans on even a voluntary basis.

Contemporary Issues

With the reversal of support from the Supreme Court, a rapid rise in resegregation can be seen in schools today. Researchers from the Civil Rights Project at Harvard University have documented this change. Some school districts are actually more segregated than they were before desegregation was implemented, even as schools today are more diverse than ever. Black and Latino students are the most segregated students, and many of these students find themselves in "apartheid" schools where over 99 percent of the student body is Black or Latino.

In addition to these segregation issues, known as between-school segregation (or first-generation segregation), there is also a phenomenon of within-school segregation (or second-generation segregation), which includes tactics that perpetuate segregation at the classroom level. For example, tracking, abuse of suspensions and expulsions, and inappropriate gifted and special education placements are all methods that can segregate students by race. African American students are disproportionately represented in low-track and special education classes, as well as among disciplinary cases.

Today's schools continue to struggle to best meet the needs of African American students. The legacy of the historical and contemporary disenfranchisement of these students can be seen in the achievement gap that exists between African American and, in particular, White and Asian students. It remains to be seen how schools will honor the legacy of passion for and dedication to education historically shown by the Black community and successfully support the learning needs of all students.

Terah Talei Venzant

See also Achievement Gap; *Brown v. Board of Education;* Desegregation; Educational Equity: Race/Ethnicity

See Visual History Chapter 7, The Education of African Americans; Chapter 13, Exhibit of American Negroes: *Exposition Universelle de 1900*; Chapter 24, The Farm Security Administration's Photographs of Schools; Chapter 25, Civil Rights

Further Readings

Anderson, J. D. (1988). *The education of Blacks in the South, 1860–1935.* Chapel Hill: University of North Carolina Press.

Kluger, R. (1975). *Simple justice: The history of* Brown v. Board of Education *and Black America's struggle for equality.* New York: Knopf.

Ladson-Billings, G. (1994). *The dreamkeepers: Successful teachers of African American children.* San Francisco: Jossey-Bass.

Walker, V. S. (1996). *Their highest potential: An African American school community in the segregated South.* Chapel Hill: University of North Carolina Press.

Williams, H. A. (2005). *Self-taught: African American education in slavery and freedom.* Chapel Hill: University of North Carolina Press.

AFRICAN AMERICAN EDUCATION: FROM SLAVE TO FREE

The resiliency and determination of African Americans to become literate, as part of a long historical struggle against slavery and racism in favor of freedom and equality, gives testimony to the value they placed on education. During the period of slavery, the desire for literacy was in itself an act of resistance. The quest for book learning served as a direct challenge to the repressive law and social customs that strove to keep both enslaved and free African Americans illiterate, as literacy meant empowerment and freedom from enslavement.

Such appreciation for the written word was passed down for generations in the slave community until slavery's abolition. After slavery, this cultural appreciation for book learning among freed Southern Blacks flourished and took on new forms. As an ideal, literacy still equated with freedom, only this time it related to the extension of personal freedoms as citizens in a democracy and it served as the foundation for citizenship and individual and collective improvement for Blacks. This entry recalls that history.

During the Slavery Era

On the eve of the Civil War (April 1861), less than 5 percent of the 4.5 million African Americans living in the United States had ever attended school. Consequently, the vast majority of African Americans, 90-plus percent, were deemed illiterate. The primary reason for the lack of literacy and schooling opportunities among African Americans was slavery (4 million African Americans were still enslaved on the eve of the Civil War) and the various antiliteracy laws established to deny or restrict them from learning.

The Role of Literacy

Nearly every American colony, and later state, prohibited or restricted teaching free and enslaved African Americans to read or write. South Carolina was the first. As early as 1740, the colony enacted a law that forbade the teaching of enslaved African Americans. Thirty years later, colonial Georgia enacted a similar statute.

In the American South restrictions against African American literacy grew worse during the antebellum or pre–Civil War era. The laws against teaching enslaved African Americans to read and write during the first half of the nineteenth century grew out of a variety of fears and concerns, the most straightforward concern being the use of literacy as a means to freedom (such as the forging of passes for escape).

By 1840, the slave-sanctioning states of Alabama, Georgia, Louisiana, North Carolina, South Carolina, and Virginia imposed punishment such as fines, public whippings, and/or imprisonment on anyone caught teaching enslaved or free African Americans. Arkansas, Kentucky, and Tennessee never legally forbade the teaching of enslaved African Americans, but public opinion against African American literacy had so hardened that the actual opportunities for enslaved Blacks and free persons of color to learn decreased as much as in states where illiteracy was legally mandated. Mississippi, Missouri, and Maryland never statutorily penalized anyone associated with teaching African Americans. Rather, they barred public assemblages of African Americans for educational purposes and strongly discouraged Whites from assisting Blacks in "book learning."

Harsh Repression

Local sentiment served as an additional impediment to Southern-born African Americans becoming literate during the antebellum era. Proslavery ideologues assumed only madmen would teach their slaves to read or mingle with literate free Blacks. Most believed that slaves should only receive instruction that would qualify them for their "particular station" in life. These sentiments were ingrained points of view by the 1840s, and they complemented the growing number of aforementioned laws banning or hindering literacy among African Americans. Similarly, they served not only as a rationale for the continued maintenance of hereditary slavery and *de jure* (by law) segregation of African Americans in a democratic society, but also to validate the pseudoscience of the day that determined African Americans to be by nature genetically inferior and accordingly incapable of learning.

Enslaved African Americans who aspired to become literate had to learn in secrecy or among individuals they trusted or assumed were uninformed of the law. Many learned firsthand the horrors that awaited a slave able to obtain some book learning. As a child during slavery, William Heard personally witnessed the punishment inflicted on a slave who secretly learned the rudiments of literacy. Heard starkly remembered that any slave caught writing would have his forefinger cut from his right hand. Disfigurement was to ensure that a literate slave never wrote again, because a slave able to write could literally write his or her own pass to freedom. Former slave Lucindy Jurdon had similar recollections. Correspondingly, Arnold Gragston of Macon County, Kentucky, recalled that when his master suspected his slaves of learning to read and write, he would call them to the big house and severely beat them. Still, despite the dangers and difficulties, countless slaves learned to read and write.

In fact, historians speculate that by 1860, 5 to 10 percent of enslaved African Americans had acquired some degree of literacy without ever attending school. Some would learn from the slaveowners themselves, or from a fellow enslaved person who learned to read or write earlier in life, but most would learn to read and write from the slaveowner's children, who were not cognizant of the antiliteracy laws or local sentiment that discouraged teaching their young Black friends what they had learned in school.

The Civil War and Reconstruction

The fact that a small percentage of African Americans acquired a rudimentary education during enslavement was significantly important during and after the Civil War. These literate African Americans would serve as some of the first teachers to the masses of former slaves who aspired to become literate during enslavement but were not allowed because of slavery and the law. When various Southern states seceded from the Union to form the Confederacy, the nation no longer recognized the laws or sovereignty of these states; accordingly, the antiliteracy laws that hitherto denied African Americans opportunities to become literate or attend school became null and void.

Educating Themselves

Formerly enslaved African Americans throughout the South apparently were well aware of the changes. This was particularly true after 1863 when the nation ratified the Emancipation Proclamation. Liberated Blacks throughout the South immediately demonstrated their lifelong desire for acquiring an education by building and attending schools. Their goal was to use schooling as a means to obtain liberty and literacy for citizenship. But even before the Emancipation Proclamation, as early as 1861, free, freed, fugitive, and enslaved African Americans throughout the South established churches and schoolhouses for individual and collective improvement, and former slaves and freeborn Southern Blacks, literate and barely literate, served as these schools' first teachers.

All the same, the most impressive history of African Americans attempting to educate themselves came after emancipation. Between 1863 and 1870, countless former slaves rushed to the schoolhouse with the hopes of learning how to read and write. In his 1901 autobiography *Up From Slavery,* Booker T. Washington, a part of

this movement himself, described most vividly his people's struggle for education: "Few people who were not right in the midst of the scenes can form any exact idea of the intense desire which the people of my race showed for education. . . . It was a whole race trying to go to school. Few were too young, and none too old, to make the attempt to learn" (pp. 30–31).

Most attended what was called a freedmen school, or a school started by Northern teachers who migrated south to assist freedpeople in their transition from slavery to citizenship. By 1870, more than 9,500 teachers, with the assistance of the Bureau of Refugees, Freedmen, and Abandoned Lands—a governmental agency commonly referred to as the Freedmen's Bureau—taught nearly 250,000 pupils in more than 4,300 schools.

Freedom Schools

Another type of grassroots school that arose in the immediate emancipation years was what the late historian Herbert Gutman called "schools of freedom." "Freedom schools" were established, financed, and maintained by former slaves, with only the minimal assistance of others. These virtually self-sufficient schools arose in every locale following the Civil War and historians are finally giving them the attention they deserve.

The collective effort on the part of formerly enslaved African Americans in these freedom schools served as the catalyst for the aforementioned educational activities of Northern freedmen aid and missionary organizations. These agencies and organizations went south to "uplift" and educate former slaves only to find them already engaged in the processes of learning in every state they entered. This surprised some Northerners who maintained preconceived and generalized notions that all enslaved African Americans were downtrodden and in desperate need of guidance and assistance.

Nonetheless, the combined energies and educational activities of Northerners, freedpeople, and the Freedmen's Bureau, systematically educated a people who had been historically denied an education, so much so that by the end of the nineteenth century nearly 60 percent of all African Americans in the South over the age of ten were deemed literate. This meant that in less than forty years literacy rates among African Americans had increased sixfold.

Christopher M. Span

See also Freedmen's Bureau; Slave Codes and Literacy

See Visual History Chapter 7, The Education of African Americans

Further Readings

Anderson, J. D. (1988). *The education of Blacks in the South, 1860–1935.* Chapel Hill: University of North Carolina Press.

Anderson, J. D. (1995). Literacy and education in the African-American experience. In V. Gadsden & D. Wagner (Eds.), *Literacy among African-American youth: Issues in learning, teaching, and schooling* (pp. 19–37). Creskill, NJ: Hampton Press.

Cornelius, J. (1983). We slipped and learned to read: Slaves and the literacy process, 1830–1865. *Phylon, 44,* 171–186.

Cornelius, J. (1991). *When I can read my title clear: Literacy, slavery, and religion in the antebellum South.* Columbia: University of South Carolina Press.

Genovese, E. (1974). *Roll, Jordan, roll: The world the slaves made.* New York: Pantheon Books.

Gutman, H. G. (2000). Schools for freedom. In T. C. Holt & E. Barkley Brown (Eds.), *Major problems in African-American history* (Vol. 2, pp. 388–401). Boston: Houghton Mifflin.

Heard, W. (1924). *From slavery to the bishopric in the A.M.E. church.* New York: Arno Press.

Irons, P. (2003). *Jim Crow's children: The broken promise of the* Brown *decision.* New York: Viking.

Rawick, G. (1972). *The American slave: A composite autobiography* (19 vols.). Westport, CT: Greenwood Press.

Span, C. M. (2002). Alternative pedagogy: The rise of the private Black academy in early postbellum Mississippi, 1862–1870. In N. Beadie & K. Tolley (Eds.), *Chartered schools: Two hundred years of independent academies in the United States, 1727–1925* (pp. 211–227). New York: Routledge.

Span, C. M. (2002). I must learn now or not at all: Social and cultural capital in the educational initiatives of formerly enslaved African Americans in Mississippi, 1862–1869. *Journal of African American History, 87,* 196–205.

Span. C. M., & Anderson, J. D. (2005). The quest for "book learning": African American education in slavery and freedom. In A. Hornsby, Jr., D. P. Aldridge, & A. Hornsby (Eds.), *A companion to African American history* (pp. 295–311). New York: Blackwell.

Washington, B. T. (1967). *Up from slavery* (Reprint). New York: Airmont. (Original work published 1901)

Williams, H. A. (2005). *Self-taught: African American education in slavery and freedom.* Chapel Hill: University of North Carolina Press.

AFRICAN AMERICAN PRIVATE ACADEMIES

Dissatisfied with a second-rate education, Africans in America and African Americans historically have opened independent schools or private academies in attempts to either integrate segregated schools or gain influence over the policy, curriculum, and instruction of schools operated for them by European Americans.

In the 1800s, Black parents complained that private schools operated by White religious and benevolent societies did not expect enough of Black students. Frustrated, African Americans established charitable societies (African Woolman Benevolent Society, The Phoenix Society, and the Society for the Promotion of Education Among Colored Children, Savannah Education Association, the American Missionary Association), which in turn established over 150 thriving private academies.

These academies provided high quality education for Black youth in an inhospitable South where a poor establishment view of Black intelligence denied educational opportunity to African Americans. The instruction in academies was highly structured and inclined toward college preparation. In fact, this schooling led easily to college admission. The typical academy did not emphasize industrial education, but did focus on respect for the dignity of labor.

Today half a dozen private academies for African Americans are still in operation, forming the Association of African American Boarding Schools. The schools are Laurinburg Institute, Laurinburg, North Carolina; Piney Woods Country Life School, Piney Woods, Mississippi; Southern Normal School, Brewton, Alabama; Pine Forge Academy, Pine Forge, Pennsylvania; and Redemption Christian Academy, Troy, New York.

Paul Green

See also African American Education

Further Readings

Institute for Independent Education. (1991). *On the road to success: Students at independent neighborhood schools.* Washington, DC: Author.

AFROCENTRIC EDUCATION

Afrocentrism is a multifaceted "racial project" that seeks to reorient how all children (though, most importantly, African American children) learn about the roots of Western civilization. Pointing to the miseducation that African Americans have received throughout the history of the United States, Afrocentrism aims to decenter Eurocentric biases in the standard social studies and history curriculum by establishing Black Egypt as the cradle of Western culture. Scientific discoveries, medicine, philosophy, mathematics, and art are said to have emerged in northern Africa and to have been stolen by the ancient Greeks, who then represented these accomplishments as their own. By teaching children a corrected history of their ancestors, Afrocentrism's advocates intend to improve the educational achievement of African American children.

Based on the scholarship of several key figures, including Molefi Asante, Asa Hilliard, and Maulana Karenga, Afrocentrism is known as an "essentialist" philosophy of race, which argues not only that ancient Africa's great accomplishments have been overlooked in the standard curriculum, but also that all descendants of Africa—no matter where they now live, following the Black diaspora—are essentially similar in terms of cognitive, cultural, and aesthetic characteristics. In keeping with this philosophy, Afrocentrists argue that African-descended school children must be taught new content about their history in the curriculum, using new pedagogical methods. Among the different teaching methods proposed are more cooperation than competition, an emphasis on rhythm, and repetition.

Afrocentrism differs from the more widely recognized multiculturalist curriculum supported by most educators. While multiculturalism has many variations, its proponents generally seek to infuse standard history and social studies curricula with a pluralist appreciation of the contributions of all cultures, while also encouraging students to view history from multiple perspectives. Afrocentrists consider the reforms advocated by multiculturalists to be both inadequate for solving the problem of African American inequality and ideologically suspect. Rather than placing a few sporadic and disconnected items about African Americans into a fundamentally biased curriculum—the charge Afrocentrists make against multiculturalism—Afrocentrism's supporters argue that public school curricula must be fundamentally transformed to emphasize the uniqueness of African peoples and the impact of African people on world civilization. Afrocentric scholars believe that their mission is revolutionary, rather than reformist, and as such, irreconcilable with the conventionally pluralist claims of multiculturalism.

A spate of Afrocentric curriculum challenges occurred in the 1980s and 1990s, mainly in school districts with majority African American students and teaching staff. Some of the most visible sites for challenge were in Washington, D.C.; Detroit, Michigan; Atlanta, Georgia; and Camden, New Jersey. The first district to seriously incorporate Afrocentric materials into its curriculum was Portland, Oregon, where the baseline essays attracted national attention, both from supporters and detractors. A related challenge also occurred in Oakland, California, where school district officials received widespread criticism for proposing to teach Ebonics (Black English vernacular) as a recognized language.

Amy J. Binder

See also Black English Vernacular; Curriculum Challenges in Schools; Multiculturalism, Philosophical Implications

Further Readings

Asante, M. K. (1990). *Kemet, Afrocentricity, and knowledge.* Trenton, NJ: Africa World Press.

Binder, A. J. (2002). *Contentious curricula: Afrocentrism and creationism in American public schools.* Princeton, NJ: Princeton University Press.

Marable, M., & Mullings, L. (1994). The divided mind of Black America: Race, ideology, and politics in the post civil rights era. *Race and Class, 36,* 61–72.

AFTER-SCHOOL EDUCATION

After-school education consists of structured time outside of formal schooling at youth-serving agencies that offer academic activities (homework help and tutoring, field trips, community service) as well as nonacademic activities such as cooking, sports, crafts, and unstructured playtime. Frequently aimed at low-income, minority urban youth, after-school programs incorporate both enrichment and protectionist aspects and function either independently of (or supplemental to) school activities. This entry recalls the history of after-school education and current issues related to practice.

Nineteenth-Century Programs

After-school programs began in the United States during the nineteenth century in response to the following social trends: (a) the increasing population of children, (b) the gradual decline in the need for child labor, (c) the growth of schooling resulting from the passage of compulsory education laws, and (d) immigration. There was, in particular, a growing fear of children who lived in tenements and slums who had nothing to do and nowhere to go except the streets. During this period, "the street" became known as a gathering place for working-class and immigrant boys and, eventually, girls.

Most early programs were informal, unstructured, and not particularly educational, although some provided religious and moral instruction along with a good dose of middle-class values such as cleanliness, punctuality, and honesty. During the Progressive Era, children's out-of-school time made the transition from unstructured time spent on the street to semistructured opportunities created by social reformers intent on rescuing children from the physical and moral hazards of the streets.

Most after-school programs shared the following aims: to protect children and control their activities, to provide order and a safe space, to socialize children and enrich their lives, to Americanize immigrant children and support their pride in "home" cultures, to reinforce the work of schools, and to nurture children's individuality and help them adjust to societal demands. On the one hand, social reformers wanted to protect children and families from the rampant poverty, dangerous working conditions, and poor health that accompanied urbanization and industrialization. On the other, they were influenced by the child study movement, which, during the late nineteenth century, considered childhood to be a distinct stage of life. John Dewey and other Progressive educators argued that, as a result, children needed real-life problems and interaction with the social environment. In addition to focusing on the individual, Progressives expressed a concern for society. After-school programs were supposed to keep society safe from boys and girls who would otherwise engage in crime, sex, school truancy, and other socially unacceptable behaviors.

Boys' and Girls' Clubs

By the late 1890s, nascent after-school programs generally expanded to include playrooms and gymnasiums. Around 1900, continued worry about unsupervised and undersocialized working-class boys prompted the addition of "boys' work" or manual training and shop classes. Between 1900 and 1920, boys' and girls' work continued to expand, sponsored by settlement houses, private sources, and churches. In 1905, approximately fifty local after-school programs in Boston formed a national organization that came to be known as the Boys' Clubs of America, with reformer Jacob Riis as its first president.

By the late 1920s, 120 boys' clubs in 87 cities were members of the Boys' Club Federation. Most of the programs operated five or six days a week, from after school until the evening. A nominal membership fee was charged, and Saturday activities (particularly field trips) were common. Activities were arranged in terms of "classes" or focused group activity, or clubs (photography club, history club, science club, dance club, etc.). In order to keep children busy by involving them in constant activity, some classes lasted only twenty minutes. There was some attempt to separate older and younger children because of their different interests. Most boys' clubs originally had playgrounds as well as a game room and other activity rooms. Then as now, the gym was the center of activity and basketball was a popular sport.

By the early 1920s, girls made up as many as one third of the participants in some programs, although the activities were gender specific. First involved in drama, music, and domestic crafts such as sewing and cooking, girls began to engage in gymnastics and sports. Although girls were allowed to attend, the clubs were not coeducational. Girls' Club was a separate entity. When membership began dropping at both boys and girls independent organizations, however, girls were finally invited to join boys' clubs as full-fledged members. The Boys' Club would not officially acknowledge girls as members until 1990, when the organization's title was changed to the Boys and Girls Clubs of America, Incorporated.

Postwar Growth

During the post–World War II period, after-school programs positioned themselves as a "safe haven" during a time when Cold War fears predominated. Responding to the national agenda, such programs focused on science clubs just as the federal government appropriated money to schools to promote science, math, and foreign language in the national interest.

It was also during this time that low-income children began to use the streets as a form of resistance rather than survival. The rise of urban housing projects—which were often high-rise apartments with no green (or play) space whatsoever—concentrated poor children into a different kind of tenement. The term *juvenile delinquency* began to be used to identify children who were poor, marginalized, and disaffected from school. Rather than situate clubs in areas away from racial minorities, clubs now moved toward them, often locating in storefront facilities in the middle of the inner city.

During the 1960s, the War on Poverty domestic policy declared by U.S. President Lyndon B. Johnson stimulated modest growth in after-school programming. An emphasis was placed not only on preventing juvenile delinquency but also on equalizing educational opportunities. The 1966 Coleman Report suggested that the child's home and community environments and extracurricular experiences were as important as school

experiences in determining educational success. After-school programs began to focus on literacy and academic achievement. This caused a shift in funding from private sources (including individual donors, corporate donors, community chests, and United Way agencies) to federal sources and grants from philanthropic foundations. Spurred by the civil rights movement, programming addressed ethnic pride and identification and expanded opportunities for girls.

The role and purpose of after-school programs changed once again in the 1970s and 1980s. The programs became more involved in school-age child care because of an increase in single-parent households due to divorce and numbers of women entering the workplace. Children taking care of younger siblings or family members and lack of supervision left young children vulnerable to victimization and neglect.

Contemporary Challenges

The Back to Basics movement of the schools during the 1980s and 1990s tightened up accountability and administrative control and reemphasized basic skills and direct instruction. Once again, after-school programs were asked to address the problem of educational failure by concentrating on basic skills tutoring and homework help. After-school programs have generally resisted these attempts, citing their commitment to the development of "the whole child" while at the same time providing accountability to donors and sponsors. After-school programs once provided a safe haven from the drugs and gangs of the inner cities. More recently, clubs are considered to be a stable place for children living in poverty whose lives are marked by mobility and instability.

During the late 1990s, after-school programs were considered to be a partner in the effort to meet the needs of low-income children. Due to changes in the welfare laws, more children were left alone while the primary caregivers worked two or more low-paying jobs. Although the distinction is still made between being a day care center and an after-school program, more clubs are providing care for students below the age of five. Yet with economic downturns, some agencies have been forced to consolidate their activities because of shrinking donations.

Governmental entities that contribute to the operational funds of after-school programs are searching for ways to combine the services of programs and community centers in order to be cost efficient. The problem then becomes one of maintaining institutional identity. At the same time, higher education classes that require students to engage in service learning often approach after-school programs as a kind of laboratory or field experience. The end result is that after-school programs have become more burdened and bureaucratic and less free and unstructured.

Although the clubs could be a bridge between family and school, schools (both public and private) have been reluctant to mesh their activities with those of after-school programming and to capitalize on their knowledge of the child's environment. Club staff members are generally not credentialed teachers, are often part-time employees, and have short tenures with long hours and low pay. Schools criticize them for not knowing how to discipline children or for being too empathetic to them. Clubs and schools continue to disagree over the meaning and role of "play," and clubs continue to consider themselves to be more child-centered than schools.

Jayne R. Beilke

See also Economic Inequality; Progressive Educaton

Further Readings

Halpern, R. (2003). *Making play work: The promise of after-school programs for low-income children.* New York: Teachers College Press.

Noam, G. G., Biancarosa, G., & Dechausay, N. (2003). *Afterschool education: Approaches to an emerging field.* Cambridge, MA: Harvard Education Press.

Web Sites

Boys and Girls Clubs of America, Inc.: http://www.bgca.org

ALTERNATIVE ACCREDITATION FOR TEACHERS

Alternative certification allows individuals who have undergraduate degrees in fields other than education to obtain a teaching certificate through participation in training and/or on-the-job learning experiences. These programs are usually shorter in length and more intense than traditional programs. They provide many different routes to certification, and are characterized by the fact that they offer individuals opportunities to teach without graduating from a traditional teacher-preparation program, fulfilling student teaching obligations, or passing certification exams. Many districts and states around the country are using alternative certification as a means of coping with growing teacher shortages, concerns about quality and quantity of teachers, increased student enrollment, mandates for smaller class size, and the lack of diverse teachers.

Alternative certification programs and the number of people choosing to pursue these avenues are growing. In 2002, forty-five states had alternate routes to teacher certification. Today, more than one in ten teachers enter the profession through alternative certification programs. According to the National Center for Education Information, there are more than 125,000 teachers today who were certified through an alternative certification program, which is three times what it was more than ten years ago.

In recent years, several organizations have provided leadership in the field of alternative certification. Perhaps the most well known of these organizations is Teach for America. Created by Wendy Kopp in 1989 as an extension of her senior thesis at Princeton University, Teach for America recruits recent college graduates, provides them with a five-week summer training session, and then places them in low-income U.S. communities where they agree to teach for at least two years. In the last ten years 5,000 individuals have participated in Kopp's program, teaching largely in urban and rural public schools. Based loosely on the model of the Peace Corps, Teach for America has been funded in part through President Clinton's National Service Initiative, Americorps, and most recently it has received funding through the Bush administration.

There have been many spin-offs of Teach for America, some created by Kopp or by former recruits or managers in the Teach for America organization. These include the Knowledge Is Power Program (KIPP), Knowledge Empowers You (KEY), The New Teacher Project, and TEACH! In addition to national programs, state programs are creating ways for teachers to obtain teaching certification in nontraditional ways.

In some cases, the requirements are very similar to those in traditional programs.

Some educators support whereas others oppose alternative accreditation programs. Some educators in favor of these programs suggest that colleges of education are producing mediocre teacher candidates; alternative approaches that allow people to become certified without graduating from these programs offer the opportunity to recruit highly skilled people from the private sector who have developed real-world experience, they say.

Critics of alternative certification argue that these programs deskill and deprofessionalize teachers by providing them with inadequate training and by taking the education of teachers out of the hands of colleges and universities. Critics view alternative accreditation as employment programs for liberal arts graduates on their way to a real job, and they fear that this rationale affords no protection to the pupils, who are often the most disadvantaged students. It is common for alternative-certificate holders to be assigned to disadvantaged neighborhoods where students are frequently subjected to substitute teachers and inexperienced, unsupported recruits, many of whom don't last a year in the classroom.

It is likely that opinions of accreditation programs for teachers differ because the programs themselves vary greatly—ranging from full-fledged education programs with stringent entry criteria to programs with nonexistent entry requirements that make unsupervised emergency placements.

Jodi C. Marshall

See also Deskilling

Further Readings

Berry, B. (2001). No shortcuts to preparing good teachers. *Educational Leadership, 58*(8), 32–36.

Haberman, M. (1991). Catching up with reform in teacher education. *Education Week, 11*(10), 29–36.

Kopp, W. (2000). Ten years of Teach for America. *Education Week, 1*(41), 48–50.

Legler, R. (2003) *Alternative certification: A review of theory and research.* North Central Regional Educational Laboratory (NCREL). Retrieved from http://www.ncrel .org/policy/pubs/html/altcert/intro.htm

Mabry, M., & Gordon, J. (1990). The new teacher corps. *Newsweek, 116*(3), 62–64.

ALTERNATIVE SCHOOLS

Throughout its history, American education has included alternative forms of schooling that provide choices to parents, students, and teachers. Over the years, alternative schools have provided opportunities beyond those offered by traditional public, religious, and independent schools. In many different formats and motivations, they have met evolving needs.

Public schools did not exist during the Colonial Period (1607–1783). Lawrence Cremin has described the period as the golden age of alternatives. These alternatives ranged from formal Latin grammar schools to academies, dame schools, moving schools in the South, the use of tutors, and the apprenticeship system, reflecting the strong religious beliefs of the colonists.

Following the formation of the United States, the focus was on nationalism and patriotism. During the National Period (1783–1876) of immigration, industrialization, and urbanization, the common school movement was publicly supported and controlled. Private academies attracted the wealthy. Experimental educational ideas were part of the newly created utopian communities. Examples are Robert Dale Owen's vocational education in New Lanark, Scotland; Joseph Neef and William McClure's Pestalozzian School in New Harmony, Indiana; and Brook Farm in West Roxbury, Massachusetts, which offered an idealistic form of schooling within a utopian community. Catholic parochial schools also developed during the nineteenth century as religious alternatives.

During the Progressive Period (1876–1957), the individual student became the focus of alternatives to public schools. Parents, teachers, and communities utilizing Dewey's progressive teaching ideas led these efforts. Examples include the Walden School and Caroline Pratt's play school in New York and the Park Schools in Baltimore, Buffalo, and Cleveland.

During the social and political ferment of the 1960s and 1970s, parents demanded choices in the schooling of their children. These alternative schools were not state accredited or funded. An alternative schools directory listed about 350 schools with about 15,000 students and 3,000 staff. These schools symbolized the radical reform movements of the time.

They focused on changing the structure and process of education, influencing public schools. The spectrum ranged from schools as part of communes in rural settings to urban-centered, storefront schools. The middle-class White community was seeking unstructured opportunities for their children to acquire traditional academic skills.

People of color emphasized their culture and parental involvement. Examples were the Harlem Prep School, Born Free, the Unschool, Someday School, and the Sante Fe Community School. They ranged from suburban to rural, Black inner-city to multicultural schools. They could be found in churches, storefronts, homes, and old barns. Such notables as George Dennison, Nat Hentoff, and Jonathan Kozol were leaders in the movement. Kozol ran a free school in the Roxbury ghetto. Learning also began to take place within the community, like at the Cleveland Urban Learning Community, a school without walls. "Schools within public schools" were started, like that at the New School in New York. More recent efforts have focused on such alternatives as homeschooling and voucher and charter schools.

Alternative schools since the 1970s have taken on many guises, including school choice programs and independent and home-based education. They not only provide a test bed for innovation, but an alternative choice for those parents and children not interested in more traditional models of schooling.

Sally H. Wertheim

See also Charter Schools; Free School Movement

Further Readings

Brown, L. H. (2007). *Building community in an alternative school: the perspective of an African American principal.* New York: Peter Lang.

Cremin, L. A. (1970). *American education: The colonial experience.* New York: Harper & Row.

Graubard, A. (1973). *Free the children: Radical reform and the free school movement.* New York: Pantheon.

Neumann, R. (2003). *Sixties legacy: A history of the public alternative schools movement*, 1967–2001. New York: Peter Lang.

AMERICAN EDUCATION, THEMES IN THE HISTORY OF

Since the institution of schooling directly reflects a culture's essential characteristics, there are meaningful and recurrent patterns—persistent themes—in the history of American education. An understanding of these key themes, which are described in this entry, helps to explain the social and political issues that shape public schooling.

One defining theme is nationalism. Teaching children how to be "Americans"—and, indeed, defining what this means—has been a consistent fundamental purpose of public schooling. Since the early years of nationhood, influential Americans have viewed the school as a primary agency for training in citizenship, loyalty to the state, and personal identification with the national heritage, mythology, and interests. Early American intellectuals (such as Noah Webster and Benjamin Rush) realized that the United States lacked a traditional, distinctive culture, language, and historical identity, and had grown out of a national ideal or ideology that needed to be deliberately instilled in each new generation.

The common school initiatives of the mid-nineteenth century gained support in large part because the rise of immigration seemed to threaten this national identity. The launching of the *Sputnik* satellite by the Soviet Union in 1957 galvanized school reform in the interest of national defense, and the landmark 1983 report *A Nation at Risk* zealously restated this theme, charging public education with the task of safeguarding the very survival of the American nation.

Schooling has also been shaped significantly by the distinctive features of the economic system of capitalism. In essence, capitalism is a social order based on meritocracy—a presumably open competition in which winners achieve high status, wealth, and influence and losers are expected to accept the conditions of their roles as employees and consumers. Capitalism measures success primarily in economic terms (profit, income, gross national product, etc.) and tends to push aesthetic and spiritual concerns to the margins of the culture. Education is consequently defined in terms of effective management and productivity.

Since the 1840s, when Horace Mann persuaded the emerging industrialist elite to support public education because it would provide a supply of dependable, sober, disciplined factory workers, schools have been used to cultivate a compliant and productive workforce. Increasingly since the start of the twentieth century, business leaders and policy makers have steered education toward values of "social efficiency," standardization, and management of what is often called "human capital." The testing, grading, labeling, and ranking of students reflect a competitive, materialistic, production-oriented economic system. Many young people and their families value education above all else for the vocational opportunities it can open for them, if they are successful in school.

Historically, the rise of capitalism was linked to the modernist philosophy of scientific reductionism, which views the world from a materialist and utilitarian perspective. Nature is best understood, according to this perspective, through objective observation, measurement, and abstract reasoning. Complex, holistic processes are reduced to their most basic components and discrete functions. Through such analysis, modern society can develop powerful tools and technologies to manage natural resources, and human energies are viewed as such resources. In the early years of the twentieth century, social scientists and educators began to apply this technocratic approach to social institutions, especially schooling. Intelligence tests, behaviorist psychology, "scientific management," and other presumably objective techniques were developed and increasingly used to provide more consistent control of teaching and learning.

At the same time, American culture has been shaped by a religious ideology that has resisted the secular worldview. What might loosely be called a Puritan theology draws a firm distinction between the natural, material world and the realm of the divine or sacred, and sees humanity as "fallen" or sinful because we are immersed in the physical world. Only through personal religious faith can one be "redeemed" or spiritually rescued. American religious life is complex and diverse, and this theology has been expressed through numerous forms, sects, and beliefs. Together, they constitute a powerful element of American culture that has influenced educational philosophy and policy.

Ongoing political arguments over evolution and creationism, the role of prayer or Scripture in schools, and the teaching of morally controversial subjects or texts demonstrate this influence. On a more subtle cultural level, the view of the child as an intellectually and morally empty vessel, needing instruction and discipline in order to properly mature, is at least partly rooted in this theological heritage. In addition, historians have shown how Puritan morality was closely aligned with capitalist values of individual initiative and the virtue of the "work ethic"; in this view, success and wealth naturally flow to deserving individuals. Schooling is then construed as a public arena for testing and grading to determine who deserves success.

Interwoven with these cultural themes in American history is an ongoing struggle for democracy. The *ideal* of democracy, expressed in soaring notions such as "freedom," "liberty," "equality under the law," and "government of the people," is widely venerated, but the implementation of this ideal has been irregular, due to social, political, and economic conflicts that have led to an inequitable distribution of opportunity and privilege. Race, class, gender, ethnic, or religious identity and other human differences have been exploited to permit some individuals access to higher status and to deny such access to others. Paradoxically, the success of capitalism, although rooted in an ideal of fair competition, has led to substantial disparities of wealth, status, and influence that provide significant advantages to a minority of society.

Schools have been greatly affected both by the democratic ideal and by the failure of American society to fully attain it. From Thomas Jefferson to Horace Mann and down to recent times, public education has in part been conceived as a mechanism for attaining a more fully participatory, democratic society—a way to equalize opportunities for personal advancement. Yet throughout the history of American education, democratically oriented policies and reforms have faltered against the biases and interests that perpetuate social divisions and inequality. Segregation of the "common" schools by race and class, even when legally banned, has continued due to patterns of neighborhood settlement and distribution of property taxes. Some of the most intractable, and sometimes violent, conflicts over education have arisen over different interpretations of, or commitment to, the democratic ideal.

Ron Miller

See also Democracy and Education; Philosophy of Education; Politics of Education

See Visual History Chapter 4, The Common School Movement; Chapter 15, Progressive Reform and Schooling

Further Readings

Miller, R. (1997). *What are schools for? Holistic education in American culture* (3rd ed.). Brandon, VT: Holistic Education Press.

Spring, J. (2005). *The American school, 1642–2004* (6th ed.). New York: McGraw-Hill.

AMERICAN FEDERATION OF TEACHERS

The American Federation of Teachers (AFT) was founded in 1916 by classroom teachers who believed that the National Education Association (NEA), founded in 1857, did not represent teachers who were interested in negotiating for better salaries, professional working conditions, and the protection of basic civil rights such as free speech and political participation. Early organizational efforts were led by activists in Chicago, such as Margaret Haley, and by Henry Linville in New York City. Linville became the first president of the AFT, and John Dewey became an honorary member. The AFT became a union under the broad umbrella of the American Federation of Labor led by Samuel Gompers. Today, it is an affiliated international union of the AFL-CIO with more than 3,000 local affiliates nationwide and 43 state affiliates.

The ineffectiveness of efforts within the NEA to democratize its organization and give a stronger voice to classroom teachers provided an impetus for the newly formed AFT. The NEA scorned the practice of collective bargaining and considered affiliation with working-class unions to be unprofessional.

It maintained an organizational structure that was controlled by school administrators who were unsympathetic to teacher-defined initiatives.

Nevertheless, early growth of the American Federation of Teachers was slow, although some organizational success was achieved in larger urban areas and in cities and towns that had histories of labor organization. The AFT adopted a platform of social progressivism that some teachers found too liberal. During the 1930s, the AFT was scandalized by the presence of Communists in their association. Though these individuals were eventually rooted out under the union presidency of George S. Counts, organizational growth had been damaged by the public perception that the AFT was a radical organization.

Societal events of the later 1950s and 1960s had an impact on teacher organization. The crush of the baby boom generation on the schools led to severe problems with overcrowding, inadequate school facilities, and difficulty in attracting teachers into careers with poor pay and benefits. The AFT's successes in collective bargaining successes enhanced its growth. The 1961 New York City strike of teachers, organized by the United Federation of Teachers and its president, Albert Shanker, closed down the city's schools and established the ability of a teachers union to carry out a work stoppage. State court rulings that removed classroom teachers from the "critical health and public safety employees" category, which included police officers and firefighters, meant that injunctions against teacher union strikes were no longer easy to obtain. One by one, the states introduced laws allowing teacher strikes. Shanker led the AFT until his death in 1997.

The NEA's adoption of collective bargaining, its inclusion of classroom teachers in the administrative structure of the organization, and its political influence through the political action committees of its state affiliates stole some of the thunder that historically had belonged to the AFT. Today, NEA membership stands at 3.2 million, while AFT membership is 1.4 million.

William Edward Eaton

See also National Education Association

Further Readings

Bascia, N. (1994). *Unions in teachers' professional lives: Social, intellectual and practical concerns.* New York: Teachers College Press.

Eaton, W. (1975). *The American Federation of Teachers: A history of the movement, 1916–1961.* Carbondale: Southern Illinois University Press.

Web Sites

American Federation of Teachers: http://www.aft.org

AMERICANIZATION MOVEMENT

Americanization has been defined as the instruction of immigrants in the English language and U.S. history, government, and culture. The push to Americanize immigrants has continually been a part of American society and education. However, at no time in the history of the United States was this effort as widespread as in the early decades of the twentieth century, particularly between the years 1914 and 1924, an interval referred to as the Americanization period. This entry looks at the roots of assimilationist ideas, the proponents and opponents of the movement, and the implementation and goals of Americanization.

Historical Roots

Americanization has been a key educational issue since Horace Mann's early nineteenth-century introduction of the concept of the common school. Mann believed the central and fundamental purpose of the public school was to teach good citizenship and democratic participation in order to produce a common culture for the good of society.

The first manifestation of Americanization occurred in the 1850s when large numbers of Catholic, Celtic, and Teutonic immigrants arrived in Protestant, Anglo-Saxon America. Nativists, Americans advocating stricter immigration laws, called attention to the increasing numbers of "undesirables," predominantly Irish and German immigrants. The "Know Nothings," named for their refusal to answer questions about their group activities, worked to prohibit undesirable immigrants from acquiring citizenship. Political Nativism reached its peak when supporters of the movement gained control of several state legislatures in the mid-1850s. However, interest in Nativist groups waned as national attention turned to the pre–Civil War debate over slavery and secession.

Immigration numbers did not increase dramatically until the first decade of the twentieth century. Immigration reached a historical high between 1901 and 1910, with 8,795,386 immigrants recorded. The next decade saw the second highest number of immigrants (5,735,811) despite the advent of war, with 93 percent of those immigrants coming from Eastern, Southern, and Central Europe. This influx of European immigrants, whose customs, languages, and traditions were different from those practiced in America, raised concern among the citizenry. Anglo-American citizens responded to their suspicion, fear, and wartime hysteria with a new nativistic movement. Americanization was seen as the way to strengthen the country by compelling immigrants to assimilate and become naturalized citizens.

The height of the Americanization period began with World War I and ended with the enactment of the Johnson Immigration Act of 1924. The beginning of war in Europe precipitated a return of U.S. resident aliens and naturalized citizens to Europe for the purpose of supporting those countries they considered their homelands. This exit caused many Americans to question the loyalties of all immigrants. The purpose of the Johnson Immigration Act of 1924 was to strictly curtail the number of immigrants from any one country.

Movement Proponents

Americanization was advocated by citizens in all levels of government and social strata. As early as 1904, Theodore Roosevelt used assimilation as a theme in his campaign for president, stating, "We have room for but one language here, and that is the English language . . . and we have room for but one soul loyalty and that is a loyalty to the American people." Woodrow Wilson, in a speech to new citizens in 1915 contended, "You cannot become thorough Americans if you think of yourselves in groups. America does not consist of groups. A man who thinks of himself as belonging to a particular national group in America has not yet become an American." Calvin Coolidge in his state of the union address in 1923 said, "America must be kept American." Elwood P. Cubberly, Dean of the Stanford University School of Education, defined the purpose of the movement as that of breaking up ethnic groups and helping individuals assimilate to American culture, thereby instilling in them an understanding of the concepts of law and order propagated in Anglo-Saxon countries, as well as a respect for the democratic form of government.

Beginning in 1915, citizens were urged to turn annual Fourth of July celebrations into a celebration of American citizenship. The National Americanization Day Committee sponsored by *The Immigrants in America Review,* a quarterly publication, along with the U.S. Department of Labor, Immigration Service, urged communities across the country to organize local Americanization Day celebrations for the purpose of dissolving the boundaries between native-born Americans and newly naturalized citizens. The event, advertised through foreign language newspapers, was promoted as an opportunity for native-born citizens to honor naturalized citizens.

The Americanization theme took different forms. Royal Dixon, Vice President of the League of Foreign Born Citizens and author of *Americanization* (1916), urged the Americanization of both recent and not-so-recent immigrants. Emory Bogardus, author of *Essentials of Americanization* (1919) and a professor at the University of Southern California, advocated the Americanization of minority groups, including American Indians, Negroes, and Appalachian Mountaineers. Gino Speranza, author of *Race or Nation: A Conflict of Divided Loyalties* (1923), urged a return to the nation's original Anglo-Saxon Protestant principles. In *Reforging America: The Story of Our Nationhood,* Lothrop Stoddard, a professor at Harvard University, urged all citizens to unite with one national loyalty.

Perhaps the most prolific writer and strongest advocate of Americanization was Frances Kellor, lawyer, settlement worker, editor of *The Immigrants in America Review,* secretary of the National Americanization Committee, and unofficial spokeswoman

for myriad committees, divisions, and bureaus. Kellor promoted Americanization for both citizens and immigrants, clarifying America's immigration policy as one of racial assimilation. She also interpreted the immigration influx as an economic asset, but proposed strict immigration policies and subsequent naturalization of immigrants in order to lessen exploitation.

Autobiographies from the period were replete with the Americanization themes of freedom and opportunity based in hard work and perseverance. *The Autobiography of Edward Bok* tells how an immigrant from the Netherlands rose from a modest beginning to become the long-time publisher of *The Ladies' Home Journal.* Bok made reference to his desire to take advantage of all America had to offer, no matter how much work was involved, while relying on honesty, perseverance, speaking English, giving back to the country, and patriotism to bring him success.

In a similar vein, autobiographies by Mary Antin, a Jewish immigrant from Russia, and Michael Pupin, a Serbian immigrant and eventual professor at Columbia University, told of the "American Miracle." For Antin, the United States provided the miracle of free education, the beneficence of the police, and the equality of all. Pupin recounted his amazement at being treated with respect and kindness by a farmer, which taught him more about the spirit of democracy than any classroom. He learned more about the democratic election process when he saw the peaceful resolution of a disputed presidential election.

Culturally Pluralistic Ideas

Many, however, objected to the all-out assimilation of immigrants, and called for the unification of diversity, not its obliteration. Jane Addams and Ellen Gates Starr of Hull House saw Americanization as an opportunity to help disadvantaged immigrants attain a higher standard of living. Immigrants could learn English at Hull House, but were encouraged to maintain their native languages and unique cultural practices. Addams contended that a person's character should be valued above his or her ability to assimilate cultural norms. Addams and Starr hoped to see American society become more cosmopolitan through the convergence of old and new cultures.

Similarly, Horace Kallen and John Dewey saw Americanization not as assimilation, but as an opportunity to combine cultures. Dewey rejected the concept of the American race, noting that no single culture could provide a standard of conformity for other cultures. Kallen coined the term *cultural pluralism* to describe the United States as a commonwealth of combined cultures seeking common goals. He believed that ethnic diversity could enrich American civilization, and argued that one's cultural heritage could not be abandoned in the manner that one might change one's clothes, politics, or religion. Dewey and Kallen saw the American as a person who had successfully integrated two cultures to form a distinctly new culture.

Opposition to the Americanization movement hardly impacted popular opinion. The Americanizers were able to strike a chord in the hearts of the American public, convincing them that the assimilation of the immigrant was necessary for the well-being of the country. However, disorganization at the national level prevented the movement from attaining its goal of reaching all immigrants.

Implementation

The general consensus of government agencies was in favor of the Americanization movement; however, no single agency was given full control over the establishment of a nationwide Americanization program. A bill enacted in 1915 provided federal monies to any organization, public or private, that desired to provide Americanization classes and established the National Americanization Committee, which organized the first Americanization Day. However, this committee was not given authority to coordinate the organization of classes at the national level.

There were at least ten governmental agencies and thirty private agencies that provided some form of Americanization training for immigrants, but without federal guidance, these agencies became rivals in the establishment of programs, often overlapping in services provided. Eventually, in 1924, at the same time the Johnson Immigration Act was passed, Congress made the Americanization movement official, with the U.S. Bureau of Education leading the program. The National Americanism Committee and the Division of Americanism were established by the Bureau of Education for the purpose of providing Americanization education for all immigrants.

Despite its leadership role in the waning days of the movement, the federal government did not attempt to manage the details of all Americanization programs, choosing to leave most plans and decisions to the local agencies that already had established Americanization programs. State and city governments as well as private organizations sponsored Americanization classes and were allowed to dictate their own standards for teaching English, democracy, and citizenship.

Church groups, civic organizations, local boards of education, and industries offered classes for the adult immigrant, while immigrant school-age children were immersed in mainstream American school classrooms, without the opportunity for special language programs. Publishers and authors, both private and public, offered many new textbooks designed to teach adult immigrants to read and write English in order to become naturalized American citizens. English language instruction was considered to be the quickest and most effective route to assimilation, "a door into your souls through which American life may enter" as noted by Judge Charles F. Amidon, while passing sentence on sedition.

Goals

The aim of the Americanization movement was to impose assimilation of all things American on immigrants, requiring them to abandon the cultures and languages of their homelands in favor of American culture and language. Three elements were considered necessary for immigrants to assimilate. Immigrants were expected to change the precepts within themselves that determined their attitudes and actions in order to adopt a spirit of democracy. In addition to inward change, immigrants had to change outwardly, putting on the habits and lifestyle of typical Americans. Lastly, and perhaps most importantly they had to learn the English language and use it regularly in all dealings, both public and private.

Full and complete assimilation was accepted as outward proof of an inner allegiance to the country. The goal of Americanization was to create a nation solidified in purpose and aspiration, which would allow the country to be impregnable to its enemies.

The purpose of Americanization classes was to mold immigrants into politically, culturally, and linguistically ideal Americans in order to become part of the American race.

Annis N. Shaver

See also Immigrant Education: History

Further Readings

Bogardus, E. S. (1919). *Essentials of Americanization.* Los Angeles: University of Southern California Press.

Carlson, R. A. (1970). Americanization as an early twentieth-century adult education movement. *History of Education Quarterly, 10*(4), 440–464.

Dixon, R. (1916). *Americanization.* New York: MacMillan.

Kellor, F. (1916). *Straight America.* New York: MacMillan.

McClymer, J. F. (1978). The federal government and the Americanization movement, 1915–1924. *Prologue, 10*(1), 23–41.

Olneck, M. R. (1989). Americanization and the education of immigrants, 1900–1925. *American Journal of Education, 97*(4), 398–423.

Speranza, G. C. (1925). *Race or nation: A conflict of divided loyalties.* Indianapolis, IN: Bobbs-Merrill.

Stoddard, L. (1927). *Re-forging America: The story of our nationhood.* New York: Scribner's.

Thompson, F. V. (1920). *Schooling of the immigrant.* New York: Harper Brothers.

AMERICAN LABOR COLLEGES

The independent labor colleges represented the most radical form of workers' education in the early twentieth century. Work People's College (1903–1941) located in Duluth, Minnesota; Commonwealth College (1925–1939) in Mena, Arkansas; and Brookwood Labor College (1921–1941) in Westchester County, New York, earned the most notoriety. They grew out of the American noncommunist left, namely the Socialist Party and the Industrial Workers of the World, which flourished during the late nineteenth and early twentieth centuries. Educational progressives also provided intellectual support by serving as trustees and guest lecturers. Although uniquely American, labor college students and teachers knew about the workers' education efforts of their British counterparts.

The labor colleges maintained two educational goals: creating a new social order and preparing worker-students for active service in the labor movement as organizers, lawyers, and writers, not as labor bureaucrats. Full-time studies at these residential labor colleges involved classroom work as well as experiential learning. Instructors generally came from the ranks of agricultural and industrial workers themselves. The formal curriculum fell into two categories: theoretical (or background) subjects and tool (or utilitarian) courses. The former critiqued capitalism in classes like labor history and economics. Guided by the notion of direct action, the latter gave students practical, organizing skills through journalism to publish newspaper reports on working conditions and strikes, public speaking to communicate with large crowds, proletarian drama (borrowing the agitprop tradition) to raise the consciousness of workers, and organizing experience through field work among sharecroppers and unskilled factory workers. The labor colleges made no explicit claims about cultivating a communal environment, but nevertheless they did. Teachers and students worked together to construct and repair buildings, cook meals, launder clothes, maintain gardens, and wash dishes, among numerous other tasks.

The labor colleges provided many of the leaders who organized the Congress of Industrial Organizations during the 1930s. Longstanding internal stresses combined with this newfound visibility contributed to their demise. Usually restrained, dogmatic differences between socialist and communist students and instructors became strident during the fluid 1930s, spawning school strikes and irreparable political and personal divisions. Because of their anticapitalist views and labor organizing activities, local and federal law enforcement agencies monitored the schools, ultimately pressuring them to close.

Richard J. Altenbaugh

See also Highlander Folk School

Further Readings

Altenbaugh, R. J. (1990). *Education for struggle: The American labor colleges of the 1920s and 1930s.* Philadelphia: Temple University Press.

Bloom, J. D. (1978). *Brookwood Labor College, 1921–1933: Training ground for union organizers.* Unpublished master's thesis, Rutgers University.

Howlett, C. F. (1982). Brookwood Labor College: Voice of support for Black workers. *Negro History Bulletin, 45,* 38–39.

AMERICAN SIGN LANGUAGE

In the early twentieth century, most schools for the deaf across the nation used the "natural" sign language, now called American Sign Language (ASL). Most of the administrators and teachers who ran these schools were deaf. Not until 1880, after an international conference in Milan, Italy, did educators decide that the oral approach was the best way to teach deaf children. The rationale was that to assimilate the deaf children into the society of hearing people, the children must learn to speak and understand the language of their hearing community and to read and write it well.

From the perspective of many deaf communities, this reflects a dark period of deaf education. One by one, schools for the deaf all over the nation abolished ASL, forced deaf educators out of their jobs, and radically changed the classroom atmosphere forever. Deaf students in the classrooms were forced to speak and write in English only. Oralism continued well into the twentieth century; ultimately, however, the effort to teach deaf students to speak, read lips, and be literate was a dismal failure. Today strictly oral schools are rare; however, oral methods are still used to teach students to become bilingual and bicultural.

In the 1960s William Stokoe, a scholar of ASL, was instrumental in shifting perceptions of ASL from a substandard form of English to a thriving, complex natural language of the deaf with a rich syntax and grammar. For the first time, ASL was deemed an important and viable mode of communication for deaf students. While it was recognized that manual communication was essential in educating deaf students, hearing professionals created sign systems that mirrored oral English rather than using ASL. Many believe this occurred because manually coded (oral) English is easier for the hearing individual to use than to learn a new language for educating deaf students. The next thirty years promoted educating the deaf through total communication—the use of sign systems and oral methods. As a result, ASL became influenced by these other sign systems and many deaf individuals experienced language confusion

as they graduated from school and became socialized into the deaf community.

In 1988, the deaf community organized a rally, Deaf President Now (DPN), to protest the newly appointed hearing president of Gallaudet University, the world's only deaf university. The protest quickly became a national platform for the deaf community to raise public awareness about the rights and abilities of deaf and hard-of-hearing individuals. In the years following the protest, many bills and laws were passed that advanced the rights of deaf and hard-of-hearing individuals to include the recognition of ASL as the natural language of the deaf.

Today, many colleges and universities accept ASL as part of the foreign language requirement, and interpreting programs have been established. According to recent reports, ASL is the fourth most-used language in the United States and thirty-five states officially recognize ASL as a language. As well, the push to accept ASL as a viable mode for teaching deaf students has been advanced through the bilingual-bicultural (bi-bi) movement, whereby deaf students are taught first in their native language and learn oral English as a second language. The goal of this approach is to create fully literate deaf students who are proficient in ASL and written English.

Barbara J. Dray and Lee Dray

See also Disabilities and the Politics of Schooling

See Visual History Chapter 21, Students With Special Needs

Further Readings

Lane, H., Hoffmeister, R., & Bahan, B. (1996). *A journey in the deaf-world.* San Diego, CA: Dawnsign Press.
Laurent Clerc National Deaf Education Center. (2006). *Deaf President Now for teachers and students.* Washington, DC: Gallaudet University. Retrieved September 12, 2006, from http://clerccenter.gallaudet.edu/DPN/index.htm

ANNA T. JEANES FOUNDATION

The Anna T. Jeanes Foundation, also known as the Negro Rural School Fund, was established by Quaker heiress Anna T. Jeanes in 1907. She directed that her estate of $1 million was to support the "rudimentary education" of African Americans in the rural South. The foundation or fund, administered by the Rockefeller Foundation's General Education Board, supported special supervisory teachers who offered guidance to Black rural school teachers, who might be poorly trained and lacking other support. More than one half of the salary was paid by the fund, and the remainder was paid by the county board of education. The initial plan was to employ a Jeanes teacher at a demonstration center in the county, one who would also serve as a supervisor of the rural Black schools within the county school system.

But it was the work of one Black teacher, Virginia Randolph, in Henrico County, Virginia, that would ultimately define the role of the Jeanes teacher. The daughter of slaves, Randolph began teaching at sixteen after she graduated from high school. She then established her own Mountain Road School where she paired the teaching of industrial arts of cooking and sewing with the moral values of cleanliness and orderliness. Jackson Davis, Henrico school superintendent, applied for a grant from the Negro Rural School Fund and adopted Randolph's model for the rural Black schools. The leaders of the fund were so impressed with Randolph's work in Virginia that they hired her as the first supervising industrial teacher in 1908.

Randolph's instructional model became known as the Henrico plan and formed the basis for the work of the fund in each of the Southern states that allowed Jeanes teachers into their Black rural schools. For Jeanes teachers, education was about the whole community and its welfare, with the school as the agency that would teach people how to live better. Under the guidance of the Jeanes teachers, Black schools came to resemble settlement houses where students and their parents learned more than just "the 3Rs"—they learned about health, sanitation, and nutrition, and homemaking skills as well. The teachers also worked outside of the schools by consulting with ministers and speaking at churches on school-related issues, and they lobbied White politicians on school boards for financial support of Black teachers and their students.

By 1911, the fund employed 129 teachers across the South, most of whom were Black women; the first group of Jeanes teachers had no college training. By the mid-1930s, 45 percent had obtained their bachelor's degrees, paid for by the fund, through summer courses at Hampton Institute. While the number of Jeanes teachers had grown to about 500 by 1950, their role was being impacted by the societal and cultural changes occurring across the nation. The *Brown v. Board of Education* Supreme Court decision declared segregated schools unconstitutional; the passage of the Smith-Hughes Act provided funding for vocational education at rural high schools; the civil rights movement had begun; and industrial training for African Americans was viewed as outdated. The fund and its teachers stopped their work in 1968.

Louise Anderson Allen

See also African American Education; African American Education: From Slave to Free

Further Readings

Jones, L. A. (2002). *Mama learned us to work: Farm women in the new South.* Chapel Hill: University of North Carolina Press.

Leloudis, J. L. (1996). *Schooling and the New South: Pedagogy, self, and society in North Carolina, 1860–1920.* Chapel Hill: University of North Carolina Press.

Woodfaluk, C. S. (1992). *The Jeanes teachers of South Carolina: The emergence, existence, and significance of their work.* Unpublished dissertation, University of South Carolina, Columbia.

ANTIRACIST EDUCATION

Antiracist education, also referred to as antiracism education, has emerged within the broader field of multicultural education. Its explicit focus on power relations, institutional structures, and identity distinguish it from more traditional forms of multicultural education. Antiracist education emphasizes the need to address systemic barriers that cultivate and sustain racism, particularly within educational settings. Similarly, at the theoretical level antiracist education seeks to support social justice and equity by understanding and dealing with the complexity of identity and the intersection of diverse forms of difference and marginalization, including social class, gender, ethnicity, ability, linguistic origin, sexual orientation and religion, among others. This entry addresses the theoretical, conceptual, and applied aspects of antiracist education.

The Context

Antiracist education was born in the UK over two decades ago in response to an anti-immigration backlash from right-wing conservatives. Key figures that shaped the field were Barry Troyna and Bruce Carrington, and there was some important work in schools by David Gillborn. In the United States, antiracist education has direct links with the civil rights movement and has been advanced by a number of contemporary educational scholars who adopt a critical stance toward multicultural education; influential researcher activists leading the field include James Banks, Cherry McGee Banks, Christine Sleeter, Carl Grant, and Sonia Nieto. Their focus is on honoring difference and correcting differential learning experiences and outcomes, especially among minority and marginalized students. This has also been referred to as "antibias" or "antioppression" education, following Kevin Kumashiro, and there is an explicit connection to various forms of difference in social justice education in the United States.

The term *antiracist education* is more contested than *multicultural education* because it specifically mentions the word *race,* now understood to have no biological significance. While race no longer holds salience as a genetic concept, society has long been organized around categorizations of people based on perceived racial identity. The fact that Aboriginal peoples have lived on the land known as North America for some 20,000 years underscores the antiracist vantage point that power relations and identity need to be problematized within the context of colonization. Similarly, the infamous legacies of slavery, segregation, Jim Crow and myriad discriminatory laws, policies, and social practices have divided the United States along racialized lines. The reality that more African American males are in prison than in university, combined with the illustrative socioeconomic and educational context, are further evidence of the effects of discrimination based on racial identities in contemporary American society.

Antiracist education seeks to correct inequities within this social context. On the one hand is the concrete reality of underachievement, marginalization, and discrimination, and on the other is a pervasive ideology of individualism, merit-based achievement, and an education system that has historically ignored social justice issues. For the past two decades, the National Association for Multicultural Education (NAME) has been one of the leading organizations articulating a vision for antiracist education, and it includes social justice and the struggle to eradicate inequity and discrimination in its official definition of multicultural education.

The Foundation

In their conceptualization of antiracist education, Canadian scholars George Sefa Dei and Agnes Calliste have questioned the notion of a color-blind society and argue in favor of a more transparent and equitable sharing of power. The history of race relations is never neutral, and antiracist education requires surveying and critiquing textbooks, curricula, policies, outcomes, and general conditions related to education to better understand and take action on inequity and racism. As Paul Carr and Darren Lund's recent work concludes, this must include recognition of Whiteness, the understanding that White people have acquired and exercised power and privilege based on their racial identity. The role and implication of White teachers in classrooms with diverse student bodies has been a growing area of interest for antiracist educators, including Gary Howard in the United States.

The premise of antiracist education is that excellence and equity are intertwined. To achieve equity, explicit and implicit efforts, strategies, and resources must be concentrated and activated in a coherent manner. Frances Henry and Carol Tator have written about the "colour of democracy," documenting how supposed democratic structures and systems work to support racism. For antiracist education to be realized, it is imperative that systems, structures, and institutions are critically assessed and reformed.

Neo-Marxist antiracist theorists have linked racism and marginalization in society with capitalism and the economic exploitation of the working class and marginalized groups. Following the work of Paulo Freire, Henry Giroux and others have promoted the need for political literacy and critical pedagogy, widely considered important elements of the antiracist education movement. Antiracist education, therefore, seeks to cultivate critical thinking and an appreciation among students for the lived experiences of all people. Giving voice to those who have traditionally been marginalized is a key step in making schools more inclusive and representative.

Antiracist education seeks to develop an inclusive curriculum that encourages critical reflection and action, infused throughout subject areas and school culture. As Julie Kailin has argued, all teachers must be able to present concepts, examples, lessons, and activities that foster social justice and equity, and that support high academic achievement. Antiracist educators understand that all education is political, and their approach to inequity includes the need to address power imbalances for the benefit of all students.

Complementing the field of antiracist education are a number of group-specific disciplines, including Latino/a Studies, Asian American Studies, African American Studies, and Aboriginal/First Nations Studies, all of which deal with the legacy and implication of race playing a role in histories, cultures, and social conditions.

Moving From Multicultural Education to Antiracist Education

While critical pedagogues and scholars in the United States usually refer to multicultural education, this differs from conceptualizations of the term in other English-speaking countries, namely Canada, Australia, and the UK. In Canada in the mid-1990s, Earl Mansfield and Jack Kehoe characterized the multicultural-antiracist schism by noting that multicultural education is usually focused on intergroup harmony, celebration of diversity, and cultural heritage and pride, while antiracist education attends to educational disadvantage, systemic racism, power relations, politics, and critical analysis. Likewise, Stephen May has been critical of the unfulfilled promises of multicultural education, particularly the limited perspective on inequitable power relations. He has taken aim at the Eurocentric curriculum that pervades teaching and learning, and calls for broader understanding of the social context shaping the education experience.

Antiracist education raises issues that often elicit discomfort and tension, and its supporters understand this conflict as a necessary part of the learning process. They believe that education should not avoid dealing with systemic issues but, rather, should require that students become engaged in understanding and acting on controversial issues. Antiracist education presupposes a commitment to the praxis of education—the intersection of theory and practice—extending earlier practices of multicultural education that were limited to fostering tolerance and respect.

Antiracist education critically analyzes both the development and implementation of educational policy. While the process for developing policy is important, antiracist education considers closely the outcome of such policies. For example, the dropout—or as George Sefa Dei calls it, the "push-out"—rate of Black/African American students in education must be problematized at several levels. Rather than pathologizing the role of the Black/African American family, antiracist educators are critically focused on how teachers, principals, education officials, and decision makers are complicit in this situation.

Antiracist Education Policies

A number of jurisdictions, particularly in Canada, the UK, and Australia, have developed school-based antiracism policies. However, the overall commitment and emphasis on antiracism appears to take place in a patchwork manner, with some school boards and provinces or states embracing the approach more than others, as results from large nationwide studies by Patrick Solomon and Cynthia Levine-Rasky in Canada have shown. Antiracism policies are often fraught with the very issues that they are intended to dismantle, namely systemic discrimination, passive resistance, and marginalized status in competition with a curriculum focused on achieving high academic standards. In addition to the formal policy articulating guidelines for action, jurisdictions with such policies customarily provide resource documents, training, and dispute-resolution mechanisms to monitor and support progress.

In the United States, there are numerous initiatives addressing academic underachievement. The No Child Left Behind legislation requires data collection based on race, but this has been critiqued because school boards have flexibility in reporting differential outcomes. There are a number of research centers, resources, initiatives, programs, grants, and projects targeting racism in the United States, many of which form part of the antiracist education movement. With the debate over the utility and legality of affirmative action, in light of *Brown v. Board of Education,* race remains a controversial issue in education circles. Despite the achievement gap in education between racialized groups, there is still much resistance to adopting antiracist education as a means to advancing educational outcomes for all students.

Criticism of Antiracist Education

Some criticize antiracist education as being too overtly political and, moreover, as focusing too narrowly on race. Others refute the notion that White people universally oppress Black people, arguing that antiracist education often distorts the complex lived reality of people within diverse demographics. The emphasis on race is also criticized for subverting other forms of difference, especially gender, social class, and culture. Similarly, critics contend that the overidentification of race may reinforce negative stereotypes related to racial identity.

Antiracist Education Programs

Some common features to groups, schools, institutions, and researchers developing antiracist education approaches and pedagogies include the following:

- The notion that good teaching must take into account the varied perspectives and experiences of diverse student-bodies and society
- The need for a full analysis of school climate, diagnosing and remedying systemic barriers
- The importance of robust involvement and engagement from all sectors forming the school culture, including teachers, principals, guidance counselors, psychologists, lunchroom and custodial staff, parents, and others
- The need to problematize how questions of race, culture, and identity in relation to differential educational outcomes and experiences

Antiracist education seeks to infuse learning with an explicit social justice agenda that reinforces academic achievement. It is concerned with accessibility, power imbalances, identity, and reversing the perception that students from marginalized groups constitute a "deficit culture." Antiracist education more directly focuses on race and the intersections of identity than has traditional multicultural education. There are many commonalities and convergences between antiracist and multicultural education that depend on conceptual, jurisdictional, and ideological factors, in addition to the specific groups involved. Through the meshing of various tenets, strategies, resources, and leadership, antiracist education, in collaboration with more critical forms of multicultural education, aims to render schools and educators better equipped to deal with equity issues in rapidly changing demographic and social conditions.

Paul R. Carr and Darren E. Lund

See also Educational Equity: Race/Ethnicity; Multicultural Education

Further Readings

Banks, J. A., & McGee Banks, C. A. (Eds.). (2004). *Handbook of research on multicultural education.* San Francisco: Jossey-Bass.

Carr, P., & Lund, D. E. (Eds.). (2007). *The Great White North? Whiteness, privilege and identity in education.* Rotterdam, The Netherlands: Sense.

Dei, G. J. S. (1996). *Anti-racism education: Theory and practice.* Black Point, Nova Scotia: Fernwood.

Dei, G. J. S., & Calliste, A. (Eds.). (2000). *Power, knowledge and anti-racism education: A critical reader.* Black Point, Nova Scotia: Fernwood.

Gillborn, D. (1995). *Racism and antiracism in real schools.* Buckingham, UK: Open University Press.

Henry, F., & Tator, C. (2005). *The colour of democracy: Racism in Canadian society.* Toronto, ON, Canada: Thomson Nelson.

Howard, G. R. (2006). *We can't teach what we don't know: White teachers, multiracial schools.* New York: Teachers College Press.

Kailin, J. (2002). *Antiracist education: From theory to practice.* Lanham, MD: Rowman & Littlefield.

Kumashiro, K. (2004). *Against common sense: Teaching and learning toward social justice.* New York: RoutledgeFalmer.

Mansfield, E., & Kehoe, J. (1994). A critical examination of anti-racist education, *Canadian Journal of Education, 19,* 418–430.

May, S. (Ed.). (1999). *Critical multiculturalism: Rethinking multicultural and antiracist education.* Philadephia: Falmer Press.

Nieto, S. (2004). *Affirming diversity: The sociopolitical context of multicultural education.* New York: Allyn & Bacon.

Sleeter, C. E. (1996). *Multicultural education as social activism.* Albany: State University of New York Press.

Sleeter, C. E., & Grant, C. A. (2005). *Making choices for multicultural education: Five approaches to race, class, and gender.* San Francisco: Jossey-Bass.

Troyna, B. (1993). *Racism and education: Research perspectives.* Buckingham, UK: Open University Press.

ARCHIVES AND LIBRARY COLLECTIONS ON EDUCATION

Archives and library collections for the field of education vary widely in purpose and scope. While different archives and collections may be housed in the same building at an institution, students and researchers use them to achieve a variety of goals. This entry looks at some of these institutions.

Archives and Special Collections

Archives hold records from persons or organizations. Archival documents are unique, for they are typically unpublished collections of papers, records, or manuscripts. For instance, the College of Charleston acts as the archive for the Charleston High School, one of the oldest public secondary schools in the United States, and holds the school's papers dating from 1843 to 1976. The Boston College Libraries are home to the archives of the Citywide Coordinating Council of Boston, an organization involved in the desegregation of Boston public schools.

Special collections, which may be administered by the same department as the archives at an institution, focus on specific subject areas, formats, time periods, or other factors to create comprehensive collections. Examples include materials on John Dewey and other Progressive educators in the Special Collections Division of the Morris Library at Southern Illinois University; manuscript, textbook collections, and other materials about the education of women in the United States in the early nineteenth century at Mt. Holyoke College Library; and the Marguerite Archer Collection of historical children's books at San Francisco State University.

Extensive historical textbook collections can be found at the Library of Congress, the Monroe C. Gutman Library at the Graduate School of Education at Harvard University, the Plimpton Collection of textbooks at Columbia University, the Nila Banton Smith Historical Collection in Reading in the Joan and Donald E. Axinn Library at Hofstra University, and the Nietz Old Textbook Collection at the University of Pittsburgh Library.

Holdings in archives and special collections can be especially enlightening for scholars doing original research. While many materials in archival and special collections may not appear in library catalogs, great efforts at digitization have brought publicity to many of these previously hidden collections. Due to the nature of these collections, they are often not available through interlibrary loan, meaning that one must visit their depositories in person to utilize these materials.

Research Libraries

Research libraries hold collections of books, journals, databases, datasets, and other materials to support a broad range of intellectual discourses and discovery of new knowledge, while good small college libraries focus on supporting the course work at their institutions. The first efforts at building collections specifically to support teacher education began at colleges and universities in the United States in the late 1830s. Today, many colleges and universities collect materials in dedicated education libraries.

Columbia University led the way in this regard with the establishment of the Milbank Memorial Library at Teachers College in 1887. This remains the largest education library in the world. Other examples of this type of library include the Cubberley Library at Stanford University, the Peabody Library at Vanderbilt University, and the University of Illinois Education and Social Science Library.

Other libraries house education resources within their main libraries. University of North Carolina, Chapel Hill, and Syracuse University provide examples of very strong education collections contained within the main library. Education librarians, usually professionals with degrees in both library and information science as well as education or a related field, work to build collections in this subject area and provide guidance for students and researchers.

Assessment of collections and other forms or library support is a complicated process, making it difficult to directly compare these resources at different libraries in a general way. However, as schools of education are accredited by regional or national bodies, the quality of library support for their programs is invariably considered as part of that process and can meaningfully impact the perception of a program's quality.

Most libraries at institutions with teacher preparation programs house juvenile and young adult literature to support courses in these areas. Persistent questions with these collections include the shelving and retrieval problems that arise when these books are housed according to the classification systems at use in college and university libraries. This is especially problematic in the Library of Congress classification system which is used at most university libraries, because most children's books will be given call numbers beginning with PZ, representing the class juvenile literature. That can make it difficult to locate a particular title within the collection.

Textbook adoption collections are also often found at universities with schools of education. Textbook adoption collections hold textbooks in use or under consideration for use at either the local or state level in K–12 school districts. The intent of these collections is to give students in education an opportunity to examine and create curriculum around textbooks they will likely encounter in schools.

Education curriculum collections are distinct in that they house materials not specifically designed for scholarship or research for students of education, but rather for use in K–12 classrooms. These collections may include multiple copies of readers, workbooks, models, and toys for teaching and learning, as well as DVDs and videos. Depending on the administrative structure and library system, curriculum libraries can be administered by their respective schools of education or through the library system. Innovative programs in this area include attempts to create online curriculum collections.

John P. Renaud

See also Libraries, History of; Schools of Education

See Visual History Chapter 17, Reading and Libraries

Further Readings

Ash, L., & Miller, W. G. (Eds.). (1993). *Subject collections.* New Providence, NJ: Bowker.

Christo, D. H. (Ed.). (1990). *National directory of education libraries and collections.* Westport, CT: Meckler Corporation.

ARTS EDUCATION POLICY

Arts education policy refers to the decisions that legislators, funders, and administrators make with respect to teaching and learning in the arts. Policies on arts education address not only in-school course work in art, music, drama, and dance, current attention is also aimed at out-of-school arts programming offered by community organizations and arts providers. In the last two decades, proactive policy related to arts education has become increasingly important as accountability and high-stakes testing prompt mandates for school learning that exclude time for the arts.

This entry looks at the primary policy issues facing arts education in four topic areas: (1) equity in access and opportunity for the arts in diverse communities; (2) preparation and training for in-school arts teachers, visiting teaching artists, and performing artists who work in schools; (3) the roles and responsibilities of external providers and community organizations; and (4) students learning in arts-specific instruction and integration of the arts.

Equitable Access

Policy in arts education is informed by the engagement of ethnic communities in urban school districts that advocate for the inclusion of arts history and culture in the curriculum. Local museums and performing arts organizations in urban and suburban school systems often have incentives through private and public funding options to partner with public schools and offer services to school children and their parents. Groups that traditionally have had reduced access to arts curriculum, including those in rural and isolated areas, now have more opportunities through Web-based and distance learning. The content of arts curriculum that addresses the histories and cultures of diverse populations of students and their families is increasingly essential in a multicultural society. Equity in access represents a consistent issue for policy makers at the local, state, and national levels.

Preparation and Training

A consistent debate that affects policy decisions in the field focuses on who should teach the arts. Recruitment and retention of arts teachers for arts-specific instruction remains an issue, particularly for school districts in which funding has been directed away from arts teaching and toward reading, math, and science content. In this climate of diminishing resources, arts councils and school districts are also considering the merits of integrating the arts into the existing math, science, social studies, or literacy curriculum. Classroom teachers and visiting teaching artists then teach the arts, often without the support of a certified arts teacher in the building. This practice has raised questions about how to advocate for more arts funding while supplying arts education through classroom teachers.

Endorsement, certification, and other means of licensure required by states and school districts for artists and arts teachers working in schools remain a topic for policy makers. Just as in nonarts subject fields, there are persistent questions about teachers' content expertise, experience in making and performing art, and preparation for teaching in and across art forms. How and whether noncertified teaching artists can contribute to arts curricula in schools is a focus for research and evaluation. There is a need for research that addresses the interrelationships and continuity of arts teaching and learning from preschool through higher education. Policy research can only be addressed if funders are willing to support such initiatives.

Outside Providers

A third arena for policy discussion focuses on the role of external providers, particularly in the major metropolitan areas of the United States. It is not clear whether the engagement of theater companies, symphony orchestras, dance companies, and museums has contributed to learning in the arts disciplines or to students' nonarts academic achievement. As community arts organizations form partnerships to deliver arts curricula in schools, they are increasingly involved in providing evidence that what they offer contributes to student learning.

Arts and the Curriculum

Has arts integration, implemented by noncertified visiting artists or nonarts classroom teachers, enhanced specific learning in nonarts disciplines as defined by state standards? Has arts integration maintained the integrity of the art form engaged? Some arts education proponents claim that increasing arts integration in financially strained districts is a means of avoiding hiring of faculty specialists in the arts. Others claim that arts integration programs raise the visibility of the arts in communities, thereby encouraging more arts-specific programming in schools.

Arts education proponents are being asked to document how the arts contribute to nonart learning through questions such as, "What is the effect of the arts on literacy?" Arts researchers are also raising the inverse question, "What is the effect of literacy on the arts?" Indicators of student learning in the arts are examined by researchers and program evaluators in response to the demand for accountability. Government-funded programs and private funding agencies continue to support research that examines the impact of arts education on student learning. As compelling research emerges that underscores the important role of teacher expertise on student learning, arts educators are also considering how teacher learning through arts-based professional development contributes to student achievement. Both research programs suggest the challenge and opportunity for balanced curricula in an era of teacher shortages, resource scarcity for the arts, and standards-based learning in schools.

Researchers and program evaluators are informing policy makers, district administrators, arts administrators, and teachers about arts learning, using mixed methods that include intensive multimedia documentation, teacher action research on arts practices, and assessments of student achievement through performance. The development of research programs that investigate the possible transfer of student learning in the arts to nonarts academic achievement and social development continues. The question of what is convincing, yet also authentic, research regarding arts curricula and effective teaching in school and after-school programs remains a challenge.

Gail Burnaford

See also Politics of Education; Teacher Preparation

Further Readings

Burnaford, G., Aprill, A. & Weiss, C. (2001). *Renaissance in the classroom: Arts integration and meaningful learning.* Mahwah, NJ: Lawrence Erlbaum.

Chapman, L. H. (2004). No child left behind in art? *Arts Education Policy Review, 106*(2), 3–17.

Eisner, E. W., & Day, M. D. (2004). *Handbook of research and policy in art education.* Mahwah, NJ: Lawrence Erlbaum & National Art Education Association.

Fiske, E. B. (Ed.). (2000). *Champions of change: The impact of the arts on learning.* Washington, DC: Arts Education Partnership & The President's Committee on the Arts and the Humanities.

Stevenson, L. M., & Deasy, R. J. (2005). *Third space. When learning matters.* Washington, DC: Arts Education Partnership.

ASIAN AMERICAN EDUCATION

Asian American education has changed from a time when Asian American children were often not welcome in U.S. public schools to a time when they have become the mythic "model minority." As in other areas, education has been an arena where Asian Americans have often had to fight for their rights. In addition, their diversity of origins reflects a broad range of educational achievement. This entry looks at the demographic and historical background and current educational attainment of Asian Americans and some research studies focusing on this population.

Historical Background

Asian American education can be divided into three historical periods. In the first (1850–1941), Chinese and Japanese settled mainly along the West Coast and Hawai'i. Between 1882 and 1941, state and federal laws restricted immigration, voting rights, land ownership, and educational rights for Asians in America. Persons of Asian descent born in the United States successfully challenged discriminatory citizenship regulations in *U.S. v. Wong Kim Ark* (1898) and *Weedin v. Chin Bow* (1927), though courts upheld restrictions on foreign-born Asians in America in *Takao Ozawa v. U.S.* (1922) and *Bhagat Singh Thind v. U.S.* (1923).

Racial segregation of Asian Americans in public schools followed national trends in the late 1800s and early 1900s. Chinese students were barred from public schools in San Francisco in 1859. Their parents responded by opening a private "Chinese school," which later admitted Korean and Japanese students. The California Supreme Court ruled in *Tape v. Hurley* (1885) that San Francisco public schools must admit Asian Americans, though the state legislature created a parallel "Oriental School" system the same year. In Hawai'i, Japanese, Chinese, and other Asian Americans were discouraged from attending schools by plantation owners, and were generally segregated from Whites until Hawai'i became a state in 1959. Asian American school enrollment matched that of Whites by 1920, and exceeded that of Whites by 1930.

The second period, between 1941 and 1965, began with wartime hostilities, which led to the incarceration of over 100,000 West Coast Japanese Americans in ten detention camps in 1942. Through 1945, tens of thousands of Japanese Americans attended ill-equipped camp schools, though some were allowed to attend a university away from the West Coast. After World War II, Asian Americans benefited from the slow integration of public schools and the expansion of postsecondary institutions. Economic growth also helped propel second- and third-generation Asian Americans into professional occupations at rates higher than the national average.

The Immigration and Nationality Act of 1965 initiated the current period of Asian American education. After 1965, immigration increased rapidly from the Philippines, China, Korea, Vietnam, Laos, Cambodia, and India. Many "second-wave" immigrants were well educated and prosperous in their home countries. However, immigrants from Laos, Cambodia, and Vietnam were often war refugees with few educational credentials or financial resources. Unlike the Japanese and Chinese immigrants of the late nineteenth century, many second-wave immigrants brought children, who enrolled in public schools unprepared for linguistic and cultural diversity. Chinese Americans in San Francisco challenged local segregationist practices and limited language and course offerings in the late 1960s. As a result, the U.S. Supreme Court ruled in *Lau v. Nichols* (1974) that the city's lack of bilingual programs prevented 1,800 Chinese American students from "meaningful participation" in public schools.

Over time, bilingual and culturally appropriate courses expanded across California and the United States. Also, in the wake of the civil rights movement Asian American Studies programs were established, primarily in the Pacific states, and later in the Midwest and Northeast.

Asian American students have generally not benefited from race-based admission criteria. In the 1980s, several elite universities were criticized for tightening admissions criteria for Asian American students. By 1990, Asian Americans were being portrayed along with Whites as victims of affirmative action for Black and Latino students, reinforcing the "model minority" myth. In *Ho, Wong & Chen v. SFUSD* (1999), Chinese American plaintiffs successfully sued for the end of a 1983 desegregation consent decree that used race as a criterion for measuring integration. Critics have argued that this action will lead to a racial resegregation of San Francisco schools and hurt poorer students.

Educational Attainment in 2000

Asian Americans trace their ancestry to East, Southeast, and South Asia. According to the 2005 American Community Survey (ACS) conducted by the Census Bureau, 5 percent of the U.S population, or 14.4 million people identified as Asian American. The same year, 13.1 million people, or 4.4 percent, identified as "Asian alone." The Asian American population increased 21 percent from 2000 to 2005. A majority of Asian Americans live in California, New York, and Hawai'i, and 95 percent of Asian and Pacific Island Americans live in metropolitan areas.

Because the U.S. Census does not disaggregate for nationality, figures on the Asian American and "Asian alone" categories obscure the educational attainment within and among Asian American communities. According to the 2005 ACS, 49 percent who identified as "Asian alone" aged 25 or older had completed a bachelor's, graduate, or professional degree, compared with 27 percent of the same U.S. population. However, 10.68 percent of those who identified as "Asian alone" had reported less than a ninth-grade education in the 2000 Census, compared with only 7.55 percent of the U.S. population. Female Asian Americans both registered higher postsecondary education completion rates and were more likely to have completed less than nine years of formal schooling. Studies that have disaggregated data by ethnicity have consistently found that school completion and educational attainment rates for Southeast Asian Americans are lower than for other Asian Americans.

These data are far more complex than myths about a model minority, which developed after World War II as a result of educational and economic attainment

Table 1 Ten Largest Asian American Populations, 2000

Chinese (except Taiwanese)	2,734,841
Filipino	2,364,815
Asian Indian	1,899,599
Korean	1,228,427
Vietnamese	1,223,736
Japanese	1,148,932
Cambodian	206,052
Pakistani	204,309
Laotian	198,203
Hmong	186,310

SOURCE: U.S. Census, 2000.

among some—but not all—Asian Americans. Despite its generally positive nature, this myth obscures the educational underachievement of many Asian Americans, and reinforces beliefs about African American and Latino failure.

Recent Research

Studies in the 1980s attributed Asian American success to the convergence of Asian and middle-class U.S. cultural characteristics like ambition, persistence, delayed gratification, and social mobility. Other studies suggested limited and selected immigration in the early twentieth century and the "middleman minority" thesis as explanations. Cultural, familial, and even genetic explanations of Asian Americans' achievement remain popular explanations for Asian American success.

Contrary to the "model minority" myth, research has shown that many Asian American students struggle in school. One study found that overworked parents and limited social capital contributed to working-class Korean American students' leaving school. Another study found that Chinese American parents' participation in the mainstream economy helped them to secure the social, cultural, and human capital necessary for their children to attend and achieve in high-performing schools. In contrast, the same study found that low-income Chinese American parents had less opportunity to exploit network connections and lacked the means to relocate for educational opportunities. High educational expectations from parents can be a source of motivation and of conflict for Asian American students. A study of two Chinese American families found that children in both lower and upper income households became estranged from their immigrant parents because of the dissonant cultural expectations about money and appropriate adolescent behavior. High expectations among Korean and Chinese Americans may also be a tactic to avoid racism.

Research on Southeast Asian American students finds much higher levels of poverty than other Asian groups, and some of the lowest per capita incomes in the United States. Though many Southeast Asian American students are successful in school, studies show that significant numbers are isolated from American culture and are more likely to join gangs. Cambodian and Lao students, in particular, are more likely than Vietnamese students to struggle with English, score lower on standardized tests, and leave school.

Another area of research has focused on Asian American career choices. A 2000 study found reticence among Asian Americans, especially recent immigrants, to enter the teaching profession. Another study argued that Asian American overrepresentation in the hard sciences stems from family expectations and attempts to limit awkward social interactions.

Research has suggested that isolation and stereotypes create social pressures for Asian American students, who are sometimes reluctant to seek special services because of the stigma of the "minority" label. Administrators have been shown to neglect focused services, courses, and programs for Asian American students because of the stereotype of overachievement.

Christopher J. Frey

See also Bilingual Education, History of; Immigrant Education: Contemporary Issues; Immigrant Education: History; Japanese Detention Camps, Education in

See Visual History Chapter 14, Immigration and Education

Further Readings

Coloma, R. S., & Kumashiro, K. K. (Ed.). (2006). Asian Americans and Pacific Islanders: The state of research [Special issue]. *Race Ethnicity and Education, 9*(1).

Ng, J. C., Lee, S. S., & Pak, Y. K. (2007). Contesting the model minority and perpetual foreigner stereotypes: A critical review of literature on Asian Americans in education. *Review of Research in Education, 31,* 95–130.

Park, C. C., Endo, R., & Goodwin, A. L. (2006). *Asian and Pacific education: Learning, socialization and identity.* Charlotte, NC: Information Age.

Park, C. C., Endo, R., Lee, S. J., & Rong, X. L. (2007). *Asian American education: Acculturation, literacy development and learning.* Charlotte, NC: Information Age.

Weinburg, M. (1997). *Asian American education: Historical background and current realities.* Mahwah, NJ: Lawrence Erlbaum.

ASSISTIVE TECHNOLOGY

The Individuals with Disabilities Education Act of 2004 (IDEA) defines assistive technology as devices and services, such as visual aids, communication tools, and specialized equipment for accessing a computer, that are used to increase, maintain, or improve the functional capabilities of children with disabilities, allowing them to benefit from special education and promoting their independence. Other examples of typical assistive technology include Braille readers, wheelchairs, augmentative communication devices, electronic dictionaries/spellers, alternative keyboards, and computer software programs. IDEA mandates that assistive technology be considered in the development of individualized education programs (IEPs) for all students with disabilities, with special emphasis on facilitating students' access to the general education curriculum.

In addition to IDEA, two additional pieces of legislation relate specifically to technology for individuals with disabilities. The Technology-Related Assistance for Individuals with Disabilities Act of 1988 (known as the "Tech Act") provides states with funding to develop comprehensive programs to meet the assistive technology needs of individuals with disabilities. In this law, Congress noted that there have been significant advances in technology, that technology benefits all individuals, that technology is a necessity for some individuals with disabilities because it enables them to engage in life's tasks, that using assistive technology devices and services with exceptional individuals ultimately can reduce the overall costs of disabilities, and that many individuals with disabilities lack access to the assistive technology devices and services requisite for their functioning in the school and community at a level commensurate with their abilities. Because of these concerns, Congress identified a number of objectives in this legislation, including increasing awareness of the needs of individuals with disabilities for assistive technology devices and services; improving the availability of, and funding for, assistive technology; expanding the knowledge of well-organized applications of assistive technology devices and services; and promoting collaboration among state agencies and public and private entities that provide assistive technology devices and services.

The Assistive Technology Act of 1998 (ATA) expands its predecessor and affirms that technology is a valuable tool that can be used to enhance the lives of individuals with disabilities. It also confirms the role of the federal government in promoting access to assistive technology devices and services for individuals with disabilities. The ATA is intended to support states in strengthening their ability to address the assistive technology needs of individuals with disabilities. It requires states to engage in public awareness programs that provide information on the accessibility and benefits of assistive technology devices and services, facilitate interagency coordination that improves access to assistive technology for individuals of all ages who have disabilities, and provide technical assistance and outreach support to statewide community-based organizations that provide assistive technology devices and services.

Technology supporting students' progress may be high or low tech. Computers or other complex devices using multifunction technology may not always be needed, depending on the students' presenting characteristics and needs. Often, relatively low-tech supports (such as pencil grips, calculators, and graphic organizers) can greatly facilitate the learning of children with disabilities. Regardless of the level of technology offered, these supports enable students to communicate, receive instruction, and participate in the academic, recreational, and social activities of school and the community, ultimately promoting independence.

Instructional and assessment accommodations, which may involve some form of assistive technology, are required by IDEA for all students with disabilities, and these accommodations must be described on each student's IEP. Any number of instructional and assessment accommodations may be employed for students, depending on their unique needs. These accommodations may relate to the types of instructional methods and materials used (e.g., highlighters, diagrams, graphic organizers, books on tape), testing arrangements (e.g., using a computer to have items read aloud, allowing students to respond orally, using a calculator), and use of specialized communication systems (e.g., augmentative communication boards).

These are just a few of the accommodations whereby assistive technology can enable students to access the same material as their nondisabled peers.

Innovations in technology continue to shape how educators can better meet the needs of their students with disabilities. Assistive technology can be skillfully incorporated as a part of instruction and delivered to enhance the education and life functioning of individuals with disabilities. This technological enhancement, called the "great equalizer" for students with disabilities, requires that educators keep in step with new developments in the technology for the betterment of the exceptional students they teach.

Juliet E. Hart

See also Individuals with Disabilities Education Act; Least Restrictive Environment; Mainstreaming; Special Education, Contemporary Issues; Special Education, History of

See Visual History Chapter 21, Students With Special Needs

Further Readings

Assistive Technology Act, P.L. 105-394 (1998).

Behrmann, M., & Jerome, M. K. (2002). *Assistive technology for students with mild disabilities: Update 2002*. Available from http://www.cec.sped.org

Individuals with Disabilities Education Act, P.L. 108-446 (2004).

Technology: The great equalizer. (n.d.). Available from http://www.cec.sped.org

Technology-Related Assistance for Individuals with Disabilities Act, P.L. 100-407 (1988).

Web Sites

Center for Applied Special Technology: http://www.cast.org

Journal of Special Education Technology: http://jset.unlv.edu

ATHLETICS, POLICY ISSUES

The influence of the sport industry on the social, moral, and economic makeup of American society and its schools has rapidly expanded in the last quarter century. From the incorporation of sport-related terminology into everyday speech to the acceptance of athletic apparel as daily wear, to the role of sports in creating school identity and conformity, the impact of the sport industry is undeniable.

Athletic programs mirror the values and beliefs of the society. In doing so, sport reflects things that are good about U.S. society, as well as its problems. In this context, it is important that those interested in social and cultural issues in education identify key issues that shape athletic policy in school settings. Three themes that are of critical interest to educational policy makers are the value of participation and competition; the state of inclusiveness in sport; and the concern for the well-being of participants in sport.

Value of Participation

From its inception, sport participation and competition has been touted as an accelerant for the development of desirable character traits. Throughout history, governmental leaders have pointed to the inclusion of sporting activities and accompanying competition as a means of developing desirable character traits in future leaders. Previous research has been divided regarding the actual ability of sport and/or competition to foster the development of these desirable character traits.

B. L. Bredemeirer and D. L. Shields found that in some cases duration of participation in sports actually impeded the development of moral reasoning skills. Further, these authors also established that continued participation at more intense levels of competition actually caused regression of these abilities. Additional studies have identified the ability of sport participation to serve as a vehicle for the acquisition of desired traits, but only to the extent that those traits are emphasized throughout the athletic program and organization. This particular finding magnifies the issue of establishing expectations regarding the value of sport participation.

In a recent series of studies, John Gillentine and his colleagues found that over 92 percent of the general public indicated that they believed sports helped foster the development of desirable character traits in participants. The establishment of this baseline expectation raises the issue of whether coaches and administrators have the ability to teach these skills. It is incorrect to assume that all coaches have the aptitude to teach and/or model the desirable traits expected by the general public, or that the schools and other educators desire.

Further, the identification of what specific traits participants are expected to develop has also been subject to debate. A 1999 study identified eight specific characteristics that the general public believed were developed through sport participation: teamwork, sportsmanship, self-discipline, self-esteem, self-sacrifice, work ethic/habits, diligence, and respect for authority. The only practical way to ensure that these traits are learned through sport participation is to ensure that the coaches and administrators of these activities are educated in the appropriate methods to teach these traits.

The United States is the only major industrialized nation that does not require the certification of athletic coaches. If coaches are expected to instruct participants in the acquisition of these traits, they must be properly prepared to teach them. The only way to adequately prepare these individuals is to establish policies detailing the educational requirements and expectations of coaches and administrators. Preliminary research studies have indicated that the general public supports the required educational certification of coaches and sport administrators.

It is therefore the duty of the federal and state regulatory bodies to establish these certification requirements and determine the implementation strategy. The resistance to this concept appears to stem from two major concerns: (1) that sport is not considered by some as an integral part of the educational process, and (2) that current coaches would not qualify for certification under new expectations and guidelines. First, sport must be recognized as having a significant influence on society, including educational systems. Failure to recognize the influence of sport will only further allow for it to grow unbridled, and then society must bear any consequences from it. The other concern regarding existing coaches can be addressed through a system that allows for the "grandfathering" of current coaches who have exhibited acceptable abilities, without additional certification. While this may slow the certification process to some extent, it is a manageable strategy through which the transition can be handled. If we are to substantiate the value of sport participation and competition, the issue of preparing those charged with its instruction must be addressed.

Inclusiveness

The appropriate preparation of coaches and sport administrators will also better prepare these groups to ensure the inclusiveness of sport participation. Sport has evolved through the years to include a wide variety of participants. Through the years of desegregation the racial barriers once prominent in our schools and our sporting activities have receded. The participation of African Americans has steadily risen through the last quarter century, as has that of other racial groups. Likewise, the number of females participating in sports has also risen significantly due to the implementation in 1972 of Title IX, the federal law prohibiting sex discrimination by educational institutions.

While in each of these cases it has taken federal legislation to promote change within our sport programs, the appropriate preparation of coaches and administrators may equip them to be more proactive in creating participation opportunities for groups that historically have had limited access to sport. As previously addressed, the recognition and establishment of the values of participation and competition foster additional concerns regarding the inclusiveness of sport programs.

If the positive benefits identified through previous research can be empirically verified, then the acquisition of desirable traits must be seen as a positive outcome of sport participation for any individual of any skill and ability level. From this vantage point, coaches and administrators are more likely to establish programs that focus on these positive outcomes than to overemphasize winning or losing. This focus could promote the inclusive nature of sport to include those individuals who previously may have felt uncomfortable or even inadequate while participating in sport activities. This may encourage males and females of all races to participate in sports that had previously been viewed as racially or gender biased.

Making sport more accessible to all groups would also help eliminate the misconception that particular sport opportunities are available only to certain races, well-bodied individuals, or persons with a particular sexual orientation. Either from fear of exposure or peer group pressure, some individuals have often opted out of competition rather than fight the misconceptions regarding their participation. Only through the appropriate preparation of the coaches and administrations of these programs can sport become truly accessible to all persons.

Well-Being of Participants

Finally, the development of governing policies establishing the preparation expectations of coaches and administrators will also promote and protect the general state of well-being of participants. Through the implementation of programs that promote the acquisition of identified character traits, the concept of social justice and fairness can be promoted through sport participation. In order to help participants develop into socially conscious individuals, it is important to incorporate them into a system that promotes fairness.

Coaches and administrators may accomplish this through the development of programs in which participants have a voice in what is happening to them and a clear understanding of their role in the sport program. While this does not mean that participants will be directing the management of the programs, it does indicate that a system in which they feel empowered and invested must be established. The implication of participation in such a program could be that participants will take this understanding of social justice and fairness and apply it in other areas of their lives. This could only lead to a positive impact on all aspects of our current way of life.

This "trickle down" effect may further establish the positive benefit possible through sport participation and competition. If this is truly the desire of the general public, then it is mandatory that appropriate policies be implemented to ensure the appropriate training of coaches and sport administrators. Without such policies, sport is destined to aimlessly grow and influence society and participants in positive and negative ways.

John Andrew Gillentine and Jeremy Jordan

See also Ethical Issues and School Athletics

See Visual History Chapter 24, The Farm Security Administration's Photographs of Schools

Further Readings

Bredemeirer, B., & Shields, D. (1986). Moral growth among athletes and non-athletes: A comparative analysis. *Journal of Genetic Psychology, 147*(1), 7–18.

Cossel, H. (1991). *What's wrong with sport?* New York: Simon & Schuster.

Edwards, H. (1973). *Sociology of sport.* Homewood, IL: Dorsey Press.

Fraleigh, W. P. (1982). Why the good foul is not good. *Journal of Physical Education, Recreation and Dance, 53,* 41–42.

Gillentine, A. (2000). Character development through sport participation. *Mississippi Alliance of Health, Physical Education, Recreation and Dance Journal, 17*(1), 25–28.

Gillentine, A. (2003). An examination of the perceptions of the general public regarding the certification of coaches. *Research Quarterly, 74*(1), A44.

Gillentine, A., Danna, J., & Bender, J. (2001). *Coaching education revisited.* Birmingham, AL: Southern District American Alliance Health, Physical Education, Recreation, & Dance.

Jordan, J., Gillentine, A., & Hunt, B. (2004). Using fairness to improve team performance: An extension of organizational justice theory to a team sport setting. *International Sport Journal, 8*(1), 139–149.

Lapchick, R. E. (1996). *Sport in society: Equal opportunity or business as usual?* Thousand Oaks, CA: Sage.

Lupcia, M. (1996). *Mad as hell.* New York: Putnam.

Pitts, B. (2001). Sport management at the millennium: A defining moment. *Journal of Sport Management, 15*(1), 1–9.

AUDIOVISUAL EDUCATION, HISTORY OF

Audiovisual education became a prominent movement during the period immediately following World War I. In the decade after the war, filmstrips, motion pictures, audio recordings, and radio programming began to be widely integrated in educational settings. Classroom uses of film and 16-mm projectors lent an aura of modernity and innovation to classrooms, becoming symbols of progressive teaching practices.

In higher education, the first official credit course in visual instruction was offered at the University of Minnesota in 1918. Other courses were established at the University of Kansas and North Carolina State University Teachers College in 1921. When introduced into normal schools, the curricula provided courses of study that gave teachers the opportunity to learn the advantages and disadvantages of visual instruction through formal and informal training. Over time, many courses were offered for teachers at the college and university level, related journals and professional organizations appeared, and the first systematic research studies were reported within the emerging audiovisual field. This entry summarizes those developments.

The Audiovisual Era

With the introduction of recorded sound and radio broadcasting, sound recording was integrated with film during the 1920s, beginning the transition from the *visual instruction movement* to what was soon to be known as the *audiovisual era.*

In 1920, the Radio Division of the U.S. Department of Commerce was established, and it began to license commercial and educational radio stations. Later, during the 1920s and the early 1930s, radio became the focus of a number of educational endeavors throughout the nation as colleges and universities experimented with educational radio and began to integrate audio technology with film and visual instruction methodologies. Among these was the Ohio School of the Air in 1929, launched in a joint effort by the State of Ohio, Ohio State University, and a Cincinnati radio station.

Classroom broadcasting to enhance instruction spread rapidly during the decades preceding World War II. Typical broadcasts included lectures and performances by college bands and orchestras. Likewise, university extension divisions offered on-site and correspondence courses and in-service training, sponsored conferences, and published texts and materials in audiovisual education.

The advent of film with sound in the late 1920s introduced a critical period in instructional film history from another perspective: Just as educators were becoming convinced of the educational merits of the silent film, the advocates of film with sound realized that they would have to fight the old battle all over again to gain acceptance for this new technology, especially since they believed many educators feared that film with sound would make their silent film equipment obsolete. Aside from this battle, the commercial education film enterprise was failing at an alarming rate during the late 1920s and early 1930s due to the Great Depression.

Audiovisual Education During War

World War II gave a big boost to the emerging field of instructional design and to the audiovisual era, and the need to rapidly train tens of thousands of new military personnel created a heightened interest in applying educational research in a systematic way.

Many educational researchers participated in the war training effort, and this helped to propel forward systematic efforts to design instruction. During the war, the benefits of this effort to audiovisual media were seen primarily in increased use of educational media to train military personnel and to satisfy the demand for training millions of industrial workers as rapidly and effectively as possible. This spurred an unprecedented production of educational films for training purposes.

The army and navy introduced training films and began to establish procedures for the instructional uses of such media as slides, filmstrips, and models. Instructional media and materials used by the military included projected motion pictures, graphics (illustrations and cartoons), posters, sound, and charts—supplemented by manuals, self-instructional devices and materials, handbooks, bulletins, and other training-related literature. Educational films, in particular, became an integral part of the military training effort during the war and a part of the official training policy of the War Department.

One training device that was especially popular was the filmstrip projector—the filmstrip was a medium that answered the demand for a fast, efficient, mass training of mechanics to serve in industry and the military. Another useful device was the microfilm reader, used by the U.S. military and industries for storing and duplicating data for research and testing purposes during and after the war.

Peacetime Applications

The numerous training aids that were developed during the war were used in the civilian sector following the war. These include the Link trainer, which provided a cadet pilot with a moving view of the earth, accompanied by realistic sounds of aircraft on recordings; mockups, exhibit rooms, and "breadboards" of simulated maps, equipment, battle-front layouts, and equipment operation. Audio-recording and playback devices developed during the war were especially prominent in foreign language training after the war. Microfilm and microfilm readers were used to preserve important records and duplicate library materials in such a way as to save valuable storage space.

World War II provided impetus for audiovisual instruction and was instrumental in the evolution and development of visual aids as instructional media. The widespread use of these media to accelerate military and industry training during the war was an influential endorsement of the instructional value of visual aids. The audiovisual era reinforced a principle that developed during the preceding visual instruction movement: Visual aids can teach more people more things in less time.

J. José Cortez

See also Visual Instruction Movement

See Visual History Chapter 11, International Expositions; Chapter 18, Educational Cartoons and Advertisements

Further Readings

Cuban, L. (1986). *Teachers and machines: The classroom use of technology since 1920.* New York: Teachers College Press.

Dent, D. (1969). *Landmarks in learning: The story of SVE.* Chicago: Society for Visual Education.

Newby, T. J., Stepich, D. A., Lehman, J., & Russell, J. D. (2000). *Instructional technology for teaching and learning* (2nd ed.). Englewood Cliffs, NJ: Merrill.

Saettler, P. (1990). *The evolution of American educational technology.* Englewood, CO: Libraries Unlimited.

AUTHENTIC ASSESSMENT

Authentic assessment enables educators to determine students' skills, knowledge, and competencies and to provide evidence of their learning. Utilizing a variety of performance-based measures, complex rubrics, and real-world tasks, authentic assessment encourages greater understanding of concepts in a meaningful context. Developed in response to the rote memorization and less complex assessments of objective measurements such as multiple-choice tests, which have been traditionally employed in education, authentic assessment provides a more engaging and effective way to measure students' learning while promoting understanding and valuing the process of learning. This entry looks at how the process developed and how it works.

How It Developed

In the 1990s, renewed interest in holding public education accountable led state legislatures and the U.S. government to require ongoing and in-depth testing at various points in students' educational careers. Performance-based funding initiatives in states across the nation ensured that testing would become standardized in an attempt to homogenize the curricula and the depth and breadth of student learning in various disciplines. Proponents of mandatory standardized testing also endeavored to create normalized benchmarks of student competencies across school districts and state lines in the nation.

Teachers soon discovered that standardized testing did not engender the in-depth understanding that their students would need for lifelong learning. Grant Wiggins, a former secondary school English and philosophy teacher, has been at the forefront of the authentic assessment movement for the past twenty years. In his 1993 book, *Assessing Student Performance: Exploring the Purpose and Limits of Testing,* Wiggins challenged the morality of standardized testing and multiple-choice tests, which involve discrete and simple facts and assess student learning on a superficial level of understanding. Wiggins posed authentic assessment as an antidote to these less effective types of tests. Authenticity produces greater student achievement and learning while providing relevant, contextual, real-world applications of curricular concepts that incorporate problem-solving and critical thinking skills.

Wiggins also has suggested that to design appropriate assessments, teachers need clearly defined curricular goals; then, they can figure out what to assess and what data they need to do so. In 1998, Wiggins and coauthor

Jay McTighe further developed this idea in *Understanding by Design,* which employs "backwards design" in curriculum and assessment planning. This design encourages teachers to determine the results they seek, then identify appropriate evidence of those results. After completing the steps, teachers plan learning activities and determine instructional methods. Ultimately, teachers establish "curricular priorities" based on their instructional objectives regarding three levels of knowledge, including material "worth being familiar with," followed by knowledge "important to know and do."

The ultimate goal, Wiggins and McTighe have suggested, is that teaching will lead to "enduring understanding," whereby students are able to absorb more in-depth knowledge, producing performances or exhibiting critical thinking skills that exceed in quality the products of traditional instructional experiences. A focus on enduring understanding stresses ideas, principles, and processes rather than simple facts, ensuring that students are able to apply their knowledge in new ways and in different contexts.

How It Works

Teachers design successful authentic experiences when students employ a complex array of critical thinking and problem-solving skills that involve independent research, analysis, and application of knowledge. Students engaged in applying knowledge in new and meaningful ways are expected to achieve enduring understanding, a characteristic of authentic assessment.

Authentic assessment focuses on contextual learning in an environment that fosters inquiry and enduring understanding using evidence collected by the teacher in ongoing evaluations of student learning. The evidence of authentic learning involves documenting performances and products developed during a unit or over a period of time, which may include observations, dialogues, and students' self-evaluations. To employ authentic assessment methods, teachers design open-ended, complex assignments.

As Wiggins and McTighe have noted, these tasks and projects replicate issues and challenges faced by adults in real life and include short-term tasks as well as longer and more complex projects requiring performances and production. Characteristics of performance tasks and projects include a real or simulated setting, a targeted audience, a specific purpose that has meaning or is of importance to the audience, the personalization of the students' experiences, and the "task, criteria, and standards" for students before and during the learning activities.

Further, Wiggins and McTighe have explored the various qualities of authentic assessment in six levels of understanding. They have suggested that students who truly understand concepts are able to explain, interpret, apply, see in perspective, demonstrate empathy, and reveal self-knowledge, with clearly defined criteria for performance and production. As Wiggins explained in *Assessing Student Performance,* authenticity is thus characterized by intellectually challenging learning experiences that require students to be creative and that involve and engage them with worthwhile problems and questions. Other examples of authentic assessment include contextual learning, which replicates real-life situations or employs actual problems that require students to apply a repertoire of skills and knowledge that lead to a sound judgment or an effective solution.

Students who engage in tasks that require the development and creation of an actual artifact or product according to preestablished criteria and standards are providing evidence of authentic assessment. In addition, such assessment involves interactions between teachers and students about the evaluation process itself and provides students with opportunities to justify responses and to explain further through follow-up questions and challenges that allow for feedback, correction, and improvement. These projects and performances also increase students' engagement with both the process and the product, ensuring that students have greater motivation and responsibility for their learning and teachers get feedback in order to design ever more effective tools for evaluating them.

Ultimately, authentic assessment provides students with enduring understanding in a meaningful context that replicates the experiences of living in a complex, ever-changing society. In this way, as Wiggins and his colleague have suggested, authentic assessment prepares students to negotiate the challenges of everyday life, the complex world of careers and work, and the diverse needs of individuals and societies both now and in the future.

Roxanne Newton

See also Standardized Testing

Further Readings

Burke, K. (2005). *How to assess authentic learning* (4th ed.). Thousand Oaks, CA: Sage.

Darling-Hammond, L., Ancess, J., & Falk, B. (1995). *Authentic assessment in action: Studies of schools and students at work.* New York: Teachers College Press.

Wiggins, G. (1993). *Assessing student performance: Exploring the purpose and limits of testing.* San Francisco: Jossey-Bass.

Wiggins, G. (1993). *Educative assessment: Designing assessments to inform and improve student performance.* San Francisco: Jossey-Bass.

Wiggins, G., & McTighe, J. (1998). *Understanding by design.* Alexandria, VA: Association for Supervision and Curriculum Development.

Web Sites

University of Wisconsin-Stout School of Education Online Assessment Resources for Teachers: http://www.uwstout.edu/soe/profdev/assess.shtml

B

BILINGUAL EDUCATION, HISTORY OF

Bilingual education, or instruction in more than one language, has occurred throughout history and around the world. A review of that history reveals that practices and beliefs related to languages in education are intricately connected to attitudes toward linguistic and cultural diversity, and especially toward indigenous, ethnic, and foreign groups. Perhaps it is for these reasons that bilingual education inspires controversy and raises questions not only of pedagogy, but also of politics and ideology.

The history of bilingual education is not a steady movement in a single direction; rather, there is a constant flux of policies, practices, and ideology. Proponents of bilingual education stress the academic, cognitive, and cultural advantages that accrue to individuals and to society when children maintain and develop their home language and attain academic competence in another language as well. Opponents of bilingual education stress the need for cultural and linguistic assimilation, and posit that time spent learning in a minority language detracts from academic and linguistic development in the majority language. Struggles between these two views, as well as conflicting beliefs about the nature of diversity and the goals of education, are sure to continue. This entry looks at the development of bilingual education over the course of U.S. history and reviews contrasting international approaches.

Program Descriptions

The term *bilingual education* is popularly used for a wide variety of educational models, including some in which the only "bilingual" component is that some or most of the students are bilingual. This entry will consider educational settings in which more than one language is used in instruction, but this definition too covers a wide range of practices and goals.

Bilingual programs around the world serve immigrant and indigenous speakers of minority languages, as well as children of middle-class and affluent parents who seek bilingualism for enrichment. Among different types of programs, an important distinction is between *transitional* and *maintenance* bilingual education. In transitional programs, the use of native languages is encouraged only in the short term, for the purpose of helping students learn the majority language (i.e., English in the United States). By contrast, in maintenance programs the goal is not only second language acquisition, but also language and literacy skills in the native language. One type of maintenance program is the *dual-language* or *two-way* model, in which both languages are used, often (and ideally) with approximately half the students proficient in one language, and the other half proficient in the other, with both groups learning language and content in both languages.

Yet another type of bilingual education is heritage language instruction, in which lessons are delivered in a minority language, often one that is in danger of extinction. It is significant that the terms *majority language* and *minority language* refer not to the relative number of speakers, but rather, to the relative power and dominance of the speakers of that language.

U.S. History

Although bilingual education was common in the early history of the United States, it was virtually eliminated in the first half of the twentieth century, until a renaissance of bilingual education occurred in the 1960s both in the United States and around the world.

Early Bilingualism

As early as 1694, German-speaking Americans were operating German-language schools in Philadelphia, some bilingual, some monolingual German. By the mid-1800s, schools in Baltimore, Cincinnati, Cleveland, Indianapolis, Milwaukee, and St. Louis used both German and English in instruction. The first law in America pertaining to language use was enacted in Ohio in 1839, authorizing instruction in English, German, or both languages, according to parents' requests. Similar laws were passed soon after in other places. In 1847, Louisiana adopted the same law, substituting French for German. The Territory of New Mexico, two years after its annexation in 1848, authorized Spanish-English bilingual education.

Bilingual education grew in the 1800s in the United States. In the second half of the 1800s, schools in German, Swedish, Norwegian, Danish, Dutch, Polish, and Italian were set up by communities in several additional states. A surprising statistic is that in the year 1900, 600,000 American children—about 4 percent of the elementary school population at the time—received instruction either partly or exclusively in German. While this openness to other languages was at least partially motivated by competition for students between public and private schools, it also reflects tolerance of linguistic and ethnic diversity. Acceptance of children's home culture and language was generally believed to be emotionally and culturally advantageous to children, and the most effective route to their cultural and linguistic assimilation.

An English-Only Movement

This is not to say that such beliefs were held universally, as English-only laws were promoted as well. Both Illinois and Wisconsin adopted English-only laws in 1889, and this English-monolingual approach gained momentum at the turn of the twentieth century. One reason for the shift in attitude at that time is that the number of new immigrants increased dramatically. These new arrivals (largely Jews and Italians) were unlike previous groups, whose appearance and customs had been similar to those of other European Americans. In addition, the new immigrants headed not to the frontier, but to cities, overwhelming public schools and engendering fears of foreigners as well as increasing calls for integration and assimilation. English proficiency came to be seen as a sign of political loyalty to the United States, and the loss of home language and culture was seen as part of the Americanization process.

In 1919, the Americanization Department of the U.S. Bureau of Education adopted a resolution recommending that states prescribe that all schools, public and private, conduct instruction in English. With the entry of the United States into World War I, anti-German feeling increased, and the pressure for English monolingualism grew. Schools were viewed as instruments of assimilation, with no role for other cultures or for languages other than English. Interest in learning foreign languages declined as well.

By 1923, thirty-four states had enacted laws requiring that English be the only language of instruction in elementary schools, both public and private. A Supreme Court ruling in the same year (*Meyer v. Nebraska*) overruled a state law prohibiting the teaching of foreign languages to elementary students. The Court's ruling is significant for referring to languages other than English as "foreign" rather than "ethnic"; this terminology reflects a shift in ideology, where speakers of languages other than English came to be seen not as ethnolinguistic minorities, but instead as foreigners or aliens, outsiders in the United States. By the late 1930s, bilingual instruction in the United States had been virtually eliminated.

Ethnic Awareness

The 1960s brought new awareness of ethnic identity and civil rights, contributing to renewed attention to the education of language minority students. The success of a dual-language program at the Coral Way Elementary School in Miami, Florida, also fueled interest in bilingual education. Coral Way enrolled middle-class Spanish-speaking children recently arrived from Cuba, along with native English speakers, and achieved bilingualism, biliteracy, and strong academic attainment among both groups. The school received national notice, and served as a model for the establishment of other bilingual programs elsewhere in Dade County and in the Southwest.

In spite of the success of Coral Way and other dual-language programs, a view emerged of bilingual education as a compensatory, remedial program for disadvantaged children. The U.S. Bilingual Education Act (BEA) of 1968 saw the role of native languages primarily as a means to teach children English. It is this "deficit" view of bilingual education, rather than a "language as resource" view, that has generally informed policies and discussions of bilingual education in the United States.

Services for language minority students grew in the 1970s. In the landmark case *Lau v. Nichols,* the U.S. Supreme Court ruled in 1974 on behalf of Chinese students in San Francisco that schools must make accommodations for students who do not speak English. While the decision did not specify what actions school districts had to take, subsequent guidelines developed by the Office of Civil Rights (the Lau Remedies) did describe specific evaluation and instructional methods. In New York City in the same year, Aspira, a Puerto Rican advocacy group, reached an agreement with the city's Board of Education to provide bilingual education in classes with a specified number of students who spoke the same minority language. Nevertheless, the 1980s saw a preference for English-only classes, and a shift away from bilingual education.

Opposition Groups

Groups opposed to bilingual education, such as U.S. English, English Only, and English First, have contributed to the ideological climate. In 1998, Proposition 227 passed in California, virtually outlawing bilingual education in that state. Proponents of this law argued that teaching children in their native language served only to hold them back in their acquisition of English and therefore in their future educational success. Although a comparable initiative in Colorado failed in 2002, similar measures were approved by voters in Arizona in 2000 and Massachusetts in 2001.

In 2001, the Bilingual Education Act was replaced by the federal No Child Left Behind Act (NCLB), which requires states to measure outcomes for groups of students including English language learners. School districts may apply for funding for bilingual education, but the focus is on the use of the native language strictly as a means to proficiency in English. The high stakes assessments mandated by NCLB mean that English language learners will be assessed for English fluency and content knowledge every year, and that students and teachers will focus immediately and intensely on the skills measured on the tests.

In both a further setback for and a reflection of public disapproval of bilingual education, the federal government's National Clearinghouse for Bilingual Education changed its name in 2002 to expunge the term *bilingual education,* and is now known as the National Clearinghouse for English Language Acquisition and Language Instruction Educational Programs.

Continued Growth

Nevertheless, bilingual education programs have grown recently in the United States. The Center for Applied Linguistics (CAL) reports a doubling of the number of dual-language programs between 1996 and 2006. This growth is credited to research that has consistently documented the academic value of first-language literacy as well as the effectiveness of bilingual education for both native-language and second-language speakers, a recognition of the need for multilingual citizens, and a dramatic increase in the number of English language learners in American schools.

Interest in indigenous-language bilingual programs is also growing. Title VII of NCLB authorizes and provides funds for native-language education programs for

American Indian, native Hawaiian, and native Alaskan education.

International Experiences

Bilingual education is not a recent innovation. The earliest evidence of children's schoolwork in two languages comes from cuneiform tablets from Mesopotamia between 3000 and 2000 BCE, where Akkadian was spoken alongside Sumerian. In Ancient Rome, education was routinely bilingual in both Latin and Greek, setting the precedent still found most widely in the world: education takes place primarily in the language of the elite. Then, as now, it is most often the language of government and economic power that is the medium of instruction.

In many countries, the expected outcome of formal education is bilingualism or multilingualism; for example, instruction in Brunei, Nigeria, Singapore, and Taiwan is delivered in one or more national languages as well as in English, with the aim of full bilingualism and biliteracy. In Europe, bilingual education is called Content and Language Integrated Learning (CLIL), in which the medium of instruction is students' native language as well as an additional international language. Most European countries also provide home language support for immigrant students. While proficiency in the language of the host country is the highest priority, there is particular concern that students from other European Union member countries maintain their home language as well.

In 1951, UNESCO (the United Nations Educational, Scientific, and Cultural Organization) considered the question of language in education, and concluded that children's early education should take place in their mother tongue. Governments were encouraged to print textbooks and other materials in native languages, and to prepare native speakers to teach in those languages. UNESCO also recommended transitioning to a second language, to be taught gradually through the use of the first language.

The Canadian bilingual education movement is often traced to 1965, and the creation of an experimental kindergarten class in St. Lambert, Montreal, spurred by the activism of a relatively small number of English-speaking parents who wanted their children to become bilingual, biliterate, and bicultural, while maintaining cognitive and academic achievement. A distinctive feature of this program, known as immersion bilingual education, is that it involved speakers of the majority language, English, who received instruction in the minority language, French. English language arts were introduced gradually, beginning in the second grade. The success of the immersion program at St. Lambert led to the spread of this educational model in Canada, and to several European countries as well.

In the 1960s and 1970s, other countries that had previously offered education only in the majority language adopted the use of minority languages in instruction. For example, English-Welsh bilingual education became prevalent in Wales as a result of the Welsh Language Act of 1967. The new Spanish Constitution of 1978 recognized Catalan, Basque (or Euskera), and Galician as official languages in their communities, and mandated the use of those languages in schools in those regions.

In Peru, the indigenous language Quechua was recognized as an official language in 1975, leading to a Spanish-Quechua bilingual education project throughout the 1980s that was emulated elsewhere in Latin America in the 1990s. In Bolivia, where indigenous-language speakers comprise 63 percent of the population, the Bolivian Education Reform, launched in 1994, aims to transform the educational system by instituting bilingual education programs in all thirty of Bolivia's indigenous languages.

New Zealand, which had previously banned the Maori language from schools, has endeavored to preserve the language of the indigenous Maoris since the 1970s by creating bilingual English-Maori schools, as well as schools in which Maori instruction is supplemented by limited time in English.

South Africa's 1993 constitution explicitly recognizes language as a basic human right. Breaking with the previous view of multilingualism as a societal problem, the government now approaches linguistic diversity as a national resource. The constitution recognizes African languages as official national languages (in addition to English and Afrikaans), and schools have been charged with including the use of "own-language" instruction. Efforts are underway not only to develop and publish literature in the indigenous languages, but also to produce television broadcasting and dictionaries in these local languages.

Nancy Stern

See also English-Only Movement; Foreign Language Instruction; Hispanic Education; Immigrant Education: Contemporary Issues

See Visual History Chapter 11, International Expositions; Chapter 14, Immigration and Education

Further Readings

Baker, C. (2006). *Foundations of bilingual education and bilingualism* (4th ed.). Clevedon, UK: Multilingual Matters.

Baker, C., & Jones, M. P. (1998). *Encyclopedia of bilingualism and bilingual education.* Clevedon, UK: Multilingual Matters.

Crawford, J. (1999). *Educating English learners: Language diversity in the classroom* (5th ed.). Los Angeles: Bilingual Educational Services.

García, O. (1997). Bilingual education. In F. Coulmas (Ed.), *The handbook of sociolinguistics* (pp. 405–420). Oxford, UK: Blackwell.

Hornberger, N. H. (1988). Language policy, language education, language rights: Indigenous, immigrant, and international perspectives. *Language in Society 27,* 439–458.

BILITERACY

Biliteracy is a term used to describe competencies in reading and writing, to any degree, developed either simultaneously or successively, in two linguistic systems. It is widely accepted that the development of literacy in childhood is a transformative and emancipating accomplishment. Literacy is consistently associated with educational achievement and continues to be a part of the cultural capital valued by our society. Becoming literate has significant intellectual advantages, including the development of metalinguistic awareness (i.e., the ability to talk and think about language), access to valued cultural resources, and the strategic use of linguistic and literacy resources as tools for thinking. In the case of bilingual children, learning to read and write in only one language does not suffice since bilinguals need to function in two

linguistic communities. If becoming literate represents such a remarkable achievement, then the development of biliteracy seems to be an extraordinary feat. This entry looks at the characteristics of biliteracy and the process in which it is developed.

Characteristics

Biliteracy is a complex phenomenon of bilingualism, a ubiquitous but often misunderstood construct. Although there is no simple definition of bilingualism, François Grosjean has discussed several features of bilinguals that are relevant to understanding children who are developing biliteracy. First, bilinguals usually acquire and use their languages for different purposes, in different domains of life, with different people. Second, bilinguals are rarely equally fluent in all language skills in all their languages, as the level of fluency largely depends on the need and use of a language. Third, few bilinguals possess the same competence as monolingual speakers in either of their languages. Fourth, some bilinguals may still be in the process of acquiring a language whereas others have attained a certain level of stability. Fifth, the linguistic repertoire and language proficiencies of bilinguals may change over time. Finally, bilinguals interact both with monolinguals and with other bilinguals and adapt their language behavior accordingly. These characteristics highlight the complexities involved in defining and understanding individual bilingualism, while at the same time belie the existence of great within-group diversity.

Biliteracy is a special form of literacy that must be understood as distinct from that of monolinguals. This is because bilinguals can experience a range and variety of literacy practices and transact with two literate worlds to create knowledge and transform it for meaningful purposes through their participation in multilingual and multicultural social networks that are not accessible to the monolingual. Regardless of the pervasiveness of bilingualism in the world, including in highly literate settings, biliteracy remains a relatively unexamined phenomenon.

Biliteracy is important because it may amplify bilingual children's linguistic and intellectual possibilities by providing them with access to a broader range of academic, social, and cultural resources. Evidence from the growing research base in emergent, or early, biliteracy acquisition suggests that bilingual children have the potential to develop literacy in two languages, and that these literacies can develop more or less simultaneously in supportive classroom settings. The evidence also suggests that there are multiple paths to children's biliteracy development and that these multiple paths are normal aspects of bilingual development. Further, when biliteracy is encouraged and promoted, literacy skills and strategies learned in either language appear to influence, or transfer to, the other language. This means that biliteracy involves a bidirectional process rather than one that only involves transfer from the first language to the second. Finally, the context in which biliteracy acquisition and development occurs is an important factor that has tremendous implications for the maintenance and continued support for dual-language literacy.

Process Issues

Some bilingual children learn to read and write in both languages simultaneously. Many two-way immersion or dual-language programs in the United States follow this type of model for dual-language and literacy acquisition. Other young bilinguals learn to read and write in their second language before they learn to read and write in their first, as in the case of French immersion programs in Canada where native English-speaking children are introduced to literacy through their second language, French. Both of these approaches tend to result in high levels of biliteracy as children continue to develop both languages and literacies to high degrees on a longitudinal basis.

A third approach is where children develop literacy first in their native language, and later in a second language. In the United States, this is a common route to English-language literacy for language-minority children. This can be a successful route to biliteracy only if the native/minority language continues to be promoted and developed to high degrees once English (second language) literacy is achieved and not abandoned before it is fully developed.

As researchers have observed, multiple paths are possible for becoming bilingual and biliterate, and no single sequence is best or more appropriate for all children. For example, many emergent bilinguals write in their second language before demonstrating oral ability in that language. This pathway questions the common assumption that literacy is always dependent on progress in the spoken language. Second, a number of emergent bilinguals can write better than they can read in their second language. This pattern is also found among young monolinguals. Third, some emergent bilinguals are more proficient speakers in their first language but better readers in their second language. Formal instruction in native-language literacy, or lack thereof, may play an important role in these instances. These examples highlight the tremendous diversity in the ways in which children progress and develop in their biliterate abilities.

A growing body of research suggests that the relationships between bilingual children's languages and uses of English and Spanish within and outside of school are fluid and reciprocal. Similarly, biliteracy development is a dynamic, flexible process in which children's transactions with two written languages mediate their language and literacy learning in both languages. Emergent bilinguals employ literacy behaviors and skills cross-linguistically and bidirectionally. In other words, bilingual readers and writers apply what is learned in one language to the other language. Bidirectionality plays an especially important role in young bilinguals, as language and literacy in the two languages develop simultaneously, and development in each language supports advances in the other language.

With continued encouragement, support, and instruction in two languages, bilingual children learn to control the writing systems of both languages. That is, if children are placed in classrooms and instructional programs where their bilingualism and biliteracy are encouraged in additive contexts, dual-language literacy can thrive. For example, in Canadian immersion programs and dual-language (or two-way immersion) programs in the United States, children develop linguistic and literacy skills, often to high degrees, in two languages at no cost to either of the languages. In contrast, in subtractive environments that threaten the status and maintenance of one of the languages, usually a minority language such as Spanish or Chinese in U.S. contexts, the development of bilingualism and biliteracy is limited and often only serves as a temporary bridge to monoliteracy in English.

Biliteracy is a complex phenomenon that requires further study. This topic is only just beginning to receive more attention from educational researchers in bilingual education, literacy research, and linguistics. Children become literate in two languages not only though acquiring and developing a set of skills or abilities but also through becoming competent in a range of practices and uses of literacy that constitute the experience of living, going to school, and being successful in a bilingual community. The growing research base in the field suggests that if children have access to and opportunities to function in both languages and writing systems, they will be more likely to *maintain* and continue to *develop* their bilingualism and biliteracy at school and beyond. As such, biliteracy offers multiple lenses through which to interpret, navigate, and negotiate the world in ways that are unique to bilinguals.

Mileidis Gort

See also English-Only Movement; Hispanic Education; Immigrant Education: Contemporary Issues

Further Readings

Barnard, R., & Glynn, T. (2003). *Bilingual children's language and literacy development.* Clevedon, UK: Multilingual Matters.

Edelsky, C. (1993). *Writing in a bilingual program: Habia una vez.* Norwood, NJ: Ablex.

Gort, M. (2006). Strategic codeswitching, interliteracy, and other phenomena of emergent bilingual writing: Lessons from first-grade dual language classrooms. *Journal of Early Childhood Literacy, 6*(3), 323–354.

Hornberger, N. H. (2003). *Continua of biliteracy: An ecological framework for educational policy, research, and practice in multilingual settings.* Clevedon, UK: Multilingual Matters.

Oller, D. K., & Eilers, R. E. (2002). *Language and literacy in bilingual children.* Clevedon, UK: Multilingual Matters.

Perez, B. (2004). *Becoming biliterate: A study of two-way bilingual immersion education.* Mahwah, NJ: Lawrence Erlbaum.

Reyes, I. (2006). Exploring connections between emergent biliteracy and bilingualism. *Journal of Early Childhood Literacy, 6*(3), 267–292.

BIOGRAPHY

Biography is a useful way to focus on the major educational theories that have shaped Western education and schooling across the last 2,500 years. Tying educational theorists' and philosophers' work to their lives connects the abstract to the practical, for life includes the internal realities of the mind as well as the daily practice of living. As Barbara Tuchman has pointed out, biography is similar to a prism because it keeps people's attention on the larger subject through their interest in other people. The biographies and theories included in this entry are representative of those who have left a substantial written legacy of important ideas and theories that have helped to shape the educational landscape.

Greco-Roman Traditions

The ancient Greek and Roman philosophers had and continue to have a major impact on educational traditions in Europe and the Americas.

Plato

Plato (428–347 BCE) came from an aristocratic Athenian family and had one sister, Petone, and two brothers, Glaucon and Adeimantus, whose names appear in *The Republic.* His nickname, Plato (meaning "broad shoulders"), soon replaced his given name of Aristocles. He received an aristocratic boy's education of grammar, music, gymnastics, and poetry, which should have led him into the life of a leader and/or politician. Instead, history remembers him for his skill as a writer of numerous dialogues with Socrates as the protagonist.

Plato's thinking was strongly influenced by Socrates and Pythagoras, whose work he encountered while traveling in Egypt. His travels took him to most parts of the Mediterranean world. He returned to Athens after ten years away, and settled on land that housed a gymnasium known as the Academy where members engaged in philosophical, religious, and political discussions and conversations during dinners, or banquets, that were known as *symposia.* He died at the age of about eighty-one and left his land

and four of his five slaves to his brother, Adeimantus. He set free a female slave in his will.

Plato's social, political, and educational ideas were developed in his dialogues, especially *The Republic*. He maintained his intellectual connections with Pythagorean tenets, believing in "ideas" as universal organizing principles that undergird all sensory perceptions in the physical world. This is the theme of his allegory of the cave where the physical world is no more "real" than the shadows on the wall of the cave. To understand these organizing principles or ideas was the key to education, but everyone was not going to be able intellectually to understand them, Plato thought. Hence, in his view, education must be able to separate those who will be the leaders or philosopher-kings from those who will be the artisans, military officers, merchants, and other members of society.

This is the essence of his "myth of the metals," in which Socrates describes how God has made individuals different from one another. Education must sift out the various metals that correspond to different social occupations, leaving only the gold destined to be philosopher-kings. In the early twentieth century when testing was becoming important, some psychologists and educators thought that the IQ test was the realization of the Platonic ideal.

Aristotle

One of Plato's students, Aristotle (384–322 BCE) was the son of a Macedonian king and the tutor of Alexander the Great. He came to the Academy when he was seventeen and stayed for twenty years. Plato was said to have called him *nous* (mind) or the intellect of the school, while Aristotle regarded Plato as living by his own words in leading a life of contemplative happiness or "good"ness. (Aristotle was said to be the only Academy fellow who could comprehend Plato's concept of the "good.")

Aristotle became interested in his physical surroundings and studied them through scientific observation. For him education was the road to moral and rational virtues and moderation—the keys to happiness. These were inherent in human beings and not tied to a Platonic, transcendental ideal.

The Romans

Roman leaders were interested in the rational and philosophical to the degree that it made them good orators. Hence, the Greek study of grammar, rhetoric, and logic (*trivium*) became the most important course of study. The other four subjects or *quadrivium*—music, arithmetic, astronomy, and geometry—that rounded out the seven liberal arts were not as important to the Romans.

Cicero (106–43 BCE) was lucky to have had a Greek tutor (pedagogue), and he also studied philosophy and rhetoric and oratory in Greece and Rhodes. Upon his return he entered politics and remained until he was falsely accused of being part of the plot to kill Julius Caesar—an accusation that resulted in his beheading in 43 BCE. Twelve years earlier, however, he wrote his famous treatise on education, *De Oratore*, which called for a well-rounded broad course of study with history at the center instead of the narrow trivium.

While it had little influence on Roman schooling, it became the Renaissance ideal of education. A century after Cicero's death, a Spanish-born Roman named Quintilian (35–95 CE) patterned his *Institutes of Oratory* on Cicero's work. Quintilian came to Rome as the first imperially financed teacher, and then became the tutor to the son of one of the Roman emperors. In his treatise, good literature replaced history as the vehicle for learning, with the goal of producing good people. He was one of the first on record to speak out against corporal punishment or "flogging" as it was called. Instead, he thought children should learn to love study, and that would only happen if they were treated well and rewarded for their accomplishments.

Renaissance Transformations

Many aspects of Greco-Roman education were Christianized in the remaining centuries of the first millennium of the Common Era through the works of St. Augustine; Charlemagne and his teacher, Alcuin; and St. Thomas Aquinas. By the early part of the second millennium, those traditions that had been lost in the Christian world were rediscovered during the period known as the Renaissance.

In Florence under the direction of the Medici family, Greek and Roman literature and art were valued for their own sake instead of religious purposes. Humanism or the "new learning" was born, and the classics were read as inspiration for the cultivation of personal virtues including civic duty. Vittorino de Feltre (1378–1446) was a humanist teacher who believed in the Renaissance ideal of preparing individuals to lead a virtuous life through the study of the Greek and Roman classics.

Desiderius Erasmus

For the most part, women were not part of this Italian rebirth of learning, but as it spread to northern Europe, they found an advocate in Desiderius Erasmus (1466–1536). Known as "the Prince of Humanists." Erasmus was born in Deventer in Holland, the illegitimate son of a priest and a physician's daughter. He was educated for the priesthood by the Brothers of Common Life and the Augustinians, and continued his study at the Sorbonne in Paris. He regarded himself as a "citizen of the world" and became the friend and confidante of Sir Thomas More and other humanists in England.

His major work, *In Praise of Folly* (1911), is a satire on the ills of society, and in some of his other works he called for reform of the Christian/Catholic church. In fact, many have pointed to these latter works as the signal that began the Reformation. He made no distinction between being a Christian and being a humanist scholar and called for a well-ordered society through the study of a classical liberal arts education. In his educational scheme, he included the education of girls through a carefully developed curriculum.

John Amos Comenius

Like Erasmus, John Amos Comenius (1592–1670) was seen as a "citizen of the world" and a man of peace during a period of the religious wars of the Reformation. He was born Jan Kominsky in Moravia, Czechoslovakia, the youngest child and only son of five children born to Protestant parents of modest means. Orphaned by the age of sixteen, he attended a grammar school operated by the Unity of Brethren, a Protestant group following the beliefs of John Hus. The rector of the school supported Comenius's education and sent him to the Calvinist gymnasium (secondary school) of Herborn in central Germany.

Comenius was a supporter of education for the masses, not just the more academic secondary form of education found in grammar schools and gymnasiums. By the middle of the nineteenth century his works had been translated into German, English, and French. He became known as the "pioneer of modern educational science" because he thought that children should study things, or objects, before learning to read, and that the curriculum should be carefully organized around experiences that reflected the "natural" sensory order of things. Hence, play and enjoyment would replace the dreary grind of schooling in his time.

Comenius was one of the first to use pictures in reading texts. He also agreed with most of the reformers of the day that children needed to be able to read the vernacular in addition to Latin. In other words, he was advocating universal literacy in the vernacular along with the teaching of arithmetic skills. He included girls in this education, although he thought their roles in the household called for less of a classical or secondary preparation.

Enlightenment Thinkers

Protestant reformers such as Comenius, Martin Luther, and John Calvin provided strong voices for educating the masses. However, the class structure was still forcefully maintained in Europe. This resulted in a two-track form of schooling: basic vernacular literacy for the masses in elementary, folk, common, or petty schools and the elite liberal arts education for the upper-class leaders of society to be found in secondary schools such as gymnasia, lycées, grammar schools, and academies. Euro-American struggles in the seventeenth century provided competition for this elitist socioeducational structure and influenced the thought of Enlightenment philosophers such as Immanuel Kant (1724–1804), John Locke (1632–1704), and Jean-Jacques Rousseau (1712–1778), but it did little to transform the thinking on the education of girls and women.

Kant's *sapere aude* ("dare to know") gave the signal to individuals to use their intelligence to take charge of their lives, without the guidance of a controlling socioeconomic class. And John Locke developed a theory of constitutional law and democratic form of government along with a theory of education.

John Locke

Born to a country physician, Locke was educated at Oxford, where he also tutored and lectured in medicine and experimental science. He became the personal physician to the Earl of Shaftsbury and lived a comfortable life in England, and in Holland when his opposition to the king made it difficult to stay in London. It was during his period in Holland, when a friend asked his advice on educating his son, that he wrote *Some Thoughts Concerning Education* (1692).

Here Locke criticized the current schools for relying on corporal punishment and advocated tutorial arrangements with a curriculum that did not stress the rote memory of Latin and Greek, but focused on more practical subjects such as, geography, history, geometry, and astronomy, along with civil law and language. The focus of his educational theory was the theory of the mind as a blank tablet, or *tabula rasa,* at birth, which is filled through the child's sensory experiences.

Locke's stress on the practical along with the rejection of inborn intellectual talent found support in American colonial society, as well as in the twentieth century with American Progressives—as did the ideas of Rousseau, who was born in France shortly after Locke's death.

Jean-Jacques Rousseau

Jean-Jacques Rousseau's mother died giving birth to him, and he spent his young years in the care of his father's unmarried sister and a nursemaid. His father had wanderlust and was rarely home with his two sons. When he was home, he would read romance-type novels to his younger son that left the boy, from age seven on, with a confused sense of adult passion. As a boy Rousseau loved the countryside, and one night when he was sixteen, he chose not to return to the city of Geneva before the gates closed.

In his *Confessions,* Rousseau cites this incident as the beginning of his vagabond life, wandering between various Swiss towns and Paris. He ultimately made his living copying music in Paris. He met and befriended a rather pathetic and ignorant seamstress named Theresa, who became the mother of his five children—all of whom were given away to be raised in foundling homes. Rousseau is unclear about his motivation for doing this, other than to say that he was not cut out to be a father, and ignorant Therese seemed ill equipped to raise children.

In Paris he became friends with the French philosopher Denis Diderot and entered an essay contest at his suggestion. Rousseau argued that human nature is basically good and that it is society that corrupts. To his amazement he won the contest and began attending fashionable dinner parties where he continued to dress in his peasant fur hat and robe to remain true to his beliefs. Under the patronage of elitist society members, he wrote *The Social Contract* (1762), and *Émile* (1762), a novel about the proper education of a boy. *Émile* ultimately came under censorship from the French government and Rousseau fled to England, where he became friendly with David Hume. In 1767, he decided to return to Paris under a pseudonym. He finished his *Confessions* and began some other writing, working until 1778, when he suffered a brain hemorrhage and died.

In *Émile,* Rousseau calls for the boy to be raised in nature with a tutor and not parents who might be too controlling. In nature, Émile could explore his surroundings safely and move freely without any of the swaddling clothes that were still being used at that time. Once the child developed muscle control, moral education began, and it was taught by example. There was no punishment involved, and a boy's intellectual education came after his moral training. Knowledge was to come from studying natural science and reading books such as *Robinson Crusoe.* Subjects dealing with society were avoided until his later teen years when his character was strong enough to handle social corruption. Many of Rousseau's ideas were the basis for future Progressive reformers' theories, but the tension in his work between individual freedom and social responsibility was problematic for many of his followers.

The education of women was the last chapter in *Émile* and was the only part that did not cause a stir at the time. It described an education that taught subservience to men and epitomized the attitudes that women such as Mary Wollstonecraft (1759–1797) found so abhorrent. Her best known work, *A Vindication of the Rights of Woman* (1792), called for an end to this subservient education and proposed a more egalitarian curriculum that included females and males.

Progressive Educational Ideas

Rousseau's ideas set the ball in motion for followers such as Johann Pestalozzi (1746–1827), with his pedagogical study of objects, and Friedrich Froebel (1782–1852), founder of the kindergarten movement. Johann Herbart (1776–1841) developed many of these ideas into formal steps with his theory of apperception, which posits that any new idea is understood in terms of material and sensory experiences already known to the individual.

Nineteenth-century America was ripe for these ideas as the new United States began to think about the type of schooling that would be available to all citizens. Common school advocates—such as Massachusetts Secretary of Education Horace Mann (1796–1859); educational reformer Henry Barnard (1811–1900), who held political positions in Connecticut and Rhode Island; and Quincy, Massachusetts' superintendent, Colonel Francis W. Parker (1837–1902)—studied these continental theorists as they planned for state and local school systems. Colonel Francis W. Parker's "theory of concentration," outlined in his *Talks on Pedagogics,* was an outgrowth of his study of Herbart, Pestalozzi, and Froebel; and Clark University President G. Stanley Hall implemented Rousseauian natural growth concepts in his child study movement.

John Dewey: Early Years

The person to bring these ideas into a unified, coherent system of thought was John Dewey (1859–1952). Born in Burlington, Vermont, to fourth-generation New Englanders, Dewey grew up during the Civil War and learned at an early age the negative outcomes of prejudice and suffering. The family followed his father as he fought in the cavalry, and his mother's strong abolitionist and liberal religious views made an impression on the young boy. After the war the family returned to Burlington, where they owned a grocery store. Dewey finished his early schooling and matriculated at the University of Vermont.

Upon graduation he moved to Oil City, Pennsylvania, to teach at the high school where his cousin was principal. He taught algebra, Latin, and the natural sciences and published his first article, "The Metaphysical Assumptions of Materialism," in William Torrey Harris's *Journal of Speculative Philosophy.* Encouraged by this foray into philosophy, Dewey returned to Burlington and began a tutorial study of philosophy while he taught at the local academy. He applied to the Johns Hopkins University Ph.D. program, and because he was not awarded a fellowship, an aunt supported him financially. Influenced by the logic of Charles Sanders Pierce, the psychology of G. Stanley Hall, and the idealism of George Sylvester Morris, he graduated in 1884, having written his dissertation on Kantian epistemology and psychology.

Dewey was hired to teach philosophy at the University of Michigan, where he met and married Alice Chipman. He moved to the University of Minnesota in 1888, and taught there for one year before being hired back to the University of Michigan as the Chair of the Philosophy Department. He became friends with George Herbert Mead, who helped him secure the Chair of Philosophy, Psychology and Pedagogy at the University of Chicago.

Dewey on Education

In 1904, under Dewey's direction, the University of Chicago published a decennial series titled *Contributions to Education.* The publication caused Harvard psychologist William James to claim that under Dewey's leadership the University of Chicago had developed a new school of thought. James (1842–1910) had redefined the old Platonic idea in terms of its "workability" or utility. He had argued against absolutes and described a world that was in a state of change. This theory fit with Pierce's logic that defined concepts in terms of their human consequences, and defined knowledge as that which is validated by human experiences.

To these concepts Dewey added his theory of instrumentalism, which views ideas as instruments to be used to solve problems—psychological, social, educational, or physical/environmental. This new school of thought came to be known as pragmatism, and with the help of Ella Flagg Young, a doctoral student and future superintendent of the Chicago public schools, he implemented these progressive practices in his Laboratory School at the University of Chicago.

Dewey left the University of Chicago in 1904 and joined the philosophy and education faculty at Columbia University and its Teachers College. In 1915 his *Democracy and Education* was published, followed by many other articles and books, including the revised edition of *How We Think* (1933) and *Experience and Education* (1938). Together with his wife, Alice, he advocated equality for women and African Americans. In 1927 Alice died, and in 1930 he retired from teaching. He continued to travel, and lectured in the Soviet Union and throughout the world, becoming the first internationally renowned American philosopher. In 1946, Dewey married a much younger woman, Roberta Lowitz Grant, a widow whose family he had been friendly with during his Oil City years. He died on June 1, 1952 after a brief illness.

One of Dewey's students at the University of Chicago was John B. Watson (1878–1958), who developed a new experimental branch of psychology published as a book entitled *Behaviorism* in 1924. At Columbia, Dewey's colleague Edward L. Thorndyke (1874–1949) was working on a more experimental form of behavioristic psychology known as connectionism, which focused on observable and measurable animal responses to various stimuli.

Existential Themes in Postmodern Times

As various forms of behaviorism controlled mid-twentieth-century American schools, some educators instead embraced existentialist ideas of human freedom and turned to the 1962 book *Summerhill* by A. S. Neill (1883–1973). Published in 1960 it called for freedom from these controls and described a school in England that Neill had been running since the 1920s under the premise that children should be free "to be themselves." Nel Noddings, while concerned with issues similar to Neill's, specifically calls for schools to become caring environments, in which teachers and students are mutually dependent.

A. S. Neill

Born to strict Calvinist parents, in rural Scotland, Neill attended the local school and worked as a teaching apprentice and then an assistant teacher, although he never felt that he was a good student. At the age of twenty-five, he managed to pass exams that allowed him to enter the University of Edinburgh, where he graduated with a major in English literature.

He took a temporary position as a schoolmaster while waiting to enter the military and began keeping a log of his teaching activities. He broke with the traditions of flogging and rote memory learning in favor of allowing students to use their imaginations in the learning process. After the army, Neill came in contact with an American named Homer Lane who was running a penal colony for young delinquents. Lane ran the institution using Freudian psychoanalytic principles, along with the belief that one must always find a way of understanding and supporting the child. To practice these principles Lane had weekly meetings where every teen and adult member of the community had a vote.

After a brief period teaching at a progressive school in Germany, Neill opened his own school there based on the above principles along with the practice of weekly meetings. He ultimately relocated the school—Summerhill—near London and ran it with his wife until she died in 1940. Then he ran it with his second wife until he died. His students tended to be those who had had trouble in schools, and many of them were Americans. Students had the freedom to play and do what they pleased within safe boundaries, but once they tired of that form of freedom and opted to attend classes, they had to make the commitment to continue those classes. In Neill's estimation, it was the best education for reaching the universal aim in life of happiness. Even though the school continues today, the international attention that it received during Neill's later years has waned.

Another educational philosopher who has drawn on existentialist ideas is Maxine Greene (1917–). In her many books and articles she has articulated a freedom of choice in creating oneself, and the importance of choosing freedom that brings relations with others in order to avoid the dilemma of forlornness.

Nel Noddings

Human relationships are also the basis of Nel Noddings's care theory. Noddings was born in Irvington, New Jersey, on the eve of the Great Depression, January 19, 1929. She graduated from Montclair State Teachers College with a B.A. in 1949, and upon graduation, married James Noddings. She taught at the junior high school in Woodbury, New Jersey, for four years, then spent several years raising her family (which ultimately grew to include ten children). From 1957 to 1969, she became a high school math teacher, department chair, and finally assistant principal. Noddings received her M.A. from Rutgers in 1964, and completed her work for a Ph.D. at Stanford University, graduating in 1973. She was a member of the faculty at Stanford University from 1977 to 1998, and was the Lee L. Jacks Professor of Child Education at Stanford from 1992 to 1998. She subsequently held appointments at Columbia University, Colgate University, and the University of Southern Maine, and she is Jacks Professor of Education, Emerita, at Stanford.

In 1984 she set forth her ethics of care in *Caring: A Feminine Approach to Ethics and Moral Education.* The theory is ontologically based in the relationship between the "one-caring" and the "cared for," and the relationship is one of mutual dependence. The one-caring becomes completely absorbed or engrossed in the situation of the cared for as she receives into herself the thoughts, feelings, and circumstances of the cared for. Noddings differentiates this reality from empathy, in which a person projects herself or himself into the other's situation to understand the other's thoughts and feelings. She points out that caring on the part of the one-caring is "always characterized by a move away from self," which means that the caring individual needs to move out of the realm of assigning blame, credit, or any other rational assessment of the

particular situation, and this leads to the ethical dimension of caring.

Traditionally, ethics has involved reason and logic or *logos,* the masculine spirit. The ethics of caring, on the other hand involves a more natural affective domain and is connected to *Eros,* the feminine spirit. Noddings qualifies Neill's aim of happiness in life by defining that aim as relational: caring and being cared for. In a caring relationship, when teachers engage students through questions and discussions, they are working to engage students, and not just looking for the correct answers or responses.

Finally, Noddings differentiates between "caring for" and "caring about," with the latter being more inclusive and distant. One can care deeply about global hunger and contribute to alleviate the condition through the contribution of one's time or money or both. However, this is a broader type of caring than the one caring–cared for relationship.

Caring is also a theme in the 1992 book *Schoolhome* by Jane Roland Martin (1930–). It is one of the "three Cs" that need to be present for children to learn: caring, concern, and connection. She draws upon the work of Maria Montessori (1870–1952), who used the concept of home (*casa*) for her learning environment, known as *Casa dei Bambini.* Roland Martin's emphasis is on understanding how learning occurs, rather than on how teaching or instructional elements can be identified. Thus, she calls for an image transition from the American "schoolhouse" to the American "schoolhome."

Joan K. Smith

See also Intelligence, Theories of; Philosophy of Education

Further Readings

Comenius, J. A. (1896). *The great didactic* (M. W. Keating, Trans. & Ed.). London: Adam and Charles Black.

Dewey, J. (1916). *Democracy and education.* New York: MacMillan.

Dykhuizen, G. (1973). *The life and mind of John Dewey.* Carbondale: Southern Illinois University Press.

Locke, J. (1947). *Some thoughts concerning education.* New York: Oxford University Press. (Original work published 1692)

Martin, J. R. (1992). *The schoolhome: Rethinking schools for changing families.* Cambridge, MA: Harvard University Press.

Neill, A. S. (1962). *Summerhill.* New York: Hart.

Neill, A. S. (1972). *Neill, Neill, orange peel: An autobiography.* New York: Hart.

Noddings, N. (2003). *Caring.* Berkeley: University of California Press.

Noddings, N. (2006). *Critical lessons: What our schools should teach.* New York: Cambridge University Press.

Oates, S. B. (Ed.). (1986). *Biography as high adventure.* Amherst: University of Massachusetts Press.

Plato. (1942). *The republic* (I. A. Richards, Trans.). New York: W. W. Norton.

Quintilian, M. F. (1921). *The instituto oratoria* (H. E. Butler, Trans.). London: William Heinemann.

Rousseau, J.-J. (1979). *Émile.* (A. Bloom, Trans.). New York: Basic Books. (Original work published 1762)

Smith, L. G., & Smith, J. K. (1994). *Lives in education: A narrative of people and ideas.* New York: St. Martin's.

Woodward, W. H. (1964). *Desiderius Erasmus concerning the aim and method of education.* New York: Teachers College.

Biracial Identity

Biracial individuals are those people who have racial heritage from more than one socially or legally recognized category (the U.S. government considers Hispanic or Latino ethnicity and five races: African American or Black, American Indian and Alaska Native, Asian, Native Hawaiian and Other Pacific Islander, White). Also called, among other terms, multiracial, mixed race, hapa, or mixed heritage, individuals reporting more than one race comprised 2.4 percent of the total population estimate of the 2000 U.S. Census, and 6.3 percent of the Hispanic/Latino population. Four percent of the population under age 18, and 7.7 percent of those under age 18 with Hispanic/Latino ethnicity, reported more than race. A substantial number of these multiracial youth are school age, and the percentage of primary, secondary, and postsecondary students who are multiracial is expected to continue to grow throughout the twenty-first century. Because changes in the collection and reporting of data on race and ethnicity in education

mandated by the federal government in 1997 are still in process, it is difficult to estimate the exact number of multiracial students in K–12 and postsecondary education.

Multiracial individuals may identify themselves in a number of ways, and research suggests that there is no one most healthy or more correct identification. Biracial youth and college students may identify with just one of their heritage groups, with both or all of their heritage groups, as part of a biracial or multiracial group, outside of racial categorization, or in some other way, according to the context. Gender, social class, religious, and sexual orientation identities may interact with biracial identity by contributing to the contextual cues. Physical appearance is also a major factor in multiracial identity, possibly more so for women than for men.

Biracial Students

Biracial students of any identity find that educational settings may provide challenges and supports. In primary and secondary schools, biracial children may be unclear how to respond to "choose one race only" demographic questions on standardized tests, or may feel forced to choose an identity that they do not personally hold. Other children may ask, "What are you?" in their efforts to sort people into monoracial categories. Teachers and other adults in the school setting (e.g., classroom aides, administrators) may not recognize a person as a child's parent when that person does not appear to be of the same race as the child. These everyday occurrences reinforce the dominant societal view that monoracial identity is "normal" and bi- or multiracial identity is not. Potentially positive outcomes of school life for biracial youth include an awareness that identity is not fixed, that there are other people who do not fit into one category, and that they are unique and special.

Multiracial college students report experiences on campus that similarly reinforce the predominance of monoraciality, but these students also express a more complex understanding of their identities in relation to those messages. On some campuses, biracial students experience pressure from members of organizations based on monoracial identity (e.g., Black Student Alliance, Asian Caucus) to conform to social norms of the group or risk ostracism. A lack of cultural knowledge or language may keep some biracial students from associating with peers from one of their heritage groups, and the perceived availability of support services for underrepresented students may depend on how or whether a biracial student identifies strongly with a particular heritage.

Colleges and universities are also sites for identity exploration and support. Courses related to a heritage or to multiracial issues support identity exploration, and the growing number of campus organizations and intercollegiate conferences for bi- or multiracial students provide opportunities to gather with others who may have similar experiences. Academic, social, and political experiences related to having more than one racial heritage seem to support development of confidence and comfort in a range of racial identification among multiracial college students.

The Use of Data

Public schools represent one of the largest sectors required to collect and tabulate data on race and ethnicity. The data are used to allocate resources, to fund educational programs to promote success of underrepresented students, to assist in enforcement of school desegregation plans, and to examine trends in student ability grouping, promotion, and graduation. Before 1997 schools were stipulated by the federal government to assign only one race per person. The 1997 revisions in federal policy have resulted in changes to state and local practices in data collection in the K–12 schools; changes in postsecondary education data collection are expected to begin in 2009. The implications of the policy shift are not yet clear, but educational researchers and leaders are cautioned to be aware of how the changes impact the appearance of trend data.

As important as the shift in policy regarding collecting, aggregating, and reporting data on student race and ethnicity is the possibility for biracial individuals to change their self-identification over time.

Although it is unlikely for such shifts in identification to have a widespread impact in national or state-level data, it is possible that local and institutional data will show some variance based on individual choices in self-identification. Self-identification is the federal government's preferred method for assigning categories of race and ethnicity, and it is recommended that whenever possible, students (or their parents, in the case of younger children) be permitted to self-identify.

Kristen A. Renn

See also Educational Equity: Race/Ethnicity

Further Readings

Jones, N. A., & Smith, A. S. (2001). *The two or more races population: 2000.* Census 2000 Brief. Washington, DC: U.S. Census Bureau. Available from http://www.census .gov/prod/2001pubs/c2kbr01–6.pdf

Lopez, A. M. (2003). Mixed-race school-age children: A summary of Census 2000 data. *Educational Researcher, 32,* 25–37.

Office of Management and Budget. (1997, October 30). Revisions to the Standards for the Classification of Federal Data on Race and Ethnicity. *Federal Register Notice.* Retrieved August 25, 2006, from http://www .whitehouse.gov/omb/fedreg/1997standards.html

Renn, K. A. (2004). *Mixed race students in college: The ecology of race, identity, and community.* Albany: State University of New York Press.

Black English Vernacular

The term *Ebonics,* from the words *ebony* ("Black") and *phonics* ("sounds"), was coined by social psychologist Robert Williams in 1973. Also known as Black English Vernacular (BEV) or African American Vernacular English (AAVE), Ebonics is a social dialect spoken mainly by African Americans in the United States. It has long been a subject of controversy within K–12 education, since schools in the United States tend to view the replacement of students' nonstandard speech with standard English as one of their main tasks.

However, as perhaps the most widespread and salient nonstandard dialect of English, and one with strong cultural associations to a historically subjugated and educationally marginalized population, Ebonics has proved impervious to official attempts to eradicate it. It has thus come to symbolize both the persistent crisis of inner-city communities of color and the persistent failure of public schools to adequately serve those communities. In more recent years, recognition of its systematic nature, and of its importance as a marker of ethnic identity and cultural resistance, has spread among many educators, resulting in attempts to shift assimilationist school policies toward a more tolerant view. Nonetheless, well-meaning attempts by linguists and educators to address the educational needs of African American children have clashed with powerful language ideologies associating Ebonics with poverty, ignorance, and delinquency. This entry discusses its history and chief characteristics, the related social and educational debate, and the outlook for its continued use.

Origins

Black English Vernacular emerged from the crucible of the Southern plantation life of millions of enslaved Africans. They had been forcibly abducted and brought to North America during the seventeenth, eighteenth, and early nineteenth centuries and spoke various West African languages, and slaveholders often purposely intermingled slaves from different languages and regions, fearing that fluid communication might foster attempts at rebellion or escape. As subsequent generations of slaves grew up in this creolized context, English became their native language, albeit an English acquired informally and under conditions of intense repression and social segregation.

Sociolinguist John R. Rickford compares three different hypotheses concerning the evolution of Ebonics. The Afrocentric view holds that most of the distinctive phonological and grammatical features of Ebonics reflect features of the Niger-Congo languages spoken by the original enslaved Africans in the New World. The Eurocentric (or "dialectologist") view holds that African slaves quickly lost their original languages and that the distinctive features of Ebonics evolved through contact with the English dialects spoken by English, Irish, and Scotch-Irish settlers (including many indentured servants, who were in closer contact with African slaves). Rickford critiques both of these hypotheses in favor of the creolist view, which holds that as African slaves acquired English, they developed a pidgin that combined features of English and African languages; this pidgin eventually evolved into Ebonics. Evidence in support of this view includes the many similarities between Ebonics and English-based creole languages of the Caribbean, as well as Gullah, an English creole spoken by African Americans on the sea islands off the coast of Georgia and South Carolina.

Following the abolition of slavery, millions of former slaves and their descendants moved north, seeking employment in the burgeoning industrial centers of the North and freedom from the violent Jim Crow regime of the South. However, continued racial segregation prevented African Americans' linguistic assimilation into Northern White speech communities. Later, as the United States expanded westward, Ebonics persisted and spread as a distinct dialect, although with regional variations.

Characteristics

The distinctive features of Ebonics are commonly recognized even by those who deride them as evidence of "lazy speech" or "bad English." Linguistic research has shown these features to be systematic and rule governed; in some cases (e.g., verb tense and aspect) they encode subtleties that are absent from standard English. A much-cited example is the sentence *He be runnin,* which indicates an ongoing or habitual action. (In standard English, it would be rendered as "He is usually running.")

Simplification of certain word-final consonant clusters is another salient feature, giving rise to such forms as *tes'* for *test* and *han'* for *hand.* Copula deletion (absence of linking verbs *is* or *are*) is a common feature of many creole languages, and appears in Ebonics utterances such as *She married* ("She's married") or *They goin' now* ("They're going now"). The word-final suffix /-s/, which in standard English is used to mark both possession and the third person singular, is omitted in Ebonics, giving rise to forms such as *John house* ("John's house") and *He feed the dog* ("He feeds the dog").

Many of these features have been mistakenly interpreted (by schoolteachers and others) as evidence of Ebonics speakers' failure to grasp abstract concepts such as past tense. Not surprisingly, those features of Ebonics that express semantic or grammatical distinctions that are absent from standard English generally go unrecognized by standard English speakers.

Social Status

As is true of the speech of ethnic minority groups the world over, Ebonics is highly stigmatized. Although its grammaticality, phonological regularity, and overall utility as a communicative system have been amply demonstrated, it continues to be perceived by the general public (and even sometimes by its speakers) as slovenly, lazy, and incorrect. This perception is continually reinforced by the social barriers to nonstandard speech that are maintained by the dominant (White) speech community, through institutions like schooling, the media, and the occupational structure.

At the same time, Ebonics has strong positive associations for its speakers, as a marker of ethnic identity, community membership, and resistance to White domination. Ironically, the gate-keeping function of standard English in both education and the more prestigious forms of employment means that speakers' linguistic loyalty to Ebonics becomes yet another rationalization for their continued educational and economic marginalization. Many speakers learn to fluidly code-switch between Ebonics and standard English; however, even the nonexclusive use of Ebonics is thought by many to mark speakers as uneducated and coarse.

The Oakland Controversy

Ebonics became a focus of controversy in early 1997 when the Oakland, California, School Board passed a resolution calling for the acknowledgment of Ebonics

(or "African Language Systems") *not* as a mere dialect of English but as a valid, autonomous language that is the primary language of African American students. The resolution stressed the similarity between African American students and others with limited English proficiency (e.g., students whose home language is Spanish, Mandarin, or Punjabi), and evoked the Federal Bilingual Education Act of 1968 in calling for special programs to help African American students achieve English proficiency while respecting their primary language. In fact, the original form of the resolution recommended that Ebonics be used (along with English) as a medium of instruction for African American children and that it be not only respected but maintained. However, these provisions were later deleted under pressure, in favor of passages emphasizing the need to transition students from their home language patterns to (standard) English.

Predictably, the resolution provoked heated debate and even outrage from across the political spectrum. Some critics denounced it as an attempt to pander to African Americans by granting legitimacy to a clearly deficient speech variety and accused the Oakland School Board of succumbing to "political correctness" and/or divisive identity politics. Others, including notable African American leaders such as Jesse Jackson, called the move "disgraceful," and accused the school board of embracing low standards for African American students and condemning them to a lifetime of linguistic and cognitive inferiority. The voices of linguists and educational researchers failed to carry over the din of (often uninformed) public debate, and the resolution was eventually withdrawn without being implemented.

Future Prospects

Although the Ebonics debate has largely died down within education, it has not completely disappeared. For the most part, teachers continue to "correct" students' use of Ebonics, to lament its use by parents and public figures (e.g., professional athletes and musicians), and to enforce standard English norms and practices in the granting of educational credentials. On the other hand, the public airing of questions of race and language provoked by the Oakland controversy, combined with the diffusion and sociolinguistic research on Ebonics, led many Americans toward a more tolerant, relativistic view of African American Vernacular English and an acknowledgment of its importance to the cohesion and identity of African American communities. While U.S. society is still far from a consensus as to the legitimacy of Ebonics, recent debates have served to highlight the relationship, however muddy, between school language policies and other educational and civil rights issues.

Furthermore, through its association with certain forms of popular culture, such as rap and hip-hop music, Ebonics has gained considerable ground among U.S. youth subcultures, particularly those of White and Hispanic working-class and middle-class males. While such usage retains the air of countercultural resistance associated with inner-city minorities, this may change as the corporate culture industry appropriates this symbol of youth and rebellion for its own purposes. The literary use of Ebonics by Pulitzer-prize-winning authors such as Alice Walker and Toni Morrison has also increased its social capital in more prestigious circles.

Within urban schools, however, African American children continue to suffer severe educational inequities, manifested in high dropout rates, low college enrollment, and disproportionate failure on various measures of academic achievement. The language, history, and culture of the White majority continue to constitute the backbone of the public school curriculum. With schools currently more racially segregated than they were in the 1970s, Ebonics is unlikely to disappear anytime soon. The role of dialectal variation in explaining academic achievement gaps among ethnic groups remains unclear but is probably not negligible. For the time being, educators will continue to seek solutions that are scientifically and pedagogically sound, informed by a concern for educational equity, and compatible with the predominant language ideologies of the larger population.

Aurolyn Luykx

See also African American Education; Discrimination and Prejudice; Literacy in the South; Rap Music and Oral Literacy; Urban Education; White Privilege

Further Readings

Baugh, J. (2000). *Beyond Ebonics: Linguistic pride and racial prejudice.* New York: Oxford University Press.

Labov, W. (1998). *Language in the inner city: Studies in the Black English Vernacular.* Philadelphia: University of Pennsylvania Press.

Perry, T., & Delpit, L. (Eds.). (1998). *The real Ebonics debate: Power, language, and the education of African-American children.* Boston: Beacon Press.

Rickford, J. R. (1999). *African American Vernacular English: Features, evolution, educational implications.* Malden, MA: Blackwell.

Smitherman, G. (1999). *Talkin that talk: Language, culture, and education in African America.* New York: Routledge.

BLIND, EDUCATION FOR THE

Historically, *blind education* has referred to those facilities, programs, techniques, and practices designed to maximize formal learning for persons with significant to total loss of vision. Such education has taken place in a variety of formal and informal instructional settings, including the home, private tutoring sessions, segregated and integrated classrooms in public schools, public and private day schools, and public as well as private residential institutions. As a modality impairment, blindness has existed throughout history and in all societies. The bulk of practices in the United States, however, have evolved from origins and developments specific to the Western world. As this entry considers the education of blind persons, information on its historical development in Europe, Canada, and the United States complements descriptions and discussion of current education theory and practice regarding ways to compensate for a loss of vision through specific technologies, materials, subject matter, and instructional practices.

Historical Development

The key European figure in developing teaching methods for the blind was Valentin Hauy (1745–1822), a French aristocrat who championed more humane treatment for all disabled persons but focused on developing instructional techniques for blind persons. He played a leading role in developing raised print for use by blind readers. He also encouraged vocational training for the blind, arguing that gainful employment would permit more authentic and effective participation in a mostly sighted society.

Hauy's methods and priorities underscored a growing belief among those working with the disabled that blind persons were certainly capable of formal academic instruction and deserved more humane treatment from their fellow human beings. Education of blind persons, which typically occurred in private tutorials or in institutions, spread from France to England by 1800, where the emphasis again fell on vocational or trade training. In addition, music instruction was often featured to enhance learning through senses other than sight.

European beliefs about and approaches to the education of the blind migrated to the United States primarily via the efforts of two individuals: Dr. John Fischer and Dr. Samuel Gridley Howe, both from the Boston area. Fischer's visits to the school for the blind in Paris prompted him to work to establish a similar school in the United States. His efforts led to the 1832 opening of what became known as the Perkins Institution and the Massachusetts Asylum for the Blind, located in Boston and headed by Howe. The school quickly assumed a national leadership role and enrolled students from all regions of the country by the late 1800s.

Perkins not only educated blind students but also trained many of the teachers for other institutions and schools for the blind. Such settings increased steadily in number throughout the nineteenth and into the twentieth century, with over three dozen institutions providing educational services to blind students by the early 1900s. Many of these combined educational services with those for deaf students, while others were segregated by race. High profile cases such as Laura Bridgman (Howe's first prominent deaf-blind student) and Annie Sullivan (Helen Keller's famous teacher) drew attention to Perkins in particular and efforts to educate the blind in general.

By the early 1900s public schools had joined residential institutions as providers of formal education for the blind. In 1900 Chicago opened the first class designated specifically for children with total blindness. Most large urban school systems, however, established classes for children whose vision loss was significant but not complete. Often called "sight-saving" or "semi-blind" classes, these settings created an environment

considered optimal for students with significant vision loss, including specialized lighting, raised print (usually Braille) texts, and other instructional accommodations. Most of these classes were segregated from the regular classes but held in the local public school according to demand. These classes combined academic content with an emphasis on music instruction and vocational training. Meanwhile, the residential institutions continued with their educational mission of basic academic instruction and solid vocational training that could lead to employment upon leaving the institution.

Educational Issues

With large-scale, segregated, residential institutions as well as numerous public school systems around the country providing formal, specialized instruction for students with all levels of significant—including total—vision loss, discussion intensified over certain assumptions and practices that defined approaches to educating the blind. Such discussions continue to this day. Issues have included the propriety of segregated instruction, whether in schools or institutions; the appropriate balance of academic, vocational, and functional instruction; and the effective integration of technology into specially adapted curricula.

Segregation

The debate over integrating or segregating for instructional purposes students who are blind from their nondisabled peers has played out heatedly for generations. Advocates for residential institutions for the blind argue that the specialized settings allow more opportunities for appropriate, individualized instruction in a supportive, caring environment. Such facilities permit more effective and efficient use of what can be very expensive resources, such as large print or raised-text books, optical enhancement equipment, and audio technology. They offer comfortable environments where the teachers are trained in specific, appropriate methodology and where students share needs, abilities, and interests that may be quite limited or even nonexistent in a public school classroom.

In short, it has been argued, residential institutions for students who are blind offer the best opportunities for providing the education such children need and deserve. Separate classes in public school buildings for children who suffer severe vision loss also offer such nurturing and specialized environments and have the advantage of closer proximity to the students' nondisabled peers for events at which they can fully participate, such as lunch, festivals, or other appropriate events.

On the other hand, according to critics of segregation, the practice of intentionally separating children who are blind cannot help but contribute to long-held prejudices and misunderstandings that have confronted the blind literally for centuries. Critics contend that no amount of fiscal or instructional efficiency can justify the purposeful exclusion of any child from the mainstream of society. Too, the notion that segregated instruction provides a more comfortable and supportive environment may well be applicable in the short term but arguably makes it much more difficult for children—indeed all persons—with blindness to become socially integrated and functionally independent, given their intense isolation for years and society's relative absence of familiarity with the conditions and ramifications of the condition. Clearly, the relative merits and drawbacks of inclusion and segregation in the education of all children on the margins certainly apply to children who are blind.

Content

Discussions regarding the appropriate content and balance of formal instruction for the blind also have captured much interest among those involved in the process. For the most part, the blind long ago overcame very early prejudices that most were incapable of learning standard and advanced academic content. Nevertheless, curriculum development for blind children must consider several features unique to blindness and adapt instruction accordingly. For example, many have argued for instruction that theoretically enhances the blind child's ability to use her or his four other senses to compensate for the lack of sight. A strong emphasis on oral instruction and the use of itinerant teachers who could work with a blind child individually in her or his regular classroom have become common features of teaching children who are blind.

Moreover, a discussion as to the "best" form of text reading continues to this day. The development of practical social and vocational skills remains central to this specialized curriculum: cooking, personal hygiene, mobility, and interpersonal interactions often accompany specific training in a particular trade or skill of the child's choice. In recent decades technology designed to assist children who are blind has become increasingly sophisticated, requiring more specialized training for teachers of the blind and additional "reasonable and appropriate" expenditures for residential institutions and for school districts. As with other disabilities that can be effectively addressed through the use of highly expensive equipment or other technology, blindness raises issues as to just how much a public school district should be expected to spend on a child with the condition.

Today families, friends, and advocates of and for the blind join with educators and the general public to assure a "free and appropriate" education for the blind in a variety of settings. Nevertheless, issues of curriculum, policy, and school practice continue to raise important questions, ideas, and debates designed to address—and assure—the most effective education for children who live daily with severe or total vision loss but who also have much to contribute to their peers and to society if given sufficient opportunity and support.

Robert L. Osgood

See also Disabilities and the Politics of Schooling; Disability Studies; Mainstreaming; Special Education, Contemporary Issues; Special Education, History of

See Visual History Chapter 17, Reading and Libraries; Chapter 21, Students With Special Needs

Further Readings

Barraga, N. C., & Erin, J. N. (1992). *Visual handicaps and learning* (3rd ed.). Austin, TX: Pro-Ed.

Best, H. (1934). *Blindness and the blind in the United States.* New York: MacMillan.

Castellano, C. (2005). *Making it work: Educating the blind/visually impaired student in the regular school.* Greenwich, CT: Information Age.

Osgood, R. L. (2008). *The history of special education: A struggle for equality in American public schools.* Westport, CT: Praeger.

BOARDS OF EDUCATION

Local school boards have guided American public education for well over a century. Electing school board members to govern local schools embodies U.S commitment to democracy and the nation's desire to have some influence over the education of children who reside here. While these values still resonate with the American public, changes in society and the way schools are governed have stripped these institutions of much of their power. Instead of deciding fundamental policy issues, these institutions are now left to implement the priorities and polices of the state and the federal government.

The reasons for the diminished role school boards now play reveal much about the legitimacy of the institution as a means of democratic participation and about its ability to address issues of concern such as inequality, poverty, and diversity. This entry examines some of the historical and contemporary forces that have influenced school board structure, composition, and function. From a historical perspective, there have been many forces at work that have tended to limit the participation of citizens in school board elections and have insulated these institutions from the publics they were supposed to serve. In the contemporary context, the inability of school boards to adequately represent increasingly diverse constituents coupled with the growth of the federal and state role in education has led some to conclude that boards have outlived their usefulness.

Tracing the history of school boards can provide new and important insights into ongoing debates about the governance of public schools. For example, the Center for Education and the Economy has advocated for school governance reforms that would radically limit the role of local boards in educational decisions by turning the ownership of local schools over to limited-liability corporations. Such proposals only make sense when they are viewed as part of an ongoing transformation in societal values and interests.

The Progressive Era

Small boards of education separated from municipal government and elected at large came into existence during the progressive reform movement of the 1890s. Prior to this time schools were often run as an extension of the municipal government or by large committees of laymen. During the mid-1800s, examples of large boards included Boston with 24 members, and Philadelphia which was broken into 24 separate areas each with its own school board. These boards had significant authority over the ways schools were run including issues of curriculum, finance, and assessment. Corruption and graft in local school politics were not uncommon during this period and as the nineteenth century came to a close, reformers and muckraking journalists joined hands to expose the political spoils system that often drove local school governance.

These reformers predominately consisted of elite community members such as businessmen and lawyers who sought to centralize control of schools for the purpose of improving efficiency and imposing corporate practices on the schools. Smaller boards and at-large elections were sought as a way to insure that elites would be elected to leadership positions, rather than ward representatives who might be too closely associated with an undesirable class or ethnicity. Such changes were supported by school superintendents who enjoyed increased power over issues such as the hiring and firing of teachers. Rather than focus on the day-to-day running of the schools, corporate style boards began to focus more on policy.

By the 1920s, school districts across the nation had adopted similar forms of governance characterized by small, policy-oriented boards, whose primary responsibility was hiring and evaluating the superintendent. These changes increased accountability by focusing authority in the office of the superintendent. At the same time, schools became more insulated from the general public and less attentive to the interests of poor and minority citizens.

The Limits of Administrative Control

The power of school administrators continued to grow during the first half of the twentieth century as the nation more fully adopted the belief that educational decisions were largely technical matters best left to educational professionals rather than the lay public.

During this period, rapid population growth coupled with school district consolidations increased pressure on school boards to represent ever larger constituencies. For example in 1937 there were 120,000 school districts, a number that had shrunk to 40,000 by 1960. This pressure, coupled with consistently low voter turnout during school board elections threatened the legitimacy of these boards as governing institutions.

As problems of representation and legitimacy grew more pronounced, it became increasingly difficult for boards of education to balance competing interests and to deal with politically charged issues. In addition, the changes brought about by the Civil Rights Movement created greater political awareness, and placed even more demands on the educational system. In the new politics of the 1960s, educational interest groups became better informed, better organized, and better at using the media to their advantage. Many groups called for increased minority representation on school boards, and many of the largest urban districts sought to address their concerns by decentralizing their governance structures. Bucking the trend toward consolidation, cities such as Philadelphia, Washington, D.C., Los Angeles, Chicago, and New York were divided into smaller districts with regional superintendents and/or policy boards. The hope was that increased democracy might serve as a check on administrative authority and increase the probability that minority concerns would be addressed.

While decentralization held promise for better representation, the end result was significant infighting among interest groups over material and symbolic resources. Rather than solve the problem of racial discrimination and segregation, the more politicized environment may have worked against change as groups sought to protect their interests in the short term. Many groups seemed to lose sight of the fact that failure to come to an adequate resolution of these issues at the local level would result in unilateral federal action.

Despite many districts growing experience with federal intervention in the form of desegregation orders, or financial support through programs such as the National Defense Education Act of 1958 (NDEA) (which focused on science education), and the Elementary and Secondary Education Act of 1965 (ESEA) (which focused on children in poverty), few school boards could have predicted the degree to which federal and state intervention would eventually eclipse local control.

A Crisis in Local Governance

Federal and state involvement in education has consistently increased since the 1960s. The passage of ESEA in 1965, and Public Law 94-42, the Education for All Handicapped Children Act in 1975 set the stage for increased federal influence in the form of leveraged funds. These laws created procedures and rules that needed to be followed in order for local districts to receive the funding and subjected schools to an increased level of federal oversight.

This trend toward centralized control was reinforced by a number of school-funding lawsuits that forced states to pay an increasing share in the cost of schooling in order to help equalize differences in the tax base between local districts. This shift in funding resulted in a greater state authority over education. These changes were followed by a number of influential national reports such as *A Nation at Risk* (1983) that argued for national solutions to our educational problems. This trend continued to intensify in the 1990s culminating with the passage of No Child Left Behind (NCLB) which gives the federal government unprecedented reach into areas formerly controlled by local districts such as program design and testing.

Despite limited evidence of real improvement resulting from federal intervention, support for ever more radical changes in local governance structures continues unabated. A noted authority, William Boyd, points out that elected school boards are under fire, especially in cities, and some have proposed confining them to policy-making and planning roles. Proposals such as these proceed from logic similar to that used by reformers in the 1890s which viewed local ward-based control as inefficient and ineffective. This time however, the problem has been characterized as the limiting influence of centralized bureaucracy (i.e., school boards) on creativity and choice. Interestingly, the proposed remedy to this is, most often, increased federal or state control of education with decentralized responsibility for implementing programs and procedures.

The pressure for these changes comes from what Boyd terms, "a double crisis of both performance and legitimacy." With respect to performance, large numbers of students, particularly those from disadvantaged backgrounds are failing to meet expectations for achievement. In terms of legitimacy, the "common school" established to meet the needs of a fairly homogeneous society in the mid-1800s is having difficulty coping with growing ethnic and religious diversity. One result of this change has been a growing demand for more choices in the kinds of education available.

Given these challenges, the future role of local school boards in this nation is far from clear. The race is on for an alternative institution to run our public schools and while democracy remains an important touchstone in symbolic terms, many current proposals for reform actually serve to limit citizen participation in school governance. Current governance reform proposals include options such as school choice and vouchers, mayoral control of schools, state takeovers, charter schools, and systems of schools owned by private corporations. Each of these will be discussed in turn.

Mayoral Control

These models of governance are a return to the pre-reform-era politics that blended educational and municipal governance. Moving to mayoral control would do away with school board elections altogether and replace them with an appointed system of governance. In cities such as Chicago, Boston, Detroit, Cleveland, and New York, mayors have significant power over schools. Proponents of these plans believe that high profile mayors provide greater accountability and responsiveness.

State Interventions

States now regularly intervene in "failing" districts. State takeovers are made for a number of reasons including poor student performance, fiscal mismanagement, and administrative incompetence. States typically only intervene when problems are persistent. Proponents of these measures believe that state intervention is the only way to help a struggling district regain its footing. Critics claim that state intervention usually does little to address the underlying problems such as racial tension and poverty.

Market-Driven Models

Market-driven models of school governance have gained popularity with growth in the neoconservative movement. In general, neoconservatives typically view governments as wasteful and inefficient and strive to replace the government provision of services with market-based solutions, believing that competition is the key to improving productivity. In education, this has meant growing support for a variety of market-oriented reforms such as charter schools, vouchers, and contracting for services.

Charter Schools

Charter schools represent a limited market-based reform as the schools continue to be public in nature and are financed through tax dollars. In general, charter schools are public schools that are formed by groups of people who want to provide an alternative to traditional public schools. Some proponents argue that charters will create competition for traditional public schools and force these schools to innovate and become more efficient if they hope to survive.

The role of school boards in this reform proposal is unclear. School boards may have some attenuated control over charters as they often have the authority to accept or reject charter proposals. However, once a charter school is established, it is the tenets of the charter that govern the school rather than the district school board.

Vouchers

The arguments for vouchers are similar to those offered in support of charter schools in that vouchers are hoped to stimulate competition. Unlike charter schools, however, voucher plans provide families with a monetary allowance or tax credit that they may spend on an educational institution of their choice. Under some plans, this money could be spent on public or private schools, which raises issues concerning the separation of church and state.

The role of school boards in a system with vouchers would essentially remain the same but would only focus on the public schools in the community. Few voucher proposals discuss the oversight of public moneys spent on private institutions though this is a potential role for the school board as well. Voucher proponents would likely argue that school board involvement of this type would create too much governmental regulation.

Contract for Services

Finally, contracting for services takes numerous forms including school district contracts for food service and maintenance as well as larger contracts for management services. While contracting for auxiliary services is common and largely accepted, contracting for management is still quite controversial. Like supporters of charters and vouchers, supporters of contracted Educational Management Organizations (EMOs) believe that hiring management companies to run schools will create greater efficiency and lead to reduction in educational costs.

Similar to charter schools, EMOs are often sheltered from certain regulations applied to public schools and are thought to provide opportunities for experimentation not possible in traditional public schools. The role of school boards in the case of EMOs is similar to their role with charter schools. Boards initially negotiate contracts with EMOs but then are largely uninvolved except in monitoring the terms of the contract. This is the approach favored in a recent report from the National Center for Education and the Economy which envisions school boards as data collection agencies and emissaries working out relationships with other governmental services. In this case, the schools themselves would be owned and run by the teachers.

While each of these proposals is different, they share an emphasis on accountability, choice, and efficiency. What is often lacking in these proposals seems to be is a sincere interest in the practice of democracy at the local level.

Outlook for Boards

Will school boards remain the primary means of governing public education in the years to come?

The probable answer is no. David Conley, an authority on the issue, suggests that local control will soon be more symbolic than real. Communities will continue to play a ceremonial role, but true policymaking will take place in state and federal legislatures. While such a conclusion seems warranted given the incursion of state and federal interests into school board business, school boards still represent a desire for popular governance that is not found in other institutions.

Such an aspiration speaks to the optimism of individuals and groups striving to work together to develop common aims. Unlike other more distant forms of governance, school boards have the potential to promote dialog and create forums for public discourse. Such interactions are necessary to reveal shared goals and aspirations. Without local boards, such a forum would not exist.

Over the next decade, the nation's commitment to the concept of local control in education will be deeply challenged. School boards will only remain viable if local citizens reclaim their stake in the common good by demanding a forum in which such issues can be addressed.

Abe Feuerstein

See also Charter Schools; Commercialization of Schools; Federal and State Educational Jurisdiction; Politics of Education; School Governance; State Role in Education

Further Readings

Callahan, R. E. (1975). The American Board of Education 1789–1960. In P. Cistone (Ed.), *Understanding school boards.* Lexington, MA: D.C. Heath.

Conley, D. T. (2003). *Who governs our schools? Changing roles and responsibilities.* New York: Teachers College Press.

Feuerstein, A. (2002). Elections, voting, and democracy in local school district governance. *Educational Policy, 16*(1), 15–36.

Fraga, L., Meier, K., & England, R. (1986). Hispanic Americans and educational policy: Limits to equal access. *The Journal of Politics, 48.*

Iannaconne, L., & Lutz, F. W. (1994). The crucible of democracy; the local arena. In J. Scribner & D. Layton (Eds.), *The study of educational politics.* Washington, DC: Falmer Press.

Kirst, M. (2000). "New, improved" mayors take over city schools. *Phi Delta Kappan, 81*(7), 538–546.

Murphy, J. (1999). New consumerism: Evolving market dynamics in the institutional dimension of schooling. In J. Murphy & K. S. Louis (Eds.), *Handbook of research on educational adminstration* (2nd ed.). San Francisco: Jossey-Bass.

National Center on Education and the Economy. (2007). Tough *choices or tough times: The report of The New Commission on the Skills of the American Workforce.* San Francisco: Jossey-Bass.

Orfield, G., Eaton, S. E., et al. (1996). *Dismantling desegregation: The quiet reversal of* Brown v. Board of Education. New York: New Press.

Plank, D., & Boyd, W. L. (1994). Antipolitics, education, and institutional choice: The flight from democracy. *American Educational Research Journal, 31*(2), 263–281.

Selznick, P. (1994). *The moral commonwealth.* Berkeley: University of California Press.

Timar, T., & Tyack, D. (1999). *The invisisble hand of ideology: Perspectives from the history of school governance.* Denver, CO: Education Commission of the States.

BOSTON LATIN SCHOOL

When the Rev. John Cotton arrived in the colony of Massachusetts Bay in 1633, he brought with him the idea of the English type of free grammar school, the school he had attended as a child in Derby, England. The "free school" in England was a publicly supported institution open to all boys on the basis of academic merit. The English "grammar school" was a secondary institution offering a seven-year course of study devoted to the Greek and Latin classics and designed to prepare the pupil for admission to a university.

In 1635, two years after Cotton's arrival in the fledgling town of Boston, the town made provisions for the establishment and maintenance of a free grammar school on the English model. The school's first classes were held in the home of its first master, Philemon Pormort. The Boston Latin School, as it came to be known, is generally considered to be the oldest public school in continuous existence in the United States.

The Puritan founders of the Boston Latin School, including John Cotton, believed that a knowledge of classical languages was essential for a proper understanding of Scripture. Consequently, the curriculum of the school was originally devoted entirely to acquiring a mastery of Latin, beginning with a thorough study of Latin grammar and syntax. In the eighteenth century, the most widely used elementary Latin grammar textbook in the American colonies was Ezekiel Cheever's *A Short Introduction to the Latin Tongue* (commonly known as *Cheever's Accidence*). Cheever served as Master of the Boston Latin School from 1670 until his death in 1708. Students who had mastered the *Accidence* went on to read classical authors such as Ovid and Cicero.

Although four years of Latin are still required of graduates, the school gradually modernized its curriculum during the nineteenth and twentieth centuries, offering elective courses to supplement the core courses in English, math, science, history, Latin, and modern foreign languages. Boston Latin School is now an "examination school" of the Boston Public Schools, with admission based on a student's academic record and score on the Independent School Entrance Exam (ISEE).

In the twentieth century, the school's admissions policy, which recognized academic merit rather than class or race, provided the children of immigrants in Boston with an important stepping-stone to advancement in American society. The school became coeducational in 1972, and reached another milestone in 1998 when Cornelia Kelly became the first female headmaster in the school's 363-year history.

Notable alumni of the Boston Latin School include Cotton Mather, Samuel Adams, John Hancock, Ralph Waldo Emerson, Charles Sumner, George Santayana, Bernard Berenson, Joseph P. Kennedy, and Leonard Bernstein.

Rob Hardy

See also Classical Curriculum

See Visual History Chapter 1, Colonial Beginnings

Further Readings

Cremin, L. A. (1970). *American education: The colonial experience, 1607–1783.* New York: Harper and Row.

Feldman, R. T. (2001). *Don't whistle in school: The history of America's public schools.* Breckenridge, CO: Twenty-First Century Books.

Gould, E. P. (1904). *Ezekiel Cheever, schoolmaster.* Boston: Palmer.

Wernick, R. 1985. At Boston Latin, time out for a 350th birthday. *Smithsonian, 16*(1), 122–135.

Web Sites

Boston Latin School: http://www.bls.org

Boy Scouts of America

Founded in 1907 in England by Lord Robert Baden-Powell, the Boy Scouts of America (BSA) began in the United States in 1910 and were chartered by Congress in 1911, becoming the only national organization charged by Congress to educate American boys. The Boy Scouts were founded by Baden-Powell as a response to what he saw as a crisis of masculinity in the British Empire.

Boy Scouting teaches masculinity by focusing on five strategies: character building, handicrafts, bodily development, promoting a sense of happiness, and service to others. Baden-Powell emphasized these in *Aids to Scoutmastership.*

Throughout the United States, BSA troops are sponsored by schools, churches, synagogues, and popular social organizations. As the international Boy Scout movement has evolved over time, the BSA has in significant ways parted company with the larger boy scout community. Other boy scout organizations throughout the world have evolved in a more humanistic direction, becoming more inclusive in membership. The BSA has not. This narrower educational philosophy becomes clear in court cases addressing membership issues and changes in educational texts. The BSA requires members to be male, theistic, and heterosexual.

While many national scouting organizations welcome girls as members, the BSA insists that the Congressional charter would be violated by such a choice. Two prominent cases are *Schwenk v. Boy Scouts of America,* 551 P.2d 465 (Or. 1976) and *Quinnipiac Council v. Commission on Human Rights & Opportunities,* 528 A.2d 352 (Conn. 1987).

The BSA excludes gay adult leaders and boys from membership. In curricula regarding sexuality prepared for boys and adult troop leaders in recent years, they have shifted the context of sexuality education from health to vocation (and theology).

Other boy scout organizations in the world welcome theistic as well as nontheistic boys. Some even drop the customary reference to God from the scout oath. The BSA seems to have narrowed the religious aspect of its teaching. Baden-Powell often explained that the essence of religion was caring for nature and doing good for others, a sort of romantic pantheism. It is doubtful that the BSA would find that acceptable.

While the BSA exposes boys to other viewpoints through interaction with the wider world, the BSA sets boundaries in terms of what can and cannot be addressed and explored inside the organization. Rather than exposing a boy to ways other cultures have lived with similar issues, this educational agency limits exposure.

Baden-Powell built his boy scout movement around service to those values necessary for the British Empire. In the decades since, boy scouts, internationally, have decided to expand the inclusiveness of the organization to girls as well as gay and nontheistic youth.

Charles Joseph Meinhart

See also Compulsory Heterosexuality; Educational Equity: Gender

Further Readings

Jeal, T. (2001). *Baden-Powell.* New Haven, CT: Yale University Press.

MacDonald, R. H. (1993). *Sons of the empire: The frontier and the boy scout movement, 1890–1918.* Toronto, ON, Canada: University of Toronto Press.

Rosenthal, M. (1986). *The character factor: Baden-Powell and the origins of the boy scout movement.* New York: Pantheon Books.

Brown v. Board of Education

In the years leading up to the *Brown v. Board of Education* decision, public schools were both unequal and racially segregated—by law in the South and in practice in the Northeast and West. In 1950, the

National Association for the Advancement of Colored People (NAACP), long concerned with education, decided to mount a direct challenge to state-sanctioned segregation in schooling. The result was the *Brown* case, which joined together lawsuits begun by Black parents and students in Delaware, Washington, D.C., South Carolina, Virginia, and Kansas. Many of these plaintiffs paid a price for their advocacy. Indeed, the NAACP struggled to find Black parents willing to join lawsuits, given the possibility that workers would be fired from their jobs and their children attacked on the streets.

In its 1954 decision in *Brown v. Board of Education,* the U.S. Supreme Court ruled unanimously that "separate educational facilities" for Black and White students are "inherently unequal" and therefore unconstitutional. This ruling overturned a decision by the Court in 1896 in *Plessy v. Ferguson* that segregation in public facilities through "separate but equal" accommodations would satisfy the Equal Protection Clause of the Fourteenth Amendment of the Constitution. The *Brown* Court initially declined to specify a remedy for the public schools. When it took up the case again the next year, in *Brown II,* the Court rejected a request by the NAACP to order immediate action and counseled instead that desegregation should proceed "with all deliberate speed."

More than a half century later, public schooling in the United States continues to function as a two-tier system. In large metropolitan areas across the nation, students in central cities attend high-minority, high-poverty schools with very few White students. Many of these schools are overcrowded, lack the resources they need to meet students' needs, and are struggling to meet federal student achievement benchmarks. This entry focuses on the short- and long-term impacts of the landmark ruling.

Immediate Impact

Not surprisingly, school districts throughout the South interpreted the Court's open-ended "all deliberate speed" timetable as "never." Virtually no desegregation took place in the eleven states of the Old Confederacy during the first decade after *Brown.* On the tenth anniversary of the decision, only about 1 percent of Black children in the South attended racially integrated schools. Not until Congress passed the Civil Rights Act in 1964 and the Johnson administration used its authority to cut off funds and initiate lawsuits did school districts take steps to dismantle segregation.

The Supreme Court stood behind *Brown* for several decades. For example, in *Green v. School Board of New Kent County* (1968), the Court ordered "root and branch" eradication of segregated schooling and specified several areas, including students, teachers, transportation, facilities, and extracurricular activities, in which desegregation was required. In *Swann v. Charlotte-Mecklenburg* (1971), the Court struck down allegedly race-neutral student-assignment plans that produced segregated schools as a result of residential segregation and legitimated the use of busing to desegregate urban school districts. Between 1968 and 1972, the percentage of Black students in predominantly minority schools in the South dropped from 81 percent to 55 percent, and in intensely segregated minority schools (more than 90 percent) from 78 percent to 25 percent, which made the schools in the South the most integrated in the nation.

A critical blow to desegregation efforts came in 1974 with the Supreme Court's decision in *Milliken v. Bradley.* The case involved public schools in Detroit, where an exodus of middle-class families had created an overwhelmingly Black district in the city, surrounded by overwhelmingly White suburban districts. Because almost no White people lived within the city limits, integrating the schools was impossible. Parents in the city sought approval of a plan to merge the urban and suburban districts into one metropolitan system that would allow for integration.

A 5–4 Supreme Court majority acknowledged "disparate treatment of White and Negro students" but objected to an "interdistrict remedy" in the absence of evidence that the suburban districts had expressly intended to discriminate against students of color in Detroit. In holding that the suburbs could not be involved in a desegregation plan unless it was clear that they had participated in a segregation scheme, the Court effectively let heavily White suburbs off the hook—and rendered *Brown* almost meaningless for most of the metropolitan North and West.

Throughout these regions, city limits coincide with school district boundaries, with city schools serving largely students of color and suburban schools serving largely White students. If district boundaries could not be crossed, desegregation could not be accomplished. The Supreme Court sent the Detroit case back to a federal district court and three years later approved a modified desegregation plan that affected only schools within the city limits and required the state to help pay for some remedial and compensatory programs.

Reversal and Resegregation

The *Brown* court not only declined to provide a timetable for desegregation but also left open the interpretation of educational opportunity, which it called "a right which must be made available to all on equal terms." Was this a directive simply to end state-mandated segregation in public schooling, or a directive for states and districts to act affirmatively to integrate public schools? Supreme Court decisions in the late 1960s and early 1970s tended to affirm the broader interpretation; later decisions did not, and so paved the way for the subsequent resegregation.

With *Milliken,* the goal shifted from integration to some form of reparations for the damage allegedly caused by segregation. The question was no longer how society could realize the promise of equal educational opportunity for all, but rather how school districts could return to the status quo. In a series of decisions in the 1990s, the Supreme Court essentially answered this new question and laid out a procedure for dismantling desegregation. As a mandate for desegregation, *Brown* was over. Allowed to jettison busing plans in favor of a return to neighborhood schools, many school districts did.

In *Board of Education of Oklahoma City v. Dowell* (1991) and *Freeman v. Pitts* (1992), the Supreme Court outlined the conditions under which desegregation orders can be lifted. For example, a court supervising a school district's desegregation plan can free the district from oversight if it meets some, but not necessarily all, of the requirements laid out in *Green.* In *Missouri v. Jenkins* (1995), the Court then said that a district need not show that changes have actually improved minority students' academic achievement.

Racial and ethnic segregation in the nation's public schools intensified throughout the 1990s and early years of the twenty-first century, as the nation's diversity increased. Although schools in parts of the South have been the most integrated for many years, and schools in metropolitan areas in the North the most intensely segregated, Black communities in every part of the country are now experiencing increasing segregation. In addition, segregation of Latinos has increased steadily since the late 1960s, when the first national data were collected. More than one out of every three Black and Latino students now attend schools that are overwhelmingly (90 to 100 percent) minority.

The resegregation of the nation's public schools reflects economic as well as racial isolation. More than three quarters of the intensely segregated schools are also "high-poverty" schools, which on the whole have less funding and lower student achievement than "low-poverty" schools. Nationwide, during the 2002–2003 school year, the highest poverty school districts had $907 *less* to spend in state and local revenues per pupil than the lowest poverty districts. Disparities are particularly stark in major metropolitan areas. For the 2002–2003 year, per-pupil spending in the Chicago schools (87 percent Black and Hispanic, 85 percent low income) was $8,482, but in the nearby New Trier district (2 percent Black and Hispanic, 1 percent low income), it was $14,909. In the Philadelphia area, per-pupil spending in the city schools (79 percent Black and Hispanic, 71 percent low income) was $9,299, but in the nearby New Hope-Solebury district (1 percent Black and Hispanic, 1 percent low income), it was $14,865. This pattern holds for large metropolitan areas across the nation. Students of color in high-poverty city districts have less than students in White, wealthier suburban districts of almost everything money can buy for schools: state-of-the-art buildings in good repair; well-qualified and adequately compensated teachers; and opportunities to participate in art, music, and sports programs as well as rigorous college-prep classes.

Although a direct correlation cannot be drawn between student achievement and integration, achievement measures have fluctuated with desegregation and resegregation patterns. Reading and math achievement among African Americans and Latinos climbed substantially during the 1970s and 1980s, a period of school desegregation and relatively well-funded antipoverty programs, and the Black-White achievement gap narrowed by more than half. Progress stopped in the mid-1990s, however, and the gap reopened.

The National Assessment of Education Progress (NAEP), widely regarded as the "Nation's Report Card," shows that Black and Latino twelfth graders' achievement in reading and math is on a par with White eighth-graders' achievement. Nationally, only about half of all Black, Latino, and American Indian students graduate from high school in four years. Under the federal No Child Left Behind (NCLB) law, schools receiving Title I funding must show annual improvements in student test scores or risk sanctions. In many districts, poor children of color are bearing the brunt of this accountability "stick." Schools in Houston, New York City, and Orlando have been called to task for retaining ninth graders regarded as unlikely to boost a high school's overall test scores or of pushing low-performing students into GED programs—without counting them as dropouts. In starkly disproportionate numbers, these are poor and minority students.

Brown's Legacy

Arguably both the 1954 Supreme Court decision that gave the dream of racial equality the stamp of the nation's highest court and the White resistance to the declaration of an end to segregated schooling fueled the civil rights movement, which continues to shape life in the United States. At the same time, although considerable progress was made in the South after elected officials threw their weight behind *Brown,* there have been no significant policy initiatives to foster desegregated schooling for more than thirty years. The movement instead has been toward resegregation. Although no longer mandated by law, "separate" schooling for Whites and students of color is the predominant experience in public schools.

The *Brown* court did not address inequities in school funding. Nevertheless, its strong affirmation of education as "perhaps the most important function of state and local governments" and its belief that no "child may reasonably be expected to succeed in life if he or she is denied the opportunity of an education" invited attention to disparities. Forty-five states have now faced, or are facing, challenges to their systems of school funding,

and plaintiffs have prevailed in more than half these cases. Nevertheless, funding gaps remain.

NCLB has refocused attention on the equity and adequacy of resources, in light of new accountability expectations. Intended to end what President Bush called "the soft bigotry of low expectations" and to close the racial achievement gap by holding all students to the same high standards, the law requires schools to show steady progress in student achievement toward a goal of 100 percent proficiency by the year 2014. Initial studies show little change, however, either in overall student achievement patterns or in racial/ethnic achievement gaps since 2001—that is, on the NCLB watch.

Propelled by the dream affirmed in *Brown,* some activists, such as Gary Orfield, director of the Civil Rights Project at Harvard University, continue to work toward a vision of desegregated schooling. Others, such as Derrick Bell, visiting professor at New York University's School of Law, argue that it's time—past time—to focus instead on "desegregating the money," whether or not schools are racially integrated. Given decades of "White flight," Bell believes fairer funding is the best hope for millions of poor students of color still waiting for the equal opportunity that *Brown* promised but that the nation has not yet delivered. The ambiguous *Brown* decision—given its erratic and contested implementation, its heralded place in U.S. history, and persisting inequalities in educational opportunity—supports both commitments.

Sue Books

See also African American Education; Civil Rights Movement; Desegregation; Economic Inequality; Educational Equity: Race/Ethnicity; No Child Left Behind Act

See Visual History Chapter 25, Civil Rights

Further Readings

Bell, D. (2004). *Silent convenants:* Brown v. Board of Education. New York: Oxford University Press.

Education Trust. (2005). *The funding gap: Low-income and minority students shortchanged by most states.* Washington, DC: Author.

Kozol, J. (2005). *The shame of the nation: The restoration of apartheid schooling in America.* New York: Crown.

Lau, P. (Ed.). (2004). *From the grassroots to the Supreme Court:* Brown v. Board of Education *and American democracy* (pp. 340–360). Durham, NC: Duke University Press.

Lee, C. (2006). *Tracking achievement gaps and assessing the impact of NCLB on the gaps: An in-depth look into national and state reading and math outcome trends.* Cambridge, MA: The Civil Rights Project, Harvard University.

Orfield, G., & Eaton, S. E. (1996). *Dismantling desegregation: The quiet reversal of* Brown v. Board of Education. New York: New Press.

Orfield, G., & Lee, C. (2004, January 17). Brown *at 50: Plessy's nightmare?* Cambridge, MA: The Civil Rights Project, Harvard University.

Wald, J., & Losen, D. (2006). Out of sight: The journey through the school-to-prison pipeline. In S. Books (Ed.), *Invisible children in the society and its schools* (pp. 23–37). Mahwah, NJ: Lawrence Erlbaum.

BULLYING

School bullying is a phenomenon that affects a large population of students in many countries. In a 2001 study of over 15,686 U.S. students enrolled in public and private schools, T. R. Nansel and colleagues found that 29.9 percent of the students in Grades 6 through 10 reported moderate to frequent involvement in bullying at school. The 2001 National Crime Victimization Survey indicated that 14 percent of American children ages twelve through eighteen in public and private schools had been bullied in the last six months. Bullying is often defined as a form of aggression that occurs between individuals and groups of students, and it differs from normal student conflict because it is repetitive and involves a social or physical power imbalance. Bullying can be verbal (e.g., name-calling), physical (e.g., shoving), social (e.g., rumor spreading), and electronic (e.g., name-calling through text messaging).

Often using a social-ecological approach to understanding, researchers have identified features of individuals and aspects of the family, peer group, school, and community environment that contribute to or deter bullying. School bullying is a problem that needs to be addressed through targeted prevention efforts that take into account both risk and protective factors.

Research has documented the fact that children experience bullying differently, in terms of both behavioral patterns and psychosocial adjustment. Differences among children involved in bullying have been conceptualized into categorization of four groups: bullies, bully-victims (who are victimized and also bully others), victims (who do not report bullying others), and nonaggressive children. The discrimination between bully and bully-victim groups has aroused particular interest because these subgroups appear to display different patterns of aggression. Bullies exhibit a more goal-oriented aggression, entailing more control and planning. In contrast, the bully-victims tend to display a more impulsive aggression, manifesting poor regulation of affect and behavior, which is perceived as particularly aversive by their peers. Bully-victims as a group report attention deficits, hyperactivity, and academic and conduct problems in the classroom and have higher depression and anxiety.

The Social-Ecological Perspective on Bullying

Involvement in bullying and victimization is the result of the complex interplay between individuals and their broader social environment. Urie Bronfenbrenner's (1979) classic ecological theory is often used to illustrate the interrelated nature of the individual, multiple environments, and engagement in bullying behaviors. The social-ecological theory of bullying posits that perpetration is reciprocally influenced by the individual, family, peer group, and school.

Individual Characteristics

For decades, males have been considered the more aggressive sex. In hundreds of studies, most of the research on aggression has found that, as a group, boys exhibit significantly higher levels of aggression than girls do. Recently, however, a number of researchers have begun to question whether males are the more aggressive sex. Several different terms have been used to describe female-oriented types of aggression, including *indirect aggression, relational aggression,* and *social aggression.* Relational aggression includes behaviors that are intended to significantly damage another child's social standing or reputation. In numerous studies, relational aggression has been shown to be more prevalent among girls than boys because boys typically engage in more overt forms of aggression. However, some research results have contradicted these findings by producing data in which no significant sex differences have emerged. Therefore, there is no consensus as to whether boys bully more than girls do.

Bullies often report adverse psychological effects and poor school adjustment as a result of their involvement in bullying. Whereas victims tend to report more internalizing behaviors, bullies are more likely than their peers to engage in externalizing behaviors, to experience conduct problems, and to be delinquent. Furthermore, long-term outcomes for bullies can be serious; compared to their peers, bullies are more likely to be convicted of crimes in adulthood. One study conducted in the United States revealed that youth identified as bullies in school had a one in four chance of having a criminal record by age thirty. Anger has also consistently emerged as an important correlate of bullying perpetration.

Empathy seems to play an important role in bullying. Research has consistently found negative associations between empathy and aggression, and a positive correlation between empathy and prosocial skills. *Empathy* is defined as one's emotional reaction to another's state and consists of experiencing the perceived emotional state vicariously. However, it appears that children's positive attitude toward bullying mediates the relation between empathy and bullying.

Family Factors

With respect to the family context, bullies, as a group, report that their parents are authoritarian, condone "fighting back," use physical punishment, lack warmth, and display indifference to their children. Parents can also contribute to a *decrease* in children's aggression over time; aggressive children who experienced affectionate mother-child relationships showed a significant decrease in their aggressive-disruptive behaviors. Furthermore, these positive parental connections appeared to buffer the long-term negative consequences of aggression. Children who have

insecure, anxious-avoidant, or anxious-resistant attachments at the age of eighteen months are also more likely than children with secure attachments to become involved in bullying at the age of four and five years.

Peer-Level Characteristics Associated With Bullying

Given the social-ecological perspective that individual characteristics of adolescents interact with group-level factors, many scholars have turned their attention to how peers contribute to bullying. Several theories dominate the literature in this area, including the homophily hypothesis, attraction theory, and dominance theory. These theories taken together present a complex picture of how peers influence each other during early adolescence. The homophily hypothesis suggests that students hang out with peers who are similar in attitudes and behaviors, as in the saying, "birds of a feather flock together." Studies examining peer networks have found support for the homophily hypothesis in that peers not only affiliate with students with similar levels of aggression but also start bullying more if their peers are bullying. Dominance theory indicates that bullying is used as a method to establish power among peers. Indeed, bullying is seen as a way to establish the pecking order as students transition from elementary to middle school. Attraction theory posits that students entering early adolescence are attracted to qualities that are indicative of adulthood and a sense of independence from parents. Studies supporting this theory indicate that girls' and boys' attraction to aggressive peers and students who bully increases when they enter middle school.

School Factors

Much of the research on school factors and bullying has focused on components of school climate. School climate is a particularly important variable to consider because adult supervision decreases from elementary to middle school. In turn, less structure and supervision are associated with concomitant increases in bullying rates among middle school students. For instance, at particularly salient times such as recess, diminished supervision can have important ramifications. Classroom practices and teachers' attitudes are also relevant components of school climate that contribute to bullying prevalence. Aggression varies from classroom to classroom, and in some instances aggression is supported. Bullying tends to be less prevalent in classrooms in which most children are included in activities, teachers display warmth and responsiveness to children, teachers respond quickly and effectively to bullying incidents, and parents are aware of their children's peers relationships.

Risk and Protective Factors

Both individual and group characteristics influence the likelihood of bullying. Risk factors for bullying perpetration include individual characteristics such as being male, having less empathy, being morally disengaged, and having positive attitudes toward bullying. In some cases, perpetration is associated with other forms of delinquency. The ability to feel morally engaged with others is a protective factor, while moral disengagement appears to be associated with a positive attitude toward bullying. Risk factors also include less perceived social support from family members and insecure and/or anxious parental attachments. Peer group affiliation also plays an important role, as members appear to socialize one another to bully others through group norms that support bullying perpetration. Characteristics of teachers and of the classroom environment also serve as both risk and protective factors. Only programs that consider these factors will be successful in impacting the ecology surrounding bullying.

Dorothy L. Espelage

See also Gender and School Violence; Violence in Schools

Further Readings

Bronfenbrenner, U. (1979). *The ecology of human development: Experiments by nature and design.* Cambridge, MA: Harvard University Press.

Espelage, D. L., & Swearer, S. M. (2003). Research on bullying and victimization: What have we learned and where do we need to go? In S. M. Swearer & D. L. Espelage (Eds.), Bullying prevention and intervention: Integrating research and evaluation findings [Special issue]. *School Psychology Review, 32,* 365–383.

Espelage, D. L., & Swearer, S. M. (Eds.). (2004). *Bullying in American schools: A social-ecological perspective on prevention and intervention.* Mahwah, NJ: Lawrence Erlbaum.

Nansel, T. R., Haynie, D. L., & Simons-Morton, B. G. (2003). The association of bullying and victimization with middle school adjustment. *Journal of Applied School Psychology, 19,* 45–61.

Nansel, T. R., Overpeck, M., Pilla, R. S., Ruan, W. J., Simons-Morton, B. G., & Scheidt, P. (2001). Bullying behaviors among U.S. youth: Prevalence and association with psychosocial adjustment. *Journal of the American Medical Association, 285,* 2094–2100.

National Gay and Lesbian Task Force. (1984). *National anti-gay/lesbian victimization report.* Washington, DC: Author.

BUREAUCRACY

The original French word *bureau* denoted the baize material used to cover the top of a desk. The Greek suffixes *kratia* and *kratos* mean "power" or "rule." Thus, *bureaucracy* literally means to rule from a desk or office to conduct governmental affairs. Alternatively, bureaucracy is an instrument used by big business to define means of production. As a sociological concept, bureaucracy specifies the objective discharge of business, through hierarchical administrative structures, according to calculable rules without regard for personal prerogatives or preferences, transforming social inclinations into rationally organized action. This entry briefly describes how bureaucracy works and then looks at the most prominent explanatory theories.

How Bureaucracy Works

In bureaucracies, complex tasks are broken into individual activities and assigned as official duties that clearly define the responsibilities, rights, scope or authority, and competencies of the office. Rationality determines rules and procedures that are administered by trained experts, and objective purposes guide the conduct of both officials and their subordinates. Notably, documents are used extensively to facilitate a flow of information throughout the organization and to establish fixed rules and procedures for each individual task.

Bureaucracy operates under strict principles of hierarchy. A chain of command organizes superior offices, which supervise lower offices. Discharge of authority is based on rules without regard to personal judgment or favoritism. The correctness of authoritative rules is rationalized and well established. Procedures are established for the regulated appeal of lower offices to corresponding superior authorities for additional information and direction.

Thus, in the modern office, management is reduced to a standardized set of rules and procedures administered abstractly and impersonally. Employees are hired after prescribed special examination and according to predetermined qualifications, usually tied to educational certifications. Compensation is based on the specific duties of an office and not the individual characteristics of the person who holds the office. Conditions for career advancement are clearly delineated.

Official business is the primary concern of officials; their duties demand their complete attention, whatever the length of obligatory working hours. Officials do not own their means of production. Regulations require the clear separation of an official's private funds and personal property from public funds and resources, with clear and public accounting for resources used to discharge official business.

Theoretical Background

Early use of the term *bureaucracy* includes a letter, dated July 15, 1765, wherein Baron Grimm and the French philosopher Denis Diderot said that bureaucracy in France meant that officials of all kinds were appointed to benefit public interests and that public interest is necessary for offices—and officials—to exist.

Weber's View

The characteristics of bureaucracy were articulated first quite fully by German sociologist Max Weber early in the twentieth century. Weber described bureaucracy as technically superior to all other organizational forms because it levels economic and social differences while providing administrative functions or services. Accordingly, he thought that public bureaucratization increases as the possession of consumption goods rises,

raising the basic standard of living shared by a society: As communications, technology, and public infrastructures become more complex, the need for personally detached, objective experts becomes greater, and bureaucratic offices or officials fulfill this function.

Further, Weber viewed bureaucracy and capitalism as highly compatible, with capitalism acting as a catalyst for the growth and development of bureaucracy because it benefits from an administration that can be discharged precisely, unambiguously, continually, and quickly. With regard to the state, these characteristics constitute a bureaucratic agency; with regard to the private economy, they constitute a bureaucratic enterprise.

Weber also thought that bureaucratic systems would operate efficiently because employees know their duties precisely, allowing for quicker, more efficient task performance. Standardized rules enable the organization to respond readily to a variety of demands and aid decision making. Rules and procedures based on rationality allow a greater sense of purpose and direction.

Further, Weber identified historical examples of clearly developed, though not pure, "big state" bureaucracies: (a) Egypt, during the period of the New Kingdom (the oldest bureaucratic state administration); (b) the Roman Catholic Church; (c) China, from the time of Shi Hwangti to the twentieth century; and (d) modern states in Europe, the United States, and elsewhere. He suggested that states with a political organization utilizing officials to perform specific duties were the genius of modern bureaucracies. Bureaucracy's origins are traced to the creation of standing armies; to power politics; to the development of public finance and commerce; and, with the modern state, to increased complexity of and demands for order and safety. According to Weber, the modern state requires six types of bureaucratic structures: the judiciary, the modern government agency, the military, religious communities, states, and economies.

Marx's Vision

From another perspective, Karl Marx traced the historical origins of bureaucracy in his theory of materialism to four similar sources: religion, the formation of the state, commerce, and technology. Marx differs with Weber in that he did not see bureaucratization and rationalization as the ultimate organizational structure, but only as a transitional stage from a world of necessity to a world of freedom through communal means. He did, however, agree with Weber that rationalization and bureaucratization are inescapable and that they can produce individual alienation. Also, both viewed bureaucracy as increasing the efficiency and effectiveness of organizations.

However, Weber was not naive about bureaucratic challenges. As he saw it, bureaucratization is limited by the tendency to have bureaucracies assume more tasks than they can manage or that they have funds to support. Cultural influences, such as manipulation by political forces for personal benefit, might also create difficulty. Given the ubiquity of bureaucracy, challenges to Weber's theories are legion. Elements insufficiently or altogether unaddressed by traditional conceptions of bureaucracy include, for example, external competition, collaborative decision making, the quality of performance and product, innovation, management characterized by emotional intelligence, customer-driven outcomes, protection of minority rights, and teamwork. These gaps have led to the evolution of new forms of bureaucratization: total quality management, new public management, and digital-era governance. Inevitably, most concepts are refined or replaced in time, yet Weber's conception remains active and descriptive of small to large organizations and governments worldwide.

Susan Krebs and Rodney Muth

See also Hawthorne Effect; School Governance

Further Readings

Albrow, M. (1970). *Bureaucracy*. London: Pall Mall Press.

Draper, H. (1979). *Karl Marx's theory of revolution: The state and bureaucracy*. New York: Monthly Review Press.

Fredrickson, G., & Smith, K. (2003). *Public administration theory primer*. Boulder, CO: Westview Press.

Hawkesworth, M., & Kogan, M. (Eds.). (1992). *Encyclopedia of government and politics*. New York: Routledge.

Weber, M. (1947). *The theory of social and economic organization*. New York: Oxford University Press.

Weber, M. (1968). *Economy and society: An outline of interpretive sociology*. New York: Bedminster Press.

BUSING

Busing is the means by which public school systems across the United States have sought to achieve proportionate representation in student enrollment of disparate racial groups. Patterns of residential segregation in public school districts where policy required students to attend schools in their local area made achieving a diverse student body a challenge. Transporting K–12 students via school buses to schools outside of their neighborhood to satisfy court-ordered mandates became a source of great tension among various school communities. In addition, typical school funding formulas that depend upon local property taxes raise questions about who can benefit from school district resources. This entry looks at the origins of busing and resulting protests and assesses the outcome.

Ordering Desegregation

The U.S. Supreme Court initiated the process of school desegregation with its 1954 decision in *Brown v. Board of Education,* which held that separate schools were inherently unequal. The cognate 1955 *Brown II* decision was rendered to expedite the process by proposing that school desegregation be carried out with "all deliberate speed." What followed in the years (even decades) post *Brown I* and *II*—confusion about how to comply as well as massive resistance—revealed the depth of emotion people attach to retaining the power to control their children's schooling experience.

The *Brown* decisions were particularly directed at segregated schools in the Southern region of the United States. Many all-White public schools in the South employed a number of tactics to get around the demand to desegregate, including closing schools and establishing private schools, where they could realize their desire to maintain "racial" homogeneity. However, the Civil Rights Act of 1964 gave *Brown* more muscle to encourage Southern school districts to desegregate because it included a threat to cut off funding to schools that practiced racial discrimination. By the end of the 1960s, the percentage of Black students attending desegregated schools in the South had increased substantially, partially due to busing.

Intervention by the Supreme Court was still necessary to attempt to resolve the problem caused by continued resistance to school desegregation efforts and reinforced by residential segregation. In 1971, in *Swann v. Charlotte-Mecklenburg Board of Education,* a unanimous Supreme Court held that busing children beyond their immediate residential areas was a legitimate means to desegregate schools. Within a year of the *Swann* decision, more than forty federal judges promptly entered orders directing the use of busing to eliminate school segregation.

Resisting Change

Searing media images of violence, protests, and civil disobedience captured the sentiments primarily of White families who did not want their children bused out of their neighborhoods or Black children bused into their neighborhoods. Popular polls taken during the early 1970s found more than three out of four respondents opposed busing. Black respondents were about evenly split on the issue. Southern school districts that opposed busing found allies in Northern schools districts when lower federal courts began ordering busing to remedy school segregation nationwide. The alliance sought antibusing legislation as a way to resist what some perceived as interference with their right to run their local schools, including the right to allow residential patterns to determine school profiles. Northern school districts in cities like Detroit, Michigan; Denver, Colorado; Boston, Massachusetts; and Milwaukee, Wisconsin, are on record for their very public opposition to court-ordered busing mandates.

Metropolitan Boston earned a notorious distinction for its particularly violent response to court-ordered busing. Massachusetts U.S. District Judge W. Arthur Garrity, Jr.'s ruling in 1974 found that consistent and recurring patterns of racial discrimination in how Boston public schools were being operated resulted in unconstitutional segregation. A busing plan developed by the Massachusetts Board of Education was used to rectify the situation and implement the state's existing Racial Imbalance Law. The law required all schools to seek racial balance by achieving a student enrollment that was at least 50 percent White. The Boston school committee openly disobeyed orders from the state board of education to obey the law.

The desegregation plan sparked such violent criticism among some Boston residents that Judge Garrity himself was physically attacked. A photographer won a Pulitzer Prize for capturing a shot of a Black attorney named Theodore Landsmark leaving Boston City Hall and being attacked by a White youth who used an American flagpole as a lance. The televised images of riotous protesters hurling insults and rocks at buses during the start of the 1974 school year were reminiscent of 1950s and early 1960s Southern school desegregation protests.

Today's Strategies

The violent responses to busing during the mid-1970s occurred during a period of time when a federal judge supervised the city's desegregation plan. When supervision of the plan ended fifteen years later, the Boston School Board began using a "controlled choice" system of assigning students to schools throughout the city, which it continued for the next ten years. Since September 2000, Boston has used a race-blind admissions policy. The 2000 Census recorded Boston's White population at 54.48 percent and the Black and Hispanic populations together at 39.77 percent. Interestingly, Boston public schools are 86 percent Black and Hispanic.

Similar trends have occurred in other urban school districts. San Francisco, California, requires students to attend schools outside their own neighborhoods to promote racial diversity. Asians, primarily Chinese Americans, are the ones who actively oppose this kind of educational engineering.

In 1974, Prince George's County, Maryland, located in the east suburbs of Washington, D.C., became the largest school in the United Stated to adopt a busing plan. The White population at the time was 80 percent and growing. Busing effectively eliminated that growth to the point that now the county's residential population is less than 25 percent White and more than 65 percent Black. The school district's numbers reflect even more dramatic shifts. The more than 136,000-student school district is now less than 8 percent White and more than 77 percent Black.

Chicago, New York, and many other metropolitan public school systems have experienced demographic changes not only from busing but from immigration and economic shifts as well.

Evaluating the Outcome

To determine the success of busing as a tool for desegregation requires consideration of several intersecting factors. Some cite the Supreme Court's limit on interdistrict remedies for segregation as a feature that boded failure of the plans. Most desegregation plans have favored intradistrict remedies. While that may have worked for many Southern urban school districts, with their majority White and majority Black schools, it has not worked so well for many Northern school districts, which contain only majority Black schools. Detroit is an example of a Northern school district that attempted to use interdistrict remedies to desegregate all Black city schools by busing exchanges with mostly White suburban schools. The plan was not successful, and widespread protests led to a reversal of the court plan.

Court-ordered busing for desegregation purposes also met its demise because of an increasing tendency of the federal courts to find that the effects of past intentional discrimination and segregation had been eliminated. Persistent segregated residential patterns in the 1980s and beyond became an acceptable reason to release school districts from their court-ordered busing plans. The rationale of nonintentionality was successfully argued. Although busing for desegregation continues, the strategies used to maintain it as a viable tool have been broadened to include magnet schools, charter schools, and similar controlled-choice plans that allow parents to choose the schools their children will attend.

The popular criticisms of busing, some more legitimate than others, include concern for student safety, loss of traditional community, stress of long-distance travel, limits on student participation in extracurricular activities, and compromises on educational quality. All of these prompt educators and stakeholders to rethink the concepts of school and community. Busing joins a long list of controversial strategies, such as affirmative action, that have been used with mixed success to enforce judicial and legislative policy. Promoting social, political, and economic equality in American society is a complex task of monumental proportions. Schools will continue to be at the forefront of that struggle.

Jonathan Lightfoot

See also Affirmative Action; African American Education; Antiracist Education; Boards of Education; Charter Schools; Civil Rights Movement; Desegregation; Discrimination and Prejudice; Economic Inequality; Politics of Education; School Choice; Social Justice, Education for; Sociology of Education; Urban Education; Urban Schools, History of

See Visual History Chapter 22, Transportation

Further Readings

Armor, D. (1995). *Forced justice: School desegregation and the law.* New York: Oxford University Press.

Clotfelter, C. (2006). *After "Brown": The rise and retreat of school desegregation.* Princeton, NJ: Princeton University Press.

Formissano, R. (1991). *Boston against busing: Race, class and ethnicity in the 1960s and 1970s.* Chapel Hill: University of North Carolina Press.

Menkart, D., Murray, A., & View, J. (Eds.). (2004). *Putting the movement back into civil rights teaching.* Washington, DC: Teaching for Change.

Patterson, J. (2001). Brown v. Board of Education: *A civil rights milestone and its troubled legacy.* New York: Oxford University Press.

C

CARDINAL PRINCIPLES OF SECONDARY EDUCATION

A thirty-two-page booklet published in 1918, *Cardinal Principles of Secondary Education,* radically changed the curricular and social objectives of the nation's public secondary schools. Largely due to mass immigration, urbanization, and industrialization, the nation's relatively young, public, secondary institutions began to see a sharp increase in enrollment. Concerned with the democratic education of the growing industrial nation, the National Education Association appointed twenty-seven members to the Committee on the Reorganization of Secondary Education, which produced the booklet.

In the wake of World War I, the nation's political and economic climate was peculiarly conducive to the social agenda set forth in *Cardinal Principles of Secondary Education.* The publication outlined seven principles meant to guide the social, moral, and intellectual development of American public school children between the ages of twelve and eighteen and sought to educate both emergent self and citizen to best realize the nation's democratic ideals.

The first principle, *Health,* undertook to educate youth about the habits necessary to promote and maintain a hygienic, physically active nation. Acknowledging the need for students to master remedial academic skills including reading, writing, and arithmetic, *Command of Fundamental Processes* followed as the second principle. The third principle, *Worthy Home Membership,* sought to prepare young men and women, through "household arts" and academic disciplines, to value the home and family as the foundational institution of the larger society. *Vocation,* the fourth principle, was concerned with training future workers in specific manual occupations and "right relations" with coworkers so that they might better support their families and contribute to society. Rather than a study of "constitutional questions and remote governmental functions," the fifth principle, *Civic Education,* was primarily concerned with instilling students with a sense of civic pride and duty from the local to the national level. An objective made possible by the relative national prosperity, the sixth principle, *Worthy Use of Leisure,* sought to teach young adults to balance the interests of culture and the arts with those of vocational obligations. Informing all of the preceding principles, the seventh, *Ethical Character,* intended to shape an individual's code of moral conduct that she or he might better serve democratic principles.

During the early part of the twentieth century, sweeping social, political, and economic changes gave rise to a cultural dynamic that demanded reform of established institutions. The nation's public schools retain the ideological vestiges of the *Cardinal Principles of Secondary Education* derived almost a century ago.

Kristen Ogilvie Holzer

See also Committee of Ten; Democracy and Education

Further Readings

Beck, R. (1976). A history of issues in secondary education. In W. VanTil (Ed.), *Issues in secondary education* (pp. 30–64). Chicago: University of Chicago Press.

Department of the Interior, Bureau of Education. (1937). *Cardinal principles of secondary education* (Bulletin, 1918, No. 35). Washington, DC: U.S. Government Printing Office.

Educational Policies Commission. (1938). *The purposes of education in American democracy.* Washington, DC: NEA of the U.S and the American Association of School Administrators.

CARLISLE BARRACKS SCHOOL

In 1879, U.S. Army Captain Richard H. Pratt persuaded the federal government to allow him to establish an off-reservation boarding school for American Indians at the abandoned cavalry barracks at Carlisle, Pennsylvania. The Indian Industrial School at Carlisle became the model for the hundreds of government-run American Indian boarding schools developed after 1879 as the government policy shifted from supporting religious organizations schools, often on or near where the native peoples lived, to government-run, off-reservation schools.

Removal from family, tribe, language, place, and culture was intended to speed the assimilation of the native children into the dominant Anglo society. Besides its total immersion of native people in Anglo culture and its militaristic methods, the school is noted for its Indian arts program taught by natives; the system that placed native students in Anglo homes, businesses, or farms to work; and an athletic program that produced football teams that beat the best college teams. Olympic gold medalist Jim Thorpe attended Carlisle and was voted the greatest athlete of the first half of the twentieth century in the United States.

The school closed on September 1, 1918, with pressure from U.S. senators in the West pushing for more schools in the West, congressional investigations of mismanagement at Carlisle, and the need for hospitals for soldiers fighting during World War I. The old barracks reverted to an Army hospital. Although it has been closed for nearly a century, the Carlisle Indian Industrial School continues to have an effect into the present. The school became the model for the residential school system and the lynchpin for destruction of native cultures, which has adversely affected the lives of native peoples for generations.

Pratt commanded African American cavalry troops and American Indian scouts in Indian Territory after the Civil War. He became convinced that the natives could be like the Whites if given the proper training. He volunteered to be in charge of seventy-two Native Americans charged with various crimes and imprisoned at Fort Marion in Florida. He started language instruction, drill, and other educational activities. These successes allowed him to convince General Armstrong to establish an Indian Department at Hampton Institute in Virginia, which had been established for freed slaves. Success there combined with local support in Carlisle, and concerns over the mixing of the two races at Hampton led to approval of the Carlisle Barracks School.

Native students' physical appearance was quickly transformed by haircuts in Anglo style and military cadet-style uniforms. For many native males, hair length had cultural significance, with cutting often associated with mourning. Pratt proudly displayed before and after photographs.

Students were prohibited from speaking their own languages, were given English names, and were instructed in language by copying and imitating. Half their day was spent in academics and half at work or industrial training. Church attendance was required.

For many students, Carlisle was the end of their life. Disease and despair caused many deaths. For instance, the school reported that 21 out of 637 students died in 1889. In Pratt's twenty-four years at Carlisle, less than 160 students graduated. Many students were sent to Anglo homes under the outing system. Originally, they were paid for their work, but later they became a source of cheap labor, especially in schools out West.

After Pratt's departure, Indian culture became more acceptable at the school, and Angel De Cora, a mixed-blood Winnebago with degrees from Hampton, Smith, and Drexel, was hired to teach art. Sports began to rule the school, especially football. The football team played the big colleges and was coached for a number of years by Glenn S. "Pop" Warner. The team produced many All-American selections, including Jim Thorpe in 1912. Other sport champions included Louis Tewanima in track and Charles Bender in baseball, who later pitched in a World Series. Yet, it was the highly successful football team, with its ability to raise big funds, which helped stir the congressional investigation in 1914 over alleged mismanagement that eventually led to the school's closing.

Michael W. Simpson

See also Hampton Model; Hegemony; Native American Education, History of

See Visual History Chapter 8, The Education of Native Americans

Further Readings

Pratt, H. (1964). *Battlefield and classroom: Four decades with the American Indian, 1867–1904.* New Haven, CT: Yale University Press.

Reyhner, J., & Eder, J. (2004). *American Indian education: A history.* Norman: University of Oklahoma Press.

Witmer, L. (1993). *The Indian Industrial School, Carlisle, Pennsylvania, 1879–1918.* Carlisle, PA: Cumberland County Historical Society.

Web Sites

Cumberland County Historical Society Carlisle Indian Industrial School: http://www.historicalsociety.com/ciiswelcome.html

CATECHISMS

An instructional tool for teachers and students of religious education, a catechism is a textbook whose primary goal is to provide clear, precise, and brief answers to fundamental questions. Typically structured in the question-and-answer format, a catechism proposes a basic question, and then proceeds to answer it immediately. Catechisms thus provide a quick but exact summary of religious doctrine in a highly accessible and easy-to-understand layout.

The word *catechism,* and its cognates, *catechesis* and *catechetical,* have their origin in the Greek verb *katechein,* which is often associated with the theater and the ancient agora or marketplace; it means, "to make resound or echo." Thus, oral instruction is suggested in the etymology of the verb. While Christianity popularized the common use of catechisms, the pedagogical technique is rooted in both the Greek Socratic method and the manner of instruction found in rabbinical schools and synagogues. The question-answer format invites the participation of two, a master and a follower, a teacher and a student, a parent and a child. The use of catechisms was popular in the early days of Christianity, especially in the education of children and converts.

Catechisms tend to merit greater attention and receive wider distribution during difficult and challenging times. Martin Luther authored a famous catechism called the *Small Catechism* (1529), followed by his *Large Catechism* (1530), both of which figured prominently in the Reformation and are still available and widely used today.

Peter Canisius wrote a popular catechism in the Roman Catholic tradition in 1555. However, the Council of Trent published the most authoritative catechism of this era in 1566. Intended as a tool to combat the influences of the Protestant Reformation, the Catechism of the Council of Trent served as a reference work for clergy preparation for over 400 years.

The Baltimore Catechism was a popular presentation of Roman Catholicism that served as a classroom text in many Catholic schools from its publication in 1885 through the 1960s. The catechism took its name from the council or meeting of bishops which produced it—the Third Plenary Council of Baltimore.

Other Christian denominations have produced catechisms. The Heidelberg Catechism (1563) originated as a work of Calvinism and is the most widely used catechism in the Reformed churches. A catechism for the Anglican Communion can be found in the Book of Common Prayer. The most popular Catholic catechism in the United Kingdom for many years was the Penny Catechism.

Modern-day catechisms have tended to serve as major reference works and compendia of doctrine rather than as pedagogical instruments. The first new universal catechism of the Roman Catholic Church since the Council of Trent, *The Catechism of the Catholic Church* (1994), is not structured in the traditional question-and-answer format. It contains mostly highly annotated essays of theological depth, serving as a primary reference for educated, sophisticated readers. More recently, abbreviated versions of this catechism have been produced to provide easier access for more readers.

Ronald J. Nuzzi

See also Catholic Education, History of

Further Readings

Catholic Church. (1885). *A catechism of Christian doctrine: Prepared and enjoined by order of the Third Plenary Council of Baltimore.* New York: Benziger.

Catholic Church. (1994). *Catechism of the Catholic Church.* Ligouri, MO: Ligouri.

Catholic Education, History of

The first Catholic schools were founded in the early seventeenth century in what are now the states of Florida and Louisiana, predating the schools of Puritan Massachusetts. Beset by conflicts with public officials and anti-immigrant nativist forces, to say nothing of internal disputes, Catholic education nevertheless prevailed. While the Catholic school population peaked in the 1960s, the schools have enjoyed a considerable revival at the turn of the twenty-first century, often serving non-Catholic students with lay teachers. This entry discusses that history and record of achievement.

Early History

Catholics constituted a minuscule portion of the country's population when the nation's first Catholic bishop, John Carroll, called for the instruction of Catholic youth in 1792 with the goal of insuring their religious commitment. Catholics had often been victims of religious persecution in the early years of nationhood, and the Church's U.S. leaders looked to the often gender-specific schools—some day schools, and others for boarders—to preserve the faith of young Catholics.

Common schools, the forerunners of today's public schools, were begun in the 1830s in Massachusetts under the leadership of Horace Mann and existed in most of the Northern states by the time of the Civil War. Established at the elementary level and supported by public taxation, the schools were nominally nonsectarian but broadly Protestant, their moral foundations resting on the King James version of the Bible and what Mann termed "common core Christianity."

Insistence on the use of Protestant practices in these schools, however, created difficulties for Catholics who attended them. At the Fourth Provincial Council of Baltimore in 1840, the Catholic bishops first took note of these problems, which included devotional reading of the King James version of the Bible, anti-Catholic curricular materials, and Protestant personnel in charge of the schools. Tensions between Catholics and their fellow Americans grew as immigration swelled the Catholic ranks. Between 1821 and 1850, nearly 2.5 million Europeans entered the country, many of whom were Catholic. The punishment of Catholic children who refused to follow Protestant practices in the schools was one expression of this hostility.

The establishment of a separate system of Catholic parish (parochial) schools, founded to educate Catholic children in faith and morals as well as letters, was one result of this conflict. Not all Catholics concurred with this policy, as some felt that the Church's efforts should focus on social problems. German-American Catholic bishops were especially committed to providing Catholic schools to preserve the faith and customs of their people. They admonished parents of the dangers to their children inherent in the public school system, which could lead to religious indifference and a consequent abandonment of their faith.

After the Civil War

The growth of the secular "American" public school was seen as the major threat to the faith and morals of Catholic children after the Civil War. No longer was the main menace the pan-Protestant, allegedly nonsectarian public school.

In 1875, the Catholic population in the United States, fed by immigration, exceeded 5.7 million, served by 1,444 parishes. With mounting costs and a largely poor membership, Catholic bishops sought public funds for their schools, arguing that the state had the duty to assist parents to meet their God-given responsibility to educate their young. Many Americans resisted these efforts. President Ulysses S. Grant publicly insisted that free public schools should be the sole recipient of public funds. Shortly thereafter, Congressman James G. Blaine introduced an amendment that would have prohibited any state funds being used for religious purposes, including schools. His amendment passed in the House but failed in the Senate. Between 1877 and 1917, however, the "Blaine Amendment" was enacted by 29 states.

Meanwhile, dissent arose within the Catholic hierarchy over the need for Catholic schools. In 1875 the Vatican's Congregation of the Propagation of the Faith, which was in charge of the U.S. church at the time, called on Catholic leaders to build Catholic schools and on the laity to support, maintain, and have their children educated in them. Local bishops were left to decide if it would be permissible for Catholic children to attend local public schools.

This position was underscored by leaders of the American church meeting at the Third Plenary Council of Baltimore in 1884. The bishops passed two decrees that set official Catholic policy regarding education for decades: (1) each parish was to have a school within two years, unless the local bishop allowed otherwise; and (2) Catholic parents were to send their children to those schools unless exempted by the local bishop. The driving force behind these decrees was the belief that the future of the Church in the United States rested on the success of these schools. The impact of the decrees was limited; the percentage of parishes with schools increased from 40 percent to 44 percent in the decade after the Baltimore council. Thus, the goal of "every Catholic child in a Catholic school" was never close to being met in the nineteenth century.

A New Century's "School Question"

"Americanism," or citizenship education, based on the English language, became the watchword in public education as the nineteenth century neared its end. Moral education had become divorced from religious education; the former was the province of the public school, the latter the terrain of home and church in this framework. Public schooling had become more centralized, bureaucratized, and systematized. At the same time, immigration increased the American Catholic population from 6,143,222 to 17,735,553 between 1880 and 1920. American nativists saw this as a threat, and the public school was increasingly seen as the means of assimilating Catholic children.

On the Catholic side, Pope Leo XIII declared that the state should respect the rights of the Church in those areas that it considered its field, which included education. Catholics were instructed to follow the teachings of the Church, which led to the charge by some Americans that Catholicism and Catholic schools were "foreign" entities. Although they faced religious penalties, including being refused the sacraments, some Catholics, lay and clerical, opposed the Church's official position on Catholic schooling. This was true even within the Catholic hierarchy. Liberals, like Archbishop John Ireland of St. Paul, Minnesota, attempted to work out viable compromises with government, whereas conservatives, such as Archbishops Michael Corrigan of New York and Frederick Katzer of Milwaukee, urged total commitment to Catholic schools and denounced the public schools in rather harsh terms. The struggle, which was featured in the public press, became heated.

Dedication to Catholic schools was to some degree rooted in the wish to preserve their ethnic heritage among certain groups of Catholics, for example, Germans and Poles. Some American government officials, public educators, and religious leaders saw the ethnic Catholic commitment to parochial schools as "un-American" and called for means, including legislation, to control or perhaps destroy them. Nonetheless, enrollment in Catholic schools, which like public schools of the period was mostly at the elementary level, continued to grow, from 405,334 in 1880 to 1,701,219 in 1920.

The World Wars

World War I released passions hostile to anything "foreign" in the country, especially anything German.

As a result, the American hierarchy and prominent Catholic educators worked to eliminate old world customs, including teaching in a foreign language, in Catholic parochial schools. Catholic schools were becoming assimilated.

Nonetheless, there were attempts to curtail or even eliminate them, the most threatening of them an Oregon law that would have required attendance at public schools by all children between the ages of eight and sixteen on the grounds that attendance was necessary for citizenship. The U.S. Supreme Court ruled the law unconstitutional, stating that "the child is not the mere creature of the state"; parents retained the right to send their children to private schools as long as those schools offered secular as well as religious education (*Pierce v. Society of Sisters,* 1925).

During this period, two men improved the quality of Catholic schools. Thomas Edward Shields of the Catholic University of America (CUA) endeavored to apply the ideas of progressive education to Catholic schools, writing several textbooks, but he was not able to obtain the support of conservative Catholic clerics and educators. One of Shields's students, George Johnson, earned the title of "bridge-builder" (for building bridges among Catholic groups and between Catholic and governmental agencies) and spearheaded Catholic participation in professional educational activities at the national level.

Issues related to school accreditation and teacher certification confronted Catholic schools. Who was going to have the basic responsibility for preparing the teaching staffs of Catholic schools, made up overwhelmingly of religious women? After some discussion, the preparation of teachers was left to the respective religious orders.

With a world awash in a sea of totalitarianism from the left and right, Pope Pius XI issued his encyclical "The Christian Education of Youth" in 1929. Recognizing that three societies have rights in education—the family, the Church, and the state—the Pope reiterated Catholic teaching that parents, not governments, are the primary educators of children. Education, he averred, must be God centered and directed to humans' last end. Attendance at a Catholic school was the ideal for all Catholic children.

In the 1920s, American secondary school education experienced a huge spurt in enrollment, and Catholic schools were not unaffected. Interparish high schools and parish high schools joined the private Catholic schools that usually were owned, operated, and staffed by a religious order; these were often segregated by gender. In 1936, 1,945 Catholic secondary schools had an enrollment of 284,736, and 7,929 elementary schools had 2,102,889 students.

After World War II

Between 1940 and 1959, non–public school enrollment increased by 118 percent compared with a 36 percent gain in the public sector. Catholic schools were crowded, and suburban parishes were hard-pressed to meet the demands of parishioners for Catholic schools. This growth led to renewed interest in governmental financial aid to Catholic schools, either indirectly through the parents or directly to the school itself. In 1947, the Supreme Court upheld, by the narrowest of margins (5–4), the constitutionality of providing transportation at public expense to children who attended a faith-based school (*Everson v. Board of Education,* 1947).

Parishes continued to face severe financial pressures, however, made worse by the small number of nun teachers whose limited financial compensation made the schools possible. Citizens for Educational Freedom, composed mainly of Catholic laity under the leadership of Virgil C. Blum, S.J., a political scientist, was founded to obtain public support for Catholic schools. Arguing that children (and their parents) should not be penalized for their choice of school, the group aggressively sought funds as a constitutional right for those who chose religiously affiliated schools under the Fourteenth Amendment.

Internal Turmoil

The second Vatican Council, convened by Pope John XXIII on October 6, 1962, shook the foundations of the Catholic Church worldwide and Catholic schools in the United States in particular. In *Are Parochial Schools the Answer: Catholic Education in the Light of the Council,* a lay Catholic, Mary Perkins Ryan, argued that the clerical-dominated parochial schools had worked well for an immigrant, poor Catholic minority in the nineteenth century, but they had served their purpose and were now anachronistic. Catholic education should focus on adults, not roughly half of Catholic children, and on the liturgy, she argued, and parents should assume their rightful role in the religious education of their children.

Reaction to Ryan's book was swift, with some Catholic educators attacking her orthodoxy. In the 1965–1966 school year, Catholic K–12 enrollment reached an all-time high of 5.6 million pupils, about 87 percent of non–public school enrollment and 12 percent of all K–12 students in the nation. Then, enrollment plummeted; by 1971–1972, it had reached little more than 4 million, a drop of over 1.5 million students in six years. Accompanying this decline was the growing question about the effectiveness of Catholic schools. The source of these questions included several of the religious orders that had heavy investments of personnel and money in the schools, along with leading prelates, such as Cardinal Joseph Ritter of St. Louis.

As Catholics moved from central cities to the suburbs, a sizable number of Catholic schools in the inner cities were closed. This led some, including Monsignor James C. Donohue, an executive of the United States Catholic Conference, the official arm of the U.S. Catholic bishops, to wonder if the closings meant the Church was abandoning the poor. Meanwhile, Monsignor O'Neill C. D'Amour, an official of the National Catholic Educational Association (NCEA), was calling for Catholic school boards at the diocesan and local levels, with real, not simply advisory power. The Church needed to emphasize the professional over the pastoral and religious aspects of Catholic schools, he believed.

Attempts to obtain government financial aid to bolster the monetarily strapped schools received a setback in 1971, when the Supreme Court ruled that the purchase of secular services, which had been approved by the states of Pennsylvania and Rhode Island, amounted to "excessive entanglement" and thus were unconstitutional under the Establishment Clause of the First Amendment (*Lemon v. Kurtzman,* 1971).

At this critical juncture, the nation's Catholic bishops issued a declaration emphasizing the religious mission of the Catholic schools to teach doctrine, build community, and serve all humankind. The Catholic school was a "faith community," the bishops said. This goal was made more difficult because the percentage of nun teachers, steeped in religious traditions, dropped constantly during the 1970s, decreasing from 56.7 percent in 1968–1969 to 24.6 percent in 1981–1982. New means had to be found to develop spirituality in the largely lay staff, if the schools were to be "faith communities."

The presence of lay teachers gave rise to a new phenomenon for Catholic schools—collective bargaining. Catholic social teaching had long upheld the right of workers to join unions and to strike as the final means for their rights. The 1970s saw the institutional Church pitted against some of its own members in strikes like the one that took place in Chicago's Catholic schools.

In 1976, a group of authors concluded in *Catholic Schools in a Declining Church* that Catholic schools still enjoyed the support of the Catholic laity, but in the controversial afterword, Father Andrew Greeley recommended that the hierarchy get out of the school business and turn the running of the schools over to the laity. The bishops did not heed Greeley's unsolicited advice.

A Comeback in the 1980s

In 1981–1982, Catholic school enrollment had declined to 3,094,000, down approximately 1 million from ten years earlier. Catholic educators were issued a threefold challenge by Alfred McBride, a former NCEA official: to keep Catholic schools Catholic in all aspects, to maintain academic excellence, and to achieve financial stability. The American bishops praised the schools for what they had done for the Church and called on them to provide a high quality education in a setting infused with Gospel values. The support of Catholic schools by bishops and priests, however, was not overwhelming.

The Catholic presence remained in the inner cities. The Milwaukee-based Catholic League for Civil

Rights in 1982 reported sixty-four schools in eight central cities with a student population that included 54 percent Title I recipients, a third of them non-Catholic and nearly 79 percent minority. Catholic schools provided these pupils a safe environment, emphasized basic learning skills, and fostered moral values, the report said. The cause of Catholic schools was furthered in the 1980s by the work of James Coleman and associates, who attested to the academic achievement of Catholic schools and underscored their community support, what Coleman called the "social capital" that gave them a distinct advantage over public schools. Another endorsement from an "outside" source came in 1993, with the publication of Anthony Bryk, Valerie Lee, and Peter Holland's *Catholic Schools and the Common Good*. Decentralization, a shared set of moral beliefs, a shared code of conduct, small size, and emphasis on academics were the traits said to distinguish Catholic secondary schools.

In 1989–1990 there were 8,719 Catholic schools operating in the country, 7,395 at the elementary level and 1,324 secondary; 23 percent of the total enrollment were minority youth, and 64 percent of African American students were not Catholic. The growing non-Catholic presence among students and staff led to questions about the Catholic identity of these schools that had never arisen previously. During the 1990s, new Catholic schools opened at the rate of 21 per year; since 1985, 230 Catholic schools had opened of which 204 were elementary and 26 were secondary. Catholic schools' enrollment had also increased by a rate of 3.8 percent, but their market share had dropped from 6.3 percent to 5.6 percent during that decade.

Thomas C. Hunt

See also Catholic Schools, Contemporary Issues

See Visual History Chapter 6, Catholic Schools and the Separation of Church and State; Chapter 13, Exhibit of American Negroes: *Exposition Universelle de 1900*; Chapter 24, The Farm Security Administration's Photographs of Schools

Further Readings

Bryk, A. S., Lee, V. E., & Holland, P. E. (1993). *Catholic schools and the common good.* Cambridge, MA: Harvard University Press.

Buetow, H. A. (1970). *Of singular benefit: The story of U.S. Catholic education.* New York: Macmillan.

Cibulka, J. G., O'Brien, T. J., & Zewe, D. (1982). *Inner-city Catholic elementary schools: A study.* Milwaukee, WI: Marquette University Press.

Coleman, J. S., & Hoffer, T. (1987). *Public and private high schools: The impact of communities.* New York: Basic Books.

Coleman, J. S., Hoffer, T., & Kilgore, S. (1982). *High school achievement: Public, Catholic, and private schools compared.* New York: Basic Books.

Greeley, A. M., McCready, W. C., & McCourt, K. (1976). *Catholic schools in a declining church.* Kansas City, KS: Sheed & Ward.

McCluskey, N. G. (1959). *Catholic viewpoint on education.* Garden City, NY: Hanover House.

Nuzzi, R. J. (2004). Catholic schools in action. In T. C. Hunt, E. A. Joseph, & R. J. Nuzzi (Eds.), *Catholic schools in the United States: An encyclopedia* (pp. 120–122). Westport, CT: Greenwood Press.

Ristau, K. (1992). Current concerns. In M. A. Grant & T. C. Hunt (Eds.), *Catholic school education in the United States: Development and current concerns* (pp. 234–250). New York: Garland.

Ryan, M. P. (1964). *Are parochial schools the answer? Catholic education in the light of the council.* New York: Guild Press.

Simon, K. A., & Grant, W. V. (Eds.). (1987). *Digest of educational statistics.* Washington, DC: U.S. Department of Health, Education, & Welfare.

Walch, T. (1996). *Parish school: American Catholic parochial schools from colonial times to the present.* New York: Crossroad Herder.

Walch, T. (2004). The Education of Catholic Americans. In T. C. Hunt, E. A. Joseph, & R. J. Nuzzi (Eds.), *Catholic schools in the United States: An encyclopedia* (pp. 245–246). Westport, CT: Greenwood Press.

CATHOLIC SCHOOLS, CONTEMPORARY ISSUES

Contemporary Catholic schools face major challenges at the beginning of the twenty-first century, the most basic being money—or lack of it. This is particularly true in the urban areas where, in the decade between 1986 and 1996, the number of Catholic elementary schools declined from a total of 3,424 to 3,139, about 8.3 percent; their suburban counterparts dropped from 2,232 to 2,150, a decrease of almost 3.75 percent. The number of urban secondary schools declined from 750 to 613, whereas suburban secondary schools recorded a smaller loss, decreasing from 420 to 413.

The situation has grown worse since then, as the recent announcement by the National Catholic Educational Association (NCEA) revealed. In the 2004–2005 academic year, 173 Catholic schools, many in urban areas, were either closed or consolidated, constituting a decline of 2.6 percent, due to rising costs, changing demographics, and declining enrollment. Subsequently, the Archdiocese of Chicago announced that 5 of the 23 elementary schools designated for closing would reopen in the fall of 2005 due to positive financial developments. In 2004–2005, 37 new Catholic schools opened, and one third of existing Catholic schools had a waiting list. Many of these schools were in urban areas, such as Chicago, Detroit, Brooklyn, and St. Louis. The preceding year, 123 Catholic schools were closed or consolidated, while 34 new schools were opened.

This entry describes the present challenges facing Catholic elementary and secondary schools.

Professional Personnel

Historically, the vast majority of principals and teachers were members of religious orders (nuns or brothers) or clergy. At the elementary level, they were overwhelmingly nuns. In 2004–2005, however, the full-time professional staff at Catholic elementary schools was 95 percent laity and 5 percent religious or clergy.

This change has had several crucial consequences for Catholic schools. The financial burden is obvious; personnel from religious orders contributed services to Catholic schools in the past at little cost. The salaries and benefits for lay teachers, while they pale in comparison to those of public school personnel, nonetheless place a heavy burden on the operation of Catholic schools. In addition, the religious were steeped in the traditions of their respective orders, nurturing the schools' Catholic identity. Non-Catholic staff, as well as Catholics who have not had the opportunity to grasp the nature of the Catholic school's religious mission, can put that identity at risk.

Students

Catholic school enrollment in 2004–2005 was 2,420,590 students, of which 1,779,639 were in elementary or middle school. Minority students totaled 655,949, or 27.1 percent of the total, and 328,778, or 13.5 percent of the enrollment, were non-Catholics. The presence of non-Catholics, or Catholic children whose families are not members of the parish, can lead to difficulties with the traditional parish support of such schools. Further, some sources within the Catholic Church have questioned the schools' mission as well as the allocation of resources to schools in the inner cities, especially when a considerable number of the students are not Catholic.

Catholic schools, especially at the elementary level, have the well-earned reputation for educating the poor. Recent statistics point out that the increasing costs of tuition have led to a changed student population, economically speaking. For instance, in 1992, 5.5 percent of students in attendance at Catholic high schools were from the lowest socioeconomic quartile, while in 1972 that population was 12.3 percent. Meanwhile, the percentage from the upper quartile had risen from 29.7 percent to 45.8 percent. This change has led some to label Catholic schools as "elitist."

Financial Support

Financial problems have without question been the major factor in the decline of Catholic school attendance. The support of the parish, combined with the low-cost service of the religious faculty, at one time covered all or nearly all of the costs to the parish elementary school. In 2000–2001 parish support made up 24.1 percent of the total cost per student. Tuition exceeded parish subsidies as the major source of support by 1985–1986. Help is desperately needed.

Some have looked to publicly funded vouchers, which give parents money and let them choose which school their children will attend. Ruled constitutional in 2002 by the U.S. Supreme Court in *Zelman v. Simmons-Harris,* vouchers face major political battles across the land. Voucher programs exist in various forms in Cleveland, Milwaukee, and Washington,

D.C., to name leading examples. In January 2006, vouchers were ruled unconstitutional at the state level in Florida. The impact of this decision may well adversely affect the future of vouchers across the nation.

In thirty-eight states, legislation along the lines of the nineteenth-century Blaine Amendment, which prohibits state aid for religious purposes, is a major obstacle to the school choice cause. Teacher unions are in the forefront of the opposition to vouchers; parental groups are among their strongest supporters. Proponents argue that parents, not the government or educational personnel, are the primary educators of their children; the government should support parents' choice of schools for their children, a choice not viable for poor families without the voucher. There is a concern, however, that increased government involvement in the operation of Catholic schools through vouchers or other means might lessen, or even destroy, their autonomy of operation or their Catholic religious identity.

Privately funded vouchers are another means of support for Catholic schools. The Children's Scholarship Fund (CSF) was started in 1998. In 2004–2005, CSF partnered with thirty-four organizations across the country, and together they have provided scholarships to low-income families that have enabled thousands of those families to select a private or parochial school. In 2004–2005 alone, CSF spent or granted $17 million on scholarships, and the partners will spend another $11 million of locally raised money. Parents Advancing Choice in Education (PACE) in Dayton, Ohio, is one of these local partners. Scholarships to the children are determined by some combination of family size and income, on the one hand, and the school's tuition; the family pays some portion of the tuition; donors, large and small, contribute to the various funds. Other agencies that are independent of CSF, such as the Big Shoulders fund in Chicago, also provide scholarship money to qualified children.

Endowment efforts, especially at the secondary level, have provided a growing source of income. In 1997–1998, for instance, 57.7 percent of Catholic high schools had a full-time endowment director.

Elementary schools, as they become less affiliated with parishes, will likely follow the lead of secondary schools in seeking alternate sources of revenue, including endowments and private vouchers.

The role of the laity in Catholic educational affairs will likely grow with the shrinking number of priests and the diminishing parish support of elementary schools. Catholic boards of education, at the diocesan, local, and school levels, have become realities since the 1960s. Based in part on the right and responsibility of the laity to participate in the activities of the Church by virtue of their baptism, these boards have assumed policy making, as well as consultative and advisory roles.

New Strategies

Several recent developments merit mention. One is the founding of new forms of Catholic schools. Perhaps the best known of these are the Cristo Rey high schools and the Nativity middle schools. Begun in Chicago in 1997 for Hispanic/Latino youth, Cristo Rey schools combine work and study and are supported by a combination of donations, tuition, scholarship, and financial aid. Founded by the Jesuit order, The Cassin Foundation has been crucial to their existence. The concept has been replicated by other religious orders, such as the Christian Brothers and Daughters of Charity. In January of 2006, eleven Cristo Rey schools had an enrollment of 2,449, and three more were scheduled to open in the fall of 2006. In addition, as of January 2006, there were forty-three Nativity middle schools in operation, with a reported enrollment of 2,950, 56.1 percent African American and 28.1 percent Latino. About 90 percent of these students qualify for the federal government free/reduced lunch program. Seven more schools are being developed.

There are other institutional developments. The National Association of Private Catholic and Independent Schools (NAPCIS) was founded in 1995. In 2004–2005, they counted fifty-seven institutions in twenty-eight states. They are described as "independent schools in service to the Church." NAPCIS itself is advertised as "an accreditation, teacher certification and support organization for independent Roman Catholic schools."

At the beginning of the twenty-first century, home-schooling was growing about 7 percent per year. Estimates range from 1.1 million to 2.1 million students home schooled in 2002–2003, certainly including some Catholic youth. The Seton Home Study School in Virginia offers a wide variety of services to aid parents in carrying out their educational responsibilities.

Finally, Catholic schools have been the recent beneficiaries of dedicated young Catholics who have volunteered their professional services for a specified time period to underresourced Catholic schools. Prepared to teach at twelve Catholic universities in the nation in 2004–2005, these young people live in a community, take part in a communal spiritual life, and participate in professional development activities while teaching.

Beset with serious challenges, Catholic schools are truly at a crossroads.

Thomas C. Hunt

See also School Choice; School Funding

Further Readings

Baker, D. P., & Riordan, C. (1998). The "eliting" of the common American Catholic school and the national education crisis. *Phi Delta Kappan. 80*(1), 16–23.

McDonald, D. (2004). *Annual report on Catholic elementary and secondary schools: United States Catholic elementary and secondary school statistics* 2003–2004. Available from http://www.ncea.org

Riordan, C. (2000). Trends in student demography in Catholic secondary schools, 1972–1992. In J. Youniss & J. J. Convey (Eds.), *Catholic schools at the crossroads: Survival and transformation* (pp. 35–54). New York: Teachers College Press.

Savage, F. X. (2004). Socioeconomic status (of students). In T. C. Hunt, E. A. Joseph, & R. J. Nuzzi (Eds.), *Catholic schools in the United States: An encyclopedia* (pp. 613–615). Westport, CT: Greenwood Press.

Walch, T. (1996). *Parish school: American Catholic parochial schools from colonial times to the present.* New York: Crossroad Herder.

Youniss, J., & Convey, J. J. (Eds.). (2000). *Catholic schools at the crossroads: Survival and transformation.* New York: Teachers College Press.

CHANNEL ONE

Channel One is a commercial news and media service viewed by approximately one third of America's middle and high school students. The service was established in 1989 as part of entrepreneur Christopher Whittle's Whittle Communications. Since its establishment, Channel One has been sold to other media corporations, such as Primedia. Under Whittle's management, schools received the service by way of a contractual agreement. The agreement arranged for schools to receive equipment from Whittle, such as televisions, videotape recorders, and satellite dishes. Schools, in return, would commit to airing Channel One's twelve-minute news and advertising program everyday of the school year to at least 90 percent of the school's student population. Similar policies have continued since Channel One's sale to Primedia.

Advertising

One of the great controversies surrounding Channel One's airing in public schools has to do with the two minutes of advertising in the program. Students, teachers, parents, scholars, and public officials have expressed concern over the use of advertising in education. The concern has spanned the political spectrum, bringing together such figures as conservative political pundit Phyllis Schafly and consumer advocate Ralph Nader. Most of the criticism centers on the kind of commercialization of public schools Channel One represents. Some distinguish television advertising as different from other forms of advertising permitted on school grounds due to the level of sophistication of the commercials and their delivery.

While schools regularly permit advertising in the school newspaper or on billboards in school stadiums, critics argue that these are not required viewing and are not as persuasive as television commercials. Others focus on the captive audiences required to watch television at all. Since students are required by law to attend school, the state thereby compels those students who attend schools with Channel One to watch news and advertising. The content of the ads have also drawn criticism. With the dramatic rise of obesity as a public health concern, many question the ethics of using public schools as vehicles for encouraging the sale of soft drinks, candy, and other "junk food."

News Content

While the content of the Channel One news programming has received satisfactory ratings from students and teachers, it has been targeted by critics as problematic. The intended purpose of the news segment is to offer a child-friendly news source that keeps students abreast of current developments and speaks to them on their level. The news anchors and correspondents are of similar age to students watching Channel One in schools. The language, tone, and style of the programming are also intended to cater to middle and high school students.

To investigate the effectiveness of this approach, researchers have conducted surveys of student and teacher satisfaction with the news program. The studies have indicated that they are largely satisfied with the ten minutes of news offered by Channel One. Critics, meanwhile, contend the news offered is of little substance. Content analyses of the program suggest that Channel One news items include pop culture trivia about celebrities. Dissatisfied with such content, opponents of the service question the quality of the enterprise and its place in public education.

Technology Resource

The economics of the service has also provoked debate between supporters and critics. Supporters contend that the Channel One agreement provides much needed technological resources to public schools. With state support for education at all levels declining, school administrators see in the agreement an opportunity to provide resources for students and teachers that otherwise would not be made available. Critics counter by citing analyses of the use of technology and the expense of airing the program. Historical and contemporary studies have long suggested that technology has not had a significant impact on day-to-day teaching activities. Thus, they see administrators as overvaluing the need for technology. Moreover, the expense of airing the program, according to one study, outweighs the gains made in the technology received. Critics state that the twelve minutes of school time throughout the year, when added together and across all participating schools, amounts to billions of dollars in lost tax-supported instructional time.

Despite the controversies and mixed reception, Channel One continues to thrive. It is well received by most students, teachers, and administrators. It is well supported by commercial advertisers, who may pay up to $200,000 for one thirty-second commercial. And much of the attention the service initially received has diminished. Renewed critical attention to Channel One, however, has resurfaced largely in the form of legal challenges over private profiteering from public education as well as concern over "junk food" advertising in public schools.

A. J. Angulo

See also Corporate Involvement in Education; Technologies in Education

Further Readings

Johnston, J., & Brzezinski, E. (1994). *Channel One: A three year perspective*. Ann Arbor: University of Michigan Institute for Social Research.

Sawicky, M. B., & Molnar, A. (1998). *The hidden costs of Channel One: Estimates for the fifty states*. Milwaukee: Center for the Analysis of Commercialism in Education, University of Wisconsin, Milwaukee.

Richards, J. I., et al. (1998). Children and television: The growing commercialization of schools: Issues and practices. *Annals of the American Academy of Political and Social Science, 557,* 148–163.

Solomon, L. D. (2003). Edison schools and the privatization of K–12 public education: A legal and policy analysis. *Fordham Urban Law Journal, 30,* 1281–1340.

Chaos Theory

Chaos, a word whose origins go back millennia to creation myths in both the Hebraic-Christian and Greco-Roman traditions, has emerged in the latter part of the twentieth century as one of the "new sciences": chaos, fractal geometry, complexity. As part of the new sciences, mathematical chaos theory—still rich in fecundity and creation—is the study of equations which model the turbulence now found as natural to our universe. The nature of chaos and its implications for education are discussed in this entry.

Whereas Isaac Newton, in the seventeenth century, saw a simple order reigning in the universe—"Nature is pleased with simplicity"—scientists now find the starry skies filled with "dark" energy, pulsars, galaxies forming and exploding, and "black holes," devouring all they ensnare. On Earth, an increasing number of earthquakes, tsunamis, hurricanes, tornadoes, and global warmings are devastating—and all unpredictable. This is the sort of turbulence in nature that chaos theorists model and try to predict. Hence the term, deterministic chaos.

Deterministic chaos is not an oxymoron but, rather, is recognition that the universe and world are basically dynamic in nature—not stable in a simple sense but full of "orderly disorder." There is in nature a complexity that makes long-term prediction impossible and short-term prediction (as in weather forecasting) short range and only probabilistic. Further, this complexity, studied mathematically, shows an interweaving of order with chaos. Chaos concepts not only challenge traditional views of cause-effect (deterministic, predictable) and an either/or frame of order versus chaos, but carry educational implications for ways we teach and design curricula.

The concept that long-term prediction is impossible—*prediction devient impossible*—comes from Henri Poincaré's realization in the late 1890s that the mathematics of calculus, useful for Newton's theory of gravitation between two objects, does not work when a third object (sun, moon, earth) is introduced into the relationship. Nonlinear mathematics is needed to solve such interactions. Nonlinear relationships in a simple X–Y equation are different from the commonly used first order [X^1] and second order [X^2] equations, *where the X's are predetermined,* with the Y's (as functions of X [F(x)]) being solved for set Xs.

Nonlinear mathematics, by contrast, is recursive in nature; operating by feeding the Y (or function of X [F(x)]) answer back into the equation for an iteration. Thus the "answer" (Y or F(x)) to the first statement of the equation becomes the next X. And so the

process continues, continually recursing: the ninth statement of X depending on the eighth function of X (its Y). In this manner, the results of the iteration are deterministic—by tracing back the X/Y statements to the original X—but nonpredictable, except for a probable guess as to the next iteration. The educational implications of teaching and designing curricula from a nonlinear viewpoint challenge entrenched notions of preset syllabi, lesson plans, and methods of direct instruction.

In the 1960s, Edward Lorenz, a meteorologist with a feeling for the nonlinear, was doing mathematical simulations of weather patterns on his computer—old and slow by today's standards. Wanting to relook at his data, he submitted the old data back into the computer, but, to save time, rounded off his 6-digit equations to 3 digits. Such a minor difference (.001) should have, according to a 1:1 linear, cause-effect correlation, yielded a minor, almost unnoticeable, difference in the new printout. Using the new printout, Lorenz could check his original work. To his surprise, the new 3-digit equations produced a different set of patterns. Small differences (causes) yielded major differences (effects). Thus, was born chaos theory's famous dictum: "A butterfly flapping its wings in Rio can cause a typhoon in Tokyo." Such an accelerated and accumulated sense of development throws into doubt an educational fixity of IQ and even brings into question the "averaging" of grades.

Supercomputers have allowed nonlinear mathematics to venture where mathematical theory has not gone before—into environmental biology, population dynamics, and information theory. All these deal with interactive relationships, where factors are proactive not merely reactive. Examples include population growth (birth-death relations), predator/prey, and message-noise relations. Such system dynamism, far from states with an equilibrium or central focus, is often framed in a logistic equation. This equation, following the nonlinear X/F(x) frame, already described, is $F(x) = rx(1-x)$, where r is a constant—amount of food, space, information—and $1-x$ is an inversion of the original x, limiting (but not centering) the interactive relationship. Thus the relationship is bounded but still dynamically interactive. Again, the notion of a system being bounded but not centered, and dynamically changing, offers challenges and opportunities in the social sciences. Here the name of Niklas Luhmann stands out.

An interesting aspect of the logistic equation is that as r increases from 1 to 2, doubling occurs (the output in the equation vacillates between two numbers—a boom/bust, seven good years/seven bad years bifurcation). Another doubling occurs as r moves to 3; while at 3.57 (where the doublings are fast and furious) chaos sets in—hence mathematical chaos came from James Yorke's "Period Three Implies Chaos." Within this chaotic area (3.57 and above), there are spaces of regular order. Thus, nonlinear dynamics, in a metaphorical sense, asks social theorists to see that chaos and order are not opposed but actually are entwined within one another. Such a worldview encourages moves beyond modernism's dichotomous framings—Black/White, good/bad, either/or, right/wrong—to look at a "third space" where new possibilities emerge.

Chaos theory, the mathematical study of the non-periodic order found in nature (as in the slight fibrillation of a healthy heart), provides new insights into nature's way of being, insights which show creativity as part of that being. Its implication for education is potentially profound.

Wm. E. Doll, Jr.

See also Complexity Theory

Further Readings

Bird, R. (2003). *Chaos and life.* New York: Columbia University Press.

Doll, W., Fleener, J., St.Julien, J., & Trueit, D. (2005). *Chaos, complexity, curriculum, and culture.* New York: Peter Lang.

Gleick, J. (1987). *Chaos: Making a new science.* New York: Penguin.

Hall, N. (1991). *Exploring chaos.* New York: W. W. Norton.

Kiel. L., & Eliot. E. (1997). *Chaos theory in the social sciences.* Ann Arbor: University of Michigan Press.

Lorenz, E. (1993). *The essence of chaos.* Seattle: University of Washington Press.

Luhmann, N. (1995). *Social systems* (J. Bedartz, Jr. & D. Baecker, Trans.). Stanford, CA: Stanford University Press.

Tien-Yien, L., & Yorke, J. A. (1975). Period three implies chaos. *The American Mathematical Monthly, 8*(10), 985–992.

Web Sites

Chaos Theory and Education:
    http://www.libraryreference.org/chaos.html
Society for Chaos Theory in Psychology and Life Sciences:
    http://www.societyforchaostheory.org

CHARTER SCHOOLS

Charter schools are *public schools* established by a contract between a public agency and charter school organizers. Most charters are granted by a local school district or a state education agency such as a board of education. In some states, public colleges and universities are also authorized to grant charters. In exchange for being exempt from some of the state regulations placed on public school operators, charter school organizers agree to be held accountable for the set of educational outcomes outlined in the school's charter. There are two main types of charter schools, conversion charter schools and start-up charter schools. Conversion charter schools are existing public schools that have elected to convert to charter school status. Start-up charter schools are new schools. This entry looks at the history, organization, and impact of charter schools.

Historical Background

Charter schools have been a prominent item on the U.S. educational reform agenda since Minnesota passed the first charter school law in 1991. At the beginning of the 2005–2006 school year, forty states and the District of Columbia had charter school laws. In 2003–2004 approximately 3,000 charter schools were in operation in thirty-nine of these areas; just over 789,000 students, or 1.6 percent of all public school students nationwide were enrolled in charter schools, although enrollment varied considerably across states.

For example, the District of Columbia had the highest percentage of students enrolled in charter schools (16.6 percent) followed by Arizona (8 percent) and Delaware (5.3 percent). With only one school enrolling 196 students, which amounted to a fraction of its 869,113 public school students, Maryland had the lowest enrollment of students in charter schools. Not surprisingly, as the state with most public school students, California had the highest share of the total charter school students in 2003–2004 (20.2 percent), followed by Arizona (10.4 percent) and Michigan (9.1 percent).

Legal and Policy Issues

Charter school laws are not only constantly evolving, but they also differ widely from state to state. This is illustrated by a comparison of a few aspects of the charter school legislation in effect as of May 2005 for the three states that enroll the greatest number of charter school students—California, Michigan, and Arizona. There are similarities and differences across the three states in (a) the types of public agency empowered to authorize charter schools, (b) the certification requirements for charter school teachers, and (c) provisions allowing private schools to convert to charter school status.

In California, most charters are granted by local school districts, although county boards of education and the state board of education can also approve charter schools if a charter is denied by a local school district or if the school provides countywide or statewide services that are not provided by local school districts. In Michigan, charter schools are called Public School Academies (PSAs) and can be authorized by local school boards and the governing boards of community colleges and public universities. In Arizona, charters can be granted by school districts, the state board of education, and the Arizona State Board for Charter Schools, the state agency charged with overseeing charter schools.

Both California and Michigan require charter school teachers to hold state certification. Arizona's charter school law does not require that charter school teachers be certified.

California specifically prohibits existing private schools from converting to charter schools; Arizona and Michigan allow such conversions. Arizona requires that private schools converting to charter school status have an admissions policy that is "non-selective and nondiscriminatory." Michigan requires such schools to demonstrate a "good faith" effort that 25 percent of their students be new students.

Given this variation, charter school reform is a coherent policy in name only. The federal government has supported charter schools since 1994 through the Public Charter Schools Program. The Public Charter Schools Program provides funding for charter schools that is channeled through state departments of education. Federal funds are also used to support research on charter schools and to provide informational resources for constituents ranging from parents to educational researchers.

Charter schools are also a prominent component of the 2002 No Child Left Behind Act (NCLB), the most recent reauthorization of the Elementary and Secondary Education Act of 1965. In the final NCLB legislation, charter schools were suggested as an option for students in underperforming schools. Students whose schools are identified as underperforming by state standards must be provided with the option to transfer to other schools within their districts, including charter schools. In addition, the law outlines a timetable for interventions within schools identified as underperforming, which could ultimately entail reorganizing underperforming schools as charter schools.

The Research Debates

Two hotly debated issues are: Do charter schools increase racial segregation, and do charter schools produce higher student achievement than conventional public schools? Using largely national-level comparisons, some researchers claim that the racial composition of charter schools tends to mirror those of all public schools. Other researchers find that disaggregating the data to state and local levels and using better segregation measures shows that charter schools increase racial segregation.

The findings on achievement are mixed. For example, the National Center for Educational Statistics included a sample of charter schools in the 2003 administration of the National Assessment of Educational Progress (NAEP). On average, charter school students scored roughly equal to or lower than students in conventional public schools with similar backgrounds.

Jeanne M. Powers

See also No Child Left Behind Act; School Choice

Further Readings

Cobb, C. D., & Glass, G. V. (1999). Ethnic segregation in Arizona charter schools. *Education Policy Analysis Archives, 7*(1).

Frankenberg, E., & Lee, C. (2003). Charter schools and race: A lost opportunity for integrated education. *Education Policy Analysis Archives, 11*(32). Available from http://www.epaa.asu.edu/epaa/vol11.html

Manno, B. V., Vanourek, G., Chester, E., & Finn, J. (1999). Charter schools: Serving disadvantaged youth. *Education and Urban Society, 31*(4), 429–445.

Miron, G., & Nelson, C. (2004). Student achievement in charter schools: What we know and why we know so little. In K. E. Bulkley & P. Wohlstetter (Eds.), *Taking account of charter schools: What's happened and what's next?* (pp. 161–175). New York: Teachers College Press.

National Center for Education Statistics. (2004). *America's charter schools: Results from the 2003 NAEP Pilot Study.* Washington, DC: Author.

CHAUTAUQUA MOVEMENT

The Chautauqua movement that swept the United States during the late nineteenth and early twentieth centuries was one of the most innovative developments in the history of adult education. Following the philosophy of mainstream liberal arts colleges by offering workshops and lectures in the arts and humanities and eschewing mechanical, technical, and practical education, the movement brought liberal education, culture, and later entertainment to adults in small towns and rural communities. The Chautauqua movement also adapted the new fields of natural and social sciences and modern literature to its academic curriculum and experimented with radical programs that brought together the sacred and secular as a cultural response to a changing world in which science challenged religious authority, labor conflicted with management, women questioned their prescribed roles, and the nation grew progressively more heterogeneous. This entry looks at the history and impact of the movement.

An Educational Movement

The movement began inauspiciously in 1874 when Methodist minister John Heyl Vincent and Ohio inventor Lewis Miller conducted a two-week summer institute for Sunday School teachers at Lake Chautauqua in western New York. Two years later, the program was expanded and diversified into an eight-week liberal education experience for adults. The Chautauqua Institution offered courses in the arts, humanities, and sciences and featured lectures by the most renowned authors, explorers, and political leaders, as well as performances by acclaimed musicians and dramatists. Headliners such as Mark Twain, William Jennings Bryan, and Charles Dickens attracted huge throngs, and eventually all of the U.S. presidents from Ulysses S. Grant through William McKinley made appearances. Richard T. Ely, Jane Addams, Jacob Riis, and others expressed progressive ideas for resolving the conflicts of American life, and William Rainey Harper initiated critical scriptural analysis of the Holy Bible.

The Chautauqua idea spread rapidly, and 292 communities from Maine to Florida and Texas to California formed local independent Chautauquas attempting to copy the Chautauqua Institution by reproducing the program of lectures and entertainment, and to a lesser degree, the academic program of liberal education courses or workshops within a summer resort setting. Although the independent Chautauquas were not affiliated formally with the Chautauqua Institution, many of the speakers, artists, and musicians from the Chautauqua Institution traveled great distances to take lectures and performances across the country. Thousands of adults attended the summer programs of the Chautauqua Institution and the independent Chautauquas.

In addition to the summer programs of the Chautauqua Institution, William Rainey Harper developed a year-round home study program called the Chautauqua Literary and Scientific Circle. The Circle was a four-year correspondence course consisting of intensive home reading in history, literature, sociology, and science—the first integrated program of adult education organized in the United States on a national scale. The Circle encouraged learners to form local reading circles to discuss the texts, and between 1878 and 1894 boasted over 225,000 students and over 10,000 local reading circles. The Chautauqua Institution's leadership conceded that the Circle education was not a college equivalent, but argued that it fostered a "college outlook": exposure to liberal education for adults.

Its Influence

The Chautauqua Movement reflected a nationwide interest in the professionalization of teaching and popular liberal education for self-improvement. The Chautauqua Institution's founder, John Vincent, believed in the universal right to knowledge and insisted that continued learning in adulthood was a religious obligation. Vincent's ideas shaped the movement as a whole, which reflected belief in traditional moral authority, Enlightenment rationalism, and democratization of higher learning for adults, albeit with a Protestant purpose. Maintaining that education could occur throughout adulthood, Vincent believed that experiential learning was the best road to intellectual improvement, an idea that anticipated philosophies prevalent a half century later.

The Chautauqua Institution's and movement's detractors, such as philosopher William James and English author Rudyard Kipling, dismissed the brief summer sessions, roundtables, and public lectures as academically superficial. However, even critics who questioned the course quality did not challenge the scholarly credentials of its lecturers. Furthermore, lower- and middle-class women, who made up the majority of the Chautauquas' learners, were largely excluded from higher education: the residential Chautauquas and the Circle provided a coherent training ground for them at an affordable price.

The influence of the Chautauqua Institution and independent Chautauquas declined steeply during the early twentieth century because of the emergence of "circuit" or "tent" Chautauquas that traveled from town to town. Because of more affordable ticket prices, they soon ran most of the independent Chautauquas out of business. However, because tent chautauquas were purely commercial ventures, they changed the entire face of the movement from "education with entertainment" to "entertainment with or without education." At its peak in the mid-1920s, circuit Chautauqua performers and lecturers appeared in more than 10,000 communities in forty-five states to audiences totaling 45 million people. Even so, the tent Chautauquas served as an opportunity for rural communities to come together to watch musicians and performers that they would never have seen otherwise.

The movement died out by 1932 because of two significant factors. The spread of automobiles, radios, and motion pictures made entertainment and education more accessible. Further, the onset of the Depression made even tent Chautauquas economically impossible for organizers and audiences.

The national influence of the Chautauqua Movement on higher and adult education was immense. Under the direction of John Vincent and William Rainey Harper, the Chautauqua Institution pioneered summer sessions, correspondence courses, extension services, and the university press. Harper, as the first president of the University of Chicago, transmitted these and other Chautauquan innovations that influenced American higher education as a whole. While now less national in scope, the Chautauqua Institution still offers a thriving eight-week summer program of lectures, arts, and music and serves as a respected center for adult education and Christian religion.

Susan Birden

See also Adult Education and Literacy; Correspondence Schools

Further Readings

Johnson, R. L. (2001). "Dancing mothers": The Chautauqua movement in twentieth-century American popular culture. *American Studies International, 39*(2), 53–70.

Scott, J. C. (2005). The Chautauqua vision of liberal education. *History of Education, 34*(1), 41–59.

Vincent, J. H. (1975). *The Chautauqua movement* [Reprint]. North Stratford, NH: Ayer. (Original work published 1886)

CHEERLEADING

Cheerleading originated on Ivy League campuses with male cheerleaders who performed during football games in the late 1880s. Today, 3.8 million people participate in cheerleading in the United States, and 97 percent of them are female. The impact of gender, race, ethnicity, social class, and sexual orientation can be seen in the way cheerleading operates in elementary and secondary schools, in higher education, and in society at large.

Throughout its first fifty years, cheerleading was an exclusively male activity and represented normative masculinity. Being a cheerleader or yell leader was understood as a noble endeavor that helped prepare young White men for their rightful place as leaders in the emerging industrial order. Women began entering collegiate cheerleading in small numbers in the 1920s, but as late as the 1930s, cheerleading was still considered a male activity and was associated with athleticism and leadership. Most high school and collegiate squads were resistant to young women entering this masculine sphere, and it was feared that female cheerleaders would become loud and unladylike. When men left college campuses to fight in World War II, females stepped into the vacant spots on the squads, and by the 1950s, cheerleading had become a feminized activity. With her physical attractiveness, peer popularity, and wholesomeness, the cheerleader typified ideal American girlhood.

Cheerleading, as the symbol of ideal girlhood, became a contested activity with the implementation of school desegregation. The selection of cheerleaders in desegregated schools resulted in riots, walkouts, and one death in Burlington, North Carolina. In addition to racial politics, the women's rights movement, passage of Title IX, and the introduction of the professional Dallas Cowboys Cheerleaders in 1972 all challenged the idea that cheerleaders still represented ideal femininity. Cheerleaders became characterized as young women who conformed to oppressive notions of femininity. By the mid-1970s, the National Cheerleaders Association and the newly formed Universal Cheerleaders Association helped revitalize cheerleading by introducing a more athletic form that included gymnastics tumbling. National competitions were introduced in the early 1980s with their eventual international television broadcast.

By the 1990s, an entirely new form of cheerleading was introduced—competitive or All-Star cheerleading whose squads were affiliated with private gyms and not public schools. They exist solely to compete against other private squads. This is the fastest growing segment of cheerleading in the United States, and males have returned to the activity in order to compete.

Cheerleading remains popular with girls because it allows them to acquire many of the traits once associated with masculinity (e.g., athleticism, self-discipline, assertiveness, and risk taking) while still participating in an activity firmly entrenched in heterosexualized femininity. In recent years, cheerleading has been adapted as a political vehicle by radical cheerleaders, gay and lesbian groups, and senior citizens. Outside of the United States, cheerleading can be found around the world, although it has been modified frequently to reflect the culture that has adopted it.

Natalie G. Adams and Pamela J. Bettis

See also Athletics, Policy Issues; Physical Education, History of; Sports Mascots

See Visual History Chapter 24, The Farm Security Administration's Photographs of Schools

Further Readings

Adams, N. G., & Bettis, P. J. (2003). *Cheerleader! An American icon.* New York: Palgrave.

Davis, L. (1990). Male cheerleaders and the naturalization of gender. In M. Messner & D. Sabo (Eds.), *Sport, men, and the gender order.* Champaign, IL: Human Kinetics Books.

Fine, G., & Johnson, B. (1992). The promiscuous cheerleader: an adolescent male belief legend. In G. Fine (Ed.), *Manufacturing tales: Sex and money in contemporary legends.* Knoxville: University of Tennessee Press.

Grundy, P. (2001). *Learning to win: Sports, education, and social change in twentieth-century North Carolina.* Chapel Hill: University of North Carolina Press.

Merten, D. (1996). Burnout as cheerleader: The cultural basis for prestige and privilege in junior high school. *Anthropology and Education, 27,* 51–70.

Child Abuse: Issues for Teachers

Child abuse is the intentional infliction on children of physical, sexual, and emotional mistreatment by a parent, guardian, or other adult entrusted with their care. Teachers are among the most important people needing to be able both to identify and defend against child abuse since they are in close daily contact with their students. As mandated reporters, teachers need to better understand the wide variability of situations and behaviors that might suggest child abuse. This entry provides an overview.

Prevalence Data

According to a U.S. Department of Health and Human Services report in 2004, 64.5 percent of child abuse survivors suffered neglect (including medical neglect), 17.5 percent are physically abused, 9.7 percent are sexually abused, and 7.0 percent are emotionally or psychologically abused. Not all children survive their abuse. Approximately 1,500 children died in 2004 as a result of abuse or neglect.

Completely accurate figures are difficult to obtain because evidence of abuse and neglect is not necessarily clear-cut. Most cases of abuse and neglect never get reported because there are no outward physical effects in the case of neglect or psychological and emotional abuse, or there are attempts to cover up or hide these physical effects. In the case of sexual abuse, there is secrecy and shame that surrounds the survivor, and potentially the family, and often prevents the survivor from coming forward to tell his or her story.

The Reporting Role

There is one commonality in almost all cases of child abuse—abused children go to school. In all fifty states, teachers and other school officials are mandated reporters, as are doctors, nurses, any law enforcement official, and a long list of other professionals who come into contact with children in various capacities. Through its legislature, each state defines abuse and prescribes the rules for those who report cases.

Teachers and other school officials who have a reasonable suspicion that a child is being abused must file a report with the appropriate social service agency for their particular state, such as Child Protective Services (CPS) in California or the Department of Children and Families (DCF) in Florida. Some schools and/or districts have a policy that states that the teacher or other school official first report their suspicion to the school's principal, while others expect the teacher or school official to contact the social service agency on their own.

Whichever is the case, a report of suspected child abuse must be filed in a timely fashion—typically between twenty-four and seventy-two hours after becoming aware of the suspected abuse either by phone or face-to-face. This is followed by filing a written report within seventy-two hours of the original report. Once the report is on file with the appropriate social service agency, a determination is made whether or not to investigate the allegations of abuse or neglect by child protective services based on the information provided.

Because teachers and other school officials are mandated reporters of child abuse, each state provides the mandated reporter with immunity from the civil and criminal prosecution that may arise from reporting suspected child abuse and neglect, as long as the report was done in "good faith" and "without malice." This immunity is given so that teachers or other mandated reporters will be more willing to file a report if they do not fear being held criminally or civilly liable.

The Caregiving Role

Even though the investigation of the alleged child abuse is out of the hands of the classroom teacher, it is by no means the end of it. For the classroom teacher, this is only the first step since the abused child is a member of a classroom learning community that spends six to eight hours together five days a week. During the week, children spend more of their waking hours in school with their classmates and their teacher than they do with their families.

An abused child is a wounded child. Depending on the type of abuse he or she has suffered, his or her wounds may not be visible, but those emotional scars are still very much a part of the child's psyche. This emotional pain of abuse may present itself in a multitude of ways and depending on the age and situation of the survivor. Children may act aggressively with their peers or be disruptive in the classroom. They may be hypervigilant, constantly on the lookout for possible danger, or they may dissociate by mentally separating their minds from their bodies in order to escape the emotions running through their heads.

In terms of the responsibility of the teacher, first and foremost he or she needs to create for the abused child a classroom community that is loving and supportive. Having an established classroom routine and a predictable, stable environment where the abused child (and every child) feels safe and secure is extremely important.

The teacher should also have fair and consistent rules and consequences where children understand the limits of inappropriate behavior in the classroom. The teacher can also teach problem-solving skills and ways to deal with anger to help empower these children that allows them to regain at least a small portion of control back in their lives.

Child abuse is a basic problem that must be confronted by educators in a well-thought-out and systematic manner. It is a problem that almost every teacher will have to confront in his or her career, and it needs to be well understood from both a policy and a practical perspective.

Lisa L. Repaskey

See also Sexual Misconduct by Educational Professonals

Further Readings

Administration of Children and Families, a branch of the U.S. Department of Health and Human Services. *Child maltreatment.* Available from http://www.acf.dhhs.gov/programs/cb/pubs/cm04/cm04.pdf

Gootman, M. E. (1993). Reaching and teaching abused children. *Childhood Education, 70,* 15–19.

Hopper, J. (2007). *Child abuse: Statistics, research and resources.* Retrieved on April 15, 2007, from http://www.jimhopper.com/abstats

Lowenthal, B. (1996). Educational implications of child abuse. *Intervention in School & Clinic, 32,* 21–25.

Michigan State University. (n.d.). *MSU Chance at Childhood program.* Available from http://www.chanceat childhood.msu.edu/pdf/MandatedReporter.pdf

Yell, M. L. (1996). Reporting child abuse and neglect: Legal requirements. *Preventing School Failure, 40,* 161–163.

CHILD LABOR

By the end of the nineteenth century, industrialization had swept the United States and the employment of children had become an increasingly visible practice and a controversial problem, as an estimated 2 million children toiled in factories, mines, and offices around the country. Frequently, countless children no older than six or seven found themselves thrust into factory work that destroyed their health, stunted their social development, and left them prepared only for a life of more of the same. Working at jobs that were solitary and incessant, they were constantly tired and depressed, were denied the natural expression of childish joy and excitement, and soon began to feel and look prematurely old. For decades, church and government officials struggled to outlaw the worst excesses of the child labor system, but only the combination of protective legislation and compulsory education instituted by the end of World War I began to loosen the tight grip of work on the lives of millions of American children. This entry recalls the history of child labor and its conclusion.

Children at Work

Child labor resulted from several interrelated factors. To many observers, the employment of children in factories and other workplaces served a philanthropic function, as work kept poor children from becoming public charges, taught them the Puritan values of industry, and protected them from the sins of idleness. As industry developed more opportunities for low-skill and low-wage labor, factory officials began to aggressively seek out child workers who could do the work of adults but could not demand the same compensation. At the same time, throughout the country, family income was often so low that parents had little choice but to send their children to full-time employment to supplement their own meager earnings.

Even in agricultural regions, family welfare often took priority over the interests and aspirations of individual family members, with children helping out on the farm as soon as they could do the work. Still, these children often received at least minimal education, as their work was part time and seasonal, while industrial jobs demanded full-time attention, leaving urban children the clear choice between work and school. Also, while difficult, farm labor required tasks that varied from time to time, occurred mainly in the fresh air and sunlight, and allowed for occasional periods of rest. Industrial work was steady and year-round, making it difficult to reconcile work and school, and generally demanded mind-numbing attention to repetitive hand motions in an enclosed environment too often deafeningly loud, dirty, and dangerous.

To many, the solution to the problem of child labor appeared to be the passage and implementation of protective legislation that outlawed the employment of children in certain locations and at specific ages. Such laws evolved from pity for the exploited children, the sense that they were being prepared to act as informed citizens, and the recognition that the stunted intellectual and social skills that came from such labor cheapened and impaired industry itself. By the late 1920s every state had enacted some form of child labor legislation, even if it was honored only in the breach. Children under the age of sixteen were prohibited from engaging in most forms of dangerous factory work, and many companies had concluded that unschooled children were of marginal employment value in any case.

From Factory to School

Still, it was soon evident that legislation to eradicate child labor would not be enough to keep many children in school, as the education itself appeared disconnected from their lives and occupational needs. Students often found the curriculum boring, the discipline extreme, and the environment similar to the factories from which they had been excluded, leading many children to drop out completely; rates of absenteeism were high among those who remained.

In response, most states initiated mandatory attendance plans, and the effect was immediate. Enrollments and attendance improved, and countless children found their lives transformed by the new emphasis on the expansion of childhood in environments that were increasingly congenial. Nevertheless, schooling left children with little more than the rudimentary skills of reading and writing, and many were in danger of quitting even without the job opportunities that might have otherwise drawn them away. Wishing to be more physically active while earning money of their own, others did eventually leave school to pursue whatever employment the new laws had ignored.

The solution was a change in the direction and purpose of early education. Soon, countless elementary schools offered practical work with an industrial bent, high schools modified their curriculum to include manual skills, trade schools emerged to provide vocational training to help those who would later find skilled work, and continuation schools developed programs for those who had already entered industry with insufficient preparation. With these changes, schools began to appear as a larger part of real life, while parents and children could see that school attendance and academic achievement might eventually lead to better compensation and more pleasant working conditions. At the same time, industrial leaders came to appreciate employees who had learned specific job skills while in school and who demonstrated higher levels of industrial discipline that reduced the need for constant and close supervision. Educated workers were thrifty, efficient, and loyal and brought with them much more than the simple skills children had earlier learned while on the job.

While employment kept unruly children in check, provided additional income to struggling families, and offered cheap labor for American industrialists and merchants, it also left children injured and incomplete. Only education provided an opportunity for many to escape the worse of industrial jobs and to learn the skills and discipline required for advancement in the work they eventually found.

Bart Dredge

See also Compulsory Educational Attendance Laws

See Visual History Chapter 16, Lewis W. Hine and the Child Labor Movement

Further Readings

Fuller, B. (1983). Youth job structure and school enrollment, 1890–1920. *Sociology of Education, 56,* 145–156.

Landes, W., & Solmon, L. (1972). Compulsory school legislation: An economic analysis of law and social change in the nineteenth century. *Journal of Economic History, 32,* 54–97.

Mayer, J. W. D., Tyack, J. N., & Gordon, A. (1979). Public education as nation-building in America: Enrollments and bureaucratization in the American states, 1870–1930. *American Journal of Sociology, 85,* 591–613.

CHILDREN'S AND EDUCATIONAL MUSEUMS, HISTORY OF

Children's museums represent important sites for learning that can operate either in conjunction with or independently from schools. Their hands-on approach and play-based inquiry have the potential to draw students into learning in ways that are not as easily achieved in the public schools.

The idea of the museum as an educational force is taken for granted today by most educators and museum personnel. Yet it is a relatively modern concept dating from the second half of the nineteenth century, one that came to be realized in 1899 with the founding of the first children's museum in the United States, the Brooklyn Children's Museum, and with the organization in 1905 of the first American educational museum to be sponsored by a school system, the Educational Museum of the St. Louis Public Schools. This entry looks at the history and contributions of children's educational museums.

Museum as Educator

The concept of the museum as educator reflected not only a new approach to learning, but also a new approach to the organization of knowledge. No longer a "cabinet of curiosities," the museum in the United States increasingly became a popular educator. The growth and development of children's and educational museums and their association with the schools was a logical extension of this concept. Implicit in the idea of the museum as educator was the notion of the museum as a "mass" educator. More than any other formal educational institution during the late nineteenth century (including libraries), the museum was perceived as being capable of teaching all classes of society.

It was the great international expositions that were primarily responsible (during the nineteenth century) for popularizing the idea of the museum as a means of mass education. The Great London Exhibition of 1851 was the first of these "world fairs." Its purpose was to promote and encourage English industry by comparing it with that of the other major industrial nations of the world. The Centennial Exposition held in Philadelphia in 1876 was the first international exposition to be held in the United States. Not only did the Centennial Exposition encourage the extensive development of industrial and natural history exhibits, but it also demonstrated their educational value to a large cross-section of the population.

The Centennial Exposition directly contributed to the establishment of several major museums throughout the United States, including the United States National Museum (Smithsonian Institution) and the Philadelphia Museum of Art. Later expositions (including the 1893 World's Columbian Exposition in Chicago and the 1904 Louisiana Purchase Exposition in St. Louis) also contributed to museum development in the United States.

By the 1890s there was an increasing realization, however, that a museum differed from an exposition or fair in both its aims and methods. The exposition was primarily concerned with the promotion of industry and commerce, whereas the museum had as its primary purpose the teaching of a lesson inherent in an exhibit. Both museum curators and educators in general became increasingly aware of the need for people to learn not only through the written and spoken word, but also through objects.

School Museums

The possibilities of the museum as a vehicle for object lessons, and as an integral part of the curriculum of the schools, is most clearly evident in the work of the American educator and philosopher, John Dewey

(1859–1952). He argued that a small museum should be an integral part of every school. However unfeasible the idea of the school museum was, it did not die. Two highly successful extensions of the idea were developed: the children's museum and the traveling school museum.

The Brooklyn Children's Museum was originally conceived as a pedagogical museum where teachers could come see displayed apparatus and other materials that they could use in their classrooms. It was soon realized, however, that it would be impossible to provide teachers with the types of apparatus and materials on display. Therefore, a new purpose for the children's museum soon developed. It would be not simply a repository of pedagogical ideas and practices, but also a vital center of learning that would supplement the instruction of the public schools and also represent an important alternative for teaching, instruction, and learning. The potential of the children's museum to improve the quality of life for children living in the city was quickly realized.

Under the leadership of Anna Billings Gallup (1872–1956), the Children's Museum became an active educational center that helped children with their daily school studies and suggested new subjects for thought and pursuit in their leisure hours. By 1911, the average daily attendance had jumped to 160,000. Originally, the museum was primarily concerned with awakening an interest in nature. Throughout the museum, storytelling exhibits were displayed in cases at the proper height for children and were simply labeled. Soon, realistic miniature dioramas peopled with costumed dolls were created in an attempt to make the past come alive in the History Room.

By the 1920s, community groups such as the Women's Auxiliary were using the History Room and its miniature scenes for educational experiments in Americanization: Lessons were developed with the express goal of encouraging civic and national spirit among immigrant children. It was hoped that the Americanization program would stimulate discussions in the children's homes and even encourage their foreign parents to visit the museum—especially to see their own children perform in the plays that were being presented. Other special features such as a library, daily lectures, clubs, games, the publication of

the *Children's Museum Bulletin,* and the loan of materials to schools and the children themselves, helped make the museum a dynamic educational force in the local neighborhood and community.

Broader Scope

Unlike the Brooklyn Children's Museum, the Educational Museum of the St. Louis Public Schools was not neighborhood oriented but instead was primarily concerned with distributing supplementary educational materials such as lantern slides, natural history specimens, and objects from foreign countries throughout the public school system. "Bring the world to the child" was the museum's motto. The idea was clearly an outgrowth and a continuation of the spirit of the Louisiana Purchase Exposition.

Officially opened on April 11, 1905, the museum is commonly recognized as being the first audiovisual program in a city school system in the United States. Many of the ideas and approaches developed as part of the curriculum of the Educational Museum closely paralleled the types of activities John Dewey and his colleagues had put into effect during the late 1890s at the University of Chicago Laboratory School. The assistant superintendent, Carl Rathman; the museum's curator, Amelia Meissner; and the staff managed to find a means by which to practically implement a "hands-on curriculum" of the type that Dewey was advocating throughout an extensive urban school system.

Like the Brooklyn Children's Museum, the Educational Museum of the St. Louis Public Schools recognized the potential of the museum to help the child to better understand the community and world in which they lived. Efforts to integrate the work of the museum and the schools increased during the early decades of the twentieth century. In 1911, for example, the trustees of the Field Museum of Natural History in Chicago created a traveling museum, which contained over 1,000 cases of botanical, geological, zoological, and economic specimens.

Other museums, such as the Commercial Museum of Art in Philadelphia, the Cleveland Museum of Art, and the Carnegie Museum in Pittsburgh, not only sent exhibits out to the schools but also had teachers stationed in the museums who were paid by their school boards to give talks and conduct tours for school children. By the beginning of World War I, museums and the public schools had combined their forces in the development of a new type of curriculum emphasizing visual instruction and object teaching.

A New Era

By the end of World War I, it was clear that school and pedagogical museums were not particularly powerful movements in American education. In large part their function was taken over by the field of instructional technology. Museums such as the Brooklyn Children's Museum and the Indianapolis Children's Museum continued their efforts, however, becoming important educational institutions and community centers in their regions. By the mid-1970s there were just a small number handful of children's museums across the country.

Among the most visible were the Exploratorium, a "hands-on museum of science, art, and human perception" in San Francisco and the Please Touch Museum in Philadelphia, which has been encouraging learning through play, not just for children of all socioeconomic backgrounds, but for their teachers, parents, and caregivers as well. During the late 1970s, there developed a renewed interest in the establishment of children's museums, and by the late 1990s, there were approximately 300 such institutions in the United States.

The power of the children's museum, and much of its promise in years to come, is as a popular educator that integrates concrete experiences with science, history, and art. Increasingly, many of these activities will take place online, either in a child's home or at a desk at school. As a result, the role of the children's museum as a developer of innovative curriculum and as a mass educator becomes even more important.

Asterie B. Provenzo and Eugene F. Provenzo, Jr.

See also Museums

See Visual History Chapter 11, International Expositions

Further Readings

Farmer, D. W. (1995). Children take learning into their own hands. *Childhood Education, 71*(3), 168–169.

Gardner, H. (1992). Howard Gardner on psychology and youth museums: Toward an education for understanding. *Hand to Hand, 6*(3), 1–6.

Marsh, C. (1987). The Discovery Room: How it all began. *Journal of Museum Education, 12*(2), 3–5, 13.

Provenzo, E. F., Jr. (1979). The Educational Museum of the St. Louis Public Schools. *Missouri Historical Society Bulletin, 35*(3), 147–153.

Zucker, B. F. (1987). *Children's museums, zoos and discovery rooms: An international reference guide.* Westport, CT: Greenwood Press.

CHURCH AND STATE

The question of the relationship between church and state is and has been a pervasive problem that pervades all aspects of education in all countries and is not peculiar to this generation. In the United States the relationship is complicated by many religions and the constitutional perspective. The issue should be considered from the perspective of the one and the many, *e pluribus unum. One* signifies unity and cohesion; *many* signifies diversity and division.

Though a religious nation since its inception, the United States has believed in the separation of church and state and used the public schools to bring different religious faiths together. The First Amendment to the Constitution, the nonestablishment clause, is the basis for court decisions involving church and state questions. There was nothing in the Constitution that set limits on what the states could do in the field of education. At first the Bill of Rights only guaranteed religious freedom and due process at the federal level. In 1868 the states ratified the Fourteenth Amendment, which applied the Bill of Rights to the state level. This entry looks at how the relationship of church and state has evolved and how the Supreme Court has attempted to decide issues.

Early Years

During the colonial period in American history, church and state were united. Though the colonists came to America seeking religious freedom, their form of government only provided rights to those who practiced the state religion. In New England, the fundamental law was the Bible. In the South, the church was different, Anglican, but the practices were similar. The state enforced financial support for the established church. It gave moral and legal support to doctrines of worship resulting in no freedom of worship. Other colonies had more liberal practices.

As the United States developed after the Revolutionary War, the founders had to reconcile these opposing thoughts and traditions as they brought about the separation of church and state. Thomas Jefferson advocated religious freedom in his "Bill for Religious Freedom," which was enacted by the Virginia legislature in 1786. The First Amendment to the newly enacted Constitution calls for a separation of church and state and states that Congress cannot legislate the establishment of religion or limit its practice. Subsequently, the First Amendment became the basis for many Supreme Court decisions regarding the relationship of church, state, and schools.

The church's influence on education continued in the early part of the National Period, which began in 1789. The number of churches rose, as did the number of different religious groups and denominations. This movement was happening as the state legislatures were moving to separate from the church's influence. There was a lot of discussion about the relationship between the church and the state and the support of disestablishment. In 1833, Massachusetts became the last state to disestablish religion.

The common school movement began in the first part of the nineteenth century. The common school, a school that was publicly supported and controlled, was to be the place to bring students of different backgrounds together to provide a type of "melting pot" for different religious groups. As the common school movement grew and prospered, and as the numbers of Catholic immigrants increased, the Catholic bishops began to be concerned about what they called secularism in the schools. The number of Catholics increased from 1789, the time of the appointment of Bishop John Carroll, the first Catholic bishop in America, to 1884 when the Third Plenary Council of Bishops mandated the establishment of Catholic schools.

Catholic Schools

The bishops' concerns focused on the following public school practices: the reading of the King James version of the Bible, the saying of Protestant prayers, the singing of Protestant hymns, and anti-Catholic textbooks. They were also concerned about secularism and godlessness in the schools. While voicing these concerns, the bishops were attempting to gain public funds for parochial schools. They argued that the Catholics were taxpayers and were entitled to have public funds for their own system of parochial schools.

In 1884, the Third Plenary Council met and called for the establishment of parochial schools. A school had to be built near every Catholic Church within two years and all the parents in the congregation were required to send their children to these schools, unless the bishop approved another form of Catholic education. The bishops also expected the teachers to be qualified and certified.

The Protestants reacted strongly to these mandates, and anti-Catholic publications such as Josiah Strong's *Our Country* appeared. Strong complained that the American Catholics' allegiance was only to the pope. Nonetheless, the parochial school movement flourished and other religions also established their own schools. The United States became a pluralistic country made up of Protestants, Catholics, Jews, Muslims, and those of other religious faiths. There were also agnostics and atheists adding to the common mix. The schools tried to meet the needs of these diverse groups, moving beyond the idea of a melting pot to being guided by cultural pluralism, including not only religious groups but also different racial and ethnic groups.

Supreme Court Rulings

As the public schools grew and changed, the issue of the relationship of church and state also came into focus more, as evidenced by the increasing number of Supreme Court cases which dealt with church and state issues. These cases took many forms and can be categorized as follows: free exercise, public financial aid to church-related schools, religious education in public schools, and religious exercises in public schools. It was established that in order for any religious activity in a public school to be constitutional, it must pass three tests. It must have a secular purpose; it must have a primary effect which neither advances nor prohibits religion; it must avoid excessive entanglement between religion and the public school.

The Supreme Court case of *Pierce v. Society of Sisters* (1925) is a good example of a test of the free exercise of religion. This case dealt with the question of whether nonpublic schools have the right to exist. It involved the Hill Military School and the Society of Sisters parochial school. Oregon passed a law in 1922 mandating that every child between the ages of eight and sixteen must attend public school. The Court ruled against Oregon, saying the state could not destroy private schools and that parents have the right to choose their child's education. Other cases that followed upheld students' right to freely exercise their religion.

The Catholic bishops tried to obtain public funds for Catholic schools beginning in the nineteenth century. Though unsuccessful overall, they were able to make some inroads. Good examples of these successes are the early public financial aid Supreme Court cases. The case of *Everson v. Board of Education of Ewing Township* in 1947, which allows for free bus transportation for all schools, was decided based on the child-benefit theory. This means that when aid is given, it is not given to benefit the school directly, but rather to benefit the child. The court has ruled over the years that there can be no reimbursement for teacher salaries, but auxiliary services can be provided through the local public school. It is also allowable for the state to provide vouchers to students to attend religious schools.

The Supreme Court also addressed the issue of released time during the school day for religious education. In the *McCollum v. Board of Education* in 1948 in Illinois, the Court ruled that there could be no released time given for religious instruction in public schools. Later, in 1952, the Court ruled in *Zorach v. Clauson* in New York that time could be given to students for religious instruction off site. Religious groups are also permitted to meet in schools as a result of the Equal Access Law that was passed in 1984, even though the Court had ruled earlier that this was not constitutional.

Many school prayer cases have been heard by the Court. The best known case is that of *Engel v. Vitale* in 1962. The New York Board of Regents required a nondenominational prayer in the schools. Engel complained that this violated the First Amendment, and the Court ruled that no government agency can require prayer in the schools. Other cases involving prayer at graduation, sports activities, and moments of silence followed with similar results.

The issue of the relationship between church and state in education continues to present challenges in a diverse country with many religious faiths. The questions recur in different forms and are reconsidered and sometimes reinterpreted by the courts because the Constitution remains a living document.

Sally H. Wertheim

See also Americanization Movement; Catholic Education, History of; Values Education

See Visual History Chapter 6, Catholic Schools and the Separation of Church and State

Further Readings

Fellman, D. (Ed.). (1976). *The Supreme Court and education.* New York: Teachers College Press.

Hitchcock, J. (2004). *The Supreme Court and religion in American life.* Princeton, NJ: Princeton University Press.

Marty, M. (2004). *The Protestant voice in American pluralism.* Athens: University of Georgia Press.

McCluskey, N. (Ed.). (1964). *Catholic education in America: A documentary history.* New York: Teachers College Press.

Pfeffer, L. (1967). *Church, state, and freedom.* Boston: Beacon Press.

CITIZENSHIP EDUCATION

Citizenship typically refers to the relationship between the individual and the community, state, or nation. Encompassing aspects of membership, identity, civic knowledge, civic values, dispositions, and civic skills, citizenship education is often narrowly defined as taking place in civics, government, and history classes. But citizenship education is far broader than civics;

here, it is defined as *any educational experience that promotes the growth of individuals in regard to their civic capacities.* The civic realm, the world of political and community work, requires particular kinds of knowledge, skills, and dispositions. This is particularly true in a democracy, where the role of the citizen takes on special importance in governance.

This entry looks at citizenship education from the perspective of the social foundations discipline, which has conceptualized itself from the beginning as a field concerned with promoting schools relevant for a democratic society. Education for democratic citizenship, therefore, is both a key commitment for many in the field and source of inquiry across the range of disciplinary perspectives in the foundations of education. Whereas researchers in social studies education and political science do much work in the area of citizenship education, particularly in regard to the formal curriculum taught in schools, social foundations scholars have contributed to the inquiry and knowledge of citizenship education by pursing questions that are broader. Foundations scholars have been concerned with social contexts beyond the school, and they are more explicitly critical in their inquiry than are other kinds of education scholars. The contributions of social foundations scholars to citizenship education theory and practice are described in this entry by focusing on four overarching questions that have been central throughout the field's history.

Role of Citizenship Education

What is unique and important about citizenship education in schools that are to promote and sustain a democratic society? Citizenship education can take place in any sort of society: fascist, communist, or democratic. Education for democracy, and democratic citizenship, is perhaps one of the most fundamental issues occupying social foundations scholars since the field's inception. This question has particularly concerned philosophers of education, since the question is not empirical but a normative and interpretive inquiry into the meanings of democracy and the best ways to prepare students to contribute to a society aspiring to democratic ideals.

John Dewey led the way in positing that citizenship is not something people learn in one kind of classroom or course, but all through the home, community, and school life. For Dewey, democracy is more than a political system or a technical description of the way government is run; it denotes a way of living, teaching, learning, and doing. Democracy is a moral ideal; he said in his 1939 book *Freedom and Culture* that democracy is moral in that it is based on a fundamental faith in the ability of humans to respect the freedom of others while creating a social and political system based on cohesion rather than coercion.

Democratic education, in Dewey's writings, represents the task of unleashing the powers of each individual citizen in association with the various communities and societies of which people are part. Education for democracy involves a "freeing of individual capacity in a progressive growth directed to social aims," he said in his 1916 work, *Democracy and Education.* Students learn both through disciplined study and through the experiences of living in a school connected to the concerns and work of their own community, that democracy is the process of cooperatively solving shared problems.

Some contemporary philosophers of education have argued against this view, challenging Dewey's broad conception of democratic education as connected with human freedom. Educational philosophers such as Kenneth Strike suggest that the schools of a democratic society must balance between the individual rights of students and parents in a pluralistic society and the more minimal requirements of a democratic society. Citizenship, in this view, requires learning valuable knowledge through the disciplines, as well as learning skills for critical thinking and shared deliberation among diverse learners and future citizens. Dewey's emphasis on shared problem solving remains a key point of consensus for many foundations scholars, but since Dewey's time, the increasingly diverse society in the United States and other nations has brought about changes in the way democratic education is conceptualized.

Access to Civil and Social Rights

This question has been of special importance to historians of education, since their work has been a cornerstone for understanding how and why full citizenship has been long denied to many groups in the United States and elsewhere. Scholars in the foundations of education have particularly focused on realizing greater equity and civic participation. This question, therefore, has interested not just historians but also scholars working in curriculum studies and philosophical studies of education, as well.

Noted historian of education James Anderson has documented the education for second-class citizenship received by generations of African Americans in the United States. Historians join sociologists and philosophers of education in documenting the many forms of unequal education provided to Blacks, Hispanics, women, and American Indians. Assuming the role of equal citizenship necessitates that an equal education must be available to all children, social foundations scholars have revealed and analyzed the great disparities in educational opportunities and the corresponding lack of access to civil and social rights among many groups in the United States and other democracies.

For example, after the conquest of Native American lands and parts of Mexico, the U.S. government implemented educational programs focused on deculturalization; being a Native American or a Mexican American was, in the view of the time, not congruous with being a democratic citizen. In segregated schools designed to train children from these groups for work as laborers, students were assimilated but not socialized or educated for full democratic citizenship. Similarly, being a woman and being a citizen were, since ancient times, seen as incompatible identities. Recent feminist scholarship in philosophy has analyzed how our very conceptions of "citizen" and "the public" are gendered, and have proposed a revisioning of these terms to include a wide array of political identities and political work.

On the fiftieth anniversary of the first *Brown v. Board of Education* decision, many educators in the United States reflected upon the significance of that decision in terms of full citizenship under the law for Blacks, as well as upon the continued challenges to full racial integration in the United States. Foundations scholars have also taken up these important questions. Does a democratic society require integrated public schools? Can students learn about participating in a diverse democracy without experiences in schools that reflect the diversity of the civic body itself?

Socialization for Citizenship in Schools

In the classic sociological study of schooling, *Life in Classrooms* (1968), Philip Jackson analyzes the magnitude of the 7,000 hours spread across an elementary schooler's existence in schooling. Contributing to the scholarship engaging the question how schools *socialize* students, Jackson documented some of the very fundamental characteristics of school life, which he summarized as crowds, praise, and power. Schools teach people how to live in crowds, to be one among many, and to learn to accept the features of this existence (e.g., standing in lines, the importance of keeping quiet). Schools are also places of constant evaluation—of behavior and academic activities. Students learn that their work is evaluated by others—what becomes important is not what they think of their own work, but the mark that the teacher puts upon it. Third, school is a place where there are sharp distinctions between weak and powerful, Jackson showed. Institutions are places where students are under the control and authority of others.

Jackson's study became a classic in the foundations of education, though directly as a text about citizenship; however, this study and others confirmed that schools are not places where students can learn democratic citizenship through experience, discussion, and shared inquiry. Jackson's work argues that the hidden curriculum of schooling often teaches students to be passive and controlled rather than learning how to understand, through practice, the engagement and work of democratic citizenship.

Historiography has also contributed much to the question of how schools as institutions have shaped citizens. Not unlike the findings of Jackson's study, many other historical and sociological studies in the foundations of education field confirm that schools have often been places of social control and monocultural assimilation rather than achieving the Deweyan democratic ideal of realizing individual freedom within the contexts of diverse communities and disciplined inquiry. A central civic mission of early twentieth-century schooling in the United States, for example, was the "Americanization" of immigrants, and while the integration of new immigrants has always been a central aim of schools, "Americanization" was often carried out through blatantly sectarian and untruthful methods. Textbooks, for example, have long emphasized heroic, celebratory themes of American history, and historical scholarship reveals a century of school districts prohibiting books that were critical of American policy or leadership. Schools, it was thought, should teach a history of progress, loyalty, and heroism if new immigrants were to be assimilated as proper patriots. Thus, the history taught in the schools reflected the views of history desirable by those groups in power but not necessarily the real history of the nation or all its people.

In general, schools often socialize students for various norms that can work *against* the cultivation of good citizenship. Consistently deferring to those in power; or working primarily on individual tasks rather than in cooperative groups on shared, relevant problems; or learning about history through a very slanted and partial interpretation of historical events, all fail to promote democratic citizenship among students. A question that has accompanied these critical studies is, therefore, how *should* schools educate for citizenship, particularly in the way classrooms and schools are run? Philosophers and curricularists have developed responses to this question. A shining example of philosophical inquiry that has strongly shaped teachers' ideas on how we might best shape school practices toward democratic aims is found in the work of Maxine Greene. Among her contributions to the field has been her focus on how the arts and arts education can help students learn about meanings of human freedom in democratic societies. The arts can help people understand and empathize with diverse others, can help them imagine alternatives to "what is," and can help them take risks that promote human growth as learners and teachers.

Contrasting with the pervasive classroom norm characterized by teacher-talk and student-listening, educational philosopher Nicholas Burbules has written on the centrality of dialogue in the teaching and learning process, focusing on dialogue as a communicative relationship we enter with others. Not unlike Dewey's conception of democracy that is embedded in notions of communication and community, Burbules discusses dialogue with the hopes of expanding the ways that teachers and learners can come to know both as individuals and in the social realm, gaining both relational virtues such as respect, patience, and trust, as well as technical skills such as listening and the articulation of one's ideas.

Citizenship in a Pluralistic, Globalized Society

Globalization—the political, economic, social, and technological interdependencies that order the world—has implications for how people understand citizenship. Philosophers of education now debate whether and how globalization should change the way citizenship education is conceptualized and taught in schools. As the world becomes smaller through technological innovations (airplanes, the Internet, communications technologies), the concept of citizenship as one strictly encompassing one nation-state is challenged. That is, increasingly, people have multiple identities, loyalties, and political involvements that may cross national borders.

What does this mean for how schools prepare students to be citizens? Many scholars have argued that a more cosmopolitan citizenship necessitates a greater knowledge of the world and its peoples, a greater understanding of human diversity, and the recognition that one's worldview is shaped by one's own cultural and historical traditions. Other scholars emphasize the increasing role that knowledge of the ecosystem and biodiversity must play in educating citizens for a global society.

Planetary citizenship, according to C. A. Bowers, whose work involves education and ecology, involves a revitalization of the commons, of shared public spaces and practices in local communities. Bowers suggests that educating for planetary citizenship involves far more than understanding the harms that the current consumer society brings to the earth, its resources, and its inhabitants; it involves nurturing alternative economic, political, and social systems which are more sensitive to local cultures and ecologically sustainable practices. What all these scholars do agree upon, however, is that globalization and its positive and negative effects require rethinking citizenship to suit this new age. Education for democratic citizenship is a concept that may have to be reinvented in this new age of globalism, with all its technological wonders and environmental problems.

Kathleen Knight-Abowitz

See also Democracy and Education; Globalization and Education

Further Readings

Anderson, J. D. (1988). *The education of Blacks in the South, 1860–1935.* Chapel Hill: University of North Carolina Press.

Bowers, C. A. (2004). Revitalizing the commons or an individualized approach to planetary citizenship: The choice before us. *Educational Studies, 36*(1), 45–58.

Burbules, N. C. (1993). *Dialogue in teaching: Theory and practice.* New York: Teachers College Press.

Dewey, J. (1916). *Democracy and education.* New York: Free Press.

Dewey, J. (1939). *Freedom and culture.* New York: Capricorn Books.

Jackson, P. W. (1968). *Life in classrooms.* Chicago: Holt, Rinehart & Winston.

Strike, K. A. (1993). Professionalism, democracy, and discursive communities: Normative reflections on restructuring. *American Educational Research Journal, 30*(2), 255–275.

CIVIL RIGHTS MOVEMENT

Although the story of federal protection of civil rights is conveniently told chronologically, two themes predominate. First, federal protection of civil rights has a paradoxical relationship with states' rights. All civil rights legislation has been opposed or limited in response to the argument that the federal government should not involve itself in areas of state responsibility. The Supreme Court repeatedly voiced this concern and, in the past, invalidated civil rights legislation partly on this ground. Deference to state law enforcement prerogatives always has been a centerpiece of Justice Department civil rights enforcement policy. For decades, Congress repeatedly rebuffed so basic a measure as antilynching legislation in the name of states' rights.

Yet the original federal civil rights statutes, and their underlying constitutional amendments, were responses to outrages by states or to private outrages that states failed to ameliorate. Given the origins of the need for federal protection of civil rights, states' interests often received undue weight in shaping federal civil rights policy.

Second, there is a seedy underside to the topic of federal protection of civil rights. For many years, the federal government was more involved with denying Blacks rights than with protecting them. The quest for civil rights in education dates back to the founding of the United States as a country. In 1787, the Reverend Prince Hall and Black citizens petitioned the Massachusetts State Legislature for equal educational facilities. Their petition was not granted.

This entry highlights those themes as it reviews U.S. history in the areas of civil rights and education.

The Reconstruction Era

It was not until the Civil War that anything looking like federal involvement in civil rights and education took place, with the creation of the Bureau of Refugees, Freedmen, and Abandoned Lands (Freedmen's Bureau). The Bureau's statutory charge, "the control of all subjects relating to refugees and freedmen from rebel states," enabled it to perform a variety of educational and social welfare functions. Its greatest success was education. It established or supervised many kinds of schools: day, night, Sunday, and industrial, as well as colleges. Many of the nation's Black colleges were founded with aid from the Bureau, including Howard University, Hampton Institute, St. Augustine's College, and Fisk University, to name a few. This initial effort on the part of the Freedman's Bureau to assist Blacks was tainted by, among other factors, its role in establishing the oppressive system of Southern labor contracts. With few exceptions, federal protection of Blacks via the Freedmen's Bureau terminated in 1868.

Congress's other Reconstruction legislation employed a variety of techniques to protect civil rights. The Civil Rights Act of 1866 and the Force Act of 1870 imposed penalties on those who enforced discriminatory features of the Southern Black Codes, and the 1870 act made it a crime to conspire to hinder a citizen's exercise of federal rights. The 1870 act also provided special protection for Black Voting Rights Act and the Force Act of 1871 went further by providing for the appointment of federal supervisors to scrutinize voter registration and election practices. The Civil Rights Act of 1871 authorized civil actions and additional criminal penalties against those who violated constitutional rights and authorized the president to use federal forces to suppress insurrections or conspiracies to deprive "any portion or class of . . . people" of federal rights.

The Civil Rights Act of 1875, the culmination of the Reconstruction period civil rights program, imposed civil and criminal sanctions for discrimination in public accommodations, public conveyances, and places of amusement. Armed with the criminal provisions of the civil rights program, federal prosecutors brought thousands of cases in Southern federal courts and established criminal actions as the primary vehicle through which the federal government protected civil rights. This protective legislation ended with the compromise of 1877 engineered by President Rutherford B. Hayes and the attendant withdrawal of federal troops from the South. In 1878, only twenty-five federal criminal civil rights prosecutions were brought in Southern federal courts.

There are many reasons why federal criminal prosecutions during this period were ineffective in protecting civil rights—including equal access to education and schooling. First, shortly after enactment of the post–Civil War antidiscrimination legislation, the Supreme Court limited Congress's power to protect civil rights and narrowly construed constitutional provisions and statutory provisions that were not struck down. The entire federal statutory civil rights program, therefore, depended upon those provisions that, almost by happenstance, survived judicial scrutiny.

Separate But Equal

The principal criminal provisions that survived, now sections 241 and 242 of Title 18, United States Code, are not well suited to protecting civil rights. Enforcement of these provisions has been plagued by doubts about the specific rights they protect and the conduct they reach, and by doubt about the federal government's role in law enforcement. Similar difficulties characterized federal civil remedies to protect civil rights. For example, the Supreme Court, in *Plessy v. Ferguson* (1896), declared "separate but equal" the law of the land, providing legal justification for six decades of Jim Crow segregation, including the segregation of Black and White students in public schools.

From the Compromise of 1877 until World War II, reference to federal "protection" of civil rights was misleading. Until the war, federal employment policy included racial segregation and exclusion. *De jure* segregation in politics and the armed forces, government participation in segregated and racially isolated housing projects, racially prejudiced federal judges, and segregated public services and education all demonstrate the depth of federal involvement in discrimination. Examples of federal complicity in educational discrimination were widespread.

In 1904, for example, Kentucky enacted a "separate but equal" statute that made it illegal "for any person, corporation or association of persons to maintain or operate any college, school or institution where persons of White and Negro races are received as pupils for instruction." Berea College, a private institution in Kentucky, was found guilty of accepting White and Black students and fined $1,000. In *Gong Lum v. Rice* (1927), the court ruled that a child of Chinese descent could be required to attend a Black school in Mississippi under the separate but equal doctrine.

In *United States v. Carolene Products Co.* (1939), the Court employed deferential scrutiny in the economic realm and even greater scrutiny in the areas of civil liberties and civil rights. Six months after the *Carolene Products* decision, this approach was applied to a case involving higher education segregation, *Missouri ex rel. Gaines v. Canada* (1939). Since Missouri law required separate schools and universities for Whites and Blacks, Missouri law also required for the arrangement of tuition and fees for Black students at adjacent state institutions. Gaines brought suit against the University of Missouri to compel the university to admit him.

Postwar Changes

The end of World War II renewed violence against Blacks. Following a Democratic party defeat in the 1946 congressional elections, President Harry S Truman, in

Executive Order 9008, created a presidential civil rights committee to conduct inquiries and to recommend civil rights programs. In its report, *To Secure These Rights,* the committee made far-reaching recommendations in the areas of voting, employment, and federally assisted programs, many of which would be enacted in the 1960s. Truman, like other presidents, promoted civil rights most effectively in areas not requiring legislative action. Southern political power in Congress precluded significant civil rights legislation. Most of Truman's initiatives had to do with housing and employment, rather than education.

A focus on education was reemphasized by the Court and the federal government in the case of *McLaurin v. Oklahoma State Regents for Higher Education* (1950). In this case, Oklahoma's law requiring segregated higher education was challenged, and the Court ruled that state-supported institutions of higher education could not provide different education to students based only on their race. The Court held that such segregation deprived the individuals of their Fourteenth Amendment rights of due process.

Civil rights enforcement received little attention early in the administration of Dwight D. Eisenhower, but there were important exceptions to this pattern. Executive Order 10479 (1953) extended the antidiscrimination provisions previously required in defense contracts to all government procurement contracts. After the Supreme Court's 1954 ruling in *Brown v. Board of Education* (*Brown I*), however, Eisenhower and the federal government could no longer avoid civil rights issues. Southern recalcitrance in the face of *Brown II* (which required that desegregation proceed "with all deliberate speed") led to a federal-state confrontation in Little Rock, Arkansas, which was settled through the presence of federal troops who forced local officials to allow Black students to attend previously segregated schools (*Cooper v. Aaron,* 1958).

The Civil Rights Era

But Little Rock marked no general turning point in the administration's enforcement efforts. Legislation passed during this period included the Civil Rights Acts of 1957 and 1960, involved voting rights. However, even when armed with increased authority to investigate

denials of voting rights by the Civil Rights Act of 1957, the Justice Department brought few cases. President John F. Kennedy's administration also began with little impetus toward substantial civil rights achievement. But the rising tide of private civil rights activity, increased public awareness, and continued Southern resistance to desegregation made new federal and state confrontations inevitable.

In May 1961, federal marshals were employed to protect freedom riders. In September 1962, in connection with efforts to integrate the University of Mississippi, heavily outnumbered federal marshals and federalized National Guard troops withstood an assault by segregationists. Only the arrival of thousands of federal troops restored order. In the Birmingham crisis of 1963, which gained notoriety for the brutal treatment of demonstrators by state and local law enforcement officers, the federal government tried to act as a mediator.

The administration's inability under federal law to deal forcefully with situations like that in Birmingham led President Kennedy to propose further federal civil rights legislation. In November 1962, President Kennedy issued an executive order prohibiting discrimination in public housing projects and in projects covered by direct, guaranteed federal loans. And in executive orders in 1961 and 1963, Kennedy both required affirmative action by government contractors and extended the executive branch's antidiscrimination program in federal procurement contracts to all federally assisted construction projects.

Soon after Lyndon B. Johnson succeeded to the presidency, he publicly endorsed Kennedy's civil rights legislation. Due in part to his direct support, Congress enacted the Civil Rights Act of 1964, the most comprehensive civil rights measure in American history. The act outlawed discrimination in public accommodations, in federally assisted programs, and by large private employers, and it extended federal power to deal with voting discrimination. Title VII of the act created a substantial new federal bureaucracy to enforce antidiscrimination provisions pertaining to employment. The 1964 act also marked the first time that the Senate voted cloture against an anti–civil rights filibuster. Educational institutions receiving federal funding were profoundly affected by the act.

Despite the efforts of the Kennedy and Johnson Justice Departments, the Civil Rights Acts of 1957, 1960, and 1964 proved inadequate to protect Black voting rights. Marches and protests to secure voting rights led to violence, including an infamous, widely reported confrontation in Selma, Alabama, in which marchers were beaten. In March 1965, President Johnson requested new voting rights legislation. He included in his speech to the nation and a joint session of Congress the words of the song of the civil rights movement, "We shall overcome," thus emphasizing the depth of the new federal involvement in civil rights. By August, the Voting Rights Act of 1965 was in place. Within ten years of its passage, large numbers of Black voters were registered without great fanfare, but with corresponding gains in the number of Black elected officials. In 1968, after the assassination of Martin Luther King, Jr., Congress enacted a fair housing law as part of the Civil Rights Act of 1968.

Unlike the Reconstruction civil rights program, Congress's 1960s civil rights legislation survived judicial scrutiny. In a series of cases from 1964 to 1976, the Supreme Court both sustained the new civil rights program and revived the Reconstruction-era laws. These rulings involved public accommodations and voting rights. In *Jones v. Alfred H. Mayer Co.* (1968) and *Runyon v. McCrary* (1976), the Court interpreted the Civil Rights Act of 1866 to fill important gaps in the coverage of the 1964 and 1968 acts.

With the passage and sustaining of the 1964, 1965, and 1968 acts and the revival of the 1866 Act, the legal battle against racial discrimination at least formally was won. The federal civil rights program encompassed nearly all public and private purposeful racial discrimination in public accommodations, housing, employment, education, and voting. Future civil rights progress would have to come through vigorous enforcement, through programs aimed at relieving poverty, through affirmative action, and through laws benefiting groups other than Blacks.

Enforcing the Law

The fight for educational equality and civil rights was by no means over. For example, President Richard Nixon's 1968 "Southern strategy" included campaigning against busing, which was deliberately intended to decrease the segregation of schools. Within six months of Nixon's inauguration, the Justice Department for the first time opposed the NAACP Legal Defense and Education Fund in a desegregation case. But despite this seeming setback, under the pressure of Supreme Court decisions, and given the momentum of the prior administration's civil rights efforts, the Nixon administration did finally promote new levels of Southern integration—despite its continued opposition to "forced busing."

The period from 1970 to 1986 represents an era of ambivalence and uncertainty in terms of civil rights enforcement. During this period enforcement efforts became engulfed in the constitutionality of desegregation remedies—for example, whether to bus schoolchildren for purposes of desegregation. State-mandated school segregation was addressed in *Swann v. Charlotte-Mecklenburg Board of Education* (1971); *Davis v. Board of School Commissioners of Mobile County* (1971); *Moore v. Charlotte-Mecklenburg Board of Education* (1971); *North Carolina State Board of Education v. Swann* (1971); *Keyes v. School District No. 1 Denver, Colorado* (1973); *San Antonio School District v. Rodriguez* (1973); *Milliken v. Bradley (Milliken I;* 1974*); Pasadena City Board of Education v. Spangler* (1976); *Milliken v. Bradley (Milliken II;* 1977); and *Plyler v. Doe* (1982).

New means were provided for the enforcement of legislation. In the 1970s, for example, the Internal Revenue Service (IRS), under the pressure of court decisions, began to foster integration by denying tax benefits to private segregated academies and their benefactors. This process, however, was curtailed by other sectors of the federal government. Congress, for example, intervened to limit the IRS's use of funds for such purposes. Similarly, Congress also restrained executive authority to seek busing as a remedy for school segregation.

The comprehensive coverage of federal civil rights law did not eliminate the inferior status of Blacks in American society. Pressure mounted for assistance in the form of affirmative action or preferential hiring and admissions in higher education. Court cases ensued: *DeFunis v. Odegaard* (1973), *Regents of the University of California v. Bakke* (1978), *United Steel Workers of*

America v. Weber (1979), *Fullilove v. Klutznick* (1980), and *Wygant v. Jackson Board of Education* (1986). These divided even the liberal community that was traditionally supportive of civil rights enforcement.

School desegregation also triggered a legal backlash under Presidents Ronald Reagan, George Herbert Walker Bush, and George W. Bush. From 1986 to 2006, an era of retrenchment and unpredictability directed a more conservative policy direction for civil rights law and legislation. During this period, the Supreme Court narrowly interpreted constitutional provisions and federal statutes that provided protections for civil rights of racial and ethnic minorities. Minorities experienced setbacks in many areas, including education. Decisions related to desegregation include *Missouri v. Jenkins* (1991); *Board of Education of Oklahoma City Public Schools v. Dowell* (1991); *Freeman v. Pitts* (1992); *United States v. Fordice* (1992), and *Parents Involved in Community Schools v. Seattle School District No. 1* (2002). Other rulings involved affirmative action: *United States v. Paradise* (1987), *City of Richmond v. J. A. Croson* (1989), *Metro Broadcasting Inc. v. FCC and Astroline Communications Company* (1990), *Limited Partnership v. Shurberg Broadcasting of Hartford, Inc.* (1990), *Hopwood v. Texas* (5th Cir., 2000), *Gratz v. Bollinger* (2003), and *Grutter v. Bollinger* (2003).

Federal involvement in civil rights legislation has both hindered and advanced the process of achieving more equal schools. Since the 1954 *Brown* decision, the principle of educational equity for all citizens has predominated, but not without significant attempts to curtail the general movement toward a universal equality for all citizens.

Paul E. Green

See also African American Education

See Visual History Chapter 25, Civil Rights

Further Readings

Birnbaum, J., & Taylor, C. (1999). *Civil rights since 1987.* New York: New York University Press.

Brauer, C. M. (1977). *John F. Kennedy and the Second Reconstruction.* New York: Columbia University Press.

Carr, R. K. (1947). *Federal protection of civil rights: Quest for a sword.* Ithaca, NY: Cornell University Press.

Davis, A. L., & Graham, B. L. (1995). *Supreme Court, race, and civil rights.* Thousand Oaks, CA: Sage.

Gressman, E. (1952). The unhappy history of civil rights legislation. *Michigan Law Review, 50,* 1323–1358.

Konvitz, M. R. (1961). *A century of civil rights.* New York: Columbia University Press.

CLASSICAL CURRICULUM

The classical curriculum was intended to prepare the children of the Greek and Roman privileged classes for a life of limited self-government. To meet that goal, the student studied grammar, rhetoric, and dialectic, which medieval scholars labeled the trivium, and music, arithmetic, geometry, and astronomy, later called the quadrivium. If the Greek or Roman student intended to practice medicine or law, he would enter into an apprenticeship following his formal schooling. Trades, including any form of manual labor, were strictly taboo for the Greek and Roman aristocracies.

The classical curriculum is historically important for being the first systematic program of intellectual, physical, and spiritual development. It is of particular cultural importance for perpetuating the Greeks' advanced knowledge of mathematics and astronomy and for laying the groundwork for most contemporary academic disciplines. Because it is the oldest systematic approach to education, the character of classical education has in the past been, and continues to be, gender specific. The education of girls and young women occurred at home in Ancient Greece as well as in Rome, and the practice went unchallenged in much of the Western world until the eighteenth century. The most well-known exception is Sparta, where young women endured difficult physical training as warriors.

Latter-day proponents of the classical curriculum have a somewhat broader meaning in mind than did their ancient and medieval counterparts. Getting at that meaning has opened the field to theoretical speculation about the boundaries of philology, history, area studies, and the canon. Today, many classicists fall into one of two methodological camps, divided by conflicting ideologies as much as national boundaries:

(a) philologists, led by Cambridge and Oxford scholars who wish to take texts at face value; and (b) text theorists, largely American, who apply Freudian, Marxist, and postmodern methods to an evaluation of content.

Declining enrollment in classics departments has prompted many scholars to question the future of classical studies. The source of the West's philosophical, moral, and legal systems is bound up in the tradition of classical education—a fact that raises questions about present capacity to comprehend basic principles still guiding Western culture. Because the study of Ancient Greek and Latin is intellectually challenging, a measure of elitism may be built into classical education. It is therefore possible that classical education is essentially contrary to contemporary egalitarian sensibilities, and so its demise may come as a matter of zeitgeist rather than irrelevance.

Shawn Pendley

See also Great Books of the Western World; Trivium and Quadrivium

Further Readings

Bloom, A. (1988). *The closing of the American mind.* New York: Simon & Schuster.

Hanson, V. D., & Heath, J. (1998). *Who killed Homer? The demise of classical education and the recovery of Greek wisdom.* New York: Free Press.

Kopff, E. C. (1999). *The devil knows Latin: Why America needs the classical tradition.* Wilmington, DE: ISI Books.

CLASS SIZE

Class size has been defined as the number of students who regularly appear in a teacher's classroom and for whom the teacher is primarily responsible and accountable. It has also been referred to as the number of students for whom a teacher is primarily responsible during a typical lesson. In its simplest form, *class size* is the number of students in each teacher's classroom each day.

The reduction of *class size* has been a topic of heated debate in America. It has taken center stage both in the political and social arenas of American lives. A clearer understanding of issues surrounding class size has significant implications for educational and economic policy. Arguments for reducing class size include increasing individualized instruction, higher quality and more innovative student-centered instruction, increased teacher morale, fewer disruptions, decreased behavioral issues, and greater student engagement. Yet, the majority of the research on class size appears inconclusive at best. This entry explores the research on class size and its implications for educational policy.

History of Class Size Research

Research on class size began as early as the 1970s and quickly identified a connection between class size and achievement scores. In 1978, Gene V. Glass and Mary Lee Smith synthesized using a meta analysis of seventy-seven studies and their subsequent 725 effect sizes. *Effect sizes* measure the strength of a relationship between two variables. *Variables* are constructs of interest that can be measured, such as class size and achievement (i.e., via test scores).

According to Glass and Smith, reducing class sizes from forty or more to twenty students led to a very small increase in achievement. However, when class sizes dropped to fifteen students or less, there were larger effects on achievement. Yet due to the fact that the studies looked at were of short duration and included non-school-related cases such as tennis coaching, this analysis faced much criticism.

In 1989, Robert E. Slavin reevaluated only the studies that met higher criteria: lasting at least one year, involving a substantial reduction in class size, and random assignment or matching of students across larger and smaller classes (characteristics of scientific research that ensure differences in classrooms are not due to other factors aside from class size). Slavin concluded that substantial reductions in class size have small positive effects on students. These effects were not found to be cumulative, and disappeared within a few years.

In 1985, due to the stir caused by Glass and Smith's compilation of studies, and positive news coming from the state of Indiana regarding their class-size reduction program, a landmark study emerged. For Tennessee's Project STAR (Student Teacher Achievement Ratio), about 6,500 students in 329 classrooms in 79 schools (from rural, suburban, urban, and inner-city settings) entering kindergarten, were randomly placed in either a regular class (twenty-two to twenty-six students), a small class (thirteen to seventeen students), or a regular class with a full-time teacher aide. Participation in this study was voluntary. However, schools had to be large enough to support one control group and two treatment groups at any grade level.

Students involved in this $12 million project were to stay in classes of the same size for three years, and then move to "regular"-size classes afterwards. Teachers were also assigned at random to the various class groups without any special instructions. The study found that in each grade, the benefits of additional years in a small class were greater. Interestingly, after the students returned to regular-size classes, the effects began to decrease. In addition, when looking at gains over time, John Hattie found that the greatest gains in reading were made by the students in regular-size classes. One should note however, that for this project, as mentioned previously, regular-size classrooms consist of twenty-two to twenty-six students.

A notable finding that emerged was that effects sizes were greater (almost double) for minority students compared to White students in all achievement areas, and zero effects were found for student motivation and self-concept. Once again, flaws in the project raised questions. Bias may have been evident due to the fact that the schools participating were not random, but voluntary. Also, teachers' awareness of the project and desire for smaller classes may have caused them to work harder for more positive results.

Nonetheless, other states followed in Tennessee's footsteps. Unfortunately, when California tried a similar study in 1996, it was suffering from a shortage of teachers. The speed in implementation of California's initiative resulted in lax standards for hiring educators. Thus, in 2003, 15 percent of California teachers in Grades 4 through 12 were not fully certified. Nonetheless, the results were positive for smaller classes. However, researchers found that due to uncontrollable factors in the study, gains could not be attributed directly to reduced class sizes.

The history of class size research has been plagued by inconsistencies and contradictions. Factors contributing to the difficulty in equally considering studies on this matter include the use of pupil-teacher ratio as a definition for class size in some studies, the context-embedded nature of educational research, and the fact that class size interacts in complex ways with a range of other variables.

Findings

Nonetheless, it appears that attending smaller classes for three or more years increases the likelihood of long-term carryover effects. When analyzing small versus large classes, the literature appears to consider the class with fifteen to twenty students a smaller, more ideal class size. Small classes can provide conditions for better academic performance in content area subjects for bilingual students. In addition, smaller class sizes appear to be especially beneficial for at-risk or struggling students.

Teachers and parents strongly advocate small classes. Thus, other benefits of small classes are content parents and higher teacher morale. In fact, private "elite" schools advertise smaller classes as a bonus. Market research reveals that this advertisement is indeed an attractive feature for parents.

However, studies have also found that teachers that get smaller classes may be holding on to the same teaching methods they used with larger classes, and thus need to be trained in more effective methods that can be used with smaller classes.

Smaller classes have also been linked to higher attainment in reading in the "early" years of school. And at the high school language arts level, smaller classes create a more feasible workload for teachers grading writing assignments.

Factors to Consider in Class Size Reduction

There are many factors to consider when looking at reducing class sizes for public policy. It is a very expensive intervention, requiring more teachers, buildings, and supplies. In addition, a rapid expansion of the policy may lead to a deterioration in average teacher quality in schools. This is a significant facet to consider when the literature shows that the quality of teachers appears to have a larger impact on student achievement than any other school-related factor. The literature also points to the fact that disruptive students can disrupt a small class just as badly as a large one.

The average number of pupils per teacher in American public and private elementary schools between 1969 and 1997 fell from 25.1 to 18.3, a decline of greater than 27 percent. In secondary schools, class sizes also dropped from 19.7 to 14.0. The National Assessment of Educational Progress, however, showed no significant or consistent gains in academic performance during this time period.

Many studies look to these small improvements on standardized tests as a reason why reducing class sizes may prove unfruitful. However, those in favor of smaller classes argue that better work-related conditions for students and teachers and other beneficial factors affected by a smaller class size (i.e., high school dropout rates) may not translate into effects on student learning as measured by these standardized tests. Demographic shifts in our country also make it difficult to isolate effects of reductions in pupil-teacher ratios.

Class size is not only a topic of interest in America but abroad as well. Ideal class sizes appear to be culturally connected. Societies that focus on collective group identity may function better with larger class sizes as opposed to individualized cultures. Thus, in Japan, for example, there are substantially larger class sizes than in the United States.

In conclusion, class size remains a highly political issue for policy makers. Research findings are not necessarily conclusive, although the general trend seems to be to consider smaller classes as being better.

Maribel G. Mora

See also School Finance

Further Readings

Addonizio, M. F., & Phelps, J. L. (2000). Class size and student performance: A framework for policy analysis. *Journal of Education Finance, 26*(2), 135–156.

Ehrenberg, R. G., Brewer, D. J., Gamoran, A., & Willms, J. D. (2001). Does class size matter? *Scientific American, 285*(5), 78–85.

Finn, J. D., Gerber, S. B., Achilles, C. M., & Boyd-Zaharias, J. (2001). The enduring effects of small classes. *Teachers College Record, 103*(2), 145–183.

Finn, J. D., Gerber, S. B., & Boyd-Zaharias, J. (2005). Small classes in the early grades, academic achievement, and graduating from high school. *Journal of Educational Psychology, 97*(2), 214–223.

Gilman, D. A., & Kiger, S. (2003). Should we try to keep class sizes small? *Educational Leadership, 60*(7), 80–85.

Glass, G. V., & Smith, M. L. (1978). Meta-analysis of research on the relationship of class size and achievement. San Francisco: Far West Laboratory for Educational Research & Development.

Harris, S. (2002). Children with special needs and school choice: Five stories. *Preventing School Failure, 46*(2), 75–78.

Hattie, J. (2005). The paradox of reducing class size and improving learning outcomes. *International Journal of Educational Research, 43,* 387–425.

Nye, B., Hedges, L. V., & Konstantopoulos, S. (2004). Do minorities experience larger lasting benefits from small classes? *Journal of Educational Research, 98*(2), 94.

Ozerk, K. (2001). Teacher-student verbal interaction and questioning, class size and bilingual students' academic performance. *Scandinavian Journal of Educational Research, 45*(4), 353–367.

Pong, S., & Pallas, A. (2001). Class size and eighth-grade math achievement in the united states and abroad. *Educational Evaluation and Policy Analysis, 23*(3), 251–273.

Simmons, J. (2005). Improving writing for college: The conditions to do it well. *English Journal, 94*(6), 75.

Slavin, R. (1989). Class size and student achievement: Small effects of small classes. Educational Psychology, 24, 99–110.

West, S. S., Westerlund, J. F., Stephenson, A. L., Nelson, N. C., & Nyland, C. K. (2003). Safety in science classrooms: What research and best practice say. *Educational Forum, 67*(2), 174–183.

CLOTHING, BANNING OF SYMBOLIC

Dress codes and uniform policies have been enforced in very different ways by various schools. Schools' rationale for banning symbolic clothing may include protecting students' health and safety, minimizing social class indicators between students, and creating cohesion and uniformity. However, schools have been faced with an increasing number of controversial cases when they have banned certain clothing representative of students' political, social, or religious identities. The inconsistent and *ad hoc* approach to addressing this issue is noticeable.

The recent ban of conspicuous religious symbols in French state schools has received international attention.

Justification for the ban was that there should be a strict separation between church and state (*laïcité*). Defenders point to a policy of neutrality inside the boundaries of the school. Unlike the United States, where the separation of church and state is based on a notion of neutrality of equal inclusion—meaning that schools accommodate all conceptions of the good (at least in theory)—France bases its notion of neutrality on equal exclusion. Thus, students and teachers are to shed their private conceptions as public equals once they enter the school.

A number of cases in the United States have challenged the right to freedom of expression regarding attire worn to school. In Detroit, Bretton Barber chose to wear a t-shirt to school with a picture of President George W. Bush on the front along with the caption, "International Terrorist." The school insisted that Bretton remove the shirt, turn it inside out, or return home, for fear the shirt would cause "disruption" among students at school. Elsewhere in Michigan, Timothy Gies, a high school student in Bay City, was repeatedly suspended for wearing t-shirts with a peace sign, anarchy symbols, an upside-down American flag, and an antiwar quote from Albert Einstein. When the student attempted to defend his right under freedom of expression, the administrator said that this right did not apply to students. The court reversed that decision.

In Canada, a different court decision occurred regarding a child being allowed to bring the Sikh ceremonial dagger (*kirpan*) to school. The case went to the Supreme Court of Canada, where in March 2006, the Court ruled in favor of the Sikh family, overturning the ban in a unanimous consent of 8–0 allowing the *kirpan* in schools (*Multani v. Commission scolaire Marguerite-Bourgeoys*). The main consideration before the Court was the extent of the infringement of freedom of religion and whether this infringement should outweigh concerns about potential safety. The judges felt that a symbolic ceremonial dagger was not a trivial or superficial religious symbol but an essential part of the student's identity and faith. The second major consideration was the potential safety risk that the dagger posed to students and staff; the judges ruled that the dagger was no more dangerous than common school equipment such as sports equipment or scissors.

Divergent education policies regarding banning symbolic clothing are evident and increasing in prevalence. These tensions parallel greater societal dilemmas in balancing multicultural policies with greater societal cohesion.

Dianne Gereluk

See also Dress Codes; Multicultural Education

Further Readings

Gereluk, D. (2005). Should Muslim headscarves be banned in French schools? *Theory and Research in Education, 3*(3), 259–271.

Gereluk, D. (2007). What not to wear: Dress codes and uniform policies in the common school. *Journal of Philosophy of Education, 41*(4), 643–657.

Judge, H. (2004, November). The Muslim headscarf and French schools. *American Journal of Education,* 1–24.

Multani v. Commission scolaire Marguerite-Bourgeoys, 2006 SCC 6, [2006] 1 S.C.R. 256.

Coeducation

Coeducation refers to the practice of educating both sexes in the same setting. In its thinnest sense, this term coined in the nineteenth-century in the United States, need not signify that both sexes teach, or that the curriculum represents or addresses both sexes, or even that both sexes learn together rather than apart within that setting. The only requirement this otherwise vaguely descriptive term signifies in both popular and professional usage is both sexes' presence as learners in a setting, perhaps not even in nearly equal numbers, nor with nearly equal value.

This theoretically naive way of discussing coeducation may owe some of its currency even among professional educational theorists to John Dewey's strong polemical advocacy for coeducation in a 1911 *Ladies' Home Journal* (*LHJ*) article where he asserted the absurdity of developing a theory of coeducation. Yet he demonstrates the need for subtler coeducational thought when his own cogent *LHJ* critique of sexual essentialism with regard to elementary education and his administrative argument for coeducational classrooms at the

University of Chicago seem to contradict his *LHJ* defense of higher education in home economics for women only. Like most twentieth-century philosophers of education, he ignores coeducation's philosophical history, which is ancient: Plato, whose Academy was coeducational, includes in the *Republic,* V, Socrates' argument for providing both sexes the same education within a Guardian class organized without families.

But in its thinnest, descriptive sense, as Dewey's own self-contradictory polemic and Booker T. Washington's also influential conception of racially segregated coeducation for ex-slaves at Tuskeegee both illustrate, coeducation need not denote the same education for both sexes. Washington's coeducational curriculum includes home economics for women and other vocational training for men, whereas W. E. B. Du Bois constructs implicit premises for a more radical concept of coeducation in *The Souls of Black Folk,* by narrating the tragic case of an intellectually hungry woman's poverty, educational deprivation, domestic enslavement to family cares, and early death from overwork, largely because of her brothers' uneducated domestic skills and responsibility. These three pragmatists' theoretical differences on gender questions in education following abolition of slavery suggest a seldom noted need for interracial theorizing about coeducation. This entry looks at coeducation as viewed by some key female thinkers.

Rationale

The most substantial English-speaking tradition of coeducational thought originated in 1791 to 1792 with Mary Wollstonecraft's *A Vindication of the Rights of Woman,* which critiques slavery as it formulates coeducation in a thick normative sense. Admiring Catherine Macaulay's 1790 argument for coeducation in *Letters on Education,* Wollstonecraft constructs her revolutionary rationale for coeducation, without ever having experienced its formal practice, by critiquing the monarchist property system's moral miseducation of both sexes: patriarchal, sex-segregated education premised upon both an essentialist conception of sexual difference and an imperialist dependence upon slavery. Following her coeducational thought experiment, feminists have grounded their rationales for coeducation in their own reflective responses to Wollstonecraft's and their other forebears' coeducational thought as well as their own different cultural landscapes. Thus, her coeducational inquiry set an agenda for subsequent practical experiments and thought experiments, as well as critical treatises, concerning coeducation across the English-speaking world. Despite some differences among feminists, the feminist tradition's rationales for coeducation are all rooted in philosophical concerns to foster just societies and good lives for all.

Louisa May Alcott's March family trilogy, for example, gives fictional narrative form to many of Wollstonecraft's philosophical ideas about coeducation. Although obviously not concerned with monarchism in the United States, Alcott does portray both sexes' miseducation vividly, endorsing the moral validity of Wollstonecraft's opposition to slavery and implicitly also her concern about the likely moral failures of a republic that fails to educate women for economic independence, competent motherhood, and full democratic participation as citizens, or to teach men to value them.

Among the first generation of women to enjoy access to higher coeducation and earn a Ph.D., African American, educator-orator Anna Julia Cooper amends Wollstonecraft's and Alcott's republican rationale for coeducation by insisting also upon its value for racial development through women's generously compassionate sisterhood and men's respect for their leadership, through a coeducational curriculum grounded in both the law of love and the law of reason.

In England on the eve of World War II, Virginia Woolf, in *Three Guineas,* accepts such earlier arguments for coeducation's democratic necessity with her own satiric accounts of higher education that fails to civilize men because it overlooks how an "unpaid-for" education does civilize some otherwise uneducated women; she updates Wollstonecraft's moral skepticism about a patriarchal domestic and political economy organized around property and empire, and constructs a cogent caveat about coeducation's strategic sufficiency for preventing war and protecting culture and intellectual liberty within such a morally questionable context.

Most recently, having studied Wollstonecraft's ideal of the educated woman and then invoking both Alcott's and Woolf's educational thought in *The Schoolhome,* Jane Roland Martin cites boys' brutalizing miseducation and girls' domesticating miseducation in the late twentieth century to retheorize the U.S. Constitution's concept of "domestic tranquility" as a foundation for rethinking coeducation's purposes relative to both sexes' education for morally responsible lives in the private family home, the public nation home, and the universal planetary home.

A New Vision

Affixing the prefix *co* to *education* thus may signify not just education of both sexes in one place but, as Cooper argues, the education of both sexes situated interdependently within social relationships, political-economic systems, cultural diversity, and moral responsibilities that construct their differences from each other as well as their nation's character. Proposing coeducation as one nonviolent revolutionary strategy necessary for a republic's moral health, Wollstonecraft theorizes a multi-institutional, culturally complex context for coeducation, simultaneously private and public. Critical of private education, such as that advocated by John Locke and Jean-Jacques Rousseau, and of public education, such as that offered by unregulated residential schools, she nonetheless advocates coeducation that combines both sexes' education to love with both sexes' education to reason: the former within loving, egalitarian homes and the latter within government-financed day schools for the rich and poor of both sexes. But no less concerned about imperial economic oppression than about sexual oppression, Wollstonecraft casts severe doubt upon the notion that education can remedy social ills without revolutionary politics, recognizing print media and churches as consequential agents of public education (and miseducation).

More optimistic about coeducation's power to address social problems, Alcott's coeducational thought experiment revises Wollstonecraft's multi-institutional context by conceptually integrating an egalitarian home that teaches loving life-practices with an inclusive school that teaches academic subjects by Socratic

method into a single private institution with a public conscience: Plumfield (in the book *Little Men*). Less optimistically, Woolf acknowledges practical difficulties in establishing and changing higher education institutions for moral purposes, theorizes their complicities with fascism and war, and advocates anarchic emphasis on critical moral education about comparable tyrannies and servilities in both private house and public world. Much as Wollstonecraft, Alcott, and Cooper do, but with more theoretical elaboration, therefore, Woolf advocates women's conscientious educative participation in print media and other extra-institutional cultural activities as an unofficial "Society of Outsiders" that may distinctively foster a civilizing coeducational culture in which men and women learn to speak honestly with one another.

Most recently, Martin acknowledges coeducation's multi-institutional configuration and theorizes a broadly applicable "gender-sensitive educational ideal," proposing a new concept of multicultural public coeducational schooling, the "schoolhome," as a "moral equivalent of home"; advocating "actions great and small" that academic women might take to transform higher coeducation; and conceptualizing "multiple educational agency" as effective means of cultural transmission that require ongoing systematic moral evaluation.

Coeducational thought following Wollstonecraft has also addressed, from various perspectives, the ends and means she claims for coeducation: (1) to confound the sex distinction, (2) to renounce sex privilege and foster equality, (3) to cultivate friendly intersex mutuality, and (4) to value childrearing as educational work that requires educated intelligence and that, to be morally sound, must meet the equality and mutuality conditions. Controversies among many twentieth and twenty-first century coeducational theorists have in various ways, to different extents, and for diverse purposes addressed those four coeducational ends and means postulated by Wollstonecraft—controversies that coeducation's commoner thin sense mystifies.

Susan Laird

See also Women, Higher Education of

Further Readings

Cooper, A. J. (1998). The colored woman's office. In C. Lemert & E. Bhan (Eds.), *The voice of Anna Julia Cooper* (pp. 50–117). Lanham, MD: Rowman & Littlefield.

Dewey, J. (1911). Is co-education injurious to girls? *Ladies' Home Journal, 28*(22), 13.

Laird, S. (1995). Rethinking coeducation. *Studies in Philosophy and Education, 13,* 361–378.

Laird, S. (1998). Learning from Marmee's teaching: Alcott's response to girls' miseducation. In J. Alberghene & B. L. Clark (Eds.), *"Little Women" and the feminist imagination* (pp. 285–321). New York: Garland Press.

Martin, J. R. (1992). *The schoolhome.* Cambridge, MA: Harvard University Press.

Martin, J. R. (1999). *Coming of age in academe.* New York: Routledge.

Martin, J. R. (2002). *Cultural miseducation.* New York: Teachers College Press.

Showalter, E. (Ed.). (2005). *Alcott: Little women, Little men, Jo's boys.* New York: Library of America.

Todd, J. (Ed.). (1999). *Mary Wollstonecraft: A vindication of the rights of woman, a vindication of the rights of men.* Oxford, UK: Oxford University Press.

Woolf, V. (1938). *Three guineas.* San Francisco: Harcourt Brace Jovanovich.

COLORBLINDNESS

Colorblindness is an individual and social idea based upon two primary notions: (1) that to overtly ignore a person's race alleviates the possible racism that might otherwise operate and (2) that the equal opportunity structure of U.S. society means that failures among various racial groups to achieve can be best explained by deficiencies in individuals rather than by inequities that result from group membership. Notions of colorblindness operate throughout educational policies and in all levels of personnel. Its pervasiveness makes it a critical educational issue, both within individual classrooms and in the interactions between students and teachers, as well as in understanding educational policies such as "zero-tolerance" discipline approaches.

Many people believe that *colorblindness*—the idea that racial and/or ethnic group affinity ought to be irrelevant to how one is treated in social and interpersonal interactions—is the natural response to *racism,* which is often defined as the antipathy for or inferiorization of other people based on race. The notion of operating from a colorblind point of view has a long history in the United States, the rhetoric for which can be found embedded in several important American ideals such as universal meritocracy and the idea that "all men are created equal."

These ideas are manifest in the Thirteenth Amendment ending slavery and the Fourteenth Amendment offering equal protection under the law to all U.S. citizens. Colorblindness is an ideology frequently held by individuals but one that also works at the level of social policy due in large part to this historical legacy and rhetorical confirmation.

Historical Origins of Social Applications

During slavery, racism was overt and emerged from the notion of genetic inferiority of Blacks and other non-White races. Also known as "evolutionary" racism, slavery-era racism grew and was legalized during the Jim Crow era, which saw the undoing of much of the progressive social policy found in the Thirteenth and Fourteenth amendments to the Constitution. With legalized segregation supported by the *Plessy v. Ferguson* U.S. Supreme Court decision, Blacks and other racial minorities began to protest and initiated court cases that challenged legalized segregation in various arenas of public life. These cases culminated in the 1954 *Brown v. Board of Education* decision, which found that the separation was inherently unequal. The civil rights era continued, breaking down the practices of evolutionary racism and promoting Black empowerment.

Racism in the twentieth century did not ebb, however; rather, a new incarnation of racism emerged. Colorblind racism, or aversive racism, led to the public's rejection of overtly racist statements. Political movements of the late twentieth century, countering outright racist acts and beliefs, used as their foundation the liberal notion of impartial and equal treatment of individuals and led to the pervasive idea of individual merit as the primary determining factor in one's success. Contemporary views of colorblindness arise from this set of beliefs. The dominant idea here was that if one could squelch racist laws by eliminating racist talk and the belief systems that underlie such ideas, then race would no longer matter and individuals could be judged as individuals separate from their racial category.

These hopes, however, did not become reality. In fact, some argue that colorblindness as a social policy has maintained and exacerbated racism to epidemic levels. With regard to educational practice, Michelle Moses argues that while the civil rights era initiated important programs in bilingual education, multicultural curricula, affirmative action in higher education admissions, and remedial education, colorblindness is an insufficient philosophical foundation upon which to maintain one's support of these important programs. Instead, she and other authors argue that the present problems with racism and racial discrimination in the United States, particularly those affecting education, require *race consciousness,* if social justice is to remain the ultimate aim.

Colorblindness at the Individual Level

Colorblindness is also a philosophical and attitudinal position held by individuals. People working from a colorblind point of view generally believe that the safest interpersonal policy is not to notice or acknowledge someone's race; they claim that operating from a "colorblind" point of view inoculates them from possibly enacting deep-seeded racism. Essentially, a colorblind point of view purports to be an antiracist point of view. Thus, people working from this perspective may say to someone of color, "You're just my friend, I don't even notice that you're _____ (fill in race)."

Rather than reflecting an authentic, cultivated antiracist stance, Beverly Daniel Tatum argues that a colorblind perspective is more about civility and manners. She suggests that colorblind individuals have primarily learned that it is impolite to mention or discuss race, thus avoiding talk about race altogether. Such an outcome is only one of several detrimental results that multiculturalists commonly argue arises from harboring a "colorblind" perspective.

In addition to the taboo that is placed upon race and racial talk and dramatically limiting individuals' ability to explore this pressing educational and personal issue, colorblindness denies that race as a social construct (versus a biological one) influences the quality of one's life experience. If social conditions such as race no longer exist in a qualitative way, then colorblindness holds that essentially "we are all just individuals." Arising from this perspective is the idea that when people of color do not succeed, it must be due to individual deficits rather than the differential quality of educational, social, political, and economic resources and experiences that people of color endure. It purports that racial discrimination has ended and that racism is no longer problematic in U.S. society.

In addition, in this point of view intent, rather than effects, is emphasized, which puts enormous burden on the victims of racism to prove their case, while offering near immunity to transgressors because of a built-in benefit of the doubt. If, for instance, a colorblind individual says something a person of color finds racist, the colorblind person simply says "I couldn't possibly have meant that statement in that way, I'm colorblind to racial differences. We're all just human." Thus the victim of the racial epithet is left with the responsibility of defending the position in a nearly impossible situation.

Equally problematic is that colorblindness tends to "see" other racial groups while remaining blind to White as a racial category, effectively limiting the type of intense self-examination that most multiculturalists agree is key for White people in order to unlearn racism. Consequently, when mainstream Whiteness is not interrogated, mainstream culture is reified and assimilation becomes the key practice in creating racial integration, an idea that most multiculturalists would find deeply problematic.

Perhaps most damaging is the concomitant claim in colorblindness that color consciousness and race consciousness are inherently racist. Using the White supremacist as their example of an individual who is racially conscious, colorblind individuals suggest that to acknowledge race means to operate with antipathy and inferiorization as primary principles. Multiculturalists calling for race consciousness argue that instead of replacing "evolutionary" or overt racism with the equally powerful yet more subtle form of colorblindness, U.S. society should move toward acknowledging the ways in which race influences the lives people lead and promote the ability to discuss openly these effects so that authentic solutions to the problem of racial segregation, discrimination, and hatred can be found.

Understood by some as progressive social policy, the notion of colorblindness is a historically charged, individually and socially detrimental ideology that is often used to frame educational policy. Ostensibly, colorblindness argues for omitting race as one among many factors when allocating educational resources. Such a position may appear like good policy for educational decision making. However, in a society where racism exists in countless ways and is prevalent throughout all public spheres, the notion of retreating from using race is completely implausible, if not impossible. Colorconsciousness, rather than colorblindness, is the educational policy that actually contains the greatest power in addressing the most pressing issues of educational equity that continue to worsen over time.

Sue Ellen Henry

See also Antiracist Education

Further Readings

Blau, J. (2003). *Race in the schools: Perpetuating White dominance?* Boulder, CO: Lynne Reinner.

Blum, L. (2002). *I'm not a racist, but. . . .* Ithaca, NY: Cornell University Press.

Carr, L. (1997). *Color-blind racism.* Thousand Oaks, CA: Sage.

Cose, E. (1997). *Color-blind: Seeing beyond race in a race-obsessed world.* New York: HarperCollins.

Hitchcock, J. (2002). *Lifting the White veil.* Roselle, NJ: Crandall, Dostie & Douglass Books.

Moses, M. (2002). *Embracing race: Why we need race: Conscious education policy.* New York: Teachers College Press.

Tarca, K. (2005). Colorblind in control: The risks of resisting difference amid demographic change. *Educational Studies, 38*(2), 99–120.

Tatum, B. D. (1997). *Why are all the Black kids sitting together in the cafeteria?* New York: Basic Books.

COMMERCIALIZATION OF SCHOOLS

Over the past two decades, business leaders have gradually instituted commercial logics and practices across the educational landscape for the purposes of making a profit, attracting a generation of loyal customers, and creating a positive image of the corporate involvement in social affairs. The commercial involvement in schooling has had a profound influence on how educators, students, and the general public view the purpose of schooling, on the state's role in relationship to its citizens and institutions, and on the nature of life inside classrooms. This entry examines the constitutive forces behind the commercialization of schools; documents how commercial imperatives are altering institutions of higher education, specific programs such as teacher education, and K–12 schools; and documents how educators, socially conscious students, and concerned citizens have taken action against this trend.

The Roots of Commercialization

The commercialization of schools is not a new phenomenon; businesses leaders have earned a profit from selling textbooks for many decades. However, a new tide of corporate involvement began in the 1970s and 1980s. During the Ronald Reagan administration, the Commission on Excellence in Education prepared a report, *A Nation at Risk* (1983), which found that U.S. students had fallen behind their counterparts elsewhere in academic achievement and placed the blame on schools. Critics of the report said that it unfairly targeted schools for outcomes that were really owing to the globalization of capital and deindustrialization.

From this point forward, a marked shift took place in the influence corporations would have in the domain of schooling. Under conservative administrations in the 1980s and 1990s, Western governments cut funding to their public school systems, which opened avenues for increased corporate involvement in the education system. Increasingly, educational institutions turned to corporations for funding, resources, and guidance. In the case of underfunded K–12 schools and urban community colleges, this outside funding was needed to meet students' basic needs. In the case of public colleges and universities, these business linkages were needed to remain on a par with competing private institutions across the region or country.

Commercialization and Higher Education

Within the context of higher education, corporate policies, practices, and market ideologies have braided together to infiltrate all aspects of campus life. For instance, many public institutions of higher education in the United States have lost significant amounts of funding from state governments and face strong competition for student dollars from the growing pool of for-profit higher-education institutions. University administrators are compelled to base hiring decisions, the utility of academic programs, faculty research, and student learning with a "bottom line" mentality. Not coincidently, contingent adjunct faculty members are growing as the dominant teaching force; teaching assistants are used to replace full-time faculty members; prospective faculty are compelled to secure grants to obtain tenure-track positions; and programs that are not economically attractive are generally eliminated.

Meanwhile, university personnel often feel pressured to treat their students as "customers." They must meet student demands or face the possibility of losing needed resources with their institution, which may translate into losing their own positions. Since students have often come to view education as merely another commodity, deeming education as important to the extent it provides value in the marketplace, faculty modify their pedagogy to keep them "happy." They teach students what they find practical, rather than preparing them to become active citizens in the pursuit of forging a society predicated on justice and democracy.

Teacher Education

Looking more specifically at one academic program, teacher education, provides a view of how corporate dominance is now woven into the fabric of higher education. Over the past decade, business and government leaders have instituted an array of business-oriented policies and practices for the purposes of making a profit and blocking teacher educators from guiding pre-service and in-service teachers to challenge institutional forms of oppression inside and outside of their classrooms.

For example, in 2001, President George W. Bush, with support from corporate leaders, proposed and later implemented the No Child Left Behind Act, which has had the effect of linking K–12 teaching expertise with mastering a fixed body of knowledge on corporate-sponsored examinations. While corporations gain financially from the standardization of teaching "expertise" by producing "teacher-proof" curricula, teacher educators are in turn compelled to redirect their pedagogies. This is done by forcing them to focus on helping students who plan to be teachers to internalize the basic facts and skills needed to pass certification examinations and demonstrate potentially questionable "accomplished practices" in the classroom instead of creating pedagogical projects that help future teachers become better teachers.

Likewise, teacher accreditation agencies, such as the National Council for Accreditation of Teacher Education (NCATE), have supported a market-driven approach to teacher education. They support Bush's NCLB and aim to regulate teacher-educators' labor in a similar manner. Such accreditation agencies envision teaching and learning as exercises with simple, quantifiable "outcomes," while concomitantly instituting learning standards that keep in-service and pre-service teachers from examining the social, philosophical, and historical dimensions of schooling.

Many corporations have also been behind the proliferation of market-driven teacher programs instituted across North America. For example, corporations, such as Kaplan Inc. and Sylvan Education Solutions, have designed technical coursework, computerized examinations, and professional development initiatives to help in-service and pre-service teachers earn their teaching credentials as quickly as possible. Schools of education and other corporate conglomerates have created similar, fast-track, alternative route programs. As a result, many future teachers are earning credentials without taking *any* courses that might help them orchestrate classroom practices which might reveal or discuss social and economic inequalities.

K–12 Schooling

Irrespective of context, the vast majority of schools in North America have been forced to secure resources from corporations to meet students' needs. In exchange for monetary compensation, school districts have given corporations the exclusive rights to sell, market, and advertise their products to teachers and students.

Private firms have promised the antidote to decaying public schools and communities. They have gone into the business of building, financing, and wiring new, state-of the-art schools in economically depressed areas. Corporate leaders argue that building technologically enhanced institutions will help marginalized students and communities lift themselves out of poverty. These school structures, however, may be challenged to overcome conditions such as urban blight, crime, and violence, or to destroy institutional practices that inhibit the educational performance of marginalized youth.

Reaction

Some working-class people and educators have argued that commercial involvement in schools is part of a much larger agenda to commodify all social life. On a large scale, global citizens have protested against international policies and institutions that have supported commercial over public interests, such as the WTO (World Trade Organization), International Monetary Fund (IMF), and NAFTA (North American Free Trade Agreement). On a micro-level of education, teacher unions, other labor councils, and socially conscious university students in Canada and the United States have written position papers, launched strikes and demonstrations, and adopted policies that oppose corporate involvement in public schools. Finally, teacher educators, schoolteachers, progressive organizations, and concerned parents have created online resources, hosted international conferences, and developed curricula aimed at challenging these forces and reconstituting the notion of education as a public good.

Bradley Porfilio

See also Charter Schools

Further Readings

Bracey, G. W. (2003). *On the death of childhood and the destruction of public schools: The folly of today's education policies and practices.* New York: Heinemann.

Giroux, H. (2004). *The terror of neoliberalism: Authoritarianism and the eclipse of democracy.* Aurora, Ontario: Paradigm.

Hinchey, P. A., & Cadiero-Kaplan, K. (2005). The future of teacher education and teaching: Another piece of the privatization puzzle. *The Journal for Critical Education Policy Studies, 3*(2). Retrieved September 27, 2005, from http://www.jceps.com/?pageID=article&articleID=48

Lipman, P. (2003). Cracking down: Chicago school policy and the regulation of Black and Latino youth. In K. J. Saltman & D. Garbbard (Eds.), *Education as enforcement: The militarization and corporatization of schools* (pp. 81–101). New York. Routledge.

McLaren, P. (2005). *Capitalists and conquerors: A critical pedagogy against empire.* New York: Rowman & Littlefield.

Molnar, A. (2005). *School commercialism.* New York: Routledge.

Saltman, J. K. (2004). Coca-Cola's global lessons: From education for corporate globalization to education for global justice. *Teacher Education Quarterly, 31*(1), 155–172.

Washburn, J. (2005). *University Inc.: The corporate corruption of higher education.* New York: Basic Books.

COMMITTEE OF EIGHT

In 1905, the American Historical Association commissioned the first conference on the teaching of history in American elementary schools. The resultant report was titled, *The Study of History in Elementary Schools: Report to the American Historical Association by the Committee of Eight* (1912). It advanced a plan that increased the number of hours devoted to teaching elementary history, with a clear emphasis on U.S. history.

In the early 1900s, the teaching of history in U.S. primary grades remained largely unexplored. The reports of the Committee of Ten and the Committee of Seven, other American Historical Association committees, which researched secondary school history teaching, served as blueprints for this later investigation of history teaching in elementary schools.

The Committee of Eight employed novel social science methods for its study of elementary history teaching methods. The Committee of Eight sent circulars of inquiry to approximately three hundred superintendents of schools throughout the United States and examined the replies, analyzing the existing condition of elementary history teaching. Suggestions and recommendations were made to enhance the teaching of history in first through eighth grades. Members of the Committee of Eight included James Alton James, Henry E. Bourne, Eugene C. Brooks, Mabel Hill, Julius Sachs, Wilbur Gordy, J. H. VanSickle, and Henry W. Thurston.

Chara Haeussler Bohan

See also Educational Research, History of

Further Readings

Bohan, C. H. (2005). Digging trenches: Nationalism and the first national report on the elementary history curriculum. *Theory and Research in Social Education, 33*(2), 266–291.

COMMITTEE OF FIFTEEN

In 1893, the National Educational Association (NEA) established the Committee of Fifteen, whose purpose was to revise the elementary curriculum in American public schools in much the same way that the NEA's Committee of Ten was revising the secondary school curriculum. Groups such as the American Herbartians, under the leadership of Francis W. Parker and Frank and Charles De Garmo, called for an elementary school curriculum that was child centered and focused on the moral development of the child. More conservative approaches, led by figures such as William Torrey Harris, argued that the curriculum should be primarily concerned with preparing the child for his or her place in society.

The arguments of the committee are important in that they reflected tensions at work within American schools that would be debated for years to come. Should the schools and their curriculum focus first and foremost on the development of the child, or should they simply train students to meet the basic social needs of the culture? The conservative, less child-oriented stance predominated, setting a tone for years to come, and was further reinforced by the social efficiency movement, which viewed schools as "factories" that turned out students to meet the commercial and cultural needs of American society.

While on the surface, the decisions of the Committee of Fifteen may seem obscure, they represent the codification of an important trend in the history of American education—one involving the emphasis in public education on the needs of society to predominate over the needs of the personal development and growth of the child. This trend has continued into the contemporary era, as manifested in recent educational reforms such as the No Child Left Behind legislation.

Eugene F. Provenzo, Jr.

See also Committee of Ten; National Education Association

Further Readings

Button, H. W. (1965). Committee of fifteen. *History of Education Quarterly, 5*(4), 253–263.

COMMITTEE OF SEVEN

The Committee of Seven's (1896–1899) report, titled *The Study of History in Schools: Report to the American Historical Association by the Committee of Seven,* had a significant and lasting impact on the practice of history and social education in American schools. Concerned about the status of historical studies in secondary education, August F. Nightingale, Chairman of the National Education Association's Committee on College Entrance Requirements, asked historians at the 1896 meeting of the American

Historical Association to provide a report detailing the practice of teaching history in American schools. As its charter, the committee planned to make recommendations about the teaching of history and to foster more uniformity in secondary school history.

A committee was appointed, and to make an accurate evaluation, they conducted a nationwide survey of the subject of history in schools, analyzed the resultant data, and made appropriate recommendations based upon the social science findings. The Committee of Seven considered the scope and sequence of history offerings in secondary schools and suggested college entrance requirements. The report recommended a four-year course of study that included ancient history, medieval and modern European history, English history, American history, and civil government. The report also proposed that amount of time students engaged in historical studies increase and supported a broadened conception of citizenship. The report had a lasting impact upon historical studies in secondary schools, as a four-year course of study remains typical of many curriculum offerings.

Members of the committee, all members of the American Historical Association, were: Andrew McLaughlin (chairman), Herbert B. Adams, George L. Fox, Albert Bushnell Hart, Charles H. Haskins, H. Morse Stephens, and Lucy M. Salmon. Six members were prominent historians. George L. Fox, Headmaster of the Hopkins Grammar School in New Haven, Connecticut, was the only individual practicing in a secondary school. The only woman on the committee, Lucy Maynard Salmon, was chair of the history department at Vassar College.

Chara Haeussler Bohan

See also Citizenship Education; National Education Association

Further Readings

Bohan, C. H. (2004). Early vanguards of progressive education: The Committee of Ten, the Committee of Seven, and social education. In C. Woyshner, J. Watras, & M. Crocco (Eds.), *Social education in the twentieth century: Curriculum and context for citizenship* (pp. 1–19). New York: Peter Lang.

COMMITTEE OF TEN

The Committee of Ten was convened in 1892 by the National Education Association. The purpose of the committee was to develop recommendations for a standardized high school curriculum. Leading educators of the time were worried that too great a degree of variance existed in basic high school curricula across the country, resulting in a lack of consensus on what an educated person should know and generating confusion in college entrance requirements. Charles W. Eliot, president of Harvard University, was appointed chair of the task force. All but one member, William Harris, then U.S. Commissioner of Education, were at the time college/university presidents or secondary school principals or headmasters.

Nine subcommittees were formed, each to study a specific academic area: Latin, Greek, English, other modern languages, mathematics, physical sciences (physics, astronomy, chemistry), natural sciences (biology, botany, zoology, physiology), civics (history, civil government and political economy), and geography (physical geography, geology, meteorology). Each of the subcommittees was comprised of ten members, mostly college professors or presidents and secondary-school principals and headmasters. Per the guidelines of the Committee of Ten, each of the subcommittees convened three-day conferences in separate cities (except for Latin and Greek, both of which met in Ann Arbor, Michigan) from December 28–30, 1892. The conferences were designed so that each subcommittee would respond to a standard set of eleven questions regarding how a course of study should be designed and implemented at the secondary school level. Each subcommittee was to produce a conference report for the committee based on the assigned questions.

The conference reports were submitted to the committee in October 1893. Chairman Eliot prepared a draft report, and in November 1893 the Committee of Ten met at Columbia University in New York City to prepare the final draft, which included a minority report authored by James Baker, president of the University of Colorado. The final report was the subject of much discussion from the moment it was released. The initial circulation of 30,000 copies, published by the U.S.

Bureau of Education, was distributed free of charge. An additional 10,000 copies were published and sold out within six years.

The final report included multiple sample courses of study. Committee recommendations included the amount of time spent per day, week, and year on each subject, as well as the proportion of time that each subject should occupy in the high school curriculum. These recommendations influenced later work by the Carnegie Foundation for the Advancement of Teaching that resulted in the standard unit of credit for high school work. Though ostensibly a project designed to recommend standardization in the high school curriculum, the final report included recommendations for the first eight years of schooling in preparation for high school. The report was noted for the recommendation that all students in a high school, whether college-bound or not, should take the same course of study.

Greg Dubrow

See also Committee of Fifteen; National Education Association

Further Readings

Johanek, M. (2001). *A faithful mirror: Reflections on the college board and education in America.* New York: The College Board.

National Education Association. (1894). *Report of the Committee of Ten on secondary school studies, with the reports of the conferences arranged by committee.* New York: Author.

COMMUNITY OF PRACTICE

The idea of community of practice (CoP) has been appropriated by agencies whose enterprise is concerned with teacher education. Its use as a unit of analysis has been limited. However, the Finnish activity theorist, Yrjö Engeström, has developed a theory of activity systems that may be useful for modeling a CoP. Engeström argues that a CoP is an activity system by another name. Members of an activity system transform the shared objects to produce individual and shared

outcomes, learn to solve problems that disrupt their activity, transform existing practices, and develop new practices to sustain the activity system. This entry looks at the theoretical background of these ideas and then examines their implementation in education.

Intellectual Roots

Since the early 1900s, behaviorism, led by Edward Thorndike and B. F. Skinner, and social constructionism, led by John Dewey and Lev Vygotsky, have competed to influence the education of children and teachers. Behaviorists view learning as a process of enhancing individual cognition *inside* the heads of individual learners and reduce the learning environment to a minor role. Teaching is understood as the transmission of skills and subject matter to learners through instructional scripts and repeated exposure. The focus of instruction is on engaging learners in attending, listening, viewing, reading, and recalling, and processing information taken in. Assessment of learning is usually based on criterion-referenced, norm-referenced, and high-stakes tests.

Learning to teach is generally conceptualized as the sequential mastery of decontextualized skills and subject matter presumed to enable the performance of behaviors associated with effective teaching. The certification of teachers is based on standardized measures of subject matter and pedagogy and the evaluation of artifacts produced during courses, field experiences, and student teaching.

In contrast, social constructionists view learning as the outcome of participation in socially organized, goal-oriented activity. Learners interact with their environment, indicate to themselves what information is important, and construct its meaning through social interaction with others. Material and social resources *outside* the individual are given primacy. Learning is understood as the internalization of cognitive structures located, first, in the structures of social interactions. The process of internalization hierarchically restructures the contents of memory and cognitive processes. Teaching is conceived as arranging the distribution of learning resources so that they are accessible to learners and coordinating social interactions among learners.

Although behaviorism has exerted the most influence on education, educational theory and practice have been making a gradual turn to a social constructionist view. Based on the work of John Dewey and Lev Vygotsky, a family of theories has emerged that include sociocultural studies, distributed cognition, community of learners, situativity, and community of practice. Common threads of these theories include the ideas that (a) learning is accomplished through participation in activity that emphasizes social and environmental factors, (b) learning and development are the outcomes of culturally mediated (tool-mediated) activity, (c) learning occurs across multiple contexts, and (d) knowledge is created in communities.

Definitions

The current interest in CoP has been energized by the Institute for Research in Learning at Stanford University and the work of Jean Lave, Entenne Wenger, Ann Brown, and Joseph Campione. While the others were more interested in adult learning, Brown and Campione were interested in explaining classroom learning. Broadly conceived, the idea of CoP represents the fusion of two concepts, community and practice, to explain learning and development.

Community

The origin of community is Latin, *communitatem* and *communitas,* meaning community and fellowship, and *communis,* meaning common, public and shared by many. The meaning of *community* evolved in a variety of senses (e.g., coming together; unity of collective will; holding something in common, such as interests, goods, and identity; and bringing forth a feeling of agreement and a unified participation). Communities have often been referred to as thought communities, communities of concept users, discourse communities, speech communities, virtual communities, communities of reflective practitioners, communities of memory, and communities of practice.

The German sociologist Ferdinand Tönnies described two kinds of communities. *Gemeinschaft*

communities are informal communities constituted of informal, self-regulated collective relationships. Members, who are inducted informally, share common values, rituals, and meanings and engage in cooperative activity to attain a common goal. Examples of informal communities include collectors of baseball cards, dance clubs, little league baseball teams, community bands, and bowling leagues. Informal communities regulate themselves on the local level.

In contrast, *gesellschaft* communities involve contractually coordinated, formal relationships. Members are inducted formally. The most common idea of a formal community refers to the aggregate practices of a professional group. The group displays a sign pointing to the professional activity in which it engages, for example, the practice of law, medicine, or architecture. Communities such as departments of education, safety, health, and schools are communities legislated and funded by the public to assist in meeting needs of the public. Services and goods provided by formal communities have value and meet standards generally set by the larger professional communities to which they belong. The larger professional communities are responsible for their codification and certification and are empowered to evaluate and sanction performance.

Practices

Practices are observable actions. However, not all actions are practices. Swerving a car to miss a pothole and dashing to the sink to turn off the spigot before the sink overflows are responses to environmental stimuli rather than practices. Greeting a dinner guest by saying, "Come in! We are glad you could come!" or the habits of an actor preparing for a role are practices. Institutions, such as schools, are constituted of practices, for example, organizing students by grade levels, changing classes, assigning lockers to students, requiring students to take end-of-semester exams. Examples of teacher practices include writing interim reports, completing report cards, and convening parent-teacher conferences and back-to-school nights. As practices are repeated again and again, they come to be expected to normatively recur.

Characteristics of Community of Practice

A CoP is a cultural-historical-social space defined by a set of shared objects that glue its members together and provide direction for its central activity and by the *practices* that mediate its activity. Members of different backgrounds, professional preparation, and expertise complement each other as they enact practices to accomplish personal and collective goals. A common discourse coordinates the activity of members and brings forth the thoughts, actions, values, attitudes, and objects for the generation of practice. The discourse provides a framework for what thinking, speaking, and writing counts as meaningful, expected, and acceptable performance, and provides opportunities for members to make their knowledge and skill explicit, to argue, and to challenge each other's beliefs.

The membership of a CoP reflects levels of expertise, ranging from that of novices to experts. Categories such as old timer and newcomer are ways of organizing mutual participation rather than identifying levels of performance. The desire of novices to increase their skill levels and understandings leads to their acquisition of new practices.

There is an explicit and agreed-upon relationship between the newcomer seeking membership in a CoP and an old timer of the community. The old timer possesses a license to interpret and evaluate the performance of the newcomer in relation to the performance of practices of the CoP. In turn, the newcomers agree to be apprenticed to and evaluated by the old timer. Apprenticed participation provides members with identities, tool kits, ideologies, discourses, values, and ways of thinking that characterize one as a practicing member of the particular CoP.

Teacher Education

Teacher education is an enterprise that involves movement back and forth across contextual boundaries. Institutions of higher education and local education agencies collaborate to arrange university and classroom experiences that provide teacher education students with learning experiences across multiple contexts. The CoP of teacher education is organized to develop and implement teacher education programs and to communicate about teacher education in ways that make sense to prospective teachers, classroom teachers, researchers, policy makers, and the public. The CoP of classroom teaching is organized to provide pupils with learning experiences leading to the attainment of educational outcomes. Both CoPs collaborate to provide the route by which teacher education students acquire teaching practices.

The practice and practices of classroom teaching include most everything teachers do that contributes to their planning and interactions with students; their interactions with colleagues, administrators, and parents; and what they think, believe, and value about professional teaching. The major practices of classroom teaching are to (a) provide instruction, (b) establish meaningful relationships with students, (c) develop meaningful relationships with colleagues and administrators, (d) establish meaningful relationships with parents, (e) maintain continuous professional growth and development, (f) engage in reflection, (g) and transform practices.

Teaching practices are enacted by the application of the common declarative (what), procedural (how), and conditional (when and why) knowledge to accomplish bundles of tasks. Classroom teaching provides a good example of practices. As an illustration, the practice of providing classroom instruction is expected of teachers of every subject matter at every level of schooling. Planning is accomplished by skill in coordinating the application of declarative, procedural, and conditional knowledge necessary to accomplish a bundle of *tasks* that include (a) deciding about goals of instruction, (b) determining students' instructional needs and learner characteristics, (c) deciding what to teach and how much time to allocate for instruction, (d) identifying students' instructional levels, (e) selecting instructional materials and strategies, (f) grouping students for instruction, (g) deciding how to measure the effects of instruction, and (h) anticipating problems that might occur during the lesson and planning solutions that are held in abeyance.

An Activity System by Another Name

Teacher education and teacher education candidates' acquisition of teaching practices are the outcomes of collaboration between two CoPs, the university and a local school. The professional trajectory of prospective teachers is a gradual transition from peripheral participation to full participation in professional practices. In the beginning, core education foundations courses and early field experiences, followed by methods courses and clinical teaching experiences, and student teaching enable prospective teachers to begin their participation in both CoPs. Their professional trajectory moves on to a beginning teacher-induction period that is often supported with a teacher-support network that opens the gateway to a professional teaching career.

Yrjö Engeström argues that a CoP is actually an activity system that is organized around the shared objects of its central activity. The shared objects shape and provide direction for individual and collective activity. Figure 1 applies Engeström's model to two interacting CoPs collaborating on teacher education.

As can be seen, the mediating components of each CoP include: (a) *members,* the diverse subgroups and individuals who transform the shared objects into collectively and personally shared outcomes; (b) *objects* consist of the material, ideal, and social material that is transformed into outcomes; (c) *outcomes,* the collectively and individually expected and desired products produced and received by members; (d) *tools,* the set of instrumental and psychological tools used by members to mediate activity directed toward objects; (e) *division of labor,* the organization and roles of members and what tasks are performed, by whom, when, how, and where; (f) *rules and procedures,* the explicit and implicit rules and procedures that coordinate performances and govern interactions within, between, and among CoPs; and (g) the *community of practice,* all members who share the outcomes and values of the main activity. In addition to collaborating on teacher education, both CoPs interact with a diverse group of

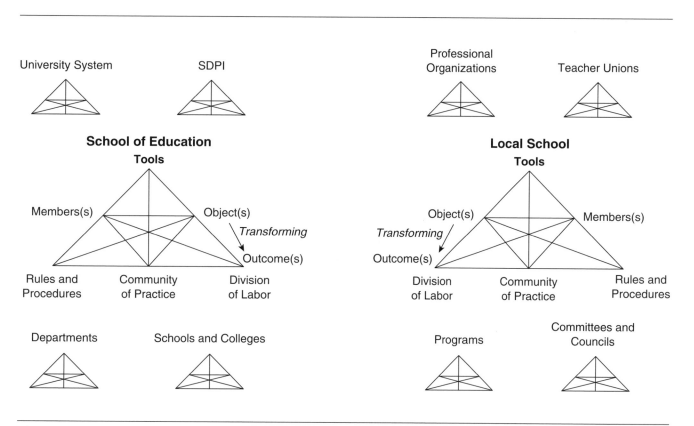

Figure 1   Interacting Communities of Practice

local and distant CoPs that affect their individual activity and their collaboration on teacher education.

Figure 2 provides a model of the teacher education program as a CoP. As can be seen, the main outcome is certified beginning teachers who can enact the practices of professional classroom teaching. The objects to be transformed into outcomes are undergraduates who seek teacher certification, information, experience, understanding, reflection, and social justice. The tool set used to mediate transformation of objects into outcomes include a conceptual framework; professional discourse; state and national assessment tools; portfolio assessment; telecommunications; digital technology; multimedia; and a database management system for analyzing data, developing reports for state and national agencies, and archiving artifacts created by undergraduates of the program. The curriculum is aligned with national and state standards. Rules and procedures are comprised of traditional academic rules, compliance with national and state

standards, performance of supervised field experiences and student teaching, and the presentation of a professional portfolio by undergraduates. The division of labor includes university and school of education faculties, departments, committees, and school of education professors who assume the role of professors-in-residence at the school site and supervise field experiences and student teaching, and cooperating classroom teachers who are trained to provide clinical supervision to apprentice undergraduates. The members of the CoP consist of all the subgroups with a central interest in or a key responsibility in the teacher education program and its outcomes.

Figure 3 models the local school collaborating with the teacher education program. Like most schools, the expected outcomes include improved basic knowledge and skills underlying performance on statewide measures of achievement and an in-service education program to improve classroom teaching. The objects to be transformed include students and

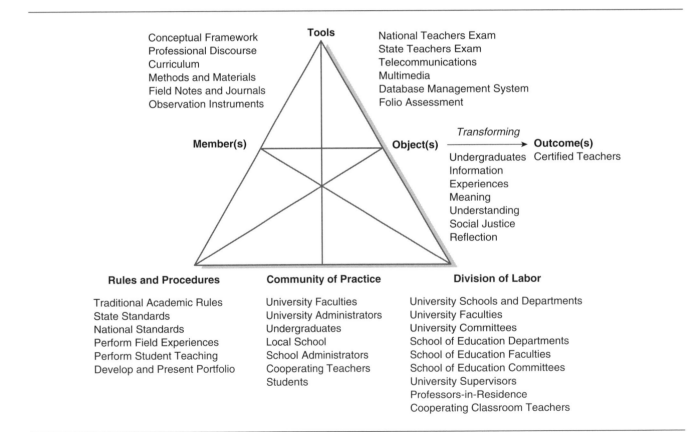

Figure 2   Teacher Education Program

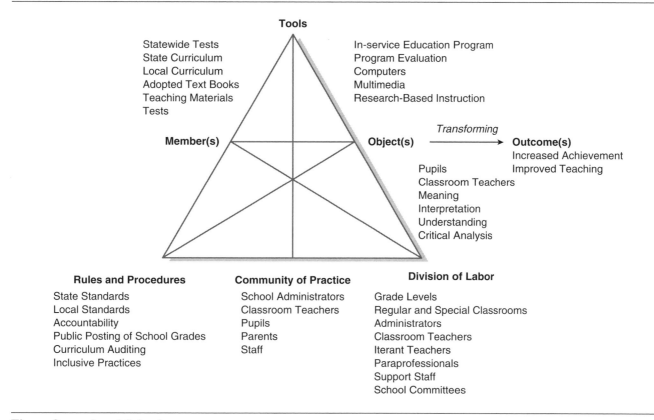

Tools

Statewide Tests
State Curriculum
Local Curriculum
Adopted Text Books
Teaching Materials
Tests

In-service Education Program
Program Evaluation
Computers
Multimedia
Research-Based Instruction

Transforming

Member(s)   **Object(s)** ⟶ **Outcome(s)**

Increased Achievement
Improved Teaching

Pupils
Classroom Teachers
Meaning
Interpretation
Understanding
Critical Analysis

Rules and Procedures

State Standards
Local Standards
Accountability
Public Posting of School Grades
Curriculum Auditing
Inclusive Practices

Community of Practice

School Administrators
Classroom Teachers
Pupils
Parents
Staff

Division of Labor

Grade Levels
Regular and Special Classrooms
Administrators
Classroom Teachers
Iterant Teachers
Paraprofessionals
Support Staff
School Committees

Figure 3   Local School

classroom teachers, meaning, interpretation, understanding, and critical analysis. The rules and procedures governing the CoP include the requirement that instruction focuses on state standards; schools receive publicly posted grades based on the performance of students on statewide achievement test performance, curriculum auditing, and inclusive practices. Tools include a system for evaluating the professional performance of teachers, statewide criterion- and norm-referenced tests, research-based instruction, curriculum, local testing program, in-service education, computers, and, multimedia.

Communities of practice and their collaboration are not tranquil and stable states. Disequilibrium and perpetual change is more like their normal state. They are riddled with problems created by the dynamics inherent in social systems. Communities of practices are constantly colliding with each other, creating endless issues that must be resolved.

Contradictions, disruptions, and breakdowns occur between the components mediating their activity and must constantly be repaired. The multiple intentions and motivations of individual and collective members who share the same resources are also problematic. The engine that transforms and sustains CoPs is fueled by motivation of their members to collectively learn, invent, and import innovations to repair breakdowns and ruptures, problems, and resolve critical issues.

In summary, the CoP concept is built on a rich intellectual tradition. The application of Engeström's activity system model to teacher education is useful for understanding the inner workings of CoPs and their collaboration in teacher preparation. The model provides a way for researchers and evaluators to analyze the contradictions, breakdowns, and disruptions and shuttle qualitative and quantitative data back and forth to explain how CoPs attain or fail to attain their outcomes as they churn through cycles of transformation and expansion and sustain themselves.

William E. Blanton, Adriana Medina,
and Paola Pilonieta

See also Teacher Preparation

Further Readings

Bellah, R., Madsen, R., Sullivan, W., Swider, A., & Tipton, S. (1985). *Habits of the heart.* New York: Harper & Row.

Brown, J. S., Collins, A., & Duguid, S. (1989). Situated cognition and the culture of learning. *Educational Researcher, 18*(1), 32–42.

Cobb, P., McClain, K., Lamberg, T. D., & Dean, C. (2003). Situating teachers' instructional practices in the institutional setting of the school and district. *Educational Researcher, 32*(6), 13–24.

Dewey, J. (1963). *Education and experience.* New York: Macmillan. (Original work published 1938)

Engeström, Y. (1987*). Learning by expanding: An activity-theoretical approach to developmental research.* Helsinki: Orienta-Konsultit.

Engeström, Y. (1991). Activity theory and individual and social transformation. *Multidisciplinary Newsletter for Activity Theory, 7/8,* 14–15.

Engeström, Y., Miettinen, R., & Punamäki, R-L. (Eds.). (1998). *Perspectives on activity theory.* Cambridge, UK: Cambridge University Press.

Franke, M. L., & Kezemi, E. (2001). Teaching as learning within a community of practice: Characterizing generative growth. In T. Wood, B. Nelson, & J. Warfield (Eds.), *Beyond classical pedagogy in elementary mathematics: The nature of facilitative teaching* (pp. 47–74). Mahwah, NJ: Lawrence Erlbaum.

Lave, J., & Wenger, E. (1990). *Situated learning: Legitimate peripheral participation.* Cambridge, UK: Cambridge University Press.

Nelson, B. C., & Hammerman, J. J. (1996). Reconceptualizing teaching: Moving toward the creation of intellectual communities of students, teachers, and teacher educators. In M. W. McLaughlin, & I. Oberman (Eds.), *Teacher learning: New policies, new practices* (pp. 3–21). New York: Teachers College Press.

Skinner, B. F. (1938). *The behavior of organisms.* New York: Appleton-Centuty-Crofts.

Skinner, B. F. (1968). *The technology of teaching.* New York: Appleton-Century-Crofts.

Thorndike, E. L. (1906). *The principles of teaching, based on psychology.* New York: A. G. Seiler.

Tönnies, F. (2001). *Community and civil society* (J. Harris, Ed.). Cambridge, UK: Cambridge University Press.

Wenger, E. (1998). *Communities of practice: Learning, meaning, and identity.* Cambridge, UK: Cambridge University Press.

Company-Sponsored Schooling

Beginning in the early nineteenth century and ending only after World War II, American companies frequently engaged in industrial welfare plans that included extraordinary investments in company-sponsored education. Industrial towns, with company houses, churches, recreation, and medical care, dotted the American landscape. Still, the most expensive and significant welfare programs involved company schools, which made a significant contribution to the history of education in the United States. They also helped provide a relatively smooth transition from an agrarian past to an industrial future. This entry recounts their history and assesses their impact.

Educating Good Workers

In 1913, a number of interested companies formed the National Association of Corporation Schools, an organization supporting the educational efforts of businesses as diverse as the Colorado Fuel and Iron in Colorado; Ellsworth Collieries and Cambria Steel Companies in New Jersey; Akron Iron in Buchtel, Ohio; the huge Piedmont and Pelzer textile manufacturing plants in South Carolina; and the Red Jacket Consolidated Coal and Coke Company in West Virginia. These and many other companies operated their schools to reduce absenteeism and turnover, increase workplace efficiency, defeat union organizing campaigns, and raise the moral quality of their workers. The children enjoyed what seemed to be an unalloyed benefit of free schooling, but it was often an education that also increased dependence on a single industry and failed to provide skills and knowledge that might have been taken elsewhere.

Many company schools began with a sponsored kindergarten program. Company and school officials recognized that education would be most effective if children were brought into the system at the earliest possible age, even in industrial sites such as coal mining that generally offered little work to women, who were free to stay home with their children. In addition, many industrialists recognized that their workplaces would later be more stable if the language barriers between immigrant workers could be removed. The kindergartens provided an opportunity for students, at the best possible age, to be immersed in English.

Following kindergarten, children often found themselves in company schools whose primary purpose was not general education but the teaching of the proper "habits of industry," deference to authority, and appreciation for efficiency on the job. These attributes became more crucial as technological and managerial advances allowed for the increasing recruitment of unskilled or semiskilled workers. Tending dirty and dangerous machines, these employees engaged in often repetitive and boring hours of work, which created an immediate need for "industrial discipline." Company officials throughout the country discovered that six or seven years in their schools could develop in children the discipline they needed to complete their work, and to do so while becoming progressively more efficient and loyal.

Seeing these advantages, hundreds of industrialists made substantial investments in company schools. They built the schools, often immediately next to the factory; set the curriculum; and hired, trained, and paid the teachers who often lived on the factory premises in boarding houses or "teacherages." In many cases, company officials also helped to write or design books that instructed students on typical school subjects, but in the context of the industry itself. Cotton mill workers, for example, learned math—but often only by calculating answers to practice problems that foreshadowed the work they would soon face in the mills. In every instance, company officials kept a close eye on expenditures and the effect their investments were having on the transformation of their employees into efficient, loyal, and docile workers.

Evaluating Outcomes

The quality of company education is difficult to assess. Still, evidence suggests that while company schooling

was quite effective in creating workers with the proper respect for work and authority, students gained very little beyond basic literacy in most cases. The schools were often poorly maintained, and in many cases the teachers had little or no training that might prepare them for their work with the students.

The teaching staff was also completely aware of its mission, and comprehensive general education was a fortunate byproduct for a few, not a goal of the schools or the companies involved. To compound the problem, company schools often operated on an abbreviated schedule—sometimes for only three or four months a year—and children were routinely pulled out of class to assist in the mines or mills if there was a sudden demand for more labor.

Finally, many students had no opportunity to pursue an education beyond the eighth grade. Companies often did not provide schools beyond this level because they needed the children to go to work, and many officials feared that education beyond the eighth grade might prepare students for jobs other than in the sponsoring industries. When students did have a chance for further education, it tended to be some form of advanced manual or vocational training that was suited for the particular industry that provided the opportunity. The huge Parker School District in Greenville, South Carolina, for example, featured a three-story cotton mill on its campus. Students were expected to be cotton millhands.

No discussion of industrial schooling can ignore the role of company libraries. Often reflecting the desire to "Americanize" immigrant workers, as well as ease the strain of industrial work and life, company libraries became a characteristic feature of many welfare plans. Some were small operations, while others held as many as 45,000 volumes and were operated out of the company schools. In most of these libraries, of course, the selection of books and magazines remained the prerogative of company officials, and most of the books appear to have been works of simple fiction or biographies, with a strong emphasis on "Horatio Alger" stories from which patrons learned that with the proper attitude toward work, thrift, and family, workers could rise from modest beginnings to prosperity. Naturally, of course, any literature that suggested a hint of support for organized labor or socialism was excluded, but even many other sources of ideas, such as *Harper's Weekly,* often failed to pass management censorship restrictions.

While most of the old company-owned schools are now gone, even today companies continue to educate by offering on-site courses in technical trades and vocational studies, while significantly supporting local community colleges as well. Through their efforts, working-class children by the millions have learned to adapt to the new demands of industrial life and work, and scores of companies have discovered the importance of specialized education for even the youngest of children.

Bart Dredge

See also Education, History of; Libraries, History of

Further Readings

Altenbaugh, R. J. (1981). "Our children are being trained like dogs and ponies": Schooling, social control, and the working class. *History of Education Quarterly, 21,* 213–222.

Brandes, S. D. (1976). *American welfare capitalism, 1880–1940.* Chicago: University of Chicago Press.

Cressman, L. S. (1924). The corporation school: A suggestion concerning education in industry. *Social Forces, 2,* 208–211.

COMPARATIVE AND INTERNATIONAL EDUCATION

The field of comparative and international education has a long history, although some argue that it is still in search of a distinct identity. This entry describes the individuals, organizations, and issues that have shaped the field, creating the problem or advantage of its multiple identities.

Historical Roots

In most North American and European literature, the field of comparative and international education is traced to the work of Parisian Marc-Antoine Jullien (1775–1848). Sometimes referred to as the "father of comparative education," he compiled data about education across Europe and developed a plan to promote international data collection and analysis to guide educational reform, that is, to address the problem that the physical, moral, and intellectual dimensions of schooling do not meet the needs of young people or their nations. Jullien developed a method of collecting statistics through distribution of a questionnaire to government ministries that became the compiling descriptive statistics by contemporary international agencies, such as UNESCO and OECD.

In Asia, however, the field is said to have emerged during the Han Dynasty (2006 BCE to 220 CE) and the Tang Dynasty (618–906 CE) in China, given that educational ideas and practices were borrowed and lent across nations in the region. Moreover, the scholarly study of education in other countries was initiated in 1849 by Xue Funcheng, who delineated the educational system in four countries to inform Chinese educational policy in line with broader moves to reestablish economic prosperity and political stability in the wake of China's defeat by Western forces in the first opium war in 1840.

The distinction in origins of the field is not only one of geography but also one of definition and identity—that is, what constitutes activity in and who should be considered a member of comparative and international education.

Traditions and Identity Sources

One source of identity for the field involves "travelers," who wrote up more or less systematic and in-depth "tales" of their visits to one or more countries with the intent to encourage compatriots to "borrow" the good ideas and practices they observed. An American, Horace Mann, would be a good example of this type of effort, focusing on European societies during the first half of the nineteenth century. Similarly, Englishmen Matthew Arnold and Michael Sadler and Russian Leo Tolstoy traveled abroad to observe educational systems in other countries and document their findings at home. Sadler's writing was distinct, in that he advocated against borrowing organizational and methodological educational elements from other country systems, arguing that such elements could not be divorced from their local context for use in another country context.

A second identity source for the field is associated with scholars based in Europe and North America during the first half of the twentieth century—Nicholas Hans, Isaac Kandel, Friedrich Schneider, and Robert Ulrich. They—as well as Ruth Hayhoe and Edmund King in the second half of the twentieth century—employed an idealist, humanist approach to investigate ideas and forms of education across countries in an attempt to illuminate historical trends in school systems within societal contexts. Their concern was less with borrowing educational ideas than with understanding how over time education systems are connected to societies in which they are located.

A third identity source is that associated with C. Arnold Anderson, Mary Jean Bowman, George Bereday, William Cummings, Max Eckstein, Erwin Epstein, and Harold Noah, who styled themselves as practitioners of the (social) science of comparative education. For them, the purpose of comparative education is to develop lawlike, quantitative generalizations about the relationships among different input and output variables related to education. Their perspective is often described as structural functionalism, with its faith in the application of empirical research and scientific methods to the study of education and the social sciences in general. Often such research has sought to illuminate how older and newer societies develop and modernize along a single continuum of stages.

In contrast to the structural functionalist perspectives of the "scientists," another identity source is associated with those who investigate education and society relations from a conflict perspective, a trend that developed within comparative education initially in the late 1960s. Robert Arnove, Martin Carnoy, A. H. Halsey, Gail Kelly, Vandra Masemann, John Ogbu, Nelly Stromquist, and Mathew Zachariah sought to document—and critique—how educational organizations, content, and processes functioned to preserve unequal power and wealth relations across ethnic, gender, and social class lines within countries and between core and periphery countries internationally. In addition to the kinds of inequality research undertaken within the

United States by social foundations scholars, scholarship within comparative and international education has sought to counter the thesis that all nation states "develop" or "modernize' along the lines of Western states. Moreover, these scholars argue and seek to document how the implementation of "Western" educational systems may contribute to reproducing economic and political underdevelopment and dependence on (Western) industrialized states. Finally, some of these scholars, notably Masemann, argued for the use of more qualitative methods of research, in order to examine school processes within the school and classroom, which could not be generated through large-scale, quantitative studies.

Postmodernism and poststructuralism have also informed the work and identity of comparative educationists. For instance, Rolland Paulston's "social cartography" project during the latter part of his career serves to illustrate this strand of the field. Paulston, along with Esther Gottlieb and other colleagues, sought to "map" the range of ideas and authors in the field. They and others reflecting a postmodernist or poststructuralist (e.g., Anthony Welch and Thomas Popkewitz) identity have sought to avoid privileging any particular theoretical or methodological metanarratives or the realities purported to describe and analyze through these narratives.

Another identity source for comparative and international educators is associated with the "problems" approach to comparative education and, at least in theory, what some would term international education activities. Brian Holmes draws on John Dewey and Karl Popper in articulating his approach to comparative education work: problem analysis; policy formulation; identification, description, and weighting of relevant factors in a given context; and anticipation, prediction, and monitoring the outcomes of policies.

While international education practitioners are also often informed *by* one or more of the other perspectives in comparative education, their activity appears to resonate best with Holmes's problem approach. These practitioners are those that work for bilateral or multilateral assistance organizations (the United States Agency for International Development, the Japanese International Cooperation Agency, UNESCO, World

Bank, etc.) or as consultants to such organizations, either individually or through a variety or "firms" which bid on contracts and grants from the international agencies. They do not mainly engage in scholarship to illuminate or critique educational phenomena, but rather seek to adapt (with greater or lesser degrees of caution) lessons learned in other countries to the contextual reality of another country. The more applied nature of their work does not prevent us from recognizing comparative education and international education as closely connected, "fraternal or Siamese twins," as David Wilson has characterized the two subfields.

Organizational Structures

The World Council of Comparative Education Societies (WCCES), which was established in 1970, has operational relations as an NGO with UNESCO, and (in 2007) included thirty-five constituent national, regional, and language-based comparative education societies as constituent members. National organizational members of the WCCES are from Argentina, Australia and New Zealand, Brazil, Britain, Canada, China, Cuba, Czech Republic, Egypt, Germany, Greece, Hungary, India, Israel, Italy, Japan, Kazakhstan, Korea, Mexico, Netherlands, Philippines, Poland, Russia, Spain, and the United States. A major vehicle for promoting research and policy dialogue internationally is the WCCES' triennial World Congress, which has been held in Africa (South Africa), Asia (Australia, Japan, and Korea), Europe (e.g., Bosnia and Herzegovina, Czech Republic, France, Switzerland, United Kingdom), Latin America (Brazil and Cuba), and North America (Canada) since 1970.

One of its constituent organizations of the WCCES is the Comparative and International Education Society (CIES), a U.S.-based organization with a very international membership. Founded as the Comparative Education Society in 1956 and renamed in 1969, CIES grew out of efforts to organize international study tours for U.S. educators and to improve and expand academic programs and scholarship in the field. Its journal, the *Comparative Education Review*, and its annual conference attract considerable attention, participation, and recognition among comparative education scholars, education policy makers, and international education

practitioners, many of whom are also members of other national, regional, and language-based comparative and international education societies.

As is the case in any field, comparative and international educators publish their work in a variety of books and journals. And while their work appears in more general social science and educational research journals, some of the most important work is made available through the following specialized journals (with the organizational base noted): *Asia Pacific Education Review; Canadian and International Education; Comparative Education; Comparative Education Review* (U.S. CIES); *Compare: A Journal of Comparative Education* (British Association of Comparative and International Education)*; Current Issues in Comparative Education; Globalization, Societies and Education; International Journal of Educational Development; International Review of Education* (UNESCO International Bureau of Education); *Korean Comparative Education Society Journal; Prospects: Quarterly Review of Education* (UNESCO Institute of Education); *Research in Comparative and International Education;* and *World Studies in Education.* These tend to attract authors and readers with overlapping, though somewhat different, identities in the field of comparative and international education.

The following universities in the United States are among the most recognized for offering doctoral programs that prepare comparative and international educators, although not all of them have specialized programs with either comparative or international in their names: Chicago; Florida State; Harvard; Indiana; Maryland; Massachusetts-Amherst; Michigan; Michigan State; Pennsylvania State; Stanford; State University of New York at Albany and at Buffalo; Teachers College, Columbia; and University of California at Los Angeles. And a small sampling of institutions offering similar programs in other countries includes: Ain Shams University (Cairo, Egypt); Beijing Normal University; German Institute for International Educational Research (Frankfurt); Comparative Education Research Center, Hong Kong University; Institute of Education, University of London; International Institute of Education, University of Stockholm; Ontario Institute for the Study of

Education, University of Toronto; Seoul National University; University of Havana; University of Paris; and University of Tokyo.

Comparative and international educators are employed in various national government agencies, including units of ministries or departments of education. In addition, they work within—or serve as consultants to—a variety of bilateral "international development" agencies, such as the U.S. Agency for International Development, the Japanese Agency for International Cooperation and Assistance, and the Swedish International Development Agency. Other contexts for activities that contribute to and draw on knowledge in the field are multilateral organizations, for example those associated with the UN system (UNESCO; UNICEF; UNDP; Institute of Education, Hamburg; International Bureau of Education, Geneva; International Institute of Educational Planning, Paris) as well as regionally framed organizations (European Commission, Organization of African Unity, Organization of American States, Organization for Economic Cooperation and Development). In addition, an increasing role in shaping educational policy and in funding international education projects is played by (regional/global) financial institutions (African Development Bank, Asian Development Bank, Inter-American Development Bank, International Monetary Fund, World Bank, and the World Trade Organization).

Major Topics

Besides a focus on education and national economic development and the status and work of teachers, comparative and international educators have developed scholarship in relation to the following topics: factors affecting achievement, inequalities in access and attainment in education, educational reform, democratizing education and educating for democratic citizenship, and world systems/globalization. Each of these is discussed briefly in turn.

A variety of individuals, organizations, and projects have focused on documenting and seeking to explain differences in academic achievement within and across countries, using large-scale, quantitative studies. Perhaps the most important contribution to this literature is the work organized through the International

Association for the Evaluation of Education Achievement (IEA) initiative. Having maintained a strong focus on mathematics and science, these studies involving teams of researchers from some "developing" and more "developed" countries have also examined the issues in literacy and civic education. The objective has been to provide cross-national data that enable scholars to better understand how social and educational variables (e.g., curriculum content, teacher qualifications, teacher behavior, and student characteristics) are related and inform policy debates in individual countries and internationally on how to enhance the achievement of various groups of students.

Related to the issues addressed by IEA, but usually pursued more by researchers espousing conflict perspectives, are empirical studies and policy and curriculum analyses that seek to investigate the degree to which and why various groups (females, ethnic minorities, and lower social classes) are less "successful" in gaining access to and attaining credentials from public and private schools and universities. The theoretical perspectives and the quantitative and qualitative methodological traditions that inform this work would be familiar to those who do such work in the social and cultural foundations of education focused on the United States, but an important difference—and potentially a real advantage—is that the findings are compared across societal contexts. This allows sometimes for firmer generalizations but also requires more complex and qualified accounts, such as when measures of socioeconomic status used in industrialized countries are not related to attainment in less industrialized societies. When done well such work considers carefully the local, national, and global contexts in which the quantitative and qualitative data are collected and analyzed.

Both comparative education researchers and international education practitioners are interested in the conditions and processes that constrain or enable various kinds of "reform" in education. Such reforms might concern how the system is organized (e.g., decentralization or privatization), how teachers and administrators are prepared and help to develop their capacities, the degree and forms of community participation, the nature of curriculum and examination systems, and how teachers and students interact in classrooms. Analyses of education reform tend to be framed from functionalist or conflict perspectives, with the respective approach tending to highlight the evolutionary/consensual or the conflict-laden and dialectical nature of the reform process.

Thus, the work is not unlike historical and sociological analyses of education reform in the United States, although a range of societies are included in the analysis of national case studies. What is quite different, however, is the focus on international relations in the reform of education, again differentiated by functionalist and conflict perspectives. Here the question is how more "developed" or "powerful" countries "lend" or "impose" reforms on less-"developed" or "powerful" countries. These issues are also of great interest to international education practitioners. Not only do they have to determine what policies and practices should be recommended or mandated as "conditionalities" as part of loans as well as technical assistance, or training projects. They also have to deal with the politics within international organizations and societies regarding the appropriateness of such transnational activities.

In recent years comparative and international educators have given more attention to what has been labeled as the "democratization" of education. Partly, this reflects scholars, policy makers, and practitioners appropriating "democratic" terminology to refer to long-standing concerns. For instance, equalizing access to and achievement through schooling are now sometimes referenced as democratization. Increasing participation in school affairs by students, parents, business owners, and other community members (both in terms of the number and variety of people involved and in the degree of decision-making authority) is also discussed under the rubric of democratization of education. A focus related to democratization concerns how education contributes to socializing students to become effective citizens within democratic societies. In this regard, the studies and projects broaden the conception of the purpose of education beyond producing human capital (economic roles) to include constructing citizens (political roles). For instance, the 2002 IEA study of civic education across sixteen countries examined the relationship between the curriculum, the teaching methods, and what students learn that informs their potential to participate in society as citizens. More focused studies of civic and citizenship education across and within cultures have sought to determine how political and social forces may influence what and how citizens are taught and the nature of relevant extracurricular, but school-based, activities. Such work has been undertaken both in long-standing "democracies" and in nations (including many former Soviet republics and Central and Eastern European societies) that have more recently moved toward Western democratic structures and procedures.

Finally, comparative and international educators (e.g., Robert Arnove, Nicholas Burbules and Carlos Torres, Mark Ginsburg, John Meyer and Michael Hannan, and Nelly Stromquist and Karen Monkman) have focused their attention on the world system and globalization. They have addressed economic, political, technological, and cultural forms of globalization, raising questions as to whether local and national education systems are responding effectively (whether proactively or reactively) to these dynamics as well as how education promotes understanding and actions that shape the nature of globalization and its impact on different societies. In addition, comparative and international educators have focused on whether the globalization of education policies and practices represents a convergent and/or divergent process as well as whether such developments are viewed positively and/or negatively by international agency representatives, government officials, and citizens in different regions and nations. Increasingly, "globalization" has found its way into official documents of national governments and international (bilateral and multilateral) organizations, and thus has become part of the landscape in which international education practitioners work.

It should be clear that there are multiple identities possible within the field of comparative and international education. While some might view this as a weakness of an academic or professional field, we view this as a sign of strength, enabling scholars, policy makers, and practitioners to find space and contribute based on their own multiple roles and identities.

Mark B. Ginsburg and Alison Price-Rom

See also Globalization and Education

Further Readings

Arnove, R., & Torres, C. (Eds.). (1999). *Comparative education: The dialectic of the global and the local.* Lanham, MD: Rowman & Littlefield.

Burbules, N., & Torres, C. A. (Eds.). (2000). *Globalization and education: Critical perspectives.* New York: Routledge.

Cookson, P., Sadovnik, A., & Semel, S. (1992). *International handbook of educational reform.* Westport, CT: Greenwood Press.

Ginsburg, M. (Ed.). (1991). *Understanding educational reform in global context: Economy, ideology and the state.* New York: Garland.

Hawkins, J., & La Belle, T. (Eds.). (1985). *Education and intergroup relations: An international perspective.* New York: Praeger.

Hayhoe, R. (1996). *China's universities, 1895–1995: A century of cultural conflict.* New York: Garland.

Holmes, B. (1965). *Problems in education: A comparative approach.* London: Routledge & Kegan Paul.

Kazamias, A. M., & Schwartz, K. (1977). State of the art [Special issue]. *Comparative Education Review, 42*(2/3).

King, E. (1979). *Other schools and ours: comparative studies for today* (5th ed.). New York: Holt.

Kubow, P., & Fossum, P. (2003). *Comparative education in international context.* Columbus, OH: Merrill/Prentice Hall.

Limage, L. (Ed.). (1997). *Democratizing education and educating democratic citizens: International and historical perspectives.* New York: RoutledgeFalmer.

Masemann, V., Bray, M., & Manzon, M. (Eds.). (2007). *Common interests, uncommon goals: Histories of World Council of Comparative Education Societies and its members.* Hong Kong: Comparative Education Research Centre, Hong Kong University.

Meyer, J., & Hannan, M. (1979). *National development and the world system: Educational, economic, and political change, 1950–70.* Chicago: University of Chicago Press.

Noah, H. (1998). The use and abuse of comparative education. In H. Noah & M. Eckstein (Eds.), *Doing comparative education: Three decades of collaboration* (pp. 57–67). Hong Kong: Comparative Education Research Center, University of Hong Kong.

Ogbu, J. (1978). *Minority education and caste: The American system in cross-cultural perspective.* New York: Academic Press.

Paulston, R. (Ed.) (1996). *Social cartography: Mapping ways of seeing social and educational change.* New York: Garland.

Postlethwaite, T. N. (Ed.). (1995). *International encyclopedia of national systems of education.* New York: Pergamon Press.

Schriewer, J. (Ed.). (2003). *Discourse formation in comparative education.* Frankfurt am Main: Peter Lang.

Steiner-Khamsi, G. (2004). *The global politics of educational borrowing and lending.* New York: Teachers College Press.

Stromquist, N., & Monkman, K. (Eds.). (2000). *Globalization and education: Integration and contestation across cultures.* New York: Rowman & Littlefield.

Tatto, M. T. (Ed.). (2007). *Reforming teaching globally.* Oxford, UK: Symposium Books.

Torney-Purta, J., Schwille, J., & Amadeo, J. (1999). *Civic education across countries: Twenty-four national case studies from the IEA Civic Education Project.* Amsterdam: International Association for the Evaluation of Educational Achievement (IEA).

Wilson, D. (1994). Comparative and international education: Fraternal or Siamese twins? A preliminary genealogy of our twin fields. *Comparative Education Review, 38*(4), 449–486.

COMPENSATORY EDUCATION

During the 1960s, a new approach called *compensatory education* was created to support access for academically underprepared and economically disadvantaged students. Compensatory education focuses on the individual student and the living and learning environment in which the student interacts. Proponents of this approach charge that environmental conditions, often induced by poverty, are responsible for the poor academic achievement of students. Common activities of this approach include: academic preparatory work, supplemental learning enrichment activities, higher parental involvement in school, and systemic changes in the school learning environment. During the early 1960s, national civil rights legislation established the Office of Compensatory Education within the U.S. Office of Education.

Elementary and Secondary Education

Federal legislation through the Elementary and Secondary Education Act and amended by the No Child Left Behind Act created a family of compensatory elementary and secondary education programs. These programs include: Head Start, Early Reading

First, Education for Homeless Children and Youth, Even Start Family Literacy, and Title I. Title I (now called Chapter 1) is the largest of these programs. It provides financial support through state and local education agencies to schools with either high numbers or high percentages of economically disadvantaged children.

More than 50,000 schools serving about 12 million students across the United States use Title I funds. If 40 percent or more of the children in the school meet federal poverty guidelines, a school may offer Title I services to all students, regardless of their economic background. Some schools focus on providing supplemental reading and mathematics instruction. Other schools focus on extending the learning environment and providing preschool, after-school, and summer bridge programs. Parental involvement is a key component.

Transition and Postsecondary Education

Concurrent with development of the aforementioned programs, compensatory education programs were created for eligible postsecondary students and those who desired to attend college. Among its provisions, the Economic Opportunity Act of 1964 and later the Higher Education Act of 1965 expanded access to higher education for disadvantaged students in two ways: TRIO programs and need-based financial aid for economically disadvantaged students (Pell and Perkins Grant programs).

TRIO refers to the original "trio" of programs (Upward Bound, Talent Search, and Student Support Services) funded by the federal government at hundreds of colleges to encourage access and success of previously disenfranchised students. Eligibility was limited to students who met one or more of the following criteria: neither parent completed college, were economically disadvantaged, and/or had an eligible disability. Common grant features included academic enrichment activities, career counseling, cultural enrichment activities, and setting high expectations for college graduation. Additional TRIO programs created later were Talent Search, Student Support Services, Educational Opportunity Centers, and the Ronald E. McNair Post-baccalaureate Achievement Program.

David R. Arendale

See also Civil Rights Movement; Economic Inequality

Further Readings

Frost, J., & Rowland, G. (1971). *Compensatory education: The acid test of American education.* Dubuque, IA: William C. Brown.

Ntuk-Iden, M. (1978). *Compensatory education.* Westmead, UK: Teakfield Limited.

Reimers, F. (2000). *Unequal schools, unequal chances: The challenges to equal opportunity in the Americas.* Cambridge, MA: Harvard University Press.

COMPLEXITY THEORY

Complexity theory, along with fractal geometry and chaos theory, is one of the "new sciences" that came to prominence in the latter part of the twentieth century. These three fields contribute to a new awareness that nature in its organization is complex, fractaled, and turbulent. This is quite different from the past (modernist) view that nature is simple, linear, and stable in form and organization. The new theory and its application to education are described in this entry.

Order Out of Disorder

Isaac Newton, in the seventeenth century, believed nature to be "pleased with simplicity" and "conformable to herself." Charles Darwin brought forward a different view, one wherein nature is capricious or random in its development. "Chance caught on a wing" is the way one scientist has phrased evolutionary development. In their study of nature, contemporary scientists, using the mathematical tools of nonlinear dynamics and the power of supercomputers, posit that nature is in form *self-organizing* and that the disorder observed in the cosmos, universe, and world is really an "orderly disorder." Models of this "stable" disorder are found in avalanches, economic systems, evolutionary development, galactic births and deaths, human bodily and social systems, and population dynamics—to name but a few. What looks and appears disorderly is really a new type of order, an order emerging from (and even embedded within) disorder.

The implications of this for education are immense and radical. Up to the present day, education, in its forms of curriculum design and instructional strategies, has been premised on a simple design, directly transferable. To think of learning, not as a passive, receivable act—with the mind a *tabula rasa* imprinted by teaching—but as an interactive, dynamic, and self-organizing process challenges past (and even present) methods of syllabi design, lesson plans, and instructional strategies.

Self-Organization and Emergence

Self-organization, whether in computer simulations, in ecological, environmental, information-processing models, or in social interactions is the defining characteristic of all complexity research and study. Whereas imposed organization—be it institutional (including education), political, or religious/philosophical (God as progenitor of the West's *Great Chain of Being*)—is always top-down, self-organization *emerges from* an interactive base of particulars. Life itself at the cellular, species/human, and social levels is an example of such a self-organizing system. As particulars or events interact, they do (under certain conditions) form a system: an interactive, dynamic, creating system. Complex networks arise from simpler networks, as in evolutionary theory; or conversely, simple, unifying networks emerge from complex interactions, as in galactic order, human bodily systems, or population dynamics.

Self-organization refers not to an individual self becoming consciously organized but rather to a dynamical system—sometimes large, sometimes small—organizing (even transforming) itself in particular phases of its development. Such a system, often labeled antichaotic, existent in all natural sciences but most prominent in the biological/living sciences, maintains its stability even as the interactions within itself and between itself and its environment proliferate.

Complex *adaptive* systems is another phrase used here, to indicate the system's overall ability to maintain order as events or particulars within the system experience change. Bodily immune systems or neurological systems are examples of this—as cells both die and regenerate, the system maintains its overall harmonious functioning. At a *critical* point, though—far from equilibrium or the system's center, out near "the edge of chaos"—a small perturbation or occurrence leads to a major, transformative change. In this view, chaos is embedded within complexity.

Evolution here is not simply the result of random or chance occurrences but is rather a natural, interactional, complex process. Organization emerges, freely and spontaneously—"order for free"—from what seems to be chaos. For those complexity theorists studying evolutionary development, "natural selection" is not the one and only way species evolve. Rather, development is stochastic, combining elements of randomization with those of natural emergence. Such emergence (arising more *from* than *toward*) is sporadic, spontaneous, and unpredictable (although deterministic, at least in a probabilistic sense).

Implications for Teaching

The educational implications of this emergent or self-organizing process are numerous and radical; most significant is the recognition of order emerging from interactions—it need not be imposed. In fact, imposition may well be a hindrance to development. If development is indeed a stochastic process—interactions among elements or events themselves interacting with random external events—then the educational design of curricula, teaching strategies, syllabi, or lesson plans needs to be rethought.

At the very least, flexibility needs to be built into the structure of curricular design and teaching strategies. Even better would be syllabi or lesson plans that emerge, a real challenge to any educator. "Teachable moments" would now be not a surprise but expected. Here, the abilities a teacher needs to possess go beyond the skills and methods usually offered in teacher preparation or school mentoring courses and situations. Further, to guide a situation toward a far-from-equilibrium situation—away from stability, toward "the edge of chaos," without going over that edge into an abyss—requires a sense of feeling for the situation not present in current teacher-centered (or even student-centered) designs. Situations become their own managers and guides, with teachers (and students) playing important but nondominating roles. Ambiguity, uncertainty, imbalance, chance, probability all take on importance as issues, not to avoid, but to utilize.

All the foregoing represent a major shift in curricular design, instructional strategies, and teacher-preparation courses and experiences. This shift is away from preset goals, experiences prechosen to mirror those goals, experiences organized to achieve the preset goals, and assessment as to how the preset goals have or have not been achieved. The shift is toward a curriculum *rich* in problematics, *recursive* in its (nonlinear) organization, *relational* in its structure, and *rigorous* in its application.

Wm. E. Doll, Jr.

See also Chaos Theory

Further Readings

Bak, P. (1996). *How nature works*. New York: Springer-Verlag.

Careri, G. (1984). *Order and disorder in matter* (K. Jarratt, Trans.). Menlo Park, CA: Benjamin/Cummings.

Davis, B., & Sumara, D. (2006). *Complexity and education*. Mahwah, NJ: Lawrence Erlbaum.

Doll, W., Fleener, M. J., Trueit, D., & St. Julien, J. (2005). *Chaos, complexity, curriculum, and culture*. New York: Peter Lang.

Fleener, M. J. (2002). *Curriculum dynamics*. New York: Peter Lang.

Kauffman, S. (1995). *At home in the universe*. New York: Oxford University Press.

Kauffman, S. (2000). *Investigations*. New York: Oxford University Press.

Lansing. J. S. (2003). Complex adaptive systems. *Annual Review of Anthropology, 32,* 183–204.

Lovejoy, A. (1965). *The great chain of being*. New York: Harper & Row. (Original work published 1936)

Prigogine, I. (1997). *The end of certainty*. New York: Free Press.

Prigogine I., & Stengers, I. (1984). *Order out of chaos*. New York: Bantam.

Waldrop, M. (1992). *Complexity*. New York: Simon & Schuster.

Wolfram. S. (2002). *A new kind of science*. Winnipeg: Wolfram Media.

COMPREHENSIVE HIGH SCHOOLS

The comprehensive high school is a unique product of efforts intended to serve the educational needs of a modern democratic society. Comprehensive high schools are designed to educate students and prepare them to adequately navigate employment, the duties of citizenship, and other facets of adult life. In comprehensive high schools, students have access to a vast array of course offerings (e.g., foreign language, home economics) and extracurricular activities (e.g., sports, clubs) resulting in a diploma. The diploma serves as a standard, signifying minimal competence to enter postsecondary education or to obtain competitive employment. This entry discusses the development of comprehensive high schools and their current configuration.

Historical Background

For a number of years, secondary education was confined to particular geographic areas (i.e., urban centers). The creation of secondary education, particularly high schools, was a reflection of progress in American society. Limited options for children meant little to no education after four or five years of instruction in the most basic of skills. Many children were not exposed to any formal schooling, leaving many illiterate. In response to this great need for formal education especially in large urban areas, comprehensive high schools were designed with the intent of teaching children not only basic skills for labor, but just as importantly, skills in citizenship.

The modern, large comprehensive high school can be dated to the ideas espoused by James Conant. Conant was primarily interested in the structure of high schools (e.g., four grades) and their organization (e.g., adequate course offerings to prepare children for employment). After assessing the landscape of high schools, Conant came to the conclusion that high schools had to be bigger to better serve students. This notion had its basis in several ideas about how secondary schools should operate, one of which included the lack of efficiency of smaller schools, which could not offer students a wide assortment of courses.

The notion that high schools had to be bigger has been confused and resulted in schools well beyond the notions of the earliest educators responsible for developing secondary education. In the early to mid part of the twentieth century, high schools enrolled small numbers of students (e.g., 100 to 250). As high schools grew and enrolled more than 400 students, many perceived these schools as too big and perhaps insensitive to the needs of students. In spite of the surrounding controversy, comprehensive high schools did grow much larger than 400 students and some have grown to enroll more than 5,000 students.

The combination of Conant's work and a burning desire to improve the educational lot of the greater society served as the backdrop for the development of modern secondary education. This movement began shortly after the turn of the last century with a report from a committee appointed by the National Education Association. In 1918, the *Cardinal Principles* report delineated seven guiding principles for secondary education. These principles included: (1) health, (2) command of fundamental processes, (3) worthy home-membership, (4) vocation, (5) citizenship, (6) worthy use of leisure, and (7) ethical charter. The principles were intended to be broad, to ensure that a substantial differentiated curriculum could be developed and implemented as a way to include the large numbers of students who were entering secondary school after World War I.

It is no mistake that almost any course of study could be included under any one of the seven principles. Conversations about the prevalence of varying intelligence among individuals (as described by psychologists like G. Stanley Hall) and the declining influence of parents (as described by philosophers like John Dewey) were among several factors that influenced educators to create large high schools that could accommodate the variability of the population. A comprehensive system of secondary education was necessary to prepare citizens to make meaningful contributions to society

(e.g., uphold democratic ideals) and prepare students to fill the many positions in the growing factory-based industries (e.g., automobile manufacturing).

Today's High School

High schools have long been conceived of as the pinnacle of American education, serving as an "equalizer" for society's children. The question surrounding the legitimacy of this task as well as the realistic prospect of ever providing adequate preparation for the majority of American children has been a point of contention dating back to the first days of large comprehensive high schools. The right to compulsory education is a well-established part of American history, and the delivery of that education has evolved from the limited focus on vocational tasks to include the wide array of curricular fields and other social services.

The American high school as we know it today, tuition-free, based in a larger school district, with four grades, and dividing time and space into major and minor courses, has existed for the last 150 years. Comprehensive high schools have a distinctive "presence" in most communities. Many members of the community are proud of the "look and feel" of the high school and express this civic pride with clothing and slogans; at times, they provide financial resources to support the sport teams or clubs. Large comprehensive high schools can serve thousands of students (e.g., 1,500 or more depending on the school district and geographic location) and hold fast to strict curricular divisions, intended to provide academic and vocational education.

A diverse mix of students, educational professionals, and other community members come together to provide educational experiences highlighted by a focus on preparation for participation in the local community as well as the greater society. Many of the most highly revered ideals have been incorporated into the secondary curriculum to ensure that children are exposed to some of the most sacred ideas about the American way of life. These ideals have been passed on within the classrooms, hallways, and auditoriums of large comprehensive high schools.

The increased size of high schools has coincided with a growing number of children "who fall through the cracks." It is possible that the students described in this way could have benefited from a number of different services available in schools (e.g., remedial instruction or family support services). In order to serve a large number of students with varying degrees of need, it is necessary to create schools with an unwieldy infrastructure, leading to an ironic turn of events—students left without any services.

Charles Dukes

See also Small Schools Movement

Further Readings

Kliebard, H. M. (2004). *The struggle for the American curriculum, 1893–1958* (3rd ed.). New York: RoutledgeFalmer.

McDonald, J. P. (2004). High school in the twenty-first century: Managing the core dilemma. In F. M. Hammack (Ed.), *The comprehensive high school today* (pp. 26–44). New York: Teacher College Press.

Schubert, W. H. (1986). *Curriculum: Perspective, paradigm, and possibility.* New York: Macmillian.

Sizer, T. R. (1984). *Horace's compromise: The dilemma of the American high school.* Boston: Houghton Mifflin.

COMPULSORY EDUCATIONAL ATTENDANCE LAWS

Compulsory education requires by law that all children receive some form of schooling. Compulsory education is largely seen as being a universal good for the child, as well as the society in which he or she lives. Less often, it is considered to be a means by which the state can exercise control and influence over its citizens. This entry looks at the history of this practice, relevant court rulings, and critiques.

Historical Background

The first compulsory education law was passed by the Massachusetts Bay Colony in 1642. The law removed control of education from the clergy and placed it under the direction of citizens or "selectmen" of the colony.

It required parents and craftsmen or masters to make sure that their children were able to read. In 1647 a general school law, known as "The Old Deluder Satan Act," was passed requiring towns in the colony to establish schools. The law took its name from its first line, which made reference to Satan. It was based on the belief that children had to be able to read the Bible and other religious texts in order to overcome his influence.

The first state in the United States to enact a compulsory education law was Massachusetts in 1852. Extremely limited in scope, the law required that children under fifteen years of age could only be employed if they had received a minimum of three months of schooling prior to their employment. Compulsory education laws were proposed in Illinois as early as 1838, but were only first enacted in 1883. The last state to require compulsory education was Mississippi in 1918.

Compulsory education at the high school level became widespread throughout the United States during the Great Depression. The shortage of jobs available to youth made schools a good place for them to be instead of out on the streets where they would compete with adults for scarce jobs and potentially become unruly. In this context, schools took on a greater custodial function—one that they still maintain to a large degree today.

Court Rulings

Whether or not the state has the right to compel students to attend only public schools was decided by the Supreme Court in the case of *Pierce v. Society of Sisters* (1925). In 1922, Oregon passed a law requiring all children between the ages of eight and sixteen to attend public schools. The idea was to provide all children with a uniform education subject to state control. It was argued that Oregon had an interest in making sure that its future citizens were educated sufficiently to hold jobs, to vote, and to understand and appreciate "American values." The law had the effect of closing down all private education—in particular, Oregon's Catholic schools.

It was eventually overturned on the basis that it interfered with the rights of parents to direct the upbringing and education of their own children. The decision did not interfere with the state's right to regulate, in terms of minimal standards, the teaching and content of the curriculum. Thus, it could require that teachers in a private school have a certain minimal level of education and that even a private school curriculum include subjects such as civics and American history.

In the 1972 Supreme Court case of *Yoder v. Wisconsin,* the issue of family rights and compulsory education was addressed once again. In the action, Amish parents maintained that the attendance of their children in schools beyond the eighth-grade level threatened their survival as a religious group. This was based on the Amish belief that knowledge received from books represents a distraction from the message God provides in the Bible and that attendance at school beyond a certain point would divert Amish children from the beliefs of their community.

The Court maintained that both the beliefs of the child and the parents needed to be taken into account, and various accommodations were set in place that allowed the Amish to continue to follow their religious beliefs. School attendance beyond eighth grade would not be required—thus contradicting the general rule that children attend school until the age of sixteen. In this context, the decision of the court took into account basic principles of religious freedom—specifically the rights guaranteed under the Establishment Clause of the Constitution.

The idea of universal and compulsory education for all children was reinforced on an international basis when in 1948 the United Nations issued the Universal Declaration of Human Rights, in which it called for compulsory elementary education for all children. In April 2000, 1,100 delegates from 164 countries reaffirmed this principle at the UNESCO-sponsored World Education Forum in Dakar by adopting the Dakar Framework for Action, which established the goal of free compulsory and high-quality education for all children by the year 2015.

Critiques

There have been a number of useful systematic critiques of compulsory schooling since the 1960s, including

Paul Goodman's *Compulsory Mis-Education* (1962), which argued that public schools represented a "compulsory trap"; Ivan Illich's *Deschooling Society* (1970), which called for the elimination of traditional schools through a process of deschooling; and John Holt's *Escape from Childhood: The Needs and Rights of Children* (1974), which declared that children should have the same rights as adults and not be compelled to attend institutions such as schools if they did not wish to do so.

In his book *Horace's Compromise* (1984), Theodore Sizer argued that society has made schools much more difficult places in which to teach and learn by compelling unwilling students to attend them. More recently, John Taylor Gatto in *The Underground History of American Education* (2003) has argued that the schools are part of a larger social and cultural system intended to suppress personal freedom and keep power in the hands of a political and social elite. In order to do so, mandatory or compulsory education is a requirement.

Eugene F. Provenzo, Jr.

See also Child Labor; United Nations Convention on the Rights of the Child

See Visual History Chapter 23, Compulsory Education and Truancy

Further Readings

Gatto, J. T. (2003). *The underground history of American education.* New York: Oxford Village Press.

Goodman, P. (1964). *Compulsory mis-education.* New York: Horizon Press.

Holt, J. (1974). *Escape from childhood: The needs and rights of children.* New York: Penguin.

Illich, I. (1970). *Deschooling society.* New York: Harper & Row.

Sizer, T. (1984). *Horace's compromise: The dilemma of the American high school.* Boston: Houghton Mifflin.

Web Sites

Dakar Framework for Action: http://unesdoc.unesco .org/images/0012/001211/121147e.pdf

Universal Declaration of Human Rights: http://www.un.org/Overview/rights.html

COMPULSORY HETEROSEXUALITY

Feminists conceived the term *compulsory hetero-sexuality* to signify the institutional pressures on women to be heterosexual, thereby ensuring men's rights of physical, economic, and emotional access. The term *compulsory heterosexuality* was first used at the 1976 Brussels International Tribunal on Crimes Against Women to draw attention to the worldwide persecution of lesbians.

Adrienne Rich more fully conceptualized "compulsory heterosexuality" in arguing that, despite qualitative differences in women's experiences across cultures and history, women's heterosexuality is not simply an issue of sexual "preference" or "orientation" but an ideology maintained by force that convinces women of the inevitability of marriage and sexual orientation toward men, even when unsatisfying or oppressive. Rich further argued that a wide range of legal, political, religious, social, economic, and physical barriers prohibit women from determining the forms that sexuality will take in their lives. Some customs that enforce women's heterosexuality are easily recognizable: chastity belts, clitoridectomies, foot binding, veils, rape, child marriage, arranged marriages, and pornography. However, other practices, such as taboos against homosexuality and the historical erasure of lesbian existence, obscure alternatives for same-sex bonding. Further, pervasive social, economic, legal, and educational inequalities ensure women's dependence upon men for survival.

Since Rich's work was published, queer theorists have demonstrated that compulsory heterosexuality also negatively affects healthy development of gay men and boys. Almost from birth, families teach not only acceptable gendered conduct, dress, and character traits, but disdain for cross-gendered behaviors. Compulsory heterosexuality is reinforced and expanded by religious institutions, peer groups, and the media, where heterosexual love is often presented as the only viable option and the value of nonheterosexual relationships may be omitted entirely, denounced, or denigrated.

Some school personnel, especially in religious schools, may educate for compulsory heterosexuality through the curriculum proper. More often, especially in public schools, teachers, administrators, counselors, and staff educate for compulsory heterosexuality through the hidden curriculum. Without ever openly denigrating nonheterosexuals, teachers of young children often encourage children to play in "gender appropriate" games and role-plays, reinforcing the notion that only certain ways of play or acting are socially acceptable. In fact, studies show that the worst verbal assault one can make against a young boy is to call him a girl.

When derogatory epithets surface among older children or youth, many school personnel refuse to challenge the language, intent, and misconceptions that are being wielded against gay and lesbian persons and identities. Researchers have documented that adolescents believe that being called "gay" or "lesbian" is the worst insult that can be leveled against them. Teachers' silence about lesbian and gay identity in fact speaks very loudly. Whether because of ignorance, design, or benign neglect, feminists and other scholars assert, these factors all contribute to a hidden curriculum of compulsory heterosexuality where every child is presumed heterosexual until proven otherwise and those children who are homosexual are labeled "defective."

Susan Birden

See also Hidden and Null Curriculum; Homophobia

Further Readings

Birden, S. (2005). *Rethinking sexual identity in education.* Lanham, MD: Rowman & Littlefield.

Rich, A. (1986). Compulsory heterosexuality and lesbian existence. In *Blood, bread, and poetry* (pp. 23–75). New York: W. W. Norton.

Russell, D. E. H., & Van de Ven, N. (Eds.). (1976). *Crimes against women: Proceedings of the International Tribunal.* East Palo Alto, CA: Frog in the Well.

COMPUTER-ASSISTED INSTRUCTION

American education has long incorporated technology in K–12 classrooms—tape recorders, televisions, calculators, computers, and many others. Computer-assisted instruction (CAI) refers to the use of computers and computer-related applications such as the Internet to support instruction and cognition. CAI also takes into consideration the processes involved in the integration of these technologies into existing curricula. Research on the effectiveness of computer use on educational outcomes is mixed, but suggests that computer-based instruction increases student achievement at least as much as more conventional modes of instruction. While information technologies, more specifically desktop computers, have had an enormous impact on American business and how business is transacted over the past several decades, instruction at the K–12 level has not undergone the "megachange" that technology was predicted to produce in U.S. schools. However, CAI is still an important component of curriculum in the Information Age. CAI may include: assessment of students, presentation of educational materials, repetitive drill practice, game-based drills, and tracking of student performance and progress. This entry looks at the growth of CAI from a tool used to facilitate drills to a central player in preparing students for a digital society.

Early Applications

The first computers used for instruction were computer-driven flight simulators used to train pilots at the Massachusetts Institute of Technology in the 1950s. Before the introduction of microcomputers, computer companies such as IBM pioneered efforts in helping to define the role of computers in education. In 1959, schoolchildren used IBM computers for the first time, for solving arithmetic problems.

In the early 1970s, IBM produced the first instructional mainframe with multimedia learning stations and worked with universities to develop CAI materials. For example, Stanford University's Patrick Suppes, considered the grandfather of CAI, developed the Coursewriter language to create reading and math drill-and-practice lessons, setting the standard for subsequent instructional software. After systematically analyzing courses in arithmetic and other subjects, Suppes designed highly structured computer systems featuring learner feedback, lesson branching, and student recordkeeping.

During the 1970s, another influential source of CAI was the University of Illinois PLATO system. This system included hundreds of tutorial and drill-and-practice programs. Like other systems of the time, PLATO's resources were available through time-sharing on a mainframe computer. Mainframes and minicomputer CAI systems, often developed by universities to serve school districts, dominated the field at the time. However, high maintenance costs and teachers' dislike of centralized control by district personnel eventually led to a decline in their use by the late 1970s.

With the development of the stand-alone, desktop computer in the late 1970s, control of educational computers was in the hands of teachers. Educational software became more widely available and was designed to meet teachers' classroom needs. With federal funding, the Minnesota Educational Computing Consortium (MECC) became the single largest computer software provider at the time. Teachers initially sought to be actively involved in the creation of software and other facets of computing, but interest faded as teachers realized how time consuming that would be. To make CAI more cost effective, districts purchased integrated learning systems (ILSs) that were administered via a central network and that used prepackaged curricula to support standards-based instruction, shifting control of educational computing again to a central source.

In the late 1970s, the idea of CAI developed into computer literacy, as skills in programming and word processing were seen as essential for functioning in society. Non-computer-literate students were predicted to become educationally disadvantaged. Lack of agreement on what exactly these "essential" computing skills should be and how to best measure them caused this idea to fade. In the 1980s, mathematician Seymour Papert's LOGO programming language sought to shift the focus from drill-and-practice applications of technology to viewing computers as a tool for problem solving. While some research did indicate positive effects from the use of LOGO, by the 1990s, LOGO was all but forgotten in educational circles.

In the 1970s and 1980s, drill-and-practice software was readily available and commonly used in classrooms. Often mimicking electronic flash cards or workbooks, this type of software showed math problems or tested vocabulary, giving simple feedback after a student response. However, incorrect answers often yielded more intricate or interesting forms of feedback, leading students to purposely give wrong answers. Further, issues with a limited catalog of software titles, aging hardware in the schools, inadequate staff development, and a perceived lack of direct correlation between technology and traditional school curricula led to a waning interest in educational technology.

The Internet Era

The dawning of the Internet era in the 1990s reignited teacher interest in using CAI. Mosaic, the first browser software, transformed a formerly text-based Internet, used predominantly by the engineering and scientific communities, into an easily accessible medium combining text and graphics. With the arrival of the new millennium, educators and students delighted in the connectivity that the Internet era ushered in. Further, the proliferation of educational software titles, efforts to address compatibility issues among operating systems, and successful attempts at meaningful integration of school curricula with emerging technologies spurred educators to reevaluate technology's role in classrooms. E-mail, videoconferencing, portable wireless devices, multimedia capability, and ease of access to online resources led to increases in distance learning opportunities.

While educational games and drill-and-practice software continued to be popular in schools, common uses of CAI now routinely include tutorials, simulations, and other open-ended applications to encourage divergent thinking. As new technologies were being adapted for classroom use, the International Society for Technology in Education developed the National Educational Technology Standards (NETS) for teachers, students, and administrators to provide a framework to guide classroom activities and foster the cohesion that was previously lacking.

CAI software, often called instructional software, teaches specific skills and knowledge, often narrowed to a specific content area and grade range. This is in contrast to tool software, which can be used in general to help students through problem processing at any grade level and in any content area, including word processors, concept processors for outlining ideas, spreadsheets, databases, audio-video editors, presentation programs, Web browsers, Logo programming language, and others.

Today, computers are powerful enough to act as file servers, and CAI can be delivered either through an integrated learning system or as stand-alone software. Typical CAI software provides text and multiple-choice questions or problems to students, offers immediate feedback, notes incorrect responses, summarizes students' performance, and generates exercises for worksheets and tests. CAI typically presents tasks for which there is one correct answer; it can evaluate simple numeric or very simple alphabetic responses, but it cannot evaluate complex student responses.

Outcomes Research

While the ubiquity of classroom technologies cannot be denied, clear impact on student academic achievement is not easy to determine because of sparse empirical evidence mostly due to methodological problems. A great deal of research was conducted during the 1970s, 1980s, and early 1990s on the effects of computer use on student achievement, attitudes, and other variables. Lack of depth in CAI inquiries makes generalizations difficult. Studies of effectiveness often pit one computer application against another or compare computer-based methods to teacher-directed activities. This type of "horse-race" research mentality does not yield effective data from which to draw conclusions.

Despite the lack of comprehensive studies of overall use, substantial research has examined the effects of using computers for particular kinds of instruction across a wide range of topics and age groups. Qualitative inquiries on the uses of computers in classroom instruction have documented positive effects on student affect and student and teacher motivation, as well as some positive impact on learning in specific classroom contexts.

Research clearly indicates that merely installing the hardware does not produce the desired outcomes. One of the main reasons for this is that technology has often been introduced as an addition on to an existing, unchanged classroom setting. Nowadays educators have a more integrated vision in which technology is considered together with the educational strategies, contents, and activities of the classroom, realizing that successful and effective learning with computers must rely on sound instructional practices that are congruent with how teaching and learning are viewed today.

Social Context

Historically and presently, the introduction of technologies in education has at times coincided with a need to improve educational outcomes or solve problems in U.S. schools. For example, after the Soviet launching of the *Sputnik* satellite in 1957, the National Defense Education Act sought to place overhead projectors in classrooms as a way to improve science and math achievement in public schools. In the 1960s, educational television for youngsters, often featuring culturally diverse children and themes, brought into focus a changing U.S. demographic and their social and literacy needs. Educational television flourished, capturing the interest of the American populace. After the publication of the report *A Nation at Risk* in 1983, which highlighted the shortcomings of American schools, educational reformers urged better integration of CAI to support a student-centered, inquiry-based mode of learning in classrooms.

During the 1990s state and federal initiatives sought to increase educational technology in classrooms and to link the nation's classrooms to the Information Super Highway in an effort to prepare students for the world of work in a digital society. The sophisticated educational software available today bears only minimal semblance to early electronic applications. Today, electronically linked text, or hypertext, "intelligent" computer tools that shape computer programs to suit learner needs, and integrated learning systems that monitor progress in academic subjects provide an endless number of CAI opportunities. A strong argument for increasing CAI is that computers are essential for preparing students for an increasingly digital world. Add to this the likelihood that school will be the only place the urban poor will ever use a computer before going into the job market, and it becomes even more imperative that schools maximize how CAI is used.

Presently, many state and national educational initiatives are supporting technology reform efforts in many schools. Educators realize that electronic communication is becoming less an option and more a requirement for students' success in the twenty-first century. The International Reading Association recognized this in its 2001 position statement on integrating technology into the literacy curriculum. Becoming fully literate, the association argues, includes becoming proficient in the new literacies of information and communication technology. Therefore, literacy educators have a responsibility to integrate emerging technologies into the literacy curriculum in order to adequately prepare students for their role in society. In simplest terms, information and communication technologies in and out of the classroom are redefining teaching and learning.

Lina Lopez Chiappone

See also Computing, Ethical Issues; Digital Divide

Further Readings

Barron, A. E., Kemker, K., Harmes, C., & Kalaydjian, K. (2003). Large-scale research study on technology in K–12 schools: Technology integration as it relates to the National Technology Standards. *Journal of Research on Technology in Education, 35,* 489–507.

Cuban, L., Kirkpatrick, H., & Peck, C. (2001). High access and low use of technologies in high school classrooms: Explaining an apparent paradox. *American Educational Research Journal, 38,* 813–834.

Papert, S. (1994). *The children's machine: Rethinking school in the age of the computer.* New York: Basic Books.

Roblyer, M. D., Castine, W. H., & King, F. J. (1988). *Assessing the impact of computer-based instruction: A review of recent research.* New York: Haworth Press.

COMPUTING, ETHICAL ISSUES

Ethics is the branch of philosophy that asks and addresses questions regarding right and wrong behavior. The contemporary industrialized world's heavy reliance on computers to accomplish a variety of tasks heightens the importance of ethical computer use. Schools are charged at some level with allowing students to consider the ethical ramifications of their actions in general. Computer use in schools is not exempt from this task. Indeed, it is now more important than ever for all members of the school community to ask difficult questions about how they and others can use computers in ethical ways in different contexts. Some of the ethical issues differ little from those in the day-to-day world without computers, that is, the "offline" world, but are nonetheless important in the online setting. Others are more specific to the online world in terms of the potential damage that computer misuse can bring compared to the offline context. The ethical contexts discussed in this entry include netiquette, censorship, digital copyright, and privacy.

Netiquette

Netiquette is a portmanteau of *net* for Internet and *etiquette*. Like etiquette for daily conversation in schools, netiquette is a way of establishing a more productive and respectful setting between school participants via appropriate means of expression. Common guidelines of netiquette are rooted in both notions of everyday courtesy in the offline world and the special circumstances of online communication. For instance, harassment, abusive language, and unnecessarily lengthy monologues should be discouraged just as much online as they are in the offline classroom setting. However, typing in all caps is a uniquely online version of shouting. Moreover, forwarding irrelevant e-mails and sending files too large for most computers to handle interferes with school community members' computer usage and should be avoided.

Censorship

To receive federal funds for computing equipment and Internet access, schools and libraries must abide by the Children's Internet Protection Act (CIPA). CIPA requires that these public institutions use filtering software that blocks access to online material that is "obscene, child pornography, or harmful to minors." While case law continues to evolve on defining the rights of students and teachers in cyberspace, this major statute stands in force.

Supporters of the law cite it as an efficient way of harnessing the power of the Internet for pedagogical purposes while blocking its more unsavory sections from students. Critics point out that corporations who manufacture the filtering software may have hidden political and social agendas reflected in the lists of blocked Web sites. These lists are not available to public scrutiny since they are considered trade secrets. Moreover, many Web sites, either intentionally or unintentionally blocked, do not have any objectionable content. Teachers and administrators are advised not only to monitor Web sites that students attempt to access, but also to monitor software that blocks Web sites that may be educationally benign or beneficial.

Digital Copyright and Fair Use

Generally speaking, the same copyright legislation that forbids large-scale unauthorized duplication and use of copyrighted works in the offline world applies to the Internet as well. Consequently, schools can be held liable in civil courts for students' sharing copyrighted music, movies, software, and other media over the Internet. The benefits and perils of sharing copyrighted works online are highly contested and involve their own set of ethical questions. Still, few would call the use of PreK–12 school networks to share copyrighted files for solely recreational purposes ethical.

Policies and related debates over the degree of latitude educators and students should be given to distribute or exhibit copyrighted works typically concern four factors. These include the action's pedagogical value, its impact on the work's marketability, the nature of the work in question, and what portion of the total work is used in terms of length and the specific portion. Traditionally, educators have relied on the fair use doctrine of copyright law to legally copy part or, less commonly, the whole of copyrighted works for pedagogical purposes. The doctrine itself was enshrined in the Copyright Act of 1976.

Nevertheless, Congress further tightened copyright protection in cyberspace in 1998 by passing the Digital Millennium Copyright Act (DMCA). The DMCA makes it a federal offense to interfere with any digitized anticopying mechanism put in place by the copyright owner of a digital work. Even bypassing anticopying mechanisms to garner material that is normally protected under fair use is largely illegal under the DMCA. The Librarian of Congress gave "media studies or film professor[s]" permission to bypass these restrictions to make film compilations for exhibition in college and university classrooms in November 2006. It is unclear if this relatively narrow exception applies to teachers and students in the PreK–12 school system.

Prosecutions of copyright infringement for teacher-supervised computing activities are rare, in part because the fair use doctrine presents obstacles for copyright holders to pursue legal action. Nevertheless, teachers and students should exercise discretion in the portion of the copyrighted work they copy for school use; generally the longer it is, the more likely fair use does not protect the action.

Privacy

Internet access provided by schools to their students comes with the expectations that schools own the means of this access and that students are primarily using it to perform school-related tasks. Legally speaking, student activities and correspondence on school networks are treated the same as student grade and behavior records. That is, school faculty and parents can access what their students and children have been doing on school networking equipment. Typically this is recorded on school hard drives and network servers in the form of saved e-mail messages that students have sent and received as well as logs of what Web sites students have visited. The same principle applies to faculty computing activities, which can be monitored by school administrators as well.

If these principles are not consistently made clear to students and faculty, then they may act indiscriminately on reasonable expectations of privacy regarding their Internet access. It is neither unusual nor unreasonable for members of the school community to sometimes go online for personal reasons. Moreover, students may use the Internet at school to gain information or access communities they are forbidden to retrieve at home, such as Web sites related to religion, politics, or sexual orientation.

Privacy laws heavily favor school personnel's and parents' right to access their students' and subordinate faculty's school records. However, monitoring potentially embarrassing personal messages and browsing or interfering with a student's identity formation begs difficult ethical questions for school practices.

Administrators and faculty should formulate online privacy policies that take these concerns in addition to relevant legislation, school objectives, and community input into account. In addition, all members of the school community should be made aware of those policies once they are in force. This is so that they can know what behaviors are expected of them and their children, and what input they should give in future policy revisions.

A Different Ethics?

It is debatable whether computer usage in schools raises fundamentally different sorts of ethical questions than those educators and students normally face. Some argue that the sort of misbehavior students and other members of the school community have engaged in online differs from common offline misdeeds only in their greater reach through a wider channel. The effects of decisions made in online computing can have a greater impact, but they are similar in nature to everyday actions in schools. Others argue that since students and educators increasingly participate in online activities as members of virtual communities, the nature of related ethical questions changes.

Virtual communities found on online forums, for instance, can accomplish similar pedagogical tasks. An example would be an analysis and critique of mass journalism guided by experts such as the online *Columbia Journalism Review*. This invites ethical questions of who should have control over the curriculum, what the nature of online learning should be (if) contrasted to offline pedagogy, and how complementary an online community should be to the school community.

Whether or not the nature of online computing alters fundamental questions of ethics, there are enduring issues that educators and students should be aware of. This enhances the role of computing in schooling and creates a platform for further discussion of ethics that is a cornerstone of a liberal education.

Brent Allison

See also Computer-Assisted Instruction; Technologies in Education

Further Readings

American Library Association. (n.d.). Internet filtering software. Available from http://www.pla.org/ala/pla/plapubs/technotes/internetfiltering.htm

Knowlton, D. S. (2000). A theoretical framework for the online classroom: A defense and delineation of a student-centered pedagogy. In R. Weiss, D. S. Knowlton, & B. W. Speck (Eds.), *Principles of effective teaching in the online classroom.* San Francisco: Jossey-Bass.

Nelson, I. (2006, December 6). New film copyright ruling will benefit faculty. *Duke University News & Communications.* Available from http://www.dukenews.duke.edu/2006/12/copyright.html

Provenzo, E. F., Jr. (1998). *The educator's brief guide to the Internet and the World Wide Web.* Larchmont, NY: Eye on Education.

CONFEDERATE TEXTBOOKS

Opposition to the use of school textbooks written by Northern authors—which to a large degree reflected a set of values and beliefs that were specific to the North—became a particularly prominent issue in the years immediately prior to the Civil War. This entry looks at the history of that conflict and at the creation of alternative textbooks by the Confederacy that were more consistent with their political and ideological values.

A Northern Bias

Throughout the eighteenth and first half of the nineteenth centuries, the writing and publication of textbooks in the United Stares was dominated by the North. With the exception of William Holmes McGuffey (1800–1873), the principal textbook authors prior to the Civil War were from New England. Noah Webster, Jediah Morse, S. G. Goodrich, C. A. Goodrich, S. Augustus Mitchell, Jesse Olney, and Emma Willard were all from Connecticut; Lyman Cobb, William Woodbridge, Richard Parker, and Salem Town were from Massachusetts; while John Frost was from Maine, and Benjamin D. Emerson from New Hampshire.

The South's dependence upon the North for textbooks reflected an important difference in the economy of the two cultures. During the nineteenth century, the manufacture of textbooks was a complicated and expensive process. Because of the widespread use of illustrations, major investments had to be made not only in engravings, but in the physical plants required to produce such works.

Southerners' resentment over their dependence upon Northern textbooks, authors, and publishers was very strong. Many popular writers, as well as educators, questioned the appropriateness of the information included in the texts brought down from the North. Prior to the Civil War, Southern authors argued that the textbooks produced by the Northern publishers had the earmarks of sectionalism and were clearly biased against Southern values and traditions.

In addition, textbooks produced in the North were often highly inaccurate when used in a Southern context. Northern textbooks, for example, often discussed towns and counties, when parish divisions were used in places like Louisiana. Northern crops were used to describe agriculture, but not Southern products such as cotton. Most objectionable to Southerners was the frequent criticism of slavery by abolitionist-oriented textbook authors. In the great majority of Northern textbooks, slavery was attacked as a corrupt institution that had to be eliminated at all costs.

The Southern Response

Protests over abolitionist content in textbooks written and manufactured in the North were widespread in the South during the 1850s. Popular journals such as *DeBow's Review* ran a series of articles criticizing Northern textbook content, while also calling for the establishment of a Southern textbook industry. The importance of the textbook issue was also reflected in the actions taken by the various Southern commercial conventions. The commercial convention which met in Charleston in 1854, for example, supported the publication of textbooks in the South, as did the convention in New Orleans in 1855.

Economic factors also played an important part in the South's opposition to Northern textbooks. Numerous authors argued that by buying their textbooks from the North, the South was in fact paying an indirect tax to the North, in which Southern capital was being expended on an inferior product. Many

Southerners came to believe that there was no reason that the South could not write and manufacture its own textbooks. The need for the South to manufacture its own textbooks became increasingly significant as the sectional conflict grew. Yet despite the passage of numerous resolutions and the organization of various committees at the Southern commercial conventions, little progress was made by the South prior to the Civil War in developing its own textbook industry.

With the advent of the Civil War, the South could no longer avoid the problem of manufacturing and producing its own textbooks. Various states throughout the Confederacy put forward legislation to promote the adoption of Southern texts and to eliminate any Northern materials from use in the education of their children. Georgia, for example, established a textbook competition to encourage the creation of a spelling book that could be used in the "common schools" throughout the Confederacy.

Within a relatively short period of time, numerous Southern texts were written and manufactured. A careful examination of these works shows them to be highly dependent upon Northern textbooks for much of their material. Typically, they were poorly printed and relatively brief in their content. It is unfair in many respects to use them as examples of what the South could potentially produce, since the priorities imposed by the war, as well as the shortage of materials necessary to manufacture books, precluded the production of higher quality works.

Lessons of the Conflict

The content of the Confederate textbooks can provide us with important insights into the South's perception of the North. While heroes of Southern origin such as George Washington figure prominently in Confederate texts, there is no mention of New Englanders such as Joseph Warren and John Adams. In works such as Marinda Branson Moore's *First Dixie Reader* (1863), comparisons are made between the life of the Black slave laborer and the free White laborer in the North that clearly suggest that the conditions of life are superior for the Black worker.

Both the North and the South were acutely aware of a textbook's potential to establish the values and norms of the children who read it. The conflict over textbooks in the years prior to the Civil War, and the eventual creation of distinctively Southern textbooks during the Civil War, was a reflection of the two profoundly different cultures that had emerged in the North and the South by the time of the Civil War.

Following the Civil War, there was a conscious attempt on the part of the North to develop textbooks by authors who were acceptable to the South. While the Civil War had removed the issue of slavery and abolition from American textbooks, it also forced Northern textbook authors and publishers to take into account the distinctiveness of the South as a region, its economy, geography, and traditional culture. In doing so, the textbooks published after the Civil War began to reflect not simply the regional interests and needs of the North but also those of the South, and of a previously divided nation intent upon reuniting itself and developing a more unified national consciousness.

Eugene F. Provenzo, Jr.

See also Catechisms; Curriculum Challenges in Schools; Textbooks, History of

Further Readings

Davis, O. L., Jr. (2001). Textbooks for confederate school children: Pursuit of national identity during the American Civil War. *American Educational History Journal, 28,* 13–19.

Knight, E. (1947). An early case of opposition in the South to Northern textbooks. *Journal of Southern History, 13*(2), 245–264.

Moore, M. B. (1864). *The first Dixie reader.* Raleigh, NC: Branson and Farrar.

Weeks, S. (1900). Confederate textbooks, 1861–1865: A preliminary bibliography. In the *Report of the United States Commissioner of Education for 1898–1899* (pp. 1139–1155). Washington, DC: Government Printing Office.

CONSTRUCTIVISM

In education, constructivism refers to theories of knowledge and learning. These theories state that knowledge is constructed rather than received from an objective world or external reality. For example, knowledge does not exist in a book but rather is produced by the reader in the process of reading. In day-to-day practice, however, constructivism is much more complicated; philosophers, psychologists, sociologists, scientists, and educators approach and understand this "simple" theory of knowledge and learning quite differently. Thus, constructivism perhaps is understood best as an academic construct or metaphor that describes many different ways of thinking about learning and knowledge acquisition, as summarized in this entry.

Theoretical Background

Constructivism does not have a clear beginning: No single person or movement appears responsible for developing or laying the foundation for modern-day constructivist theories. The seeds of constructivist approaches, though, regularly are traced to Giovanni Battista Vico, Paul Goodman, Jean-Jacques Rousseau, Immanuel Kant, John Dewey, and Lev Vygotsky. While these early thinkers did not label themselves as "constructivists," their key ideas have constructivist elements.

Constructivism primarily is a synthesis of ideas from philosophy, sociology, psychology, and education. For instance, the philosophy of poststructuralists such as Jacques Derrida, Michel Foucault, and Roland Barthes ushered in postmodernism and its skeptical attitude toward objectivity. In sociology, works like Berger's and Luckmann's further support the idea that knowledge is constructed, not given. But it was psychology—Jean Piaget and Vygotsky and later Jerome Bruner and Ernst von Glasersfeld—that shaped early constructivism.

Constructivism describes a theory of both knowing and learning. Even so, certain fields focus more intently on "knowing" (e.g., philosophy and sociology), whereas others focus more on "learning" (e.g., psychology and education). As a theory of knowing, constructivism is based on the idea that knowledge does not exist in an objective world, outside of the "knower." Instead, knowledge is constructed by people. This epistemology is often understood in relation or opposition to objectivism. While any nonconstructivist

epistemology is labeled objectivist, objectivism holds that the purpose of the mind or knowledge is to mirror the "objective" real world. But, based on findings in science, philosophy, sociology, math, and psychology, constructivists now hold that knowledge does not exist independently of a knower; rather, it is constructed individually or socially.

Constructivism as a theory of learning, or psychological constructivism, emerged from the work of cognitive psychologists such as Piaget, Vygotsky, and Bruner. With the rise of cultural psychology, two perspectives became dominant: individual constructivism and social constructivism. While these two schools of thought differ, perhaps as ends of a continuum (i.e., one focuses on the construction of meaning inside a person and the other focuses on the construction of meaning among people), others have argued that all learners construct meaning socially as well as individually.

Individual or cognitive constructivism initially evolved from Piaget's work, specifically on genetic epistemology. Cognitive constructivism developed as a reaction to behaviorist and information-processing theories of learning. It conceptualizes learning as the result of constructing meaning based on an individual's experience and prior knowledge.

Social constructivism grew from the work of individual constructivists as well as Vygotsky and others who took a social and cultural perspective of knowledge creation. Pure social constructivists believe that learning occurs via the construction of meaning in social interaction, within cultures, and through language. To confuse matters, in the sociology of knowledge, the philosophy of science, and the history of science, social constructivism denotes a field of study that focuses primarily on the social construction of science and scientific facts.

Implications for Education

In education, constructivism emerged formally as a theory of knowledge and a theory of learning during the 1980s with the works of Bruner and von Glasersfeld, which attracted the attention of educators during the early 1990s. While labeling oneself as a constructivist is now in vogue and the idea that knowledge is constructed is accepted widely, the emergence of constructivist learning theories and the constructivist pedagogies that followed created a major paradigm shift in education. Thus, greater emphasis has been placed on the learner's prior experience rather than the teacher's and on the active construction of knowledge rather than the passive receipt of information.

As a theory of learning, constructivism focuses on the implications of "constructing knowledge" for learning. Typically approaching constructivism from a psychological or cultural perspective, educators emphasize the role of learners rather than that of knowledge. Generally, educators are interested in implications of constructivist theories for practice and learning (and to a lesser degree of knowing) rather than their ontological or metaphysical implications.

While constructivism is not a theory of teaching, constructivists argue that pedagogy should be based in theories of learning to ensure that teaching always centers on student learning. Recently, constructivist theories of learning have sparked reforms in teaching practices, suggesting that learning environments focus directly on students, the importance of context, authentic problems and tasks, discovery learning, student's prior knowledge, group projects and discussion, student choice, and authentic assessment.

Explicit strategies or approaches to learning also have been identified that support individual and social learning: Anchored instruction, situated learning, and cognitive apprenticeship are just a few different approaches to teaching and learning that draw from constructivist theories. Anchored instruction involves lodging instruction in an authentic problem-based story, case study, or situation in which students generate and test possible problem solutions. Situated learning emphasizes learning through social interaction and collaboration in authentic contexts. And cognitive apprenticeship, like traditional apprenticeship, relies on pairing a guide or an expert with a learner in an authentic study but focuses on making thinking explicit.

Despite the implications, adopting a constructivist theory of learning does not preclude teacher-centered approaches to teaching and learning, because both knowledge and learning are the result of construction regardless of the teaching approach. In education from a constructivist perspective, teachers are encouraged to become student centered because constructivism is

first and foremost a theory of learning and knowledge acquisition, and the primary learner is the student.

Patrick R. Lowenthal and Rodney Muth

See also Active Learning; Cooperative Learning; Critical Thinking; Philosophy of Education; Sociology of Education

Further Readings

Berger, P. L., & Luckmann, T. (1966). *The social construction of reality: A treatise in the sociology of knowledge.* New York: Doubleday.

Bransford, J. D., Brown, A. L., & Cocking, R. R. (Eds.). (2000). *How people learn: Brain, mind, experience, and school.* Washington, DC: National Academy Press.

Bruner, J. (1960). *The process of education.* Cambridge, MA: Harvard University Press.

Bruner, J. (1986). *Actual minds, possible worlds.* Cambridge, MA: Harvard University Press.

Fosnot, C. T. (Ed.). (2005). *Constructivism: Theory, perspectives, and practice* (2nd ed.). New York: Teachers College Press.

Jonassen, D. H. (1991). Objectivism versus constructivism: Do we need a new philosophical paradigm? *Educational Technology Research and Development, 39*(3), 5–14.

Marlowe, B. A., & Page, M. L. (1998). *Creating and sustaining the constructivist classroom.* Thousand Oaks, CA: Corwin Press.

Philips, D. C. (Ed.). (2000). *Constructivism in education.* Chicago: University of Chicago Press.

Von Glaserfeld, E. (1996). *Radical constructivism: A way of knowing and learning.* London: Falmer Press.

CONTEXT IN EDUCATION

Human thoughts, meanings, interpretations, and understandings are basically formulated and negotiated through activity that is influenced by environmental conditions. Understanding and explaining the ways in which environmental conditions influence humans engaged in individual and collective activity within and among institutions is a major problem of educational theoreticians, researchers, and practitioners. A common perception of environment is that humans act on it rather than interact with it. However, active humans and active environments act on each other. *Context* is a unit of analysis that is often used to account for how environmental conditions shape human activity.

Definition

Context is derived from the Latin *contexere,* "to join together," and *texere,* "to weave." Context has multiple meanings (e.g., circumstances, settings, activities, situations, and events).

A context is constituted of the interweaving of elements mediating human activity, including material, ideal, and social objects; instrumental tools, such as computers, rulers, and pencils; psychological tools, such as everyday and institutional discourses and cognitive strategies; and rules and regulations, division of labor, participant roles, participation structures, and discourses. The dynamic interrelationship among these elements *is* a context. At one and the same time, human activity affects context and context affects human activity, co-constructing each other.

Courtney Cazden represents context as a set of concentric circles in which an activity of interest is located near the center, constituted by and constituting levels of context. Concentric circles reveal the embedded nature of the interactions constituting activities of interest, for example, teacher and pupils engaged in a literacy lesson arranged for the accomplishment of a literacy task lead to the acquisition of a concept or skill; teacher education candidates observing or participating in classroom literacy instruction; teachers participating in a professional development activity; or a professor and students participating in a methods class of a teacher education program.

Education Example

Figure 1 illustrates the idea of using concentric circles to analyze the interplay among levels of context and their potential effects on classroom instruction (top half of the model) and teacher education (bottom half of the model). First, consider the literacy lesson at the core of the concentric circles. The lesson is located in an instructional group, in a classroom. The lesson is structured according to the normative practices of the school in which the classroom is located and the professional practices of the particular classroom teacher. Schools

and classroom teachers vary in the way they interpret literacy curriculum and instruction. The literacy curriculum and instruction are regulated by policies of the state department of education, federal mandates, and local boards of education. Curriculum and instruction are organized and guided by the literacy curriculum of the local school system. The selection of and emphasis placed on the particular literacy task pupils are expected to accomplish in the lesson are influenced by statewide tests of achievement and the public posting of grades schools receive based on their performance on the tests. From this perspective, it is easy to understand how the literacy lesson of interest and its qualities are shaped by the interplay between and among a number of interacting contexts. In a sense, the literacy lesson is "caused" by other contexts.

Turning to the bottom half of the model, it is possible to consider the interactive effects of context on the preparation of prospective teachers. Teacher-education accrediting organizations, such as the National Council for Accreditation of Teacher Education, and professional associations, such as the International Reading Association, set standards related to teaching in general and to literacy instruction in particular that teacher education programs are expected to meet in order to be professionally accredited. Similarly, the state department of education sets performance standards that teacher education programs must meet for accreditation and standards their students must meet in order to obtain teacher certification. Teacher education candidates participate in learning experiences that are organized by a conceptual framework that specifies the philosophical and theoretical orientation guiding the program and its structure, including subject matter, instruction, and where, and how students will participate in field experiences and student teaching. Similar to classroom instruction, the teacher education is caused by the interaction of layers of context.

The literacy lesson in the core circle is the nexus where the two complementary contexts merge and co-construct both classroom literacy instruction and the education of prospective teachers. On the one hand, interactions among the layers of one context "author" the literacy lesson before teacher education students arrive to observe or participate in the lesson. On the other, teacher education students bring with them

Figure 1   Interplay Among Levels of Context

Source: Blanton, W. E., Shook, A., Hocutt, A., Medina, A., & Schumm, J. (2006). Professional development of reading teachers: Biography and context, p. 105. In K. R. Howey, Linda M. Post, & N. L. Zimpher (Eds.), *Recruiting, preparing, and retaining teachers for urban schools* (pp. 101–225). Washington, DC: American Association of Colleges for Teacher Education. Used with permission.

"authoring" effects of interactions among the layers of context of their teacher education program. As the contexts of classroom instruction and teacher education interpenetrate each other, they co-constrct a unique learning context for both students and teacher education candidates.

In summary, the interactive effects of the environment and human activity are bidirectional. Context and activity co-construct each other. Context is a useful unit of analysis for analyzing these effects. Contextual analyses can increase the understanding of what facilitates or inhibits teacher and student responses to classroom interventions and how patterns of activity within and among educational institutions affect teacher preparation.

William E. Blanton and Adriana Medina

See also Qualitative Research; Teacher Preparation

Further Readings

Bateson, G. (1972). *Steps to an ecology of mind.* London: Chandler.

Bronfenbrenner, U. (1979). *The ecology of human development.* Cambridge, MA: Harvard University Press.

Cazden, C. (1989). Principles from sociology and anthropology: Context, code, Classroom, and culture. In M. C. Reynolds (Ed.), *Knowledge base for the beginning teacher* (pp. 47–57). New York: Pergamon Press.

Cole, M., & Griffin, P. (1987). *Contextual factors in education: Improving science and mathematics education for minorities and women.* Madison: University of Wisconsin, School of Education, Wisconsin Center for Educational Research.

Erickson, F., & Schultz, J. (1977). When is a context? *ICHD Newsletter, 1*(2), 5–10.

Jacob, E. (1997). Context and cognition: Implications for educational innovators and anthropologists. *Anthropology and Educational Quarterly, 28*, 3–21

McLaughlin, M. W. (1993). What matters most in teachers workplace context? In M. W. McLaughlin (Ed.), *Teachers' work: Individuals, colleagues, and contexts* (pp. 79–103). New York: Teachers College Press.

Nelson, B. C., & Hammerman, J. J. (1996). Reconceptualizing teaching: Moving toward the creation of intellectual communities of students, teachers, and teacher educators. In M. W. McLaughlin & I. Oberman (Eds.), *Teacher learning: New policies, new practices* (pp. 3–21). New York: Teachers College Press.

Talbert, J. E., & McLaughlin, M. W. (1999). Assessing the school environment: Embedded contexts and bottom-up research strategies. In S. L. Friedman & T. D. Wachs (Eds.), *Measuring environment across the life span* (pp. 197–226). Washington, DC: American Psychological Association.

COOPERATIVE LEARNING

Cooperative learning was first proposed in response to traditional curriculum-driven education. It is a strategy in which small groups of students with different levels of ability engage in a variety of activities to improve their understanding of the topic. Each member of the group is responsible for learning what is taught, but also for helping other group members learn, thus creating an atmosphere of achievement for all. Students work through the task until all members of the group understand the concept. Inherent in cooperative learning is the assumption that learning is an active, constructive process that depends on rich context, that it is social in nature, and that it works best with diverse learners.

Cooperative learning is based on the social interdependence theories of Kurt Lewin and Morton Deutsch.

These theories and associated research explore the influence of social structure on individual interactions within a given situation, which then affect the outcome of those interactions. David Johnson and Roger Johnson (University of Minnesota), Elizabeth Cohen (Stanford University), and Robert Slavin (Johns Hopkins University) have spent years researching cooperative learning and are considered pioneers in this area.

Cooperative learning groups typically include the following key components: social interaction of students within groups, group incentives that motivate students to urge others in the group to perform well, equal opportunity for each member, specialization of tasks, individual accountability, and competition among groups. It is important that educators do not mistake this strategy as group work, in which students are merely seated next to each other and possibly create a product together. Cooperative learning, instead, is characterized by both individual and group accountability and achievement. Students should be arranged in heterogeneous groups, and should be given clear expectations for cooperative learning tasks.

Five elements are crucial to cooperative learning groups:

1. *Positive interdependence* means that the efforts of each group member are required in order for the group to succeed. It is based on the belief that each group member has something unique to contribute because of his or her resources and/or role or responsibility in the task.

2. *Face-to-face interaction* refers to the group members promoting success for each other. Group members teach what they know to the other members and orally explain, describe, and talk their way through solving problems. Each group member checks to see that other members are gaining understanding of the topic or task.

3. *Individual and group accountability* means that no one gets out of doing work and that each member is responsible for contributing. This element happens more easily when group sizes are small, when they are observed for participation, and when members are assigned roles or tasks.

4. *Interpersonal and small group skills* refers to the various social skills that must be present (and often must be taught) to cooperative learning groups. They include, but are not limited to leadership,

conflict management, communication, trust building, and decision making.

5. *Group processing* refers to the ability of the group to discuss how well they are achieving their goals, how effectively they are working, what they are each doing that is helpful, and the ability to make decisions about behaviors that are helping (or hurting) the group.

Cooperative learning is thought to be popular and easy to implement at any grade level. Results have included: improved behavior and attendance, increased motivation and self-confidence, increased liking of school and fellow students, and improved academic achievement. Cooperative learning is also thought to increase self-esteem, utilize higher-level thinking skills, increase students' appreciation of different points of view, develop social skills, and enhance students' satisfaction with their learning experiences.

Classroom activities that promote cooperative learning include: think-pair-share, round-robin brainstorming, jigsaw, numbered heads, literature circles, and reciprocal teaching.

Jodi C. Marshall

See also Sociology of Education

Further Readings

Balkcom, A. (1992). *Cooperative learning.* Washington, DC: U.S. Department of Education.

Deutsch, M. (1949). A theory of cooperation and competition. *Human Relations, 2,* 129–152.

Eble, K. (1976). *The craft of teaching.* San Francisco: Jossey-Bass.

Johnson, D. W., & Johnson, R. T. (1989). *Cooperation and competition: Theory and research.* Edina, MN: Interaction.

CORPORAL PUNISHMENT

Corporal punishment is one of the most long-standing issues in education. There is no general consensus on the measures necessary to ensure student compliance in schools. Therefore, a number of techniques have been used, and some have involved the infliction of pain to alter misbehavior. This entry looks at the history of corporal punishment in schools, the contemporary situation, and research on its impact.

Historical Background

Caution and debate about the use of corporal punishment has a long history in education. The roots of corporal punishment can be traced back to the early history of the education system. Almost from the very beginning of schooling, there have been discussions about the use of techniques intended to alter misbehavior. The religious foundation of the American education system has had a significant influence on the conception and ultimate use of corporal punishment. Conceptions about the nature of childhood, based on the King James Version of the Christian Bible (i.e., spare the rod, spoil the child), have traditionally served as one of the most frequently cited justifications for the use of corporal punishment.

The use of corporal punishment also has another interesting aspect to its history. There is a general belief that the intensity of punishment correlates with its effectiveness. In other words, if a more intensive punishment technique is used, the child is more likely to engage in more appropriate behavior in the future. Thus, one of the most intense forms of punishment that can be applied is corporal punishment. There is no empirical support for this notion nor does it seem like a favorable prospect for children attending schools.

It was not until well into the twentieth century that some began to question the validity of corporal punishment in schools. This is not to imply that educators, parents, and community members in general did not have concerns about the use of corporal punishment, but as the knowledge base of child development and the negative side effects of punishment became clearer, more questions were raised about its use in schools.

Historically, one of the most significant events took place in the mid-1970s. In two landmark cases, the U.S. Supreme Court affirmed that the use of corporal punishment in schools neither violates the Eighth Amendment protection against cruel and unusual punishment nor breaches the due process guarantees of the Fourteenth Amendment (*Baker v. Owen,* 1975; *Ingraham v. Wright,* 1977). Thus, the foundation was laid: Corporal punishment could be used in schools, and in many areas the use of corporal punishment has survived.

The United Sates is unique in a number of ways, and one distinction pertains directly to corporal punishment. The United States is one of two countries choosing not to ratify the Convention on the Rights of Child, adopted by the United Nations General Assembly in November 1989. The document calls for a number of protections of children, including protection from violence. Corporal punishment is legal in twenty-seven states and the District of Columbia. The highest incidence of use is reported in the southern region of the United States, with Alabama, Arkansas, Georgia, Louisiana, Mississippi, Missouri, Oklahoma, Tennessee, and Texas, making up the top ten. In spite of this, some major urban cities (e.g., Atlanta, Chicago, New Orleans, and New York) have banned corporal punishment and some entire school districts have banned the practice in spite the legal status of corporal punishment in the rest of the state (e.g., Broward County, Florida).

Is It Effective?

The legal status of corporal punishment does not address the core matters regarding its validity. There is little debate about the intent of corporal punishment: All generally agree that techniques to alter student misbehavior should be used to promote a safe, effective, and efficient learning environment. What is often debated is the use of a technique that is based on the infliction of pain.

Punishment, like many concepts that have been empirically evaluated, falls victim to completely different meanings in and outside of the laboratory. Social science researchers (e.g., psychologists) and the rest of general society have completely different conceptions about the meaning and appropriate use of punishment. The meaning of corporal punishment to general society is accepted as any punishment that inflicts bodily pain to alter misbehavior. While many accept such a definition as clear and concise, for social scientists, this definition is problematic. In contrast, social scientists define punishment as any action or event following behavior that results in the likelihood of that behavior not occurring in the future. It is possible for particular

actions or events to become "punishers." For example, a student may have several unpleasant interactions with a teacher, and the teacher becomes a "punisher," leading to the likelihood that the student will attend school infrequently or perhaps stop attending school at all. Thus, it is clear the meaning and intent of the term *punishment* does not necessarily coincide with past and current practices in schools.

The use of punishment is not only intended to stop the occurrence of misbehavior; many believe that the use of punishment techniques, most specifically corporal punishment, will actually teach children to discriminate between appropriate and inappropriate behavior. This has not been supported in a number of rigorous tests, resulting in weak support at best for the use of punishment in general and corporal punishment in particular. Therein lies one of the most highly debated issues in education: Should corporal punishment be used, and if it is applied, when, where, and who should apply this technique?

Punishment has been researched for a number of years and there is solid evidence to indicate that a number of side effects can result from its use. These include the following: (a) it provides a model of aggression for students to follow, (b) it teaches that physical outbursts are an acceptable way of resolving conflict, (c) it may lead to decreased learning, (d) it may result in poor attendance, and (e) it may create an aversion to those responsible for delivering the punishment. Corporal punishment is often thought to be one of the most intense forms of punishment to be applied as a measure of last resort. This should lead to the development and use of progressive steps to be used when misbehavior occurs, ensuring that corporal punishment is not the first step and is used only sparingly, as a number of techniques will be applied before corporal punishment is even considered. This does not seem to be the case in many schools, especially those in urban areas. The arguments for and against the use of corporal punishment will continue to be discussed back and forth in the absence of empirical support for its use as well as a high level of social acceptance from general society.

Charles Dukes

See also School Law

Further Readings

Hinchey, P. H. (2004). Corporal punishment: Legalities, realities, and implications. *The Clearing House, 77*(3), 96–100.

Hyman, I., & Snook, P. (1999). *Dangerous schools: What can we do about the physical and emotional abuse of our children?* San Francisco: Jossey-Bass.

Straus, M. A., & Donnelly, D. A. (2001). *Beating the devil out of them: Corporal punishment in American families and its effects on children.* New Brunswick, NJ: Transaction.

Web Sites

Parents and Teachers Against Violence in Education (PTAVE): http://www.nospank.net

Temple University–National Center for the Study of Corporal Punishment and Alternatives (NCSCPA): http://www.ruaneproductions.com/NCSCPA

CORPORATE INVOLVEMENT IN EDUCATION

The relationship between public schooling and the economic workings of capitalist society has long been a concern of social theorists, from European neo-Marxists such as Louis Althusser and Paul Willis, to American critics of industrial/corporate capitalism like Samuel Bowles, Herbert Gintis, and Martin Carnoy. Early initiatives by the business sector to reform public education usually focused on tailoring the curriculum to the needs of industry; critiques of such initiatives stressed the school's role in preparing students to be docile workers within a stratified labor market.

In the decades since these critiques evolved, however, both capitalism and public education have undergone profound changes. The U.S. economy, and public life in general, have been transformed by the advent of digital information and communications technology; corporations aggressively market their products to a huge student population with billions of dollars in disposable income; and beleaguered government entities are increasingly turning to for-profit, private corporations to manage public institutions like hospitals, prisons, and schools. Given the pervasiveness of these developments, it is hardly surprising that new and varied linkages have arisen between public education and private capital and that educational debates are increasingly articulated in the idiom of the corporate boardroom. This entry looks at this phenomenon by focusing on its evolving perspectives about students.

Students as Workers

Larry Cuban identifies two key periods of business-inspired school reform. The first, from 1880 to 1930, was a response to the economic and social transformations that accompanied the rise of U.S. industrialism and the concomitant waves of European immigration. Despite the thousands of immigrants and rural Americans flooding the cities in search of factory jobs, employers had trouble finding workers with the technical skills they needed. Around the same time, the invention of the corporation revolutionized the organization of large businesses. The increasing concentration of wealth and power in corporations, along with the professionalization and bureaucratization of management, meant that U.S. capitalists were well positioned to reform schools to better meet their labor needs.

Industrialists also began to feel the pressure of global competition more acutely and to look to the European technical schools of the time as a model for U.S. school reform. The business sector found common ground with progressive social reformers, who saw public schooling as a potential solution to the social ills of burgeoning urban slums.

Armed with new principles of "scientific management" and new technologies of standardized assessment, this alliance gave rise to the vocational education movement; within a few decades, this movement had reshaped the purposes, curriculum, and organization of public schooling. By the 1930s, high schools had ceased to be selective, elite institutions that prepared the children of the wealthy for college, and had become mass institutions that prepared more than half of all U.S. youth between the ages of fourteen and seventeen to enter the world of work.

Students as Raw Materials

Reform initiatives of this era cast students not only as future workers, but also as the "raw materials" in a technical process of refinement. The business model of educational management focused on the quality of the final product, that is, young people possessed of the skills and orientations required by business. The apprenticeship model of learning gave way to the institutionalized transmission of skills, with the attendant emphasis on bureaucracy, hierarchy, standardization, and certification. In addition to teaching technical skills, schools were expected to instill in students habits of punctuality, obedience, efficiency, and other characteristics of a "good worker."

In contrast to the "administrative progressives," with their emphasis on education's potential contributions to the national economy, "pedagogical progressives" drew on the ideas of John Dewey for inspiration. They focused on "the whole child" and on teaching and learning as a means to develop students' intellectual gifts and civic sensibilities, thus deepening their critical engagement within an expanding, democratic public sphere. Although these ideas gained an important place within educational discourse, the administrative progressives had a deeper and more lasting influence on how most modern schools—their personnel, curricula, pedagogy, and assessment practices—are organized and managed.

To this day, the business model of management holds a firm place within the discourse of educational administration and policy making. Local, state, and national panels of "educational experts" invariably include business leaders, who often argue (or assume) that the primary goal of schooling is to increase economic competitiveness, and describe students in terms of "human capital" and "value added."

From *A Nation at Risk* to No Child Left Behind

In the late twentieth century, corporations' roles expanded in many aspects of public life. In 1983, during Ronald Reagan's presidency, the link between schooling and national economic health was further strengthened with the release of *A Nation at Risk,* the report of the president's National Commission on Excellence in Education. This report warned of "a rising tide of mediocrity" in education, sounding the alarm in explicitly nationalist terms. A much-quoted

passage from the introduction reads: "If an unfriendly foreign power had attempted to impose on America the mediocre educational performance that exists today, we might well have viewed it as an act of war. . . . We have, in effect, been committing an act of unthinking, unilateral educational disarmament."

A Nation at Risk deepened the focus on educational outcomes (as opposed to pedagogical processes) and called for widespread reform based on the development of standards-based curricula, a longer school day and year, and more rigorous requirements for high school graduation and admission to college. These recommendations eventually evolved into the Goals 2000: Educate America Act, passed by Congress in 1994. However, given the limited federal role in educational decision making, the specific substance of reforms remained primarily in the hands of the states, and by the end of the century many of the stated goals had still not been reached.

It was not until 2002, under President George W. Bush, that the federal government assumed a more concrete and authoritative role in educational reform, with the enactment of the No Child Left Behind Act (actually the reauthorization of the Elementary and Secondary Education Act of 1965). NCLB, as it came to be known, set specific goals and deadlines for improving student performance and eliminating "achievement gaps" between students of different ethnicities and income levels. Critics argued that the measures established in pursuit of these goals were based on an overly narrow definition of student performance, and limited schools' options with regard to pedagogical strategies to address achievement gaps. Furthermore, NCLB was in large part an "unfunded mandate," in that it set strict requirements for school districts to continue to receive federal funding (which generally constitutes about 15 percent of their operating budget), but did not make available the fiscal resources to carry out the required measures.

The emphasis on "accountability" included sanctions at various levels if performance requirements were not met: students could be retained or prevented from graduating; merit pay could be withheld from teachers and administrators; and schools could face reduced funding or even reorganization, under which the entire teaching staff could be replaced. Simultaneously, school districts were experiencing a fiscal crisis brought on by the new federal requirements, increasing enrollments (especially of low-income and immigrant students), and squeezing state budgets. This combination of factors opened the door to a new era of corporate involvement in education.

Students as Consumers

Faced with rising costs, shrinking budgets, and the threat of sanctions, schools turned to the private sector for help. Corporations moved quickly into the gap, motivated in part by an important realization: that business had an interest in students not only as workers, but as consumers. As corporations became aware of the huge potential of the "youth market," they began to seek new means and venues through which to tap this market. Shifts in educational policy provided a range of opportunities to reach students with corporate messages, from traditional forms of advertising, to product placement in educational materials, to the publishing boom in standardized tests.

Advertising

Increasingly, businesses are "partnering" with schools, offering financial support in exchange for access to a captive student audience for their advertising. Examples include corporate sponsorships of school sports arenas and uniforms, school cafeterias serving fast food from Burger King and Pizza Hut, and soda contracts that pay schools to install vending machines in their hallways (often with "sales quotas" that put pressure on school administrators to increase students' soda consumption).

In elementary schools, students' academic performance may be rewarded with coupons for free meals at Sonic or Taco Bell. Printed materials sent home with students, such as monthly lunch menus and order forms for school book fairs, contain word games and advertisements featuring well-known cartoon characters with marketing tie-ins to movies, toys, and fast food. Forty percent of U.S. high schools also broadcast Channel One, whose daily program (which is obligatory for students under the terms of the contract) consists of twelve minutes of teen-oriented news and two minutes

of commercials; its advertising rates are comparable to those for prime-time network television.

Curriculum Materials

In addition to explicit advertising through traditional media like television ads and stadium scoreboard signs, many corporations have developed curriculum materials for use in public schools. These materials use academic subject areas as contexts for promoting commercial products; for example, teachers can use brightly illustrated books and online lesson plans to teach young students "M&M Math," with the colorful candies as counters; Revlon offers lesson plans that guide students to explore the relationship between their hair and their self-esteem; and Exxon produces classroom videos on ecofriendly oil-drilling practices.

Since these materials are sent free of charge to teachers (even teachers who have not requested them), they are often eagerly adopted by schools struggling under shrinking budgets. Furthermore, since they involve no financial outlay on the part of the school district, such materials are not subject to the (often lengthy) vetting and review process that regular textbooks undergo. Given these highly profitable developments in school-based media, it is hardly surprising that entire advertising agencies and trade journals dedicated to tapping "the student market" have sprung up.

Standarized Testing

NCLB's emphasis on "accountability" dovetails with corporate interests in less obvious ways as well. The law gave rise to an explosion of standardized testing in public schools, and the "high-stakes" consequences of students' performance on these tests leads many schools to invest thousands of dollars in test preparation materials. Schools' financial outlay around standardized testing has been a huge boon for textbook publishers. Critics stress the financial cost to schools and the educational cost to students of making standardized tests the central focus of instruction and assessment. Some have also denounced the channeling of billions of education dollars into scandal-plagued but profitable private ventures such as "Reading First" (owned by McGraw-Hill, whose

CEO Harold McGraw is a long-time friend and supporter of the Bush family) and "Ignite Learning" (owned by George W. Bush's brother Neil).

Other Indicators

In addition to school-business partnerships, ads in curriculum materials, and the publication of standardized tests and drill booklets, the incursion of private interests into public education is also reflected in educational policies favoring charter schools and vouchers (under the rubric of "parental choice" and "flexibility"). Over the last two decades, both Republican and Democratic administrations have displayed a strong commitment to free-market policies, as well as to expanded federal control over schooling; one result has been to apply the logic of the free market to education, by making schools compete with each other for students (especially "desirable" students, i.e., those who raise a school's average test scores). Standardized accountability measures, which are published in local newspapers, serve as the basis for "comparison shopping" by parents.

Numerous critics have noted the growing trend of "contracting out" to private companies such government functions as military support, administration of social services, prison systems, and, increasingly, the delivery of educational services. Many educators feel that their professional priorities—prioritizing the well-being of children, encouraging a wide range of public debate, and deepening our democracy by cultivating well-informed, critical citizens—are incompatible with corporations' inherent mission of maximizing profits and prioritizing the interests of stockholders. Nevertheless, given the growing corporate influence in all areas of public life, the corporation's role in educational policy and practice seems unlikely to diminish in coming years.

Aurolyn Luykx

See also Educational Reform; Privatization; School Choice; Scientific Management; Standardized Testing

Further Readings

Apple, M. W. (2001). *Educating the "right" way: Markets, standards, God, and inequality.* New York: RoutledgeFalmer.

Cuban, L. (2004). *The blackboard and the bottom line: Why schools can't be businesses.* Cambridge, MA: Harvard University Press.
Gerstner, L., Semerad, R., & Doyle, D. (1994). *Reinventing education: Entrepreneurship in today's schools.* New York: Dutton.
Giroux, H. A. (2005). *Schooling and the struggle for public life: Democracy's promise and education's challenge.* Boulder, CO: Paradigm.
Kohn, A., & Shannon, P. (2002). *Education, Inc.: Turning learning into a business.* Portsmouth, NH: Heinemann.
Media Education Foundation. (2003). *Captive audience: Advertising invades the classroom* [Film]. Northampton, MA: Media Education Foundation.
Molnar, A. (1996). *Giving kids the business: The commercialization of American schools.* Boulder, CO: Westview Press.
Molnar, A. (2005). *School commercialism: From democratic ideal to market commodity.* New York: Routledge.

CORRESPONDENCE SCHOOLS

What we now call "distance education" began long before computers linked students and teachers. From the 1890s on, a wide range of private companies, public universities, and enterprising individuals sold instruction by mail. State and federal regulations were so meager before the 1930s that even the sham schools thrived. The popularity of this form of education diminished after 1930, but before then more students enrolled annually in correspondence courses than entered colleges and universities. This entry looks at the history of correspondence schools: why students enrolled, what schools offered, how standards were developed, and why this educational option declined.

Student Motivations

Acquiring a better job was the reason why most people took a correspondence course. They wanted to learn the specific skills necessary for a promotion or for self-employment. The early-twentieth-century labor market changed more rapidly than the curriculum of the public high school, where only a small fraction of adolescents graduated, and vocational training was in its infancy. For an unskilled or semiskilled laborer, home study promised a brighter future in expanding sectors of the workforce. For White-collar workers, the field of business abounded with mail-order courses, especially in accounting and sales. For several professions where educational credentials were not yet a precondition of taking licensing examinations, coursework in law, engineering, and architecture could be purchased.

Not everyone sought vocational goals, to be sure. Self-improvement was pursued through courses in music, art, foreign languages, social skills, physical fitness, and hobbies such as radio repair. The popular Arthur Murray dance studios began as correspondence courses. Nearly any academic subject could be studied, from basic mathematics to Hebrew. The schools offered whatever the marketplace would buy—the largest firms had hundreds of courses—although the vocational fare outsold all else.

To help students succeed, the correspondence schools relied on concise texts. The schools often created their own materials rather than assign someone else's books and articles. Most courses had a series of sixteen- to thirty-two-page lessons. Short sentences, simple words, first- and second-person diction, copious pictures: The lessons were designed to be easier to grasp than those in traditional textbooks. The courses focused on practical applications rather than theoretical foundations, and they assumed that learning was linear: Students were expected to master each lesson before starting the next one. Examinations posed short-answer questions calling for restatement or paraphrase of specific passages in the lesson (art, drafting, and creative writing were the exceptions). Comments from the instructors were usually prompt and apt. Telephone calls and personal meetings were not provided, although a few schools offered several weeks of on-site training at the end of the coursework. Grading was generous, with far more As than Bs and very few failures.

University Home Study

Several of the premier universities included home study as part of their outreach to adults in their region. William Rainey Harper, the first president of the University of Chicago, had led a successful correspondence school, and he admired the home-study work of the Chautauqua summer gatherings, which mixed instruction, entertainment, and religion. Harper

celebrated the "extension" work of major research universities, sure that their mission of cultural evangelism should include instruction for nonmatriculated students by means of traveling libraries, itinerant lectures, evening classes, and home study. Most of the larger state universities shared his point of view, with the University of Wisconsin foremost in creating multiple educational opportunities for residents far from the campus. At Wisconsin and elsewhere, at least one year of college credits earned through the mail could count toward a bachelor's degree.

The universities' home-study departments never reached the scope and scale of their for-profit counterparts. When annual enrollments in university home study peaked in the 1920s, they were only 15 percent of the half million who bought home-study courses elsewhere. The greater prestige of a University of Chicago or Wisconsin did not offset several disadvantages. Many faculty refused to participate, and many administrators subordinated home study to other extension work. On most campuses, correspondence courses lacked the aggressive recruitment undertaken by the for-profit companies.

Advertising budgets were modest, and promotion by field agents paled in comparison with the solicitations by the salesmen employed by many for-profit schools. Universities preferred to recruit, quietly, from constituencies they knew needed and wanted their service, such as small, rural high schools eager to augment their patchy curriculum. And rarely did higher education target burgeoning sectors in the job market by introducing courses wholly unrelated to familiar academic departments—teacher education, yes; air conditioning and diesel engines, no.

Developing Standards

The legitimacy of home study suffered from the mischief of countless fly-by-night schools. Seeing quick and easy profits in this mail-order business, hundreds of unscrupulous entrepreneurs tried to lure the naive and gullible. Deceptive inducements to enroll were common—ads placed in the "help wanted" columns, claims that no talent was necessary, bogus scholarships, and other misleading incentives. Many schools' names—university, federal, association, national—distorted their small size. Overblown claims about the employment prospects for graduates were rife. Even when the advertisements were truthful, the pitch from the salesmen often promised the impossible, especially in regard to the job market.

In 1926, the Federal Trade Commission (FTC), working with eleven large schools, developed rules of ethical conduct. By 1940, the FTC had issued several hundred cease-and-desist orders, and the federal postal inspectors had prosecuted some schools for mail-order fraud. Internal regulations also took shape. Approximately 50 of the over-300 schools were founding members of the National Home Study Council (NHSC) in the late 1920s, the first association created by the proprietary schools. NHSC knew that the deceitful schools hurt the reputation of all schools, and it therefore supported the FTC guidelines.

Yet many NHSC schools continued to use one (legal) device that caused much ill will: Students signed binding contracts to pay the full tuition whether or not they persevered. Because only a small fraction ever finished their course, many schools aggressively sought payment, often relying on collection agencies and lawsuits. Whenever the dropout had a reasonable excuse to stop, the relentless enforcement of the contract generated bad publicity for correspondence courses.

For many legislators, the FTC and NHSC accomplishments were too modest. Nearly every state enacted regulations in the 1930s and thereafter. Requiring schools to secure a license was common, and that entailed the submission of advertisements, contracts, texts, financial statements, and other evidence of legitimacy. The states curbed the reach of the good as well as the poor schools by stiffening the requirements for licensure in many occupations. For instance, accounting had attracted thousands of home-study students in the early twentieth century, but by the 1930s, most states required two or four years of college, not just success on an examination previously open to anyone.

Postwar Decline

As an academic credential, home-study enrollment lost value as other sectors of American education expanded. Students who previously dropped out and wanted to return often had no better choice than home study. After World War II, they were more likely to be near a community college, a branch of the state university, or an evening class at the local high school. The expansion of enrollments left fewer stragglers by the wayside, and those who did languish now had fresh chances to catch up by earning traditional secondary and postsecondary credits and degrees.

Furthermore, there were fewer and fewer attractive jobs open to students who prepared solely through home study. Employers preferred or required other credentials when they hired and promoted, leaving the freelance market in art, writing, and photography as the one area where home study grew significantly in the 1950s and 1960s. Vendors of education through the mail still found students for the service they had always provided: convenience at a reasonable cost for anyone interested in knowing more and doing better.

The total number of students enrolled throughout the 1950s and 1960s stayed in or near the half million range achieved in the 1920s, but as a fraction of overall academic enrollments, home study declined. In the 1970s and 1980s, tighter state and federal regulations squeezed enrollments, as did the relentless growth of community colleges. In the 1990s, distance education revived the popularity of learning at home, and many vendors supplied what even the established correspondence schools could not offer: the traditional academic diplomas necessary for career mobility in early twenty-first-century America.

Robert Hampel

See also Distance Learning

Further Readings

Kett, J. F. (1994). *The pursuit of knowledge under difficulties.* Stanford, CA: Stanford University Press.

Noffsinger, J. S. (1926). *Correspondence schools, lyceums, chautauquas.* New York: Macmillan.

Woodyard, E. (1940). *Culture at a price: A study of private correspondence school offerings.* New York: George Grady Press.

CRITICAL GEOGRAPHIES OF EDUCATION

Critical geography, a distinct yet varied subfield of geography, seeks to understand how the social construction of space and place interacts with and reinforces structures of power and personal and group identity. A critical geography of education tries to understand how the lived experiences of schools (i.e., students, teachers, and the larger community) are defined, constrained, and liberated by spatial relationships. To understand how critical geography engages such a complex set of issues, one must begin with definitions.

Terms and Concepts

In traditional conceptions, the terms *space* and *place* are used interchangeably, with little to no distinction. To geographers, however, the difference between the terms is the basis of their entire field of study. Geographers begin to think of *space* as the physical attributes of the world around us or, more theoretically, the spatial forces at work on people. While this is what most of us think of as geography—things like mountains, rivers, borders, and capitals—spatial forces also include less tangible forces such as economics, politics, and culture. Geographers point out that something like a national border certainly represents the spatial but is human made, can change all the time, may have varying levels of importance, and ultimately may mean different things. Space, therefore, can be both natural and human made, with key characteristics within which humans interact with both constraints and possibilities.

Place, on the other hand, is a particular form of space—one in which people have imposed meaning onto particular locations or spatial characteristics. All people have places that hold special meaning to them for any variety of reasons, good or bad. Recent theoretical geographers, informed by parallel developments in Marxist, feminist, and poststructural social theory, have become interested in the processes involved in space becoming a place and what that might mean for the people involved. As these processes undoubtedly involve issues of power and identity and operate in simultaneous and complex ways, to take up this field of study requires some distinction; that distinction is known as critical geography.

Power, for critical geographers, is always a key component in spatial relations. For example, school spaces for young people are defined by restrictions and privileges. At certain times of the day students can be only in certain parts of the school property; simply being in a particular area can mean big trouble for adults. This shows how those that have power—in this case, teachers and administrators—can define the limits of where youth can and cannot go. This happens all the time in social relations.

Furthermore, young people themselves engage in similar practices. A common example could be how seating patterns in a school cafeteria are divided up. Although there are usually no official rules as to who sits where, students typically think of certain areas as their own or, sometimes dangerously, clearly belonging to another group. Critical geographers would think about all the factors that come into play in the process of making those spatial divisions for students and then think about what those separations might mean in the development of their identities.

Identity—commonly expressed in the question "Who am I?"—involves how people come to see themselves as individuals and as members of larger society. Critical geographers suggest that this process of identity formation always happens in spaces that both construct and limit possibilities and the places that have already been invested with meaning. A critical geography of education insists on including all the varying forces that act on young people, educators, and community members as they come to know themselves and their place in the world.

Although most education scholars would suggest that the process of identity formation takes place in dramatic ways during the period of adolescence, most contemporary thinkers describe the process of identity as one that is continual and ever-changing. This is to say that for critical geographers, place and space play a role in setting the limits for a person's process of identity and simultaneously reflect and come to have meaning in the interaction with the identities of those young people. Some might suggest that the question "Who am I?" needs to begin with the spatial twist of "Where am I?"

Looking at Schools

The geographies of schools serve as a point to begin looking at youth and educators and their intersections with power and identity within a spatial frame. Beginning at the smallest scale, some scholars study the physical geography of classrooms themselves and map out how the teachers interact with students, how the students interact—or don't interact—with each other, and how bodies themselves are arranged and arrange themselves.

Expanding the scale, other researchers study school buildings and architectural layouts to see if the experiences of students are in some way controlled by the physical nature of a school campus. Many of these thinkers, for example, suggest that racial segregation continues to happen in desegregated schools through the tracking of students through certain classes and therefore through certain parts of the building.

Other researchers offer an analysis of schools that begins with the unequal system of school funding based on property value and the taxes the states collect. How neighborhoods themselves are segregated and how resources are spread out across school systems might be the basis of their study. Critical geography, interested in coming to understand human interaction in all its complexity, would insist on an analysis that includes all these scales at once.

While schools might be a place to start such study, they should not be the markers of where to stop. Many studies of youth and education tend to stop at the doorway of the school, failing to recognize how young people bring the worlds of their homes and neighborhoods into the school everyday and also how events in the school day are carried outside the four walls of school buildings. Very often, youth culture is simply divided into studies of school experiences and studies of rebellion—or what some call "deviance." Critical geographers think that division is too simple an explanation or even description of the lives of young people. Critical geography also insists that trying to understand students' experiences in schools must include some understanding of the spaces and places that the students bring with them—in other words, educators must know where kids are coming from.

Finally, it has been suggested by some critical geographers that if an individual or group enjoys some degree of power, then they must be able to have some control of space. If this is true, then some study of the spaces that are controlled by youth should become a part of our study of human geography. How students divide up the spaces of schools and neighborhoods shows how structures of power are at work within those groups and speak to how the culture of those young people works. Assumptions about youth and what was once termed deviance no longer sufficiently explain the behaviors, cultures, or geographies of young people. Thus critical geography offers another insight into the particular ways in which identity is formed as a process, how structures of power operate on young people, and how youth culture responds to the places in which it resides.

Robert J. Helfenbein

See also Critical Theory; Cultural Studies; Marxism; Postcolonialism; Postmodernism

Further Readings

Aitken, S. (2001). *Geographies of young people: The morally contested spaces of identity.* New York: Routledge.

Harvey, D. (1996). *Justice, nature, and the geography of difference.* Cambridge, MA: Blackwell.

Hubbard, P., Kitchin, R., & Valentine, G. (Eds.). (2004). *Key thinkers on space and place.* Thousand Oaks, CA: Sage.

Massey, D. (1994). *Space, place, and gender.* Minneapolis: University of Minnesota Press.

Soja, E. (1989). *Postmodern geographies: The reassertion of space in critical social theory.* New York: Verso.

CRITICAL LITERACY

Critical literacy has its origins in progressive traditions and the Frankfurt School. It argues that, to become truly literate, students must move beyond simply decoding text and absorbing facts and information to thinking critically about what they learn and apply it to their lives. Critical literacy recognizes that learning involves power relationships, ones that are often defined by how language is used to shape discourse.

Critical literacy is most commonly associated with the work of the Brazilian educator Paul Freire (1921–1997). In works such as *Pedagogy of the Oppressed* (1970) and *Cultural Action for Freedom* (1972), Freire argues that knowledge that is imposed through a "banking model" (one that deposits facts and ideas into the learner) is of little value and often is used as a means of domination. Instead, he argues that learners need to become critically literate. In this context, learning to read represents not just a technical skill, but the development of a critical social and cultural awareness.

Thus, in his system of adult education, Freire has learners explore "generative" themes in order to learn reading and writing. These themes are drawn from real issues in adults' lives, such as work, family, taxes, and politics. In this regard, Freire's work is similar in purpose to that of the American philosopher John Dewey, which emphasized that learning be connected directly to the actual life and experience of learners, and thus provide the foundation for them to become socially and politically engaged citizens.

Models of critical literacy often challenge the status quo. An example would be the systematic critique of the work conservative educational commentator E. D. Hirsch, Jr. In *Cultural Literacy: What Every American Needs to Know* (1987), as well as subsequent works such as *The Schools We Need and Why We Don't Have Them* (1996), Hirsch argues for a model of "cultural literacy " in which being literate involves a "core" body of knowledge—ideally based around the accomplishments and traditions of American society. Eugene F. Provenzo, Jr., in his critique of Hirsch, *Critical Literacy: What Every American Ought to Know* (2005), has argued that Hirsch fails to take sufficiently into account the extent to which the ideas he emphasizes are representative of a dominant culture, which imposes its values and beliefs on individuals largely for its own purposes.

Hirsch includes in *Cultural Literacy* a list of 5,000 things "every American citizen needs to know." Provenzo challenges Hirsch and his list with an alternative collection of 5,000 words and ideas. Unlike

Hirsch, Provenzo argues that there are many "lists" that could be constructed, but that the real issue is that children should learn a process of democratic dialogue and negotiation in which they debate what is important, rather than simply have it imposed as part of a banking model by self-selected authorities such as Hirsch.

In summary, critical literacy is grounded in the idea of critical pedagogy and learning. As such, it involves an essentially democratic and dialogic process—one based on critical thinking and reflection and open to many ways of viewing culture and society. In doing so, it embraces the diversity which is inherent in contemporary American culture.

Eugene F. Provenzo, Jr.

See also Cultural Pluralism; Hegemony; Progressive Education

Further Readings

Freire, P. (1970). *Pedagogy of the oppressed.* New York: Continuum.

Hirsch, E. D., Jr. (1987). *Cultural literacy: What every American needs to know.* Boston: Houghton-Mifflin.

Hirsch, E. D., Jr. (1996). *The schools we need and why we don't have them.* New York: Doubleday.

Provenzo, E. F., Jr. (2005). *Critical literacy: What every American ought to know.* Boulder, CO: Paradigm Press.

CRITICAL MATHEMATICS

Critical mathematics education addresses three intersecting issues in educational theory: the question of a disciplinary orientation to curriculum development and design, the notion of "critical" educational approaches, and the peculiarities of mathematics itself as a nexus of educational and/or "critical educational" issues. This entry looks at the definition of mathematics from a critical perspective, discusses how critical mathematics is implemented, and examines issues of power and the impact of the new perspective.

Defining Terms

The modifier *mathematics* at once assumes a need for a special set of questions and issues peculiar to a subject area while also raising the specter of challenges to a disciplinary orientation to educational programs. Is there something special about mathematics that warrants a separate entry in this volume, distinct from, say, language arts, social studies, science, vocational education, and so on?

One might define mathematics as a subset of literacy, involving reading, writing, listening, speaking, and otherwise representing ideas that focus on patterns, numbers, shapes, space, probabilities, and informatics. If so, do we need unique approaches to teaching, learning, and assessment, or are the methods of instruction and theorizing pretty much the same as for any other subject area of a school curriculum? Such questions are of interest because of the specific history of (Western) mathematics, which has so often been used as a model of rational thought and knowledge in general. Because this history is so intertwined with the history of Amero-European thought, mathematics is in its own way a symbol of the intellectual history of colonialism and imperialism, as demonstrated in the fields of ethnomathematics and in ideological analyses of mathematics as constructed in ways that mask its relationships with power and social inequalities.

The modifier *critical* is added by theorists who are concerned with the constraining and enabling functions of mathematics education within a democratic society: As with any form of education, mathematical experiences may empower and disempower at the same time. Many mathematical innovations have been created in order to serve those who control, for example, within the development of military weapons and strategies, governmental accounting systems, and business practices. Issues of access internationally and in local contexts set up systems of social reproduction of inequality, where students of mathematics at various levels of education experience different forms of mathematics curriculum, with further implications for equity and diversity.

On the other hand, movements to introduce critical mathematics education and mathematics education for social justice enable students to use mathematics as a tool for social critique and personal empowerment. And knowledge of mathematics, as with any specific knowledge area, can be used as a cultural resource for reading the world and in the process transforming one's place within that world. Malcolm X's use of the concept of a variable for his name both represented the legacy of slavery and defined a political, cultural, and historic moment in the history of the United States. Students who invent their own algorithms for distributing governmental funds are confronted with the limitations of "mathematizing" social decisions.

Implementation

Critical mathematics education demands a critical perspective on both mathematics and the teaching and learning of mathematics. As Ole Skovsmose describes a critical mathematics classroom, the students (and teachers) are attributed a "critical competence." A century ago, mathematics educators moved from teaching critical thinking skills to using the skills that students bring with them. It was accepted that students, as human beings, *are* critical thinkers and would display these skills if the classroom allowed such behavior. It seemed that critical thinking was not occurring simply because the teaching methods were preventing it from happening; through years of school, students were unwittingly "trained" *not* to think critically in order to succeed in school mathematics. Later, ways were found to lessen this "dumbing down of thinking through school experiences."

Today, there is a richer understanding of human beings as exhibiting a *critical competence,* and because of this realization, it is recognized that decisive and prescribing roles must be abandoned in favor of all participants having control of the educational process. In this process, instead of merely forming a classroom community for discussion, Skovsmose suggests that the students and teachers together must establish a "critical distance." What he means with this term is that seemingly objective and value-free principles for the structure of the curriculum are put into a new perspective, in which such principles are revealed as value loaded, necessitating critical consideration of contents and other subject matter aspects as part of the educational process itself.

Christine Keitel, Ernst Klotzmann, and Ole Skovsmose together offer new ideas for lessons and units that emerge when teachers describe mathematics as a technology with the potential to work for democratic goals, and when they make a distinction between different types of knowledge based on the object of the knowledge. The first level of mathematical work, they write, presumes a true-false ideology and corresponds to much of what is found in current school curricula. The second level directs students and teachers to ask about right method: Are there other algorithms? Which are valued to meet needs? The third level emphasizes the appropriateness and reliability of the mathematics for its context. This level raises the particularly technological aspect of mathematics by investigating specifically the relationship between means and ends.

The fourth level requires participants to interrogate the appropriateness of formalizing the problem for solution; a mathematical/technological approach is not always wise, and participants would consider this issue as a form of reflective mathematics. On the fifth level, a critical mathematics education studies the implications of pursuing special formal means; it asks how particular algorithms affect people's perceptions of (a part of) reality, and how people conceive of mathematical tools when they use them universally. Thus the role of mathematics in society becomes a component of reflective mathematical knowledge.

Finally, the sixth level examines reflective thinking itself as an evaluative process, comparing levels 1 and 2 as essential mathematical tools, levels 3 and 4 as the relationship between means and ends, and level 5 as the global impact of using formal techniques. On this final level, reflective evaluation as a process is noted as a tool itself and as such becomes an object of reflection. When teachers and students plan their classroom experiences by making sure that all of these levels are represented in the group's activities, it is more likely that students and teachers can be attributed the critical competence that is now envisioned as a more general goal of mathematics education.

Issues of Power

In formulating a democratic, critical mathematics education, it is also essential that teachers grapple with the serious multicultural indictments of mathematics as a tool of postcolonial and imperial authority. What was once accepted as pure, wholesome truth is now understood as culturally specific and tied to particular interests. The mathematics-military connections and applications of mathematics in business decisions are examples in this sense of fantasies of power and control rather than consistently literal forms of control and power.

Critical mathematics educators ask why students, in general, do not readily see mathematics as helping them to interpret events in their lives or gain control over human experience. They search for ways to help students appreciate the marvelous qualities of mathematics without adopting its historic roots in militarism and other fantasies of control over human experience.

One important direction for critical mathematics education is in the examination of the authority to phrase the questions for discussion. Who sets the agenda in a critical thinking classroom? Authors such as Stephen Brown and Marion Walter lay out a variety of powerful ways to rethink mathematics investigations through what they call "problem posing," and in doing so they provide a number of ideas for enabling students both to "talk back" to mathematics and to use their problem solving and problem posing experiences to learn about themselves as problem solvers and posers, instead of as an indicator of their abilities to match a model of performance.

In the process, they help to frame yet another dilemma for future research in mathematics education, and education in general: Is it always more democratic if students pose the problem? The kinds of questions that are possible, and the ways that people expect to phrase them, are to be examined by a critical thinker. The questions themselves might be said to reveal more about people's fantasies and desires than about the mathematics involved. Critical mathematics education has much to gain from an analysis of mathematics problems as examples of literary genre.

And finally, it becomes crucial to examine the discourses of mathematics and mathematics education in and out of school and popular culture. Critical mathematics education asks how and why the split between popular culture and school mathematics is evident in mathematical, educational, and mathematics education discourses, and why such a strange dichotomy must be resolved between mathematics as a "commodity" and as a "cultural resource." Mathematics is a commodity in the consumer culture because it has been turned into "stuff" that people collect (knowledge) in order to spend later (on the job market, to get into college, etc.). But it is also a cultural resource in that it is a world of metaphors and ways of making meaning through which people can interpret their world and describe it in new ways, as in the example of Malcolm X. Critical mathematics educators recognize the role of mathematics as a commodity in society; but they search for ways to effectively emphasize the meaning-making aspects of mathematics as part of the variety of cultures. In doing so, they make it possible for mathematics to be a resource for political action.

Potential Impact

The history of critical mathematics education is a story of expanding contexts. Early reformers recognized that training in skills could not lead to the behaviors they associated with someone who is a critical thinker who acts as a citizen in a democratic society. Mathematics education adopted the model of enculturation into a community of critical thinkers. By participating in a democratic community of inquiry, it is imagined, students are allowed to demonstrate the critical thinking skills they possess as human beings, and to refine and examine these skills in meaningful situations.

Current efforts recognize the limitations of mathematical enculturation as inadequately addressing the politics of this enculturation. Mathematics for social justice, as advocated by such authors as Peter Appelbaum, Eric Gutstein, and Sal Restivo, uses the term "critical competence" to subsume earlier notions of critical thinking skills and propensities. A politically concerned examination of the specific processes of participation and the role of mathematics in supporting a democratic society enhances the likelihood of critical thinking in mathematics, and the achievement of critical competence.

Peter Appelbaum

See also Curriculum Theory

Further Readings

Appelbaum, P. (1995). *Popular culture, educational discourse and mathematics.* Albany: State University of New York Press.

Brown, S. I. (2001). *Reconstructing school mathematics: Problems with problems and the real world.* New York: Peter Lang.

Dias, A. L. B. (1999). Becoming critical mathematics educators through action research. *Educational Action Research, 7*(1), 15–34.

Frankenstein, M. (1983). Critical mathematics education: An application of Paulo Freire's epistemology. *Journal of Education, 165*(4), 315–339.

Gellert, U., & Jablonka, E. (Eds.). (2007). *Mathematisation and demathematisation: Social, philosophical and educational ramifications.* Rotterdam: Sense.

Gutstein, E. (2006). *Reading and writing the world with mathematics: Toward a pedagogy for social justice.* New York: Routledge.

Keitel, C., Kotzmann, E., & Skovsmose, O. (1993). Beyond the tunnel vision: Analysing the relationship of mathematics, technology and society. In C. Keitel & K. Ruthven (Eds.), *Learning from computers. Mathematics education and technology* (NATO-ASI-Series, F 121; pp. 242–279). Berlin: Springer.

Skovsmose, O. (1994). *Towards a philosophy of critical mathematics education.* Dordrecht: Kluwer/Springer.

CRITICAL PSYCHOLOGY

Critical psychologists consider society unjust for many and want to do something about it. They believe that psychology has the potential to bring about a significantly better world in keeping with its ethical mandate to promote human welfare, but it has failed to do so. Critical psychology is a movement that calls upon psychology to work toward emancipation and social justice, and it opposes the use of psychology for the perpetuation of oppression and injustice.

Thus, critical psychology is an alternative approach to the entire field of traditionally practiced psychology. It can be understood as a metadiscipline that urges the field of psychology to critically evaluate its moral and political implications. It differs from traditional psychology in fundamental ways. Generally, critical psychology emphasizes social justice and human welfare while holding that the practices and norms of traditional psychology obstruct social justice to the detriment of marginalized groups. It highlights the need to critically reflect on largely accepted psychological theories, methods, concepts, and practices and aims to transform the discipline of psychology in order to promote emancipation in society. This entry examines the field's values, beliefs, and practices and discusses implications of educational policy.

Values and Beliefs

Critical psychology considers certain values primary, mainly social justice, self-determination and participation, caring and compassion, health, and human diversity. Values such as these guide critiques of current social structures and inform proponents' visions of a better society. They direct attention beyond individuals toward institutional barriers that maintain oppressive practices. From a critical psychology perspective, the underlying values and institutions of psychology and modern societies reinforce misguided efforts to obtain fulfillment while maintaining inequality and oppression.

Critical psychologists view the good society as based on mutuality, democracy, and distributive justice. They define problems holistically in terms of psychological and social factors related to disempowering and oppressive circumstances. Health status or well-being is viewed as being embedded in collective factors in society, not just individual factors. Collective factors such as social, political, cultural, economic, and environmental conditions are thought to have a powerful influence on the well-being of individuals. Critical psychologists believe that social and political conditions free of economic exploitation and human rights abuses determine quality of life.

Critical psychologists also have distinctive views about the nature of the world and the people who inhabit it. Mainstream psychology's focus is on individualism and a belief that the individual is the proper object of study. Critical psychology views the individual and society as so fundamentally intertwined that they cannot be separated from one another in any way that makes sense.

Critical psychology critiques the presuppositions and perceptions of knowledge in psychology. Adherents view knowledge as infused with political uses and embedded within subjectivity of its creators. Knowledge is seen not as an objective reflection of reality but as dependent on varying historical social arrangements. Critical psychologists ask: Whose interests are supported by knowledge and its application? Who has the power to legitimize a particular form of knowledge over others? Liberation psychologist Martin-Baro suggests that psychology should be looking at issues from the point of view of the dominated—a *psychology from the oppressed.* The task for critical psychology is to question knowledge, to understand how it arose, and to demonstrate whose interests are served and whom it oppresses.

Practices

Given these values and beliefs, critical psychologists promote transformative *ends*—structural changes that benefit the powerless—while also considering the *means* used to achieve those ends. From a critical psychology perspective, these values and beliefs require alternative methodologies. Proponents believe that methods should be chosen based on the ability to create findings that are practically relevant in the real world and benefit the powerless. Critical psychologists depend mostly on qualitative approaches, as qualitative methodologies have several distinct features that facilitate critical analysis: an open-ended stance, reflection on subjectivity and bias, concern about relationships, and complex, open-ended questioning and analysis. It has been argued that the progress in statistics and experimental design is in reverse proportion to being able to apply results to real-world contexts. As researchers and practitioners, critical psychologists reflect on their existing practices and scrutinize their efforts. They try to understand how their own power and subjectivity influence what they do and feel and study.

The structural phenomenon of power has widely been neglected in traditional psychological discourse and research. Critical psychology defines power as the capacity and opportunity to fulfill or obstruct personal, relational, or collective needs. Practitioners make explicit the pervasive influence of power in all they do as psychologists. Particular forms of knowledge are supported by particular societal and psychological practices. These practices are in turn reinforced by particular distributions of power. Critical psychologists believe that power should be shared equally and that legitimacy comes through a democratic process that professional psychology, community and educational settings, and society at large generally lack. Mainstream psychologists and others whose activities depend upon psychology's status quo often have a personal and professional interest in maintaining and supporting particular forms of knowledge. Critical psychology is about understanding how power pervades what psychologists do and help to transform that awareness into practices that promote liberation and well-being.

Implications for Policy Studies

Methodology

An educational science influenced by critical psychology would involve students, parents, teachers, and school administrators in the tasks of critical analysis and transformation of educational situations. It would develop research partnerships to decide the means and ends of the investigation and utilize participatory action research approaches because transformation cannot be achieved without engaging the wisdom of the social actors affected. It would ask citizens and stakeholders what they would change in their settings, while promoting participants' self-determination and democratic participation in the research project. It would create a climate of collaboration and foster a sense of collective ownership to ensure that there is follow-up of research recommendations.

It would rely on qualitative approaches because these are more suited to understanding the differing perspectives of people and groups whose voices have not been adequately heard. Following this model, researchers should attempt as much as possible to accurately hear what their informants are saying. They have a duty to analyze informants' voices, but that they must do so in a way that remains accountable to them.

Focus of Research and Action

Quite possibly, the most difficult thing for researchers and practitioners to confront is the misguided belief that their work is entirely apolitical. All educational research is generally interested in educational policy, or how the educational system is organized and operated. An educational discipline influenced by critical psychology would be concerned with these questions: Does the field of education promote social justice or injustice? Do educational policies and procedures promote the status quo or equitable reform? Can research, teaching, and practice be redesigned to advance the interests of powerless groups? For whom is educational research directed? Whose interests will be served? Is there an awareness of the societal repercussions of the field's theories and practices, or is the field oblivious of its potential negative effects? Do researchers, theorists, and practitioners declare their values or do they assume that what they do is value free? What are the cultural, moral, and value commitments of the field? Researchers in the field must be well grounded in a critical perspective, aware of their own values, politically astute, interpersonally skilled, and passionately committed to the issue under study.

A critical psychology–influenced field would study content at different ecological levels of analysis and be concerned with identifying and exposing those aspects of social policies that frustrate the pursuit of empowerment, human development, and social justice. Beyond mere identification of those aspects, critical actors in policy studies would be oriented toward transforming the unjust conditions that place obstacles in the way of achieving educational goals. They would frame research topics and questions in action-oriented terms of how they will advance the interests of the vulnerable groups under study. Even at the individual level, they would examine individuals in their cultural, organizational, community, and macrosocial context. They would go beyond seeing problems in education only as technical problems to be solved with technical solutions. Thus, a critical educational science, as described by Wilfred Carr and S. Kemmis, has the aim of transforming education, not just explaining or understanding its different aspects.

Scot D. Evans and Isaac Prilleltensky

See also Policy Studies; Social Justice, Education for

Further Readings

Carr, W., & Kemmis, S. (1986). *Becoming critical: Education, knowledge, and action.* New York: Routledge.

Fox, D. R., & Prilleltensky, I. (1997). *Critical psychology: An introduction.* London: Sage.

Prilleltensky, I., & Nelson, G. B. (2002). *Doing psychology critically: Making a difference in diverse settings.* New York: Palgrave Macmillan.

Sloan, T. (Ed.). (2000). *Critical psychology: Voices for change.* London: Palgrave.

Teo, T. (2005). *The critique of psychology: From Kant to postcolonial theory.* New York: Springer.

Web Sites

Annual Review of Critical Psychology: http://www.discourseunit.com/arcp.htm

Psychologists Acting With Conscience Together (Psyact): http://www.psyact.org

CRITICAL RACE THEORY

Critical race theory posits that racism, White privilege, and historical context dominate and permeate institutions and systems, social norms, and daily practice. The U.S. judicial system, in this view, represents and institutes traditional historical narratives that disadvantage people of color. Research in critical race theory has a conceptual framework based on the experiences of people of color, rather than using the experience of Whites as the norm. Critical race theory can also be described as a movement of those who hope to study and transform the relationships among race, racism, and power. This movement includes activists and scholars in education, sociology, ethnic studies, and women's studies. In education, critical race theory challenges dominant education theory, discourse, policy, and practice by inserting the voices of students and communities of color and centering their experiential knowledge. This entry provides a brief overview of critical race theory and discusses its influence in education and education research.

Background and Tenets

Critical race theory grew out of a confrontation between critical legal studies researchers, dominated by White males, and a core group of legal scholars seeking to situate race at the center of the discourse.

Among those leading this burgeoning form of scholarship was Harvard law professor Derrick Bell, known to many as the movement's intellectual father figure. Bell was a law professor at Harvard Law School until the early 1980s, when his departure and the refusal of the school's administration to hire another professor of color to teach his class on race and constitutional law led some students to question hiring practices. The controversy impelled young scholars and law professors to convene a summer conference in 1989 in Madison, Wisconsin, where they began to outline the assumptions, arguments, definitions, and future research agenda for critical race theorists.

Scholars of critical race theory hold that racism is endemic and ingrained in U.S. society and that the civil rights movement and subsequent laws require reinterpretation. Concepts of neutrality, objectivity, colorblindness, and meritocracy must be challenged, they say, providing a space for the voices of marginalized people to be heard in discussions of reform. Whiteness is constructed as the "ultimate property" in this line of thought. Commitment to social justice and an interdisciplinary perspective are also features of critical race theory.

In addition to these central tenets, the concept of "interest convergence" is essential to an understanding of critical race theory. Bell first introduced the interest convergence concept when he expanded upon traditional interpretations of the *Brown v. Board of Education* landmark court case. In his view, African Americans' demands for racial equality will be met only when Whites believe it will serve their interests, too, and the legal system will not correct injustices if doing so poses a threat to the status of middle- and upper-class Whites.

Working from that perspective, Bell contended that the *Brown* decision was not based on a moral or human rights rationale. Rather, the decision came as a result of reasons directly affecting White citizens: (1) the threat of a spreading communist movement, which worried U.S. leaders about its standing in the foreign relations community; (2) the end of World War II, which meant that returning soldiers of color would demand an improvement in civil rights and educational opportunities; and (3) the need to promote economic growth or industrialization, which even in the South meant that segregationists had to consider changing the economic structure in ways that would maintain U.S. superiority. Bell contended that a civil rights strategy seeking change solely on moral grounds, as exemplified by desegregation of schools, may not be the best way to advance the interests of people of color.

Bell also laid the foundation for discussion of the first major tenet of critical race theory—the permanence of racism—in his book *Faces at the Bottom of the Well*. In his final chapter, "Space Traders," Bell discussed structural racism in society by writing a counterstory of fictionalized space aliens. In the story, White power brokers bargained, negotiated, and dealt away Black citizens to these fictional aliens because it ensured their own survival. The story stresses how Black citizens are relegated to an inferior or expendable status in U.S. systems, structures, and daily life. Like Bell, Richard Delgado and Jean Stefancic stated that racism is the normal routine and the everyday experience of most people of color. Charles Lawrence developed this tenet by introducing "unconscious racism" to the discourse. He noted that racism is part of U.S. history and the nation's cultural heritage and influences everyone influenced by that belief system—even if they are not aware of it.

Influence in Education

Gloria Ladson-Billings and William Tate were the first to consider the usefulness of critical race theory frameworks in the study of educational issues; they cautioned researchers about embracing the new theoretical framework. However, scholars soon began to tell the stories of students and communities of color in higher and public education, integrating critical race theory with their research agendas while promoting social change. Utilizing critical race theory methodologies to provide a space for the voices of marginalized communities and students to emerge was an important addition to the educational literature.

Others situated their research in educational policy and politics. Laurence Parker proposed a framework for analyzing policy decisions by scrutinizing them and the conditions they create for students of color. After many years of scholarship, critical race theory

has emerged as a powerful tool and one that remains to be fully explored.

Enrique Alemán, Jr.

See also African American Education; Civil Rights Movement

Further Readings

Bell, D. A. (1980). *Brown v. Board of Education* and the interest-convergence dilemma. *Harvard Law Review, 93,* 518–533.

Bell, D. A. (1992). *Faces at the bottom of the well.* New York: Basic Books.

Bell, D. A. (2004). *Silent covenants: Brown v. Board of Education and the unfulfilled hopes for racial reform.* Oxford, UK: Oxford University Press.

Crenshaw, K. W., Gotanda, N., Peller, G., & Thomas, K. (Eds.). (1995). *Critical race theory: The key writings that formed the movement.* New York: New Press.

DeCuir, J. T., & Dixson, A. D. (2004). "So when it comes out, they aren't that surprised that it is there": Using critical race theory as a tool of analysis or race and racism in education. *Educational Researcher, 33*(5), 26–31.

Delgado, R., & Stefancic, J. (2001). *Critical race theory: An introduction.* New York: New York University Press.

Ladson-Billings, G., & Tate, W. (1997). Toward a critical race theory in education. *Teachers College Record, 97*(1), 47.

Lawrence, C. R. (1987). The id, the ego, and equal protection: Reckoning with unconscious racism. *Stanford Law Review, 39,* 317–388.

López, G. R. (2003). The (racially neutral) politics of education: A critical race theory perspective. *Educational Administration Quarterly, 39*(1), 69–94.

López, G. R., & Parker, L. (Eds.). (2003). *Interrogating racism in qualitative research methodology.* New York: Peter Lang.

Lynn, M. (2006). Dancing between two worlds: A portrait of the life of a Black male teacher in South Central LA. *International Journal of Qualitative Studies in Education, 19*(2), 221–242.

Parker, L. (1998). "Race is. Race isn't": An exploration of the utility of critical race theory in qualitative research in education. *Qualitative Studies in Education, 11*(1), 43–55.

Parker, L. (2003). Critical race theory and its implications for methodology and policy analysis in higher education desegregation. In G. R. López & L. Parker (Eds.), *Interrogating racism in qualitative research methodology* (pp. 145–180). New York: Peter Lang.

Solórzano, D. G. (1998). Critical race theory, racial and gender microagressions, and the experiences of Chicana and Chicano scholars. *International Journal of Qualitative Studies in Education, 11,* 121–136.

Solórzano, D. G., & Yosso, T. J. (2001). Critical race and LatCrit theory and method: Counter-storytelling. *Qualitative Studies in Education, 14*(4), 471–495.

Taylor, E. (1998). A primer on critical race theory. *Journal of Blacks in Higher Education, 19,* 122–124.

Yosso, T. J. (2006). *Critical race counterstories along the Chicana/Chicano educational pipeline.* New York: Routledge.

CRITICAL THEORY

Critical theory was born in Europe out of concerns among scholars about the powers of fascist states in the mid-twentieth century. The legacy of the so-called Frankfurt School is embodied in many research studies, critical pedagogies, and utopian visions put forth by critical theorists in education for the past forty years. Critical theorists see education as a tool used by the ruling elite to sustain oppression along the lines of race, gender, ethnicity, and sexual orientation. They have also offered pedagogies designed to rebuild schools and social and economic institutions in what they see as more egalitarian ways. Scholars in schools of education employ various methodological tools and theoretical insights across disciplines to reveal what causes social domination and suggest ways to subvert the corporate ordering of life. This entry briefly examines the origins of critical theory, then looks more closely at the many ways it has been applied in education research.

The Frankfurt School

The ideological and philosophical underpinnings of critical theory are generally associated with the Western European philosophers and social theorists who forged the Institute for Social Research at the University of Frankfurt in 1929. By the early 1930s, scholars such as Max Horkheimer, Theodor Adorno, Herbert Marcus, Franz Neuman, and Walter Benjamin, like others across Western Europe, were deeply concerned about the rise of fascism, mass consumer culture, and the state's desire to circumscribe intellectual inquiry and critical dissent by the masses through science and technology.

Unlike other radical scholars in this era, who linked the ruling elite's power to purely the antagonistic relationship between labor and capital, the group excavated the intellectual work of scholars such as Karl Marx, Max Weber, Sigmund Freud, and Friedrich Nietzsche, to understand how the political and economic elite might cement their control over social institutions and the means of production. For instance, the group provided a complex portrait of how institutions, such as the media, schooling, and political and government bodies breed a sense of false consciousness among the masses, enabling multiple forms of oppression and domination and engendering unjust practices and systemic barriers that perpetuate asymmetrical relationships in most social contexts.

Their interdisciplinary approach to understanding the social world also concerned itself with how their intellectual contributions can breathe life into building social movements that have the critical capacity to critique what gives rise to oppression and domination in economic and social contexts. They promoted the belief that it is possible to get beyond current social realities and build social and economic institutions predicated on improving the human condition and on embracing the values of democracy, equality, and justice.

The Frankfurt School scholars' ideas inspired and informed many marginalized scholars during the 1960s and 1970s. For instance, some African American, feminist, and neo-Marxist scholars and activists in the United States examined Herbert Marcuse's critique of U.S. society to gain insight in relation to how oppression on the axes of race, class, gender, and sexuality is promulgated by the dominant economic and cultural elite as well as to find inspiration that their intellectual and cultural work had the power to forge a utopian social world. Gradually, the theoretical contributions and visions of social and economic emancipation proffered by Frankfurt scholars and other enlightened citizens infiltrated schools of educations.

Critical Theory and Education

In the late 1960s and early 1970s, a growing group of scholars in schools of education across North America came to question positivistic types of research generated by scholars in clinical laboratories. Critical scholars argued that these dominant forms of research did little to shed light on how larger institutional arrangements are inextricably linked to the conditions confronting students and teachers inside classrooms, to create instructional practices aimed to help all students learn, and to examine institutional practices and forms of knowledge embedded in schools, which often perpetuate the domination of the 'Other' at all levels of schooling.

For instance, in 1970, Ray Rist went inside elementary classrooms to pinpoint how teachers' expectations influenced impoverished students' academic performance. In his 1970 article "Social Class and Teacher Expectations: The Self-fulfilling Prophecy in Ghetto Education," he showed some ways that schools functioned as an appendage of the ruling elite. Educational institutions spawn the environment and practices that position many students to disengage from schooling, he thought. This cyclical process, in many urban school systems in North America, ensures that capitalists are supplied with a cheap source of labor to produce goods and provide services, he concluded.

Concomitantly, other scholars, such as Samuel Bowles and Herbert Gintis, interrogated the myth that children succeed in schools purely by merit or cognitive ability. In *Schooling in Capitalist America,* the authors made a macroexamination of U.S. schools. They provided evidence of how the culture of schooling prepares youth for the adult work world and ensures class relationships are maintained in the wider society. Class analysis of schooling also became predominant in Europe, through the work of scholars such as Paul Willis and Angela McRobbie.

Impact on Student Identity

Rather than focusing more heavily on how capitalist relations of production affect youths' relationships in K–12 classrooms as well as impact relationships they forge outside of classrooms, the Europeans focused on how the cultural aspects of schooling and mass consumer culture together impact working-class youths' identities, their schooling experiences, and their occupational choices and opportunities. The European researchers' investigations were also designed to gauge whether working-class youth were active participants in reproducing the same working-class status as their friends and family members. Finally, these researchers also hoped to determine whether it is possible to build a larger social movement by positioning working-class youth to understand that the larger social and economic arrangements serve the interests of political and economic leaders rather than their own interests.

The researchers found that working-class youth realize that schooling may not serve their best interest, and they actively resist the norms and values embraced by teachers, administrators, and some of their peers. They showed that despite being located within debilitating schooling structures, youth are active agents who have the power to generate a culture in opposition of the schools. Based on their findings, critical teachers and activists may be able to turn youth resistance into movements against the social and economic structures that they view as perpetuating the alienation and oppression of working-class citizens.

Freire and Oppression

During the 1970s, Brazilian educator Paulo Freire's text *Pedagogy of the Oppressed* impacted scholars across the globe in relation to unearthing what larger political and economic forces generate unjust practices that create oppression in various social contexts as well as how to use critical forms of pedagogies to help students and working-class peoples see what causes oppression in their lived worlds, in their communities, and across the globe, while simultaneously guiding them to individually and collectively tackle the unjust conditions and lived practices girding their oppressive social relationships. Arguably, Freire's work served as a springboard to modernize critical theory.

Scholars have devised new theories and conducted research specifically designed to gauge what economic, social, and political forces cause suffering and oppression in educational systems and in the wider society. Teachers and activists alike have also developed new forms of pedagogies aimed to guide students to reflect upon the totality of social reality, to struggle actively against oppression, and to dream collectively about a world without a hierarchy based on the social markers of race, class, gender, and sexuality.

Issues of Race and Gender

Rather than focusing on oppression of working-class populations, a growing group of activists and scholars have illustrated how students are marginalized in schools based upon the social marker of race. For instance, scholars taking up critical race theory have shown how unjust practices in schools, such as zero-tolerance policies, IQ testing, school-funding formulas, tracking, high-stakes examinations, curricula focusing on the dominant culture's accomplishments, and teachers' low expectations, have collectively ensured that Blacks and Latinos/as disengage or underperform in schools as compared to their White counterparts.

Scholars such as John Ogbu and Signithia Fordham also contend that castelike minorities, such as First Nation's people and Blacks who have been forced to assimilate to the dominant norms in North America, often hold oppositional attitudes toward schooling. Minorities may come to understand that schooling is set up to serve the interests of members of the dominant culture, instead of being configured to promote the intellectual and social growth of all students. Minority students who attempt to succeed in school often have to grapple with social reprisals from their peers and family members (the burden of "acting White"), as being successful in school is viewed as a negative trait. Students who are academically successful may be perceived as outcasts who are willing to denigrate their own culture in favor of embracing the values and beliefs of the oppressors.

Antiracist educators have also formulated Whiteness studies to detect how White citizens are afforded unearned privilege in schools and other social contexts. Some researchers have studied "up" to provide White youth and pre-service and in-service teachers with the reflexive outlet to think about the systemic nature of racism, institutional practices, and policies that have given them unearned power and privilege during their lifetime, and their biases and preconceptions about the Other. These educators have also created pedagogies earmarked to help White students recognize how to unpack the unearned privilege they accrue due to their skin color; they argue that the ruling elite reconfigures what is considered White or normal to keep its citizens divided. Such pedagogies also offer advice on how to become allies with citizens across the racial spectrum to promote social justice in schools and society.

Feminist scholars have examined how gender may be mediated within schools to oppress many girls and women. For instance, scholars have shown how the formal curriculum of schooling fails to focus on the contributions of women, how girls endure sexual harassment in schools' hallways and classrooms, and how young women are often positioned to downplay their intellect in order to be accepted by their peers, male counterparts, and teachers. They have also documented how male governmental officials may fail to provide the needed resources, time, and training to female teachers so as to block them from implementing pedagogies that can promote gender equity, social justice, and cultural transformation.

Some contemporary critical theorists have attempted to get beyond determining how classroom dynamics unfold and illuminating students' identity formation process by gazing through only one social category, such as race, class, or gender. Instead, they have instituted qualitative studies inside and outside of schools to gauge how race, class, gender, and sexuality braid together to disempower specific segments of the school population. These theorists develop pedagogies that are inclusive of the lived experience of all students and envision new educational policies and practices that will help eradicate what they see as oppression on the lines of the aforementioned social categories.

New Pedagogies

Others have attempted to examine the educational experiences of students within specific social groups for the purpose of finding ways to build educational institutions that serve the interest of the public over the interests of political and economic elite. Although the scholars recognize how schooling structures ensure many minority youths' alienation and marginalization inside and outside of classsrooms, they believe much is gained by highlighting how the socio-cultural processes and institutional practices embedded within certain schools help some minority students grow intellectually and socially.

Contemporary critical theorists have also taken several interdisciplinary approaches to understanding the complexity of today's border youth, to promote pedagogies for social and cultural transformation, and to illuminate how unjust institutional arrangements become reinscribed in schools. For instance, cultural studies scholars such as Shirley Steinberg, Eugene F. Provenzo, Jr., Joe Kincheloe, and Henry Giroux have shown how economic and political leaders utilize various forms of media and technologies to create debilitating cultural texts along the lines of race, class, and gender; in this way, these leaders have promulgated corporate and militaristic values over democratic impulses and imperatives and have demonized, trivialized, and commodified today's youth and the Other.

On the other hand, some scholars have shown how the cultural texts, along with the cultural work promoted by alterative youths' subcultures, can provide students culturally responsive education, pedagogies that spur them to understand the nature of the material world and the need to be active agents to promote social and cultural transformation in their schools and communities.

Curriculum Theory

Over the past several years, likewise, curriculum theory has taken an interdisciplinary approach to understand the relationship between power and knowledge and building equalitarian schools and a just society. Scholars typically foreground their experiences of what they believe curricula are, how curricula should be revamped to empower all populations across the globe, and how curricula should be configured in the future. In this vein, scholars such as Madeleine Grumet have employed historical methodologies, psychoanalysis, phenomenology, and autobiography to understand the social, personal, and political dimensions of women and teaching.

In addition, poststructural and postmodern theories have informed curriculum studies by deconstructing who has power to define "truth," by examining what groups create the "official knowledge" taught in classrooms and lecture halls across the globe, and by providing voice and space to marginalized students in classrooms, in the virtual world, and in writing projects. These outlets allow students to constitute their own form of selfhood, one that is free from social categories spawned by the cultural elite to control the Other.

Finally, queer theory and gay and lesbian studies have examined issues of masculinity in education, called into question the makeup of the teaching profession and curricula, and problematized the masculinzation of computing technology and culture.

Movement to Marxism

Several scholars, such as Peter McLaren, Dave Hill, and Nathalia Jaramillo, believe critical theorists must retool their pedagogies and research designs to focus on how class exploitation is the key force behind growing hate, hostility, poverty, racism, and environmental degradation at today's historical juncture. They also have raised concerns and highlighted how corporatist practices and imperatives are flooding K–12 schools and institutions of higher education, so as to block critical theorists from conducting research and instituting pedagogies bent on bringing awareness of oppression along the axes of class, race, gender, and sexuality and how to promote global movements that support social and cultural transformation.

Brad J. Porfilio

See also Antiracist Education; Critical Race Theory; Feminist Theory in Education; Postmodernism; Whiteness and Education

Further Readings

Apple, M. (2000). *Official knowledge: Democratic education in a conservative age.* New York: Routlege.

Bohman, J. (2005). Critical theory. *Stanford encyclopedia of philosophy.* Retrieved July 28, 2007, from http://plato.stanford.edu/entries/critical-theory

Bowles, S., & Gintis, H. (1977). *Schooling in capitalist America.* New York: Basic Books.

Brown, W. (2006). Feminist theory and the Frankfurt School: Introduction. *A Journal of Feminist Cultural Studies, 17*(1), 1–6.

Davis, A. (2004). Preface. In D. Kellner (Ed.), *The new left and the 1960s: Collected papers of Herbert Marcuse.* New York: Routledge.

Farber, P., Provenzo E. F., Jr., & Holm, G. (Eds.). (1994). *Schooling in the light of popular culture.* Albany: State University of New York Press.

Fordham, S., & Ogbu, J. (1986). Black students' school success: Coping with the "burden of 'acting White.'" *The Urban Review, 18*(3), 176–206

Freire, P. (1970). *Pedagogy of the oppressed* (M. B. Ramos, Trans.). New York: Herder & Herder.

Giroux, H. A. (1991). Postmodernism as border pedagogy: Redefining the boundaries of race and ethnicity. In H. A. Giroux (Ed.), *Postmodernism feminism and cultural politics: Redrawing educational boundaries* (pp. 217–256). Albany: State University of New York Press.

Giroux, H. A., & McLaren, P. (Eds.). (1994). *Between borders.* New York: Routledge.

Grumet, M. (1988). *Bitter milk.* Amherst: University of Massachusetts Press.

Hill, D. (2004). Critical education for economic and social justice: A Marxist analysis and manifesto. In M. Pruyn & L. M. Huerta-Charles (Eds.), *Teaching Peter McLaren: Paths of dissent.* New York: Peter Lang.

Kellner, D. (1992). *Critical theory, marxism, and modernity.* Baltimore: Johns Hopkins University Press.

Kellner, D. (1998). *Critical theory today: Revisiting the classics.* Retrieved September 28, 2007, from http://www.uta.edu/huma/illuminations/ke1110.htm

Kincheloe, J. (2004). *Critical pedagogy primer.* New York: Peter Lang.

McLaren, P. (2005). *Capitalists and conquerors: A critical pedagogy against empire.* New York: Rowman & Littlefield.

McRobbie, A. (1980). Settling accounts with subcultures: A feminist critique. *Screen Education, 34,* 37–49.

Pinar, W. F. (1998). *Queer theory in education.* New York: Lawrence Erlbaum.

Rist, R. (1970). Social class and teacher expectations: the self-fulfilling prophecy in ghetto education. *Harvard Educational Review, 40,* 411–451.

Soloman, P. (1992). *Black resistance in high school: Forging a separatist culture.* Albany: State University of New York Press.

Steinberg, S., & Kincheloe, J. (2004). *Kinderculture: The corporate construction of childhood.* New York: Westview Press.

Willis, P. (1981). *Learning to labor: How working class kids get working class jobs.* New York: Columbia University Press.

CRITICAL THINKING

Critical thinking may be defined as the art of continuous questioning and analysis of two sides of an argument, problem, or context. Furthermore, the ability to think critically requires human beings to embrace a world free of orthodox views and/or sectarian, social norms, in a continuous effort to search for the essence of truth and expand the knowledge base. Critical thinking is an imperative for a cohesive social order as well as the development of an interdependent global focus. As such, it is a priority for educational reform ventures at all levels—from K–12 through postsecondary institutions—that attempt to foster higher order thinking skills in students and provide them with a holistic framework for discerning information in all terrains of scientific inquiry and sociopolitical agendas, toward the advancement of civilization.

Thus, the critical thinking objective, vis-à-vis methods of teaching, is for students to become engaged in a critical dimension—one where analysis, synthesis, and evaluation (higher order thinking skills) are practiced—as opposed to a didactic context where only fragmentation and rote memorization prevail as hallmarks of effective teaching and learning. Clearly, a critical thinker learns how to think rather than what to think.

History of Critical Thinking

The origins of critical thinking are usually associated with the Golden Age of Athens and Socratic questioning. Indeed, philosophy, from the Greek *filo sofia*—love of wisdom—encompasses the interdependence of constructs without clear delineations between disciplines and/or subject areas. It was in this context that the Greeks practiced the *trivium*—grammar, rhetoric, and logic—and *quadrivium*—arithmetic, astronomy, geometry, and music. Socrates' teachings centered on a continuous dialogue and in-depth examination of an issue through the use of questions and answers to arrive at a quasi-finite conclusion or argument. This context served as the framework for what was to become the empirical view, practiced by Aristotle, as opposed to the idealistic or absolute world of ideas, promoted by Plato. In his painting *The School of Athens,* the Renaissance artist Raphael depicts the duality between the acceptance of absolute truths (Plato) and the questioning of static knowledge (Aristotle).

Indeed, it was the Aristotelian paradigm that eventually transcended through the ages and influenced the minds of those who played an active role in the Enlightenment; it was in this context that the adoption of skepticism and consistent intellectual debate were accepted as essentials for objectivity or accuracy in thinking. On these premises, a liberal arts education model was founded in Europe and later implemented in the colonial colleges.

Critical Thinking and Teaching

Teaching students how to think cannot be carried out in isolation. The very nature of this intellectual exercise requires the absence of what educational thinker Paulo Freire referred to as "banking education"— where knowledge is literally "deposited" in the learner's mind. Teaching students how to think calls for a reflective pedagogy or dialogue whereby the students and teacher collaborate and build on preexisting knowledge.

There are myriad teaching methods that will foster critical thinking skills. Each of these must promote the disciplining of the mind toward thinking that involves reflexivity, skepticism, and a holistic approach to teaching and learning. Teachers in the elementary grades may begin to move students beyond rote memorization and fragmentation of facts by providing them with opportunities for the appreciation of cultural diversity. At the postsecondary level, college professors must actively engage students in processes that demand the evaluation of knowledge. For example, in a college history course, students may be asked to read articles and consider the issue of "voice" within the context of historiography, given the dominant or sociopolitical forces of the period. Students in a sociology course may be required to develop an archival document that represents a specific neighborhood or community.

Thinking that does not allow one to question or analyze two sides of an argument is driven by fallacies and, thus, is nonprogressive in the human quest to advance knowledge. The first decade of the twenty-first century calls for a global citizenship platform. This requires that individuals practice a liberal education and be able to analyze, synthesize, and evaluate the very elements that constitute the social fabric.

Although educational reform must continue to respond to the call for accountability at the K–12 as well as postsecondary levels, educators must work to emphasize a critical pedagogy. Within this context, thinking that is critical aims to provide a teaching method that allows for open-ended questions, while evaluating new theories through continuous reflection and mental discipline. Critical thinking is an imperative for the human experience and the pursuit of a democratic world order.

Carmen L. McCrink and Teri D. Melton

See also Classical Curriculum; Critical Literacy; Models and Methods of Teaching; Trivium and Quadrivium

Further Readings

Freire, P. (2002). *Pedagogy of the oppressed.* New York: Continuum Press.
Gabennesch, H. (2006). Critical thinking: What is it good for? (In fact, what is it?). *The Skeptical Inquirer, 38*(3), 36–41.
McMahon, C. M. (Ed.). (2005). Critical thinking: Unfinished business. *New Directions for Community College Journal, 130.*
Paul, R. (1995). *Critical thinking: How to prepare students for a rapidly changing world.* Santa Rosa, CA: Foundation for Critical Thinking.
Yuretich, R. F. (2004). Encouraging critical thinking. *Journal of College Science Teaching, 33*(3), 40–46.

CROSS-CULTURAL LEARNING IN ADULTS

As communication technologies are connecting people from all over the world within seconds, exploding world populations are becoming more mobile than ever before, and globalization is affecting national economies, political systems, businesses, and entire cultures. As a result, there is an increasing demand for cross-cultural learning in adult education. This exponential change impacts individuals and populations daily on a global scale, confronting millions of people with different cultural values, traditions, and norms, and often finding them ill-prepared to respond.

Cross-cultural learning enables people to gain an awareness and understanding of an environment characterized by many cultures intersecting and interacting; people are then capable of functioning and problem-solving as global citizens. From a sociocultural-global perspective, this type of learning may prove essential for future coexistence of populations on both a micro and macro level. Cross-cultural learning blends the traditional types of experiential training techniques with eclectic, innovative educational teaching methods, striving to equip the adult learner with both theoretical knowledge and practical skills and competencies. Effective cross-cultural learning also requires flexible leadership that is well versed in many educational methods. A variety of cross-cultural training programs have been developed over the years to assist specific cultural groups with cross-cultural adjustments or to prepare individuals for overseas assignments.

Terminology

Cross-cultural is sometimes replaced by *intercultural* or *multicultural*. Both of these terms are used in various fields, such as education, communication, psychology, and anthropology, to refer to the exchange between two cultures or interaction between two or more differing cultures. All of these terms may also refer to the inclusion of multiple cultural groups. *Multicultural* has also been used in particular sociopolitical and educational contexts in Europe to describe a specific type of integration within communal policy and guidelines for community development programs.

The term *cross-cultural* is generally used to designate that which extends beyond one set of cultural norms, traditions, boundaries, and unspoken givens and is applicable and relevant across differing cultures or in varying cultural contexts. Hence, cross-cultural learning for members of one culture involves the inclusion of familiar and given elements in their own culture coupled with unfamiliar elements of other cultures, challenging them to travel outside their cultural conventions and personal comfort zone into unknown territory. The metaphor of "exploration" captures the essence of this type of learning experience, however, not into utter wilderness but into foreign terrain, inhabited and valued by others.

Basic Elements

The striking aspect of cross-cultural learning is that it involves the convergence of knowledge acquisition

and transferable skills and competencies, which cannot be viewed as separate entities. This type of cognitive and behavioral learning is neither provincial nor static. In contrast to traditional learning assessment in academic settings, cross-cultural learning cannot be measured by standardized tests or the amount of material successfully memorized. Effective cross-cultural learning entails critical inquiry and the subsequent transfer of theory and concepts into praxis. In other words, people develop and learn new concrete skills and competencies based on their newly acquired knowledge, experiences, and understanding.

At the micro or individual level, there are at least four components to cross-cultural learning. Initially, assumptions and facts about cultures are explored. Generally, people—students or participants—first need to understand the significance of culture and become aware of their own cultural scripts and boundaries, including common ethnocentric tendencies, assuming the universality of one cultural system.

Following self-awareness of cultural identity, people are better able to gain an appreciation for significant cultural differences, problems, and conflicts, as well as the often inevitable emotional responses such as stress, frustration, or anxiety that may accompany initial exposure to another, unfamiliar culture. This is often referred to as *culture shock*. Coupled with culture shock is the shock of a problem or a conflict erupting seemingly out of nowhere, or being interpreted and viewed in a totally different cultural context.

A third component of cross-cultural learning, which may or may not occur after the above components, is the critical identification and assessment of cultural variations such as dress and appearance, food and eating habits, body language, nonverbal communication and cues, personal sense of physical space, and individual cultural orientations of what is and what is not appropriate. In this process, individuals are sensitized to common thought and behavioral patterns of other cultures, attitudes, perceptions, interpretations, values, norms, beliefs, and even "peculiar" customs.

Following individuals' attainment of greater awareness, understanding, and possibly empathy, their observations and abstract constructs about cultural variations come to life when they are translated into specific situations to practice. Both the content and the process of this learning target cognitions, behaviors, and emotions. At this point in cross-cultural learning, individuals are challenged to practice, develop, and refine concrete strategies, skills, and competencies via exercises such as role-plays, simulation games, critical incidents, or case studies. Follow-up reflection and analysis of the effectiveness and relevance to real life, and present-day situations are essential and reinforce the learning and transfer of theory into praxis.

At the macro or societal level, fundamental cultural patterns in society such as urban development, national traditions, religious practices, health care, child care norms, patterns of consumption, gender and family dynamics, recreation, socioeconomic realities and political systems, and the role and impact of oppression including racism and prejudice are illuminated. Other specific phenomena may be addressed as well, such as high versus low cultural contexts, monochronic versus polychronic cultural time systems, past or future cultural orientations, or an individualistic versus collectivist framework. Not only information pertaining to cultures in general, but also culture-specific knowledge may be introduced. Concurrently, the spectrum of culturally approved group behaviors, meanings, and expectations might also be explored for distinct populations.

Effective Teaching Methods

Participatory, transformative, and empowering methods of teaching are necessary for cross-cultural learning. The teacher or instructor facilitates a learning process by which participants are enabled to integrate knowledge cognitively, emotionally, and behaviorally. An interactive and experiential framework is essential. Nina L. Dulabaum's evaluation research identified four major guidelines for facilitating cross-cultural learning and cross-cultural conflict transformation: (1) reach a preliminary consensus on the group's focus, goals, and pace; (2) build rapport and foster dialogue and critical exchange (everyone can become an expert, not just the teacher, instructor, or leader); (3) empower participants to take ownership of their learning process; and finally, (4) blend theory and practice continuously.

Effective leadership also includes fostering a never-ending learning cycle characterized by multiple stages

of critical analysis and reflection. As participants explore theory and praxis by experimenting with different strategies for implementation, it is a fine art to maintain the delicate balance of accepting individuals while challenging them to move outside and beyond their personal comfort zone, to think and feel anew, in order to gain greater awareness, understanding, and knowledge.

Cross-cultural learning has applications in many professions, for example in business, education, health care, and the social services where greater sensitivity and competence in dealing with the complexities of cultural differences and practices is critical. Educating people to search for solutions, creatively engineer strategies, and build bridges to members of other cultures with whom they interact at the local, city, state, national, and international level is critical. This in turn has implications and applications for the entire sociopolitical process.

Nina L. Dulabaum

See also Adult Education and Literacy; Cultural Pluralism

Further Readings

Brislin, R. W., & Yoshida, T. (1994). *Improving intercultural interactions: Modules for cross-cultural training programs.* Thousand Oaks, CA: Sage.

Casse. P. (1981). *Training for the cross-cultural mind: A handbook for cross-cultural trainers and consultants.* Washington, DC: The Society for Intercultural Education, Training and Research (SIETAR).

Dulabaum, N. L. (1996). *A pedagogy for cross-cultural transformation in germany: The development, implementation and assessment of violence prevention training seminars.* Hamburg, Germany: Dr. Kovac.

Fowler, S. M. (Ed.), & Mumford, M. G. (Assoc. Ed.). (1995). *Intercultural sourcebook: Cross-cultural training methods.* Yarmouth, ME: Intercultural Press.

Gochenour, T. (Ed.). (1993). *The experiential approach to cross-cultural education.* Yarmouth, ME: Intercultural Press.

Harris, P. R., Moran R. T., & Moran, S. V. (2007). *Managing cultural differences: Global leadership strategies for the 21st century* (7th ed.). New York: Elsevier.

Hofstede, G., & Hofstede G. J. (2005). *Cultures and organizations: Software of the mind.* New York: McGraw-Hill.

Locke, D. C. (1992). *Increasing multicultural understanding: A comprehensive model.* Newbury Park, CA: Sage.

Week, W. H., Pedersen P. B., & Brislin, R.W. (1979). *A manual of structured experiences for cross-cultural learning.* Yarmouth, ME: Intercultural Press.

CULTURAL CAPITAL

According to Pierre Bourdieu, the theory of cultural capital refers to the socially inherited economic, political, and cultural resources that inform social life and situate groups apart from one another. Ideologies and material benefits related to power, privilege, and education are tied up in the possession of these assets, which are not equally distributed among all members of a society. This capital and its allocation are connected to social locations like race, class, and gender. Those most endowed with socially valued and high cultural resources like travel, art, and financial investments represent the most powerful societal classes; thus the cultural capital of the rich, in this definition, holds more value than the cultural capital of the poor.

Educators have been concerned with cultural capital because academic success is connected to it. Cultural capital, like economic capital, has value that can be exchanged for resources that scaffold educational achievement. Schools transmit knowledge in cultural codes that simultaneously afford advantages to some and disadvantages to others. Schools follow and perpetuate the dominant society's cultural ideals and privilege traditional forms of cultural capital.

In the United States the dominant view of cultural capital as related to educational skills, intellect, and practice often highlights traditional measures of success like high standardized test scores, participation in study abroad programs, college preparatory courses, parental college education, and high grade-point averages. The relationship of these markers of academic success to social locations like race, class, and gender means that those not holding privilege in these locations are often described as having no cultural capital to exchange for academic success. Those who are underprepared for college due to attendance at underfunded K–12 schools or whose parents or guardians worked multiple jobs, leaving little time for trips to a museum or library, are less likely to be seen as academic achievers despite the capital they bring.

One of the dangers of Bourdieu's focus on high culture as most socially valuable is that the cultural capital that groups other than the described privileged elite possess, share, and utilize often goes unnoticed and unrecognized. In schooling, this oversight leads to oppressive devaluation leaving some students largely excluded from the discourse of academic success. The cultural capital of nondominant groups can only be extrapolated by a move from the focus on high culture to one more inclusive. Research on cultural capital should include more social groups, not just elites, recognizing that all social groups have cultural assets that warrant scholarly attention.

Cerri Annette Banks and Jennifer Esposito

See also Hegemony; Privilege

Further Readings

Bourdieu, P. (1984). *Distinction: A social critique of the judgement of taste.* Cambridge, MA: Harvard University Press.

Franklin, V. P., & Savage, C. J. (Eds.). (2004). *Cultural capital and Black education: African American communities and the funding of Black schooling, 1865 to the present.* Greenwich, CT: Information Age.

Lareau, A. (1987). Social class differences in family-school relationships: The importance of cultural capital. *Sociology of Education, 60*(2), 73–85.

Perry, T., Steele, C., & Hilliard, A. (2003). *Young, gifted and Black: Promoting high achievement among African American students.* Boston, MA: Beacon Press.

CULTURAL LITERACY

In the United States during the late twentieth and early twenty-first centuries, the notion of cultural literacy presupposes a common cultural ancestry, imagines a homogeneous cultural experience, and assumes a collective cultural legacy. Associated with a conservative social, economic, and political agenda, cultural literacy and related issues often carry partisan connotations. According to its conservative advocates, cultural literacy consists of "factual" information known to a majority of literate Americans. Challengers assert that the dominant culture determines the contents of the cultural canon.

Citing "universal" meaning, "common" knowledge, and historical intransigence as hallmarks of canonical worth, allies of the cultural literacy movement deem superfluous those cultural traditions seen as outside of the dominant culture. Thus, the Western cultural tradition arbitrates both the composition of the cultural canon and the debate over cultural literacy in the United States.

Appropriating the Western, culturally appraised values that inform meaning cultivates the ability to "read" the productions of the dominant culture. Under the auspices of equalizing the educational playing field, curricular perimeters and literary selections are often guided by notions of cultural literacy advanced by members of the dominant culture. According to patrons of the cultural literacy model, comprehension of a range of textual allusions must be qualified by a familiarity with fixed prior cultural knowledge. Minority perspectives and marginalized subjectivity detract from the singularity and power of Western cultural capital. Thus, mastery of this shared cultural knowledge is crucial to social communication, economic participation, and political representation.

The idea of cultural literacy has been most popularized by the University of Virginia Professor of English E. D. Hirsch, Jr. in his 1986 book *Cultural Literacy: What Every American Needs to Know*. In this work, as well as his numerous other publications, Hirsch has developed a widely used curriculum for K–12 schools based on the learning of essential or "core knowledge." Hirsch's views have been consistently criticized by people in the social foundations of education field for being elitist and antidemocratic.

Absent the rigors of critical inquiry, becoming culturally literate involves acceptance of received knowledge. To be considered culturally literate, one must possess a broad scope of superficial knowledge and understand referential allusions stated without definition or explanation within both classical texts and popular media. In order to participate and contribute to the marketplace of democratic American society, the emergent citizenry must be equipped with the cultural knowledge necessary to compete. Supporters of "core knowledge" curricula propose to elevate the perceived status and competency of subordinate cultures by insisting that public education impose the values of the dominant culture. Curricular standards established according to the ideals of cultural literacy presume the existence of a stable institution of knowledge, an invariable conception of democracy, a static definition of culture, and a narrow characterization of literacy.

Kristen Ogilvie Holzer

See also Critical Literacy; Cultural Pluralism; Culture-Fair Testing; Economic Inequality

Further Readings

Bloom, H. (1994). *The Western canon: The books and school of the ages.* New York: Riverhead Books.

Giroux, H., & McLaren, P. (1994). *Between borders: Pedagogy and the politics of cultural studies.* New York: Routledge.

Hirsch, E. D. (1988). *Cultural literacy: What every American needs to know.* New York: Vintage Books.

Provenzo, E. F., Jr. (2005). *Critical literacy: What every American ought to know.* Boulder, CO: Paradigm.

CULTURALLY RESPONSIVE TEACHING

The conceptual foundation of culturally responsive teaching is the belief that culture plays a critical role in how students receive and interpret knowledge and instruction. The pedagogical principles of this approach use cultural knowledge and students' frames of reference to facilitate learning and achievement. Concerns with how to effectively educate diverse student populations leads to conceptualizations of culturally responsive practices that situate teaching and learning within students' values, languages, and cultural orientations. This entry describes how the system works and what research contributes.

Knowledge, Roles, and Practices

The theory of culturally responsive teaching holds that incongruence between students' ethnic culture and school culture leads to dissonance, disengagement, and underachievement. Advocates argue that teachers should develop and use knowledge of diverse cultures to create classroom environments that are not in conflict with students' cultural referents.

Teachers are expected to learn about interpersonal communication styles, language, and cultural norms and incorporate facets of students' cultural life into the curriculum. In this approach, they also reflect on their biases and examine the broader social, economic, and political implications that contextualize the use of culturally responsive practices. They consider how their views of culturally diverse students affect their teaching practices. By developing self-awareness of their cultural values and norms, advocates of this practice believe teachers will better understand the worldviews of diverse student populations. They are expected to engage in cultural reflexivity in more than precursory ways and understand that difference cannot be neutralized when students are forced to adopt the hegemony of normative instructional approaches.

A responsive instructional framework places students at the center of teaching and learning. Teachers nurture students' intellectual, social, emotional, and political identities. They use cultural attributes and references to impart knowledge, skills, and attitudes. Teachers facilitate cross-cultural interaction and help students articulate their cultural assumptions and values. As they compare these with assumptions and values of the dominant culture, greater competency in understanding cultural orientations present in the classroom become obvious. Practices promote student engagement in learning and take into account value orientations, motivations, standards of achievement, and interpersonal patterns embedded in the cultures represented and studied in their classrooms.

Culturally responsive classrooms provide opportunities for students and teachers to interact with each other as a way to understand culturally diverse human beings. Cultural differences in worldviews, communication patterns, and customs are examined without perpetuating stereotypes or essentializing cultural differences. Books and other materials used are ethnically and culturally relevant and offer layered and multiple perspectives. Such exposure is believed to help students articulate their cultural assumptions and values and make comparisons across cultures.

Teachers in the culturally responsive mode incorporate culturally congruent assessments that give students the opportunity to demonstrate their learning. Instructional strategies target students' strengths, and students recognize that knowledge is subjective, value-laden, and culturally constructed. Teachers display a commitment to structure content, instruction, and assessment in ways that support student achievement and demonstrate a belief in students' abilities. Teachers assist students in negotiating conceptual bridges between cultural knowledge and new information. They recognize bias in assessment systems. So do their students.

The essential components of culturally responsive teaching are characterized as: (a) learning environments that are productive, rigorous, and aware of cultural diversity; (b) comprehensive approaches that demonstrate cultural relevance, equitable access, and instructional flexibility; (c) classroom communities based on caring, collaboration, open communication, and understanding of cultural interpersonal differences; and (d) instructional strategies that target students' strengths, habits of mind, and learning styles.

Research on Pertinent Issues

Researchers examine culturally responsive teaching and provide educators with specific strategies for addressing the needs of a diverse population of students. They document the potential salience of culturally responsive practices. By researching how cultural values, norms, and traditions affect particular learners, researchers provide information about the effect of teaching practices on particular groups of learners. In addition, researchers examine differences of individuals within cultural groups, providing rich details that help avoid stereotyping of group characteristics.

Researchers apply culturally responsive teaching principles and practices to classroom management and attitudinal work. This adds a new dimension to the literature by establishing that student resistance and behavior problems may be culturally induced. Research on the use of cultural communicative strategies affirms that students who use their native languages or dialects are significantly affected in motivation and/or achievement. The confluence of language, beliefs, values, and behavior are examined in several studies with specific populations. For example, one study focuses on acts of disclosure and demonstrates how self-disclosure is incompatible with cultural values of many Asian Americans, Latinos, and American Indians,

Researchers focus on trying to understand the impact of the high percentage of urban teachers who are middle-class, White, European Americans on minority student populations. Research studies highlight the need for a diverse teaching staff as a potential resource for advancing culturally responsive practices. Other studies examine the effects of teaching culturally responsive practices on pre-service teachers' practices. This research will be important to teacher educators and has programmatic implications.

The literature on culturally responsive pedagogy provides a compelling case for centering curriculum and instruction on what is good and just for all students with the belief that a tacit understanding of students' cultures and lives are at the center of teachers' work.

Ruth Vinz

See also Multicultural Education

Further Readings

Gay, G. (2000). *Culturally responsive teaching: Theory, research, and practice.* New York: Teachers College Press.

Hollins, E. R. (1996). *Culture in school learning: Revealing the deep meaning.* Mahwah, NJ: Lawrence Erlbaum.

Ladson-Billings. G. (1995). Toward a theory of culturally relevant pedagogy. *American Educational Research Journal, 32,* 465–491.

Macedo, D., & Bartholomé, L. (2000). *Dancing with bigotry: Beyond the politics of tolerance.* New York: St. Martin's.

CULTURAL PLURALISM

Cultural pluralism is a widely used term that has application to and relevance for education. *Culture* can be defined as a common set of values, beliefs, and social practices, as well as the group of people who share that similar identity. The word usually applies to ethnicity and race—for example, African American

culture or German culture—but more contentiously, it may apply to groups of individuals who share traits or similar beliefs, for example, the gay culture or the Christian culture. *Pluralism* describes a situation in which the diversity among the cultures of different groups is an accepted part of a civil society. This entry examines what is involved in cultural pluralism and looks at its application in education.

Defining Culture

How a cultural group is formed and identified varies significantly. Some cultures are identified by an obvious trait or characteristic: skin color, ethnicity, race, gender, and the like. Other cultures involve people who have a consciously shared aim. Whether or not the individual wishes to be associated with the first kind of culture is of little consequence; for example, people who are born Chinese are part of that culture whether or not they wish to actively partake in the group's beliefs and practices.

In a more substantial conception of culture, an individual actively participates in and wishes to be recognized as a member of a particular cultural group. Mutual identification by its members is a key element in these groups. Members identify with people who share a common interest or aim and with other people who feel a reciprocal commitment and attachment. Some individuals not only may wish to participate in the group, but also may believe that being part of the group is a constitutive aspect of their identity: The individual cannot separate personal identity from the cultural identity of the group. This position suggests that when individuals are born, they are born into a particular culture, experience, and language, all of which form an essential part of their identity.

Culture and Education

How cultural pluralism should be applied in educational contexts is unclear. Some argue that schools should create a common identity, even if students represent a diverse range of cultures, whereas others insist that this cultural pluralism should be acknowledged and promoted actively in schools.

France has taken a firm stance: All conspicuous religious symbols are banned in schools. The rationale for this decision is twofold. France wishes to uphold the civic republican tradition through the concept of *laïque*—the separation of church and state—and to actively promote the national civic republican traditions of the political public sphere. Further, through the concept of *laïque,* the aim is that students will be more able to shed their family's identity at the door and to explore alternative beliefs and traditions within the safe confines of the school. There is a concept of "equal exclusion": All individual cultures are excluded within the school setting.

In stark contrast is the U.S. interpretation of the separation of church and state. While religion is not explicitly (at least officially) taught in public schools in the United States, students may wear religious symbols into schools as an aspect of "equal inclusion": All individual cultures are equally welcome. In some cases, the rights of parents to raise their children within a particular culture come into tension with the obligations of a state to protect the future autonomy of children. A frequently cited case in this area is that of the Old Order Amish community in the United States. The 1972 *Wisconsin v. Yoder* case considered whether compulsory school attendance infringes on the religious freedom of parents to raise their children in the Amish way of life.

The Amish faith seeks to return to a simpler life, de-emphasising material success, renouncing competitiveness, and insulating members from the outside modern world. In its legal case, the community argued that integrating Amish children with other children in the mainstream culture and having them learn a curriculum that emphasizes science and technology would seriously threaten their accepted way of existence. To the Amish, survival of their way of life is important enough to limit children's attendance at public schools. Parents therefore asked the court to allow them to remove their children from schooling following the eighth grade.

The U.S. Supreme Court agreed to exempt Amish children from compulsory attendance laws after completion of the eighth grade. The justices decided that having their children attend state schooling would substantially compromise the cultural integrity of the Amish community. The Court further thought that state interference to force Amish children to go to public schools was not warranted. It should be noted that the verdict might have been considerably different if the Amish families had asked that their children be completely exempt from attending public schools. As it was, the Amish agreed that children would attend primary education through the eighth grade. They further guaranteed to continue the children's education within the Amish community, in ways that reflect the skills and training needed for their agricultural way of life. Those skills developed in the Amish community could be transferable to the mainstream world; in this way, should the teenagers wish to leave the Amish community, they could find suitable alternative forms of work within the modern world.

Defining what is deemed reasonable under the parameters of cultural pluralism in education is a difficult and often contested process. The Amish example makes explicit the tension that schools face in trying to balance respect for cultural ideals with the autonomous interests of the child. A pluralist society assumes that schools will foster respect for diversity. Schools, however, are also charged with protecting the interests of each and every child and with cultivating certain skills and dispositions to help students become fully functioning members of society. Trying to balance these two competing aims can be challenging.

Dianne Gereluk

See also Biracial Identity; Church and State; Deaf Culture; Multicultural Education

See Visual History Chapter 14, Immigration and Education

Further Readings

Feinberg, W. (1998). *Common schools/uncommon identities: National unity and cultural difference.* New Haven, CT: Yale University Press.

Gereluk, D. (2006). *Education and community.* London: Continuum Press.

Gutmann, A. (2003). *Identity in democracy.* Princeton, NJ: Princeton University Press.

Reich, R. (2002). *Bridging liberalism and multiculturalism in American education.* Chicago: University of Chicago Press.

Reich, R. (2002). *Yoder, Mozert,* and the autonomy of children. *Educational Theory, 52*(4), 445–462.

Rosenblum, N. (1998). *Membership and morals: The personal uses of pluralism in America.* Princeton, NJ: Princeton University Press.

Wisconsin v. Yoder, 406 U.S. 205 (1972).

Young, I. M. (2000). *Inclusion and democracy.* Oxford, UK: Oxford University Press.

CULTURAL STUDIES

Cultural studies is a multidisciplinary, interdisciplinary, antidisciplinary, even postdisciplinary approach to education. When viewed together, cultural studies and education, broadly, seek to reveal and analyze relationships of knowledge, power, pedagogy, and formal and informal learning production and practice in society and culture. Conveying perspectives from the humanities and social sciences to critically assess education through support, resistance, or transformation, cultural studies engages education through both critique and creativity.

Relational in nature, it is predicated upon intellectual activism as social intervention through engagement with praxis (the bridging of theory and practice) and represents a politicized engagement with society. For these reasons, this relationship is integral to considerations of the social and cultural foundations of education. This entry will provide a broad overview of cultural studies: its origins and related developments, illustrations of the kind of work cultural studies scholars/activists do, cultural studies contributions to education, and misconceptions about cultural studies.

Origins and Developments

Cultural studies practices existed before the term itself, so as with its theoretical origins, its institutional origins cannot be viewed as definitive. Cultural studies may be theorized and historicized in multiple locations, and while those mentioned here are by no means exhaustive, some particular movements and institutions are generally associated with cultural studies and education, and within these, certain individuals and propositions.

Cultural studies has broad origins within the Russian culturology movement and the Harlem Renaissance in New York in the 1920s and 1930s, in addition to folk schools in Denmark and the Appalachian region of the United States in the 1930s (Myles Horton's founding of the Highlander Folk School, now the Highlander Research and Education Center, in 1932 in Tennessee), and the Negritude Movement in France, and francophone Africa and the Caribbean. The 1960s saw the development of subaltern studies in India and Southeast Asia, adult literacy and popular education movements throughout Latin America (perhaps most noted in relation to Brazil with Paolo Freire's work in the 1960s), and popular theater of resistance in Kenya (the Kamiriithu Community and Cultural Centre in Limuru, Kenya, in the 1970s).

The institutional beginnings of Western cultural studies are most often associated with the Birmingham school, originating from the Centre for Contemporary Cultural Studies (CCCS, founded 1964 at the University of Birmingham) in Birmingham, England, and the work of several associated scholars, including Raymond Williams, Richard Hoggart, and E. P. Williams in England, and Stuart Hall, Angela McRobbie, and Paul Willis, among others, at the CCCS.

The 1980s saw the development of the intersections of cultural studies and critical pedagogy, developing as a discourse in discussions of postmodern educational thought and focused on examining the power, politics, and public consumption of schooling and, within schools, exploring representational politics, constructs of student subjectivity, and the analysis of pedagogy; it is praxis oriented and intervenes in the institutional arrangements and ideologies in society that reproduce oppressions and structural inequalities. As teachers are always operating within historically, socially, and culturally situated contexts and constraints, and because education itself is so politically charged and contested, teacher roles cannot help but also be political, a link underscoring education's relationship with cultural studies.

In terms of progressive education, cultural studies has grown as a discourse that has included its institutionalization in graduate schools of education, particularly from the 1990s through today. While a foundational context of its development has been its location in class-conscious social critique and intervention outside of the "confines" of formal education, cultural studies has expanded globally in terms of university programs, conferences, and scholarly publishing.

Characteristics of Cultural Studies

Culture is neither static nor stationary, but constantly in process, creating multiplicity, and approaches to its examination are not limited to any one part of the social spectrum. Unlike other disciplines or subjects, cultural studies has no single object area, theory, or methodological paradigm to neatly or "cleanly" define it. Cultural studies is inherently variable, differing in locations, moments, projects, and areas of inquiry.

Reflecting its flexibility, in theory it does not endorse individuals or canons. Cultural studies has been taken up in various times and places, in locations where commitments were enacted to create social transformation and justice, address local and regional conditions and concerns, and co-construct knowledge in community engagement through popular approaches for purposeful political resistance. Cultural studies emerged from interdisciplinary activist projects within progressive adult education, where commitments to literacy and working-class issues and concerns were major emphases, and where academic and community research collaborations developed.

Cultural studies resists generic definition, as it is an array of many different theories, circumstances, and representations; it is renowned for being arduously difficult to define, and this in turn becomes one of its most defining elements. Along with popular, grassroots performative cultural acts that formed as resistant political expression, cultural studies emerged from several traditional, established, academic disciplines (sociology, media studies, English, and philosophy, among others), while at the same time having an underlying ambivalent, at times altogether contentious, relationship with disciplinarity, which is why it is referred to at various moments as multidisciplinary, interdisciplinary, antidisciplinary, and postdisciplinary. Within cultural studies' theoretical discourses, there are convergences and divergences, and positions are never completely concrete, final, or resolved.

Cultural studies allows concerns and expressions of experience on both personal and collective levels to be taken seriously as important indicators, interpretations, and negotiations of human existence. Because it deals generally with subjective human experience, cultural studies tends to favor qualitative research methodologies and, in particular, ethnography and textual analyses as primary methods of documenting the life and practices of "ordinary" society and culture. It has a commitment to the importance of recognizing popular culture as integral to the relationship of schooling and society, and links the creative and scholarly cultural production of the academy and community.

Continually experimenting with applications of new approaches to existing social conditions, it has been related as a successor to critical pedagogy and multicultural education. It recognizes the importance and validity of nontraditional teaching experiences, and can offer resistance to formal school instruction when applied as a tool for oppressive social reproduction and cultural transmission.

Ultimately, cultural studies may best be spoken of not in a definitive way, but more in terms of characteristics. Handel Wright offers an indicative, transient list of broad characteristics which underpin much of the work designated as cultural studies: (a) informed by and creative of theory yet praxis driven (no practice without theory, no theory without practice); (b) addresses issues of power, is concerned with social justice, examines and critically reflects on social and national identity/identification; (c) takes the popular seriously (mass-mediated or popular culture, "low" culture); (d) deals with issues of social difference and diversity; (e) is interdisciplinary and flexible (subject to radical and far-reaching change); and (f) is specific and local in its projects and never creates or endorses canons. Wright notes that these characteristics need to be treated as subject to negotiation, revision, even rejection, for cultural studies is always a contested terrain.

Examples of cultural studies scholarship that address "low culture" or popular culture are studies that look at media presentations of performers such as Madonna, in terms of gender analysis, or sports stars such as Tiger Woods, in terms of racial analysis.

Cultural studies has helped to argue for the value of sports stories, such as Lance Armstrong's story of recovery from cancer and his continued success as a professional bicycle rider, that can serve as rich examples of narrative stories that can teach students about ethics. Cultural studies makes the case that not only classic literature ("high culture") but also sports stories can serve as examples of narrative arguments for teaching ethics.

Misconceptions About Cultural Studies

There are numerous misconceptions about cultural studies that one finds when working in a cultural studies of education program and when reading student applications to the program, as well as when potential faculty apply for job openings in the program. Sharing these misconceptions may help to further clarify just what cultural studies is, in contrast.

Not a Study of Cultures

Some international students and scholars may think of cultural studies as a study of cultures. There is a tendency for them to assume that individuals from a country other than the United States or United Kingdom, particularly if they have studied in one of these Western countries, can consider themselves experts in cultural studies. It is clear from their applications and letters and e-mail that they are not aware there is a group of scholars known as cultural studies scholars, or that cultural studies worries about certain kinds of problems and seeks to address those problems in particular ways.

Just to be positioned as an outsider to the United States or United Kingdom does not qualify one as a cultural studies scholar, and it is possible to be a cultural studies scholar from the U.S. or UK, for example, and never have traveled or lived in other countries. Today, many people travel, and a good number live for extended periods of time in countries other than where they were born; everyone has the opportunity to meet international people. Still, all of this exposure to diverse cultures does not make a person necessarily or automatically a cultural studies scholar.

Some examples of recent research work might help to illustrate a cultural studies approach to the study of cultures. So Young Kang, a doctoral student from Korea, wrote a dissertation that compared White feminist care theory, Black feminist care theory, and Korean care theory as she proceeded to develop her own care theory as a contribution to the conversation on caring. Her philosophical analysis involved descriptions of the various theories and critiques of them from the varying perspectives, so that it became clear that an eastern perspective is missing from care theory. In this dissertation, power issues were exposed such as positions of marginality for Korean perspectives of caring that are influenced by Confucian ideals. The decontextualized, ahistorical nature of White feminist care theory was troubled and the race/ethnicity discussion of care theory was enlarged beyond the boundaries of Black feminism to include an Asian perspective.

Another graduate student, Zaha Alsuwailan from Kuwait, recently wrote a dissertation that examined the history of girls' education in Kuwait prior to and since the introduction of Western ideals through the discovery and development of the oil industry. Her analysis includes a comparison of Kuwaiti tribal, Islamic, and Western values and their varying influences on the national educational policy for girls' education, as well as the various people's responses to these policies. She examines the issue of girls being educated in terms of history, sociology, and anthropology and brings a cultural studies critique to the analysis in terms of gender issues as well as colonization issues. The work focuses on power issues in terms of the marginalization of women in the culture, but not necessarily in the Koran, and the hegemonic forces that create a situation where the women in Kuwait resist enrolling their daughters in schools and resist earning an education for themselves. What is taught in the all-girls' schools in terms of a genderized curriculum is also analyzed.

Not International Education

Other people apply to cultural studies of education programs who think that cultural studies of education means this is an international education program or a comparative education program. However, both international education and comparative education are fields of study that have a distinctive history of scholarship associated with them. That scholarship does not necessarily address power issues and take a social justice focus, as cultural studies work is committed to doing. One can find scholars with an international focus in most fields of study today, not just in education.

For example, at the University of Tennessee, Brian Barber in Child and Family Studies looks at the problem of children growing up in violent conditions, such as in war zones. Barber's work takes him to various countries, such as Ireland, Bosnia, and Palestine, and it has an international focus, but that does not mean he is a cultural studies scholar. In the Public Health program, Arjumand Siddiqi, an epidemiologist, looks at health care access issues at an international level. Siddiqi studies national health policies and compares, for example, national spending on health care across a spectrum of differing types of governments and economic systems. This is international work and it involves comparisons of differing cultures, but that does not make it cultural studies research.

A cultural studies approach to international studies would entail a need to address the power issues involved, with a focus on social justice issues. In Siddiqi's case, it might involve looking at classical liberal hegemony, which can be viewed as causing people to vote against national health care plans in the United States, for example, even though it would benefit them directly to have such a plan, because the United States's ideology emphasizes the value of choices and the importance of market competition in order to keep prices down and keep quality of health care up. In Barber's work on how war zones impact children growing up in them, a cultural studies scholar would need to address power issues: for example, looking at war in terms of the objectifying, marginalizing, othering process that goes on that allows us to think of the children as "them," "others," "those Iraqis," distant and separate from the United States and its children. A cultural studies focus could provide a framework to address the experiences of children living in war zones in terms of race, class, and gender, as well as degrees of impact depending on varying social status.

Not Multicultural Education

Cultural studies may be erroneously thought of as multicultural education. Multicultural education began

its development in the 1960s and 1970s in the United States with a distinct focus on power issues, in particular racism. However, many believe it has lost its critical edge as it has been mainstreamed into higher education and K–12 grade education. From the perspective of cultural studies scholars, multicultural education has evolved into a "melting pot" kind of approach to educational issues that seeks to embrace the valuing and appreciation of the experiences of all individuals, retaining its contextualizing of individual and collective identities but with less of an interventionist political focus. At one time, it had a sharper political focus that looked at issues of forced assimilation to the White majority culture and the loss of one's unique cultural identity. A cultural studies approach would examine and critically reflect on national identity/identification and the harm the majority culture imposes on various minorities, and antiracist educational approaches have developed that seek to maintain a political focus on social justice issues. Thus one finds that an antiracist approach to education is representative of cultural studies, but a multicultural approach is not necessarily representative.

Cultural Studies and Education: Always in Process

As a social project, cultural studies emphasizes the many cultural phenomena that comprise society, including moments of contention and intervention. In education, it is central to an oppositional, socially interventionist project that attempts the disruption of domination and oppression in schools and society. Even though cultural studies began with an educational focus, through adult education programs such as the Danish folk schools and Highlander Folk School in Tennessee, and extramural programs such as the Kamiriithu Community and Cultural Centre in Limuru, Kenya, over time, education has become marginalized as a topic for cultural studies, while popular culture focuses have continued to develop.

Early Focus

Adult education spaces were initially the only spaces that allowed for a broader and deeper social and cultural critique. However, as other spaces have developed, including cultural studies entering the academy with the establishment of CCCS in the 1960s and gaining legitimacy within higher education, a focus on educational issues has lessened. The world of school buildings and classrooms does not seem to be able to compete with a consumer-driven, product-oriented market, reinforced throughout media and society.

There are, of course, exceptions. Henry Giroux and Handel Wright serve as good examples of scholars who bring cultural studies to bear on educational issues, but both of them have written about the marginalization of educational topics within cultural studies, and both have noted how cultural studies has moved away from its roots.

Early on, cultural studies scholars such as Paul Willis worried about how schools treated working class lads and offered a deep analysis of schools in terms of their class distinctions. Paolo Freire was concerned about how schools create passive students who are so used to being banked, with knowledge deposited in their brains by their lecturing teachers, that they don't learn how to solve their own real problems or how to resist the forced passivity of the banking method. Myles Horton and the rest of the staff at Highlander Folk School strove to create adult centers where people could unlearn the passivity of school learning and begin to see themselves as social activists and leaders for change in a world that is unjust. Adults came to Highlander to learn how to organize and found themselves positioned as teachers teaching each other what they knew and helping each other solve their problems, with the staff at Highlander serving as facilitators and resources to aid in their organizing efforts.

Cultural studies brings to education a focus on social justice issues. It attends to forms of discrimination such as racism, classism, and sexism and how these impact children in schools, and the teachers who teach them. It is concerned with the marginalization of immigrant students, new to a country, and whether their cultural expressions are engaged and their learning styles and needs are addressed in relevant ways. Cultural studies strives to connect educational theory to educational practice as it looks at how power is used in ways that are generative as well as harmful.

Cultural studies pays attention to the formal curriculum in schools (what is present or not in terms of content), as well as the informal and hidden curricula (activities and structures of clubs and extracurricular activities, as well as daily ritual practices such as dismissal for lunch or recess, or the lack of recess or playgrounds in lower income school areas). Cultural studies examines educational policies and how they impact diverse student populations in diverse ways (for example, what are the effects of federally mandated educational policies such as No Child Left Behind and the push for standardized national testing on children and their teachers in poorer school districts?).

Cultural studies considers the commodification of education as a consumer product and attends to marketing issues such as the sponsoring of Coke machines in school hallways and television sets in classrooms, donated by Channel One in exchange for the requirement that children watch Channel One programs while in school. (Channel One is a twelve-minute current-events television program, containing two minutes of commercials, shown in participating public schools who receive free video equipment in exchange. It is often given as a primary example of the "corporatization" of public schools.) Cultural studies takes up the creative democratization of access to knowledge and technology, such as free and open source software and the free culture movement.

A Research Example

In terms of research approaches, cultural studies of education starts with a social problem and then tries to consider what discipline areas and methodologies are available to help solve this problem. It is possible to find numerous discipline contributions and a variety of research methodologies employed to try to address research problems from a cultural studies perspective. For example, one of the authors of this entry, Barbara Thayer-Bacon, recently completed a study of five collective cultures in an effort to help her develop a relational, pluralistic democratic theory that moves beyond liberal democracy, with its assumptions of individualism, rationalism, and universalism, all of which have been critiqued by cultural studies scholars. She also sought to consider how such a theory translates into our public school settings. As a cultural studies scholar, it was vital that her theory writing be informed by practice in order to keep her theory grounded in the historical, local, contingent, everyday world. If she did not turn to the everyday world of schooling practice in various cultures, she risked writing a theory that assumes/imposes a universal, abstract perspective as if it were everyone's reality. A theory that is separated from everyday practice will be unable to actually address anyone's particular reality.

Consequently, when she began working on this project, prior to trying to write any philosophical political theory that moves us beyond liberal democracy, she sought to immerse herself in particular school cultures and communities, relying on a phenomenological methodology. She realized that she was raised in an American culture that embraces classical liberal values of individualism, universalism, and rationalism.

What triggered Thayer-Bacon's concerns with the impact of classical liberal democratic theory on U.S. public schools was the realization that the students who seem to be struggling the most in U.S. schools, the ones with the highest dropout rates and the lowest proficiency exam scores, are also students whose cultural backgrounds have a more collective focus that believes the family is the heart of the community, not the individual, and that "it takes a village to raise a child." These students with the highest dropout rates include Native American, Mexican American, and African American students. Collective, communitarian values of cooperation, sharing, and fraternity, based on a belief in the interconnectedness of self to others, including nature, are in direct contrast to the individualistic values that shaped America's government as well as its schools.

Thayer-Bacon suspected that if she studied Native American, Mexican, and African cultures in depth, she would gain a greater appreciation of the values and beliefs that support a collective sociopolitical focus and a greater understanding of how these values and beliefs function in contrast to individualistic ones. In order to help her address her own cultural limitations and better understand tough questions and issues a relational, pluralistic political theory must face in our pubic schools, Thayer-Bacon designed a study that required her to spend time in U.S. schools where the majority of the students historically have been disenfranchised from the United States's "democracy." She spent time in communities where students from these three cultures are succeeding in American schools, as well as traveled to the origin countries of these three cultures to see how their collective focuses translate into the school curriculum and instruction there.

Notice that this research project is focused on social justice issues (concern for the high dropout rate of students from collective cultures) and how these students are disadvantaged within American schools (the norms of the schools being based on Western European individualistic values). Thayer-Bacon is worried about social difference and cultural diversity. Her study is praxis driven, for it seeks to connect democratic theory to the daily practice of what goes on in public schools. The study is also interdisciplinary, as it involves philosophical theory and educational research, and its research methods use qualitative research techniques through observations, interviews, collection of materials handed out to parents, and field notes, as well as a narrative style of philosophical argumentation, through its phenomenological approach of direct experience and its use of the field notes gathered at the schools as narrative stories to illustrate the philosophical ideas. The researcher went into the field not knowing what she would find and was forced to be flexible and adaptive. Going to specific schools and staying in the homes of local members of the community, made her observations local and specific to particular people in their local settings. All of these qualities are what make this study a good example of cultural studies applied to education.

Other Research Approaches

As with the issues presented in Thayer-Bacon's study, the research and social justice work of cultural studies scholars/activists reflects this range in subject matter and application. Qualitative research applications of cultural studies and education offer a wide range of research possibilities. For example, an ethnographic educational research project conducted by Rosemarie Mincey examined the perceptions of educational experience of twenty adults in Guatemala who were participating in a formal social development program that employed an application of popular education pedagogy most associated with educator Paulo Freire.

In this qualitative study, principal data collection methods were in-depth interviews and participant observations, with twenty interviews with ten male and ten female program participants providing the principal data that were analyzed for the study (participants ranged in age from sixteen to sixty-two, all with little or no prior formal schooling). Observations of classes and the interactions of the participants, both inside and outside of the classroom, were documented.

Findings indicated that, with the exception of several participants who were attending formal schools, all of the participants had their formal educational pursuits interrupted or ended due to several prohibitive factors: large families, the need to help contribute to their families' subsistence, and economic difficulties. Almost all participants indicated a desire to have acquired more formal education, in addition to feeling that better educational opportunities would be key in helping their children and future generations have a better life. Grassroots organization, community activism, and sharing what was learned in the popular education classes with their communities were identified by the participants as being particularly significant.

This study is grounded in Mincey's praxis of working for educational equity as a means of social justice, born from her experiences with formal schooling inequities she experienced as a student from a working poor family in the Appalachian region of the United States. This study draws from a number disciplines; namely, it is sociological in its view of social structures, institutions, and class, and anthropological in its use of data collection methods (ethnography). Theoretically, the study was informed by Marxist influences in the discernment of the roles class and economics may play in the translation of social power and structural schooling inequalities. The analytic perspectives of multiculturalism and feminist critical pedagogy were applied to examine the contextualizing experiences of the intersections of gender, race, class, and schooling, and explored formal education and literacy as components of participatory democracy. The design and issues of this study deeply locate it within cultural studies and education.

The relationship between cultural studies and education has strengthened the reconceptualization of education's social and cultural forms of knowledge, analysis, production, theory, and practice, supporting a foundational engagement with transformative implications for humanity. In higher education, cultural studies' relationship with education has brought the arts and humanities together with education, not just social foundational discipline areas such as sociology, anthropology, history, and philosophy, but also media studies, popular culture, literature, and film, for example, in a way that breaks down discipline boundaries and facilitates an understanding of issues in their shifting, changing complexity.

This multidisciplinary, interdisciplinary, antidisciplinary, postdisciplinary approach to research analysis insists on never losing sight of the political implications of educational practices and the impact education research has on the daily lives of local, particular, contingent human beings, students in classrooms, in daycare facilities, on playgrounds, in shopping malls, on the streets. Cultural studies asserts that classrooms are not neutral places, textbooks are not neutral descriptions of the world, tests and grades are not neutral forms of assessing what students know, and policies such as mandatory attendance and zero tolerance have differing impacts on the lives of children and their families, for they are not neutral either.

Where there are power issues, there are social justice issues, and cultural studies helps education address these issues through its contributions of critical assessment and creative possibilities, its offer of social engagement in resistance and transformation, with the hope of helping to change unjust conditions and improve the quality of people's lives as a result.

Barbara J. Thayer-Bacon, Diana Moyer,
and Rosemarie Mincey

See also Critical Race Theory; Feminist Theory in Education

Further Readings

Adams, F., with M. Horton. (1975). *Unearthing seeds of fire: The idea of Highlander.* Winston-Salem, NC: John F. Blair.

Barber, B. K. (Ed.). (2008). *Adolescents and war: How youth deal with political violence.* New York: Oxford University Press.

Casella, R. (1999). What are we doing when we are "doing" cultural studies in education—and why? *Educational Theory, 49*(1), 107–23.

Dent, G., & Wallace, M. (Eds.). (1992). *Black popular culture.* Seattle, WA: Bay Press.

Freire, P. (1970). *Pedagogy of the oppressed* (M. Bergman Ramos, Trans.). New York: Seabury Press.

Giroux, H. (1994). Doing cultural studies: Youth and the challenge of pedagogy. *Harvard Educational Review, 64*(3), 278–308.

Grossberg, L., Nelson, C., & Reichler, P. (Eds.). (1992). *Cultural studies.* New York: Routledge.

Horton, M., & Freire, P. (1990). *We make the road by walking* (B. Bell, J. Gaventa, & J. Peters, Eds.). Philadelphia: Temple University Press.

Hytten, K. (1997). Cultural studies of education: Mapping the terrain. *Educational Foundations, 11*(4), 39–60.

Kincheloe, J., & Steinberg, S. (1997). *Changing multiculturalism: New times, new curriculum.* London: Open University Press.

Lather, P. (1986). Research as praxis. *Harvard Educational Review, 56*(3), 257–277.

Storey, J. (Ed.). (1996). *What is cultural studies? A reader.* London: Arnold.

Wright, H. (1996). *Notes.* Presented in the 590 Cultural Studies Seminar, University of Tennessee, Knoxville.

Wright, H. (1998). Dare we de-centre Birmingham? Troubling the origins and trajectories of cultural studies. *European Journal of Cultural Studies, 1*(1), 33–56.

CULTURE EPOCH THEORY

Culture epoch theory holds that the civil and religious history of a people is characterized by a succession of ever more complex and sophisticated periods that are distinguishable from one another and that the study of children reveals a parallel development. The theory essentially holds that history is a record of progress from the primitive to the civilized state and that individual abilities, mental as well as physical, also progress from the simple to the complex.

Adherents of this theory believed that, as children grow, their interests and abilities are analogous to those periods their people have passed through as they progressed from early savagery to their present highly civilized state. The relationship between the historical periods and the developmental stages of the individual thus called for a curriculum that included ordered historical content that would interest children as they grew from one stage to the next.

Culture epoch theory is often conflated and confused with but is clearly distinguishable from recapitulation theory. That confusion may be attributed to the idea expressed by C. C. Van Liew in the first sentence of his article on "culture epochs" in the *First Yearbook of the National Herbart Society:* "the individual recapitulates the experience of the race in his development." This idea, which gained widespread currency in the late nineteenth and early twentieth centuries, can be traced back to Johann Friedrich Herbart (1776–1841). In the United States, the theory's acceptance and use by American Herbartians (for example, Charles De Garmo, Charles McMurry, Frank McMurry and C. C. Van Liew) was based on the interpretations of Tuiskion Ziller (1817–1882) and Wilhelm Rein (1847–1929).

E. V. Johanningmeier

See also Progressive Education

Further Readings

Darroch, A. (1901). *Alexander Herbart and the Herbartian theory of education: A criticism.* London: Longmans, Green.

Stafford, D. K. (1955). Roots of the decline of Herbartianism in nineteenth century America. *Harvard Educational Review, 25,* 231–241.

CULTURE-FAIR TESTING

Culture-fair testing, also known as culture-free testing and unbiased testing, has as its purpose the elimination of cultural bias in performance-based assessments for culturally and linguistically diverse populations. Culture-fair tests are designed to be culturally impartial and to ensure that groups and individuals of one culture have no advantage over those of another culture in the assessment process, that is, standardized measures of assessing IQ. Culture-fair testing is commonly used with non-English speakers, both nationally and internationally.

These concepts are based on utilizing measurements with content that are presumed to be common across diverse cultures, a sort of universal measurement. Culture-fair testing was developed to equally measure all participants regardless of their verbal fluency, cultural climate, and education level. This entry discusses how cultural testing came about and what it does.

Background

Culture-fair tests were first developed prior to World War I to assess the ability levels of immigrants and non-English speakers. Soon after, culture-free testing started to evolve to assess multiple intelligences (e.g., adaptable abilities, constant abilities). The concept of culture-fair testing was brought to the attention of the research community and the general public in the late 1960s and early 1970s during the civil rights movement, when cultural, racial/ethnic, and gender rights were the focus of much national concern. Currently, there is only limited research on the use and implications of this type of assessment for individuals from diverse backgrounds. However, the literature does highlight the biases of assessment/testing as evidenced by the rise in popularity of portfolio and curriculum-based measurement in schools.

Today, there is serious debate on the issues of current assessments and their appropriateness for all students, and culture-fair testing has gained popularity across fields of study (e.g., sociology, anthropology, psychology, and many of the behavioral sciences). Culture-fair testing has been proposed in many of these fields to help students deconstruct the unjustified and unfair notions of racial and cultural identity. For example, in the field of special education, the deconstruction of biases by race/ethnicity and culture is vital because of the current and historical disproportionate representation of diverse students in categories of learning disabilities and behavioral disorders.

Traditional Intelligence Tests

Proponents of culture-fair testing take issue with the standardized measures that have typically been used to assess academic success and the measurement of IQ. They believe IQ tests are culturally biased, putting culturally and linguistically diverse students at a disadvantage compared with their European American peers. They further assert that traditional aptitude assessments or IQ tests simply assess students' abilities to understand and apply knowledge of the dominant culture, not students' true abilities, intelligence, and multiple intelligences. As a part of this argument, James W. Vander Zanden maintained that IQ tests measure only recipients' cultural exposures. However, opponents of culture-fair testing contend that it is just as biased and no more reliable than traditional testing and assessments. They maintain that because of the varying complexity and the revolving characteristics of culture, no test or assessment can truly be unbiased.

Types of Culture-Fair Tests

There are two types of culture-fair tests. The first type does not examine verbal intelligence. In fact, it removes all verbal questions and consists instead of questions intended to avoid bias based on socioeconomic or cultural background. The second type of culture-fair test is a system of multicultural pluralistic assessments (SOMPA). This type of test examines both verbal and nonverbal intelligence in addition to social adjustment to school and physical health while taking into account an individual's socioeconomic background.

Within the two types of culture-fair tests, there are a variety of tests that have been created to assess individuals from different racial and ethnic backgrounds. For example, some tests have been specifically designed to assess and measure African Americans' academic success and IQ. The Dove Counterbalance General Intelligence Test was developed in 1968 to show the fundamental differences in speech patterns of African Americans and their European American peers. The Black Intelligence Test of Cultural Homogeneity was developed in 1972 by Robert L. Williams to assess the intelligence of African Americans. The test uses vocabulary common to the vernacular of some African Americans. Another test focuses on assessment of IQ of persons and groups from Hispanic backgrounds. The Australian-American Intelligence Test was based on a test first introduced in the late 1960s and early 1970s to assesses IQ in the Aboriginal culture of North Queensland.

Whether culture-fair testing can be truly fair or free from culture bias is open to debate. It does represent an important attempt to provide an assessment tool that will eliminate cultural bias for persons from culturally and linguistically diverse backgrounds that may be found in more common performance-based assessments.

Satasha L. Green

See also Cultural Literacy; Cultural Pluralism; Standardized Testing

Further Readings

Anastasi, A. (1964, Fall). Culture-fair testing. *Educational Horizons*, 26–30.

Arvey, R. D. (1972). Some comments on culture fair tests. *Personnel Psychology*, 433–446.

Benson, E. (2002). Intelligence across cultures: Research in Africa, Asia and Latin America is showing how culture and intelligence interact. *Gale Group, 56*.

Darlington, R. B. (1971). Another look at "cultural fairness." *Journal of Educational Measurement, 8*, 71–82.

Davis, R. (1993). Biological tests of intelligence as culture fair. *American Psychologist, 48*(6), 695–696.

Dove, A. (1971). The "Chitling" test. In L. R. Aiken, Jr. (Ed.), *Psychological and educational testings*. Boston: Allyn & Bacon.

Matarazzo, J. D. (1992). Psychological testing and assessment in the 21st century. *American Psychologist, 47*, 1007–1018.

Shuey, A. M. (1966). *The testing of Negro intelligence* (2nd ed.). New York: Social Science Press.

Taylor, V. R. (1968, July). Control of cultural bias in testing: An action program. *Public Personnel Review*, 3–14.

CURRICULUM CHALLENGES IN SCHOOLS

The First Amendment to the U.S. Constitution states: "Congress shall make no law respecting . . . the right of people . . . to petition the government for redress of grievances." Since public schools are part of the government, people have a right to petition schools when they have a grievance about curriculum. This right is exercised with consistency across the country.

Once a person petitions a school or district, there is an expectation that challenges will be resolved in a way that is "just." Americans' sense of fairness is founded on equality in the assignment of rights and duties. Thus, each person who challenges curriculum expects to be treated equally or fairly. The community, in turn, expects public school boards will provide equal treatment and consistency to protect citizens from unfair treatment. Social norms of fairness also prescribe just treatment. Communities look with disfavor on those in power, such as principals, if they deal unfairly with challengers.

The legal requirement for fair treatment by government agencies, including school districts, is expressed in the due process clause of the Fourteenth Amendment, which states: ". . . nor shall any state deprive any person of life, liberty, or property, without due process of law." Legal scholars point out that due process requires that citizens have a right to air their views on matters that affect them. It also requires school districts to respond to challenges by following established procedures, applying the procedures in an even-handed way, and outlining the process by which challengers can appeal decisions.

Defining Curriculum Challenges

The American Library Association defines a challenge as an attempt to remove or restrict access to materials, based upon objections of a person or group. Thus, a challenge is not just an expression of opinion, but goes further. A successful challenge would restrict or remove material from access by others not participating in the challenge.

Some complaints about school programs may be related to the performance of a particular teacher who uses unapproved materials or covers material beyond the approved scope of a class or grade. These are not curriculum challenges and are usually addressed as personnel issues following procedures outlined in employee contracts and personnel laws.

Usually curriculum challenges relate to some form of printed material, curriculum guidelines or handbooks, media, or pedagogical practice which is part of the approved curriculum of the school or district. The complaint is usually lodged by a parent of a student, but some have been made by other members of the public and even district employees.

The range of items challenged is quite varied, from *James and the Giant Peach* to *The Catcher in the Rye*.

Even J. K. Rowling's *Harry Potter* novels have been on the list of challenged materials.

Research About Challenges

There was a series of studies conducted that focused on gathering data about types of challenges. Between 1956 and 1958, Marjorie Fiske did an interview study that included school libraries in twenty-six California communities. A major finding was that libraries react in a precautionary way in book selection when highly charged and widely reported community conflicts are caused by challenges to books. A more recent study by Dianne McAfee-Hopkins surveyed school library/media specialists in secondary public schools between 1987 and 1990. The primary reasons for the complaints reported in this study were: lack of family values, sexuality of the material, and morality concerns.

A 1977 study conducted by Lee Burress for the National Council of Teachers of English surveyed secondary school teachers on censorship and found that almost half reported some kind of attempted or successful censorship based on the language use such as profanity or erotic qualities in books. In 1980 the Association of American Publishers, the American Library Association, and the Association for Supervision and Curriculum Development conducted a survey of librarians, principals, and superintendents and reported that challenges happened in all regions and types of communities. In this study only 10.5 percent of the challenged materials related to religious issues such as "moral relativism" and evolution.

In 1992, Martha McCarthy and Carol Langdon conducted a survey of superintendents to study the nature and scope of challenges for the Indiana Education Policy Center. They noted that challenges increased beginning in 1989, at the same time that the state required inclusion of AIDS instruction and drug education in the curriculum. Louise Adler conducted similar surveys in California in 1990, 1991, 1993, and 1995, which showed that the number of districts reporting challenges increased by 5 percentage points between 1990 and 1995. Forty-one percent of the responding districts reported challenges from 1993 to 1995. Concerns about religious conflicts or satanic/witchcraft issues accounted for 32 percent of challenges, and parents were the most frequently identified challengers (54 percent). A significant percentage (76 percent) of districts reported that they were experiencing the same number or more challenges.

Several organizations also collect data on reports of challenges. The People for the American Way published a list of incidents that were either reported in the media or reported directly to their organization between 1986 and 1996. The reports received wide media attention, and conservative groups challenged their accuracy. Similarly, the American Library Association (ALA) publishes the *Newsletter on Intellectual Freedom,* which also lists incidents of challenges in schools, as well as libraries and universities. The ALA reports that between 1990 and 1998, over 5,000 challenges were reported to their Office for Intellectual Freedom. Most of the challenges were to material in classrooms or school libraries. In 2002, ALA reported that they received about 900 reports of challenges per year, an increase from about 300 each year in 1978.

Herbert Foerstel is the author of *Banned in the U.S.A.: A Reference Guide to Book Censorship in Schools and Public Libraries* (2002), which lists the most frequently challenged books giving synopsis and background about selected challenges.

Recent Media Reports

A review of recent education media suggests some of the interests challengers seem to have. The arguments for inclusion of alternative theories to evolution were labeled "creationism" during the 1980s and 1990s. Now the theory being supported by challengers of evolution is "intelligent design." These challenges are taking place at schools, at the district level—even by some school board members—and at the state level.

Another type of religiously based challenge reported in the media results from attempts by districts to include the study of various religions. Attempts to find "balanced" curriculum materials can result in challenges for a variety of reasons. This happened recently in Anchorage, Alaska, when the district removed a teaching guide called the *Arab World*

Studies Notebook. In 1994, the Freedom Forum First Amendment Center at Vanderbilt University developed a resource guide to help schools find a proper constitutional and educational role for religion. It offers legal and practical advice for dealing with religiously based curriculum challenges.

Due Process Procedures

Many district policies and most model policies contain the following key provisions:

1. Challenges must be made in writing using a specified form.

2. Challengers must begin the process by discussing their concern with the principal of the school where the challenged material is used.

3. A review committee (which can be constituted either at the school or district level) conducts a study of the challenged material.

4. Challenged materials remain in use during the review period.

5. The child of a challenger may be given an alternative assignment during the process.

6. The steps of the review process are outlined in the policy and provide for an appeal process.

7. Standards used by the committee to review the challenged material must be specified in the policy.

8. A standard should be established that states how often a challenged item or service will be reviewed within a specific period.

9. Guidelines must be established for selection of review committee members.

Professional organizations such as The American Library Association, National Council of Teachers of English, and Phi Delta Kappa have developed guidelines for responding to challenges. Jonathan Weil reported on a district policy from Evanston, Illinois, which contains the provision that "no parent has the right to limit reading, viewing, or listening materials for students other than his or her own children." Once the board makes a decision on a challenge, the Evanston policy states that there will be no further review (no new challenge to that material) for three years. Challengers must answer the following questions:

1. Do you represent an organization or other group?

2. To what in the material do you object?

3. What do you feel might be the result of students becoming involved with this material?

4. Is there anything good about this material?

5. What do you believe is the theme of this material?

6. In its place, what other print or nonprint material would you recommend?

Commentators on model policies unanimously support the key provision requiring that challenged materials remain in use during the review process. While challengers must be afforded due process, the burden of proving that material should be removed rests on the challenger. This provision is designed to prevent a demand by the challenger that the district rush to judgment in order to protect their child from the "damaging" material. On a practical level, it is easiest to implement when the challenge concerns one story out of a textbook or one library book for a single child. When an entire textbook series and more than one family is involved, however, implementation of this provision can be problematic.

While the policies enunciate due process procedures, they also serve as mechanisms controlling the level of controversy typically surrounding challenges. Organizational theorists call this "buffering the technical core of an organization." Requiring that the challenge be put in writing assures that the challenger's concerns are clearly expressed. At the same time, it serves as a buffer, since some parents will not want to invest the time necessary to fill out the required form or make their concerns part of the public record. The provision for establishing review committees assures that the challenger will get a hearing—a key ingredient in due process. But the district can control the level of controversy by the way it appoints the members of the review committee.

Louise Adler reported that in 1995, 62 percent of the challenges resulted in continuing to use the challenged material or using the material but excusing the challenger's child from using it. Nineteen percent of these challenges successfully restricted use of material, while only 14 percent resulted in completely removing material.

Existence of challenge policies, while assuring due process, also constrains the controversies that typically surround challenges by defining the channel through which these must flow. Districts can develop and adopt policies during times of political quiescence so they will be in place when political storms erupt over challenges.

Louise Adler

See also Religious Fundamentalism and Public Education

Further Readings

Adler, L. (1993). Curriculum challenges in California. *Record in Educational Administration and Supervision, 13*(2), 10–20.

Adler, L. (1995). Are the public schools a meeting ground or a battleground? *Religion & Education, 22*(1), 17–26.

Association of American Publishers, American Library Association, & Association for Supervision and Curriculum Development. (1981). *Limiting what students shall read.* Washington, DC: Authors.

Burress, L. (1979). A brief report of the 1977 NCTE censorship survey. In J. E. Davis (Ed.), *Dealing with censorship* (pp. 14–47). Urbana, IL: National Council of Teachers of English.

Doyle, R. (2004). *Banned books: 2004 resource book.* Chicago: American Library Association.

Fiske, M. (1959). *Book selection and censorship.* Berkeley: University of California Press.

Foerstel, H. (2002). *Banned in the U.S.A.: A reference guide to book censorship in schools and public libraries.* Westport, CT: Greenwood Press.

McCarthy, M., & Langdon, C. (1993, June). Challenges to the curriculum in Indiana's public schools. *Policy Bulletin* No. PB-B20, pp. 2–9.

Weil, J. (1987). Policy and procedures: Dealing with censorship. *Social Education, 51*(6), 448–449.

CURRICULUM THEORY

Curriculum theory is the network of assumptions that undergirds curriculum proposals, policies, or practices, and is the critique of the same. Curriculum, and curriculum theory as a subset, is an offshoot of philosophy and social foundations of education that started in the early twentieth century.

Origins of Curriculum Theory

Curriculum theory and foundations of education, together, grew to prominence, and then starting in the 1930s began to become more differentiated at key universities such as Teachers College, Columbia University; Ohio State University; and the University of Illinois. These universities had strong early- to mid-twentieth-century social and cultural foundations faculty, many of whom became well known in curriculum theory and in foundations. Examples of some of the major contributors to the field from the first half the twentieth century include John Dewey, William Bagley, George Counts, Harold Rugg, William H. Kilpatrick, and John Childs. Among more recent figures are, to name just a few, Jonas Soltis, Dwayne Huebner, Maxine Greene, David Hansen, Janet Miller, Ralph W. Tyler, Joseph J. Schwab, William Pinar, and Sarah Lawrence Lightfoot.

Forms of Curriculum Theory

Forms of curriculum theory (often derived from philosophical and other foundations of education) include the following: descriptive theory, prescriptive theory, critical theory, hermeneutic theory, postmodern theory, and personal theory.

Descriptive curriculum theory builds upon analytic and empirical philosophical traditions. Analytic theory strives to clarify concepts and builds theory upon both philosophical conceptualization and empirical studies that are assumed to provide small pieces of large puzzles of inquiry. It draws upon realism in philosophy of education and is patterned after investigation in the natural sciences that has led to theories of the biological cell or to atomic theory, for example. Work in this tradition often draws upon psychological origins of theory and research, exemplified by early work of E. L. Thorndike, G. Stanley Hall, Charles Judd, and B. F. Skinner, and the curriculum work of Franklin Bobbitt, Ralph W. Tyler, George Beauchamp, Mauritz Johnson, Howard Gardner, and George Posner.

Prescriptive curriculum theory is often referred to as *normative,* in that it posits values that guide decisions about that which is worth teaching and learning, and then proceeds to justify such values through philosophical argument. Such argument may be made through appeal to authoritative sources of the past and usually involves the cogent construction of reasoning through deductive, syllogistic, prepositional, symbolic, inductive, or dialectical logic. Associated primarily with philosophical schools of idealism, naturalism, scholasticism, and to a lesser extent with pragmatism and existentialism, prescriptive curriculum theorists attempt to present compelling defenses of proposed or practiced responses to curriculum positions on what is worth knowing, needing, experiencing, doing, becoming, being, overcoming, sharing, and contributing. Contemporary prescriptive curriculum theorists might draw upon philosophical roots in the likes of Plato, Aristotle, Augustine, Thomas Aquinas, Peter Abelard, Martin Luther, Ignatius Loyola, Rene Descartes, G. W. F. Hegel, Immanuel Kant, David Hume, Alfred North Whitehead, William James, John Dewey, and others.

Today's versions of such theorists range from conservative proponents of the Western canon (e.g., Mortimer Adler, E. D. Hirsch), to liberals (e.g., Decker Walker, R. F. Dearden, David Hansen, Philip Jackson, Joseph Schwab, William A. Reid, and Nel Noddings), to radicals (e.g., William Ayers, James Beane, Paulo Freire), and many others whose writing is often of the essay form.

Critical curriculum theory began as an accepted curriculum discourse in the 1970s, though it has roots in radical racial and cultural scholarship and critique (e.g., Sarah Winnemucca, W. E. B. Du Bois, Horace Mann Bond, Carter G. Woodson, Jose Marti, Elizabeth Blackwell, Emily Blackwell, Franz Fanon, George L. Sanchez, Ivan Illich, Malcolm X, Cesar Chavez, Martin Luther King, Jr.). Like the work of these too often neglected theorists, the focus of critical curriculum theory is on exposing and overcoming injustice. Grounded in the work of Karl Marx and his dialectical class analysis, post-Marxists have pushed the boundaries to include inequities based on race, ethnicity, gender, language, culture, nationality, place, sexual orientation, age, ability/disability, health/illness, religion/belief, membership, and more. The legacy of neo-Marxists such as Herbert Marcuse, Theodor Adorno, Max Horkheimer, Antonio Gramsci, Erich Fromm, and Jürgen Habermas is drawn upon by contemporary curriculum theorists, such as Paulo Freire, Michael Apple, Henry Giroux, Cleo Cherryholmes, Jean Anyon, Peter McLaren, Patti Lather, William Watkins, Donaldo Macedo, and others

Hermeneutic curriculum theory stems from continental European phenomenological and existentialist origins, having roots in the work of Edmund Husserl, Søren Kierkegaard, Martin Heidegger, Jean Paul Sartre, Albert Camus, Simone de Beauvoir, M. J. Langeveld, and others. A diverse array of curriculum scholars have built upon these scholars. Some, such as Max van Manen, Ted Aoki, Ton Beekman, George Willis, Maureen Connolly, Francine Hultgren, Valerie Polakow, Terry Carson, David Smith, Stephen Smith, and Donald Vandenberg, strive to depict the meanings of lived experience They transform the literal notion of hermeneutics as interpretation of texts in the Judaic tradition to metaphorically refer to an ever-vigilant understanding of texts as the perspectives or outlooks of human beings as they encounter existence.

A figure like Maxine Greene combines existential and phenomenological with critical theory and perspectives drawn from literature and the other arts. Her work as well as that of James B. Macdonald and Dwayne Huebner has influenced William Pinar, Madeleine Grumet, Janet Miller, and others who have referred to *currere,* the verb form of *curriculum,* a term used to highlight the active portrayal of seeking to understand how one's interpretation of the past and anticipation of the future continuously reconstruct fleeting images of the present.

Postmodern curriculum theory is a rather new phenomenon that has grown from disenchantment with all organized systems of thought or metanarratives as captured in Jean-François Lyotard's central theme that postmodernism is incredulous of and should interrupt metanarratives. Other postmodern theorists, such as Maurice Merleau-Ponty, Michel Foucault, Jacques Lacan, Ferdinand de Saussure, and Paul Ricoeur, have been major contributors to curriculum theory that counters metatheory by employing the ideas of William Pinar, William Doll, Noel Gough, Patrick Slattery, William Stanley, Bernardo Gallegos, Elizabeth Ellsworth, Bernadette Baker, and others. This is done by advocating multiple narratives, deconstructing those texts, complicating reflections and conversations on what they signify via differing interpretations of their possible meanings.

Personal theory emerges largely from pragmatism, which assumes that the values of ideas reside in action based on those ideas. Thus, for John Dewey (as influenced by fellow founders of pragmatism—Charles S. Peirce and William James), the study of effective social practice yields salient theory that is continuously reconstructed by subsequent experience. Practical inquiry, as developed by Joseph Schwab, also has origins in the pragmatism of Dewey. It seeks problems in states of affairs, not generalized states of mind; its method of inquiry is more immersion and interaction than induction and hypothetical deduction, while it unveils subject matter that is situationally specific, rather than lawlike, and ends that consist of knowledge, not merely for its own sake, but for the sake of morally defensible action. Eclectically combined with autobiographical, biographical, and aesthetic narrative discourses, practical postures of inquiry facilitate personal theory—a kind of *currere* in which individuals and communities create perspectives that guide their lives. Revising such perspectives is deemed the process of education itself, a novel variation on the time-honored, but too seldom emphasized, goal of self-education.

Critics of contemporary education such as William Pinar argue that much of contemporary curriculum theory that attempts to guide practice today is too often a meager amalgam that masquerades as prescriptive and descriptive theory to justify the policies of elite groups, who design education as schooling that benefits their own social, political, and economic aims. Pinar argues that this state of affairs requires curriculum theorizing that is distanced from practice and policy, so it will not be co-opted by power, and thus be able to offer radically imaginative alternatives. Peter Hlebowitsh has argued that such distancing is an abdication of responsibility, since children come to school daily and must experience the best that curriculum theorists have to offer to the democratic process, even under oppressive and autocratic circumstances. J. Dan Marshall and his colleagues portray a kind of postmodern pastiche of how curriculum theorists have responded to the needs of curriculum work since 1950. William Schubert argues that curriculum theorizing must become instantiated in the minds, hearts, and practices not only of theorists, researchers, and consultants, but of educational leaders, teachers, parents, and learners at all levels, both in school and in the many other venues of teaching and learning in life.

William H. Schubert

See also Ideology and Schooling; Philosophy of Education

Further Readings

Connelly, F. M., He, M. F., & Phillion, J. (Ed.). (2008). *Handbook of curriculum and instruction.* Thousand Oaks, CA: Sage.

Hlebowitsh, P. (1993). *Radical curriculum theory reconsidered.* New York: Teachers College Press.

Marshall, J. D., Sears, J. T., Allen, L. A., Roberts, P. A., & Schubert, W. H. (2007). *Turning points in curriculum: A contemporary American memoir.* Columbus, OH: Pearson Merrill-Prentice Hall.

Pinar, W. F. (2004). *What is curriculum theory?* Mahwah, NJ: Lawrence Erlbaum.

Pinar, W. F., Reynolds, W. M., Slattery, P., & Taubman, P. M. (1995). *Understanding curriculum.* New York: Peter Lang.

Schubert, W. H. (1986). *Curriculum: Perspective, paradigm, and possibility.* New York: Macmillan.

Schubert, W. H. (2008). Curriculum inquiry. In F. M. Connelly, M. F. He, & J. Phillion (Eds.), *Handbook of curriculum and instruction.* Thousand Oaks, CA: Sage.

Schubert, W. H., Lopez Schubert, A. L., Thomas, T. P., & Carroll, W. M. (2002). *Curriculum books: The first hundred years.* New York: Peter Lang.

D

DALTON PLAN

The Dalton Plan was the progressive pedagogical model used by Helen Parkhurst, who founded the Dalton School in New York City in 1919. Her book, *Education on the Dalton Plan,* was published in 1922, and within six months of publication it was translated into fourteen languages.

The plan's principles were freedom and cooperation. Freedom meant the ability for individuals to function independently and autonomously. Cooperation meant the interaction of group life. Concerned with preparing students to live in a democracy, Parkhurst created an environment to balance cooperation and freedom.

The components of the Dalton Plan were House, Laboratory, and Assignment. *House* was the arrangement of students into advisory groups, which met four times per week for a total of ninety minutes with a teacher-advisor. Its purpose was to foster cooperation among students and to develop the qualities of independence and social awareness. Blocks of time were set aside each morning from nine to twelve o'clock and called lab time or *Laboratory.* Each teacher had a lab and students were expected to utilize the resources of their teachers in order to help them fulfill their assignment. *Assignment* was an outline of each student's coursework for the year. Students were required to discuss their plans with their teachers; they also might have discussed their plans with other students. The plans might have been modified, or students might even have abandoned their plans and started over. Students participated in planning their studies with both faculty and peers, interacting with the community in a spirit of cooperation.

Flexibility was the keystone of the Dalton Plan. The school during Helen Parkhurst's time exuded informality, spur-of-the-moment decision making, enormous energy, high-level engagement, and the element of surprise. Parkhurst's greatest contribution to education was her emphasis on process rather than product. She saw the Dalton Plan as a vehicle for teaching the curriculum. It was far from perfect. Former students complained of lack of structure. Teachers had to be reeducated in Dalton ways. Often, because of the emphasis on process, they were insecure with regard to the curriculum. How the student was to realize his or her potential as an individual and to be a contributing member of a community remained a problem largely unsolved. The Dalton Plan's House system, however, has been rediscovered by the contemporary small-school movement and called *Advisory Groups,* although contemporary reformers do not acknowledge Parkhurst's influence.

Susan F. Semel

See also Dalton School; Progressive Education

Further Readings

Cremin, L. A. (1961). *The transformation of the school.* New York: Alfred A. Knopf.

Dewey, E. (1922). *The Dalton laboratory plan.* New York: E. P. Dutton.

Parkhurst, H. (1922). *Education on the Dalton plan.* London: G. Bell.

Sadovnik, A. R., & Semel, S. F. (Eds.). (2002). *Founding mothers and others: Women educational leaders during the Progressive era.* New York: Palgrave.

Semel, S. F. (1992). *The Dalton School: The transformation of a progressive school.* New York: Peter Lang.

Semel, S. F., & Sadovnik, A. R. (Eds.). (1999). *"Schools of tomorrow," schools of today: What happened to progressive education.* New York: Peter Lang.

DALTON SCHOOL

The Dalton School is a coeducational, K–12 independent school located on the Upper East Side of Manhattan, founded by Helen Parkhurst as a progressive school in 1919. Today, Dalton is a competitive, elite, college preparatory school with tuition over $30,000 per year.

The school followed Helen Parkhurst's philosophy, embodied by the Dalton Plan for education, which was designed to individualize instruction and create community. Parkhurst's Dalton reflected the child-centered progressive movement of its time: often chaotic and disorganized, but at the same time caring and familial. It focused on child growth and development, community, and social service, and it strove to synthesize the affective and cognitive domains of the child. In 1942, Parkhurst was forced to resign due to financial irregularities. By the time she did, the Dalton Plan was internationally accepted as an important model for schooling.

Charlotte Durham, a teacher and administrator under Parkhurst from 1922, was headmistress from 1942 to 1960. Under her leadership, Dalton retained its child-centered pedagogy and its caring orientation, while placing more emphasis on academic rigor. It was more orderly and less experimental and more a part of the traditional New York City independent school community. Her genius was to create a tradition out of a progressive experiment, using the Dalton Plan as its guiding ritual.

Donald Barr served as Dalton's headmaster from 1964 to 1974. Although a product of progressive education, Barr had developed an educational philosophy closer to conservative critics of progressivism. He thought progressive education was anti-intellectual and permissive, and he injected a rigorous and traditional curriculum into the Dalton Plan. Reflecting antipathy for progressive education, Barr began the transformation of Dalton into a large, academically competitive and trendy institution. His administration was rife with controversy, and in the end, he resigned under a cloud.

Gardner Dunnan served as Dalton's headmaster from 1975 to 1997. The first head to come from the public school sector, he continued Dalton's transformation into an efficient, selective, and academically rigorous institution. He initiated the Dalton Technology Plan, which he promoted as the link between the progressivism of Helen Parkhurst and the Dalton of modernity. The school's graduates entered prestigious universities, reflecting the goals of its parent body. By the time Dunnan resigned amid financial and personal problems in 1997, the Dalton School had become a traditional, elite college preparatory school with only vestiges of its progressive past.

After four years of uninspired leadership, Ellen Stein, a former Dalton student, became head in 2001. Stein has attempted to reconnect Dalton with its progressive past. Although the school still refers to the Dalton Plan, and the school is more progressive than most public schools, it is different from the school Helen Parkhurst founded.

Susan F. Semel

See also Dalton Plan; Progressive Education

Further Readings

Semel, S. F. (1992). *The Dalton school: The transformation of a progressive school.* New York: Peter Lang.

Semel, S. F. (1999). The Dalton school. In S. F. Semel & A. R. Sadovnik (Eds.), *"Schools of tomorrow," schools of today: What happened to progressive education* (pp. 171–212). New York: Peter Lang.

Semel, S. F. (2002). Helen Parkhurst. In A. R. Sadovnik & S. F. Semel (Eds.), *Founding mothers and others: Women educational leaders during the progressive era.* New York: Palgrave.

DEAF, EDUCATION FOR THE

Although the first known reference to deafness was found in the Egyptian Ebers in 1500 BCE, it was not until 1578 CE that the world's first school for the deaf was established in Spain. The late 1700s saw the start of the so-called Hundred Years War, with disagreement over classroom communication modes arising in Europe: the Abbé Charles-Michel de l'Eppé of France believed sign was the natural language of the deaf (manualism), while Samuel Heinicke of Germany declared that deaf people must be taught via aural/oral means because thought was only possible through speech (oralism).

In the United States, education for deaf children began in 1817 when a wealthy community leader, Mason Cogswell, sought to provide formal schooling for Alice, his deaf daughter. Cogswell sent Thomas Hopkins Gallaudet to Europe to research the best practices. After being rejected by the oralist teachers in England, Gallaudet studied with the manualist teachers in France. Gallaudet persuaded a deaf teacher, Laurent Clerc, to return to the United States to help found the Connecticut Asylum for the Deaf and Dumb, now known as the American School for the Deaf.

Within the next few decades, regionalized schools cropped up across the United States. In 1864, Congress authorized the addition of a collegiate department to the Columbia Institute in Washington, D.C., creating the only liberal arts college for deaf people in the world, the National Deaf Mute College, now called Gallaudet University.

Until the late 1860s, about half of the teachers were deaf and all classes in schools for the deaf were taught via American Sign Language (ASL). Change came with the establishment of the New York Institution for the Improved Instruction of Deaf-Mutes, now known as the Lexington School for the Deaf, which prohibited the use of signs and followed the oralist model.

The battle over modes of communication had found its way to North America and was reflected most clearly in the public feuding between the president of the National Deaf Mute College, Edward Miner Gallaudet (son of Thomas Hopkins Gallaudet), who supported signs and speech in the classroom, and the famous inventor, Alexander Graham Bell (whose mother and wife were both deaf), who strongly advocated for the exclusive use of speech.

Culturally Deaf people contend that the "Dark Days" of deaf education began in earnest in 1880 at the International Congress on Deafness, held in Milan, Italy. Oralism was chosen as the sole method allowed in educational settings. Due primarily to the efforts of E. M. Gallaudet, manual methods continued to be used in the United States. In response to this defiance of the Milan decision, Bell used his influence to foster a rapid increase of programs teaching deaf students through oral methods, rising from 7 percent in 1882 to a peak of 80 percent by 1919. It was during this time that signing became covert, with older deaf children passing the language to younger children in the dorms of residential schools.

The "Dark Days" ended in the 1960s when Gallaudet University Professor William Stokoe conducted research on the linguistic and grammatical structure of signs used in the deaf community, finding that ASL is indeed a separate and unique language. The tide turned and by the mid-1970s, sign language was once again permitted in schools. However, ASL was not used then, nor is it used in most academic programs today. Instead, various forms of voiced artificial sign systems designed to follow English word order are the means of providing a "total communication" learning environment. In the past ten years, however, there has been a growing movement toward a bilingual-bicultural approach.

Supported by federal legislation in the 1970s, placement patterns shifted from regionalized schools to local public school programs. However, due to the low incidence of deafness, all too often only a few deaf children are placed amid hundreds of nondeaf students in these programs. Therefore, this change has not occurred without controversy, as some people believe that such isolation does not satisfy the intent of the least restrictive environment component of the federal mandate.

The field of deaf education has been and continues to be a highly volatile entity, charged with emotional, political, and philosophical disagreements.

Jean Theodora Slobodzian

See also Deaf Culture

See Visual History Chapter 17, Reading and Libraries;
    Chapter 21, Students With Special Needs

Further Readings

Marschark, M., Lang, H. G., & Albertini, J. A. (2002).
    Educating deaf students: From research to practice.
    New York: Oxford University Press.
Spencer, P. E., Erting, C. J., & Marschark, M. (Eds.). (2000).
    *Essays in honor of Kathryn P. Meadow-Orlans: The deaf
    child in the family and at school.* Mahwah, NJ: Lawrence
    Erlbaum.

DEAF CULTURE

A cultural community arises when a group of people, communicating through a common language, develops a set of beliefs, social behaviors, and norms. Deaf people who use American Sign Language as their primary language form such a cultural community. Hailing from all races, religions, socioeconomic classes, and geographical regions across the United States, culturally deaf people hold the view that deafness is a social phenomenon rather than a disability. They take pride in their shared social/political organizations, literature, visual works of art, history, and group norms.

Deaf children born to deaf parents begin language and cultural learning at birth, but these children are far and few between. More than 90 percent of all deaf children are born to two nondeaf parents, many of whom have probably never met a deaf person in their lives. In cases where the diagnosis of deafness is not made for months or even years after the baby is born, the critical time for language development is irretrievably lost. The early years for the undiagnosed deaf child of nondeaf parents will probably be filled with rich experiences that lack the appropriate language accompaniment to foster intellectual and cultural understandings.

After the diagnosis of deafness is made, nondeaf parents are forced to make an immediate decision regarding communication. If they continue utilizing aural/oral methods, they will need to accept that, despite the intensity of direct instruction, their child may make relatively slow progress in speech, listening, and speech-reading skill development. If they decide to implement signed communication methods, they will need to learn sign language and consistently use it when their child is in their presence. In either case, the consequences of this delayed language input are serious and long reaching. Schools serving deaf students often find it necessary to supplement social-emotional, linguistic, and cultural development in addition to the traditional role of transmitting academic information.

The federal government, through the enactment of Public Law 94-142, the Education for All Handicapped Children Act, and the recent reauthorization of Public Law 101-476, the Individuals with Disabilities Education Act (IDEA), guarantees the educational rights of all children. However, parents, students, concerned deaf adults, court judges, and educational professionals disagree as to what actually constitutes the mandated free and appropriate education in regard to deaf students. Less than 1 percent of all school-age children are classified as deaf, yet it is impossible to find one educational setting that satisfies all involved.

There is a wealth of public school placement options currently available from which to choose. At one end of the continuum is full-time care in a boarding school that serves only those who are deaf, while at the other end is total inclusion in a class of deaf/nondeaf peers in a local public school. Between these two extremes lie options such as day classes in a regionalized school for the deaf; a self-contained classroom in a public school; part-time placement in a Resource Room; tutorial pull-out classes with an itinerant teacher trained to work with deaf children; or at-home instruction.

Regionalized schools bring together larger numbers of children who are deaf, have a culturally dedicated focus that normalizes deafness, and provide numerous deaf role models, though the deaf child may be taught far from home, thus causing separation from family and neighborhood nondeaf peers. Local public schools reduce the physical distance between deaf and nondeaf students, increase the potential for interaction between the two cultural groups, and offer an environment where mutual appreciation and respect can be fostered, though the deaf child may be alone among hundreds of hearing schoolmates and not meet any deaf role models until adulthood.

No one type of communication mode or program is ideal for all deaf children, whose needs are as diverse as the contributing factors to the condition. It would be incorrect to use a single model to try to satisfy the needs of all deaf children. Ideally, each child's situation should be individually evaluated and addressed.

Jean Theodora Slobodzian

See also Deaf, Education for the

See Visual History Chapter 17, Reading and Libraries

Further Readings

Lane, H., Hoffmeister, R., & Bahan, B. (1996). *Journey into the Deaf world.* San Diego, CA: DawnSign Press.

Marschark, M., Lang, H. G., & Albertini, J. A. (2002). *Educating deaf students: From research to practice.* New York: Oxford University Press.

Spencer, P. E., Erting, C. J., & Marschark, M. (Eds.). *Essays in honor of Kathryn P. Meadow-Orlans: The deaf child in the family and at school.* Mahwah, NJ: Lawrence Erlbaum.

DECLARATIONS ON WOMEN'S RIGHTS

Important declarations concerning the rights of women were promulgated in France and England during the late eighteenth and mid-nineteenth centuries. These included the 1791 French Declaration of the Rights of Woman and the Female Citizen, and the 1848 Declaration of Sentiments.

Declaration of the Rights of Woman and the Female Citizen

The feminist manifesto Declaration des Droits de la Femme et de la Citoyenne, written by Marie Gouze, who was known as Olympe de Gouges, was a response to the French Republic's Declaration of the Rights of Man and Citizens (1789), which de Gouges challenged as not applying equally to women. She charged that this declaration fell short of equal treatment of the sexes in matters of law, marriage, property, employment, and education, and she called upon the National Assembly to work toward obtaining a woman's right to vote. She also placed particular emphasis on the need for an accessible and rigorous education for women.

De Gouges dedicated her tract to the queen, Marie Antoinette. In her preamble, de Gouges called for a national assembly of women to reform French society, based on laws of nature and reason. She set forth seventeen principles, articulated in her articles of equality. Among her assertions one finds that men and women should be equally admitted by ability to all honors, positions, and public employment. Freedom of speech and assembly should be guaranteed to women, and they should have the right to demand an accounting of the tax system. Article 16 declared the constitution of the state null if the majority of the people, including women, had not cooperated in drafting it. De Gouges ended with a social contract for women, proposing new laws of marriage and property.

Throughout her adult life, de Gouges wrote about the position of women, and the quality of their education, while other women of the period were addressing similar concerns in more tolerant societies. While education was a primary issue addressed in her many pamphlets, plays, novels, and political tracts appearing from 1788 to 1793, this remarkable and unpretentious woman, like the majority of females in her day, would not have received a rigorously academic or scholarly education. Education notwithstanding, she encouraged women of her time to become involved, to speak openly and publicly in support of her Declaration of the Rights of Woman and the Female Citizen. As Benoite Groult theorizes in her 1986 work on de Gouges, the unfortunate reality is that the women who participate in revolutions are hardly ever awarded the benefits of change. De Gouges write in 1791 that if "woman has the right to mount the scaffold; she must equally have the right to mount the rostrum, provided that her demonstrations do not disturb the legally established public order." With these words, she foretold her own story. Because of her audacious, passionate, and radically conceptualized Declaration of the Rights of Woman and the Female Citizen, and the sociohistorical context in which she lived, de Gouges was found guilty of treason and sentenced to death by guillotine on November 3, 1793.

Declaration of Sentiments

In the United States, a similar declaration was put forward over fifty years later as part of the first American women's rights convention was held in Seneca Falls, New York, on July 19 and 20, 1848. The convention had as its purpose the examination of the social, civil, and religious condition and rights of American women. The convention was led by Susan B. Anthony (1820–1906) and Elizabeth Cady Stanton (1815–1902). On the second day of the convention, a Declaration of Sentiments (largely written by Stanton and modeled after the Declaration of Independence) was approved by the sixty-eight women and thirty-two men who attended the convention. The declaration had as its main assertion that "all men and women are created equal." Besides arguing that "He" (a general reference to male-dominated society) had not permitted women to vote, to have a voice in the creation of laws, or the right to property in marriage, the declaration maintained that women were denied the facilities for obtaining a proper education—specifically collegiate instruction.

Like de Gouges's declaration, the Seneca Falls Declaration of Sentiments challenged the notion that the rights afforded to women should be any different than those assigned to men. Also like the Declaration des Droits de la Femme et de la Citoyenne, the Declaration of Sentiments used a male-created revolutionary document as a template for its creation. In doing so, it made clear the hypocrisy of making all men free while excluding half of humanity in the form of women.

The 1848 meeting at Seneca Falls and its Declaration of Sentiments is widely considered the beginning of the feminist movement in the United States, as well as the foundation for the passage the Nineteenth Amendment to the Constitution in 1920, which enfranchised women by declaring that: "The right of citizens of the United States to vote shall not be denied or abridged by the United States or by any State on account of sex."

In 1948, the UN Universal Declaration of Human Rights called for universal and equal suffrage for all people. Its principles were further reinforced with its Convention on the Elimination of All Forms of Discrimination Against Women, which was passed by the UN General Assembly in 1979. Interestingly, the

United States is the only developed nation that has not ratified the convention. At the beginning of the twenty-first century, women's suffrage has been largely achieved throughout the developed world, with notable exceptions in countries such as Saudi Arabia.

Connie Titone, Shannon White, and Meghann Fee

See also Education, History of

Further Readings

Flexner, E. (1996). *Century of struggle: The women's rights movement in the United States.* Cambridge, MA: Belknap Press of Harvard University Press.

Groult, B. (1986). *Olympe de gouges: Oeuvres.* Paris: Mercure de France.

Levy, D. G., AppleWhite, H. B., & Johnson, D. M. (Eds.). (1979). *Women in revolutionary Paris, 1789–1795.* Urbana: University of Illinois Press.

Macaulay, C. (1790). *Letters on education with observations on religious and metaphysical subjects.* London: Dilly.

Murray, J. S. (1798). *The gleaner: A miscellaneous production.* Boston: I. Thomas and E. T. Andrews.

Wagner, S. R. (1998). *A time of protest. Suffragists challenge the republic, 1880–1887.* Aberdeen, SC: Sky Carrier Press.

Wollstonecraft, M. (1975). *A vindication of the rights of woman.* Harmondsworth, UK: Penguin Press. (Original work published 1792)

Web Sites

Convention on the Elimination of All Forms of Discrimination against Women: http://www.un.org/womenwatch/daw/cedaw/cedaw.htm

Declaration of Sentiments: http://www.nps.gov/archive/wori/declaration.htm

Universal Declaration of Human Rights: http://www.un.org/Overview/rights.html

DELINQUENCY EDUCATION

School experiences are connected to issues of delinquency, and for adjudicated youth, negative experiences in school are common. As institutions of socialization and stratification, schools frame student behavior in the language of normal or deviant. Schools label students and student learning as successful or unsuccessful and stratify student achievement into separate curriculums. Research indicates that low school performance, experiences with truancy, and school leaving at a young age are factors related to delinquency; students who experience low school performance are more likely to engage in delinquent behavior. The educational history of incarcerated youth reveals low grades in school, behavior problems, and school leaving.

In the United States, less than half of the prison population has either a high school diploma or a GED. And although the majority of state prisons offer secondary education programs, less than one fourth of the prison population participates in GED and high school classes.

Education programs for youth in prison are cost effective, increase life skills and job skills, and reduce recidivism. Participation in education programs has been linked to decreases in the level of violence in crimes committed by youth after release from prison. Although education programs generate positive effects, historically, support for correctional education has waxed and waned, as this entry shows.

In the Beginning

The history of "delinquency education" extends back to the late eighteenth century. During the Revolutionary War, more revolutionaries died as prisoners in overcrowded and unhygienic conditions than as soldiers in combat. Unwavering in their defense of the ideals put forth in the Declaration of Independence, revolutionaries criticized the inhumane treatment perpetrated by the British during the war and worked diligently among White populations to use incarceration and the judicial system in constructive ways. Benjamin Rush, a signatory, along with Quakers from Pennsylvania, supported the idea of rehabilitation in prison. The idea of rehabilitation and reeducation expanded in the 1800s, particularly in regard to children; however, many prisons instituted rules of silence, restricted mobility, and abusive control of those who were incarcerated.

In the early 1800s as the concept of childhood developed, states began to distinguish differences between adults and children and founded separate institutions of incarceration. States established refuge houses and reformatories for boys and girls, separating them from the adult prison population. By the end of the 1820s the legal community recognized children who violated the law as belonging to a special category, and the first refuge houses opened in New York, Boston, and Philadelphia. Boys and girls were both sent to refuge houses, although always to separate quarters.

The judicial system framed the illegal activities of children as uncontrolled and unguided behavior that needed modification. Supporters of refuge houses recognized the problem of severe poverty and advanced the idea of giving young offenders education and vocational training rather than punishment. They hoped civilized instruction in reformatory schools and work in reformatory factories would alter the behavior of the children. Religious studies, vocational training, and hard labor defined the educational programs for delinquents. The reformation of the child, not punishment, became the goal. Unfortunately, many refuge houses exploited the labor of the children, and often staff abused the children.

The Reform School Era

During the latter half of the 1800s, reform schools grew with continued state support. In 1854 the Lancaster Industrial School for Girls in Massachusetts established the first reformatory exclusively for girls and introduced a new structure to reform schools—the cottage plan. Over the next fifty years, cottage plan systems emerged at reform schools across the country. Supporters of the schools believed that society needed to save children from poverty in industrialized urban centers. They sought to train children to work and become good citizens. Typically located in rural areas and often on farms far from urban centers, cottage plan reform schools provided surrogate homes for children as young as six years old. The cottage parent or parents, usually a matron or married couple, supervised about twenty children in a cottage.

Many reformatories identified themselves as training schools and scheduled the children for a half-day of work and a half-day of school. Vocational training dominated the education at most schools, and often consisted of the maintenance of the school and grounds. Many schools ran farms. Typically, boys worked on the farms, in the kitchen, or in print, wood, or auto shops. Girls worked on the farms, too, as well as in gardens and greenhouses. Some reform schools became almost entirely self-sufficient. Although the work boys and girls completed was similar, the amount of time they spent under state control differed significantly. Whereas the boys left reform schools often at age 16, at some schools, girls stayed until the age of 25. At many reform schools, like the refuge houses that preceded them, juveniles faced exploitation, corporal punishment, and abuse, and staff used solitary confinement and food deprivation as punishments. Maintaining control and order at these institutions often preceded secondary commitments to education.

States began to found training schools for White boys and boys of color, and for White girls and girls of color. In the North, most training schools were integrated; girls of color and White girls often shared the same cottage. During the same period in the South, training schools only accepted White children. Eventually, Southern states founded separate institutions for girls of color, and White girls, and boys of color, and White boys. Most schools provided an academic education that reflected the curriculum in public schools. Tragically, many training schools excluded boys of color from academic programs. Some schools failed to educate boys of color beyond the eighth grade. If boys of color arrived at a school with an eighth-grade education, staff forced them to work rather than continue their education. Similarly, when compared with their White counterparts, girls of color received substandard academic and vocational training. Often they served school staff in domestic capacities and lived in overcrowded conditions in their cottages.

A New Movement

By 1900, juvenile court laws made distinctions between youth and adult offenders, and many states adopted a parental role over children charged with juvenile offenses, the same role they had assumed with children suffering from neglect. The Progressive Era reformers worked from the early 1900s through the 1920s to improve the conditions of reform schools.

They believed fervently that boys and girls could not control their environments or their experiences. Believing that modifications would lead to social adjustment, they argued that training schools altered both the child's behavior and the environment to positive ends. Focusing on the misbehavior of the individual child, reformers introduced the concepts of parole, probation, and intermediate sentencing.

The introduction of clinical psychology and clinicians to reform schools during this time individualized treatment and advanced the study of casework. Although some White training schools used psychological assessment tests in admission procedures, individualized assessments of a child's mental health were not a part of integrated services. The tests redistributed the population along new lines of classification; test results labeled the majority of juveniles in reform schools as morons and dullards. The classifications reorganized custody responses to juvenile populations. Those juveniles whom the tests classified as capable received educational programs, vocational training, and recreation. In contrast, those juveniles whom the tests classified as dullards, administrations excluded from the educational programs and recreation.

Training schools using the cottage plan became widespread, and as schools developed, some progressive schools incorporated psychotherapy into their trade and professional training. Supporters of psychotherapeutic work critiqued the label "delinquent" and believed that individualized attention, nurturance, and community building would alter the ways in which boys and girls behaved.

In the 1930s the Hawthorne-Cedar Knolls School in New York established a groundbreaking psychotherapeutic guidance clinic with psychiatrists, psychologists, and case workers who became an integral part of their rehabilitation program. Demonstrating commitments to psychotherapy and individualized attention, the school allowed boys and girls to create their own combination of academic education, vocational education, and work programs. Believing that negative experiences in former classrooms and emotional instability prevented classroom learning, the administration provided flexibility in school and work schedules to increase overall student engagement. Although each student received instruction in English and arithmetic, all other areas of study became elective. Some electives included drama, music, photography, creative arts, and woodwork. Individualized assessment accompanied individualized plans. Students received qualitative feedback on their progress in ungraded classes, and the administration abandoned report cards. They situated learning within the larger context of social adjustment and rehabilitation.

Contemporary Programs

Although most training schools mirrored the public school curriculum in some way, with the rise of clinical case work and individualized treatment, the primary concern in many schools became the diagnosis and treatment of behavior. For the next forty years, systematic evaluation, the use of case workers, and therapeutic treatment became typical elements in rehabilitation programs. For although images of juvenile delinquency increased in the 1950s and 1960s, rehabilitation programs remained much the same until the 1970s.

In the 1970s reviews critical of rehabilitation programs challenged the traditional perspectives in correctional education. Citing high recidivism rates, conservatives attacked the ideal of rehabilitation and curtailed education programs and funding. The policy of incapacitation dominated the prison system, and emphasis on punishment and not rehabilitation emerged for the first time in over 100 years. The policy continued into the early 2000s. During that time, funding for prison construction increased dramatically. In contrast, funding and support for correctional education programs declined, even though the relationship between low performance in school and delinquent behavior remains strong.

In the late 1990s the education of young African American boys committed to correctional institutions reflected a fourth-grade reading level. Assessments revealed that most of the boys needed special education classes. Minority children, who are only one third of the population, were two thirds of the children who were incarcerated, and over one fourth of girls who were incarcerated had learning disabilities. In the early 2000s almost 100,000 juveniles were incarcerated in public and private facilities in the United States.

Although educational programs have been truncated, research on education services has continued to reveal that the replication of traditional schooling in correctional programs is ineffective, and that individualized attention and cooperative learning are essential. Other research has documented struggles with overcrowding in juvenile facilities, verbal and physical abuse of children by staff, education programs that are lusterless and incomplete, and policies that allow custody to call students from class to work.

Resocialization programs combined with academic and vocational work remain central components in delinquency education, and recent research findings have documented that interpersonal skills training, and the combination of psychotherapeutic work with an academic education, generates the lowest recidivism rates.

Allison Daniel Anders

See also Economic Inequality; Educational Equity: Race/Ethnicity

Further Readings

Fine, M. (1991). *Framing dropouts: Notes on the politics of an urban public high school.* Albany: State University of New York Press.

MacKenzie, D. L. (2006). *What works in corrections: Reducing the criminal activities of offenders and delinquents.* Cambridge, UK: Cambridge University Press.

Noblit, G. W., & Collins, T. W. (1978). Order and disruption in a desegregated high school. *Crime and Delinquency, 24*(3), 277–289.

Polk, K., & Schafer, W. E. (1972). *Schools and delinquency.* Englewood Cliffs, NJ: Prentice Hall.

Reeves, M. (1929). *Training schools for delinquent girls.* Philadelphia: Russell Sage Foundation.

Slavson, S. R. (1961). *Re-educating the delinquent: Through group and community participation.* New York: Collier Books.

Tueba, H. T., Spindler G., & Spindler, L. (1989). *What do anthropologists have to say about dropouts? The first centennial conference on children at risk.* New York: Falmer Press.

Weeks, A. H. (1958). *Youthful offenders at Highfields: An evaluation of the effects of the short-term treatment of delinquent boys.* Ann Arbor: University of Michigan Press.

DEMOCRACY AND EDUCATION

Education and democracy are inextricably linked in American social thought and practice. Democracy, in all of its historic and contemporary forms, has played a pivotal role in shaping conceptions of public education. How public education is imagined, scripted, and enacted is contested along philosophic, programmatic, and pedagogic dimensions in relation to competing conceptions of democracy.

Classic contributors to modern political thought and commentary, as well as those who framed modern arguments, have dealt specifically with the educational necessities of establishing and maintaining a democratic polity. They have generally reflected on the tensions between the socialization of a democratic nation's *subjects* (as acculturated, law abiding members) and the education of its *citizens* (as critically thinking, active participants). Both education and democracy in the United States have evolved in response to historic geographic-based concerns (persistent regionalism, westward expansion, rapid urbanization, and globalization), significant demographic shifts (especially the cultural diversity brought by immigration), and economic growth (mostly the imperatives of industrial technologies).

Capitalism in all of its historic forms (e.g., preindustrial, industrial, postindustrial globalization) and through its dominant technologies (e.g., mechanized agriculture, mass commodity production, transportation, and global information networks) sets limits (such as what's acceptable for critical analysis in curricula), provides objectives (such as agile job-readiness, rational consumer skills), and shapes policy and practice (such as corporate bureaucratic form, economic incentives, market-based curriculum, emphases on individual choice) in public education.

This entry examines three different concepts of democracy and how they envision the role of education. Then it looks at how a more radical democracy—called "deep democracy"—might transform social and political life and what that would portend for education.

Complex Interplay

Along with the cultural, social, and economic factors shaping contemporary public education, specific goals and their programmatic implications are intertwined in three partially overlapping forms of American democracy: institutional republicanism, popular democracy, and deep democracy. Each embodies general American cultural values (e.g., liberty, equality, and justice; free expression and tolerance for competing ideas; and the rule of law). All three democratic forms support specific institutional arrangements (e.g., power sharing among legislative, executive, and judicial branches; free and frequent elections; majority rule with minority rights). All three promote universal education as necessary for effective citizenship. There are, however, important differences for both democracy and education in each form.

Institutional republicanism understands the Constitution as establishing a republic with a limited representative government. Public education is understood as necessary to support government-centered institutions. The focus is on preparing citizens for orderly civic participation centered on obeying the law and voting in national, state, and local elections. Public education's role is primarily one of promoting *social stability* to ensure political continuity and economic growth. Young people are to acquire the knowledge, skills, and dispositions necessary for informed and responsible consumption of material goods (economic productivity) and nonmaterial civic benefits (individual rights).

Popular democracy emphasizes broad and active involvement in civic life that goes beyond dutiful voting in periodic elections. Public education is needed to ground young citizens in democratic values (especially equality and social justice) and to inform them about central institutional structures and processes. But education must also include critical analysis of contemporary ideas, conditions, and events. Interwoven with instructional efforts to shape social stability are programs designed to promote *social mobility* to overcome persistent structural barriers to status and opportunity. Young people are prepared to move through critical awareness toward principled action.

Deep democracy advocates full participation in all aspects of social and civic life—not only those conventionally identified as political. Beyond the teaching of core democratic values and dominant institutional arrangements, public education is to provide direct experience with practices of collective civic engagement. Young citizens are to enact complex processes of teaching and learning that lead to deliberative competence, social imagination, and inclusive participation in *social transformation.*

The Challenges of Civic Education

All three democratic forms and their public education priorities have coexisted and often competed with each other throughout the twentieth century and into the twenty-first century. In different contexts, places, and times, one or another version of democracy and education has seemed predominant. While they are in competition over recognition and resources, each form generates internal conflict.

Most government officials and business interests understandably favor public education that legitimates their roles and therefore advocate the values emphasized in institutional republicanism. This understanding of democracy supports civic education that promotes the traditional values of patriotism, social unity, and economic growth; that provides extensive institutional descriptions; and that champions individual responsibility. Tensions within this mix of education and governance include conflict over state and local control versus national policies and standards, and public school adequacy versus privatization.

Advocates of popular democracy criticize persistent and growing social, economic, and political inequalities and point to a politically disengaged and often cynical citizenry. A government largely ineffective in reducing social and economic inequalities is insufficient for a vibrant democracy, they say. Civic education must include responsible critique, engagement with perennial problems, strategic understanding of institutional processes, and learning experiences that promote civic action. Tensions within this approach include trenchant, often dismissive, social criticism rather than attempts to broaden understanding and build coalitions. Progressive paradoxes also involve advocacy for more inclusive forms of action rather than continuing reliance on small elites and special interest group politics.

Deep democracy and its educational imperatives have yet to be widely established and sustained. Despite enduring and often valiant efforts, there have been few instances of profound and integrative restructuring of public education and democratic governance. Confronted with fundamentally nondemocratic social structures such as entrenched bureaucracies, persistent status hierarchies, dominant religious organizations, and even traditional family structures, civic education for deep democracy faces formidable resistance. Given aspirations for full and inclusive participation across all aspects of social life, civic educators must address tensions between the instructional requirements of individual versus social learning along with recognition of private achievement versus collaborative accomplishment.

Education for Deep Democracy

Democracy, in all of its forms, is a continuing project. The development of its necessary elements, including public education, is uneven. Competitive individualism as the exclusive method for achievement in learning and life restricts both instructional and civic practice. The dominant result has been a shallow American democracy with voter indifference, elite-dominated public discourse, and growing citizen disengagement. With some situational differences, shallow democracy reinforces voters as passive consumers of candidates, parties, and policies that are advanced in ways indistinguishable from those used in the retail marketplace. Public education that emphasizes market-centered learning results in low-intensity citizenship with personal civic responsibilities that can be discharged by preferred ignorance, fragmentary complaints, and episodic votes.

Drawing from and moving beyond the well-intended efforts associated with institutional republicanism and popular democracy are real prospects for deep democracy. A deep democracy is *radically social, persistently exploratory,* and *compellingly aesthetic.* These distinguishing criteria are recognizable in many versions of the good society. There are long-standing aspirations for a social order that supports the establishment of justice, the pursuit of truth, and the experience of beauty.

A deep democracy is radically social when it is broadly inclusive and authentically collaborative.

Politics and education, at all levels and in all venues, involve dominant elites and a limited set of special interest groups. Reliance on these established patterns supports isolation, drives alienation, structures a narrowed discourse, and solidifies established forms of opposition in schools and society.

Developing a deeper set of democratic processes would expand the number of active participants across their life span and at all stages of social inquiry, decision making, and implementation. Such movement requires broad engagement of school-age youth, adult citizens, and disadvantaged groups to support border crossings between disparate positions and expectations. In finding such pathways, difficult encounters and negotiations will occur. These are necessary to engage and possibly integrate what may appear to be sharply conflicting goals, values, and behavioral styles.

This challenge is approachable when democratic processes are persistently exploratory. Shallow democracy offers a sense of certainty with minimal effort by students and adult citizens. Yet the realities of constant change flowing from the dynamics of our experienced world signal pervasive uncertainty. Deep democracy requires persistent collaboration in teaching and learning to maintain openness, support principled risk taking, and yield an adaptive response. Deep social inquiry requires creativity over caution, vision over constraint, and deliberation over the convenience of closure. It is difficult, but necessary, to encourage and sustain conceptual divergence and multiplicity in adapting both to the turbulent and to the subtle changes in our multileveled lives. In education for deep democracy, there are no easy answers.

Deep democracy is *compellingly aesthetic* as it engages the emotions and energies necessary to persevere through the challenges of change. Intuition and inspiration, prophecy and poetry, enchantment and emotion, mystery and movement, silence and spirit are concepts seldom associated with problem solving in education, politics, or governance. Teaching, learning, and decision making for public purposes require much more than objective analysis and linear problem solving. Inseparable rather than distinct from highly individualized cognitive processes are human capacities for social empathy and intuition. Emotions shape our thinking, often focusing attention, sometimes exerting decisive influence. Empathy, a feeling-based capacity, makes it possible to establish meaningful connections. Its continuing development allows us to sustain collaborative relationships not only with like-minded others, but even more importantly, with those whose experiences and commitments are quite different from our own.

Fulfillment of deep democracy's transformative purpose would require continuing innovation in civic education. Civic education must emphasize pedagogies that support movement beyond illusions of certainty, convenience, convergence, and control. Civic education for a deeper democracy must engage diversely valid meanings, perspectives, possibilities, and plans. Such pedagogies must (a) extend collective wisdom concerning significant social issues, (b) expand possibilities for thought and action beyond those initially brought by individuals, (c) enrich relationships by increasing the number and variety of meaningful connections among diverse participants, and (d) enhance capacities for continued engagement in civic learning and public life that narrow the gap between democratic aspirations and real-world accomplishments.

Deep democracy is a dynamic, multifaceted social composition. It can be shaped to create sites for the expression of strategic intuition, imaginative policy, and artistic advocacy. A more inclusive, more widely exploratory, and more aesthetically informed public education broadens opportunities for richer experiences of democratic life.

Ruthanne Kurth-Schai and Charles R. Green

See also Citizenship Education; Philosophy of Education

Further Readings

Barber, B. R. (1992). *An aristocracy of everyone: The politics of education and the future of America.* New York: Oxford University Press.

Dahl, R. A. (1998). *On democracy.* New Haven, CT: Yale University Press.

Dewey, J. (1944). *Democracy and education.* New York: Macmillan. (Original work published 1916)

Gutmann, A. (1987). *Democratic education.* Princeton, NJ: Princeton University Press.

DESEGREGATION

Desegregation entered the standard American English lexicon in about 1951 to describe the process of removing racial and other minorities from isolation or sequestration in society. The related terms *segregation* and *integration* are found in sixteenth-century texts and have broader generic meanings that require contextual understanding. Using the modern civil rights movement as the context with which to frame an understanding of these terms can provide the means for critical analysis of relevant issues. This entry reviews the context in which desegregation became policy, examines its progress in the particular instance of schools, and looks at the larger question of whether desegregation is necessary to achieve equality.

Historical Context: Overview

From the beginning of intergroup contact among Europeans, Africans, indigenous Americans, and Asians on American soil, there has been an ongoing struggle for human rights and later civil rights between the dominant and subordinate groups. Desegregation was but one aspect of the modern civil rights movement that looked to the U.S. Constitution, Declaration of Independence, Supreme Court decisions, and related state and federal legislation for support to fuel its goal of equal opportunity and social justice for all U.S. citizens.

Desegregation should not be confused with social integration; they are not the same. Desegregation relies on quantitative measurements to determine effectiveness, whereas social integration is assessed qualitatively according to the degree to which differentiated pairs and groups express bonding and commonality, as in friendships, marriages, and organizational memberships. A school may in fact meet the quantitative standards of desegregation—that is, no single group comprises more than 50 percent of the student body and at least one other group is 25 percent—but fail to meet the qualitative standards of social integration because students attend separate proms and exercise minimal contact with one another outside of the classroom. The legacy of American slavery, White supremacy, and Jim Crow apartheid appears to continue to determine school outcome profiles despite legal and political efforts to promote both desegregation and social integration.

Efforts to "racially" desegregate American society were made in virtually all areas of society, including but not limited to schools, housing, employment, the military, criminal justice, entertainment, sports, and public service. Current research and statistical evidence indicates that the success of these efforts is mixed at best. For example, several scholars note that American schools are more segregated today than they were in 1954, when the Supreme Court declared that separate schools were inherently unequal, and in 1955, when schools were admonished by the same Court to desegregate with "all deliberate speed."

After overcoming massive resistance to court-ordered busing and other strategies to get Black and White students into the same classrooms, schools seem to have reached a peak of quantitative desegregation and now are experiencing a reverse trend toward resegregation. In retrospect, it seems that the vagueness of the 1955 "all deliberate speed" mandate has encouraged school districts to deliberate long and act slowly as a form of resistance to desegregating their schools.

Court Rulings and Social Response

When the Supreme Court rendered the *Brown v. Board of Education* decision in 1954 and its companion ruling in 1955, it officially ended the era of Jim Crow apartheid ushered in by the 1896 Supreme Court ruling in *Plessy v. Ferguson*. *Plessy* was a case involving interstate travel that set the precedent that separate facilities for Blacks were constitutional so long as they were not inferior to White ones. It was not long before the "separate but equal" doctrine was quickly extended to cover many areas of public life, such as restaurants, theaters, restrooms, and public schools. The *Brown* case was a suit that specifically argued against segregated schools, establishing that separate educational facilities are inherently unequal; it initiated a protracted struggle to desegregate transportation systems, park facilities, retail establishments, water fountains, and other public venues.

At the time of the 1954 decision, laws in seventeen Southern and border states and the District of Columbia required that elementary schools be segregated. Four other states had laws permitting segregation. While segregation and school discrimination existed in other parts of the nation, law did not sanction it. As expected, the most violent and heated resistance to desegregation came from many of the Southern states. Governor Orval Faubus of Arkansas is noted for his open defiance of federal orders to desegregate schools in Little Rock in 1957. He called out the Arkansas National Guard to prevent nine Black students from entering Central High School. President Eisenhower responded by sending federal troops to enforce the Court order.

In 1958, Virginia chose to close nine schools in four counties rather than desegregate them, prompting Virginia and federal courts to rule these moves illegal. In 1962, two people were killed when James Meredith opposed Mississippi Governor Ross Barnett and attempted to enroll at the University of Mississippi at Oxford. Another governor who became famous for his resistance to desegregation was George Wallace of Alabama. He stood in a doorway at the University of Alabama in a failed symbolic attempt to prevent two Black students from enrolling there in 1963.

Even in the North, Black parents had to file a lawsuit in 1960 against the school system of New Rochelle, New York, because of its policies permitting racing segregation. In 1961 a federal judge ordered the schools to be desegregated. Black parents in other cities had to do the same to get full access to their public schools. Boston, Massachusetts, long a haven of intellectual progressivism, as late as 1974 had White members of its community exposed on national television in riot mode, fighting court orders against busing and school desegregation.

Television was still in its infancy during the 1950s and early 1960s, but cameras captured a good deal of the chaos and vitriol directed at freedom fighters who upset the status quo by attempting to fulfill recent court orders aimed at desegregating public life. Archival footage shows how racist taunts, spitting, rock throwing, dog attacks, and fire hose power were used to create fear and intimidation among those in the Black community who tried to desegregate schools and other public facilities. Some even credit television with giving the civil rights movement much needed momentum because the country and even the world got to see how Black citizens were being treated in a free democratic society such as that of the United States.

Affirmative Action and Legal Response

A number of court cases have arisen over the decades since *Brown* that depart from debates specifically aimed at desegregating school systems and institutions of higher education to become debates arguing issues of affirmative action and diversity. Critical to the analysis of theses cases is the important distinction between mandatory K–12 public education and competitive admissions into postsecondary public and private colleges and universities. Any institution that accepts federal funding such as financial aid for students is subject to federal legislative rulings used to guide access to equal educational opportunity.

In the mid-1970s, Allan Bakke, a White graduate student, filed suit against the California Board of Regents, charging reverse discrimination and arguing that affirmative action programs were responsible for denying him admission to the University of California at Davis medical school and thus violating his Thirteenth and Fourteenth Amendment rights under the Constitution. The case reached the Supreme Court and was settled in 1978 in a split 5–4 decision in favor of Bakke. The decision allowed affirmative action policies to continue but with a caveat: racial quotas were to be eliminated and race-based admissions allowed only when other factors were used to determine qualifications for acceptance.

The assaults against affirmative action and other diversity initiatives since *Bakke* have increased. Scholarships and other financial incentives earmarked for underrepresented groups are challenged for being discriminatory against Whites. Some legal analysts have touted the 2003 Michigan affirmative action case *Grutter v. Bollinger* as a plan to minimize the importance of race while offering maximum protection to Whites. Affirmative action was once lauded as a means to achieve institutional desegregation and redress past discrimination and denial of equal educational opportunity against Blacks and other students of color; the tenor has changed to now view affirmative action as a tool to facilitate institutional diversity with less regard to the social barriers created by the historical legacy of racial bias.

Colorblind Policy

When Justice John Harlan declared in his lone dissent in *Plessy v. Ferguson* in 1896 that "Our Constitution is colorblind and neither knows nor tolerates classes among citizens," he unwittingly gave support to the current conservative position advocating colorblindness as the future of American policy. Those in favor of colorblind approaches to policy argue that taking cognizance of racial group membership is illegitimate and likely to lead to further discrimination and reinforces the perceived inferiority of people of color. They also believe that a once unfair system has been made fair and that continued recognition of race disrupts the mechanisms now in place to insure equality and equity. Opponents of colorblind approaches to policy argue that ignoring race is the antithesis of fairness and obstructs the creation of mechanisms needed to achieve equality and equity.

The American tradition suggests that in the United States justice is administered to all citizens without regard to race or skin color. The historical and statistical evidence suggests otherwise. Scholarly research on equal educational opportunity should help us understand how and why racial segregation has persisted in spite of federal and state decrees making racially discriminatory schooling illegal. Contemporary movements toward colorblindness and meritocracy, which emphasize individual merit without consideration of group membership, appear to frustrate desegregation efforts and diversity initiatives. Elementary and high school resegregation and increased postsecondary competition for coveted admissions point to America's dilemma of legal and cultural contradiction.

A pluralist society believes that different cultural groups can maintain their integrity and still enjoy equality with the dominant culture. Actually achieving true pluralism in American democratic society will require an effective reconciliation of the movement from liberal to conservative legal rulings with the movement from conservative to liberal sociocultural values. Whereas most Americans no longer believe in legal segregation, de facto segregation is allowed to develop unopposed or is responded to with weak policies that are unable to reverse it.

Equality Without Integration?

So the larger philosophical question is whether racial equality is achievable without racial integration. Critics of school desegregation, both Black and White, have argued that court-enforced desegregation efforts were unnecessary and maybe even self-defeating. Many Blacks would have been satisfied if the state had made more of an effort to ensure that their schools were on a par with the White schools when it came to teacher's pay, student resources, and funding. These Blacks had little interest in having their children sit next to White children just for the sake of it. However, they saw the futility in trying to get the state to make their schools "equal" to White ones and thought it easier to "integrate" White schools, thereby giving their children access to the better facilities and resources.

The downside of *Brown* and its legacy was that thousands of Black teachers and principals throughout the South lost their jobs and were never absorbed into the newly desegregated schools. White resistance to highly qualified Black teachers and administrators teaching and having administrative capacity over their children was clear. Poorly maintained Black schools were shuttered and some razed along with the memories of alumni who had attended them. Communities that regarded their schools as central features had to reconceptualize their understanding of and connection to schools. Desegregation is also blamed for the loss of Black businesses and loss of community cohesiveness in all Black towns and segregated urban neighborhoods.

America's commitment to a desegregated society is evidenced by legal policy and politically correct social policy. The means by which America has sought to achieve desegregation has been painful for many people, and the verdict is still out on the best way to get the job done. One thing is clear: The desegregation story must be recounted with bold accuracy. Sanitized and revisionist accounts will not enable scholars to help answer many of the unanswered questions or resolve many of the unresolved issues. So when contemporary students read textbooks that fail to mention that the plaintiffs and the attorneys in the *Brown v. Board* decision were Black or that the National Association for the Advancement of Colored People (NAACP) had argued a number of cases around the country that led to *Brown*, then the foundation upon which critical analysis is built is weaker. Crediting the federal government as a benevolent innovator of actions initiated and nurtured by Blacks and their White allies disempowers people who believe that power belongs to the people and the way to social change is through the people.

Jonathan Lightfoot

See also Affirmative Action; *Brown v. Board of Education*; Colorblindness; Cultural Pluralism; Desegregation Academies; Discrimination and Prejudice; Education, History of; Educational Equity: Race/Ethnicity; Hegemony; Minority Student Access to Higher Education; Politics of Education; Urban Schools, History of

See Visual History Chapter 25, Civil Rights

Further Readings

Anderson, J. D. (2006). Still desegregated, still unequal: Lessons from up North. *Educational Researcher, 35*(1), 30–33.

Armor, D. (1995). *Forced justice: School desegregation and the law.* New York: Oxford University Press.

Bankston, C. J., III, & Caldas, S. J. (2005). *Forced to fail: The paradox of school desegregation.* Westport, CT: Praeger.

Bell, D. (2004). *Silent covenants:* Brown v. Board of Education *and the unfulfilled hopes for racial reform.* New York: Oxford University Press.

Menkart, D., Murray, A. D., & View, J. L. (2004). *Putting the movement back into civil rights teaching: A resource guide for classrooms and communities.* Washington, DC: Teaching for Change.

Morris, V. G., & Morris, C. L. (2002). *The price they paid: Desegregation in an African American community.* New York: Teachers College Press.

Ogletree, C. J. (2004). *All deliberate speed: Reflections on the first half-century of* Brown v. Board of Education. New York: W. W. Norton.

Wolters, R. (1989). Segregation, integration, and pluralism: Approaches to American race relations. *History of Education Quarterly, 29*(1), 123–130.

DESEGREGATION ACADEMIES

Of the hundreds of independent African American schools that exist today, many were founded as desegregation academies between 1964 and 1984. The Black Power movement and the civil rights movement were the driving forces behind the establishment of these institutions. The initial impetus, however, was more pragmatic: When communities adamantly objected through massive resistance to desegregated schools, even closing entire school systems down, desegregation academies served as a reliable and independent source of ongoing education from a perspective that fostered African American values. This entry looks at the origins and current status of these academies.

The spirit of desegregation academies was derived from the philosophy of cultural revolt taking place in universities and colleges around curriculum issues. Black college students wanted to change the European-centered curriculum; they believed that it produced students who did not serve the Black community, either because they had no desire to do so or because their White-oriented education made it impossible to communicate with African Americans. Graduates from these programs established desegregated and independent academy schools in their communities.

These schools were also an outgrowth of parents' struggles over control of their children's education in existing public schools. During the 1960s and 1970s parental and community protest fueled the formation of independent schools. The result was the creation of a Pan-African educational movement. The Malcolm X Liberation University in Durham, North Carolina, and the Center for Black Education in Washington, D.C., for example, defined their primary educational mission as supplying skilled technicians to the African continent. While important, both of these efforts failed to properly understand the central nature of the Black Liberation movement in the United States.

Today, the Institute for Independent Education reports that over 400 independent Black inner-city or neighborhood academies serve children of color nationwide. More than 200 of these academies are owned and operated by African Americans. These schools are located primarily in urban areas and mostly in the Northeast, with the remaining scattered across the Southwest, South, Southeast, central United States, and the U.S. Virgin Islands. They are typically directed by individuals committed to social change, leaders who aim to promote academic excellence but can work within a small budget.

One half of the schools have waiting lists. The tuition is often weighted based upon the family income. While the schools tend to be racially homogenous, no school denies access to any child based on race, creed, religion, ethnicity, or political affiliation. The student-teacher ratio for all schools is 14:1, slightly higher in religious or parochial schools and slightly lower in private secular schools. Most of the students who attend live in the immediate vicinity of the school.

Many teachers are employed at these schools an average of two years or less. Most hold bachelor's degrees, while a few hold master's degrees and/or doctorates. Teachers' mean salaries range from $11,273 to $23,142 per year.

Paul E. Green

See also African American Education; Desegregation

Further Readings

Lomotey, K. (1992). Independent Black institutions: African-centered education models. *Journal of Counseling Development, 61,* 454–462.

Shujaa, J. M. (1992). Afrocentric transformation and parental choice in African American independent schools. *Journal of Negro Education, 61,* 149–157.

Deskilling

Deskilling, as it pertains to the teaching profession, refers to the reduction of the teacher's role in the classroom to that of a conveyor of information. The teacher is expected to iterate assigned information to students, and the students are merely to reiterate this information back. Tests are employed to determine the degree to which a teacher has prioritized this process, and a teacher is rewarded depending on how well his or her students produce the information on the tests. In this process, the teacher is seen as a laborer, a nonvariable in the classroom, one who simply follows the prescribed curriculum without input. Pedagogy becomes irrelevant. Pedagogic skill not only is not required, but is not undesirable. The result is the deskilling and deprofessionalizing of the teacher and teaching.

Joe Kincheloe has explained how the phenomenon of deskilling the factory worker and the teacher are comparable. He has pointed out that the deskilling of teachers and deintellectualizing of the curriculum occur when teachers are considered receivers rather than producers of knowledge. In this arrangement, information deemed important by school or government officials is simply given to teachers to distribute. Just as the factory worker in many ways became an accessory to the machine, teachers are an accessory to the curriculum in that they are bound by what the predetermined curriculum allows. This entry looks at how the deskilling process was first initiated and examines current practice for deskilling potential.

Historical Background

The notion of deskilling the worker comes from the growth of industry of the nineteenth century, and in particular, from the model for industry laid out by Frederick Taylor. Like many of his contemporaries, Taylor believed that there was one best way to do any job. He devised a process to find this one best way by comparing how the quickest and best workers would complete a task and then making this method the standard required of all workers. Taylor also devised a bureaucratic, hierarchical chain of command to optimize productivity. The worker would perform small tasks as directed by superiors, a manager class would coordinate workers, middle management would be the liaison between the floor and upper management, which in turn would report to the factory owner.

Joseph Mayer Rice, a doctor turned educator, promoted this model for industry as being advantageous for school in order to assure a standard, consistent quality of teachers and education. To the many in power who venerated the ideals of social efficiency (a belief that schools should serve society and the economy by "socializing" and "Americanizing" immigrants to the norms of American society and produce a docile workforce), this approach was very attractive. As a result, schools of the late nineteenth and early twentieth centuries adopted Taylor's model for industry. In this approach, the superintendent became the controller of schools and under him fell a bureaucratic system of supervisors, principals, vice principals, and teachers. The teacher was seen as a worker expected to run the classroom with military order and ensure the imposition of assigned tasks.

Ivan Illich saw this process also being implemented to society at large. What he called a "radical monopoly" was the aim of making individual skills less useable through schooling that deskills the individual. The result is a society where people are less able to translate their personal understandings and skills into valuable attributes.

Today's Practice

Many believe that the corporate-friendly 1980s marked a return to seeing teachers as workers rather than educators. As evidence, they assert that standards-based education policy discourages teachers from engaging in constructivist, child-centered education in favor of strict adherence to a prescribed curriculum. The increase in standardized testing since that time is viewed as an effort to ensure teacher compliance with prescribed curricula, thus deskilling the teacher.

Under the system established by the No Child Left Behind Act, teachers are provided with a prescribed distribution of what may be fragmented and decontextualized pieces of information, fragmented so that they may be easily quantified and assessed through positivistic testing methods. Such multiple choice and true or false tests further reduce the role of the teacher as a decision maker in terms of grading. By basing judgments of the teacher's competence on how well his or her students perform on standardized tests, teacher compliance is encouraged, if not assured.

Opponents of the standardization movement see the teacher who behaves as a nonvariable, distributing information without discussion or question, is most highly rewarded in this system. The deskilled teacher is not asked to be a creative, nurturing teacher striving to instill a love for learning and the ability in students to understand and shape the world around them, they

argue. Rather, the deskilled teacher is asked to distribute information and tasks as prescribed by the school hierarchy without interruption.

Donal E. Mulcahy

See also Scientific Management

Further Readings

Illich, I. (1971). *Deschooling society.* New York: Harper & Row.

Kincheloe, J. L. (2001). *Getting beyond the facts: Teaching social sciences in the twenty-first century.* New York: Peter Lang.

Kincheloe, J. L. (2003). *Teachers as researchers: Qualitative inquiry as a path to empowerment* (2nd ed.). London: RoutledgeFalmer.

Kleibard, H. M. (1992). *The struggle for the American curriculum, 1893–1958.* New York: Routledge.

Kohn, A. (2000). *The case against standardized testing.* Portsmouth, NH: Heinemann.

Tyack, D. B. (1974). *The one best system: A history of American urban education.* Cambridge, MA: Harvard University Press.

DIGITAL DIVIDE

The term *digital divide* refers to the distance between those people with access to computers and digital sources of information, such as the Internet and the World Wide Web, and those who lack such resources. This division includes not only hardware and software, but also access to training and technology based on geographic location. What Eugene Provenzo refers to as "posttypographic textuality" and George Landow calls "hypertextuality" relies on digital technology; thus, it is prudent to explore how computers are used to instill a sense of cultural inferiority.

In this context, Tamara Pearson notes that in many educational settings, computers are used primarily for drill and practice exercises, preparing students for standardized tests. This poses a problem for economically and ethnically marginalized groups, as their opportunities for high-order thinking exercises, such as problem solving and creative movie making and narration, are fewer when compared to computer practices in more affluent schools with socially dominant demographics. Pearson also notes that marginalized groups are much less likely to have home computers and home Internet access than privileged groups. According to research by Craig Peck, Larry Cuban, and Heather Kirkpatrick, this aspect of the digital divide is telling because much of the active computer experimentation occurs in the home.

Roy Bohlin and Carol Bohlin concur that among Latino and African American student populations, computers are used much more often for drill and practice applications than for higher order learning, such as simulations and applications. Latino students they interviewed recognized that knowing how to use computers was important to get a job in the digital age workplace, but they didn't understand how they would use computer technology in their intended work.

Michael Mazyck notes that computer-based instructional models such as Integrated Learning Systems (ILS) have been instituted predominantly in schools within economically disadvantaged areas. In this context, what is significant to many is that ILS grew out of social efficiency's wunderkind, the teaching machine, and the instrumental conditioning models of figures such as the behavioral psychologist B. F. Skinner. The utopian logic underlying teaching machines proposes to replace haphazard teaching by substandard teachers for chronically underachieving school populations. The ideal for teaching machines is a perfected curriculum that substandard teachers cannot misappropriate as they become little more than technicians within the teaching process. However, after four decades of ILS integration into economically disadvantaged schools, no independent research can confirm the rosy picture painted by ILS advocates and the research conducted by the ILS providers.

The results of this research, then, suggest that computers used for traditional curricular designs do not improve education, particularly for those learners who have been historically marginalized by such positivist pedagogies. It's not computers that are to blame, but how they are used. Simply providing minority or economically needy students with access to computers is an inadequate solution to meeting their educational needs. Instead, a much deeper understanding of how people have access to computing, and the type of training provided them, is essential if the digital divide that clearly exists is to be closed.

James S. Dwight

See also Computing, Ethical Issues

Further Readings

Bohlin, R. M., & Bohlin, C. F. (2002). Computer-related effects among Latino students—educational implications. *TechTrends: For leaders in education & training, 46*(2), 2.

Landow, G. P. (1992). *Hypertext: The convergence of contemporary critical theory and technology.* Baltimore: Johns Hopkins University Press.

Landow, G. P. (1994). *Hyper/text/theory.* Baltimore: Johns Hopkins University Press.

Landow, G. P. (1997). *Hypertext 2.0* (Rev., amplified ed.). Baltimore: Johns Hopkins University Press.

Landow, G. P., & Delany, P. (1993). *The digital word: Text-based computing in the humanities.* Cambridge: MIT Press.

Mazyck, M. (2002). Integrated learning systems and students of color: Two decades of use in K–12 education. *TechTrends, 46*(2), 33–39.

Pearson, T. (2002). Falling behind—a technology crisis facing minority students. *TechTrends: For leaders in education & training, 46*(2), 6.

Peck, C., Cuban, L., & Kirkpatrick, H. (2002). Techno-promoter dreams, student realities. *Phi Delta Kappan, 83*(6), 472–480.

Provenzo, E. F., Jr. (2002). *Teaching, learning, and schooling: A 21st-century perspective.* Boston: Allyn & Bacon.

DISABILITIES, PHYSICAL ACCOMMODATIONS FOR PEOPLE WITH

Physical and health disabilities have always existed yet have been treated differently across civilizations, cultures, and settings. Students with physical disabilities were initially educated in institutions that could provide a centralized place for equipment and treatment. The first of these institutions was the Industrial School for Crippled and Deformed Children in Boston, established in 1890. Beginning in the 1900s public schools for "crippled children" were established but were self-contained, typically housed in a separate facility or classroom, and did not allow children to interact with their peers without physical disabilities. Through advocacy, legislation, shifts in attitudes, and advances in medical practices, more inclusive settings became available for all children, including those with physical and health needs.

Today, federal laws protect individuals and outline the accommodations that are required to ensure access and participation for all individuals regardless of ability or disability. Most physical accommodations can be implemented with minimal cost and are likely to benefit all individuals with or without disabilities. This entry looks at the laws that establish criteria for the education of children with disabilities and examines how those guidelines are implemented in today's schools.

Laws

Three federal laws most readily pertain to the education and care of children with disabilities. They are described briefly in this section.

Education for All Handicapped Children Act (1975), renamed *Individuals with Disabilities Education Act* (IDEA, 2004). IDEA is a federal law (most recently reauthorized and amended by Congress in 2004) that governs all special education services for children in the United States from birth to age twenty-one. In order for children to receive special education services under IDEA, they must be in one of the following categories or have one of the following disabling conditions: autism, deaf-blindness, emotional disturbance, hearing impairment (including deafness), mental retardation, multiple disabilities, orthopedic impairment, other health impairment, specific learning disability, speech or language impairment, traumatic brain injury, or visual impairment (including blindness). This law stipulates that all children are entitled to a free, appropriate, public education.

Section 504 of the Rehabilitation Act of 1973. Section 504 is a civil rights statute that prohibits discrimination against individuals with disabilities. Schools must ensure equal access for children with disabilities and also provide them with reasonable accommodations. The law covers all programs or activities, whether public or private, that receive federal financial assistance. Reasonable accommodations may include providing a computer, seating students in the front of the class, modifying homework, or providing necessary services. Typically, children covered under Section 504 have disabilities that do not fit within the eligibility categories of IDEA or that are due to accident or illness, which is not permanent. Under Section 504, any person who has an impairment that substantially limits a major life activity is considered disabled. Learning and social development are included under the list of major life activities.

Americans with Disabilities Act (ADA, 1990). Like Section 504, the ADA is civil rights legislation for individuals with disabilities. Unlike Section 504, the ADA applies to almost every entity in the United States, regardless of whether it receives federal funds; churches and private clubs are the only two entities that are exempt from the ADA. For instance, private schools that are not associated with a religious organization have to comply with the provisions of the ADA. Schools that may be exempt from Section 504 because they do not receive federal funds are not exempt from making accommodations based on ADA. The ADA contains several titles that focus on various aspects of disability discrimination. Title I prohibits discrimination in employment. Title II prohibits discrimination in state and local governmental entities, including schools. Title III addresses public accommodations, including hotels, restaurants, department stores, grocery stores, and banks. In all instances, entities delineated are required to make *reasonable accommodations* or modifications necessary to ensure persons with disabilities have access to goods and services.

Physical Accommodations

Some students have disabilities that they are born with or have acquired and may be unable to undertake the same physical activities as their peers. This includes individuals who have difficulty walking, individuals who have difficulty using their hands or arms, or individuals with restricted growth. Etiology is varied and includes conditions affecting bones, muscles, nerves and tendons, spinal cord, and the brain. The effect of the disability will also vary, and students may experience weariness or pain, which may become worse when they are fatigued. Several types of physical accommodations may be necessary.

For Learning

For students with limited, or no use of their hands, arms, or legs, a range of physical accommodations and technology may be of assistance. Students may benefit from someone to take notes, undertake experiments, carry or open books or physically write assignments for them. Some students experience excessive fatigue or may have medical conditions that require providing a place to rest during the day. Students who are wheelchair users or who have conditions affecting their backs may need specially designed chairs, desks, or positioning equipment.

Tape recorders and adapted keyboards or software can be critical for note taking and other assignments for students who cannot write or write as quickly as others. Keyboards can be adapted for size and shape or include a pointer or switch device operated by any part of the body that moves. Software is available that will predict what a student is writing from input of the first few letters of the word. This word prediction capability is particularly useful for those whose writing speed is severely impacted. Voice recognition software allows students to dictate, and the software will type in their response. Both word prediction and voice input may be useful for other students.

For Access

For many students, the physical environment may form the greatest barrier, and accommodations will be necessary. The academic setting includes areas where students typically congregate, including libraries, dining rooms, and social areas, as well as classrooms and labs. In the academic setting, access accommodations may include installing ramps or lifts, moving lift buttons to an accessible height, removing areas with fixed seating to allow wheelchair access, and installing accessible toilets. It may be necessary to modify rooms to ensure access to certain lectures,

seminars, or other sessions, including altering entries, the height of lab benches, or seating.

For college and university students living in residential facilities, accommodations may include larger rooms to allow entry and maneuvering of wheelchairs, guide animals, and other mobility devices; appropriate surface heights and hoists or rails in bathrooms, kitchens, bedrooms, and study areas; designated parking spaces; nearby rooms for personal assistants; and access to telephone and laundry facilities.

Universal Design

Universal design refers to an environment that can be used by people with or without disabilities, eliminating or minimizing the need for special accommodations. Creating an environment accessible to people with disabilities usually benefits others and can greatly increase access. For example, curb cuts in sidewalks are designed to make sidewalks and streets accessible to those using wheelchairs, yet benefit parents with strollers, children and adults using bicycles, rollerskates, or skateboards, and delivery persons with rolling carts. There are a number of design changes that are cost effective to implement.

These are the major components of universal design. Equitable use means that the design is useful and marketable to people with diverse abilities. Flexibility in use means that the design accommodates a wide range of individual preferences and abilities. Simple and intuitive designs are easy to understand, regardless of the user's experience, knowledge, language skills, or current concentration level. Designs with perceptible information communicate necessary information effectively to the user, regardless of ambient conditions or the user's sensory abilities. With tolerance for error, designs minimize hazards and the adverse consequences of accidental or unintended actions. Designs should also involve low physical effort, so they can be used efficiently and comfortably with a minimum of fatigue. Size and space for approach and use must be provided so that users can approach, reach, manipulate, and use a facility regardless of their body size, posture, or mobility.

Michelle Larocque

See also Disabilities and the Politics of Schooling; School Law

Further Readings

Cedar Rapids Community School District v. Garret F., 526 U.S. 86 (1999).

Fadiman, A. (1997). *The spirit catches you and you fall down.* New York: Farrar, Straus & Giroux.

Heller, K. W. (1999). *Classroom modification checklist for students with physical and health impairments.* Atlanta, GA: Bureau for Students with Physical and Health Impairments.

Rapport, M. J. (1996). Legal guidelines for the delivery of special health care services in schools. *Exceptional Children, 62,* 537–549.

Web Sites

National Center on Accessible Information Technology in Education: http://www.washington.edu/accessit

DISABILITIES AND THE POLITICS OF SCHOOLING

Discussions of disability in educational contexts commonly equate disability with individual tragedy, individual deficit, and individual dysfunction rooted in oppressive medicalized and clinical discourses that offer little space for alternative, empowering discourses of resistance and of possibility. In contrast, the field of disability studies has theorized disability as a social and political construct and theorized disabled people as a minority group engaged in a political struggle for civil rights. Disability studies' scholarship foregrounds social difference as its central analytic and deconstructs the social hierarchies society creates between the normal and the pathological, the insider and the outsider, and the competent citizen and the ward of the state.

Similarly, some discussions on the politics of the everyday practices of educational institutions, in their functions of sorting, organizing, educating, and evaluating students, also serve to foreground the social, political, and economic impact of disciplining a diverse student population into conforming to a mythical but rigid norm. It is in this context, then, that a disability-studies perspective is useful to the politics of education in foregrounding why and how the social construction of the disabled Other is used to organize social difference (i.e., race, class, gender, and sexuality) along the axes of normative ability in educational contexts. This entry provides a brief overview of that perspective.

Education as Control

The historical role of public education has been one of social control. Students are subject to a normative code of behaviors, attitudes, skills, and dispositions through the use of standardized, objective, and scientific evaluations that demand homogeneity from an otherwise heterogeneous student population. According to disability studies, those whose bodies challenge the norm are defined as "unruly bodies" and are subject to punishment, physical segregation, and/or exclusion.

Student populations that are designated as social outcasts of education are as heterogeneous as the identities they embody. Students of color from low-income neighborhoods are segregated on account of presumed academic and behavioral "deficiencies" that differ from White suburban aspirations and lifestyle. Pregnant teens, who may be seen as an embodiment of moral deviance, are often exiled to alternative programs outside the school, presumably because their pregnant condition is seen as socially contagious to other teenage girls. Legislation—for example, California's Proposition 187 passed in 1994 to deny public benefits and therefore public education to the children of "illegal" immigrants—and the debate about the legitimacy of bilingual education programs across the country have made linguistically diverse students cultural outcasts in some public school contexts. Lesbian, gay, bisexual, and transgendered students are often enshrouded in educational discourses of deviancy, isolation, and silence, even by those policy makers who have attempted to combat the violence the youngsters face in school on a daily basis. And last but not least, notwithstanding the Individuals with Disabilities Education Act (IDEA), many students labeled as disabled continue to be ostracized and warehoused in self-contained classrooms on account of their significant physical/cognitive/behavioral differences.

From the disability-studies perspective, public education has used the concepts of difference, deviance, and disability synonymously to justify the exclusion of certain student populations in an attempt to adhere to demands of normativity, even while claiming that their practices are democratic. Disability therefore plays a critical role in contemporary educational politics.

Educational discourses may support their adherence to normativity by constructing disability as the antithesis of educational practice and therefore a condition that must be rejected, avoided, and (if need be) excluded. However, because difference (on the basis of race, class, gender, sexual orientation, and disability) is also an integral part of public education in a democratic society, disability scholars assert that educational practices support difference if and only if difference can be controlled, disguised, or rendered invisible—in other words, if difference is "prostheticized."

Disability-studies scholars David Mitchell and Sharon Snyder define a prosthesis as a device that accomplishes an illusion that enables people to fit in and de-emphasizes their differences so that they can return to a state of imagined normativity. In most educational contexts, they argue, students identified as different because of their race, class, gender, ethnicity, or sexual orientation are validated if and only if they can deploy "prosthetic practices" that enable them to "pass" themselves off as not really that different from the norm by hiding their "dis/ability." As a result, disability becomes the discursive link that simultaneously explains and exposes the social construction of difference in education along the axes of race, class, gender, ethnicity, and sexual orientation, in this view.

How It Works

The logic of normativity is easily identified in the daily workings of the educational bureaucracy: the battery of standardized tests that students take, the detailed records of any infringement of school policy that teachers complete, the carefully spelled out and controlled curriculum, the codes of acceptable behavior even in extracurricular activities such as the school prom. These bureaucratic functions, from the disability studies perspective, are an effort to sort students out on the basis of their dis/ability to conform to the normative requirements of schooling.

Put more simply, to be labeled as disabled in an educational context implies that one is both a disruptive presence and an embodiment of deficiency, according to disability scholars. Disability, therefore, serves as the raw material that is utilized to make other differences visible by requiring all students to exhibit particular skills/behaviors/dispositions (prosthetics) that minimize their difference and distance from the norm, in this view. Failure to do so results in punishment, segregation, or expulsion and therefore relegation to the special education or alternative school bureaucracy.

Nirmala Erevelles

See also Disability Studies

Further Readings

Danforth, S., & Gabel, S. (Eds.). (2007). *Vital questions facing disability studies in education.* New York: Peter Lang.

Erevelles, N. (2000). Educating unruly bodies: Critical pedagogy, disability studies and the politics of schooling. *Educational Theory, 50*(1), 25–47.

Gabel, S. (Ed.). (2006). *Disability studies in education: Readings in theory and method.* New York: Peter Lang.

Linton, S. (1998). *Claiming disability: Knowledge and identity.* New York: New York University Press.

Mitchell, D., & Snyder, S. (2000). *Narrative prosthesis: Disability and the dependencies of discourse.* Ann Arbor: University of Michigan Press.

Watts, I., & Erevelles, N. (2004). These deadly times: Reconceptualizing school violence using critical race theory and disability studies. *American Educational Research Journal, 41*(2), 271–299.

DISABILITY STUDIES

Disability studies refers to the interdisciplinary investigation of how social, political, and economic factors interact to construct the phenomenon of disability. It has emerged within the last two decades as a new academic discipline that critically analyzes the construct of disability. Scholars who align themselves with this discipline regard disability as a basic human condition that should be studied and investigated as part of the diverse fabric of human experience. They highlight the importance of infusing a critical understanding of disability throughout the entire academic curriculum. How people with disabilities have been perceived and treated in different societies throughout history; the representation of disability in film, literature, and the arts; and the relationship between built environments and social participation are but a few examples of the interdisciplinary nature of this field. This entry looks at traditional views of disability and how this new field offers an alternative perspective.

The Traditional View

If you asked ordinary people to define disability studies, chances are most would say that it is about the study of disability: what causes "it," how "it" can be cured, and how people who have "it" (or are "afflicted with it") can be helped. Common to such answers is an unquestioned conception of disability as a cognitive, sensory, or physical deficit that inevitably leads to a diminished quality of life for afflicted individuals and their families. A logical conclusion of such a conception would be that disability studies is about curing, managing, and/or rehabilitating disabling conditions.

Applied fields such as medicine, rehabilitation, and special education have historically studied disability as a biomedical condition. Disability was narrowly perceived as a physical, sensory, or cognitive impairment that resides in certain individuals and needs to be treated or otherwise managed. Individuals whose minds or bodies differed from the norm were perceived as victims of their condition and in need of professional care. Their marginalization and social exclusion was seen as inevitably linked to their respective impairments. Disabled activists, academics, and their supporters have challenged such conceptions of disability. They have argued that disability is not simply a deficit inherent in individuals, but rather a condition aggravated by preventable, socially created barriers.

A New Model

Disability studies is closely linked to the social model of disability, which highlights oppression and discrimination as primary barriers in the lives of people with disabilities. Disability rights activists have challenged prevailing perspectives of disability as a tragedy that inevitably constricts the lives of individuals. Rather than focusing on the impairment itself, they have highlighted the issues of poverty, poor education, lack of affordable and accessible housing, and low employment rates that often characterize the lives of people with disabilities.

Such conditions cannot be directly linked to physical, cognitive, or psychological impairments. Rather, they result from unaccommodating societal structures that systematically exclude people with disabilities and prevent them from active participation in society. Ramps in public buildings and laws that prohibit explicit discrimination have been highly instrumental in increasing access and enhancing social participation for people with disabilities. Nonetheless, negative attitudes and more subtle forms of marginalization are more resistant to change.

Related Research

A paradigm shift that increasingly emphasizes the social, cultural, and economic determinants of disability has important implications for research. Disability-studies scholars and activists have pointed a collective and blaming finger toward most of the past research on disability. They have claimed that, by and large, it has reinforced the dominant idea that disability is an individual problem and has thus contributed to the problems faced by people with disabilities. They have brought to the forefront a host of critical but previously unexamined questions pertaining to research on disability, such as who determines the research questions worthy of inquiry and controls the process and product of the research; how research agendas are determined and funded; and, most importantly, what are the often hidden biases and assumptions that undergird much of this research.

This claim is well exemplified by critical perspectives on psychological research on disability. Recent critiques within psychology have highlighted the discipline's historical focus on pathology and mental illness and neglect of strengths and well-being. This is highly applicable to the study of psychosocial aspects of disability that has largely focused on negative emotional reactions of affected individuals and has all but neglected the study of how people can live well with a disability. The insider experience of disability is quite different from what is assumed by the outsider looking in.

Insiders are familiar with their disability, have learned how to cope with it, and, thus, often report a much higher level of well-being than what an outsider would assume. Traditional psychosocial research has also been criticized for the often unquestioned assumption that the impairment itself presents a major obstacle or source of distress. This rarely resonates with individuals with disabilities, who often identify social barriers and negative societal attitudes as the biggest impediments to well-being.

People with disabilities increasingly demand more than token participation in research projects. They are interested in research projects that go beyond the personal experience of disability to explore the impact of ableist policies and practices. They want to see research projects that expose, examine, and attempt to transform disempowering and ableist policies and practices in schools, hospitals, and other organizations.

Finally, critical disability theorists and activists are interested in exploring and challenging dysfunctional societal practices that perpetuate ableism, oppression, and discrimination. The multidisciplinary field of disability studies has been highly instrumental in advancing these goals, and its messages have been heard both within and outside the disability community.

Ora Prilleltensky

See also Politics of Education; Sociology of Education.

Further Readings

Dunn, D. (2000). Social psychological issues in disability. In R. G. Frank & T. R. Elliot (Eds.), *Handbook of rehabilitation psychology* (pp. 187–224). London: Sage.

Linton, S. (1998). *Claiming disability: Knowledge and identity.* New York: New York University Press.

Olkin, R., & Pledger, C. (2003). Can disability studies and psychology join hands? *American Psychologist, 58*(4), 296–304.

DISCRIMINATION AND PREJUDICE

While often used interchangeably in everyday dialogue, *prejudice* and *discrimination* actually refer to two different yet interrelated concepts. *Prejudice* refers to a value judgment either in favor of or against a person or a thing and stems from the Latin root for "prejudgment." It is an attitude. *Discrimination,* on the other hand, refers to the active exclusion of a group of people from a desired benefit or advantage. It is an action. Prejudicial attitudes, even when negative, do not always result in discrimination. Therefore, for example, two employers who are prejudiced against Irish people may manifest their prejudices differently. One person, even though he or she in private may tell jokes about Irish people, may still hire an Irish employee. Nevertheless, the person is prejudiced because of his or her attitude toward the Irish. The other employer, however, may not only tell jokes about the Irish, but also adopt a policy of not allowing the employment of any Irish people in his or her firm, thus participating in the action of discrimination. Prejudice and discrimination lead to what is commonly referred to as the "isms," including sexism, racism, and ageism. This entry provides a basis for understanding the origins, consequences, and policy implications of prejudice and discrimination.

Theoretical Perspectives

Among social scientists, there are three main theoretical frameworks used to analyze prejudice and discrimination. Symbolic interactionists argue that the way people label the world determines their perception of it. According to these theorists, prejudice and discrimination result from selective perception through which a person ignores certain facts and focuses on others. Thus, distinctions between in-groups and out-groups become exaggerated. Detrimental labels further serve to perpetuate prejudice and discrimination.

Functionalists analyze prejudice and discrimination based on costs and benefits. From this perspective, ethnic stratification, for example, is functional for society because it provides categories of workers who will do menial jobs and thus keeps wages for this category of jobs low within the division of labor. Conflict theorists analyze prejudice and discrimination from a Marxist perspective. From this perspective, prejudice and discrimination stem from the capitalist system itself, which requires conflict among groups in order to extract greater profit from production.

Causes

All societies have experienced or perpetrated both prejudice and discrimination, because in every society on earth a dichotomy exists between the "us," meaning the in-groups, and the "them," referring to the out-groups. In-groups include those within a given social and economic system who can access important resources such as education, employment, and food supplies. In-groups have power and are often referred to as part of the "dominant group." Out-groups include those within a given social and economic system who cannot or cannot easily access these same resources. Out-groups have less power and are often referred to as "minorities."

In-groups and out-groups can be based on many factors, including race, ethnicity, gender, sexual orientation, geographical origin, language, and physical or mental abilities. Therefore, in Northern Ireland, Protestants discriminate against Catholics; in the United States after September 11, 2001, non-Muslims discriminated against Muslims; in Mexico, heterosexuals discriminate against homosexuals; in Japan, native Japanese discriminate against immigrant Koreans; many companies discriminate against older workers; and throughout the world, some men discriminate against women.

Prejudice and discrimination are intricately linked to ethnocentrism. Ethnocentrism refers to the use of one's cultural, personal, and societal values to judge other cultures, people, and societies. Social scientists have found that nearly every racial and ethnic group considers itself superior to other groups in at least some ways. When taken to extremes, however, such ethnocentrism creates prejudice and discrimination, which often lead to fanaticism and tragedy.

Throughout the world, for example, ethnocentrism led to the racial prejudice and discrimination that contributed at least in part to the perpetuation of slavery and all its horrific ills. In Nazi Germany, ethnocentrism led to the racial and religious discrimination that helped Hitler rise to power. In South Africa, it led to apartheid. In short, the ills caused by extreme ethnocentrism and the resultant prejudice and discrimination include genocide, murder, starvation, and others.

Types

Social scientists distinguish various types of prejudice and discrimination: individual, institutional, *de jure,* and *de facto.* Individual prejudice and discrimination occur between individuals and are manifested through the tone of their interpersonal relationships. Usually, this type of prejudice and discrimination does not go beyond the individual level. Institutional prejudice and discrimination, on the other hand, refers to the very fabric of society, including educational institutions, lending institutions, housing opportunities, and employment opportunities. Institutional prejudice and discrimination is widespread and is not confined to individuals but rather encompasses entire groups. *De jure* discrimination refers to formalized prejudice and discrimination through law. Such legislation may include restrictions on physical movement, access to schooling, and expression of cultural mores. *De facto* prejudice and discrimination is not legislated, but rather, is supported by social custom and business practice.

There are many factors that lead ordinary people to develop prejudices and to participate in overtly discriminatory actions. Sometimes, the out-groups are portrayed as less than human and referred to in animalistic terms, thus facilitating and justifying horrors such as genocide. In the 1800s, the U.S. government referred to Native Americans as "savages," thus facilitating and justifying their decimation in the pursuit of resources for White settlers. Similar patterns of dehumanization are found in many countries, including South Africa, Tasmania, and Mexico. Other times, economic depression, anger, and the simplification of complex social issues lead to prejudice and discrimination. Studies of organizations such as the Ku Klux Klan and neo-Nazi leaders in the United States have found that the membership of such groups consists mainly of disenfranchised Whites who consider their well-being as having been negatively influenced by the presence of non-Whites. The members justify the groups' violent philosophies and acts by dividing the world into segregated in-groups and out-groups. In this worldview, survival depends of the triumph of one group over the other in the struggle for scarce resources, such as employment, housing, and education.

Responses

Not all societies recognize, acknowledge, and condemn prejudice and discrimination. Yet, in those that do, the desired patterns of intergroup relations fall into two main nonexclusive categories: assimilation and multiculturalism. Assimilation refers to the absorption of minority groups by the dominant group and can be voluntary or forced. It is multidimensional, and can include aspects of culture, outward appearance, and behavior. Assimilation is often referred to as an "ization," such as "Americanization," "Arabization," and "Italianization," based on the group into which the minority group is being absorbed. Multiculturalism refers to the encouragement of racial and ethnic diversity by the dominant group. Switzerland is the country most often considered a model of multiculturalism. After a history of divisions among bureaucratic regimes, religions, and languages, Switzerland now emphasizes linguistic equality, proportional representation in politics, and consensual decision making.

The issues of prejudice and discrimination are intricately related to issues of civil and human rights. Civil rights refer to the rights of individuals by virtue of citizenship. In the United States, such rights include freedom of speech and association. Human rights refer to the basic rights to which all human beings are entitled and which any government may not violate. Such rights include the right to life and equality before the law. Yet, prejudice and discrimination often interfere with the respect of civil and human rights for out-groups.

Education

Worldwide, education occupies a central position in the dialogue about issues of prejudice and discrimination and in its policy implications. Education is considered especially important because of its role in reinforcing cultural norms and in distributing scarce resources. Prejudice and discrimination in education take many forms, including segregation, linguistic isolation, and tracking. Likewise, the remedies to prejudice and discrimination in education can take many forms, including desegregation, bilingual education, multiculturalism, and affirmative action programs. While there are many landmark cases in different countries, an analysis of the *Brown v. Board of Education* case in the United States illustrates both the detrimental effects of segregation on educational opportunities and the role of legislation in addressing prejudice and discrimination.

The case started in 1951 when Oliver Brown, the father of the African American third-grader Linda Brown, requested that his daughter be allowed to attend a White elementary school in Topeka, Kansas, because of the proximity of the school to the child's home. After the school principal rejected his request, Brown went to the Topeka branch of the National Association for the Advancement of Colored People (NAACP) for help. The 1896 *Plessy v. Ferguson* case allowed separate but equal schools for Blacks and Whites; generally, however, Black schools did not enjoy the same resources as White ones. Yet, finally in 1954, the Supreme Court ruled in favor of the plaintiffs—now from various states—in the *Brown v. Board of Education* case, thus opening the door to the desegregation of the U.S. school system.

Yet, the importance of the case is not only in its legislative impact on school desegregation, but also in the expectations of society that it changed. Prior to *Brown v. Board of Education,* children studied in schools which replicated the norms and values of a divided society. Yet, with this landmark case, though limited initially only to the educational sphere, the groundwork was set to change the very socialization process of U.S. society. The separate but equal credo, so accepted in the country at the time, began to crumble, and the issues of prejudice and discrimination got pushed to the forefront of the U.S. political, social, and legal agenda.

More recent U.S. legislative remedies to prejudice and discrimination in education have included policies aimed at improving access to education and retention rates among minority populations. The policies, lumped under the term "affirmative action," tend to spark great controversy with claims of reverse discrimination by dominant groups, mainly White males.

Conclusion

Prejudice and discrimination exist in every society in the world. Prejudicial attitudes often, although not always, result in discriminatory acts. In its extreme forms, discrimination can result in genocide, population transfers, and other acts of violence.

Prejudice and discrimination can occur on the individual or the institutional level. On both levels the result is negative consequences, but institutional prejudice and discrimination affect many more people and negatively affect their life chances, rather than simply their interpersonal relationships. Racism, sexism, and ageism are just some of the forms of prejudice and discrimination prevalent in the modern world.

Prejudice and discrimination are not recognized, acknowledged, and condemned in all societies. Once they are acknowledged, however, policy responses vary. Prejudice in the realm of education is usually considered especially detrimental because of education's impact on life opportunities and distribution of resources.

Moira Murphy

See also Activism and the Social Foundations of Education; African American Education; Culture-Fair Testing; Dropouts; Economic Inequality; Educational Indicators

Further Readings

Allport, G. W. (1954). *The nature of prejudice.* New York: Addison-Wesley.
Ezekial, R. (1995). *The racist mind: Portraits of American neo-Nazis and Klansmen.* New York: Penguin Books.

DISCURSIVE PRACTICES

Briefly defined, discursive practices in education are the uses of language in an educational context (e.g., the typical pattern of teacher question, student answer, teacher feedback) or the use of language in context relating to education (e.g., state legislators' talk when making new educational laws). Language includes spoken, signed, and written forms of communication. Context includes the aspects of the situation in which such communication takes place that affect the meaning of the communication either in its production or its reception. Part of the context of language use is the relevant language that comes before and after the particular discursive practice in question. Thus, discursive practices generally encompass language chunks larger than one sentence.

Discursive practices in education are increasingly of interest to a number of academic disciplines. Some of the discursive practices that have been examined include Rosemary Henze's work on the metaphors used by school leaders use when discussing equity; Felecia Briscoe's studies of the discourse of professional educational associations; patterns of conversational turn taking in classroom lessons; the frequency and relative positioning of men and women in history textbooks; the distancing, exclusion, or inclusion of some groups but not others; and even who should produce discourse about the different groups.

This entry discusses why educational discursive practices are important, how they can be researched, and finally how discursive practices might become part of the school curriculum.

Why Discursive Practices Are Important

Discursive practices are of interest to educational researchers because the social world is largely constructed through language. This includes the organization of social actions, practices, and structures of education. In order for groups to act in concert, communication between the members generally must take place. Human beings communicate with each other largely through language use. However, not only is language used to coordinate action, it is also the means by which groups develop a shared understanding of the world, that is, their ideology.

A group's ideology largely determines which actions seem reasonable or unreasonable. Most discursive scholars contend that language always carries with it political or ideological implications. That is, there is no such thing as ideologically or politically neutral language. So when discursive practices are analyzed, both the actions directly proposed and the ideologies supported explicitly and implicitly by language use are investigated. Although preexiting ideologies constrain what sorts of discursive practices are possible, they do not determine which discursive practices might emerge, and it is primarily through new discursive practices that preexisting ideologies may be transformed. Given the integrality of discourse in developing, maintaining, or transforming shared ideologies, the discursive practices of schools are particularly important—especially the importance of understanding not only the ways that they induce particular ideologies, but determining what sort of ideologies are promoted by the discursive practices of schools.

Research Approaches

Educational discursive practices can be investigated through either discourse analysis or critical discourse analysis (CDA). CDA is of especial interest in that it specifically incorporates an examination of both ideology and power. CDA is both cross-disciplinary and interdisciplinary: incorporating research methods of linguistics, cognitive psychology, ethnography, anthropology, communication, media studies, literature analysis, and/or media studies as well as others. However, no matter which disciplinary method or combination of methods is used in CDA, establishing the relevant context is problematic.

The problem is that it is impossible to describe the entire context; it would in fact be like describing reality. Thus, the researcher must pick out the relevant aspects of the context. However, different aspects of the context will affect both the meaning and the effect of the discourse according to the producer or consumer's identity (e.g., gender, ethnicity, economic status, nationality, and so on) that is the particular individual's history. Thus, the researcher must rely upon generalizations produced by quantitative studies (generalizations that will not fit a portion of discourse participants), rely upon explanations by the producers and consumers of the discourse, rely upon the ensuing

social actions (including discourse), or rely upon all three to determine which aspects of the context are relevant. For critical discourse analysts, power relations inherent in the context are always relevant. Rebecca Rogers in *An Introduction to Critical Discourse Analysis in Education* discusses the problem of determining which aspects of context are relevant. Ruth Wodak and Michael Meyer in *Methods of Critical Discourse Analysis* provide systematic research procedures for CDA. Other well-known authors who provide alternative methods of CDA include Norman Fairclough, Tuen van Dijk, and James Gee.

Curriculum Issues

Aside from researching the discursive practices of education, many have proposed that CDA ought to be an integral part of the school language curriculum. Authors such as Tuen van Dijk maintain that public schools should focus on teaching students the analytic skills necessary to understand the implicit as well as explicit content of texts. His proposed objectives for secondary students also provide a rudimentary model for the aspects of language use that ought to be considered when analyzing discourse. By the final grades of secondary school, he proposes, students should have been educated such that they are aware of and capable of analyzing the following aspects of discourse:

1. The relationship between a particular discourse and its historical and contemporary social context

2. Discourse incorporating speech acts, social acts, and will—all of which occur strategically in interactions

3. Different discourse types that are linked to and regulated by particular social contexts, situations, or circumstances and in which participants have different statuses and partake of different roles and functions

4. The intentions, wishes, preferences, interests, and goals of the speakers that appear in their discourse

5. The several levels of discourse: morphophonology, sentence structure, and semantics

6. The dimensions of style of these levels, which are determined by personal and social context, perspective, and so on

7. Different rhetorical flourishes that will enhance or detract from the goals of the discourse

8. Nonverbal communication, which also forms part of the frame of a given discourse

Discursive practices are important in educational settings such as schools, and are of fundamental importance to our understanding of how schools work as social, political, and cultural systems within larger social, cultural, and political systems.

Felecia Briscoe

See also Curriculum Theory; Educational Research, History of

Further Readings

Borman, K., & O'Reilly, P. (1989). The eighties image of girls and women in the educational reform literature. In C. Shea, P. Sola, & E. Kahane (Eds.), *The new servants of power: A critique of the 1980s school reform movement* (pp. 175–183). New York: Greenwood Press.

Briscoe, F. (2005). A question of representation in educational discourse: Multiplicities and intersections of identities and positionalities. *Educational Studies, 38*(1) 23–41.

Briscoe, F. (2006). Reproduction of racialized hierarchies: Ethnic identities in the discourse of educational leadership. *Journal for Critical Education Policy Studies, 4*(1). Retrieved from http://jceps.com/index.php?pageID=article&articleID=60

Duzak, A. (Ed.). (2002). *Us and others: Social identities across languages, discourses and cultures.* Philadelphia: John Benjamin.

Fairclough, N. (2003). *Analyzing discourse: Textual analysis for social research.* New York: Routledge.

Gee, J. (2005). *An introduction to discourse analysis.* New York: Routledge.

Henze, R. (2005). Metaphors of diversity, intergroup relations, and equity in the discourse of educational leaders, *Journal of language, identity, and education, 4*(4), 243–267.

McCollum, P. (1989). Turn-allocation in lessons with North American and Puerto Rican students: A comparative study. *Anthropology & Education Quarterly, 20*(2) 133–156.

Rogers, R. (2004). *An introduction to critical discourse analysis in education.* Mahwah, NJ: Lawrence Erlbaum.

Santa Ana, O. (2002). *Brown tide rising: Metaphors of Latinos in contemporary American public discourse.* Austin: University of Texas Press.

van Dijk, T. (1981). Discourse studies and education. *Applied Linguistics, 2,* 1–26.

van Dijk, T. (1997). Discourse as interaction in society. In T. van Dijk (Ed.), *Discourse studies: A multidisciplinary introduction* (Vol. 2). London: Sage.

Wodak, R., & Meyer, M. (2002). *Methods of critical discourse analysis.* London: Sage.

DISTANCE LEARNING

Terms like *distance learning* and *distance education* are largely associated with recent developments in computing—specifically the growth of the Internet and World Wide Web, but the reality of distance learning is much older. Isaac Pittman taught shorthand by mail as early as the 1840s. In 1858, the University of London had created an external degree program using the mail as a means by which students and teachers could exchange materials. Modern distance learning and education has its origins in the beginning of the twentieth century and the pioneer efforts of the French educator Célestin Freinet and Italian educators Mario Lodi and Bruno Ciardi.

Freinet started his teaching career in 1921 in a small village in the coastal Alps near the Mediterranean. In October 1924 he introduced the "learning printing technique" into his class. It was a process where the pupils used a printing press to reproduce texts and projects they had created freely based on personal experience inside and outside the classroom. Later these texts would be compiled as a class journal and a school newspaper.

School printing to reproduce pupils' texts was already used by several teachers in the nineteenth century. In 1926, Freinet began regular exchanges of his class productions, especially the school newspapers, with other elementary school classes in France. He called it the technique of "school correspondence," whose purpose was for students to practice critical literacy skills by comparing worlds and realities. This technique later spread throughout other European countries, as well as in Africa, Asia, and Latin America.

In the 1950s and 1960s, Mario Lodi's and Bruno Ciardi's elementary school classes collaborated on various student journalism projects although the classes were hundreds of miles apart. The teachers taught their students how to use the printing machinery, but the students did more than that. They wrote, edited, and published *Il Mondo* ("The World") and *Insieme* ("Together") as nearly everyday newspapers and had a readership of fellow students, parents, and even subscribers in ten countries for years. The goal of Lodi and Ciardi was to adapt Freinet's pedagogy to the Italian schools.

Film, radio, and TV made possible new approaches to distance learning during the 1960s and 1970s. The Internet, however, transformed the field. In 1991, when the first Internet search and navigation tools were released, the Internet began to be widely used in distance education.

Today, Internet-supported or -supplemented teaching is widespread. Distance education is now practical on a wide-scale basis. Distance education programs are increasingly found in K–12 settings, higher education, business and industry, and the military and government. Individuals who are geographically isolated can have regular instruction provided to them, as can individuals who are homebound because of illness or family needs. Instruction can occur in real time, or at the convenience of teachers and learners, who communicate through the exchange of e-mails or other electronic media.

Freinet's dream of technology extending the reach of the classroom throughout the globe is a reality. As new and more efficient technologies come into wider practical use, such as streaming video and real-time netcasting and texting, educational institutions will increasingly function in cyberspace. In doing so, the nature of instruction at all levels from K–12 to university and college, will inevitably be profoundly changed and redefined.

Li Ma

See also Internet, Social Impact of; Technologies in Education

Further Readings

Cummins, J., & Sayers, D. (1995). *Brave new schools: Challenging cultural illiteracy through global learning networks.* New York: St. Martin's.

Moore, M. G., & Anderson, W. G. (Eds.). (2003). *Handbook of distance education.* Mahwah, NJ: Lawrence Erlbaum.

Dress Codes

Guidelines directing student dress requirements are common in public and private schools. Dress codes include hair length and color, clothing, school uniforms, body art and piercing, insignias, and jewelry. Dress guidelines or codes have their historical beginning in the English private schools, but have recently permeated schools in the United States. This entry looks at regulation of student apparel and grooming, including the imposition of school uniforms, and discusses related legal cases.

Regulating Dress

The history of dress codes in the United States receives little attention in the literature. However, there is evidence that student dress was predicated upon cultural and economic predispositions until the social upheaval of the 1960s. The burgeoning baby boom generation, with a growing disposable income, became a focal point of clothing marketers. As a result, fashion became a means of student expression and identity.

Developing dress codes to meet the fast-changing fashion industry has become problematic for policy makers. In *Tinker v. Des Moines,* the U.S. Supreme Court affirmed students' right to freedom of speech by striking down a school district policy prohibiting students from wearing black arm bands in protest of the Vietnam War. Consequently, school district dress guidelines began to consider students' right to expression. Then, with the growth in conservatism in the 1980s, combined with the rising public concern about student discipline and safety in the schools, the courts became more receptive to increasingly dogmatic school dress policies, such as school uniform policies. Although the idea of implementing school uniform policies in the public schools began in the late 1980s, President Clinton added credence to the practice in

1996 when he endorsed school uniform policies as a means of reducing school violence and disciplinary problems.

How Dress Codes Work

Specific dress codes for students are universal. Commonly, the codes attempt to prevent the promotion of drug and alcohol use, gang-related insignias, sexually provocative clothing, and hate-related clothing. Empirical evidence regarding the effectiveness of dress codes is inconclusive. Proponents of dress codes argue that dress codes improve the learning environment, enhance student safety, place less stress on the family, particularly low-income families, and eliminate student preoccupation with fashion. Opponents of dress codes counter that dress codes are discriminatory, focusing on females and minorities. In addition, opponents argue that dress codes violate students' fundamental right to free speech and are oversimplified solutions to much larger systemic problems.

Acceptable student dress codes are flexible and avoid restricting constitutionally protected freedoms, like religious expression. Dress codes devised as an attempt to affect disciplinary problems or gang violence should be developed as part of an overall school safety program. If the dress code has economic implications, some assistance may need to be provided to economically disadvantaged students. Finally, the dress code should pass the review of legal counsel, and the policy makers should ensure that the employees possess the necessary resources to fairly and effectively enforce the policy.

School Uniforms

In the late 1980s, public schools began to mimic many private schools by requiring school uniforms. Interestingly, during this same time period, many private schools chose to abandon the practice of school uniforms in favor of less rigid dress guidelines. Often controversial, school uniform policies have become popular with state-level policy makers. Currently, many states allow, and encourage, local public school policy makers to implement school uniform policies.

Much like the research regarding dress codes in general, the research on the effectiveness of school uniforms is inconclusive. Whereas dress code policies are often viewed as restrictive, detailing what may not be worn, school uniform policies are often viewed as directive, detailing what must be worn. This minor distinction in difference can play a significant role in how the courts view the legality of uniform policies.

The Courts

The seminal court case on student dress guidelines is the 1969 case *Tinker v. Des Moines*. In this case, several students were suspended from school because they chose to wear black arm bands in protest of the Vietnam War. The students successfully argued before the U.S. Supreme Court that their First Amendment right to freedom of expression had been violated. The Court held that students do have the constitutional protection of freedom to express themselves as long as the expression does not disrupt the educational process.

More recently, the courts have been inclined to uphold reasonable student dress codes as long as the policies allow students to legitimately express themselves on political issues. However, the courts have held that the right to wear fashionable clothing is not, in itself, a fundamental right protected by the Constitution. In addition, the courts give wide latitude to policy makers to develop dress codes that regulate obscene or lewd speech and gang-related clothing.

The courts have been inclined to support school uniform policies, allowing local-level policy makers to determine what is best for their schools. However, because school uniform policies tend to be viewed as directive, an "opt out" policy is a common means of avoiding potential litigation.

A persistent dress code issue is the matter of hair length and color. Viewing this issue as an educational one, the Supreme Court has not ruled on hair length or color restrictions. Thus the controversy remains unsettled, with the outcome of cases being dependent upon the persuasion of the courts and varying from region to region.

Mark Littleton

See also Clothing, Banning of Symbolic; Gangs, in Schools; Hate Crimes in Schools; Rights of Students

Further Readings

Anderson, W. (2002, Fall). *Policy report: School dress codes and uniform policies.* Eugene, OR: ERIC Clearinghouse on Educational Management. (ERIC Document Reproduction Service No. ED 471528)

Brunsma, D. L. (2004). *The school uniform movement and what it tells us about American education.* Lanham, MD: Rowman & Littlefield.

Holloman, L. O., LaPoint, V. Alleyne, S. I., Palmer, R. J., & Sanders-Phillips, K. (1996). Dress-related behavioral problems and violence in the public school setting: Prevention, intervention, and policy—a holistic approach. *Journal of Negro Education, 65,* 267–282.

Rubenstein, R. P. (2001). *Dress codes: Meanings and messages in American culture* (2nd ed.). Boulder, CO: Westview Press.

Wilson, A. M. (1998). Public school dress codes: The constitutional debate. *Brigham Young University Education & Law Journal, 1,* 147–172.

DROPOUTS

Adolescents have left schools for as long as there have been schools, but the term *dropout* emerged in popular culture on the cusp of the tumultuous 1960s in the United States. With the use of the term came multiple political, social, cultural, and economic interpretations, each situating the label and domain of *dropout* in particular ways. Evidence from the last century about school leavers indicates that the issue of leaving school is multilayered and systemic. This entry is a historical sketch of school leaving, or dropping out, and the contexts in which schools produced students who left school.

Early History

The first public high school opened in Boston in 1820, and other high schools were opened in cities soon thereafter and competed with private academies. However, high school was a luxury, and most older children went to school only when they were not farming or working.

Early High Schools

Wealthy and middle-class White families supported the early high schools, and their affluence allowed them to extend the formal education of their children. Few adolescents living in poverty attended them. The high schools were not popular with working-class children and adolescents, who found the subject divisions in the curriculum unconnected to the lives they led and the labor they provided. Although these schools prepared students for teaching, they rarely made them ready for college or specialized professions.

Over time, each state adopted compulsory schooling laws. Massachusetts passed the first compulsory schooling law in 1852, requiring children eight years old to fourteen years old to attend school twelve weeks a year. By 1918 every state had passed compulsory schooling laws, though the age varied from state to state. Compulsory schooling began at age five in some states, and six, seven, or eight in others. Compulsory schooling ended at age sixteen or seventeen in some states and age eighteen in others. Of course truancy, or unexcused absences from school, did not exist until states passed these compulsory schooling laws. New York passed the first truancy law in 1853, prohibiting any child between the ages of five and fourteen from wandering the streets. The number of days that defined truancy varied by school, district, and state.

Although compulsory schooling laws were in place, there were high percentages of school leaving, as young men in particular, many contributing to family income, chose work over school. Throughout the late 1800s, when these young men left school, they found work opportunities without a high school education. During this time, less than 40 percent of children received regular instruction in school, and only one student in ten finished the fifth grade.

In the early decades of the 1900s, tens of thousands of working-class immigrant youth chose the same pattern. They left school to work. Many left school before completing the eighth grade. In 1902 researchers found that students reported leaving school because they did not like school, they had family and financial responsibilities, or they suffered from ill health. Social reformers concerned about the high rates of school leaving supported the implementation of a practical, differentiated curriculum, and they hoped such a curriculum would engage and retain students.

William Heard Kilpatrick (1871–1965), a philosopher of education at Columbia University's Teachers

College in New York, thought that the subject divisions of the current curriculum hurt most students, and he developed a curriculum for primary and secondary schools that promoted specializations as early as the sixth grade. In essays collected in *Remaking the Curriculum* in 1936, he described a schedule that encouraged individual interests that transcended subject divisions. As children moved from grade to grade, teachers would document their interests and consult with their future teacher. Specializations would slowly encompass more time in the school day as the student moved through the grades and link the student's interest to life experience rather than formal subject schoolwork. Kilpatrick believed that the majority of students had no need to specialize along subject lines throughout secondary school, and that those students whom teachers forced to do so dropped out.

Postwar Years

Following World War II, retention programs emerged in earnest as administrators continued to witness the production of dropouts. Successful programs echoed Kilpatrick's sentiments and suggestions from school leavers. In a New York study on retention conducted from 1946 to 1954, researchers found that school leaving could be reduced by connecting a practical curriculum to experience in the world with activities, such as field trips; increasing job counseling; providing opportunity for work experience; assisting with job placement; increasing electives; and communicating with parents through home visits.

During this time, thousands of school leavers in a Midwestern study expressed concern about schools' ability to retain students. These early school leavers proposed that students needed work experience or specialized vocational instruction, an increase in school activities, opportunity to change courses, more caring and productive relationships with counselors and teachers, and smaller classes to provide opportunities for individual attention.

In the late 1940s, a young White man could leave school and find work (much as in the late 1800s), but a decade later, unemployment rates had increased. Youth who left school before graduating had trouble finding a job. In an economy that had just begun to cut unskilled and semiskilled jobs, school leavers, without training or work experience, sometimes could find only part-time work and experienced more job insecurity than students who had completed high school and received a diploma.

By 1950, only 60 percent of youth had completed high school, and to increase the accuracy of national and state studies on school leaving, federal and state departments urged local school districts to keep records of students leaving school. As the decade began, White high school dropouts received stable employment in occupations to which Black high school graduates were denied access. White high school dropouts in 1950 comprised 65 to 70 percent of skilled and semiskilled work in industry and 40 percent in sales. By 1960, although over 40 percent of Black youth ages twenty to twenty-four had successfully completed high school, White business refused to offer them jobs. Less-educated White workers dominated industry and sales.

Unemployment among youth began to rise as the demand for unskilled and semiskilled work, especially in large urban centers, decreased. Youth faced increased job insecurity and unemployment. In the schools, one student of every three left before completing the eighth grade. Across the fifteen largest cities in the United States, researchers found that over 60 percent of the students living in neighborhoods of poverty left school, a quarter of whom could not find a job. These conditions affected mostly Black children, as urban populations had become predominantly Black in the 1950s.

School Leavers Become Dropouts

Historically, educators and social reformers used "school leavers" or "early school leavers" as labels to describe those children, and later adolescents, who left school before completing the grade that dominant, White, middle-class culture expected them to complete. In 1900 this meant completing the eighth grade. Sixty years later this meant finishing high school. In the 1960s, those students who left high school before graduating found themselves called dropouts and centered at a national crisis in education.

Framing school leaving or dropping out as a process and not an event was paramount as educators worked to understand the factors related to leaving school. And the factors were multifold. Dropping out or school leaving is generally viewed as the result of larger systemic issues of inequity in public schools. In this perspective, the public high school, although free, is a place where teachers and administrators sort, separate, and stratify children across the curriculum. The curriculum and the process of socialization alienated children who lived in poverty and children who were minorities, particularly in urban environments, where the intersection of class and race was fused for children living in impoverished and disenfranchised neighborhoods and wards. After 180 years, low socioeconomic status remained the strongest factor related to school leaving. In the United States, this meant that children of color, who were more likely to live in poverty, were therefore disproportionately more likely to leave school.

A Crisis Emerges

Educators, school reformers, philosophers of education, psychologists, and sociologists addressed the issue of school leaving through the first half of the twentieth century, but not until the early 1960s was school leaving and the dropout labeled a national crisis. In 1963, President John F. Kennedy declared school leaving a national problem, and government agencies, public and private institutions, and nonprofit organizations hastened to complete research on the national crisis of the dropout while a new economy, with requirements for specialized skills, grew.

Schools and districts embraced reform models to increase retention, many with success. A project in junior high and senior high school in Kentucky targeted at increasing students' self-concepts, providing personal and social services for students, and implementing a new curriculum generated successful results in significantly reducing dropout rates and issues of discipline. The school made structural changes giving teachers the autonomy to develop a new curriculum where needed, and provided students with free or reduced breakfast and lunch, school supplies, instructional fees, clothing, medical assistance, and counseling services. Students' self-concepts increased, and in-service training for teachers increased flexible, engaging, and encouraging pedagogical practices in the junior high school and encouraging pedagogical practices in the senior high school.

For school leavers, however, the situation worsened. By 1965, the unemployment rate for school leavers was double that of high school graduates and the highest unemployment rate for any age group. The availability of jobs involving unskilled and semiskilled labor continued to fall into the early 1970s. Although experts had documented the changing economy, and poverty remained the strongest factor related to school leaving, research in the 1960s burgeoned with formulas identifying the individual characteristics of school leavers. The U.S. Department of Education reported low grades and an inability to get along with teachers and other students as reasons students left school.

Some researchers attributed the phenomenon of dropping out to a character disorder in the dropout. Ignoring the context in which students went to school, the structure of school as an institution, and school leaving as a violation of White, middle-class expectations, these researchers cited low aspirations and goals, cynicism, family problems, and a history of school leaving in Black communities as reasons for dropout rates. They emphasized individual and community deficiencies rather than institutional and pedagogical deficiencies. Ironically, among their recommendations for change and retention were the establishment of genuine, caring relationships between teachers and students and developing relevant curricula connected to work and life experience.

Decades later, research emerging in the 1980s identified anxiety about the changing economy, race riots in Northern cities, and illegal activity among youth, as well as the conservative politics of school administrators and institutionalized classism and racism, as elements contributing to upper- and middle-class expectations that urban high schools quell urban chaos. The term *dropout* emerged as the label and domain that captured these anxieties.

School leavers faced higher rates of unemployment and health problems than those who stayed in school and were more likely to work illegally or participate in illegal activities, but whereas concern for school leavers by social reformers in the early 1900s stressed connections across curricula to employment, fear directed the worry over dropouts in the 1960s. A privileged upper- and middle-class White public heaped their anxieties about crime and race, as well as demands for institutional change from communities of color, onto the dropout and the schools he and she left.

Research that captured the articulation of students for school leaving documented responses that had been shared by school leavers for seventy-five years. Former students explained that they left school because they chose to go to work rather than to go to school, had family and financial responsibilities, and did not like school. In addition, researchers found that nonpromotion of students increased dropout rates.

School completion rates have increased since the 1970s for both White students and Black students; however, poverty remains the strongest factor related to school leaving. Research in the early 1980s revealed, counter to claims of the 1960s, that students who left urban schools were psychologically healthy and thoughtfully critical of the social and economic conditions in which they lived and their schools functioned. Demonstrably different from their counterparts who stayed in school, these students developed a sound sense of self and were less prone to depression than their peers who stayed in school.

Throughout the 1980s, conservatives continued to pathologize children instead of the system and refused to address the failings of public school systems and the responsibility of schools. The credibility of this position was challenged amid research findings that situated school leavers in systemic dysfunction and historical and material conditions. Researchers found that disempowered teachers stigmatized and discouraged students, and that schools where students cited uncaring teachers and administrators, inconsistent and unfair discipline procedures, and truancy produced more dropouts. Schools with tracking, strict nonpromotion policies, and competency examinations also produced more dropouts. Urban high schools in particular faced severe overcrowding and abysmal student-teacher ratios. Research during this period also documented the high numbers of LBGT (lesbian/bisexual/gay/transgendered) students who left school from fear of harassment and violence.

The Current Situation

By the late 1990s, the dropout rates for Black students were twice those of White students, and for Hispanic students three times that of White students. Consistent with research findings for a century, the majority of school leavers survived on less, with their incomes in the lowest 20 percent of family incomes. These students were four times more likely to leave school than their peers whose families' incomes were in the top 20 percent of family incomes.

In 2005, the national dropout rate was still about 25 percent, more than 410,000 students, but in urban high schools, the rate reached 60 to 70 percent. The same year the Urban Research Institute Education Policy Center announced that over 1.3 million ninth graders would not receive a high school diploma. Nationally, dropout rates doubled for students who had repeated a grade, signaling that the rule of nonpromotion was not working. Research continued to show that students chose work over school (illegal work for many), had family and financial responsibilities, and no longer liked school or the uncaring teachers there. Young Latinas, with the highest rate of school leaving, cited family responsibilities, motherhood, and marriage as reasons not to stay in school. School leavers continued to earn less than those students who finished high school, and a higher percentage of young women among school leavers faced motherhood than their counterparts who stayed in school. School leavers still faced higher incidents of illegal activity in addition to drug use.

Systemic issues remained: overcrowding; dilapidated school facilities; reduced resources; reduced staff, including counselors and social workers; a rigidly standardized curriculum; and school violence. And much like the preceding decades, more Native American students left school than Hispanic students, more Hispanic students left school than White students, and more White students left school than Asian students, and the strongest factor related to school leaving was low socioeconomic status. In the 2000s, researchers recommended specialized diversity training for teachers, critical multicultural education in teacher education programs, apprenticeship programs for high school students, and alternative visions for the curriculum in high schools (like Kilpatrick in 1936).

Allison Daniel Anders

See also Economic Inequality; Educational Equity: Race/Ethnicity

See Visual History Chapter 23, Compulsory Education and Truancy

Further Readings

Dorn, S. (1996). *Creating the dropout: An institutional and social history of school failure.* Westport, CT: Praeger.

Fine, M. (1991). *Framing dropouts: Notes on the politics of an urban public high school.* Albany: State University of New York Press.

Kelly, D., & Gaskell, J. (Eds.). (1996). *Debating dropouts: Critical policy and research perspectives on school learning.* New York: Teachers College Press.

Weis, L., Farrar, E., & Petrie, H. G. (Eds.). (1989). *Dropouts from school: Issues, dilemmas, and solutions.* Albany: State University of New York Press.

DRUG EDUCATION

There are many forms of drug education in American schools. Today the most commonly used drug education program is Drug Abuse Resistance Education (DARE), which operates in about 80 percent of American school districts. Hundreds of other programs designed to decrease illicit drug use also exist, some of them proven effective by vigorous, long-term research. There is no federal requirement that forces states to use DARE; however, governors are mandated to use funds toward the Law Enforcement Education Partnership (LEEP), effectively funding DARE and other drug education programs. Recent federal activity suggests that there is a push to make drug use reduction education a federal responsibility. This entry looks at drug education programs and research on their effectiveness.

Federal Support

The Safe and Drug-Free Schools and Communities Act (SDFSCA) of 1994 provided federal funding for formula grants to state agencies to be used on programs intended to decrease drug use and violence. This funding was intended to serve several functions, including programs, professional training and development, targeted resources for high drug areas, and safe passage of students from school to home. The SDFSCA was recently reauthorized through the No Child Left Behind Act, part A of Title IV. Currently, 20 percent of state SDFSCA funding goes to the governor to distribute through competitive grants, and 93 percent of all funds granted to state educational agencies must go directly to local educational agencies to use in drug prevention programs. Federal grants may also be obtained by local school administrators, nonprofit organizations, or partnerships designed to decrease drug abuse or violence that comply with the Principles of Effectiveness outlined by the federal government. The Principles of Effectiveness include needs assessment, measurable objectives/performance measures, effective scientifically based programs, program evaluation, and parent involvement.

DARE programs are generally focused on elementary school students, even though research suggests that there is no significant difference in future drug use between those who had DARE in elementary schools and those who did not. DARE is a nonprofit organization that receives funding and assistance from the Departments of Justice and Education, federal and local grants, state budgets, donations from organizations, "sin" taxes, drug recovery and forfeitures, and local law enforcement. It is a network of law-enforcement officials, school leaders, and grassroots organizations that focuses on providing information about drugs and mentoring students. DARE can be found in foreign countries as well.

Outcomes Research

Hundreds of drug education programs have recently been evaluated by the Departments of Education and Health and Human Services (HHS). Only a handful have been found effective, including ones that focus on life skills, increasing protective factors, resisting prodrug pressures, focusing on family factors, and providing community-based programs that utilize mass media, parent education, and health policy programming. According to DARE, it is currently going through a revision in order to utilize the most effective means of educating and preventing illicit drug use among youth.

While drug education has been undergoing reviews and changes, President George W. Bush has poured money into random drug testing of America's school children. This is a million-dollar industry, and its practices bring up questions about students' right to privacy and confidentiality. Scare tactics, like random drug testing, are often used to deter students from using drugs. Proponents of drug testing in schools argue that random drug testing will allow drug-abusing students to receive treatment that they would otherwise not receive. Opponents claim that it is a violation of First Amendment rights.

In addition to drug education partnerships like DARE, some schools provide drug education in health or science classes. Other schools do not provide any form of drug education. The controversy behind drug education's effectiveness is currently a major factor behind the evaluation of its success in decreasing drug use among American students. Whether or not the programs are found successful, many of them will continue to reap the benefits of the billion-dollar industry of drug education.

Mark Mussman

See also Family, School, and Community Partnerships; Federal and State Educational Jurisdiction; Gangs in Schools; Moral Education; No Child Left Behind Act; Surveillance in Schools

Further Readings

Rowe, T. (2006). *Federal narcotics laws and the war on drugs: Money down a rat hole.* Binghamton, NY: Haworth Press.

U.S. General Accounting Office. (1997, March 14). *Drug control: Observations on elements of the federal drug control strategy.* Report to congressional requesters (GAO/GGD-97-42). Washington, DC: Author.

DRUG-EXPOSED CHILDREN

Public concern about the education of drug-exposed children dates back to the mid-1980s. During that time, prenatal drug abuse among poor urban women became epidemic, which resulted in unusually high numbers of drug-impacted children enrolling in school. Many of these children demonstrated developmental impairments. Interest concerning the educational prognosis for these youngsters resulted in a public discussion about the future of children whose mothers abused drugs while pregnant and had inadequate prenatal care and poor maternal health. This entry reviews the needs of these children and describes appropriate interventions.

During the 1980s, drug-exposed children became an urban educational issue. Educators had many preconceived beliefs about what to expect from these youngsters in the classroom. School officials were bracing themselves for the worst, assuming that these children would have extremely low intellectual functioning or mental retardation and be uncontrollable, and that schools would not know how to handle these children. Most troubling was the idea that this population would consume most of the special education funding, placing further strain on school resources for children with developmental challenges.

More sophisticatedly designed research on children prenatally exposed to drugs and their developmental outcomes have given educators hope for working with this population. Studies have shown that although these children have early childhood delays, which for the majority will lead to later educational difficulties, their impairments are not as severe as was once believed. With appropriate intervention, most can reach appropriate developmental milestones. In fact, many drug-exposed children have tested within the normal cognitive range on commonly used intelligence test measures.

So, how are public schools responding to the needs of these children? In *Educating Drug-Exposed Children,* Janet Thomas points out that public school systems have not seriously addressed this issue. The book gives attention to the dilemmas teachers face in working with this population and the three key issues involved in educating these children. The first issue is behavioral and learning problems. Teachers have found that there are specific patterns that present challenges to working with these children in a regular classroom setting. Although many of these children show potential, their behavioral and learning problems cause many to be referred for special education placement, which is not always appropriate to address their needs.

The second issue is the psychosocial risk factors that present obstacles to positive educational outcomes of school-age children. These things include but are not limited to inconsistent caregiving, lack of educational continuity, frequent absences, and exposure to drug-abusing environments. Teachers have found that these factors are prevalent in the drug-impacted population and that they have as negative an effect on school performance as do behavioral and learning problems.

The third issue is the need for guidance on how schools can effectively intervene. Teachers have expressed a need to develop a professional knowledge base for dealing with this population. Public schools have no assessment tool for detecting the symptoms of prenatal drug-exposure, a problem that is often missed when using traditional measures. Teachers have no professional guidance on how to effectively intervene on behalf of this population in a special education or regular education environment. For this reason, these children are among the most educationally at-risk populations.

Recommendations

The educational difficulties of drug-impacted school-age children are best addressed in the context of school and community. Educational policies and programs focusing on these children's specific needs are necessary to effectively intervene with this population. Such interventions must take a comprehensive approach, start before these children enroll in school, address psychosocial risk factors, and provide guidance for schools working on behalf of these children.

Drug-exposed children with developmental issues should be identified for early childhood interventions before they enter school. Intervening as early as possible will help prevent their issues from developing into more serious problems. Tracking systems are especially needed in school communities where there are large numbers of children whose mothers abused drugs while pregnant.

School-based social support systems are needed in public schools to assist these children as they move through the educational system. Such services should be community oriented, extending support to the caregivers of drug-impacted, school-age children. This can be a powerful collaboration for advocating for the educational need of drug-exposed children with developmental challenges.

Building the knowledge base about drug-exposed children is the most important aspect of addressing these children's school failure. Education professionals must become more proactive in contributing to the understanding of how drug exposure impacts children and what are effective education practices. Other populations with birth-related developmental challenges have been clearly defined and appropriately studied, and the drug-impacted population deserves equal attention.

Janet Y. Thomas

See also Disabilities and the Politics of Schooling; Family, School, and Community Partnerships

Further Readings

Thomas, J. Y. (2004). *Educating drug-exposed children: The aftermath of the crack baby crisis.* New York: RoutledgeFalmer.

E

EARLY CHILDHOOD EDUCATION

Early childhood education is a field within education encompassing the knowledge base related to children from birth through age eight (third grade). Early childhood is a unique time in the development of a child, during which much learning takes place. Approaches to teaching young children cover a wide spectrum ranging from direct instruction to emergent curricula. This entry provides a brief historical background of early childhood education, discusses its roots in child psychology, summarizes outside impacts on the field, and describes its main curricular models.

Historical Background

The development of young children is addressed in historical evidence from the ancient civilizations of Greece and Rome (by the work of Plato and Aristotle and Quintillian) to the Middle Ages in Europe (by the work of Martin Luther, John Amos Comenius, John Locke, Jean-Jacques Rousseau, Johann Pestalozzi, and Friedrich Froebel).

In Colonial America it was typically the role of the parents to educate the youngest children in the family, although there is evidence of some New England families using the services of private dame schools to help their children learn basic reading skills. By the early 1800s, infant schools were established in large cities across the country (New York, Philadelphia, and Boston) as a primary means of addressing the needs of disadvantaged youth. Modeled after the schools run by Pestalozzi in Europe, these schools typically used a play-based method of teaching. Even at this time there was controversy as to the roles of rote memorization and discipline in the education of young children.

Education and Psychological Development

The phrase *developmentally appropriate practice* is commonly linked to early childhood education. Educators working with young children understand that there is a predictable sequence of growth and development and apply this knowledge of how young children grow as they develop and learn to prepare learning environments that meet the "age appropriate" educational needs of the children in their setting. As all children grow at varying rates, educators must consider the "individual appropriateness" of learning experiences. The work of Jean Piaget serves as the foundation for what today is considered developmentally appropriate practice. Piaget's work established that children's cognitive development evolves in a series of stages (sensorimotor, preoperational, concrete operational, and formal operations), with each stage bringing a unique opportunity for young children to construct their own knowledge by interacting with the environment and with those around them. By using these developmental profiles, early childhood educators can encourage unique child-centered learning experiences that highlight the development of the whole child (physical, social, emotional, and cognitive).

The work of Lev Vygotsky also contributed greatly to the study of young children. He believed that the sociocultural aspects of learning had to be considered and he highlighted the role of language in reaching higher cognitive processes. His theory supports assistance by others in helping the young child to a more complex level of development if the child is near his or her own limit of ability or zone of proximal development (ZPD). The learning theory known as constructivism has its roots in the "active learning" models of both Piaget and Vygotsky.

Various Impacts on the Field

There is a great focus internationally on the development of young children, and many professional organizations address young children's needs. The National Association for the Education of Young Children (NAEYC) has brought professional leadership to the development of accreditation criteria, establishing position statements that define and support developmentally appropriate practice. Over almost eighty years, NAEYC has been a leader in promoting excellence in early childhood education, working with other organizations to enhance professional development for those working with young children. The Zero to Three organization provides up-to-date, research-based resources, with a focus on brain research, for early childhood educators. Citing work from child development professionals at the Erikson Institute, they provide "parent friendly" resources that summarize important aspects of the 2000 National Research Council and Institute of Medicine report titled *From Neurons to Neighborhoods: The Science of Early Childhood Development.*

Government has also had an impact. In the United States more and more families have both parents in the workforce, making the demand for high quality early childhood care and education even greater. In 1965, as part of President Lyndon Johnson's "War on Poverty" program, the federal government supported the establishment of the Head Start project in an attempt to counteract the effects of childhood poverty by providing high quality early childhood experiences, health education, nutritional information, social services, and parent education experiences.

Head Start and Early Head Start have served as models for other early childhood programs, and federal support has continued due to the overwhelmingly positive support from communities that have benefited from this focus. It is important to note the fact that federal dollars are used to support this initiative, and therefore there is an element of accountability that must be addressed. Many longitudinal studies have been conducted to confirm the success of these programs, resulting in a greater national focus on collecting data. Thus, even those programs geared for young children are required to assess children in order to continuously provide the evidence necessary to maintain funding.

Research and Curricular Models

The curriculum in early childhood education is determined by the philosophy of learning that is being emphasized. Therefore, many early childhood programs rely on a child-centered approach to developing the curriculum; however, it is the philosophy that establishes how this looks in practice. In addition, there are several important curricular models that have impacted early childhood education throughout history.

Maria Montessori (1870–1952), the Italian physician who worked to educate children of the working class, discovered through her observations at Casa dei Bambini that children who work in carefully prepared environments can develop a sense of independence if the self-correcting materials that they work with and the directress (teacher) who guides them emphasize practical life experiences. Her success in working with this population caught the attention of many, and the materials that she developed quickly became part of the Montessori Method, which emphasizes that children can naturally teach themselves. She made several visits to the United States beginning around 1913 to share her method of teaching, and the American Montessori Society (AMS) that was founded in 1960 still works to accredit schools and prepare teachers in this model of early childhood education.

In 1914, Caroline Pratt founded the City and Country School in New York City at a time when the progressive education movement was being emphasized in the United States. She was a firm believer that play is the "work" of children and that through the use of open-ended materials children could explore the world around them. As a result she designed wooden unit blocks to be used with two- to seven-year-olds, and the blocks are still popular today in many early childhood classrooms across the country. In 1917 she was joined by Lucy Sprague Mitchell, and together they created a community where children were passionate about learning. Their work, often called the "developmental interaction" model, was later established as the Bank Street approach to educating young children.

The High Scope approach to early childhood education emerged from the work of David Weikart at the Perry Preschool Project in Ypsilanti, Michigan. The work of Jean Piaget was influential in the development of this cognitively oriented curriculum. Teachers participate freely in activities with children, guided by "key experiences" that provide a framework for planning activities but allowing flexibility to accommodate the needs of individual learners. The "plan-do-review" sequence is used throughout the day, and gives teachers time to observe and record the progress of a child's development. Today, this method of delivering early childhood educational experiences is quite popular in that there is an extensive amount of research supporting the long-term effectiveness of this approach.

The Waldorf approach to educating young children emerged from a model of the school that was designed for the employees of the Waldorf-Astoria cigarette company by Rudolf Steiner in 1919. Steiner's vision of educating the "whole child" includes the mind, the heart, and the will of the child. All Waldorf teachers focus on the aesthetics of the educational experience, and much of the subject matter is taught through drama, art, or music. In visiting a Waldorf school today, an observer would likely notice the emphasis on nature and the surrounding world.

The newest curricular approach to early childhood education is found in the programs exploring the Reggio Emilia model. This approach began in the Italian community of Reggio Emilia through the efforts of Loris Malaguzzi and a group of women who came together to advocate for a law requiring free quality early care and education for children up to age six. Reggio educators (pedagogistas) are keenly aware of the need for documentation (photos, drawings,

recordings, etc.) of a child's development. They consider the curriculum to be 'emergent,' in that only general goals are established and the curriculum emerges around the interests of the children as they explore projects ranging from a few days to a few months. All Reggio schools have a unique space called the atelier that serves as the studio or workshop for the projects. There is an atelierista who is trained in the arts who provides guidance on projects.

Jill Beloff Farrell and Lilia DiBello

See also Education, History of; Reggio Emilia Approach

Further Readings

Bredekemp, S., & Copple, C. (1997). *Developmentally appropriate practice in early childhood programs* (2nd ed.). Washington, DC: National Association for the Education of Young Children.

Morgan, H. (2006). *Early childhood education: History, theory, and practice.* Lanham, MD: Rowman & Littlefield.

National Research Council and Institute of Medicine. (2000). *From neurons to neighborhoods: The science of early childhood development* (J. P. Shonkoff & D. A. Phillips, Eds.). Committee on Integrating the Science of Early Childhood Development; Board on Children, Youth, and Families; Commission on Behavioral and Social Sciences and Education. Washington, DC: National Academy Press.

Paciorek, K. M. (Ed.). (2007). *Annual editions: Early childhood education 06/07* (27th ed.). Dubuque, IA: McGraw-Hill/Dushkin.

Paciorek, K. M., & Munro, J. H. (Eds.). (1999). *Sources: Notable selections in early childhood education.* Guilford, CT: Dushkin/McGraw-Hill.

Peltzman, B. R. (1998). *Pioneers of early childhood education: A bio-bibliographical guide.* Westport, CT: Greenwood Press.

Piaget, J. (1950). *The psychology of the child.* New York: Basic Books.

Piaget, J., & Inhelder, B. (1969). *The psychology of the child.* New York: Basic Books.

Web Sites

American Montessori Society: http://www.amshq.org

National Association for the Education of Young Children (NAEYC): http://www.naeyc.org

National Head Start Association: http://www.nhsa.org

Zero to Three: http://www.zerotothree.org

Ecojustice and Social Justice

Educators interested in ecojustice analyze and fight to end the increasing destruction of the world's diverse ecosystems, languages, and cultures by the globalizing and ethnocentric forces of Western consumer culture. In addition, they also study, support, and teach about the ways that various cultures around the world actively resist these forces by protecting and revitalizing their "commons," that is, the shared languages, practices, traditions, and relationships (including relationships with the land) necessary to sustain their communities. By emphasizing the commons (and its enclosure or privatization), scholars using ecojustice perspectives recognize social justice as inseparable from and even imbedded in ecological well-being. Ecojustice education thus emphasizes educational reform at the public school, university, and community levels as necessary to stem the tide of both cultural and ecological destruction.

The following five priorities are central to ecojustice-based educational reforms: (1) helping to overcome the environmental and political sources of environmental racism; (2) reducing the consumer-dependent lifestyle and traditions of thinking that contribute to the current exploitation of the cultures of the southern hemisphere by the cultures of the northern hemisphere; (3) revitalizing the diversity of cultural and environmental commons as a way of reducing the environmentally destructive impact of the West's industrial culture; (4) learning to live in a way that helps to ensure that the prospects of future generations are not being diminished; and (5) contributing to a wider understanding of the importance of what Vandana Shiva refers to as "earth democracy"—that is, the right of nonhuman participants that make up the earth's interdependent ecosystems to reproduce themselves in ways that are free of technological manipulation and exploitation.

This entry looks at the ecojustice view of education from the perspective of an advocate.

The Commons and Educational Reform

Educational reforms that contribute to the revitalization of the commons, in effect, represent pedagogical practices that are achievable within different communities and bioregions. Rather than being built on abstract theories about emancipation or transformation, these practices are grounded in the diverse day-to-day relationships and needs of particular communities and built upon important knowledges and traditions passed down through many generations. Rather than arguing for universal application, this approach to educational reform begins by recognizing the specificity of local cultures—the attending languages, practices, beliefs, decision-making patterns, and so on—in relation to a particular geographical context. It also recognizes that all communities and cultures share the necessity to preserve the life systems that they depend upon to survive. Thus, while the particular ways they may go about creating these practices and relations may differ radically, all cultures create a "commons."

The commons are not a theoretical abstraction, and thus they should not be understood as a project to be achieved in the future. They represent the aspects of everyday life and of the natural world that have not yet been privatized and monetized. Scholars in this field refer to "enclosure of the commons" when the shared aspects of day-to-day life that once contributed to the general well-being of communities are transformed into privately owned money-making resources. Many taken-for-granted aspects of life are practices that have been refined and handed down through many generations, including practices as seemingly mundane as the way to make a bed, set a table, shingle a roof, or stack wood; more threatened practices like gathering and preserving seeds or protecting life in a stream; and more formalized practices and principles such as those represented in the U.S. Constitution and Bill of Rights. Freedom of speech and freedom of the press are two parts of the U.S. commons that are shared by all citizens and keeping American communities healthy.

Thus, the commons need to be understood as still existing in both rural and urban settings and in every culture and bioregion on earth. Some commons practices and relations are expressed in craft knowledge (how to farm without wearing out the soil, or how to select a tree and plane a log to become a piece of lumber), others in formal and informal rules of decision making (ward representation in community politics, or household division of labor), still others in more mundane "chores" (how to keep a house clean, a garden tidy, or animals fed and cared for).

The cultural and environmental commons thus represent the lived alternatives to money-dependent activities. They are potential sites of resistance to the spread of the consumer-dependent lifestyle that is viewed as a major cause of ecoinjustices. While not all commons practices are necessarily ecofriendly, learning about the commons in the students' own community and bioregion, as well as the economic and technological forces that threaten what remains of the local commons, helps students to identify those areas that are healthy.

Such a focus should thus be a major aim of educational reform within public schools and universities. The emphasis on the local and the nonmonetized practices of daily life that have a smaller ecological impact would require a radical shift away from the centuries of focus on progress, competition, and growth.

Conceptual Foundations

Although the commons is part of everyday experience, its complexity, as well as the ways people depend on its many life-enhancing and community support systems, go largely unnoticed. The patterns of interdependency that make up the commons are largely taken for granted. For example, speakers of English write from left to right, and speak in patterns that are organized in terms of subject, verb, and object. The embodied experiences of the commons—for example, the multisensory experience of well-being one can get from working in the garden or sharing in a community-based activity—are also difficult to recognize for reasons that have direct implications for thinking about educational reforms.

From the ecojustice perspective, corporations and other modernizing institutions such as the media expose people to a constant stream of images that connect consumerism with success, happiness, and the achievement of social status. Images of the activities and relationships that do not promote the monetized and commodified culture are largely nonexistent. Advocates of ecojustice believe that public schools and universities, for the most part, contribute to the dependency upon a consumer-oriented culture by

promoting a mix of what they see as classical liberal, Enlightenment, and industrially inspired myths. These ideas include: the individual becoming ever more autonomous, change as a constant and a sign of progress and success, literacy and other abstract systems of representation as a more reliable source of knowledge than the context-sensitive oral communication that sustains daily life in the community, and experimental approaches to knowledge and values as more empowering than intergenerational knowledge. Ecojustice advocates argue that the ethnocentrism that underlies the high-status knowledge found in universities leads to a greater dependency upon the industrial system to supply daily needs and discourages students from understanding their own cultural commons and bioregion. It also contributes to the near total silence on how non-Western cultures are attempting to sustain their commons in the face of globalization.

An example of how the combination of silences and linguistic-based misrepresentations can distort the ability to recognize the realities of daily life can be seen in how the Nobel Prize committee omitted Marie Curie's name when they awarded the Nobel Prize to her husband and Henri Becquerel, even though the scientific discovery was largely based on her research.

From the ecojustice perspective, the interpretative framework that still dominates universities and public schools makes local traditions appear as sources of backwardness and impediments to change, progress, and greater individual freedom. To make the point more directly, advocates would say that being able to recognize the commons as sources of individual and community empowerment and self-sufficiency is undermined by the way in which traditions are misrepresented in the educational process. Many teachers, for example, understand traditions simply as holidays and family gatherings, rather than as the complex collection of shared practices of everyday life. Among some social justice or multicultural educators, traditions are presented only as the harmful practices associated with social inequities related to racism or sexism, and thus needing to be overturned in the name of social progress. Most students graduate from universities without learning to use critical analysis to identify the traditions and practices in day-to-day life that need to be *conserved* to sustain healthy communities, ecojustice advocates say.

These advocates argue that most students graduate from universities having learned one primary form of critical reflection, a technical form that prevails in the corporate and/or scientific world. Beginning from the question "What will work best?"—and often devoid of the complementary ethical question, "Is it good for the society and the ecosystem?"—this approach results in the development of new technologies and new forms of dependency. To understand the cultural and environmental commons, students need language that more accurately represents the complex nature of traditions—including the continuities within the culture that are examples of nonmonetized activities, relationships, and forms of knowledge that protect the land and the human communities living on it, ecojustice advocates say.

Issues Related to Language

Ecojustice educators point out other basic misconceptions and silences that limit people's ability to understand the importance of the commons to a sustainable future. Again, what seems to underlie these is the ethnocentrism that is learned in everyday life and reinforced in the educational process, so that a number of other cultural myths are central to giving legitimacy to what is represented as high-status knowledge. One of the more important, ecojustice advocates would say, is the view of language as a conduit in a sender-receiver process of communication. This view of language supports other ideas, such as the objective nature of knowledge and the conception of the individual as an autonomous rational—even critical—thinker. As a result, individuals lack a conceptual basis for making explicit the taken-for-granted cultural practices that are viewed as undermining the commons.

In the ecojustice view, this misunderstanding of language, particularly the assumptions encoded in such words as *progress* and *development,* leads to ignoring or viewing as backward the ways in which other cultures are able to maintain a balance between their commons and market-oriented activities. Ignorance about how the metaphorical nature of language encodes a specific cultural way of knowing also leads to a state of prideful ignorance about the differences in other cultural ways of knowing, advocates assert.

For example, when the notion of progress is taken for granted, along with the idea that Western cultures are the most advanced, the conceptual and moral groundwork has been laid for cultural imperialism, which may lead to the subjugation and economic exploitation of the commons of other cultures.

Some Potential Reforms

Suggesting curricular and pedagogical reforms that focus on the different aspects of the cultural and environmental commons that have not been monetized is relatively easy. For example, having students give special attention during a typical day to the different activities and relationships that have been monetized is the first step in increasing their understanding of the differences between what is shared as part of the commons and how much of daily life has been enclosed by market forces. Similarly, having students identify the many relationships and activities within both the cultural and environmental commons that have not yet been entirely enclosed (privatized and monetized) is also a straightforward and easy task. Depending upon the cultural group and bioregion, students might identify different forms of intergenerational knowledge about food, healing, entertainment, craft knowledge, narratives, ceremonies, and traditions of mutual support within the family and community, as well as the characteristics of the natural environment that have not been degraded or turned into an exploitable resource. Even these simple, straightforward activities of mapping the aspects of daily life that do not require money, as well as the many more that do, will be affected by language.

Educational reforms that contribute to revitalizing the commons, which in turn help to address the issues that ecojustice advocates believe have worldwide importance for the future of humans and natural systems, require more. If the diversity of the world's cultural and environmental commons is being affected by a wide array of forces—ideological, economic, technological, even religious—then the commons must become a more central part of the university curriculum. This is potentially the most difficult part of the educational reforms proposed by ecojustice advocates: getting university faculty to recognize that in carrying on the traditional approaches to their respective disciplines, they are in a state of denial about how serious the ecological crisis really is. Such a revised curriculum might include issues discussed in the next section.

Issues for the Ecojustice Curriculum

One critical theme for ecojustice advocates is the many ways in which industrial culture encloses the commons, from the genetic engineering of plants and animals to the privatization of the airways and cyberspace. This should lead to an examination of the connections between the many ways the commons is being enclosed, the ecological crisis, and the spread of poverty. The impact of enclosure on the different forms of intergenerational knowledge that represent the alternative to monetized dependencies should also be considered.

Another area of inquiry should focus on how the ideology of the World Trade Organization leads to undermining local economies and democratic decision making. Western science and technology are too often introduced without a consideration of the traditions of self-sufficiency within the cultural commons that contribute to living within the limits of the bioregion. The assumptions that underlie Western educational approaches to development also need to be questioned in terms of whether they contribute to the loss of cultural and linguistic diversity and to undermining the local traditions that kept market-related activities from overwhelming the life of the community. For example, does Western science undermine the narratives that are the basis of the moral values and sense of life purpose not centered on possessing more material goods?

A discussion of how ideologies support or undermine the commons can be centered on the nature of the commons: diverse in terms of culture and bioregion, dependent upon the renewal of intergenerational knowledge that reduces the dependency upon consumerism, with patterns of moral reciprocity rooted in the different cultures' narratives. The question can then be raised as to whether Western ideologies of market liberalism, libertarianism, Marxism, and social justice liberalism support or undermine the commons. There should also be a discussion of the connections between economic globalization and the rise of fascism—including how fascism affects the local commons of different cultures.

A more accurate understanding is needed of how the metaphorical nature of language encodes and carries forward over many generations ways of thinking that are not sensitive to the importance of the cultural and environmental commons. This might show how language now reproduces the thought patterns and values of the industrial culture. Special attention should be given to understanding the nature of root metaphors that represent humans and the environment as interdependent and that take account of responsibilities for renewing the nonmonetized traditions that contribute to community self-sufficiency. The root metaphors that undermine the commons also need to be identified and discussed in terms of how they influence people to think and act in ways that contribute to their impoverishment and isolation. How the curriculum in both public schools and universities reinforces the root metaphors that contribute to undermining the commons also needs to be examined.

Ecojustice educators believe it is a myth to represent technology as a neutral tool; the expression of progress needs to be considered in terms of how it impacts the commons. Questions that should be considered include: What are the differences between the modern technologies of the West and indigenous technologies? How does the organization and use of technologies in the factory system influence human relationships, contribute to the loss of craft knowledge, and impact the local economy? Is automation inevitable, and what are the assumptions that represent it as inherently progressive? How do computers influence local language and knowledge systems that encode generations of knowledge of the characteristics of the bioregion? In what ways can computers be used to strengthen the commons, and what are the uses that contribute to undermining the commons? Do computers, by their very nature, contribute to the enclosure of different aspects of the cultural commons?

Educational reformers may base their proposals on a superficial understanding of current theories of learning that do not take account of the differences in the knowledge systems of different cultures, and the environmental crisis. The proposals need to be carefully examined. Government-initiated educational reforms, as well as reforms such as place-based education and reforms based on various constructivist theories of learning, should be assessed in terms of whether they promote the forms of learning that strengthen the mutual support systems within communities and prevent the further enclosure of the local cultural and environmental commons.

Historical Record

A number of thinkers have written on themes related to ecojustice and the revitalization of the commons, long before these terms were in common use to designate such issues. Among the earliest books to warn that unending progress might be disrupted by the industrial approach to the environment was Rachel Carson's *Silent Spring* (1962). This was followed by a report to the Club of Rome, *The Limits to Growth* (1972). Since these early warnings, a steady stream of scientifically grounded books has appeared on subjects ranging from species extinction, depletion of the world's fisheries, and chemical contamination to global warming.

Of special importance was the yearly report *State of the World,* published by the Worldwatch Institute. The warnings of these scientifically based books and reports on the deepening ecological crisis were taken seriously and led to more credibility for the social theorists who subsequently provided the conceptual basis for understanding the importance of the commons as sites for resistance to economic globalization and reducing the adverse human impact on the environment.

The understanding of the commons and dynamics of enclosure that underlie ecojustice recommendations for educational reforms was first derived from Karl Polanyi's 1944 classic, *The Great Transformation*, a new edition of which was published in 2001, and *The Ecologist*'s publication *Whose Common Future* (1993). In the past decade or so, a number of other books have made the case that the strengthening of local economies and decision making represent the most viable alternatives to economic globalization—and have influenced thinking about what should be the major focus of educational reform. Among these are *The Case Against the Global Economy and for a Turn Toward the Local* (1996) by Jerry Mander and Edward Goldsmith, and

the report of the International Forum on Globalization, *Alternatives to Economic Globalization* (2002). Joel Spring's *How Educational Ideologies Are Shaping Global Society* (2005) makes a more recent contribution to understanding how the neoliberal ideology that underlies the thinking of many educational reformers contributes to the form of global culture required by transnational corporations.

The writings of Third World activists have provided further insight into how Western colonization is contributing to the loss of identity and traditions of self-sufficiency in the Third World. These writings on how the commons are being exploited by Western corporations and governmental policies have helped ecojustice proponents to recognize both the nature and importance of the commons—understandings that had not been part of American graduate studies. In effect, their writings also helped American educators to recognize the ethnocentric foundations of their thinking. Among the most importance sources of influence about what ecojustice should encompass, and how it relates to resisting the enclosure of the commons, are the writings of Vandana Shiva, Helena Norberg Hodge, G. Bonfil Batalla, Gustavo Esteva, Grimaldo Rengifo, and the contributors to Wolfgang Sachs's *The Development Dictionary* (1992). *Vanishing Voices* (2000) by Daniel Nettle and Suzanne Romaine and *Linguistic Ecology* (1996) by Peter Muhlhausler have been especially useful in helping Westerners to understand the connection between globalization and the loss of linguistic diversity—and how conserving linguistic diversity is essential to conserving biodiversity.

Several of these Third World activists have recently given personal accounts of how their attempts to introduce Paulo Freire's approach to fostering literacy and consciousness raising led to their realization that Freire's ideas were based on Western cultural assumptions and that his approach represented yet another example of colonization—again, in the name of progress and emancipation. These essays can be found in *Rethinking Freire: Globalization and the Environmental Crisis* (2005), edited by C. A. Bowers and Frederique Apffel-Marglin.

Other sources of influence that have led to the present understanding of or approaches to educational reform centered on ecojustice and revitalization of the commons include the Peter Berger, Thomas Luckmann, and the Alfred Schutz tradition of the sociology of knowledge. *The Sociology of Knowledge* (1967) by Berger and Luckmann was especially important in that it explained the role of language in the construction of a taken-for-granted, socially shared view of everyday reality. Edward Shils's *Tradition* (1981) was essential to understanding the complexity of the everyday traditions that we rely upon—and that go largely unnoticed because of their taken-for-granted status. His book was especially important to our current effort to understand that the revitalization of the commons and the forces promoting its enclosure represent traditions that need to be made explicit so that those that are undermining the commons can be made explicit and democratically challenged. These books, along with books on the metaphorical nature of language—for example, Richard Harvey Brown's *A Poetic for Sociology* (1977), Andrew Ortony's *Metaphor and Thought*, (1979), and George Lakoff and Mark Johnson's *Metaphors We Live By* (1980)—have provided a way of understanding how language carries forward earlier patterns of culturally specific ways of thinking, as well as how language encodes and intergenerationally reproduces the moral values of the culture. They also have provided a basis for recognizing the constructivist theories of learning that assumed that knowledge is constructed by individuals, and that individual autonomy should be the goal of radical approaches to educational reform, were fundamentally at odds with the reality of culturally constructed knowledge, which the individual may question, reinterpret, and/or misinterpret but for the most part take for granted.

The origins of thinking that led eventually to making ecojustice and the revitalization of the commons the central foci of educational reforms can be traced back to C. A. Bowers's *Cultural Literacy for Freedom* (1974), which presented the argument that educators can only address the systemic causes of the ecological crisis as they help students to recognize the cultural assumptions that were contributing to overshooting the sustaining capacity of natural systems. More recent educational writings on the need to address the cultural roots of the ecolgcical crisis include David Orr's *Ecological Literacy* (1992), Gregory Smith's *Education and the Environment* (1992), and Gregory

Cajete's *Look to the Mountain* (1994). Smith's writings focused on the importance of educational reforms that strengthen the sense of connection to place and community, while Orr's work focused on the need for a more intelligent understanding of ecological design. Cajete's contribution was in presenting the indigenous approaches to environmental education that are still practiced in communities across the land. One of the first books to introduce the idea that an understanding of the environmental commons should be part of the curriculum was Mitchell Thomashow's *Ecological Identity* (1995). In *Our Common Illiteracy* (2002), Rolf Jucker combined an in-depth critique of how global capitalism is undermining the earth's natural systems with a series of recommendations for the reforms that need to be introduced at all levels of our educational institutions. Rebecca Martusewicz's *Seeking Passage* (2001) reflects her deep rootedness in the sociology of knowledge, as well as in the ideas of Gilles Deleuze, Michel Serres, and Gregory Bateson. She has been especially focused on overturning the idea of the individual as a rational agent acting on a nonintelligent world, and on highlighting the importance of context and the generative role that difference plays in human-nature relationships.

Others who have added to our understanding of how the revitalization of the commons contributes to the achievement of greater ecojustice in the world, as well as the implications for educational reforms, include David Gruenewald, who writes on the importance of connecting place-based educational reforms with the emancipatory agenda of critical pedagogy theorists, and C. A. Bowers, who has written a number of books that explain how constructivist theories of education contribute to undermining the world's commons. Bowers's work also explores how western universities are complicit in the globalization of the West's economic and consumer-dependent culture, and suggests the nature of reforms that must be undertaken in teacher education programs if the revitalization of the commons is to be taken seriously. Important contributions to how an understanding of ecojustice issues can be incorporated into teacher education courses are currently being made by Jennifer Thom, Kathleen Pemberton, Kate Wayne, Elaine Riley-Taylor, Amanda Phillips, Karen Ferneding, Bob Farrell, Eugene Provenzo, and Jeff Edmundson.

Edmundson has undertaken the most comprehensive approach to introducing an ecojustice/revitalization of the commons perspective into all of the courses being taken by students in a teacher education cohort at Portland State University.

Current Directions

Unlike place-based educational reforms, and the various approaches of constructivist learning advocates, the sociology of knowledge and the understanding of how the root metaphors of a culture reproduce earlier patterns of thinking have become central to ecojustice proposals for how teachers can become aware of how the ecological patterns of thinking that support the industrial culture are passed in the curriculum and in classroom conversation.

Educational reforms that contribute to the greater achievement of ecojustice through the revitalization of the commons can also be understood as contributing to the practice of an environmental ethic. These educational reforms are deeply moral in nature. They are also based on a tradition of both western and non-western ways of understanding moral reciprocity within the human and human-nature communities. In terms of the western tradition, Aldo Leopold's "land Ethic" and the writings of Wendell Berry, Gary Snyder, and Gregory Bateson have been the most formative. Again, our own cultural ways of understanding the practice of environmental ethics has been influenced by what we learned from the writings about non-western practices of an environmental ethic. The writings of Keith Basso, G. Bonfil Batalla, Loyda Sanchez, Grimaldo Gengifo, Vandana Shiva, and Helena Norberg Hodge have been especially useful in enabling us to see more clearly our own cultural patterns—and possibilities.

The relationship between the theory and classroom/community practices that contribute to a more ecologically sustainable future is explored in the online journal *The Ecojustice Review: Educating for the Commons*, which includes articles on the practice of an ecojustice pedagogy. The journal's Web site also contains an ecojustice dictionary that clarifies how words take on different meanings, depending upon whether their definitions are based on the assumptions that underlie the West's industrial, consumer-dependent culture or on the assumptions that take account of the nature and diversity of the world's commons.

Chet Bowers and Rebecca Martusewicz

See also Cultural Pluralism; Globalization and Education; Social Justice, Education for

Further Readings

Apfel-Marglin, F., & PRATEC (Eds.). (1998). *The spirit of regeneration: Andean culture confronting Western notions of development*. London: Zed Books.

Batalla, G. B. (1996). *Mexico profundo: Reclaiming a civilization*. Austin: University of Texas Press.

Bateson, G. (1972). *Steps to an ecology of mind*. New York: Ballantine Books.

Bateson, G. (1980). *Mind and nature*. New York: Bantam Books.

Berger, P., & Luckmann, T. (1967). *The social construction of reality: A treatise in the sociology of knowledge*. Garden City, NY: Anchor.

Berry, W. (1986). *The unsettling of America: Culture and agriculture*. San Francisco: Sierra Club Books.

Bowers, C. A. (1974). *Cultural literacy for freedom*. Eugene, OR: Elan.

Bowers, C. A. (1993). *Critical essays on education, culture, and the recovery of the ecological imperative*. New York: Teachers College Press.

Bowers, C. A. (1993). *Education, cultural myths, and the ecological crisis: Toward deep changes*. Albany: State University of New York Press.

Bowers, C. A. (1995). *Educating for an ecologically sustainable culture: Rethinking moral education, creativity, intelligence, and other modern orthodoxies*. Albany: State University of New York Press.

Bowers, C. A. (1997). *The culture of denial: Why the environmental movement needs a strategy for reforming universities and public schools*. Albany: State University of New York Press.

Bowers, C. A. (2001). *Educating for eco-justice and community*. Athens: University of Georgia Press.

Bowers, C. A. (2003). *Mindful conservatism: Rethinking the ideological and educational basis of an ecologically sustainable future*. Lanham, MD: Rowman & Littlefield.

Bowers, C. A., & Appfel-Marglin, F. (Eds.). (1995). *Rethinking Freire: Globalization and the environmental crisis*. Mahwah, NJ: Lawrence Erlbaum.

Brown, R. (1977). *A poetic for sociology: Toward a logic of discovery for the human sciences*. Cambridge, UK: Cambridge University Press.

Cajete, G. (1994). *Look to the mountain: An ecology of indigenous education.* Durango, CO: Kivaki Press.

The Ecologist. (1993). *Whose common future? Reclaiming the commons.* Gabriola Island, BC, Canada: New Society.

International Forum on Globalization. (2002). *Alternatives to economic globalization.* San Francisco: Berrett-Koehler.

Jucker, R. (2002). *Our common illiteracy: Education as if the earth and people mattered.* Frankfurt am Main: Peter Lang.

Lakoff, G., & Johnson, M. (1980). *Metaphors we live by.* Chicago: University of Chicago Press.

Leopold, A. (1966). *A Sand County almanac.* New York: Oxford University Press.

Mander, J., & Goldsmith, E. (Eds.). (1996). *The case against the global economy: And for a turn toward the local.* San Francisco: Sierra Club Books.

Muhlhausler, P. (1996). *Linguistic ecology: Language change and linguistic imperialism in the Pacific region.* London: Routledge.

Nettle, D., & Romaine, S. (2000). *Vanishing voices: The extinction of the world's languages.* New York: Oxford University Press.

Norberg-Hodge, H. (1992). *Ancient futures: Learning from Ladakh.* San Francisco: Sierra Club Books.

Orr, D. (1992). *Ecological literacy: Education and the transition to a postmodern world.* Albany: State University of New York Press.

Ortony, A. (Ed.). (1979). *Metaphor and thought.* Cambridge, UK: Cambridge University Press.

Polanyi, K. (2001). *The great transformation: The political and economic origins of our time.* Boston: Beacon Press.

Rengifo, G. (1998). The Ayllu. In F. Apffel-Marglin & PRATEC (Eds.), *The spirit of regenerations: Andean culture confronting Western notions of development* (pp. 124–145). London: Zed Books.

Sachs, W. (Ed.). (1992). *The development dictionary: A guide to knowledge as power.* London: Zed Books.

Schutz, A. (1971). *Collected papers: The problem of social reality.* The Hague, The Netherlands: Martinus Nijhoff.

Shils, E. (1981). *Tradition.* Chicago: University of Chicago Press.

Shiva, V. (1993). *Monocultures of the mind: Biodiversity, biotechnology, and the Third World.* Penang, Malaysia: Third World Network.

Smith, G. (1992). *Education and the environment: Learning to live within limits.* Albany: State University of New York Press.

Snyder, G. (1990). *The practice of the wild.* San Francisco. North Point Press.

Thomashow, M. (1995). *Ecological identity: Becoming a reflective environmentalist.* Cambridge: MIT Press.

Worldwatch Institute Report. *1984—State of the World.* New York: W. W. Norton.

Web Sites

The Ecojustice Review: Educating for the Commons: http://www.ecojusticeeducation.org

ECONOMIC INEQUALITY

The study of the relationship between economic inequality and educational opportunity has been guided by at least three assumptions. First, education is a crucial factor in improving one's social and economic status. Second, the quality of schooling one receives is related to the degree of social and economic success one achieves. And, third, the society has some level of responsibility for the type and quality of schooling available to its citizens. Following a description of the historical context of the relationship of education to economic inequality, this entry discusses two opposing perspectives from which that relationship has been interpreted. To conclude, several key legislative decisions and educational reform movements related to economic inequality and the schools are summarized here.

Historical Context

Support for publicly funded education has, from its earliest attempts, been framed largely in terms of the need to provide for equal economic opportunity through equal educational opportunities. While couched in the language of religious salvation, even early mandatory education legislation, like the Massachusetts School Law of 1642 and the "Old Deluder Satan Act" of 1647, could be considered economic legislation, given the close tie between Puritan views of salvation and a person's work ethic and the fear that the poor and unchurched might be a threat to the social and economic order.

Certainly by the time of early nationhood the notion that education was closely tied to social mobility and personal advancement and should be available to all American citizens was well established. More importantly, what was established was the inconsistency between rhetoric calling for free public schooling and new curricula and the reality that most educational ventures were actually local, erratically funded projects that were not available to large segments of society. From then on, the challenge to any claim that education can be an economic equalizer would involve understanding the relationship between the quality of schooling provided and future economic success, and coming to some agreement as to how to provide high quality educational opportunity to all citizens.

Two Conflicting Perspectives

Two perspectives have come to characterize the study of the relationship between schooling and economic inequality. One is sometimes called a functionalist perspective. This perspective, often associated with conservative political and economic ideology, assumes that one of the roles of the school is to justify inequalities in society by explaining that wealth and status are the proper rewards of educational attainment. An underlying understanding is that the degree of educational and economic success people attain is due largely, if not solely, to the choices they make and their inherent or natural gifts. From this perspective, failure to attain one's economic goals through education is due less to any societal inequity than to the personal qualities of the individual or the technical or professional failings of individual teachers and schools. Among the influential contemporary advocates of this position are Diane Ravitch, Chester Finn, and William Bennett. In recent years, this position has also provided the sociological and ideological bases for proponents of educational vouchers, school choice, and other market-based reforms.

It follows then that for schools to do a better job of bringing about economic equality, they need to strive for greater personal and institutional accountability, responsibility, and efficiency. This can happen by helping students make better personal choices and take on new skills and values, or when schools are seen as the cause of students' failures, may be a matter of correcting the school's low expectations or forcing schools to become more efficient and effective or close their doors as a result of free market competition with other schools of choice.

An alternative analytical framework is based on the notion that economic inequality is the result not so much of individual choice or limitation as of well-established societal barriers to economic advancement. From this perspective, often associated with liberal or progressive political and economic ideology, the critique of the relationship of public education and economic inequality is systemic in nature and seeks to expose those deeply rooted barriers and the role played by schools in reinforcing the cultural assumptions and values that sustain them.

The more radical statement of this perspective argues that schools are among the social institutions that reinforce the existing social and economic order and are relatively powerless to correct economic inequities. Schools reward qualities like passivity and obedience and discourage creativity and spontaneity because that is what a capitalist economy demands. Even critics sympathetic to this general position realize that such an interpretation fails to take into account the ways in which existing schools can undermine capitalist goals and overlooks the potential of individuals to actively resist the control of others and construct their own futures.

What has emerged in recent years is a more refined and empowering critique of the school's role in reinforcing economic inequality. This includes an emphasis on an analysis of the roles played by individuals in succumbing to or resisting dominant groups; the relationships between social class, race, and gender; and the development of what has been called a *critical pedagogy*. This refers to ways of teaching that are intended to help people to become more aware of their cultural, political, and economic context and those systemic factors that lead to discrimination or oppression. They then learn ways in which literacy and other intellectual tools can be used to bring about economic and political change.

Some Key Events

Perhaps the earliest, deliberate attempt to create equal educational opportunity and erase some social class barriers was Thomas Jefferson's attempt to pass his Bill for the More General Diffusion of Knowledge in 1778. In the bill he proposed a system of free schooling through the university level based solely on the merit and achievement of the students. Another important step toward equality of opportunity intended to address economic inequalities was the "common school" movement that began in the late 1830s. While the primary motivation behind the movement was to create a uniform system of schools in which all American young people, especially recent immigrants, would be steeped in common American values, it was also argued that if poor immigrant children had access to free public schooling they would be able to increase their education level and, thereby, their economic and social standing. Both efforts are not without critics who argue that simple access to schooling cannot overcome the advantages of wealth; it is clear that at least the rhetoric acknowledged existing inequalities and the need to lessen them.

Any discussion of attempts to address economic inequality through education must include the efforts of the federal government during the 1950s and 1960s. An important step was the Supreme Court's 1954 decision in *Brown v. the Board of Education of Topeka, Kansas,* which acknowledged the connection between race and economic and educational inequality and declared that racially segregated schools were unconstitutional and could not provide equality of educational opportunity. The 1966 *Equality of Educational Opportunity* study, which is often called the "Coleman Report," further documented the inequality in schools based on the economics of individual communities, and the federal government responded with a variety of well-funded legislation designed to provide additional educational opportunities and resources to children in poverty. The government's actions extended to other social spheres and institutions as well.

Few critics or defenders of public education will argue that schools have had a lasting impact on lessening economic inequalities, especially given recent data that shows the gap between rich and poor to be increasing. Recently, efforts to lessen economic inequality have gone in at least three directions. The federal government, through the No Child Left Behind Act of 2001, has turned its efforts to demanding that schools be more accountable to and have higher expectations for the achievement of poor and minority students. The government is also attempting to assist a second approach that is more populist in tone and direction, the creation of charter schools designed to use public money to create schools tailored to special interests and local needs and the funding of voucher programs that allow parents in low-achieving schools to move their children to the school of their choice. A third trend involves challenging the constitutionality of state policies that fund public education primarily through local property taxes, since that practice is considered by some to be one of root causes of inequality of educational opportunity by ensuring that schools in wealthy communities and large tax bases will always have more than those located in poor communities with little source of consistent funding.

Rick A. Breault

See also Civil Rights Movement; Compensatory Education; Critical Theory; Hegemony; Sociology of Education

Further Readings

Bowles, S., & Gintis, H. (1976). *Schooling in capitalist America.* New York: Basic Books.

Chubb, J., & Moe, T. (1990). *Politics, markets, and America's schools.* Washington, DC: Brookings Institution.

Coleman, J. S. (1966). *Equality of educational opportunity.* Washington, DC: U.S. Department of Health, Education, and Welfare, Office of Education.

Kozol, J. (1991). *Savage inequalities.* New York: Crown.

Ravitch, D. (1983). *The troubled crusade: American education, 1945–1980.* New York: Basic Books.

EDUCATION, AIMS OF

Educational aims express the social and developmental outcomes that schools hope to achieve. Herbert Spencer approached educational aims through the question, *What knowledge is of most worth?* This and the following related questions have long been central to educational scholarship. Why are certain types of learning valued over others? Should schools strive for critical thinking or cultural literacy? Should they seek practical relevance or academic rigor? Should schools prepare students to accept social norms and the responsibilities of adult life? Should they prepare students to reform society through civic participation and activism? Or are all of these aims equally important?

Some educational writers treat the terms *aims* and *objectives* as synonymous. Objectives, however, are usually more specific than aims because the former are justified largely on the basis of how they contribute to a particular discipline or subject area. Knowledge of grammar, for example, might be justified as an objective of the English language arts if it contributes to literacy. In contrast, aims typically go beyond subject matter to ask, at a more general level, who benefits and how. To what use, for example, should literacy be put? Why is it valued, by whom, and in what contexts? Must everyone learn grammar? Why or why not? This entry examines educational aims as broad statements of intended outcomes and desires. It discusses how social and developmental needs serve as key sources of educational aims, and it addresses how these aims function within education to inform both its theory and practice.

Sources of Educational Aims

Socrates was one of the earliest western thinkers to explicitly link education and social needs. He argued that a good education could not be formulated directly without first addressing the question of what constitutes a good society. A clear understanding of the good society would then provide the logical foundations for determining educational aims. This approach places education largely in the service of the state and its citizens, a perspective widely evident today as schools are called upon to address an ever increasing range of social needs—from the nation's economic security to responsible citizenship.

Jean-Jacques Rousseau and child-centered progressives such as John Dewey would later challenge the adequacy of social needs as the sole basis for education. Albeit for different reasons, both Rousseau and Dewey sought to balance the needs of society with needs of individuals. This balance is well illustrated in the National Education Association's 1918 report, *Cardinal Principles of Secondary Education*. The report lists seven educational aims: (1) health, (2) command of the fundamental processes, (3) worthy home membership, (4) vocation, (5) citizenship, (6) worthy use of leisure, and (7) ethical character. Today's curriculum may seem less generously conceived, but concerns over individual needs are still widely evident in the guise of human development training, in constructivist theories of learning, and in concepts such as self-actualization.

How Aims Contribute to Education

Theorists and the public at large rarely agree over what counts as a social need, and even developmental needs often spark controversy. Nevertheless, aims remain squarely at the center of education. The intractable importance of aims can be understood by recognizing the key roles that aims play in both the theory and practice. Theory and practice in education are closely related, much like two sides of the same coin or like the rows and columns that define each cell in the table as informed by both types of activity.

Theory, the first dimension, is used here to include the competing schools of thought that are found in common approaches to conceptualizing curriculum and instruction. These approaches include, for example, essentialism, perennialism, social adaptation, social reconstructionism, constructivism, and progressivism. Space does not allow a full description of these approaches other than to suggest that each approach is distinguished largely on the basis of the educational aims it adopts. In essentialism, for example, the primary aims of education are to bequeath our cultural heritage as it is represented in the academic disciplines. In perennialism, the aims are to cultivate the intellect and promote rational thinking. In social adaptation, schools are to prepare individuals in ways that will make them fit for the roles of adult life. In social reconstruction, schools are to promote justice and equity through social reform. Constructivism and progressivism seek individual development for participation in democratic life. Many of these aims clearly overlap. Yet, each approach possesses enough distinctiveness and coherence to give its proponents their own sense of identity and rallying points. Moreover, the aims of each approach hold far-reaching implications for the practical work of program design.

Program design is the second dimension of education, in which aims play and necessary and leading role. For more than fifty years, the chief paradigm for program design has been the "Tyler rationale," named for Ralph W. Tyler, the author of the highly influential book *Basic Principles of Curriculum and Instruction* (1950). In this slim volume, Tyler organized program design around four questions. First, what aims should schools seek to attain? Second, what experiences will be useful in attaining these ends? Third, how can these experiences best be organized? Fourth, how can the effectiveness of these experiences be evaluated? In this approach, aims not only come first, but they require almost half of total number of pages that Tyler's book devotes to the whole design process. Moreover, the four steps are sequenced so that experiences and organization follow directly from program aims, and the program itself is finally evaluated by comparing its outcomes with its original aims. Thus, one could argue that once aims are determined, the remainder of the design work is largely mechanical or at least prefigured by the first step of specifying aims.

The preceding discussion is meant to highlight two key functions of educational aims. First, aims tether education broadly to social life and individual well-being. Second, aims guide the basic approaches and processes of educational design. Because contemporary education is dominated by talk of standards and high-stakes testing, aims talk seems to be on the wane. In particular, content standards and test scores are often assumed to be important without questioning why, for whom, or under what circumstances. But if history is our guide, the perennial and complex questions that surround educational aims will not quickly yield to simple and expedient remedies.

David J. Flinders

See also Philosophy of Education

Further Readings

Kliebard, H. (1995). *The struggle for the American curriculum.* New York: Routledge.

Noddings, N. (2004). The aims of education. In D. J. Flinders & S. J. Thornton (Eds.), *The curriculum studies reader* (2nd ed.). New York: Routledge.

Peters, R. S. (1960). *Authority, responsibility, and education.* London: George Allen & Unwin.

Tyler, R. (1950). *Basic principles of curriculum and instruction.* Chicago: University of Chicago Press.

Whitehead, A. N. (1967). *The aims of education.* New York: Free Press. (Original work published 1929)

EDUCATION, HISTORY OF

The history of education is the study of the origin and evolution of organized learning in the lives of individuals, groups, institutions, and nations. The field attempts to assess the values and behaviors of systems of education, their achievements and dysfunctions. In this sense, the field is akin to other social scientific approaches to education, such as sociology, anthropology, economics, and political science. It is not too much of an overstatement to say that the field is concerned with the vast cultural terrain between theories about how education should work and what children and adults actually do with what they have learned. Rather than recounting the history of education, this entry looks at the field of study and its principal scholars.

Describing the Subject

How and why did education arrive at this contemporary set of conditions, structures, and policies? This is the driving question of History of Education. To make sense of the present, historians of education research questions about the grand plans, events, and controversies of the past. The point is to describe and explain how those educational heritages have shaped contemporary assumptions and practices.

Historians ask, for example: Who and what have exerted the most influence on the way we currently conceive educational problems and solutions? Which groups have enjoyed access to quality education? Who has been denied equality of educational opportunity and why? How and why have movements to reform schools succeeded or failed? These are the kinds of inquiries that motivate historians to discover the past and organize it into coherent narratives.

A Humanistic Inquiry

But historians are not focused exclusively on contemporary educational problems. A second important aspect of the field is less related to the social sciences and is a kind of humanistic inquiry. In this frame of mind, historians of education ask questions about educational traditions—attempting to address the past on its own terms and for its own sake. The human condition presupposes intergenerational communication and training for the young. The humanistic study of the educational past takes this intergenerational encounter as its starting point. Connecting the past to the present becomes, therefore, a secondary consideration, a minor concern.

This humanistic purpose is served by investigating the unfamiliar educational worlds of the past. The point is to better understand the circumstances educators have faced and the cultural forms they have adopted to prepare their children for an uncertain future. Bernard Bailyn believes that historians should not apologize for these humanistic and at times antiquarian inclinations. For Bailyn, the study of history begins with the idea that the past was essentially different from the present.

What all of these historians assume is that education was and remains a complicated, mediating, moral, and political human invention. Education is complicated by the fact that historically it has taken many forms and served many purposes. It is a mediating institution, shaped by assumptions about what makes for good lives within the context of a good and evolving society.

Education is a moral enterprise in that its justification proceeds from elders' desire for a better future in an improved world for "favored" members of a younger generation. Education is political in the sense that educational resources are not distributed in isolation from a political process. Political interests define who is favored and who is neglected in the conflicted allocation of financial, social, and intellectual capital to communities, schools, and students. Historians begin their work, therefore, with the assumption that education cannot be researched in isolation from the visions of preferred ways of living, model communities, and idealized futures that are embedded in educational theory and political realities.

Admittedly, this agenda is grand and perhaps grandiose. Historians of education alternate between granular, empirical analysis of single high schools and rarefied interpretations of national reform movements. They ask about the connective tissues among a single community's students, textbooks, teachers, and schools. They inquire about systems of thought and

institutional arrangements at an expansive societal level. They do their work on unwieldy, multileveled stages, hoping to understand the many functions education has served.

Historians of education operate with theoretical premises that inform their choices of researchable questions and influence how they categorize data and reach conclusions. Carl Kaestle argues that these premises usually occupy a "middle ground" between overarching social theories and antitheoretical narratives that purport to stick to the facts for the purpose of telling a good story.

No Single Version

The expression "*the* history of education" is misleading, since the manifold circumstances of time and place, to say nothing of the daunting archives of evidence, have made comprehensive narratives virtually impossible. The most encompassing single interpretation is James Bowen's exceptional *A History of Western Education* (three volumes). Bowen offers a transcontinental tour of educational ideas and institutions from ancient Mesopotamia to Alvin Toffler's *Future Shock*.

A single, definitive narrative of education in a nation as old and diverse as the United States has been difficult to conceive and implement. What exists are *histories* of education, analytic chronicles that are thematically organized and set in a national or regional context. Historians value both the majestic synthesis and the revelatory case study, and the lack of the latter is cause for concern.

Historians worry about "presentism" in their work, the fallacy of mining the past to justify a desired version of the present or imagined model of the future. The historian's dilemma is a real one. Isolate oneself too far from the present and the field becomes anachronistic. Adhere too closely to the issues of the month, and the field's well-earned temporal detachment and hard-earned perspectives are compromised.

Ruminating on this dilemma in 1978, Warren Button foresaw no easy way out. The dilemma, in Button's view, is a historian's professional fate. He argued that historians could not extricate themselves from the dual responsibility of understanding the past on its own terms and using their expertise to provide better ways to think about current educational problems.

Problematics of the Field

Academic fields are defined and bedeviled by their "problematics," and the history of education is no exception. "Problematics" are those core questions, disciplinary boundaries, methodologies, and instances of "specified ignorance" that guide the research agendas of practicing scholars.

When there is substantial agreement among practitioners about core problematics, a field can mature by generating knowledge, resolving important questions, renewing its research agenda, and gaining the regard of scholars outside of the field. If there is substantial disagreement, then a field may be absorbed by other fields, fail to train a next generation of researchers, or become irrelevant to contemporary scholarly exchange.

The history of education is a field in which there is both significant agreement and disagreement about problematics. A consequence is that the field occupies an ambiguous position in the larger conversation about the exasperating intergenerational challenge known as education. As the educational historian John Rury has argued, the field is somewhat odd and isolated, not entirely embraced by either the professional world of teaching or academic history departments and their major professional organizations.

On the one hand, there has been a rough consensus that the history of education is a project focused on schooling within nations, although some attention has been paid to cross-national comparisons. It is commonly assumed that historians of education will publish their work in traditional genres: biographies, case studies, scholarly articles, thematic monographs, institutional histories, grand narratives, and documentary histories. Periodization, at least in the context of the United States, has not been a cause of significant contention.

But there have been sharp disagreements over core disciplinary issues. The publication of Lawrence Cremin's *American Education: The Metropolitan Experience, 1876–1980,* the third and final volume of his grand narrative on the history of American education, provided the occasion for an intense and unsettling exchange. In a *History of Education Quarterly* Forum on *The Metropolitan Experience,* Robert Church criticized Cremin's work, recognizing it as the most comprehensive existing history of American education but voicing chagrin that it expressed ambivalence and distaste for the political project of providing equal education opportunity. British historian Harold Silver concurred with Church, calling Cremin the "ultimate de-schooler," and concluding that *The Metropolitan Experience* looked to the future more than the past.

Cremin vigorously defended his interpretation and the definition of education that he had steadfastly employed throughout his career. Cremin offered a broad view of education as the systematic and ongoing effort to communicate knowledge, skills, and values, as well as its results. This formulation is only slightly narrower than that of Bernard Bailyn, who had defined education as the process in which a culture reproduces itself into the future.

Cremin's definition gave him wide latitude to connect people, events, and institutions to the intellectual and cultural climate of their times. He argued that the field of the history of education needed to liberate itself from the narrow institutionalism, anachronism, and moralism of teacher training institutions. Cremin rejected the laudatory "lives of the saints" approach to history of education. Concerned about the field's isolation, he demonstrated one strategy for connecting the field to a larger landscape of European and American ideas, ideals, and institutional arrangements. In the end, Michael B. Katz posed the most serious challenge to Cremin, arguing that Cremin's broad definition actually impeded research and had brought the field to a state of crisis. Its broadness posed an impossible challenge for historians.

Cremin and his critics had reached a stalemate. School curricula and soap operas both engage in the deliberate transmission of attitudes, values, and sensibilities. Which of the two is more important to study and why? Without a clear and compelling answer to these questions, what was to prevent the history of education from dissolving into cultural studies? On the other hand, if school agendas expressed the political agendas of dominant groups writ small and camouflaged with manipulative rhetoric, then what else was there to understand?

Given these issues, it is reasonable to ask: What is the payoff for undertaking this research, for studying this field? What value can the history of education deliver to other disciplinary investigations and scholarly exchanges about education? The answers to these questions require elaboration but can be stated concisely. Historians can describe and explain the influential, the significant, change and structure, and contradictory trends and offer a detached and reasoned perspective.

Historians disentangle complicated, cross-cutting historical trends. They sort out events that seem to contradict each other and establish distinctions and contexts in which the contradictions can coexist and be connected by a new historical logic. In a nation such as the United States, a climate of national crisis overlaps with local moods of relative contentment about public education. Historians can therefore provide valuable perspectives on the nature of educational criticism itself. When is it on target and fair? When is it misinformed and excessive?

What Merton calls strategic research materials (SRMs) are also an important aspect of problematics. A field's evidence makes up the most significant part of what it brings forward for public and professional consideration. These discovered and organized data are what scholars present in support of their claims, arguments, and conclusions.

The Future of the Field

To speculate about the future of the field is to ask whether it consists of a disorganized mass of case studies, institutional histories, and single-issue, regional monographs or whether it provides some depth of knowledge or breadth of understanding that might engage the interest of scholarly or public audiences. The history of the field suggests that no single structure or perspective unites the diverse field. Historians will continue to work in areas where their talents and their intellectual interests merge. The questions are these: Can those talents and interests be better directed at defining and enriching the field, and can historians negotiate a more central role in scholarly and public debates about the future of education?

It is important for the professional credibility of historians to participate in scholarly and public deliberations about how current educational problems are framed and which solutions are being considered. Without these engagements, historians' valuable perspectives on influence, significance, and contradictory trends and criticism will be lost.

But the quality of historians' participation will depend on the quality of the field's problematics: the core questions, the specified ignorance, the definitions, explanatory models, and the strategic research materials. Energetic attention to and some degree of consensus about these foundational issues can yield useful directions for the history of education.

It will continue to be important for scholars and the public to understand the various ambitions, implementations, and results of educational reform. Historians are uniquely positioned to engage scholars and the public in discussions of how and why change has proceeded well and badly. Diane Ravitch's *Left Back: A Century of Failed School Reforms* is a cautionary tale. She emphasizes how often reforms have become paths of least resistance, lowering academic standards, embracing social problems and passing along underprepared students to the next tier in the system.

Larry Cuban and David Tyack's *Tinkering Toward Utopia* is insightful about the stages of reform—policy talk, policy action, and implementation. And it details how schools change reforms, sticking to the plan without taking care of unintended outcomes. In American education there will be continuing tensions between systems and reforms, and historians have the expertise to ask whether schools have the capacity, the focus, and the commitment to avoid faddish programs where durable solutions are needed.

Historians who employ a developmental framework will find that their work dovetails with the longitudinal studies of social scientists interested in questions of when and how education matters over the life course. Sociologist Katherine Newman, for example, has completed a third set of follow-up studies of Harlem's working poor, *Chutes and Ladders,* which provides multiple perspectives on how some students succeeded while others did not.

Similarly, the work of David Lavin and David Hyllegard suggests that educational interventions later in the life course of adults, such as those offered by the City University of New York (CUNY) in its open admissions programs of the early 1970s, can have an impact on a city or region's social structure by increasing the number of people in minority communities who have a college degree. Henry Drewry and Humphrey Doermann's *Stand and Prosper* documents the role that historically Black colleges and universities have played in building a civic leadership class in urban centers such as Atlanta and Charlotte.

Finally, it will be important for historians to develop ways of understanding the emerging interplay between globalization and education. Thomas Friedman's "flat world" envisions a future in which anyone can take part in communications, both creative and not. If brick and mortar institutions lose their hold on future generations of students, how will the history of that dramatic change be researched and written?

John G. Ramsay

See also Educational Research, History of

See Visual History (all)

Further Readings

Bailyn, B. (1960). *Education in the forming of American society: Needs and opportunities for study.* Chapel Hill: University of North Carolina Press.

Bowen, J. (2000). *A history of Western education* (3 vols.). London: Methuen.

Button, H. W. (1979). Creating more useable pasts: History in the study of education. *Educational Researcher, 8*(5), 3–9.

Cremin, L. A. (1965). *The genius of American education.* New York: Random House.

Cremin, L. A. (1977). *Traditions of American education.* New York: Basic Books.

Cremin, L. A. (1988). *American education: The metropolitan experience, 1876–1980.* New York: Harper & Row.

Cuban, D., & Tyack, L. (1995). *Tinkering toward utopia: A century of public school reform.* Cambridge, MA: Harvard University Press.

Donato, R., & Lazerson, M. (2000). New directions in American educational history: Problems and prospects. *Educational Researcher, 29*(8), 4–15.

Dougherty, J. (2000). Are historians of education "bowling alone"? Response to Donato and Lazerson. *Educational Researcher, 29*(8), 16–17.

Drewry, H., & Doermann, H. (2003). *Stand and prosper: Private Black colleges and their students.* Princeton, NJ: Princeton University Press.

Friedman, T. (2000). The world is flat: A brief history of the twenty-first century. New York: Farrar, Straus & Giroux.

Kaestle, C. F. (1992). Theory in educational history: A middle ground. In R. K. Goodenow & W. E. Marsden (Eds.), *The city and the education in four nations* (pp. 195–204). Cambridge, UK: Cambridge University Press.

Kliebard, H. M. (1992). *Forging the American curriculum: Essays in curriculum history and theory.* New York: Routledge.

Labaree, D. F. (2006). Mutual subversion: A short history of the liberal and the professional on American higher education. *History of Education Quarterly, 46*(1), 1–15.

Lavin, D., & Hyllegard, D. (1997). Changing the odds: Open admissions and the life chances of the disadvantaged. *Social Forces, 76*(2), 705–707.

Menand, L. (2001). *The metaphysical club: A story of ideas in America.* New York: Farrar, Straus & Giroux.

Merton, R. K. (1987). Three fragments from a sociologist's notebook: Establishing the phenomenon, specified ignorance, and strategic research materials. *Annual Review of Sociology, 13*, 1–28.

Merton, R. K. (1994). A life of learning (Charles Homer Haskins lecture). *American Council of Learned Societies, Occasional Paper*, Vol. 25.

Newman, K. S. (2008). *Chutes and ladders: Navigating the low-wage labor market.* Cambridge, MA: Harvard University Press.

Ravitch, D. (1983). *The troubled crusade: American education, 1945–1980.* New York: Basic Books.

Ravitch, D. (2000). *Left back.* New York: Simon & Schuster.

Rury, J. L. (1984). Vocationalism for home and work: Women's education in the United States, 1880–1930. *History of Education Quarterly, 24*(1), 21–44.

Samuels, E. (Ed.). (1973). *The education of Henry Adams.* Boston: Houghton Mifflin.

Tyack, D. B. (1976). Ways of seeing: An essay on the history of compulsory schooling. *Harvard Educational Review, 46*(3), 355–389.

Vinovskis, M. A. (1983). Quantification and the analysis of American antebellum education. *Journal of Interdisciplinary History, 13*(4), 761–786.

Vinovskis, M. A. (1996). An analysis of the concept and uses of systemic educational reform. *American Educational Research Journal, 33*(1), 53–85.

Vinovskis, M. A. (1999). Do federal compensatory education programs really work? A brief historical analysis of Title I and Head Start. *American Journal of Education, 107*(3), 187–209.

Vinovskis, M. A. (2000). An elusive science: The troubling history of education research. *American Journal of Education, 108*(3), 253–256.

EDUCATIONAL ANTHROPOLOGY

Like any discipline, educational anthropology is a network of individual scholars, a kinship group, linked by common theoretical frameworks and research interests as well as reflected in the professional organization's structure through which it disseminates scientific inquiry. The field begins, grows, and changes through the work of these scholars as knowledge and methodologies of research are passed down through formal and informal mentoring of the next generation of scholars. These networks of researchers are reflected in the organizational structure of the field, in this case, in the Council on Anthropology and Education (CAE), a unit within the American Anthropological Association (AAA). This entry examines the history, organization, and key theoretical, methodological, and empirical contributions of the field.

The Formative Years

The anthropology of education is an interdisciplinary field that has its roots in nineteenth-century anthropology and became structured over the course of the twentieth century through the engagement of anthropologists and educators as they examined notions of culture, particularly in non-western groups.

Anthropological interests in educational problems, practices, and institutions can be traced back to Edgar I. Hewett's articles in the *American Anthropologist* titled "Anthropology and Education" (1904) and "Ethnic Factors in Education" (1905). In these papers, Hewett recommended the incorporation of ethnological and cultural history within the course of study in public schools, joint meetings of national education and anthropology societies to discuss mutual problems, and the inclusion of anthropological studies in the training of teachers.

As early as 1913 Maria Montessori drew on work in physical anthropology to inform her work with children, which stressed a developmental process, respect for individual differences in growth and function, and the study of local conditions in the development of her notion of "pedagogical anthropology." In his 1928 *Anthropology and Modern Life,* Franz Boas, the father of American anthropology, argued for anthropological research to be used by educators to better understand cultural notions of child development.

From the 1890s through the early 1950s anthropologists engaged in intensive fieldwork in small communities using participant observation of everyday life to understand the culture or ways of life of a particular group. Using these ethnographic methods enabled researchers to detail what they believed to be the "total way of life" of a group including the use of language, enculturation of their young, and ways formal and informal education took place within these groups. Anthropologists working during this time period were particularly interested in cultural maintenance (how cultures were continued across generations) as well as cultural acquisition (how people got culture). These researchers often reported on the life-cycle development from birth through childhood, adolescence, young adulthood, and elderhood and focused on learning and teaching in all aspects of the culture. Much of this early descriptive work was an effort to capture indigenous cultures before they were transformed through contact with other cultures, particularly western cultures.

Elizabeth Eddy (1985) described 1925 through 1954 as the formative years of anthropology and education, when many anthropologists were engaged in studies documenting formalized systems of education and the enculturation of the child. Major anthropologists contributing to this body of work include Gregory Bateson, Ruth Benedict, Franz Boas, John Dollard, John Embree, E. E. Evans-Pritchard, Felix Keesing, Ralph Linton, Bronislaw Malinowski, Margaret Mead, Hortense Powdermaker, Paul Radin, Robert Tedfield, Edward Sapir, W. Lloyd Warner, and John Whiting.

Social anthropologist Ruth Benedict, a student of Franz Boas at Columbia University, wrote *Patterns of Culture* (1934), a major work in the personality and culture school, arguing that each culture had a "personality" consisting of certain traits that were encouraged or enculturated into individuals within the culture.

When Benedict was on the faculty at Columbia, she worked with Margaret Mead, whose research also focused on personality and culture as well as childrearing in works such as *Coming of Age in Samoa* (1928) and *Sex and Temperament in Three Primitive Societies* (1935).

In the 1940s when studies of culture and personality were central to anthropological work, a six-year social-action research program on Indian personality, education, and administration was initiated by the U.S. Department of the Interior and Commissioner of Indian Affairs John Collier. It was first established in cooperation with the Committee on Human Development, University of Chicago, and later with the Society for Applied Anthropology. This interdisciplinary study to collect scientific data from 1,000 Indian children in twelve reservations representing five tribes became the basis for preparing recommendations to improve policies in Indian education and administration.

The work of these anthropologists who examined education within cultures was shared in a series of conferences between 1930 and 1954, thus facilitating the growth of the field of anthropology and education. In 1930, Edward Sapir and John Dollard conducted a seminar on the impact of culture on personality at Yale University. This initiative was followed in 1934 with the Hanover Conference on Human Relations, in which researchers examined enculturation and socialization of the child, and in that same year, the Education and Culture Contacts Conference at Yale where A. R. Radcliffe-Brown and others addressed the theme of adapting education to individual and community needs. Two years later, Felix Keesing organized a five-week study conference at the University of Hawaii in which sixty-six educators and social scientists from twenty-seven nations examined problems of education and adjustment among peoples of the Pacific.

While much of the early work was done with non-western groups, anthropologists and sociologists began ethnographic examinations of educational settings in the United States with mainstream communities. Two examples of early work within these school and community settings are Robert and Helen Lynd's classic *Middletown: A Study in Modern American Culture* (1929) and August Hollingshead's *Elmtown's Youth* (1949).

During the first half of the twentieth century, relationships between anthropologists and educators in major universities laid the groundwork for the field of anthropology of education. Hervé Varenne noted that by the 1930s courses in anthropology were offered as part of the foundations of education, with anthropologist Margaret Mead establishing a long association with Columbia University's Teachers College. After World War I, researchers increasingly turned their attention to communities, schools, and other institutions in industrialized societies with the aim of understanding the structures and socialization of youth in these community and school contexts. Work in culture and personality diminished as psychological anthropology and cognitive anthropology became a focus of study among anthropologists. For example, the work of John and Beatrice Whiting, cultural anthropologists at Harvard University, documented comparative child development and the influence of culture on human development. Perhaps their most well-known work, *Children of Six Cultures: A Psycho-Cultural Analysis* (1963), which examines childrearing and children's behavior through ethnographic data collected in Mexico, India, Kenya, New England, Okinawa, and the Philippines, is a classic study in the field.

There was a growing interest in the social sciences on inequalities in education for specific cultural groups of children and the role of educators in perpetuating these unequal consequences of schooling. Anthropologists used ethnographic methods in educational contexts to critically examine how schooling was enacted in communities for different groups of students. In 1949, Mead organized the Educational Problems of Special Cultural Groups Conference at Teachers College. Solon Kimball joined the faculty in 1953, as did other anthropologists, to establish a strong anthropological presence at that institution that continues in its current program in anthropology and education. Stanford, Harvard, and the University of Pennsylvania developed in parallel, with anthropologists working within schools of education training the next generations of researchers and K–12 teachers equipped with anthropological understandings of schooling for diverse groups of children.

Organizational History of the Council on Anthropology and Education

From 1950 to 1970, the field of anthropology moved to a more formal organizational structure first through a series of conferences and finally to the founding of the Council on Anthropology and Education in 1970. This section describes events within this period, incorporating discussions of major themes and research contributions within this emerging field.

A figural event for the field of anthropology and education was the June 9–14, 1954, conference sponsored by the Carnegie Corporation at Carmel Valley Ranch, California, which brought together twenty-two anthropologists and educators to examine the relevance and relationships between these two fields and explore ways each could contribute to the other. Formal papers were presented by James Quillen, George Spindler, Bernard Siegel, John Gillin, Solon Kimball, Cora DuBois, C. W. M. Hart, Dorothy Lee, Jules Henry, and Theodore Brameld. Anthropologists who participated in the discussions included Margaret Mead, Alfred Kroeber, Louise Spindler, and Roland and Marianne Force. Participants included educators William Cowley, Lawrence Thomas, Arthur Coladarci, Fannie Shaftel, Lawrence Frank, Hilda Taba, and Robert Bush, and psychologist William Martin.

According to George Spindler, the 1954 conference consolidated and systematically focused attention on educational issues that had been raised in earlier anthropological work, but not pursued. In that sense, the conference was the beginning of the formal period of an anthropology of education. The original papers presented at the conference, as well as the substance of the discussions, were compiled in Spindler's *Education and Anthropology* (1955). In his introductory chapter, Spindler summarized ways anthropology could contribute to understanding educational problems, arguing for more analysis of the interrelationships between educational systems, educative processes, and social structures, as well as for inclusion in the foundations of education courses within teacher and administrator training programs. He argued that since anthropologists in the United States had only recently been interested in their own society, anthropological contributions to understanding educational problems in American society had yet to be made.

The American Anthropological Association (AAA), with support from the U.S. Office of Education, the National Science Foundation, and other foundation sources, held a series of conferences in the 1960s where anthropologists and educators began to systematically focus on educational issues and contexts. At the request of Francis A. J. Ianni, Deputy Commissioner for Research in the U.S. Office of Education, Stanley Diamond (Syracuse University) initiated the Culture of Schools Program, sponsoring a 1966 Culture of Schools Conference at Syracuse University, the first of two conferences sponsored by the AAA. The program included statements from participants who provided early organizational leadership to the emerging field of anthropology and education: Jacquetta H. Burnett (University of Illinois), John H. Chilcott (University of Arizona), Elizabeth Eddy (Hunter College), Estelle S. Fuchs (Hunter College), Fred Gearing (University of California, Riverside), Solon T. Kimball (Teachers College, Columbia University), Eleanor Leacock (Polytechnic Institute of Brooklyn), and Murray Wax (University of Kansas).

After a year and a half, the Culture of Schools Program was transferred to AAA, while maintaining the support of the Office of Education, where it became the Program in Anthropology and Education (PAE), which was directed by Fred Gearing and Murray Wax from 1967 to 1969. Under the auspices of PAE, Gearing and Wax used Wenner-Gren funding to initiate a set of major and minor conferences including AAA's second sponsored conference, the National Conference on Anthropology and Education, which was held in Miami Beach on May 9–12, 1968. The organizing committee was composed of Malcolm Collier (AAA's National Science Foundations funded Anthropology Curriculum Study Project), Charles Frantz (AAA), Frederick Gearing (University of California, Riverside), and Murray Wax (University of Kansas).

Nine papers were presented at this conference by early leaders in the field: Daniel G. Freedman (University of Chicago), Frederick Gearing, John C. Holt (Boston University), Dell Hymes (University of Pennsylvania), Vera John (Yeshiva University), Martin Orans (University of California, Riverside), Theodore

Parsons (University of California, Berkeley), Sherwood Washburn (University of California, Berkeley), and Murray Wax. Anthropologists Solon Kimball (Teachers College, Columbia University), Eleanor Leacock (Polytechnic Institute of Brooklyn), Robert Textor (Stanford University), and Harry Wolcott (University of Oregon) served as respondents.

Conference participants proposed two specific tasks that were aimed at continuing to articulate this emerging field of anthropology of education to a broader audience: (1) a bibliography of source materials in the field of anthropology of education, and (2) a summer institute. These sponsored conferences established a system of communication among anthropologists and educators interested in the emerging field of anthropology and education.

A significant event in the formation of the field was the 1968 meetings of AAA in Seattle, Washington, where a session called the Ethnography of Schools was organized by John Singleton and chaired by George Spindler. This session brought together educational anthropologists from the Stanford and Columbia groups around the anthropological study of educational settings. An ad hoc group on Anthropology and Education was established and chaired by Solon Kimball. Over 120 AAA fellows and members formally constituted this group and established procedures for the immediate election of a permanent steering committee. Conrad Arensberg, Dell Hymes, George Spindler, Robert Textor, and Sherwood Washburn served as members of the temporary steering committee. While senior scholars known for their work in educational anthropology such as the Whitings, the Spindlers, Mead, Robert Havighurst, and Hollingshead were not participants in this meeting, some were represented by their students, Harry Wolcott and Charles Harrington. The ad hoc group formally established four working committees of persons whose special interests involved research and development work in (1) the cultural, linguistic, and biological study of school and community; (2) minority curricula improvement; (3) the training of anthropologists and educational anthropologists; and (4) the preparation of teachers and school administrators and curriculum planning incorporating anthropological perspectives.

This organizational meeting at the fall 1968 AAA conference was followed up by a February 8, 1969, steering committee meeting in Chicago where Murray Wax served as the chair and first president of the newly formed Council on Anthropology and Education. He wrote the final draft of CAE constitution that was published in May 1970 in the first volume of the *Council on Anthropology and Education Newsletter.* This inaugural newsletter summarized the history of the field of anthropology and education by stating that CAE members had carried out John Napoleon Brinton Hewitt's 1904–1905 recommendation that anthropologists and educational researchers work together in the areas of their common interests. These activities included organizing symposia presentations for the American Anthropological Association, the American Educational Research Association, and other professional associations. The newsletter listed the group's research interests as the following: minority-group educational programs built on cultural difference rather than cultural pathology models, schools as social and cultural systems, relationships of education and poverty, generational conflict and cultural transmission, teaching of anthropology, linguistic and cognitive aspects of education, and what might be called "applied educational anthropology" in school systems, teaching materials, and teacher-training programs. It was the stated expectation of those involved in the organization of the Council on Anthropology and Education that research from those areas should contribute significantly to the development of anthropological theory and to the practical improvement of education.

In March 1970, in an effort to share their work with the educational research community, a number of anthropologists presented an overview of the field at the American Educational Research Association meeting through a symposium organized by Harry Wolcott, Anthropological Approaches in Educational Research, which included work representing major themes of the anthropological research at that time: sociolinguistic analyses of classroom interaction, cultural conflict in classrooms, ethnographic approaches to teacher education, and ethnographic methods in curriculum evaluation.

By 1971 the interest groups identified by the fledgling CAE in 1968 became the first four standing committees of the Council on Anthropology and Education: (1) Anthropological Studies of Schools and Culture, (2) Cognitive and Linguistic Studies, (3) Graduate and Undergraduate Education in Anthropology (changed to Teaching Anthropology in 1972 and later to Anthropology of Post-secondary Education), (4) Minority Affairs (with divisions, including Black, Chicano, Native American, Women's Studies). Two more committees were later added: (5) Anthropology, Education, and the Museum, and (6) Preparation of Educators and Educational Materials.

Over the years, these committees changed names, and new committees were added to reflect the research interests of constituent members. The committee structure of the organization has remained relatively stable since its inception in the early 1970s and has served to provide its membership a means to contribute to the scientific program at the national meetings of CAE within the larger American Anthropological Association. Many of the papers presented were published in the *Anthropology and Education Quarterly,* the official journal of the CAE that is disseminated to a broader academic community. This journal began as the council on *Anthropology and Education Newsletter* in 1970, became the *Council on Anthropology and Education Quarterly* in 1974, and four years later was renamed *Anthropology and Education Quarterly,* a name it has maintained today.

The group committed to teaching of anthropology in PreK–12 settings as well as the preparation of resources and curricular materials began its work immediately with two annotated bibliographies, *Anthropology and Education: A General Bibliography* (1970) and *Anthropology and Education Annotated Bibliographic Guide* (1974), both intended to survey the anthropological research focused on formal and informal education. Those scholars committed to infusing anthropology throughout the K–16 curriculum organized sessions on undergraduate and graduate education in anthropology and teaching anthropology, as well as sessions for teachers on the contributions of anthropological research on education for their work in the classroom. Sessions like these continue to be offered by members of the Council on Anthropology and Education community.

Establishing the Field

While the field was engaged in organizational development, its contributing anthropologists and educators used ethnographic methods to study informal and formal educational settings. Anthropologists examined ways culture was transmitted through teaching and learning in communities and schools. As a reaction to the models of cultural deficit and cultural disadvantage that were at the core of the 1960s "War on Poverty," anthropologists used their skills to examine cultural transmission in minority communities as well as the culture of mainstream schooling and the ways these cultures clashed.

Anthropologists of education argued that by understanding "culturally different students" research could inform teachers' work within these communities. This research took the form of more traditional ethnography in schools and other educational settings with a focus on cultural transmission and anthropological studies of cognition and learning. Other anthropologists at the time used close analysis of language and interactions in classrooms to understand cultural mismatches between students and their teachers. In addition, some researchers worked extensively with teachers to use the tools of ethnographic inquiry teachers to understand cultures within their own classrooms as a means to provide more culturally congruent schooling for students from minority communities. A related theme in the field was the inclusion of anthropology in the K–12 and higher education curriculum to more broadly prepare citizens to understand ways culture is created, transmitted, and adapted in their daily lives. A brief discussion of each of these thematic strands in the anthropology and education literature follows.

Traditional structural functionalist ethnographies conducted in schools examined school structures as well as the relationships between communities and schools. Jules Henry, an anthropologist at Columbia, was an early contributor to the field through a number of articles focused on how learning and teaching takes place in cross-cultural settings. In his classic *Culture Against Man* (1963), Henry used anthropological methods to examine American culture of the 1950s, arguing that the competitive, hierarchical processes and interactions in schools he observed limited the development of students' critical and creative abilities. This book influenced later ethnographers of schooling in work such as Estelle Fuch's *Teachers Talk* (1967), Louis Smith and William Geoffrey's *The Complexities of an Urban Classroom* (1968), Philip Jackson's *Life in Classrooms* (1968), Elizabeth Burke Leacock's *Teaching and Learning in City Schools* (1969), Elizabeth Eddy's *Becoming a Teacher: The Passage to Professional Status* (1969), and Gerry Rosenfield's *Shut Those Thick Lips!: A Study of Slum School Failure* (1971).

Harry Wolcott's *A Kwakiutl Village and School* (1967) and Alan Peshkin's *Growing Up American: Schooling and the Survival of Community* (1978), as well as his later book *God's Choice: The Total World of a Christian Fundamentalist School* (1986), provided insights into how culture is learned, transmitted, and perhaps resisted through sociocultural interactions among participants within school structures and processes. Theoretical foundations for the field at that time included George Spindler's 1963 *Education and Culture: An Anthropological Approach,* his 1974 *Education and Cultural Process: Toward an Anthropology of Education,* Murray Wax, Stanley Diamond, and Fred Gearing's 1971 *Anthropological Perspectives on Education,* Gearing's 1973 *Where We Are and Where We Might Go: Steps Toward a General Theory of Cultural Transmission,* Solon Kimball's 1974 *Culture and the Educative Process*, and Friedman Hansen's 1979 *Sociocultural Perspectives on Human Learning: Foundations of Educational Anthropology.*

The body of studies focused on the anthropology of learning or cognitive anthropological included early essays by Hansen, the Spindlers, and Erik Erickson on the centrality of learning to the concept of culture and in the discipline of anthropology. Erickson argued that deliberately taught cognitive learning should be of interest to anthropologists with a shift to the individual learning within the learning environment. Jean Lave's anthropological work on situated cognition, or how people use knowledge and problem-solving skills within formal learning contexts such as craft apprenticeships, serves as one example of the way anthropologists use observational data to understand learning and cognition in everyday life.

Another approach to educational anthropological research used sociolinguistic analyses of classroom communications to explain the relationships between classroom interactions, culturally based communications, and school success and failure. Studies looked at cultural differences and cultural congruities or lack thereof between minority students and their mainstream teachers. Courtney Cazden, Vera John, and Dell Hymes's 1972 *Functions of Language in the Classroom* served as a key text for the examination of how verbal and nonverbal language is used by teachers to communicate with students in classrooms, particularly with students from different cultural groups. Educational anthropologists used these sociolinguistic, microethnographic approaches to examine teacher-student classroom interactions. For example, Kathryn Hu-pei Au and Cathie Jordan's work at the Kamehameha Early Education Program (KEEP) in Honolulu was central to the work that used participant observation and microanalysis of videotapes to argue that poor school achievement by many minority children is related to the nature of the teacher-student classroom interactions. Gerald Mohatt and Frederick Erickson reported in 1981 how they used microethnography to examine differences in native and nonnative social interactional differences in two first-grade classrooms in northern Ontario in classrooms of Odawa and Ojibwa children. They argued that the different cultural backgrounds of the teachers established differences in the cultural organization of social relationships in that classroom, resulting in two different participation structures—with the native teacher providing a more culturally congruent setting that allowed more pauses, or "wait time," for increased student participation.

These studies all argued for a closer examination of schooling for culturally different (from mainstream White middle-class) students, and they called for culturally responsive pedagogies. Spindler's 1982 *Doing the Ethnography of Schooling: Educational Anthropology in Action* is a compilation of the first ethnographic studies in the field of anthropology and education. This volume served as a classic for students in schools of education. Frederick Erickson and Jeffrey Shultz's 1982 *The Counselor as Gatekeeper: Social Interaction in Interviews* used this microanalytic approach to interactions between educational counselors and their clients, illustrating differential treatment based on the extent to which the client shared similar verbal and nonverbal communication styles.

Shirley Brice Heath's ethnographic study *Ways With Words* (1983) analyzed styles of questioning and speech interaction between parents and their children in two communities, Trackton, a working-class Black community, and Roadville, a middle-class White community. Her study documented differential use of language in these communities and involved teachers in analyzing and using community-based interactional styles with Trackton students. Her work with teachers as inquirers of their own contexts and practices demonstrated a model for training teachers to look ethnographically at their own classrooms and communities to better understand how to interact in ways that were culturally congruent with their students.

In contrast to micro-ethnographies of social interactions, anthropologists such as John Ogbu used macro community and historical analyses to explain variations in minority student performance. Ogbu's work, spanning almost three decades, began with *The Next Generation: An Ethnography of Education in an Urban Neighborhood* (1974), which theorized variation in minority student school performance through an analysis of the historical and cultural context of the particular group. He argued that minority students vary in their status as historically subordinated or migrant groups, and categorized them into (1) autonomous minorities who were born in the United States and no longer experience systematic discrimination despite cultural differences from mainstream; (2) voluntary immigrants or immigrant minorities who moved to the United States for economic, political, or religious opportunities and buy into mainstream work ethic and success in school as a means for economic advancement; and (3) involuntary or castelike immigrant minority groups incorporated into society forcibly either through conquest or colonization, and having experienced a long history of subordination and oppression based on the historical conditions and experience of the particular cultural group in the United States, and face a job ceiling constructed by a racist society that puts limits on their economic opportunities even if they are academically successful. Signithia Fordham built on Ogbu's theories in her

1991 ethnographic study of Black students' academic success at "Capital High School," a school located in a predominantly African American section of Washington, D.C. Fordham found that many students were coping with the burden of "acting White" and did poorly because they had difficulty reconciling school achievement and maintenance of African American cultural identity. What she called "fictive kinship" or "sense of peoplehood" was a compelling reason for these Black students to assign more importance to success with their peers and community than to success in the school community.

Also utilizing Ogbu's framework in an ethnographic study, Margaret Gibson conducted an ethnography, published as *Accommodation Without Assimilation: Sikh Immigrants in an American High School* (1988), in which she found that Sikhs in America were more serious about school and attained higher academic achievement than their European American classmates. She attributed their success to parental expectations, as well as to cultural values that placed respect for family and authority at a premium and enabled them to maintain their own community culture while accommodating successfully to Western school structures and practices. These studies that examined cultural transmission, learning and cognition, cultural differences between students and school contexts, and various theories to explain differential success of minority students were shared not only with the scientific community within the anthropological and educational spheres, but also with practicing teachers and administrators.

Critical and Postmodern Anthropology of Education

Since the late 1970s, educational anthropologists have been influenced by critical and postmodern theorists who reject claims to an objective truth, call into question functionalist notions of culture, and critique anthropologists' traditional roles in the communities they have studied as well as their representations of these communities. Critiques from within mainstream anthropology have raised issues around positionality, reflexivity, objectivity, and representation in ethnographic work in works such as George Marcus and Michael Fischer's *Anthropology as Cultural Critique: An Experimental*

Moment in the Human Sciences (1986) and James Clifford and George Marcus's *Writing Culture: The Poetics and Politics of Ethnography* (1986).

During this same time period, macro-level theories of economic stratification, social class, power, and cultural structure—and the role of schooling in transmitting these class and cultural structures as well as resistance to them—shifted the focus of anthropologists of education toward more critical analyses of school contexts. Critical educational theories in the works of Michael Apple and Henry Giroux were particularly influential in the United States. In addition, theorists and researchers in the new sociology of education in Europe began using observational methods to understand how the explicit and implicit curriculum in schools transmitted cultural understandings to students. Jerome Karabel and Albert Halsey's *Power and Ideology in Education* (1977), Paul Willis's *Learning to Labour: How Working Class Kids Get Working Class Jobs* (1977), and Nell Keddie's *Classroom Knowledge* (1977) provided theoretical and empirical foundations for later critical ethnographies such as Dorothy Holland and Maragaret Eisenhart's *Educated in Romance* (1990), Michelle Fine's *Framing Dropouts: Notes on the Politics of an Urban High School* (1991), and Douglas Foley's *Learning Capitalist Culture: Deep in the Heart of Tejas* (1990). Critical, postmodern, poststructural, and feminist theories and analyses problematized traditional understandings of culture, how researchers study "the other," and the politics of representation.

Ethnography and Qualitative Research in Education

Educational research during the 1960s and 1970s was largely dominated by quantitative designs from psychology. Dissatisfied with analyses of educational problems that largely ignored local classroom and school contexts, the field of anthropology and education during this time captured the attention of educational researchers moving toward a closer examination of the culture of schooling and other educational settings. Using ethnographic and qualitative methods for this work, created a need for more attention to these methods in schools of education. Anthropologists of

education were ready to fill this need through their commitment to explicitly teach these methods to researchers and doctoral students.

Anthropologists of education have been at the forefront of the field of ethnography and qualitative research in education. The centrality of ethnographic methods in the formative years of the Council on Anthropology and Education continues to influence the work of scholars today. Anthropologists learning their craft in the early and mid-twentieth century typically received little formal training in research methods, so there were few texts to guide education researchers in ethnographic methods. Pertti Pelto and Gretel Pelto's *Anthropological Research: The Structure of Inquiry* (1978), Hortense Powdermaker's *Stranger and Friend: The Way of an Anthropologist* (1966), James Spradley's *The Ethnographic Interview* (1979) and *Participant Observation* (1980), and Rosalie Wax's *Doing Fieldwork: Warnings and Advice* (1971) provided some guidance for new ethnographers.

Frederic Erickson's 1973 essay "What Makes School Ethnography 'Ethnographic'" and his 1986 article "Qualitative Methods in Research on Teaching" articulated the ethnographic method in educational settings. Harry Wolcott's 1975 "Criteria for an Ethnographic Approach to Research in Schools" began his long involvement with training researchers in ethnographic methods. Judith Goetz and Margaret LeCompte's *Ethnography and Qualitative Design in Education Research* (1984) is now a classic text in research design grounded in anthropological traditions. Margaret LeCompte, Wendy Millroy, and Judith Pressle's 1992 *Handbook of Qualitative Research in Education* is another contribution to the field of qualitative research methods. Corrine Glesne and Alan Peshkin's *Becoming Qualitative Researchers: An Introduction* (1992) used an anthropological field-method framework aimed at beginning researchers in the field, and it continues to be used in both undergraduate and graduate introductory courses in qualitative research methods.

Since the early 1990s, there has been an explosion of resources in the field of ethnography and qualitative research more generally, with hundreds of texts available to address general qualitative research methods as well as specific approaches to research such as narrative, interview research of varying types, ethnomethodology, and arts-based research. This continually expanding literature certainly informs the way anthropologists of education now do their work, as is evidenced by the last decade of articles in the Council on Anthropology and Education's journal, *Anthropology and Education Quarterly.*

While the original research interests of educational anthropologists of the 1960s and 1970s remain—cultural transmission and acquisition, ethnographic approaches to schools and their communities, cultural contexts of language, literacy and cognition, multicultural and multilingual education as well as work focused on specific groups (e.g., Blacks, Latinos) and gender in education—the theories and methods informing this work have become more complex and nuanced, thus leading to work that is reflective, reflexive, and in collaboration with community members.

Kathleen deMarrais

See also Critical Theory; Educational Research, History of; Postmodernism; Qualitative Research

Further Readings

Cazden, C. B. (1972). *Functions of language in the classroom.* New York: Teachers College Press.

Eddy, E. M. (1985). Theory, research, and application in educational anthropology. *Anthropology and Education Quarterly, 16*(2), 83–104.

Erickson, F. (1984). What makes school ethnography "ethnographic"? *Anthropology and Education Quarterly, 15,* 51–66.

Fine, M. (1991). *Framing dropouts: Notes on the politics of an urban public high school.* Albany: State University of New York Press.

Gibson, M. (1988). *Accommodation without assimilation: Sikh immigrants in an American high school.* Ithaca, NY: Cornell University Press.

Heath, S. B. (1983). *Ways with words: Language, life, and work in communities and classrooms.* New York: Cambridge University Press.

Henry, J. (1963). *Culture against man.* New York: Random House.

Jackson, P. (1968). *Life in classrooms.* New York: Teachers College Press.

Kimball, S. T. (1974). *Culture and the educative process: An anthropological perspective.* New York: Teachers College Press.

Ogbu, J. U. (1974). *The next generation: An ethnography of education in an urban neighborhood.* New York: Academic Press.

Peshkin, A. (1978). *Growing up American: Schooling and the survival of community.* Chicago: University of Chicago Press.

Peshkin, A. (1986). *God's choice: The total world of a fundamentalist Christian school.* Chicago: University of Chicago Press.

Singleton, J. (1984). Origins of the AEQ: Rituals, myths, and cultural transmission. *Anthropology and Education Quarterly, 18*(4), 312–334.

Smith, L. M., & Geoffrey, W. (1968). *The complexities of an urban classroom: An analysis toward a general theory of teaching.* New York: Holt, Rinehart, & Winston.

Spindler, G. (1955). *Education and anthropology.* Stanford, CA: Stanford University Press.

Wax, M. L., Diamond, S., & Gearing, F. O. (1971). *Anthropological perspectives on education.* New York: Basic Books.

Wolcott, H. (1967). *A Kwakiutl village and school.* New York: Holt, Rinehart, & Winston.

Wolcott, H. (1975). Criteria for an ethnographic approach to research in schools. *Human Organization, 34*(2), 111–127.

EDUCATIONAL EQUITY: GENDER

For many years, researchers have been documenting the multiple ways in which girls and women are "shortchanged" in their schooling experiences. Today, there continue to be differences in schooling access, experiences, opportunities, and outcomes for girls and women in this country, and gender inequities can be found from grade school to graduate school. In spite of many years and many attempts to eradicate these inequities, girls and women still receive less recognition and encouragement in the classroom, fewer questions from and interactions with their teachers, and less representation—on classroom bulletin boards as well as in the curriculum.

Over the course of their schooling experiences, these inequities take their toll on female students, combining to insure that they receive less support for their academic confidence and success than male students receive. While there have been many advances for girls and women—socially, politically, economically, and educationally—these advances sometimes mask the continuing discrepancies they face.

Today, girls are getting better grades, and women are entering college in increasing numbers; however, gender equity still has not been achieved. For example, although girls are performing better on math and science achievement tests, they continue to score lower on both verbal and mathematics sections of high-stakes tests such as the SAT, Advanced Placement exams, and the GRE. And while women are entering medical schools in increasing numbers, they continue to be concentrated in particular specializations that are female friendly and lower paying. Before these gender inequities can be addressed, an understanding is needed of the subtle, and not so subtle, ways in which girls and women continue to experience discrimination in their access, experiences, opportunities, and outcomes in schools and classrooms. This entry provides some background on gender discrimination, looks at Title IX legislation and its impact, and discusses other potential ways to address continuing discrimination.

Background

Gender discrimination and inequalities have been present in U.S. schools for centuries, largely reflective of similar patterns of discrimination and inequality present in the society at large. This can result in different experiences, expectations, and outcomes for many students. The very idea that girls and women should have access to education, especially to higher education, is in itself a relatively recent development in U.S. history. Until late in the 1800s, most women had few opportunities for education beyond elementary schooling, and when they were allowed to pursue advanced schooling, their access to schools and experiences there depended upon a system that was separate and unequal, much like that experienced by Blacks in this country. Today, girls are for the most part allowed to attend the same schools, take the same classes, and do the same activities as boys. However, the "equal" access girls currently enjoy often masks the continued discrimination and inequity that girls experience in schools.

There is much evidence about how traditional curricula, school and classroom interactions, and pedagogies work to disadvantage girls. The result is often a gender-biased classroom and/or school that (1) does not represent the experiences of girls and women in teaching and evaluation material; (2) instills the development of negative attitudes toward and thus an avoidance of particular content areas such as math and science in girls; (3) reinforces lower career aspirations for girls; (4) promotes and/or maintains an acceptance of sexual harassment; (5) relies heavily on gender stereotypes in classroom and school materials, practices, and/or interactions; (6) reinforces cultural stereotypes about girls and women; and (7) contributes to lower self-esteem for girls. These gender-based disparities and forms of discrimination do not apply to all classrooms and all schools, nor do they disadvantage all girls in the same ways, in part because identity is comprised of the intersection of many different characteristics. Social class can change the dynamics and impact of some of these factors, as can race and ethnicity or sexuality. In addition, many of these same disadvantages also apply to some male students, especially those who do not conform to traditional male gender norms.

Title IX

One of the more recent attempts to address gender discrimination was the passage of Title IX of the Education Amendments of 1972. Title IX is a comprehensive federal law that prohibits discrimination on the basis of sex in any federally funded education program or activity. Its principle objective is to prohibit the use of federal funding to support educational programs that engage in discriminatory practices on the basis of sex, and to provide individual students and teachers effective protection against those practices. The law requires educational institutions to create and maintain policies, practices, and programs that do not discriminate on the basis of sex. Under the scope of Title IX, it is expected that males and females will receive fair and equal treatment in all arenas of public schooling, including recruitment, admissions, course offerings and access, financial aid and scholarships, sexual harassment, extracurricular activities, counseling, and facilities and housing.

Impact of the Law

Today, many people believe that Title IX is at the heart of efforts to create gender equitable schools for girls and women by creating equality of opportunity and access, thus leading to equal outcomes. While the link between Title IX and increased opportunities for women and girls in athletics is well known, Title IX has also played a role in improving schooling for girls and women in areas such as access to higher education, career education, employment, learning environment, math and science, sexual harassment, standardized testing, and treatment of pregnant and parenting teens. The focus on athletics is much easier to document since it is easily understood and examined in relationship to numbers: numbers of teams for boys and girls, numbers of players, numbers of dollars spent, and numbers of scholarships awarded, for example. Other areas of improvement are not so easily defined and much less easily measured. Sexual harassment in the classroom and the representation of girls and women in teaching materials are more difficult to define, to measure, and to prove—leading to less of a focus on them.

In many ways, schools have made much progress in eliminating gender discrimination from their policies, programs, and practices. However, vestiges of bias, discrimination, stereotyping, and inequities remain intact, and they continue to have a powerful and often negative influence on many students. For example, it is rare today to see a specific policy prohibiting female students from enrolling in nontraditional vocational courses like auto mechanics or carpentry, and yet few girls and young women do enroll in them. In addition, while schools may offer equal numbers of sports for girls and boys, other inequities often remain—who has access to fields, practice spaces, or equipment; who is able to play on teams traditionally associated as "male" sports; and who has access to coaching opportunities, among other things.

Ongoing Issues

Sexual harassment is yet another example of continuing gender discrimination. Large numbers of girls and women continue to experience various forms of sexual harassment in their schooling experiences. Often, teachers and administrators do little to address these infractions. This is another issue that does not affect all girls and women in the same way. Young women who adhere to more traditional forms of femininity and whose bodies represent the desired cultural norm are less likely to experience such harassment. In addition, the sexual harassment and bullying of boys, especially of those boys who are perceived to be gay, represents another way in which gender discrimination extends beyond the experiences of girls and women. While many schools meet the letter of the law in relationship to Title IX, it is clear that in many ways many students still have not achieved educational equity based on gender.

Examples of continuing gender inequities often reflect the links between educational inequities and broader social and cultural assumptions and inequities. For example, while girls often receive higher grades than their male peers, especially early in their schooling, this may represent their reward for being quiet and passive in the classroom. Female students at all levels tend to be invisible members of classrooms, spectators for their male peers who dominate classroom talk and activities. Teachers often do not recognize that they are calling on and encouraging boys more often, providing more critical questioning and probing for boys, or utilizing materials that fail to represent girls and women or represent them inaccurately or inappropriately. Sexual harassment of girls, women, and gay students also represents broader social norms where such harassment is seen as inevitable and acceptable. When something becomes accepted practice, it becomes difficult to even recognize when it is happening. And when we do not recognize something, we cannot address it.

Today, gender equity is often defined as parity in quality and quantity for girls and boys within schools and classrooms. Thus, in order to achieve gender equity, girls should be represented in equal numbers to boys in all facets of schooling—from science classes to sports to scholarships. However, focusing on equal numbers allows us to ignore broader issues related to gender equity, and is one reason that Title IX is sometimes said to have failed. Even though girls and women may sit in classrooms in equal numbers to boys and men does not mean they are benefiting equally from those experiences. In addition, focusing specifically on girls and women allows us to obscure how gender discrimination may be affecting other students in our schools. Typically, discussion of gender inequality focuses on the experiences of girls and women in relationship to the experiences of boys and men. However, it is not as simple as looking at the experiences of girls and women. In relationship to schooling, this means that not all girls experience schooling in the same way. In addition, some boys are also affected by gender discrimination and inequality. For example, boys who are perceived to be gay certainly do not experience schooling in the same ways that their heterosexual peers do.

Another way to define gender equity might be as the ability for all students to attain full and fair participation in and benefit from their schooling experiences. Thus, gender equity in schooling may reflect a broader responsibility, embodied in a social justice model, where schools have an obligation to prepare all students to participate in, contribute to, and benefit from a democratic society through their schooling. This broader goal demands more than just equal numbers and more than just a focus on girls and women—it requires a shift in how schooling experiences are created.

Corrective Proposals

In this model, equity may be achieved by focusing not on equal numbers, but on equitable representation, treatment, and outcomes. In part this may require not treating people equally (in the same ways), but treating people differently, and in ways that are sensitive to their differences. Another positive step would be contextually equitable classrooms that are representative of the fluid and multiple meanings, experiences, and identities that students bring with them to school. This demands a shift in the cultural norms associated with schools and classrooms in order to truly move toward a more inclusive and responsive practice.

Such a shift might entail a reexamination of the competitive construction of schooling, and a move toward more collaboratively focused classrooms. Collaboration, rather than competition, forms the basis for the more equitable forms of participation that could benefit all students, not just girls and women. Such

an approach has the potential to recognize the value of each person's voice and knowledge. It also helps insure that knowledge becomes the construction and possession of all participants. Schools and classrooms may also need to address the individualistic and meritocratic nature of schooling that values and rewards some students at the expense of others, as well as how power and privilege are imbued in such a system. Rather than depicting gender equity as a battle between girls and boys, or men and women, it could be reframed as negotiating the interactions between them. Such a shift could provide more students with possibilities for enhanced learning and success.

A more inclusive and responsive practice would also demand attentiveness to the actions of teachers as well as students. Self-awareness is vital to this process; it is difficult to recognize bias without it. In addition to self-awareness, teachers and administrators must be aware of their actions—instructional practices, curricular and assessment tools and materials, classroom and school management, for example. Simple instructional practices, like the use of wait time, can make for more equitable practice. Using wait time before calling on a student for a response can allow the possibility of more voices participating in and benefiting from classroom interactions. In addition, using wait time after a student responds allows teachers to consider the strengths and weaknesses of a student's answer and provide all students with feedback that will push their critical thinking and analysis.

Schools must also address the invisibility, fragmentation, and selectivity of representations of girls and women in the curriculum and in classrooms. For example, discussion about how women were "given" the vote denies the work and suffering of women who "won" the vote; the use of Women's History Month allows schools to ignore their contributions the rest of the year and integrate this information more broadly into the curriculum; and glossy multicultural covers on textbooks often mask the actual integration of multicultural perspectives and information contained within them.

To address gender equity successfully requires examining how the dominant values, assumptions, and practices of schooling contribute to the success of some at the expense of others. Recognizing how these are constructed, mediated, and perpetuated by broader social and cultural norms and expectations is also important.

Sandra Spickard Prettyman

See also Title IX

Further Readings

Abu El-Haj, T. R. (2003). Challenging the inevitability of difference: Young women and discourses about gender equity in the classroom. *Curriculum Inquiry, 33,* 401–425.

American Association of University Women. (1992). *Shortchanging girls, shortchanging America.* Washington, DC: American Association of University Women.

American Association of University Women. (1998). *Gender gaps: Where schools still fail our children.* Washington, DC: American Association of University Women.

Clewell, B., & Campbell, P. (2002). Taking stock: Where we've been, where we are, where we're going. *Journal of Women and Minorities in Science and Engineering, 8,* 255–284.

Kimmel, M. (2004). *The gendered society.* New York: Oxford University Press.

Palmer, P. J. (1998). *The courage to teach.* San Francisco: Jossey-Bass.

Rofes, E. (2005). *A radical rethinking of sexuality and schooling: Status quo or status queer?* Lanham, MD: Rowman & Littlefield.

Sadker, D., & Sadker, M. (1995). *Failing at fairness: How America's schools cheat girls.* New York: Touchstone Press.

Stone, M., & Couch, S. (2004). Peer sexual harassment among high school students: Teachers' attitudes, perceptions, and responses. *High School Journal, 88,* 1–13.

United States Department of Education, National Center for Education Statistics. (2000). *Digest of Education Statistics, 1999.* Washington, DC: Office of Educational Research and Improvement.

EDUCATIONAL EQUITY: RACE/ETHNICITY

The history of U.S. education has included a record of inequity for and discrimination against many students and communities of color. The concept and practice of educational equity has been a long-developed and sought-after goal of educators, activists, parents, and students who aim to ensure that all students have equal educational opportunities. Those working toward educational equity have attempted to highlight current and historical policies and practices that have marginalized students, while also advocating for changes in perspective.

Unequal school funding, tracking, discipline, and the lack of access to a rigorous curriculum are some of the issues that have sustained the struggle for equity. Although this struggle is long-standing, research and scholarly debate over equity in education has gained increased attention in recent years. For scholars who engage in educational research, inform policy debate, and lead from within multiple school settings, as well as those who advocate for social and community change, educational equity remains an uncompleted goal. This entry provides a brief summary of the issues and three areas of contention: school financing, deficit-based research, and subtractive schooling.

A History of Inequity

Discussion of race and racism, a complex and contentious topic, is foundational in the conceptualizing of educational equity. Although a universally accepted definition of *race* does not exist, multiple scholars have described it as a socially constructed concept in which power and a racial hierarchy lead to institutionalized and systemic inequity. Moreover, many scholars expand upon the narrow conceptualization of race or racism as discrimination or inequity based on biology or skin color. They attempt to shift the discussion to systemic, institutional, or historical notions of discrimination or oppression, such as the way funding systems have been developed and implemented in a manner that disadvantages communities and students of color. For Latinas/os, scholars point to issues of immigration, language policy, and accountability systems as examples of educational policies and practices that continue to institute racial inequity.

While African American scholars as far back as W. E. B. Du Bois have written about the "problem of the color line," accurately pointing out structural and/or systemic inequity based on race, the problem has persisted into the twenty-first century. Some educational scholars contend that the problem no longer exists, but research demonstrates that inequity remains entrenched in U.S. educational systems, policies, and practice.

School Financing

Examples of blatant racism and gross inequity are ubiquitous in the history of U.S. education, a history that informs current educational inequity. Thus analyses of state educational finance systems provide evidence of long-standing and hard-fought civil rights litigation, years of legislative stalling, and ongoing grassroots political activism striving to change school finance policies. In Texas, most districts where property values and the taxes based on them are low have historically consisted of students of color, while districts with high values and greater tax revenues have predominantly consisted of White students.

The Texas legislature resisted a shift to a more equitable system until 1995, when concerned parents from some of the poorest neighborhoods in the state initiated a campaign of litigation, social action, and legislative battles to achieve an "equalized" system. Similar actions occurred in states such as New Jersey and New York. As with school funding issues, historical inequity continues to shape the current situation in areas such as access to rigorous and culturally relevant curricula, highly qualified and caring teachers, and higher educational opportunities.

Deficit-Based Research

Educational practice, policy, and research continue to marginalize children of color. Deficit-based research focuses on students, parents, or communities of color as the primary "problem" in educational underachievement. It blames the victim, often society's least powerful members, rather than placing the onus on the educational systems developed, implemented, and administered by predominantly White educators and educational leaders. Equity-oriented scholars contend that an inherent danger to democracy and social justice exists when policy makers, education leaders, and school administrators fail to critically analyze the effects of education policy on the most vulnerable of schoolchildren. When analyses and practice are based

on deficit notions, the danger to educational equity becomes more apparent.

Subtractive Schooling

In addition, subtractive schooling processes negate the home language, culture, traditions, and knowledge that students bring with them to the classroom, resulting in what equity scholars see as another barrier to educational equity. Rather than viewing students of color and their families as "holders and creators of knowledge," subtractive schooling practices further entrench school inequity and create challenges for advocates, researchers, and educators trying to make education more equitable for all school children.

Enrique Alemán, Jr.

See also African American Education; Civil Rights Movement; Critical Race Theory

See Visual History Chapter 15, Progressive Reform and Schooling

Further Readings

Du Bois, W. E. B. (1994). *The souls of Black folk*. New York: Dover. (Original work published 1903)

Omi, M., & Winant, H. (1994). *Racial formation in the United States: From the 1960s to the 1990s* (2nd ed.). New York: Routledge.

Spring, J. (1997). *The American school: 1642–2000* (5th ed.). New York: McGraw-Hill.

Valencia, R. R., & Black, M. S. (2002). "Mexican Americans don't value education!"—on the basis of the myth, mythmaking, and debunking. *Journal of Latinos and Education, 1*(2), 81–102.

Valenzuela, A. (1999). *Subtractive schooling: U.S.-Mexican youth and the politics of caring*. Albany: State University of New York Press.

Woodson, C. G. (1998). *The mis-education of the Negro*. Trenton, NJ: Africa World Press. (Original edition published 1933)

EDUCATIONAL INDICATORS

Educational indicators are pieces of evidence that provide information about the success of educational programs, policies, or processes. The indicators used in different instances depend on the goals that are being examined and the level of education that is being evaluated. There is no universally agreed upon set of educational indicators primarily because in a diverse society there is ambiguity regarding the aims of education. Educational indicators can be standard measures that are easily compared or nonstandard assessments used to judge the value of educational outcomes.

Reports of educational successes or failures are conclusions based on analyses of the indicators that were selected for the evaluation. Educational indicators exist at the societal level, the systemic (district or state) level, the school level, and the individual level. This entry looks at various kinds of indicators and what they purport to say about education.

Indicators of Social Aims of Education

Education is a fundamental institution of society and is frequently used as a vehicle to accomplish broad goals such as social justice and equity. Social justice refers to the equal treatment of citizens under the law, regardless of social class, race, religion, disability or other characteristics. Historically, underprivileged and minority groups have not had the same opportunities as the majority to attain a high quality education. In 1896 the U.S. Supreme Court decided in *Plessy v. Ferguson* that separate schools for racial groups were permissible if they were equal. However, in 1954 this ruling was overturned when the Supreme Court ruled in *Brown v. Board of Education* that "separate but equal was inherently unequal." The Court effectively set up racial integration of schools as an indicator of social justice.

Another social aim of education is equity, or the provision of equal opportunities for all. In the 1960s a number of studies concluded that family income had a large impact upon the educational attainment of students, and that children from low-income homes did not have an equal chance of success without some form of intervention. This ushered in an era of compensatory educational programs aimed at increasing opportunities for the success of high-poverty students. The Elementary and Secondary Education Act (ESEA)

of 1965 provided funding for schools to offer programs designed to "level the playing field" for these students. Multiple factors may be used as indicators of such broad-based social aims as social justice in education, because there is no simple or obvious way to measure attainment of these complex goals.

Indicators and School Accountability

Since the 1990s, educational reforms have stressed the need for greater school, district, and state accountability for results in education. In response to this push, most school districts and states began to develop systems for tracking and reporting school effectiveness. Prior to the passage of federal legislation, each state was left to decide whether to report student achievement to the public, and if so, to determine how.

In 1994, ESEA was reauthorized under the Improving America's Schools Act. In 2002, it was again reauthorized and renamed the No Child Left Behind Act. This federal legislation requires states to report on the academic achievement of students at each individual school. In compliance with No Child Left Behind, each state developed an accountability plan for reporting academic achievement to the public. School accountability systems usually focus on student achievement in core academic areas such as mathematics, reading or English, science, and social studies.

Although educational indicators of student achievement used by the states vary somewhat, student performance on standardized tests is the primary indicator of educational success in most accountability programs. These tests can be state criterion-referenced tests that measure attainment of state standards, or norm-referenced tests that compare student achievement to national norms. State accountability plans may also include other indicators, such as attendance, graduation, and/or dropout rates. The indicators selected by the states are weighted, in some fashion determined by the state, and used to calculate a school index score that reports the mean achievement of students at each school. This score is intended to inform the public about how effective each school is. No Child Left Behind also requires that a separate score be calculated for each subpopulation within the schools; this is meant to serve as an indicator of equity.

Other Systemic-Level Educational Indicators

There are a number of indicators of educational quality that are not frequently included in school accountability reports. Some of these include: high school graduation rates, scholarships issued, grade-point averages, advanced courses taken, student attitudes toward school, suspension rates, and portfolios of student work. Post–high school indicators of school success might include college graduation rates, incarceration rates, or income, but these measures are controversial as educational indicators because there are a number of other factors that could impact them besides the educational system.

States and school districts also use indicators to signal the success of specific educational programs. The indicators selected depend on the goals of the particular policies or programs under evaluation. For example, if a drug prevention program is being evaluated, indicators of success might include student attitudes toward drugs before and after participation in the program, self-reported use of drugs following participation in the program, comparison of rates of drug use for participants versus nonparticipants, or arrests for drug use in areas that have had the program in use for a while.

Indicators of the effectiveness of particular programs include measures of whatever outcome the program was expected to impact. Usually these outcomes are compared with outcomes of similar populations that did not participate in the program. Analysts use various techniques to interpret the meaning of the indicators, for example input-output models might be used to determine the cost effectiveness of various initiatives. For example, when determining the amount of state money to be appropriated to English as a Second Language (ESL) programs, indicators of success might include comparisons of grades or graduation rates of program participants and nonparticipants. A cost-benefit strategy might be employed to determine whether the benefits derived from the program (based on the indicators selected) merit the amount of investment required.

Individual-Level Indicators of Educational Attainment

Student growth from year to year in each major discipline is frequently considered an indicator of individual student learning. Standardized tests provide an easy means of assessing growth when they report the grade-level equivalent scores. A simple comparison of student scores from year to year can indicate student academic growth. Grades are also a commonly used indicator of student achievement. College admission departments frequently rely on a combination of student high school grade point average (GPA) and student score on a standardized admissions test such as the Scholastic Aptitude Test (SAT), which measures reasoning and verbal abilities, or the American College Test (ACT), which is designed to measure mastery of various subject areas. Some colleges use other indicators of student achievement or ability such as questionnaires, interviews, or portfolios to predict a student's potential for success in higher education.

"Authentic" Assessment Indicators

Educational indicators that do not involve test scores are used less frequently, regardless of the level or program, but are considered by some to be more authentic measures of student learning. Proponents of authentic assessment argue that test scores are not the only measures of student achievement, nor are they necessarily the most valid means of assessing competence or learning. Authentic indicators of achievement might include student performances, presentations, projects, demonstrations, oral or written discourses, or other demonstrations that allow an assessment of student mastery. Authentic educational indicators are sometimes collected in portfolios.

Critics of authentic indicators cite problems with the use of portfolios in education, including lack of clarity or uniformity in determining what goes into a portfolio and difficulty in arriving at a standard means of comparing the data from student to student and from school to school.

La Tefy G. Schoen

See also Compensatory Education; No Child Left Behind Act

Further Readings

Fitz-Gibbon, C., & Kochan, S. (2000). School effectiveness and education indicators. In C. Teddlie & D. Reynolds (Eds.), *The international handbook of school effectiveness research* (pp. 257–282). New York: Falmer Press.

Newmann, F., & Associates. (1996). *Authentic achievement: Restructuring schools for intellectual quality.* San Francisco: Jossey-Bass.

Pullin, D. (1999). Whose schools are these and what are they for? The rule of law in defining educational opportunity in American public education. In G. Cizek (Ed.), *Handbook of educational policy* (pp. 4–29). San-Diego, CA: Academic Press.

Serow, R., Castelli, P., & Castelli, V. (2000). *Social foundations of American education.* Durham, NC: Carolina Academic Press.

Thomas, J. Y., & Brady, K. (2005). Equity, accountability, and the evolving federal role in public education. *Review of Research in Education, 29,* 51–67.

EDUCATIONAL POLICY AND THE AMERICAN PRESIDENCY

While U.S. presidents currently play an important role in creating and shaping educational policy in the United States, this is a fairly recent phenomenon. Prior to the 1960s, presidents played a minor or nonexistent part in the creation of educational policy. This largely stems from limited federal involvement in education and a prevalent view during the nineteenth and early twentieth centuries that education was a state, not federal responsibility. This entry offers a brief historical review and discusses how presidents make policy in this area.

Historical Review

Beginning in the 1960s, presidents grew more involved in educational policy making, although interest varied across administrations. President John F. Kennedy spoke often about educational policy and proposed several bills, but it was not until Lyndon Johnson's Great Society that significant educational policy saw realization at the federal level. With the Elementary and Secondary Education Act and the Higher Education Act, both of 1965, President Johnson substantially changed the federal role in education.

While Johnson established a new model for presidential involvement in educational policy making, his next three successors did not follow suit. Presidents Richard Nixon, Gerald Ford, and Jimmy Carter largely ignored education throughout the 1970s. Even that decade's most significant educational milestone, the creation of the federal department of education in 1979, resulted not from President Carter's leadership but from heavy pressure from the National Education Association.

It was not until the 1980s that education again played a significant role in the American presidency, but the policy ideas differed from Johnson's. Ronald Reagan entered office vowing to reduce the federal role in education. He called for greater state responsibility and the dismantling of the Department of Education. His proposed policies included school choice, an amendment for voluntary school prayer (eventually the Equal Access Act), and block grants to states. With the 1983 release of *A Nation at Risk,* a report commissioned by Secretary of Education Terrel Bell, Reagan also called for educational excellence and reform in the form of a core curriculum, stronger school discipline, greater parental influence, and higher academic standards for teachers and students.

George H. W. Bush continued the momentum of these policies, particularly educational reform through school choice, greater state oversight of education, and academic standards. Through his educational summit with all fifty state governors in 1989, the latter policy received the most attention and eventually resulted in academic standards and assessments in nearly every state and a set of national educational standards.

These same standards became the centerpiece of President Bill Clinton's Goals 2000, which became law in 1994. Clinton's other major education policy, also approved in 1994, was School to Work, a program to provide high school students the opportunity to gain job-related skills. Although Clinton continued to focus on education throughout his terms, an opposition Congress elected in 1994 limited his ability to pass policies of any substance.

It was not until the No Child Left Behind Act (NCLB) of 2001 that another major educational policy (other than reauthorization bills) passed through Congress. In NCLB George W. Bush pressed for increased accountability, the closing of the achievement gap, a greater emphasis on reading and math, expanded school choice, and increased flexibility for state education agencies working under federal law; only the first three of these remained in the bill's final version in significant form.

How Presidents Make Policy

This review of presidents and educational policy making demonstrates the vehicles typically utilized by modern presidents in shaping education. First, and by definition, legislation represents the most important function of educational policy making in the presidency. Through it, presidents can define terms, set agendas, identify priorities, and establish standards of accountability. However, the involvement of presidents in educational legislation differs significantly. Some play an active role in the creation and passage of policy, while others merely preside over bills passed on their watch.

Second, presidents set policy through budgets. Although budgets do not necessarily define terms and establish standards, they most certainly identify priorities and set agendas. For example, efforts to reduce educational spending or implement block grants to the states send a clear message and produce different effects than spending increases and programmatic and/or categorical funds.

Third, presidents shape educational policy through executive orders and vetoes. For example, President Carter issued executive order 12232 aimed at using federal resources to strengthen historically Black colleges and universities. However, because of their narrow scope compared to legislation, executive orders as a policy-making tool are restricted. The veto, too, is a limited means compared to legislation, but the ability to prohibit the passage of some pieces of legislation while allowing others unquestionably shapes the policy landscape.

Finally, presidents shape educational policy through rhetoric. With the "bully-pulpit," presidents can champion some policy ideas over others, raise the nation's collective consciousness about educational issues and priorities, and define and popularize obscure concepts. For example, until President Reagan championed it, school choice remained a largely unknown policy idea. Through his rhetoric on school reform, Reagan brought choice into the educational debate as a legitimate, albeit controversial, policy option.

Dick Michael Carpenter II

See also Achievement Gap; Educational Reform; Equal Access Act; Federal and State Educational Jurisdiction; *Nation at Risk, A*; No Child Left Behind Act; School Choice; U.S. Department of Education

Further readings

Berube, M. R. (1991). *American presidents and education.* Westport, CT: Greenwood Press.

Finn, C. E. (1977). *Education and the presidency.* Lexington, MA: Lexington Books.

Hess, F. M., & McGuinn, P. J. (2002). Seeking the mantle of "opportunity": Presidential politics and the educational metaphor, 1964–2000. *Educational Policy, 16*(1), 72–95.

Keppel, F. (1995). The presidency and education: From Washington to Johnson. In K. W. Thompson (Ed.), *Problems and policies of American presidents* (pp. 335–350). Lanham, MD: University Press of America.

McAndrews, L. J. (1991). *Broken ground.* New York: Garland.

McAndrews, L. J., & Scott, K. M. (2002). Full circle: Elementary and secondary education politics and policies of Lyndon Johnson and Bill Clinton. *Social Science Journal, 39*, 53–64.

Michel, G. J. (1980). Success in national educational policy from Eisenhower to Carter. *Peabody Journal of Education, 57*(4), 223–233

Thompson, K. W. (Ed.). (1990). *The presidency and education.* Latham, MD: University Press of America.

EDUCATIONAL REFORM

Reform is a complex concept. As a noun, the term is used to describe changes in policy, practice, or organization. As a verb, *reform* refers to intended or enacted attempts to correct an identified problem. As an educational aspiration, its goal is to realize deep, systemic, and sustained restructuring of public schooling. Throughout the history of American public education, reform has been a means of conceiving and enacting visions of the collective good. From the establishment of common schools, through struggles over John Dewey's advocacy for public education as the primary method of social reform, to the far-reaching ambitions of the No Child Left Behind Act, reform efforts have responded to conditions of broad consequence that require ethically centered and future-oriented deliberation and action. This entry looks at three key approaches to reform and the challenges each faces, then outlines one strategy that might be used to achieve comprehensive reform.

Approaches to Reform

Reform movements in American public education have been framed by declarations of *crisis,* with rhetoric of intolerable urgency, and visions of *hope,* with inspirational themes to guide principled action. What constitutes crisis and hope has been largely shaped by three competing conceptions of educational reform—essentialism, progressivism, and holism. Reform can be glimpsed in terms of the controversies raised for educational principles, policy, and practice in American public schools.

Essentialism

For essentialists, educational philosophy and policy center on providing access for all citizens to a common literacy—a core of knowledge, skills, and values applicable across time and cultures. Heavily informed by idealist and realist philosophies, the concept of learning is conceived as an individual quest for excellence. Learners are to accumulate the knowledge base and higher level cognitive skills necessary to lead an intellectually, morally, economically, and socially productive life. The learner's progress is acknowledged and rewarded by his or her achievement and maintaining of positions in competitive hierarchies.

Public schools, through teachers as primary agents, lead individuals along a clearly defined path by articulating, modeling, and holding learners accountable to universally held standards. Teachers, as respected authorities, skillfully guide learners to humanity's highest thoughts (e.g., Socratic method, liberal studies) and

most useful methods for shaping the world around them (e.g., formal logic, critical reasoning). As all are offered the same invitation to excel, and variations in needs, abilities, and interests are understood and accepted as differences in personal motivation and merit. As all receive a common grounding in prevailing traditions and expectations, learners experience a sense of shared purpose and social unity.

Contemporary essentialists are critical of most aspects of public school performance. Current reform objectives and initiatives feature national standards for student achievement and teacher preparation (citing significant discrepancies in state-based standards and requirements); the emergence of a national curriculum (emphasizing advanced placement, "cultural literacy," "numeracy," and scientific reasoning); strengthening student, school, and district accountability for academic performance (emphasizing standardized tests); expanding school choice (emphasizing open enrollment, charter schools, and homeschooling); enhancing connections between educational and economic goals (emphasizing job-readiness and consumer education); and promoting "character development" (emphasizing role modeling, patriotism, and traditional social values).

Progressivism

Progressive educators also pursue universal access to personal fulfillment, but they work to promote social justice (emphasizing civil rights) and social change (emphasizing educational, economic, and political equity). Progressives draw from a broad range of philosophical perspectives, including romanticism, humanism, pragmatism, and social reconstructionism. Education remains largely an individual journey, but one leading to a broadened self-identity and heightened sense of social responsibility. The definition of valued knowledge is expanded beyond the intellectualized priorities of the essentialists, to assert inclusion of emotional dimensions of learning and to recognize education as an explicitly political endeavor.

The central purpose of public schooling shifts from preparing "the best and the brightest" to compete academically and economically to empowering those disadvantaged by their social position to pursue their educational goals and improve the quality of their lives. Knowledge is explicitly regarded as a form of power. Learners are encouraged to acquire knowledge to strengthen their skills in self-efficacy (e.g., values clarification and affective learning) and social advocacy (e.g., feminist and critical pedagogy). The progressive teacher guides learners through carefully designed experiences (i.e., developmentally appropriate and responsive to diverse learning styles) so that they might work together to construct knowledge (e.g., constructivist pedagogy and cooperative learning). Knowledge is valued for its relevance and utility to specific persons in specific social contexts. Progressive classrooms are to extend into all aspects of community life. Communities are called upon to restructure patterns of social and economic privilege to guarantee movement from goals of equal access toward goals of equal power, participation, and performance.

Current progressive reform advocacy includes more equitable school financing (e.g., increased state and federal funding, decreased property tax dependence); power-sharing through decentralization (e.g., site-based management, charter schools); multicultural, bilingual, antibias, and gender-fair curriculum (i.e., responsive to academically and socially significant dimensions of diversity); strengthened ties between schools and communities (e.g., service learning, community partnerships); and teaching the skills of democratic deliberation and social activism (e.g., contemporary issues-driven and discussion-based curriculum, civic engagement, authentic democratic school governance).

Holism

The third approach, holism, draws from Buddhism, Taoism, Hinduism, Transcendentalism, indigenous belief systems, and ecologically centered philosophies. The primary purpose of public education is to encourage full development and integration of mind, heart, body, and spirit while promoting social and environmental communion. For holists, knowing is essentially relational—it occurs within the context of connections that are close, compassionate, enduring, and mutually beneficial. Holists work to design schooling to encourage supportive relationships across multiple dimensions

of learning, such as intrapersonal learning (promoting integration of mind/heart/body/spirit), interpersonal learning (enhancing the quality of relationships among people and building community), and transpersonal learning (connecting in life-affirming ways with non-human entities, spiritual values, and social and environmental forces).

As each individual is fundamentally connected to the whole of humanity and nonhuman nature, deep knowing is at once intensely personal and profoundly social. Personal transformation occurs in harmony with social and biophysical worlds, resonating outward through intricate webs of relationship. Its effects are strengthened when communion is created across dimensions of difference. Individual, societal, and biophysical diversity is valued and protected because it provides opportunities for creative synthesis and renewal. Holists struggle to develop and integrate a spiritual dimension along with intellectual, emotional, and moral aspects of learning and life. Spirituality is described and experienced as the inspirational moment at which elusive and complex understandings suddenly become clear. Though difficult to capture in words, such moments are characterized by intense and elegant integration of sensation, emotion, insight, and mystery.

Contemporary holist educators favor shaping public education to be more interdisciplinary (emphasizing interdependencies between fields and methods of inquiry); multisensory (emphasizing opportunities to synthesize perceptive, cognitive, emotional, and kinesthetic learning); and exploratory (emphasizing student inquiry over content coverage). Also featured are broadly conceived understandings of environmental sustainability (emphasizing environmental ethics and both social and economic consequences of consumption) and civic education (emphasizing nonviolent conflict resolution and coalition building). Holists further envision public education reform that supports spiritual development (emphasizing intuition, aesthetics, and nonmaterialism).

Challenges to Reform

Advocates of essentialist, progressive, and holistic approaches have actively engaged in reform, but remain deeply dissatisfied with the results and sharply critical of the status quo. Essentialists have attempted to influence decision elites—some target master teachers, local school boards, state departments of education, and state legislators, while others lobby national policy makers. They have generally adopted a top-down implementation style, seeking mandatory standards from higher authorities and directing their preferred changes downward through the school system. They have been frustrated, however, by incomplete compliance, which they attribute to resistance from mid-level administrators, professional curriculum developers, many classroom teachers and their unions, and special interest groups championing specific categories of students and their needs.

Progressives have also attempted to influence decision elites, often petitioning the courts to bring sweeping changes in federal-, state-, and district-level policy. Although their reform aspirations are broad and systemic, initiatives are most frequently implemented locally, as targeted demonstration projects. While much frustration flows from bureaucratic indifference and interference, at the same time progressives confront widespread public and professional ambivalence toward what is perceived as an excessively critical perspective and overtly political agenda. Transforming public education into the primary site for social change is as politically volatile as it is pedagogically challenging.

Holists have "dreamed impossible dreams" in an implementation environment that sometimes shares their broad objectives but effectively thwarts most of their programmatic attempts. Their aspirations for a fully integrated public school experience confront increasingly competitive, specialized, and segmented bureaucratic, social, economic, and political realities. Professionalized division of labor and fragmented curricula, along with entrenched hierarchies and their oppositional politics, are usually successful in resisting holism's distinctively expansive and integrative reform efforts. Most initiatives are relegated to the margins, or struggle to survive outside of traditional public school systems.

Comprehensive Reform

Essentialism, progressivism, and holism present competing educational principles, contrasting approaches to policy, and distinctive pedagogies. All three share advocacy for comprehensive, systemic change. Yet given the barriers to enacting any complex vision in large, resource-constrained, bureaucratic, and authoritarian sociopolitical systems, *deep reform is a daunting ambition.* As some education analysts see it, implemented reforms generated by all three positions have been fragmented, incremental, and programmatically fragile, and none have resulted in broadly sustained philosophical, institutional, or participatory change. In education, politics, and the economy, fundamental patterns of opportunity and interaction are difficult to alter in structural ways.

Reducing the gap between reform aspirations and their realization may require radical changes—those that are deeper and more systemic—to ensure greater equity and effectiveness in schools and society. While advocates often claim widely shared values, the politics of education reform has been divisive and oppositional. The exclusivity projected by the most ardent essentialists, progressives, and holists as they have pursued change on their own terms has limited cooperation and depleted imagination. New reform perspectives, with new political and pedagogic practices, need to be composed through collaborative discourse and hard work of proponents of the three approaches.

Comprehensive, systemic public education reform might be negotiated and implemented through local strategic coalitions of proponents of the three competing positions. Reform strategies that build from diverse perspectives are likely to support continuing participation of ideological adherents, as well as those who demand a predetermined organizational form or pedagogic design. Continuing connections could then be established linking school- and district-level initiatives to state and national policy development.

Comprehensive, systemic reform is an evolving project that brings new insights to perennial public education concerns, requires reconfiguring both human and material resources, and challenges advocates' imagination and stamina. Comprehensive educational reform must embrace deeper visions, bolder proposals, and sustained innovation.

Ruthanne Kurth-Schai and Charles R. Green

See also Holistic Education; Politics of Education;
  Progressive Education

Further Readings

Berube, M. (2004). *Radical reformers: The influences of the left in American education.* Greenwich, CT: Information Age.

Fullan, M. (2001). *The new meaning of educational change.* New York: Teachers College Press.

Miller, R. (1992). *What are schools for? Holistic education in American culture.* Brandon, VT: Holistic Education Press.

Ravitch, D. (2001). *Left back: A century of battles over school reform.* New York: Simon & Schuster.

Sarason, S. (1996). *Revisiting the culture of school and the problem of change.* New York: Teachers College Press.

Tyack, D., & Cuban, L. (1997). *Tinkering toward utopia: A century of public school reform.* Cambridge, MA: Harvard University Press.

EDUCATIONAL RESEARCH, HISTORY OF

Educational research has a long and distinguished history, closely related to the evolution of the social and behavioral sciences. It also has been centrally concerned with the improvement of instructional practice and determining better means to aid learning. Research in education has thus embraced both theoretical and practical dimensions of systematic inquiry into teaching and learning. It also has been shaped by ongoing disputes about the nature of human development and the aims of education, as described in this entry.

Early Works

Inquiry into learning and education dates from ancient times, but it became a more highly organized social activity with the advent of state-sponsored mass schooling in the nineteenth century. Perhaps the earliest forms of such research in the United States were found in comparative accounts of school systems in other parts of the world, provided by traveling educators and other observers. State and federal departments of education published reports on various educational problems, as did early journals such as Henry Barnard's *American Journal of Education.* More systematic forms of inquiry into education and learning appeared with the early development of the social and behavioral sciences in the closing decades of the century, particularly psychology.

Early psychological research and writing related to education focused on the learning process and child development and was associated with such influential figures as William James, G. Stanley Hall, and John Dewey. They contributed to the growth of "child study," a movement focusing on the observation and analysis of children's physical and mental development and the learning process.

In the opening years of the twentieth century, yet another line of inquiry focused on measuring differences in learning, leading to the development of early mental tests. Following the ground-breaking work of French researcher Alfred Binet, such American proponents of IQ testing as Lewis Terman and Edward Thorndike contributed to the growth of standardized testing as a characteristic feature of American education.

A Scientific Approach

Testing proponents were a major element of the movement to foster "scientific" approaches to educational research across much of the twentieth century. This impulse extended from psychologists to researchers studying educational administration. The former emphasized the importance of experimental methods to determining the effects of educational "treatments" or instructional strategies. The latter utilized survey research and case study approaches to assess the efficiency and effectiveness of school systems, especially those in larger cities. Both approaches were considered scientific in the sense that they relied upon the systematic analysis of data collected under "objective" criteria. The growing use of testing in schools across the country, and survey methods to assess schools and districts, meant that thousands of students were introduced to these forms of educational research at colleges and universities each year by mid-century.

Other forms of educational research existed alongside these approaches. Inquiry regarding education in the domains of history and philosophy was conducted during the nineteenth century as well, and these fields also were widely taught in universities. John Dewey was the predominant figure in the philosophy of education until his death in 1952, and beyond. Sociological research on educational topics came into currency during the twenties and thirties with such figures as George Counts and Willard Waller providing important models.

These tendencies extended into the post–World War II era, when race emerged as a critical issue in education. Allison Davis and Kenneth Clark, influential African American researchers, helped to demonstrate the impact of educational discrimination and inequality, leading to the historic *Brown v. Board of Education* decision in 1954 and subsequent efforts to desegregate schools and insure equality. The sociological tradition of educational research was reflected in the work of James Coleman, whose career spanned a wide range of topics and theoretical contributions to the field. In the domain of experimental research design and statistical methodology, such educational researchers as Donald Campbell and Julian Stanley gained worldwide renown for their technical expertise. Psychologists such as Jerome Bruner and B. F. Skinner proposed new conceptions of the learning process. The American Educational Research Association (AERA), which had been founded in the 1920s, grew to become a large, diverse organization by the end of the 1960s.

A Funded Enterprise

In the 1970s and '80s educational research became a large-scale enterprise, drawing financial support from the federal government as well as private foundations. Much of this research was quantitative, focused on racial inequities in schooling and other problems related to social inequality. Another body of work represented the growing field of evaluation research, intended to provide comprehensive assessment of educational programs and other types of systematic interventions to change human behavior. Large scale national surveys of educational questions were undertaken with federal support.

Coleman supervised an influential study of educational inequality in 1967 that revealed the importance of such nonschool factors as parental background on the educational performance of children. Christopher Jencks and other researchers followed with additional quantitative studies of social stratification, highlighting the contributions of education to individual success. This line of inquiry was supplemented with observational studies that examined the effects of race, social class, and other factors in the experiences of teachers and students in particular schools. Case studies of desegregation plans proliferated in the wake of ongoing controversy over busing and other approaches to racial integration.

Experimental studies of particular learning strategies and instructional approaches continued apace, but a new interdisciplinary approach to studying the learning process emerged in the 1960s and '70s in the field of cognitive science. Spearheaded by Jerome Bruner and his colleagues at Harvard, this line of inquiry embraced a wide variety of methodological traditions and disciplinary perspectives, all dedicated to better understanding how people think, acquire knowledge, and solve problems. Perhaps the most widely influential outgrowth of this was the work of Howard Gardner on "multiple intelligences," but it has affected many other realms of educational theory and practice as well. The development of cognitive science also helped to foster a greater degree of methodological diversity in scholarship on learning.

Dueling Paradigms

Educational researchers debated the virtues of quantitative and qualitative approaches to investigation during the 1980s, a time marked by "paradigm wars" between proponents of different research traditions. Ethnographers Harry Wolcott and George Spindler were influential practitioners of observational methods, and growing numbers of students eschewed quantitative research in favor of naturalistic inquiry. Educational historians and philosophers displayed limited interest in these debates, focusing much of their attention to questions of inequality and social justice.

The American Educational Research Association continued to grow in size and complexity as it strove to embrace a widening diversity of research modalities. The association's 1988 publication of the collection of essays titled *Complementary Methods for Research in Educational Research* marked an attempt to bring coherence to the field. Subsequent editions of the book have featured an ever-expanding array of approaches to investigation, making it difficult to identify a predominant tradition within the educational research community.

The closing years of the twentieth century were marked by a number of major developments. Perhaps the most striking was the Tennessee Student–Teacher Achievement Ratio (STAR) project, which randomly assigned thousands of students and teachers to different size classes to determine the effect on educational outcomes. Results from this massive experiment appeared in the early to mid-1990s, clearly demonstrating the advantages of smaller classes, especially for students from disadvantaged backgrounds. STAR data also showed the contributions of effective teachers. These dramatic findings, along with the availability of major new national data sets on education, children, and youth, helped to spark renewed interest in quantitative research. Increasingly, however, investigators combined qualitative methods with quantitative studies, utilizing "mixed methods" to achieve greater insight into educational problems. As the century drew to a close, debates related to the dueling paradigms of earlier years subsided audibly.

Policy Debates

Educational researchers became embroiled in critical controversies over educational policy during the 1990s and beyond. One prominent issue was school choice and the impact of vouchers, which had been aggressively promoted by conservative social critics for a number of years. As school voucher experiments were conducted in Milwaukee, Cleveland, New York, and other cities, researchers on either side of the issue exchanged barbed commentaries about their findings. Again, experimental studies were pointed to as the "gold standard" for evaluating the effectiveness of such approaches. Although this style of inquiry was favored by conservative proponents of choice, studies conducted in this fashion failed to provide much support for their cause. At the present time, there is little evidence, experimental or otherwise, that school choice promotes higher school achievement, but debates continue regardless.

At the start of the twenty-first century, educational research is once again at the center of national debates about educational change. Conservative proponents of reform in the federal government called for more "scientific" research on schooling, specifically citing the need for experimental and quantitative approaches to evaluation and other forms of investigation. The research community has responded by noting that "science" embraces many different traditions, including case studies, historical or documentary inquiry, discourse analysis, and ethnography.

Calls for greater attention to "applied" research have also prompted debates over the extent to which everyday problems in education and related fields can be "solved" by the application of systematic inquiry. In the last analysis, it may very well be the case that the principal function of educational research, in all of its varied forms, lies in the realm of informed reflection on major educational issues rather than the ultimate resolution of particular problems or practical dilemmas.

John L. Rury

See also Qualitative Research

Further Readings

American Educational Research Association. (1997). *Complementary methods for research in education* (2nd ed.). Washington, DC: Author. (Original work published 1988)

Green, J. L., Camilli, G., & Elmore, P. B. (Eds.). (2006). *Handbook of complementary methods in education research.* Washington, DC: American Educational Research Association.

Lagemann, E. C. (2000). *An elusive science: The troubling history of education research.* Chicago: University of Chicago Press.

Lagemann, E. C., & Shulman, L. S. (Eds.). (1999). *Issues in education research: Problems and possibilities.* San Francisco: Jossey-Bass.

Reese, W. J. (1999). What history teaches about the impact of educational research on practice. *Review of Research in Education, 24,* 1–19.

Richardson, V. (2001). *Handbook of research on teaching.* Washington, DC: American Educational Research Association.

Towne, L., & Shavelson, R. J. (2003). *Scientific research in education.* Washington, DC: National Academies Press.

EDUCATIONAL TRANSFER

The study of policies that have been transplanted from one cultural context to another occupies a prominent place in comparative education research. To some extent, educational borrowing and lending implies artificially isolating education from its political, economic, and cultural context. Consequently, numerous warnings have been made about this kind of educational transfer, whether it is wholesale, selective, or eclectic.

Comparative research on *policy borrowing* has undergone several major discursive shifts in the past twenty years. Arguably, the largest shift was the move from normative to analytical studies; the first being concerned with what *could* and *should* be borrowed and the latter interested in understanding *why* and *how* references are made to experiences from elsewhere. Jürgen Schriewer, noted German comparative education researcher, needs to be credited for critiquing normative or meliorist approaches to the study of policy borrowing. Using a theoretical framework of system theory, Schriewer proposes to study the local context of policy borrowing to better understand the "socio-logic" of externalization.

According to this theory, references to other educational systems provide the leverage for carrying out reforms that otherwise would be contested. Schriewer also finds it indicative of the "socio-logic" of a system that only specific educational systems are used as external sources of authority. Which systems are used as "reference societies" and which are not tells a great deal about the interrelations of actors within various world systems.

Using a similar approach, David Phillips identifies factors that account for "policy attraction" between two educational systems. By studying British interest in German education over a sustained period of time, he finds that the same educational system can be an object of attraction for different reasons at different times. Pursuing an analytical rather than a normative approach to the study of educational borrowing, a conclusion may be reached that is quite the contrary to what normative borrowing advocates have suggested: Borrowing does not occur because reforms from elsewhere are better, but because the very act of borrowing has a salutary effect on domestic policy conflict.

Several scholars have applied the concept of externalization to comparative policy studies and found that it is precisely at moments of heightened policy contestation that references to other educational systems are made. Thus, borrowing, discursive or actual, has a certification effect on domestic policy talk. Against this backdrop of system theory, three common phenomenon, which at first appear to be counterintuitive, make perfect sense: (1) very often the language of the reform is borrowed, but not the actual reform; (2) borrowing occurs even when there is no apparent need, that is, even when similar reforms already exist in the local context; and (3) if the actual reform is borrowed, it is always selectively borrowed and sometimes locally recontextualized to the extent that there is little similarity left between the original and the copy.

The concept of externalization has also been applied to *policy lending,* where the political and economic reasons for policy export have been examined. For example, Phillip Jones, of the University of Sydney in Australia, focuses on the duality of the World Bank's education portfolio: the World Bank's portfolio with regard to monetary *loans* and its portfolio with regard to the *lending* of ideas about educational reform to low income countries. Although using finance as a means to drive policy change is hardly new, the scale and global reach of international organizations raise critical questions for education theory, policy, and practice. For example, have national educational reforms gradually converged toward an international model of reform that produces a shared global belief in progress and justice? Driven by questions like this, Stanford neo-institutional sociologists John Meyer and Francisco Ramirez have greatly contributed to theory in globalization studies and to research on educational borrowing and lending.

In the context of globalization, research on educational transfer has experienced a revival in recent years, with researchers turning their attention to what the established field of comparative education can contribute to understanding the processes of local adaptation and recontextualization that occur as a result of reform import.

Gita Steiner-Khamsi

See also Globalization and Education

Further Readings

Anderson-Levitt, K. (Ed.). (2003). *Local meanings, global schooling.* New York: Palgrave Macmillan.

Baker, D. P., & LeTendre, G. K. (2005). *National differences, global similarities: World culture and the future of schooling.* Stanford, CA: University of Stanford Press.

Jones, P. (1992). *World Bank financing of education: Learning and development.* New York: Routledge.

Phillips, D. (1993). Borrowing educational policy. In D. Finegold, L. McFarland, & W. Richardson (Eds.), *Something borrowed, something learned? The transatlantic market in education and training reform.* Washington, DC: Brookings Institution.

Phillips, D., & Ochs, K. (Eds.). (2004). *Educational policy borrowing: Historical perspectives.* Oxford, UK: Symposium Books.

Ramirez R., & Meyer, J. (1985). The origins and expansion of education. *Comparative Education Review, 29,* 145–170.

Schriewer, J., & Martinez, C. (2004). Constructions of internationality in education. In G. Steiner-Khamsi (Ed.), *Lessons from elsewhere: The politics of educational borrowing and lending.* New York: Teachers College Press.

Steiner-Khamsi, G. (Ed.). (2004). *The global politics of educational borrowing and lending.* New York: Teachers College Press.

EDUCATION AND ECONOMIC DEVELOPMENT

Education is related to various kinds of development: individual human development, different dimensions of societal development (e.g., political and cultural), and national economic development. This entry focuses on the last relationship, between economic development and education, which can be understood from different perspectives, grounded in functionalist, conflict, or less structuralist social theories.

Functionalist Views

From a functionalist perspective, development is usually linked to the idea of modernization. Scholars and policy makers adopting this perspective stress that it is a normal and positive experience for undeveloped or developing nations' economies to come to model the economies of "modern" or "developed" nations (i.e., capitalist or "free market" systems). Based on assumptions of human capital theory, investment in education (schooling and nonformal education) is seen as building a nation's stock of human capital (the knowledge, skills, and values of its worker-citizens), and this along with investments in physical capital (e.g., machines) fosters economic development. Within functionalism, the education system is viewed as not only training but also selecting and sorting—meritocratically, based on their talents and motivations—future workers.

From this perspective, a developing nation's government officials, business leaders, educators, other professionals, and citizens can steer their education systems to facilitate their nation's advancement. Educational development to promote economic development is accomplished by using national human and financial resources as well as by arranging for financial and technical assistance from international organizations, such as corporations, philanthropic foundations, and bilateral and multilateral development agencies. The education systems of "developed"—and, particularly, "newly developed"—nations are taken as the models for other countries' educational development.

Debates among functionalists tend to be couched in technical terms and to focus on (a) what levels of the education system (primary, secondary, or higher) contribute most effectively; (b) what kinds of skills, knowledge, and attitudes are most productive to include in the curriculum; (c) what mix of public and private funding sources is most appropriate; and (d) whether formal or nonformal education programs represent a better investment.

Conflict Perspectives

In contrast to functionalism, which views human systems as performing certain necessary functions (determined by consensus), conflict perspectives conceive of human social relations as determined by the needs and interests of dominant groups or nations, which conflict with or contradict the needs and interests of subordinate groups or nations. At an international level, conflict perspectives include dependency theory and world systems theory and tend to employ terms like *imperialism, colonialism,* and *neocolonialism.*

Rather than assuming that some nations are "undeveloped," scholars and policy makers adopting a conflict perspective highlight that some nations are underdeveloped. That is, the economies of societies in the periphery of the world system are constructed through exploitative, dependence-inducing relationships imposed on such nations by the dominant groups in more powerful, core societies. Thus, more powerful nations "develop" and their elites accumulate capital at the expense of less powerful nations. Moreover, from a conflict perspective, socialism (rather than capitalism) is often viewed as the desired goal of economic development.

In the conflict-perspective narrative, elite groups in more powerful, wealthier nations design educational systems to serve their own interests. They seek to educate youth and adults within their own countries with the skills, knowledge, and attitudes "needed" for producing wealth that elites can accumulate, while at the same time inculcating worldviews that justify inequalities in wealth and power relations within and between countries. Individual or group achievements in education and in the economy are viewed as based not on "merit" but on the possession of cultural capital recognized and valued by elites.

Moreover, elites in core nations seek to shape the education systems of societies in the periphery to train more productive workers and to socialize citizens who view as legitimate not only their positions within their country's stratification system but also their nation's less privileged place within the hierarchically organized world system. Core country elites' interventions that create underdevelopment in societies on the periphery are facilitated by the activities of multinational corporations, philanthropic foundations, and bilateral and multilateral development agencies.

Less Structuralist Views

In contrast to the more determinist, structuralist accounts provided by functionalist and conflict theories, less structuralist perspectives highlight human agency. Rather than (a) viewing government officials, administrators, and teachers in undeveloped or underdeveloped societies as passively accepting the educational policies, curriculum, and processes "lent" or "imposed on" them by core and/or developed nations; and (b) viewing students (and their parents) as necessarily accepting and internalizing the lessons they are taught, adults or young people are portrayed as ignoring, resisting, struggling, or even strategically accepting (for purposes that contradict what was intended) "foreign" educational structures, content, and practices.

For instance, during their pre-1954 colonization of Vietnam, the French sought to use schooling to inculcate in Vietnamese youth conceptions of history and culture that characterized Vietnam as incapable of political or economic independence, but Vietnamese teachers and community members challenged this message and even set up "illegal" alternative schools to transmit other curricular messages to their children. In the 1980s, when Vietnam occupied Cambodia in the aftermath of the latter's destructive Khmer Rouge regime, Vietnamese advisers promoted the use of the Vietnamese language and curricular ideas. However, these were accepted by Cambodian leaders only selectively, temporarily, and competitively—with the languages and ideas offered through educational assistance from Cuba and the Soviet Union—in their strategic efforts to rebuild their higher education system.

Also in line with a less structuralist perspective are contingency theories, which emphasize that the links between education and the economy are always contingent and subject to readjustment. Such theories draw attention to political struggle over the selection and allocation of workers and to variations (across time and place) in employers' demands for workers with different types of knowledge, skills, and attitudes. Such theories could be combined with world systems theories to explain why different types of "educated" workers are desired by employers in different industries in core, semiperipheral, and peripheral societies, and why the formal and hidden curriculum of schooling and higher education might vary across Fordist and post-Fordist economic formations.

Finally, less structuralist theories are reflected in analyses that do not take as predetermined or natural that globalization entails certain changes in education or the economy. This creates debates regarding the contemporary relevance of the nations as economic or political entities. Scholars and policy makers in this tradition may focus attention on global dynamics and international organizations, such as the World Trade Organization, which can shape the provision of education and other economic commodities and services. However, at the same time, they highlight the agency of actors situated in various (core and periphery) nations and transnational organizations.

Mark B. Ginsburg

See also Comparative and International Education; Economic Inequality; Politics of Education

Further Readings

Altbach, P., & Kelly, G. (Eds.). (1978). *Education and colonialism.* New York: David McKay.

Clayton, T. (2000). *Education and the politics of language: Hegemony and pragmatism in Cambodia, 1979–1989.* Hong Kong: Comparative Education Research Centre.

Ginsburg, M., Espinoza, O., Popa, S., & Terano, M. (2003). Privatization, domestic marketization, and international commercialization of higher education. *Globalisation, Societies and Education, 1*(3), 413–446.

Hickox, M., & Moore, R. (1992). Education and post-Fordism. In P. Brown & H. Lauder (Eds.), *Education for economic survival: From Fordism to post-Fordism?* (pp. 95–117). London: Routledge.

Inkeles, A., & Smith, D. H. (1974). *Becoming modern: Individual change in six developing countries.* Cambridge, MA: Harvard University Press.

Meyer, J., & Hannan, M. (Ed.). (1979). *National development and the world system.* Chicago: University of Chicago Press.

Robertson, S., Bonal, X., & Dale, R. (2002). GATS and the education service industry. *Comparative Education Review, 46*(4), 72–96.

EDUCATION COMMISSION OF THE STATES

Education Commission of the States (ECS) is a nonprofit, nonpartisan, interstate organization composed of forty-nine states, the District of Columbia, Puerto Rico, American Samoa, and the Virgin Islands. Its primary purpose is to improve public education by researching, gathering, and disseminating information to inform educational policy makers and leaders across the United States. Now in its fourth decade of service to American public education, ECS supports the diverse needs of numerous stakeholders.

History and Organization

In his 1964 book titled *Shaping Educational Policy,* former Harvard University president, James Bryant Conant, called for a national educational policy partnership among the states. Early in 1965, his call was answered when John W. Gardner of the Carnegie Corporation of New York and former North Carolina governor Terry Sanford led the creation of the Compact for Education—the Congress-approved, state-endorsed, agreement that created the ECS. Two years later, ECS sprung into action as the operational branch of the Compact for Education out of its national headquarters in Denver, Colorado. Today, each state and territory that makes up the Education Commission of the States is represented by seven commissioners, including one state legislator from each house, the governor, and four others that she or he appoints. ECS is financially supported by a wide range of grants, sponsorships, state fees, and contracts.

Purpose and Goals

The primary purposes and goals of the ECS are detailed in the Compact for Education and in the ECS statement of mission, values, and goals. At its core, ECS acts as an advocate for the improvement of American public education through its varied approaches to informing state leaders and the general public about educational policy issues. These approaches include providing research, policy analysis, technical assistance, recommendations, and publications to educational decision makers, as well as creating a nonpartisan forum for interstate communication and collaboration across educational policy issues. Further, ECS acts as a national clearinghouse for all relevant research and information related to educational policy.

Contributions to Education

ECS is well respected as an educational policy resource due to its comprehensive and significant contributions to the field. In addition to its services to members of the commission, ECS offers a wide range of resources to the general public. These resources include up-to-date news and information provided on the ECS Web site and in electronic publications and newsletters; policy research and analysis on a wide range of relevant topics; national, state, and regional policy conferences, workshops, and seminars; technical assistance and technology-related services; a quarterly report, numerous print publications, and links to additional resources across a diverse set of educational issue areas; and the ECS Clearinghouse—the country's only complete database of state and national policy enactments, multistate reports, and links to detailed information across more than 100 educational policy issue areas.

Carri Anne Schneider

See also Philanthropy, Educational; Policy Studies

Further Readings

Conant, J. (1964). *Shaping educational policy*. New York: McGraw-Hill.

Web Sites

Education Commission of the States: http://www.ecs.org

EDUCATIONESE

Critics of education use the term *educationese* to describe what they consider to be the pretentious jargon educators use when, in the critics' opinions, everyday English would be more appropriate. Conservatives are the most vocal critics of educationese, as part of their general challenge to the legitimacy of public education and educators. However, educators' use of specialized language also concerns liberals and progressives because it may impede efforts to communicate with families and community members.

Linguistic Background

Educationese is a pejorative term, and educators usually would not use it to describe their language. The *-ese* suffix can be added to the name of any field

to create a term for the language used by practitioners in that field (e.g., *legalese* and *medicalese*). Such terms denote specialized vocabularies, not entirely distinctive languages. They are pejorative because they parody the use of obscure terms or euphemisms when common, everyday words might do. Academics play a major role in creating these specialized vocabularies. Practitioners in a field acquire them through professional education, and keep up to date on new terminology through continuing education.

Other terms relevant to educationese are *bureaucratese,* which disparages the technical, impersonal language that accompanied the rise of bureaucracy as an institutional type, and *doublespeak.* Bureaucratese is a barrier for people who need to communicate with staff in an organization in order to receive services. Bureaucratic jargons are also replete with euphemisms that make undesirable or mundane things sound more tasteful or important. Although George Orwell did not coin the term *doublespeak,* it is probably an adaptation of his term *Newspeak,* a political language meant to deceive the citizenry in the novel *1984.* Detractors of doublespeak believe that euphemisms (such as *downsizing* for "firing" or *collateral damage* for "dead civilians") are deliberate attempts to hide the harms of corporate or governmental actions from the public.

Specialized vocabularies need not be viewed so negatively, however. They indicate the professionalization of an occupation. For members of a profession, specialized terms facilitate communication with colleagues, because they allow more precision in description. For example, *spinal stenosis* is more precise than "aching back," and *autistic* is more informative than "acting strange and not talking." In addition, professionals today often work in bureaucratic organizations in which they must adopt technical terms and acronyms associated with government programs, the insurance industry, and/or other entities that impinge on their work.

Sociological Interpretations

Sociologist Max Weber is most associated with analysis of the rise of both professions and bureaucracies as institutional changes in modern societies. Neo-Weberian institutional theorists interpret the specialized vocabularies of the professions and bureaucracies as markers of intentional institutional advancement. For example, Murray Edelman interprets language change as a strategy in the advancement of the helping professions. As actors claim the exclusive right to certain practices and give those practices special labels, they are able to exert more power over those outside the institution. They label or frame problems in ways that give them a greater prerogative over the solutions.

Some sociologists argue that physicians, for example, medicalize more and more areas of life, so that nonphysicians become more dependent on their services. Spoofing or denouncing medicalese can be a way to question the legitimacy of such power. Ethical problems also arise when professionals communicate with those outside the profession. Lay people, especially clients, often cannot understand professional jargon, and this may impede professional-client communication or even the client's ability to receive or benefit from services.

Applications to Education

Education both fits and does not fit this general analysis. Public education in the United States and other nations did become increasingly bureaucratized during the twentieth century, and there have been calls for greater teacher and administrator professionalization. In 1975 when sociologist Dan Lortie published the book *Schoolteacher,* he reported that teachers did not use terms unfamiliar to the general public. Since that time, if critics are to be believed, educators have traded their everyday way of talking for a pedantic style loaded with jargon.

Conservative critics of educationese, such as Diane Ravitch, have been especially scathing, perhaps because of an assumption that educators neither receive the extended, rigorous education nor possess the advanced skills of other professionals, such as physicians. Thus, their adoption of specialized jargon is a mere pretense. Educators' "politically correct" euphemisms, such as "performing below grade level" and "underachieving," are attempts to prettify the harsh truth of academic failure. Education professors also regularly borrow contemporary jargon from other fields, such as business and science, and add it to their discourse. While such practices seem open to question,

educators must use certain terms and acronyms to communicate with government bureaucracies, and classroom teachers must be acquainted to at least some extent with the technical vocabularies of colleagues in special education and other programs.

At the same time that educators have been striving for more professional status, education reformers have called for more parent and community involvement in schooling, which would require educators to understand and speak the language of homes and neighborhoods. This is more complex than it may seem, because educators and noneducators in some communities may operate according to different cultural models. Special educators, in particular, have adopted more scientific models for children's behaviors that parents or community members might label "bad" and deserving of punishment. There is some evidence that homeschoolers and parent advocacy groups are advising their members to learn educationese, so that they can balance the power in conflicts with public school educators. Understanding such language differences must be part of any attempt to bridge the gaps between homes and schools.

Peggy L. Placier

See also Bureaucracy; Discursive Practices; Sociology of Education; Teachers, Professional Status of

Further Readings

Edelman, M. J. (1974). *The political language of the helping professions.* Madison: University of Wisconsin Press.
Lutz, W. (1996). *The new doublespeak: Why no one knows what anyone's saying anymore.* New York: HarperCollins.
Ravitch, D. (2003). *The language police: How pressure groups restrict what students learn.* New York: Alfred A. Knopf.

EDUCATION IN THE NEW AMERICAN REPUBLIC

In hindsight, education during the American nation's first fifty years looks like a hodgepodge. Although several of the nation's founders urged broad access to schooling, the Constitution was silent on education.

Thomas Jefferson imagined an ambitious, multilevel schooling scheme, and the Land Ordinance of 1785 dedicated one section to schools in each future township. Some states had school funds, but no state boasted a real school system. The founders' dreams evaporated as most Americans resisted school taxes. Better-off parents preferred private education; existing options plus apprenticeship met others' expectations. Yet over the next fifty years or so, the attitude toward the importance of education changed, as this entry shows, and by the 1830s, the nation was primed to offer public education for all.

In early America, as in colonial days, parents taught introductory literacy, although female literacy lagged. Young town-dwelling children might attend a "dame school," learning letters in a woman's busy kitchen. Longer-settled areas usually offered basic public schooling. As settlement dispersed after the Revolution, rural towns split schooling functions into tiny districts of perhaps twenty neighboring families, each district possessing a one-room schoolhouse and a superintending committee.

Early public schools met for three-month summer and winter terms, since farm work dominated spring and fall. Older boys attended winter schools, while younger boys and girls could attend both, except where girls were schooled separately at odd hours. Most teachers were men, ministers or college students, with widely varying teaching abilities. Learning involved solitary memorization of Bible passages, Noah Webster's "blue-backed speller," and random family-owned schoolbooks, followed by recitation— not understanding or reflection. Rural schoolhouses were drafty or hot, with rough backless benches; urban schools met in any available room. Corporal punishment was common, for both misbehavior and recitation mistakes. At term's end, "rate bills" charged parents for each day their children had appeared. Attendance was optional and spotty.

Urban education featured more private schools, although the public-private boundary blurred. Churches and philanthropic groups funded schools for the poor, including separate "African" schools. Beginning around 1810, Sunday schools targeted working children, offering literacy more than religion. In large cities, where free schooling signified genuine poverty, a motley array of academies served the majority of families. Most charity and pay schools resembled public schools in pedagogy, facilities, and teacher quality.

Since early colleges produced mostly classically trained ministers, college-bound boys studied Latin with a private instructor or attended a preparatory academy. In a few places, notably Massachusetts, towns supported Latin "grammar schools." Girls had sparse advanced schooling opportunities; most elite girls' academies spotlighted music, fancy needlework, and dancing.

As voting eligibility extended to men of little property after 1800, however, more Americans sought correspondingly broad educational access. The education of females gained importance from John Locke's childrearing ideas, which emphasized children's early impressionability, while the emerging concept of "republican motherhood" suggested that only educated mothers could raise republic-ready men of thoughtful judgment. These forces plus an increasingly complex, technical economy, demanding flexible, transferable skills and knowledge, slowly built acceptance of expanded schooling. When better schooling became more visibly useful, more parents invested in it.

By the 1810s, public and private schools began broadening their curricula. Academies offered more history, geography, modern languages, advanced mathematics, and occasionally teacher training. Boston's English High School, founded in 1821, provided a practical public education beyond the classics. Soon academies sprouted everywhere, peaking in the 1820s, when there were perhaps 6,000 (many ephemeral) by 1850. Girls enjoyed greater access to town and private schools by 1800. A few girls' academies rivaled advanced education for boys, and some towns added girls' secondary schools by the 1820s. With more women equipped to become teachers (and working cheap), district schools began hiring women, at first for summer sessions, when older boys did not attend. Imported teaching methods promoted further innovation.

Meanwhile, westward migration and Protestant denominational splits helped quadruple the number of colleges by 1820. Many colleges widened their offerings, and medical and law schools multiplied. Still, no college admitted women before the mid-1830s.

By 1830, schooling had clearly gained momentum. Challenges remained: bills and work demands that shut out poorer children; inferior opportunities for African Americans; limitations on women's higher education; unsuitable textbooks, buildings, and teachers; skimpy attendance; and skeptical taxpayers. Yet the notion that American children of all classes—if not all races—could learn together in free public schools lay just around the bend.

Rebecca R. Noel

See also American Education, Themes in the History of; Higher Education, History of; Literacy in the Colonial Era

See Visual History Chapter 2, Early Textbooks

Further Readings

Kaestle, C. F. (1983). *Pillars of the republic: Common schools and American society, 1780–1860.* New York: Hill & Wang.

Madsen, D. L. (1974). *Early national education, 1776–1830.* New York: John Wiley.

ENGINEERING EDUCATION, ORIGINS AND HISTORY OF

In standard accounts, the history of American engineering education began with the establishment of the U.S. Military Academy at West Point in 1802. This was the first institution to offer formal instruction in civil and military engineering in North America. Through the course of the nineteenth and twentieth centuries, engineering education became increasingly widespread and professional, as this entry describes.

Early Education

If the ruins left by ancient Mayan and Aztec civilizations are considered, then informal means of engineering education existed in the Americas long before colonists crossed the Atlantic. The pyramids at Teotihuacan and Chichen Itza provide evidence of early forms of engineering education in at least two ways. First, the ruins by their very structure imply a pattern of scientific organization and a familiarity with basic mathematical sciences. Central to pyramid construction were applications of principles derived from geometry and physics. Second, the structures suggest a pattern of social organization necessary for transmitting scientific or practical knowledge. A means of passing this knowledge from one group (i.e., organizers) to another (i.e., managers and laborers) required an informal process of teaching and learning engineering concepts.

Formal institutions of higher learning first appeared in the "new world" in Latin America during the sixteenth century and then in North America during the seventeenth century, but these institutions largely ignored the practical and engineering sciences. Throughout the seventeenth and eighteenth centuries, North American colonial colleges followed the classical curriculum that required studies in Latin, Greek, rhetoric, logic, and other language-related areas, with slight attention to mathematics and science. The science courses offered to students were often dated and not aligned with practical interests.

Systematic attention to engineering education, as at West Point, began to appear in the early to mid-nineteenth century within a dynamic social and cultural milieu. Developments in American society after the Revolutionary War and into the antebellum period included wars with England and Mexico, a fundamental transformation in the economy from agrarianism to industrialization, patterns of migration from rural to urban areas, and westward expansion. Wars with European and Latin American forces prompted calls for greater attention to military engineering. The founding of military academies soon followed with the establishment of the Virginia Military Institute (1839), the Citadel (1843), and the U.S. Naval Academy (1845).

Change Produces Needs

The transformation of the economy, meanwhile, resulted in a dramatic shift from agriculture to industry. At the start of the nineteenth century, there were only a handful of American factories; by 1850, there were over 140,000 producing more than a billion dollars worth of goods. The technical and technological needs of factory operation created a demand for graduates of engineering education. Rapid industrialization facilitated the process of rapid urbanization. In 1800, there were fifteen Americans in rural life to every one city dweller. By 1850, the ratio was approximately five to one.

With an increased concentration of labor in urban centers came the establishment of mechanic institutes. These organizations, such as the Franklin Institute (1824) in Philadelphia, developed curricula centered on practical and useful knowledge. Westward migration increased the need for those knowledgeable in the practical sciences. Large-scale land surveys funded by local, state, and federal governments as well as the construction of rail lines often required trained engineers and contributed to the expansion of formal engineering instruction.

Antebellum social, cultural, and educational developments are particularly important to note for historiographical reasons. Traditional, and now defunct, interpretations about higher education before the Civil War have suggested that these institutions failed to respond to the needs of society and that little, if any, attention was placed on practical or scientific studies. Recent scholarship has emphasized that many technical schools, polytechnic institutes, mechanic institutes, practical lyceums, military academies, and other institutions came into existence during this period, along with curricular reform at traditional colleges that expanded opportunities for practical and engineering studies.

Approach to Education

The conceptual foundation of many well-established American engineering institutions—such as West Point, Rensselaer in 1824 and Massachusetts Institute of Technology (MIT) in 1861—relied to a large extent on French models of polytechnic instruction. West Point's first superintendent, Sylvanus Thayer, visited the École Polytechnique in Paris and borrowed heavily from its curricula upon his return. Rensselaer's Amos Eaton practiced a laboratory model of instruction that also mirrored the French system. And MIT's conceptual founder, William Barton Rogers, was highly influenced by the École Centrale des Arts et Manufactures.

Common to the Parisian schools was an emphasis on the practical and mathematical sciences and their application to field work. Differences between French institutions largely had to do with the focus of student preparation. Graduates from the École Centrale prepared for such fields as agriculture, architecture, railroad engineering, textile manufacturing, public works, industrial chemistry, general civil engineering, machine manufacturing, metallurgy and mining, and commerce. The École Centrale was established in response to the largely mathematical, theoretical, and military training of the École Polytechnique; as a civilian, rather than military, program, it balanced theoretical training in geology, physics, and chemistry with practical laboratory exercises and the workshop. A majority of students in these laboratories and workshops came from the business, industrial, and labor classes.

During the mid- to late nineteenth century, U.S. government support for engineering education fueled the expansion of existing institutions and the founding of new ones. The Morrill Act of 1862 is often noted as the first federally funded program for American higher education. Senator Justin Morrill had as a goal for the act the establishment of college-level agricultural and mechanical programs of study. The funding came from an allotment of western lands to, at first, Northeastern states, since the act was passed during the Civil War. Southern states later received an allotment for similar purposes shortly after the war and in a federal land-grant act of 1890.

Although popular as a result of developments during the antebellum period and as evidenced by the land-grant acts, engineering schools produced a culture clash within the profession. The cultural rift occurred between those who learned their skills and knowledge through experience (i.e., shop culture) and those who learned the same through formal instruction (i.e., school culture). Thus, shop culture tended to distrust "book learning" and valued the practical experiences gained through work, whether in shops developing machinery, in open fields surveying lands, or deep within the earth mining for natural resources. School culture tended to find incomplete the learning acquired through work experience and valued the knowledge gained through formal science and engineering courses. By the turn of the twentieth century, the culture clash began to fade as the engineering community underwent a process of professionalization and engineering programs became more common.

A. J. Angulo

See also Higher Education, History of; Morrill Act

Further Readings

Calvert, M. A. (1967). *The mechanical engineer in America, 1830–1910.* Baltimore: Johns Hopkins University Press.

Day, C. R. (1987). *Education for the industrial world: The Ecole d'Arts et Métiers and the rise of French industrial engineering.* Cambridge: MIT Press.

Pfammatter, U. (2000). *The making of the modern architect and engineer: The origins and development of a scientific and industrially oriented education.* Boston: Birkhauser.

Reynolds, T. S. (1992). The education of engineers in America before the Morrill Act of 1862. *History of Education Quarterly, 32,* 459–482.

ENGLISH-ONLY MOVEMENT

The "English-only" movement (also known as the "Official English" movement) is a network of activists organized around the legislative goals of passing a constitutional amendment to make English the official language of the United States and restricting the use of languages other than English for official purposes. These would include written usage in ballots, signage, drivers' licensing exams, public safety pamphlets, and other government documents, as well as oral usages such as voting assistance, provision of social services (e.g., health care or job training), and translation assistance for crime victims, witnesses, or defendants. Some cities have passed English-only laws restricting the use of other languages on private business signs. A major area of debate has been language policies around public education, particularly for immigrant children. Correspondingly, schooling has been a major focus of the movement's campaign, and bilingual education advocates are among its staunchest opponents.

Throughout U.S. history, public enthusiasm for declaring English the (exclusive) official language has waxed and waned, largely as a reaction to the ebb and flow of immigrants from non-English-speaking countries. In earlier decades, such immigrants were mainly from Europe and China. Aggressive assimilation policies targeting Native Americans (e.g., via the forcible removal of Indian children to English-medium boarding schools) and anti-German sentiment surrounding World War I also prompted several states to pass legislation restricting the use of languages other than English in public schools.

More recently, immigration from Latin America, particularly Mexico, has spurred the English-only movement to aggressive action on various fronts. Spearheading this movement has been California businessman Ron Unz, whose "English for the Children" initiative led to the passage of California's Proposition 227 in 1998. Though it did not outlaw bilingual education outright, Proposition 227 severely restricted the educational options available to students learning English, and established various bureaucratic hurdles to the provision of educational services in other languages.

To date, roughly half of the fifty states have passed English-only laws; court challenges to these measures are ongoing in some states. Not surprisingly, the English-only movement has been most active in states with a large proportion of speakers of other languages, such as California, Florida, Nebraska, Colorado, Hawaii, and Massachusetts. On the other hand, some states with large immigrant populations (e.g., Texas) have resisted such legislation, while a few (notably New Mexico) have passed nonbinding "English plus" measures in support of multilingualism.

Although critics have charged that the English-only movement is fueled by nativist, anti-immigrant, or racist sentiments, and tenuous links have been drawn to White supremacist organizations, bilingual education advocate James Crawford argues that such links are less significant than is often believed. Rather, the movement has gained widespread public support (even among some Hispanics) by stressing the right of all immigrants, especially children, to have access to the English language. They argue that the provision of services in other languages impedes immigrants' acquisition of English, and that bilingual education, while arguably necessary for some children, should be of short duration and focused on the transition to English-medium education.

Opponents argue that such policies fly in the face of most research, which indicates that well-implemented, long-term bilingual education programs are more effective at promoting the acquisition of English than are transitional bilingual education or "sink or swim" English immersion programs. Organizations dedicated to the defense of civil liberties and minority rights have also argued that laws restricting language use are inconsistent with the Equal Protection Clause of the Fourteenth Amendment to the Constitution, as well as the First Amendment's protection of free speech. Nevertheless, English-only advocates have, for the most part, been more effective at disseminating their views among a public that is generally unfamiliar with research on second language acquisition, and tends to view monolingualism as the norm in human societies.

Aurolyn Luykx

See also Activism and the Social Foundations of Education; Bilingual Education, History of; Discrimination and Prejudice; Hispanic Education; Immigrant Education: Contemporary Issues; Immigrant Education: History

See Visual History Chapter 14, Immigration and Education

Further Readings

Baron, D. (1992). *The English-only question: An official language for Americans?* Hartford, CT: Yale University Press.

Crawford, J. (2000). *At war with diversity: U.S. language policy in an age of anxiety.* Clevedon, UK: Multilingual Matters.

Web Sites

English for the Children: http://www.onenation.org

James Crawford's Language Policy Web Site & Emporium: http://ourworld.compuserve.com/homepages/jwcrawford

Language Policy Research Unit, Arizona State University: http://www.language-policy.org

EQUAL ACCESS ACT

In 1984, President Ronald Reagan signed into law the federal Equal Access Act (EAA). This law permits student-initiated noncurricular clubs to meeting during noninstructional time, if a given public secondary school maintains a "limited public forum." In addition, if a public school permits other noncurricular organizations to meet on school grounds outside of instructional time, it cannot bar religiously oriented student groups.

EAA was passed on the heels of a thrice-defeated proposed amendment to the U.S. Constitution that would have permitted state-sanctioned prayers in public schools, and the original legislative intent behind EAA was specifically religious. However, in the midst of the legislative process, the original wording was modified to include *secular,* noncurricular groups.

EAA's constitutionality was later upheld in *Board of Education v. Mergens* (1990). At the time, religious conservatives hailed the Supreme Court's 8–1 decision. However, the *Mergens* decision also built the foundation for later conservative discontent. In his lone dissent, Justice John Paul Stevens predicted that to meet the law's requirements, school districts would have to bar most groups from using their facilities if they wanted to ban controversial organizations such as the Ku Klux Klan.

Justice Stevens's observation proved to be prophetic. By the mid-1990s, Gay-Straight Alliances (GSAs), which are student-initiated clubs for both straight and gay secondary students, formed at public schools across the United States. In some instances, public school officials permitted the groups. But in the case of Salt Lake City, Utah, the local school board chose to ban all noncurricular groups rather than permit the GSA, which was their only other option under the constraints of *Mergens* and EAA. The student group later won in federal court, and the courts have consistently maintain the right of GSAs to form if the school district in question maintains either an open public forum or limited public forum. In lay terms, thanks to the EAA, if a school district permits a Bible club to meet on school property, it must permit a Gay-Straight Alliance to also meet. It is an ironic legacy from a conservative presidency.

Catherine A. Lugg

See also Federal and State Educational Jurisdiction; Politics of Education; School Governance

Further Readings

Grattan, R. M. (1999). It's not just for religion anymore: Expanding the protections of the Equal Access Act to gay, lesbian, and bisexual high school students. *George Washington Law Review, 67,* 577–599.

Lipkin, A. (1999). *Understanding homosexuality, changing schools: A text for teachers, counselors, and administrators.* Boulder, CO: Westview Press.

MacGillivray, I. K. (2004). *Sexual orientation and school policy: A practical guide for teachers, administrators, and community activists.* Lanham, MD: Rowman & Littlefield.

Russ, J. A., IV (1997). Creating a safe space for gay youth: How the Supreme Court's religious access cases can help young people organize at public schools. *Virginia Journal of Social Policy & the Law, 4,* 545–577.

Walsh, M. (1990, June 13). School religion club is constitutional, Court rules. *Education Week.* Available from http://www.edweek.org

ETHICAL ISSUES AND SCHOOL ATHLETICS

When applied to sports, *ethics* refers to the principles and values associated with sports participation, including sportsmanship and character development. It is an important issue in K–12 school athletics. Sports participation is generally believed to teach character and leadership skills that can be applied later in life. Teamwork, communication, peaceful resolution to conflict, goal setting, motivation, and the work ethic are seen as some of the positive aspects.

In addition, certain values and principles are associated with being engaged in athletic activities, such as respect (for rules and people), integrity, competition, honesty, safety, fairness, trust, and sportsmanship. Since ethics is often thought about as "doing the right thing," then sport ethics means doing the right thing in a sports setting. Sportsmanship cannot be achieved without ethical behavior.

When an ethical dilemma occurs in a sports setting, two or more values, such as wanting to win versus safety or fairness are in conflict and the participant is forced to choose between those values. When the need to win becomes more important, unethical or unsportsmanlike behavior may occur, such as a coach playing an injured athlete simply to win a contest. This entry examines the ethical issues in school athletic programs that are confronted by athletes and their coaches and parents.

Ethical Dilemmas

The extent to which ethical issues play an important role in the climate of contemporary schools can be seen in the results of a number of recent surveys. In a 2004 survey of 4,200 high school athletes, 12 percent of males and 36 percent of females admitted to using performance enhancing drugs in the past year. In addition, 68 percent of males and 50 percent of the females in the study admitted that they had bullied, teased, or taunted someone in the past year, and 55 percent of males acknowledged using racial slurs. A 2006 survey revealed that high school students involved in athletics cheat more in school than their nonathlete counterparts.

Young athletes are increasingly the subjects of news stories about negative incidents in sports. Recently, a thirteen-year-old boy was charged with murder for a fatal attack with a baseball bat on another boy who teased him about losing a baseball game. A case that received worldwide attention involved a Dominican immigrant who became one of the biggest sensations in Little League baseball history by pitching the first perfect Little League game in forty-four years and striking out 90 percent of opposing batters with a skill level that far exceeded all of his thirteen-year-old competitors. It was later discovered that his birth certificate had been altered by two years, meaning that he was and had been ineligible during his championship run. Parents, coaches, and players were all aware that he was too old to play but ignored the rules in favor of winning games.

Ethical issues involving school settings are not limited simply to students, but also involve coaches and parents. In a recent study of 803 athletes ranging in age from nine to fifteen, and 189 parents and 61 youth sport coaches, poor behavior among parents and coaches was consistently reported. Among parents, 13 percent acknowledged angrily criticizing their child's performance.

Coaches are increasingly reported as being involved in unsportsmanlike behaviors—behaviors that often clearly have ethical overtones. For example, a 2004 study indicates that 8 percent of coaches encouraged their players to hurt an opponent, while 7 percent condoned cheating, and 33 percent admitted yelling at players for making mistakes. In addition, 4 percent of the athletes reported that a coach had hit, kicked, or slapped them.

A relatively new phenomenon, "sports rage" has developed in recent years, with an increasing number of parents and coaches stepping over the line at sporting events and engaging in aggressive and violent behavior. Examples can be found of a father shooting a football coach because of the coach's treatment of his son, a father being beaten to death by another parent at a youth hockey game, four- and five-year-olds watching parents brawling at a t-ball game, and parents poisoning the members of an opposing team.

Ethical Theory Applied to Sport

A number of important concepts drawn from the more general field of ethics have a particular application to sports ethics. These include deontology; teleology; rule, principle, and the categorical imperative; situational ethics; and the ethics of social contracts.

Deontology refers to ethical decision making based on moral obligations and responsibilities or actions that are taken for reasons other than consequences, such as telling the truth and respecting others. In sport, helping an injured opponent, equal participation, and being honest with officials or referees serve as examples of deontology.

Teleology suggests that ethical behavior is based on ends, consequences, or goals, often manifested in sports by the focus on winning. How one wins may be viewed as less important than the victory itself. The utilitarian view looks at the pursuit of pleasure and the avoidance of pain as a measure of the "rightness" of an action, and when more than one person is involved, what is best for the greatest number of people.

In youth sports, for example, when a coach chooses to play only the best players in an effort to win, and thus ignores the notion that equal participation is important at this level, a teleogical approach has been used. If happiness is achieved, especially for the greatest number of people (team, coaches, players, and parents), then the fact that a few players sat on the bench is considered unimportant.

Another aspect of teleology, and perhaps a more practical way of approaching ethical theory lies with a situational approach, or "letting conscience be your guide." In this theory, an individual views each moral episode as a separate and unique event, and decisions are based on what is right in a given situation without regard to a specific set of rules, likely consequences, or moral obligations. An example of this type of behavior might be a coach looking at another team's playbook or an athlete tampering with the equipment of an opponent.

A rule- or principle-based perspective, based on the work of the German philosopher Immanuel Kant, is predicated on the maxim that an action is acceptable as a universal law. The cheater in sports doesn't want everyone to violate the rules; otherwise, cheating would offer no rewards. This includes the virtuous aspect of sport, or what it "ought" to be, as opposed to what it is, or winning the "right way" instead of "winning at all costs."

The social contract view of ethics maintains that the community or group dictates what is ethical or not. Athletes on a team, for example, agree to the rules and parameters of their participation, and decision making takes the form of give and take. When athletes take steroids, the action violates the social contract that athletes have agreed to abide by—that is, not to have an unfair advantage over their opponents.

Sportsmanship Versus Gamesmanship

Understanding the difference between sportsmanship and its counterpart, gamesmanship, is essential to a discussion of sport ethics. Sportsmanship refers to the virtuous perspective or the way that sport participation "ought" to be. It includes winning the right way, being willing to lose gracefully, having appropriate respect for opponents and officials, understanding and abiding by the spirit of the rules, and putting competition into perspective. Gamesmanship, on the other hand, is the winning-at-all-costs mentality; it is the way that sports may be, not how it should be. It includes looking for exceptions to the rules, taunting, fake fouls, illegal head starts, taunting to gain an advantage, intentionally injuring another player, and intimidation or espionage.

While winning is commonly the goal in a sport contest, the pervasive notion that it is the most important aspect of the contest causes unethical behavior and even violence in sports. In the 1996 Olympics, a popular Nike ad sent the message that "you don't win the silver, you lose the gold," and the famous NFL football legend and coach Vince Lombard is often quoted as saying "winning isn't everything, it's the only thing." These examples perpetuate the notion that winning is the most important goal in sports, and to be successful, one must attain that goal in whatever manner available. It is also a perspective that is not necessarily consistent with what is considered appropriate ethical behavior.

The Future of Sport Ethics

The future of sport ethics at the K–12 level rests on the ability of those involved to adhere to the principles of good sportsmanship and minimize the need to win at all costs. Education of parents, coaches, teachers, administrators, and athletes is essential, and can take the form of holding sport ethics clinics and workshops, developing and implementing codes of ethics for all stakeholders, rewarding good sportsmanship, and having a zero tolerance for gamesmanship.

Susan P. Mullane

See also Athletics, Policy Issues

Further Readings

Malloy, D. C., Ross, S., & Zakus, D. H. (2003). *Sport ethics: Concepts and cases in sport and recreation*. Toronto, ON, Canada: Thompson.

Shea, E. J. (1996). *Ethical decision in sport*. Springfield, IL: Charles C Thomas.

Shields, D. L., & Bredemeier, B. J. (1995). *Character development and physical activity*. Champaign, IL: Human Kinetics.

Web Sites

Center for Character and Citizenship: http://www.characterandcitizenship.org

Charactercount.org: http://www.charactercount.org

Positive Coaching Alliance: http://www.positivecoach.org

ETHICS AND EDUCATION

Ethical questions are about right and wrong, good and bad, just and unjust. They matter because what people do affects them individually, affects their community, and can even affect those they do not know or see. Unfortunately, students often do not know how to reason about an ethical decision. This is due to the fact that they, like many adults, do not recognize when ethical reasoning is the best option for making a decision or dealing with conflict. This entry briefly describes ethics, looks at the current forms of character education, and contrasts them with ethics-based approaches.

What Is Ethics?

More often than not, ethics is erroneously constructed in and by all areas of American culture as a prescriptive set of rules that answer whether an action in a given situation is universally perceived as correct or incorrect. Such a universal dichotomy rarely exists. Rather, making ethical decisions is a complex and nuanced process requiring critical examination, reflection, and explanation.

One should not rely on ethics to argue that one's behavior is beyond reproach or scrutiny. There is rarely a single correct answer that will be appropriate for all individuals. Rather, ethics must be constructed broadly, as centuries of philosophers have done, as a branch of moral philosophy that is concerned with the study of how individuals and groups go through the process and analysis of deciding what they believe in dealing with issues of determining what is right or wrong, just or unjust. Though ethics does involve answering complicated and often nuanced questions about issues including good and evil, and the limitations of personal responsibilities and behaviors, these answers are not universal.

There are many factors that are involved in making a decision about right or wrong when it comes to ethics. These include, but are not limited to, culture, values, norms, and theology—themselves all concepts that reasonable people do not always agree on. Though these concepts may be complicated and difficult to navigate, particularly in the current political and social climate, they are of vital importance. Students need to be able to identify situations that require ethical reasoning and then be able to act accordingly. What they currently get as an alternative is not acceptable.

Character Education

American educators across the country are currently engaged, often through governmental regulatory mandates, in the delivery of character education. Though there are several different approaches and curricula, all touted by companies seeking to profit from the need to instill character in our students, there are basic tenets that bind them together. Among these is the belief that students can be told, through edicts and dictums, how to be persons of character.

The prescriptive approach embedded in these various curricula and lessons explicitly sends students the message that if they simply follow the appropriate instructions, they will possess the qualities of character. These qualities include such admirable traits as fairness, honesty, respect, citizenship, and trustworthiness. The problem is not the promotion of these traits, but the manner in which they are promoted.

Students are simply told to be fair, honest, respectful, trustworthy, and good citizens. But they are rarely given the space to question what it means to be a person who reflects these traits. Students are told what these traits mean and how they manifest, without any examination of the ambiguous nature these words often take when in the context of real situations that individuals are forced to navigate. Students are presented with a binary of a person either "being" or "not being" the human embodiment of these characteristics

as a litmus test of whether or not they are persons of character.

An Ethics Approach

Ethics differs significantly from character education in that it seeks to develop critical thinking skills that result in habits of reason, rather than of compliance. Ethical reasoning presupposes no set of rules or principles; rather, it seeks to have students consider conflicting points of view.

Engaging students in activities that include ethical reasoning promotes the idea that critically analyzed and constructed arguments and rationales for making a decision are much more valuable than a simple regurgitation of established norms. Ethical reasoning results in shared insights about the agreements people need to have to live well together. Reasonable people disagree all the time, and that is not to be discouraged. Students need to learn that when they encounter situations in which people disagree, they need to be able to sort out what they believe and why. They must focus on the different processes that lead to these varying conclusions, not demonize each other for their disagreements.

Though this is an age that often seems to determine who is right by who can scream the loudest and for the longest, ethics differentiates itself from such outbursts by promoting civil discourse. Through a mutually respectful process that embraces the value inherent in multiple points of view, students come to understand that a deviation from the values espoused by a set of rules, as in the example of character education, does not make one a deviant. Instead of promoting the answers to the question of what is simply right or wrong in a given situation, schools could work to improve the critical thinking skills necessary for engaging in rigorous intellectual endeavors such as ethical reasoning. Students need to be able to articulate what they believe, but more importantly, they need to have the skills to articulate why they believe it.

Though there is not a great deal of this type of pedagogy currently practiced, a brief overview of one of the major methods used in the practice of engaging students in ethical reasoning and critical thinking will illuminate the differences between this method and the currently more utilized character education. By examining the differences it will be clear why inclusion of activities rooted in the encouragement of the development of critical thinking skills is more appropriate for participating in activities that may legitimately be placed in the category of education concerned with ethics. As noted previously, ethics is about the exchange of ideas and does not assume that there is one right answer that will eventually be reached by all who seek the truth. It is not simply a statement of right and wrong.

Tools for Teaching Ethics

One of the primary means of including ethics in the curriculum is by using vignettes, or case studies, as examples of situations where ethical reasoning must take place. The case studies are accompanied by a generic protocol that asks students to answer some basic questions about the situation they have been presented. These questions are:

1. What do you know about this situation? What do you believe to be true? Why do you believe it and not something else?

2. What don't you know? What hasn't been asked? Is this the whole truth? What questions have not been answered?

3. Who is responsible? For what? What could be done? What are the possible (not necessarily desirable) alternatives?

4. What should be done? By whom? Why is this the best ethical decision?

Before beginning this activity, teachers should participate in training that prepares them to look at situations through the lenses of veracity, transparency, responsibility, and justice. In learning how to guide students through answering the questions posed above, teachers should be able to tease apart these questions and see how they promote civil discourse and critical thinking, resulting in students gaining confidence in their abilities to participate in ethical decision making. This process of using critical thinking skills to engage in discourse about ethical issues with the goal of improving decision making is applied ethics.

Ethical reasoning tools like those allow students to openly and honestly discuss complex issues where it is perceived as acceptable for reasonable people to disagree. But this is not without its own predictable problems. There are two general problems that students experience when attempting to investigate such issues. First, like adults, students are quick to jump to opinions and hold to them dearly even when presented with evidence to the contrary. Second, after choosing sides on an issue, students often attack their peers who hold different views, rather than spending their energy on enhancing and strengthening the rationale for their positions.

Therefore, this protocol incorporates civil discourse with a required tone of decency that expects students to use critical thinking skills to arrive at the answer to the question, "Why do you believe what you believe and not something else?" Once students can successfully articulate an answer to this question by providing a rationale that is comprised of well-developed ideas, and not merely attacks on others who disagree, this is when they demonstrate that they possess the ability to call themselves ethical members of society.

The ability to participate in such activities is paramount to becoming a civically engaged member of a democratic system. By being able to comprehend the concepts of ethical reasoning through critical thinking, students feel empowered and demonstrate personal responsibility, integrity, and other values that are impossible to instill through just the more limiting didactic methods of character education.

Joshua Diem

See also Moral Education; Values Education

Further Readings

Dixon, B. (2002). Narrative cases. *Teaching Ethics, 3*(1), 29–48.

Kohn, A. (1997, February). How not to teach values: A critical look at character education. *Phi Delta Kappan,* 429–439.

Noddings, N. (2002). *Educating moral people: A caring alternative to character education.* New York: Teachers College Press.

Pernecky, M. (2003). Faculty development for teaching ethics across the curriculum: The case of an economic justice course. *Teaching Ethics, 4*(1), 11–24.

Pring, R. (2001). Education as a moral practice. *Journal of Moral Education, 30*(2), 101–112.

Rhodes, B. (2003). Ethics across the curriculum and the nature of morality: Some fundamental propositions. *Teaching Ethics, 4*(1), 59–65.

Slattery, P., & Rapp, D. (2002). *Ethics and the foundation of education: Teaching convictions in a postmodern world.* Boston: Allyn & Bacon.

Zubay, B., & Soltis, J. (2005). *Creating the ethical school: A book of case studies.* New York: Teachers College Press.

ETHICS CODES FOR TEACHERS

Unlike other professions such as medicine and law, the teaching profession has not developed a consistent and universal code of ethics—a prerequisite for being a profession in the minds of many theorists. Figures such as Myron Lieberman, an expert on education policy and teacher bargaining, have argued that such a code cannot emerge as long as collective bargaining drives teacher–school district negotiations. The development and enforcement of ethical standards, according to Lieberman, is left to administrators and school boards. This is not to suggest that teachers, as a group, are devoid of ethical principles, only that as a professional group, they have not adopted, nor do they enforce on their peers, an ethical code of behavior.

In this context, if a teacher observes other teachers conducting themselves in what may be perceived as an unethical manner, it is not considered his or her duty to enforce a code of professional ethics. This does not mean that teachers do not have an obligation ethically, and possibly legally, to report inappropriate behavior by fellow professionals. But it is not their job to enforce such codes or rules. Instead, this is the responsibility of school administrators and local school boards. Such a model is unlike that of the legal profession, in which peers judge peers based on their conduct and are subject to deliberations by the Bar. Likewise, doctors are subject to peer review by medical boards made up of fellow practitioners.

Ethical codes for teachers are occasionally promulgated at the state and local level, and there is an ethical code that has been developed by the National Education Association (NEA), something which does not exist for the American Federation of Teachers (AFT). According to Lieberman, if teacher unions played a more active role in defining and policing the ethical behavior of their members, they would find themselves faced with two insolvable problems: (1) they could not represent the interests of the teachers who had membership in the union, since there would be a conflict of interest; and (2) there would be an unavoidable problem of accountability—the union leadership, by definition, being an organization that is not legally accountable to the school district or the local community where the ethical misconduct may have occurred.

The educational philosopher Karl Hostetler maintains that Lieberman's interpretation is based on a "conceptually inadequate notion of moral and political negotiation." Instead, he argues that the union can take an intermediary role by establishing standards for ethical behavior and seeing that they are enforced, while at the same time advocating for the rights and protecting the interests of its members. In such a scenario, it becomes reasonable for a union to put in place a code of ethical conduct.

In the case of the National Education Association's code, its basic principles are brief and to the point. According to the NEA, educators (in terms of dealing with students) should seek to help each student realize his or her potential, while at the same time stimulating the process of inquiry, acquisition of knowledge and understanding, and the formulation of worthwhile goals. The teacher shall not deny students access to different points of view; shall not suppress or distort knowledge; shall make reasonable efforts to protect the safety of students; shall not intentionally embarrass the student; shall not discriminate against the student based on race, color, creed, sex, national origin, marital status, political or religious beliefs, family, social or cultural background, or sexual orientation; shall not use his or her professional relationship with students for private advantage; and shall not disclose private or confidential information about students unless compelled to do so by a clear professional reason or by the law.

In terms of commitment to the profession, the NEA Code of Ethics maintains that teachers are public servants, and therefore expected to maintain the highest possible standard of professional conduct. In this context, teachers should not make false statements;

should not overstate their professional qualifications; should not assist the entry of unqualified individuals into the profession; should not knowingly make a false statement concerning the qualifications of a candidate for a position; should not assist noneducators in participating in unauthorized teaching; should not unnecessarily discuss information about colleagues unless professionally compelled to do so or as required by the law; should not make false or malicious comments about a colleague; and should not take gifts that will influence their behavior or professional judgment.

In conclusion, ethical issues faced by teachers are particularly complex: Teachers are public servants, they serve highly complex and diverse populations, and they work with minors. While issues of regulation and authority may be debated, reasonable principles do exist, which ultimately provide guidelines on appropriate ethical conduct and behavior.

Eugene F. Provenzo, Jr.

See also National Education Association; Teachers, Professional Status of

Further Readings

Hostetler, K. (1989). Who says professional ethics is dead? A response to Myron Lieberman. *Phi Delta Kappan, 70,* 723–725.

Lieberman, M. (1994). Professional ethics in education. In M. Lieberman, *Public education: An autopsy.* Cambridge, MA: Harvard University Press.

Peters, R. S. (1966). *Ethics and education.* Atlanta, GA: Scott, Foresman.

Web Sites

National Education Association, Code of Ethics of the Education Profession: http://www.nea.org/aboutnea/code.html

EUGENICS

Eugenics is a movement, supposedly based on scientific evidence, that holds that people are naturally superior and inferior to each other based on their racial and genetic makeup. Its political dimension, which was widespread in the early twentieth century, used this basis to recommend selective breeding of superior people and policies of restricted immigration, sterilization, and segregation of those deemed inferior. Traces of this ideology remain in behavioral determinism. This entry looks at the history of the movement, especially in the United States.

Historical Background

The American eugenics movement can be traced to Great Britain and to the work of Sir Francis Galton, who coined the term *eugenics* in 1882 to mean "well born." A member of the British upper classes, Galton thought that the social positions achieved by England's ruling elite were determined by their superior biological inheritance; nature was far more important than nurture in human development. Believing in the determinism of biology and "positive" eugenics, he recommended that society's best marry their superior counterparts and have many offspring.

By contrast, American mainline eugenics added a "negative" dimension to its policy options. By 1906 the American Breeders Association investigated and reported on just the issues that would have interested Francis Galton. Building on a rigid interpretation of the recently rediscovered research by the Moravian monk Gregor Mendel, and presuming hereditary differences between human races, the association popularized the themes of selective breeding, the biological threat of "inferior types," and the need for recording and controlling human heredity. By 1910, and under the leadership of Charles Davenport, the Eugenics Record Office served to propagandize eugenics nationally.

By 1918, the Galton Society, reflecting its namesake's interests, was formed in New York City. Concerned with policies of differential breeding and presumed human racial differences, it brought together eugenicists such as Charles Benedict Davenport, racist authors such as Madison Grant and Lothrop Stoddard, and leaders from the academy, museums, and philanthropic organizations. Consistent with its popularization mission, the society was organized into committees focused on cooperation with clergy, religious sermon contests, crime prevention, formal education, and selective immigration.

Transformed in the 1920s into the American Eugenics Society, it sponsored Fitter Families Contests and exhibits at state fairs in locations as varied as Kansas and Massachusetts. Exemplifying the tone of these exhibits, the 1926 display "The Triangle of Life," which referred to environment, education, and heritage, warned of the threat of inherited "unfit human traits," including feeblemindedness, criminality, and pauperism. "Selected parents will have better children," poster exhibits claimed. "This is the great aim of eugenics."

Impact on Education

Mainline eugenics also found support from leaders in educational statistics and education for gifted children. For example, E. L. Thorndike and Leta Hollingworth popularized eugenics in their classes at Columbia University's Teachers College throughout their careers. Using flawed racial interpretations of the World War I Army alpha and beta test data, Carl Brigham added to eugenics' temporary luster in *A Study of American Intelligence* (1923). At the same time, authors such as Edward A. Wiggam were recommending policies of controlled breeding for America's citizenry. Traveling across the country with lantern-slide presentations that linked eugenics with the rise of civilization, he proposed a new ten commandments based upon eugenic principles.

Popular eugenics was also part of the fabric of American popular culture during the twentieth century's second and third decades. For example, on a given Saturday night, high school students might go to the movies to see *The Black Stork* or *Tomorrow's Children,* films that supported eugenics-based sterilizations. On Sunday, they might join their families in church, where they could listen to sermons selected for awards by the American Eugenics Society, learning that human improvement required marriages of society's "best" with "best." Monday's newspaper might discuss the threat posed to America by a "rising tide of feeblemindedness," a tide which required restrictions on southern and eastern European immigration. And

Tuesday's paper might carry the "good" news that thousands of Americans were being sterilized for eugenic purposes. On Wednesday and Thursday, while visiting a state fair with their hygiene class, these students might sign up for a eugenic evaluation at a Fitter Families Exhibit.

By week's end, and back in the classroom, these same students would learn from their biology textbook's chapters on eugenics about the beneficial policies of immigration restriction, sterilization, and segregation. One analysis of high school textbooks determined that between 1914 and 1948, over 60 percent supported Galton's original policies of differential birth rates.

Eugenics also found its place in the college classroom; many of America's leading universities, including Harvard, Columbia, Cornell, and Brown offered courses on the topic. In fact, by 1928, 376 separate college courses included the subject, with approximately 20,000 students and the potential to influence the social attitudes of America's future leaders.

Eugenics' Decline

Mainline eugenics became a mainstay of racism in the United States, and it was used as a rationalization for the Nazi Holocaust, but by the early 1930s, its popularity in the United States had diminished. The reasons were many. By the late 1920s, it had succeeded in its policy initiatives; anti-immigration laws had been passed, the Supreme Court had legalized state-sponsored sterilization, and many states had passed antimiscegenation laws. In addition, legitimate advances in biology revealed eugenics to be a suspect science. Further, the worldwide economic depression that began in 1929 made it clear that the unemployment of millions could not simply be explained by their heredity.

While the early twentieth-century eugenics had lost its legitimacy by the 1930s, biological determinism did not, and today's public continues to read of the links between complex human behavior and genetics. There are claims that people are what their genes make them, that the basis for a market economy is genetic, that faith is inherited, and that playing fair is hereditary.

While these are reports of pioneering work, the findings are far from robust enough to serve as the basis for significant education policy and practice. Rather, schools and teachers frame a series of environments—learning, social, physical, and moral—that also shape the students entrusted to them.

Steven Selden

See also Intelligence Testing; "Scientific" Racism

Further Readings

Gould, S. J. (1981). *The mismeasure of man.* New York: W. W. Norton.

Kevles, D. (1985). *In the name of eugenics: Genetics and the uses of human heredity.* New York: Alfred A. Knopf.

Lombardo, P. A. (2003). Taking eugenics seriously: Three generations of ??? are enough. *Florida State University Law Review, 30*(2), 191–218.

Selden, S. (1999). *Inheriting shame: The story of eugenics and racism in America.* New York: Teachers College Press.

F

FAMILY, SCHOOL, AND COMMUNITY PARTNERSHIPS

The social context in which children learn and develop—their families, schools, and communities—has rapidly changed in only a few decades. Today's images of the postmodern family differ greatly from the traditional images of the modern family of the 1950s. Correspondingly, as these contextual blueprints have shifted, so have partnerships within the family and between each of these environmental settings. These relational changes bring with them perceptions of self and experiences with others. This entry examines the possible impact of cultural transitions on family, school, and community partnerships.

Schools have a vested interest in children's families since families serve as the primary agents of socialization. Likewise, schools are adapting to societal change by providing more supportive, familylike atmospheres and collaborating with community partners to form learning communities. As the demographics of schools shift, the need for multistranded partnerships is underscored by issues of poverty, transience, an aging population, and cultural diversity. All of these aspects point toward ways that schools mirror the larger culture.

Effects of Cultural Transitions on Family Partnerships

Television content in popular culture lends insight into modern and postmodern assumptions on the nature of family and the impact of cultural transitions on family partnerships. During the 1950s, family sitcoms such as the *Donna Reed Show, Leave It to Beaver,* and *Ozzie and Harriet* created images of self-perceptions and experiences with others. For example, with regularity each of these families was cast with father as breadwinner, mother as homemaker, two children, and a dog. Families were all Caucasian and lived in middle-class, suburban neighborhoods. Togetherness was valued and, many times, romanticized by scenes of family meals around the dining room table, parents reading bedtime stories to children, and families playing games on a well-groomed lawn. In general, even though this portrayal of a modern family was accurate, it was uncharacteristic of the many ethnically diverse families and even some nuclear families during this same time period.

Cultural shifts from the assumptions of the modern family to the assumptions of the postmodern family are ambiguous. There are no specific timelines between these two Western phenomena. However, the belief that scientific theory can yield absolute truths, the underestimation of technology's ability to create powerful weapons of mass destruction, and the perpetual destruction of the environment served as the impetus for questioning the given structures and the turn toward postmodern thought.

Family sitcoms such as the *George Lopez Show,* the *Fresh Prince of Bel-Air,* and *Roseanne* represent the diverse nature of postmodern family partnerships. Overnight, culturally diverse families appeared, with relatives moving in and out to form new family ties.

Issues of race, class, and gender projected families as uniquely different from families in earlier versions of modern family life. For example, in the *George Lopez Show*, a Hispanic man becomes employed in a job that gives him newfound power. His family includes his acerbic mother, working wife, dyslexic son, adolescent daughter, and newly divorced father-in-law. The modern role of "father knows best" has now transitioned to a freewheeling approach to parenthood. Family sitcoms, couched in the framework of modern and postmodern worldviews, convey the impact of cultural transitions on the nature of family life and the renewed interest in strengthening family partnerships.

The Nature of School and Family Partnership

Schools have a vested interest in children's families because the initial socialization of the child begins in the home. Schools continue the socializing process begun in the home by means of curricula. In her work on child, family, school, and community, Roberta Berns found that the school's ability to socialize the child depends greatly upon the nature of the families the schools serve and the ability of the school to develop mutual partnerships. Other longitudinal studies find close-knit partnerships between home and school result in a significant difference in children's learning and development. As schools reflect society and continue to function as society's medium for change, relations with family partners have become a critical focus.

However, public schools do not operate in a vacuum, and how to effectively preserve a diverse cultural heritage and yet prepare individuals for the future is a challenge that educators confront daily. Two major underlying societal factors that influence the decision-making process in American public schools are a political ideology that supports the democratic ideal of equal opportunity for all school-age children to gain a free public school education and an economic system that operates on the principle of cost effectiveness and accountability. Both of these factors help shape the partnerships of school, family, and community.

Currently, most public school funding comes from local property taxes and from state revenues from sales tax and income tax. In comparison, direct federal funding to public schools is limited. Most federal resources to public schools are in the form of grants to local educational agencies and entitlements such as Title I of the Elementary and Secondary Education Act of 1965, which provides support for qualifying low-income families. Nonetheless, the process by which public schools are funded means that families living in lower socioeconomic school districts may have less school funding available to prepare children for the future. Many times these children are members of minority groups, their family's income is below the poverty line, and they need additional intervention programs with more individualized accommodations in order to meet national testing requirements legislated by the No Child Left Behind Act (NCLB).

One determinant of educational revenue distribution is the change in size and distribution of the population. As an increasing population competes for resources, more people need supportive services to live. One reason for the increase in population is the fact that people now live longer. In only a few years, the baby boomers will be eligible for Social Security and Medicare health benefits. The question for schools will be whether or not this sizable group will still be interested in voting for school bond issues in support of other people's children.

Population distribution is another critical issue influencing partnerships. U.S. Census reports reveal that transience is a form of diversity that can measurably affect school funding and the ability of a school to properly nurture the school-to-family relationship. Harold Hodgkinson, Director for the Center for Demographic Policy, Institute for Educational Leadership, reported that 40 million Americans move each year, while only 3 million babies are born. These facts indicate that a teacher might get to know one group of students in the fall only to find his or her classroom filled with newcomers in the spring. Therefore, mobility becomes a larger issue than birth rate not only in funding but also in the ability of schools to create multistranded partnerships with families.

Another expanding population is homeless families. The U.S. Census has reported that families with children make up more than one third of the nation's homeless populations. Poverty continues to outpace all other issues as the dividing line in achievement. If a child is a minority but middle class, that child's chances for success are much greater than those of any other child who is stricken by poverty. The concept of creating caring communities to support the success of low-income children highlights the need for bridging the multiple worlds of families, schools, and communities. "It will take a village" to make a difference in the life of a child who lives in poverty.

The demographic shift in the size of culturally diverse populations is another critical issue influencing the development of partnerships. North Carolina alone has experienced a 394 percent increase in its Hispanic population over the past ten years, making it the nation's leader in Hispanic population growth. Even so, the percentage of Hispanics in North Carolina's population is only 4.7 percent, compared to New York at 15.1 percent, Florida at 16.8 percent, Texas at 32 percent, and California at 32.4 percent. Consequently, federal initiatives along with state and local public schools are collaborating with community colleges and four-year colleges to develop licensure programs for in-service and pre-service ESL (English as a Second Language) teachers to accommodate the needs of these culturally diverse learners.

School and Family Involvement

Typically, traditional parent-involvement programs have been composed of family resources flowing into a school for the main purpose of supporting the school's curriculum, programs, and activities. This unidirectional approach to parent involvement is, by itself, an ineffective way to connect and involve families, as far too many families are missing from this mutual endeavor. Presently, the goal of partnerships is to create learning communities where families, communities, and schools collaborate to provide the best possible educational opportunities and learning environments for children.

Cultural transitions have called our attention to the need for "outreach models" for developing family, school, and community partnerships. In *Preparing Educators to Involve Families,* Heather Weiss and others suggest that schools and communities use a combination of multiple approaches and strategies adapted to the particular needs of the learning community.

Some of these approaches and strategies developed by educators are (a) creating a familylike atmosphere at school initiated on the premise that family involvement at school is an outgrowth of family involvement at home; (b) using a school improvement model based on family outreach programs with a focus on creating caring communities of mutual trust; (c) collaborating with the "funds of knowledge" model developed by Louis Moll, which focuses on knowledge and skills found in family households as a resource for developing culturally relevant pedagogy; and (d) empowering approaches that serve low-income families, which focus on supporting parents' development of self-confidence so that they can advocate for better schools and higher expectations for children. Research from these models hypothesizes that if families value education, create home environments that foster learning, maintain positive and reasonable expectations for children, and become involved with schools, then achievement gaps tend to narrow.

Collaborating With Community

When schools function as learning communities, they form networks with various community partners in planning activities that connect school program goals to student opportunities and experiences that would not otherwise be feasible. These partners include volunteers from all sectors of the community. For example, martial arts classes and popular dance are taught by community instructors to help develop student self-esteem and interest in community programs. Community business partners defray costs for field trips, sponsor apprenticeships, serve as guest speakers, and donate computer technology to schools for career training. Health care volunteers provide students and families with wellness information and medical testing. These are only a few of many linkages between the school and the community that support children and families.

Cultural transitions within families and between the environmental settings of family, school, and community influence the nature of partnerships. Some suggestions to help strengthen these important relationships include organizing more inclusive networks for those whose voices previously have been excluded and establishing local neighborhood centers that provide a safe haven and convenient meeting place. Schools of higher education might develop tutoring and mentoring programs, or community service projects that focus on the care of others and the environment. Builders of community could begin to restructure and restore neighborhoods, with families and schools at the center of the planning process. Each of these recommendations points to the influence of cultural transitions on family, school, and community partnerships.

Frances Putnam Crocker

See also Cultural Studies; Popular Culture; Sociology of Education

Further Readings

Berns, R. M. (2007). *Child, family, school, community, socialization and support.* Belmont, CA: Thomson.

Epstein, J. L. (2001). *School, family, and community partnerships: Preparing educators and improving schools.* Boulder, CO: Westview Press.

Hodgkinson, H. (Dec. 2000–Jan. 2001). Educational demographics: What teachers should know. *Educational Leadership, 58*(4), 6–11.

Huston, P. (2001). *Families as we are: Conversations from around the world.* New York: Feminist Press.

Taylor, L. S., & Whittaker, C. R. (2003). *Bridging multiple worlds: Case studies of diverse educational communities.* Boston: Pearson Education.

Weiss, H. B., Kreider, H., Lopez, M. E., & Chatman, C. M. (Eds.). (2005). *Preparing educators to involve families: From theory to practice.* Thousand Oaks, CA: Sage.

FAMILY LITERACY

Family literacy is commonly examined in larger discussions of literacy and language and in relationship to PreK through 12 schooling, adult learning, or child-parent learning in home and school settings. As a formal area of inquiry in language and literacy research, family literacy has a relatively short history. Definitions of family literacy vary. A common definition used in the United States and the United Kingdom describes family literacy as encompassing a wide variety of programs that promote parents and children in literacy-enhancing practices and activities. This definition is often accompanied by a more purposeful and controversial goal, described later in this entry: to improve the literacy of "educationally disadvantaged parents and children," based on the assumption that parents are their child's first and most influential teachers. However, family literacy in its broad sense includes a focus on the social practices that exist within families and the ways that individual family members and the family as a unit access and use fundamental reading, writing, and problem-solving abilities to engage with each other and the world and to achieve their personal, academic, and work goals.

Historical Background

The origins of family literacy can be traced to different and equally compelling points in the larger discussion of literacy, particularly reading research in the 1960s. Delores Durkin's work on young children in low-income homes in Chicago pointed to the significant role that parents assume and play in engaging their children in reading and supporting their literacy development. Studies such as Durkin's emerged during a time when there was increasing attention to children's achievement in diverse cultural, ethnic, and language families and communities. Although they were not borne entirely from the national focus on civil rights, the studies were often intertwined with controversial discussions that coincided with the civil rights movement and questions about equality, equity, and justice for minority children and their families.

Prior to the 1960s, family literacy had long been the site of inquiry on reading and literacy—as far back as the eighteenth and nineteenth centuries. In the late nineteenth and early twentieth centuries, family literacy studies centered on the lives of children and families of European ancestry who were from upper-income homes, were literate, and were exposed to high levels of literacy within the home. Because these families shared a common social status and land of origin, there was little examination of intragroup differences and the relationship between these differences and the cultural histories that divided or connected the families. Not until the 1960s and 1970s did these studies directly address the cultural dimensions of literacy within families or the importance of exploring culture in designing and implementing instructional approaches.

The historical progression of family literacy mirrors the shifts in reading and literacy research more generally. By the 1980s, traditional foci on reading had expanded to literacy, taking into consideration social processes, sociocognitive development, and sociocultural contexts for learning. Increased attention to children's literacy within these contexts as well as increasing emphasis on adult literacy translated into a life-course perspective in which children's early literacy or emergent literacy was examined. William Teale and Elizabeth Sulzby's research on emergent literacy opened up discussions of parents' understanding of children's early expressions of reading and writing. At the same time, adult literacy was shifting its focus to consider the diversity of purposes for which adults seek to improve their literacy, the diversity of learners themselves, and the places (e.g., programs) where such literacy learning was taking place.

Despite the focus on families in family literacy, few studies at this point provided a picture of the nature of family interactions, experiences, and processes or examined in depth how the social, cultural, and societal issues associated with different levels of literacy influenced learning in families. Denny Taylor's 1983 book, *Family Literacy*, served as a catalyst for examining the ways in which families use informal and formal literacy knowledge to support themselves, their children, and their communities. Taylor's ethnographic approach to studying families and literacy also deviated from past approaches and offered observers—researchers, practitioners, and policy makers alike—a new lens into the everyday literate experiences, negotiations, and goals of families.

A range of studies was conducted subsequently, with foci that traveled between and within different methodological and conceptual frameworks. One conceptual strand included studies that were primarily interested in the ways in which families take up roles and responsibilities that require differing levels of literacy. Another examined children's literacy learning in school and the role parents play in supporting children's literacy development in and out of schools. A third focused primarily on parent-child literacy interactions. A fourth addressed family literacy within diverse language groups. A fifth examined intergenerational learning in families and the reciprocity between and among different social systems that constitute families.

The primary focus of work in family literacy today is still largely on parent-child learning, although several studies of intergenerational learning exist. Much of the public attention has focused on family literacy programs themselves. Such programs and associated projects number in the hundreds and are based in settings ranging from Head Start to other public-funded and private-funded early-childhood efforts designed to enhance reading, writing, and other literate acts in the home and school. A common mission of these programs is to address the needs of parents with low literacy, to "eradicate low literacy," and increase the literacy options and opportunities for these parents' children. Programs vary by focus and location and differ in the primary adult populations they serve. In addition to getting parents involved, some programs recruit grandparents as a way both to engage children in literacy learning and to help children learn more about their heritage. Other programs are located in schools, while still others are administered through outreach efforts and are operated by churches and faith communities. There are also programs offered in community centers or in prisons that may encourage the use of computers or may prepare parents to reconnect with their children.

Current Issues and Tensions

Several issues have been identified as areas of tension in family literacy. For example, unlike reading research, family literacy is still being defined, though there continues to be relatively limited focus on families as institutions and cultures guiding the instruction. The single focus on improving literacy is associated by many researchers with a deficit perspective that assumes that low-income and low-income minority families come to literacy learning with few resources or are empty vessels to be filled. Thus, a mismatch may exist between the findings of research on reading and literacy within families and the emphasis of family literacy programs.

At the same time, researchers and practitioners alike have focused on the social processes in literacy learning and highlighted the significance of culture and context in understanding and supporting children's literacy development. On the one hand, the field of family literacy has struggled to situate itself in broad conceptualizations and critical discourses of literacy. For example, a series of rich ethnographic studies from the 1980s to the present have pointed to multifaceted and complex relationships within home, school, and community contexts. These contexts were thought to influence how children and adults engage in formal literacy instruction, draw upon diverse linguistic and cultural practices to communicate within and across different settings, and make meaning of literacy.

On the other hand, theorists such as Brian Street and David Barton and Mary Hamilton would argue that the field has not moved far enough outside of autonomous models, in which literacy as a technique is applied across all social and cultural contexts with uniformity, to embrace more expansive models (e.g., critical literacy or new literacy studies).

Two seminal works in literacy and family literacy, Shirley Brice Heath's 1983 *Ways With Words* and Denny Taylor and Catherine Dorsey-Gaines's 1988 *Growing Up Literate*, both argue that the study of family literacy is more than the study of individual learners within a family or within programs alone. Learners typically do not leave family influences or cultural markers at home upon entering literacy instruction. Similarly, in the 1990s, Victoria Purcell-Gates and Vivian Gadsden referred to the increasing significance of studying culture in family literacy, stating that research into family literacy practices is research into cultural practice.

To organize assumptions, goals, and practices in the field, Elsa Auerbach identified three models—intervention/prevention, multiple literacies, and social change—that still hold currency. The intervention/prevention approach is consistent with historical efforts to eradicate low literacy among poor, undereducated parents, through a series of programs and approaches designed to replace home practices with school-like approaches. The multiple-literacies approach takes up this sociocultural perspective in a particular way by examining the much-discussed mismatch between the expectations and practices of school-based literacy learning and the home practices of children who are not achieving in school. Social change is focused on multiple literacies but also highlights the role of power hierarchies in sustaining political and social structures that alienate rather than engage learners and their cultural histories. From this perspective, failure to attend to these imbalances of power reinscribes inequity and inequality. For example, in a series of texts during the 1990s (*From the Child's Point of View, Learning Denied, Toxic Literacies,* and *Many Families, Many Literacies*), Taylor discusses the need for structural change in the social and political hierarchies that govern institutions and work against the inclusion of historically marginalized groups.

Possibilities and Considerations

More is known about family literacy today than a decade ago. However, challenges remain in terms of how much more there is to learn and how to disentangle the complexities that arise from problems that interfere with learning (e.g., poverty, poor schools). Although there are several issues that persist, two are highlighted here. The first is a conceptual question that ultimately contributes to methodological options: What are the ways that family literacy might be examined in the context of new models of research, including critical literacy and new literacy studies? Moreover, how do we study, understand, and serve learners as members of a family units, which they are as likely to distance themselves from as embrace? The second follows from the first: How are the issues of father involvement addressed in family literacy programs? As Gadsen and her coresearchers have observed, there are few fathers who participate in family literacy programs, and there is little information about those who do attend. Some of the problems associated with engaging fathers stem from the unavailability of some fathers who serve as the family's primary breadwinners; in other cases, fathers live outside of the home and are not considered as important by program staff, are difficult to reach, or are not accessible. The issue of father involvement raises questions about how gender is discussed and approached in programs.

As the field of family literacy grows, several questions persist, a few of which are: What are the outcomes of children and adults participating in family literacy programs, and how do we examine these outcomes to capture the range of learning that occurs? What actually occurs in programs that promote reading, writing, and problem solving? What are the activities involving reading, writing, and problem solving that are integrated within the larger life issues of parenting, parent-child interactions, and family functioning? And finally, how are issues around cultural difference, race, and poverty examined and addressed in research and practice?

Vivian L. Gadsden

See also Adult Education and Literacy; Literacy in American Culture; Reading, History of

Further Readings

Auerbach, E. (1995). Deconstructing the discourse of strengths in family literacy. *Journal of Reading Behavior, 27,* 643–661.

Auerbach, E. (1997). Family literacy. In V. Edwards & D. Corson (Eds.), *Encyclopedia of langauge and education: Vol. 2. Literacy* (pp. 153–161). London: Springer Press.

Barton, D., & Hamilton, M. (1998). *Local literacies: Reading and writing in one community.* New York: Routledge.

Durkin, D. (1966). *Teaching young children to read.* Boston: Allyn & Bacon.

Gadsden, V. L. (1995). Representations of literacy: Parents' images in two cultural communities. In L. Morrow (Ed.), *Family literacy connections in schools and communities* (pp. 287–303). Newark, NJ: International Reading Association.

Gadsden, V. L. (1998). Family culture and literacy learning. In F. Lehr, J. Osborn, & P. D. Pearson (Eds.), *Learning to read* (pp. 32–50). New York: Garland Press.

Gadsden, V. L. (2007). The adult learner in family literacy: Gender and its intersections with role and context. In Belzer (Ed.), *Defining and improving quality in adult basic education: Issues and challenges* (pp. 573–587). Mahwah, NJ: Lawrence Erlbaum.

Heath, S. B. (1983). *Ways with words: Language, life, and work in communities and classrooms.* Cambridge, UK: Cambridge University Press.

Purcell-Gates, V. (1993). Issues for family literacy research: Voices from the trenches. *Language Arts, 70,* 670–677.

Street, B. V. (1984) *Literacy in theory and practice.* Cambridge, UK: Cambridge University Press.

Street, B. V. (2001). *Literacy and development: Ethnographic perspectives.* New York: Routledge.

Taylor, D. (1983). *Family literacy: Young children learning to read and write.* Portsmouth, NH: Heinemann.

Taylor, D. (1990). *Learning denied.* Portsmouth, NH: Heinemann.

Taylor, D. (Ed.). (1997). *Many families, many literacies: An International Declaration of Principles.* Portsmouth, NH: Heinemann.

Taylor, D., & Dorsey-Gaines, C. (1988). *Growing up literate: Learning from inner-city families.* Portsmouth, NH: Heinemann.

Teale, W. H., & Sulzby, E. (Eds.). (1986). *Emergent literacy: Reading and writing* (pp. vii–xxv). Norwood, NJ: Ablex.

Wasik, B. H. (Ed.). (2004). *Handbook of family literacy.* Mahwah, NJ: Lawrence Erlbaum.

FEDERAL AND STATE EDUCATIONAL JURISDICTION

Common or public education has traditionally been a state and local concern. In the landmark 1954 desegregation case of *Brown v. Board of Education,* the Supreme Court recognized that education is "perhaps the most important function of state and local governments." While all fifty state constitutions contain variously worded provisions recognizing their responsibility to provide public education, the U.S. Constitution does not refer to schools or include any article pertaining to education. In *San Antonio v. Rodriguez,* the nation's highest court concluded that public education is not a federal fundamental right, but rather a function of the state, reserved for the states by the Tenth Amendment.

Even after the Court's decision in *Rodriguez,* debate over whether education is a fundamental right persisted. *Plyler v. Doe* revisited the issue when deciding whether the state of Texas violated the equal protection rights of undocumented children by denying them admittance into public school. The Court in *Plyler* held that education, while not a fundamental right, is an important state interest and that no rational basis exists to provide it to some children and deny it to others solely based on their immigration status.

Lack of any constitutionally expressed federal jurisdiction over education has not prevented the federal government from intervention in educational issues. It has always had sole responsibility for the

Bureau of Indian Affairs–funded school system established on or near Indian reservations and trust lands throughout the nation. In mandating other educational concerns, Congress has utilized the authority of both the Spending and the Commerce Clauses. Under the Spending Clause, the Individuals with Disabilities Education Act (IDEA) was enacted, requiring significant state action to equalize educational opportunities, but only for the disabled.

Other examples of federal involvement in state public education include the desegregation requirements in *Brown* and the antidiscrimination provisions of the Civil Rights Act of 1964, which prohibit discrimination based upon race, color, or national origin in any program receiving federal financial assistance. Subsequently, the Equal Educational Opportunity Act of 1974 forbade states from denying "equal educational opportunity" to individuals based on "race, color, sex, or national origin." Court cases relying on the federal constitutional rights of free speech, as well as free exercise and nonestablishment of religion, have had a significant impact on the day-to-day functioning of public schools.

In 2001, the federal government made a significant foray into the educational policy sphere when the No Child Left Behind Act (NCLB) was signed by President Bush. NCLB reauthorized and amended the Elementary and Secondary Education Act (ESEA), requiring all schools to set high standards, assess students for attainment of those standards, and make adequate yearly progress at the risk of losing federal funding. With more and more federal legislative incursions into public education, the question of whether a federal fundamental right to public education exists may continue to fall under court scrutiny.

Teresa Anne Rendon

See also School Governance; School Law; State Role in Education

Further Readings

Patterson, J. T. (2001). Brown v. Board of Education: *A civil rights milestone and its troubled legacy.* New York: Oxford University Press.

Brown v. Board of Education, 347 U.S. 483 (1954).
Brown v. Board of Education, 349 U.S. 294 (1955).
Civil Rights Act of 1964, 42 U.S.C. § 2000.
Equal Education Opportunity Act, 20 U.S.C. §§ 1703 *et seq.*
Imber, M., & Van Geen, T. (2001). *A teacher's guide to education law.* Mahwah, NJ: Lawrence Erlbaum.
Individuals with Disabilities Education Act, 20 U.S.C. §§1400 *et seq.*
No Child Left Behind Act, 20 U.S.C. §§ 1041 *et seq.*
Plyler v. Doe, 457 U.S. 202 (1982).
San Antonio Independent School District v. Rodriguez, 411 U.S. 1 (1973).
Zirkel, P. A., Richardson, S. N., & Goldbert, S. S. (1995). *A digest of Supreme Court decisions affecting education* (3rd ed.). Bloomington, IN: Phi Delta Kappa Educational Foundation.

FEMINIST THEORY IN EDUCATION

Feminist theory contributes significantly to the social and cultural foundations of education. This entry traces the history of the feminist movement in the United States, explores various meanings of feminist theory, and considers what feminist theory contributes to education.

In the United States the feminist movement is associated with three waves, or periods of time, with the "first wave" feminist movement (1848–1920s) representing women's efforts to get the right to vote, to own property, to divorce and receive alimony and child support, and to manage their own bodies (e.g., sexual reproductive rights). First wave feminism is associated with Seneca Falls, New York, and the sustained agitation for concrete social change of suffragettes such as Lucreta Mott, Elizabeth Cady Stanton, Susan B. Anthony, and Sojourner Truth.

The "second wave" of the feminist movement corresponds to the 1960s to '70s and to women's efforts to obtain equal access to higher education in all fields of study and to be free from discriminated in the workplace due to their gender. While second wave feminists sought equal treatment in the classroom and on the job, they continued the fight for the right to manage their own bodies (e.g., sexual reproductive rights). Second wave feminism is associated with *Ms.* magazine and with Betty Friedan, Gloria Steinem, and Mary Daly, to name a few. It was during this time that women's studies programs opened on college campuses across the country and feminist theory began to develop in earnest.

Starting in the early 1990s, a "third wave" of the feminist movement began to develop. This third wave represents an explosion of multiple, diverse perspectives as Third World, lesbian, Chicana, indigenous, and Black feminists and others add their voices to the movement. They critique the essentializing of "woman" as a category, one which has privileged heterosexuality, First World, middle-class, and White norms. Third wave feminism is associated with Audrey Lorde, Adrienne Rich, María Lugones, Gloria Anzaldúa, Judith Butler, Luce Irigaray, Donna Haraway, Gayatri Spivak, and Trinh Minh-ha, to name a few.

Beyond a general agreement that women have been oppressed and unjustly treated, and that discrimination on the basis of gender is wrong, there is much upon which various feminists do not agree. It is dangerous to assume there is a "female point of view" or that women have special resources available to them due to their experiences as females. It is also problematic to think that only women can be feminists. In fact, some postmodern feminist scholars, such as Judith Butler and Luce Irigaray, recommend that we get rid of "gender" as a general category, because of the false binary it establishes (man/woman) and the androcentric and/or heterosexual norms and standards it imposes of people's shifting sexual identities. The feminist movement, in all its waves, has helped us understand that the personal is political, that what goes on in the home is very much related to how the larger society defines individuals' gendered roles, and that those roles need to be critiqued. Feminists have demonstrated that language is not gender neutral, but in fact affects our consciousness, and that social institutions are not natural or given, and therefore settled for all time. Feminist theory reveals how gender roles are socially constructed, by showing how they have varied across time and cultures, and how they continue to adapt and change. Feminism is concerned with the forms and functions of power and how power is wielded, in particular against girls and women.

Second Wave Feminism

During the second wave of feminist research, much focus was placed on discrimination issues within educational settings. Researchers looked at tracking issues, and why it is that girls were tracked into "traditionally feminine" classes such as child care, education, home economics, and nursing, and not honors classes and higher-level math and science classes. Attention was placed on studying what teachers do in schools to discourage girls, such as not calling on them as often as boys or not giving them the opportunity to correct their mistakes before moving on to someone else (usually a boy). Attention was also placed on the curricula, and how girls were presented in pictures and stories in comparison to boys. Researchers looked at ways students were assessed and began to consider the possibility that what were taken to be gender neutral and unbiased methods of assessment might actually favor boys over girls, given that boys consistently score higher on field independent, analytically focused material and multiple-choice exams, while girls tend to do better on essay-type exams. During this time, all classes became open to both genders, and efforts began to be made to actively encourage girls to achieve at the same levels as boys.

In university settings, with the opening of women's studies programs during the second wave, faculty began to explore gender issues and to consider whether there was gender discrimination at the higher education level involving students, faculty, and/or administrators. Faculty began to critically examine their philosophies of teaching to discover if the way they taught, how they assessed students, their expectations, and their curricula, for example, were gender biased. They turned a critical eye on their curricula and discovered that women's contributions as scholars and artists were missing. It was hard to find their work included in texts, and if they were included they were relegated to the margins, as the final chapter in the book that no one seemed to get to, or in boxes on the margins and at the end of chapters. More girls were admitted to college than ever before during the second wave, but it was still not in equal proportion or under the same standards.

During the second wave of the feminist movement, much effort was placed on trying to recover women's work from earlier periods of time, and to protect that earlier work that was rescued from biased male presentations of it, to allow the women to speak for themselves. This work continues today. See, for example, Jane Roland Martin's *Reclaiming a Conversation* and Charlene Haddock Seigfried's *Pragmatism and Feminism.* Another example of the gender problem is Simone de Beauvoir's *The Second Sex,* which was translated into English by a male editor without her permission and with her disapproval in regards to the translation. Also during this period of time, scholars began to realize that most studies that were used to shape the development of fields of study, such as psychology, were based on studies of males with the theories developed assumed to be general and applicable to all human beings, regardless of gender. Research began focusing on women and girls, such as that reported in Carol Gilligan's work, *In a Different Voice,* and Mary Belenky, Blythe Clinchy, Nancy Goldberger, and Jill Tarules's study, *Women's Ways of Knowing,* which drew attention specifically to women and girls and developed theories based on interviews and observations of them. Feminist scholars began arguing for the qualities and experiences of women that are specific to their gender and have been devalued and marginalized but need to be recognized and valued in society. Care theories are examples of gender-based theories, such as those in Nel Noddings's *Caring* and Sara Ruddick's *Maternal Thinking,* as well as in Sandra Harding's feminist standpoint epistemology.

In women's studies courses during the second wave, feminist professors began to explore alternative methods of instruction and to critically examine their role as teachers as well as their students' roles. Critique was developed for the standard lecture style of teaching and the passive role in which it positioned students. It became more common to see chairs organized in circles instead of rows in college classrooms, and to have teachers encouraging their students to share about their personal lives in the public classroom space, as well as for teachers to break down the public/private split and to soften their role as authority by sharing with students about their personal lives as well in the classroom space. Questions concerning the teacher's role as authority and students' roles as active learners and co-constructors of knowledge were openly discussed in classrooms and written about in feminist theory. Small group discussions and collaborative approaches to teaching were developed, in contrast to competitive models. Performance and portfolio forms of assessment were developed, as well as group grades.

Third Wave Feminism

Third wave feminism has contributed to feminist theory in education by critiquing second wave feminist theory for its lack of attention to other power issues that influence varied gendered experiences and expressions. Attention is currently being placed on the assumed positions of power with first and second wave feminism. Earlier feminist theory is being critiqued for its lack of awareness or attention to norms of Whiteness, property-owning classes, heterosexuality, and ablebodiedness, for example. Third World women who have received higher levels of education in First World universities are now able to contribute to the conversation as scholars and have their voices heard. They are offering critiques of First World colonization and the arrogance of its assuming to know Third World women and their needs. Third wave feminists offer sharp criticisms of their earlier sisters' work, which is unfortunately causing that earlier work to disappear from conversations and classrooms, setting up again what will become the need for future recovery work of women's contributions to scholarship.

In the classroom, third wave feminists have questioned the idea that a classroom can ever be a safe environment, as second wave feminists tried to make it, for there are too many power issues involved. Not only is safety an impossibility, it is questionable whether it is even a worthy ideal, as it is through risk and discomfort that we learn to trouble the basic categories we take as a given and begin to experience the cracks and fissures and see the faults and weaknesses in our worldviews. In this space of discomfort and unease is where education as growth can take place. Third wave feminists emphasize our plurality and differences as they uncover the hidden colonization of the 1960s melting-pot metaphor, which argued for others, strangers, to become assimilated to the norms of White, property-owning, Anglo-Saxon, heterosexual Christians. For women and girls this assimilation process meant that they would be treated equally as long as they could adapt and be like the men and boys. Feminists refer to this assimilation approach as "add women and stir."

Feminist theory in education today refers to models for education that emphasize diversity and encourage us to maintain and value plurality. Metaphors such as salads and Chinese hot pots abound to describe students' unique, distinctive qualities, as well as their commonality. Feminist scholars emphasize our shifting, changing identities (Judith Butler's drag, Donna Haraway's cyborg, and Gloria Anzaldúa's *mestiza* metaphors come to mind) and our coming together in cohorts to address particular social/political problems, and then disbanding as those problems are addressed (for example, Iris Young's unoppressive city metaphor). Feminist theory in education offers some of the most exciting, cutting edge, politically and culturally aware work that contributes to our thinking about education in new ways today.

Barbara J. Thayer-Bacon

See also Cultural Studies; Education, History of; Philosophy of Education

Further Readings

Anzaldúa, G. (Ed.). (1990). *Making face, making soul/Haciendo caras: Creative and critical perspectives by feminists of color.* San Francisco: Aunt Lute Foundation Books.

Belenky, M., Clinchy, B., Goldberger, N., & Tarule, J. (1986). *Women's ways of knowing.* New York: Basic Books.

Butler, J. (1990). *Gender trouble: Feminism and the subversion of identity.* New York: Routledge.

Collins, P. H. (1990). *Black feminist thought.* Boston: Unwin Hyman.

de Beauvoir, S. (1989). *The second sex* (H. M. Parshley, Ed. & Trans.). New York: Random House. (Original work published 1952)

Gilligan, C. (1982). *In a different voice: Psychological theory and women's development.* Cambridge, MA: Harvard University Press.

Grimshaw, J. (1986). *Philosophy and feminist thinking.* Minneapolis: University of Minnesota Press.

Haraway, D. (1991). *Simians, cyborgs, and women: The reinvention of nature.* New York: Routledge.

Harding, S. (1991). *Whose science? Whose knowledge? Thinking from women's lives.* Ithaca, NY: Cornell University Press.

hooks, b. (1984). *Feminist theory: From margin to center.* Boston: South End Press.

Iragaray, L. (1985). *Speculum of the other woman* (G. Gill, Trans.) [Reprint]. Ithaca, NY: Cornell University Press. (Original work published 1974)

Martin, J. R. (1985). *Reclaiming a conversation.* New Haven, CT: Yale University Press.

Martin, J. R. (1994). *Changing the educational landscape: Philosophy, women, and curriculum.* New York: Routledge.

Noddings, N. (1984). *Caring: A feminine approach to ethics and moral education.* Berkeley: University of California Press.

Ruddick, S. (1989). *Maternal thinking: Toward a politics of peace.* Boston: Beacon Press.

Seigfried, C. H. (1996). *Pragmatism and feminism: Reweaving the social fabric.* Chicago: University of Chicago Press.

Stone, L. (Ed.). (1994). *The education feminism reader.* New York: Routledge.

Young, I. M. (1990). *Justice and the politics of difference.* Princeton, NJ: Princeton University Press.

FEMINIZATION OF THE TEACHING PROFESSION

Beginning with the common school movement in the late 1830s, teachers increasingly began to be recruited from the female population. This was in contrast to the colonial period and the postrevolutionary period when men dominated the profession. Women were teachers during this earlier period, but only at the lowest levels, as indicated by the titles given to teachers, including masters, tutors, governesses, and school dames.

Rationale for Bias

Women were recruited into the teaching profession—particularly very young women (often at the age of thirteen or fourteen)—because they were an inexpensive and malleable labor group who readily met the demands of a burgeoning school system. In many instances, teaching became a brief interlude in the lives of young women, one which took place prior to marriage and the bearing of children.

While young female teachers were clearly exploited by the society as a source of inexpensive and readily available labor, teaching, like nursing, provided access to education and respect from the community at a time when few professions were open to women. It was also a profession that was relatively easy to enter, typically requiring only a year or two of training at the high school level.

Women were often encouraged to enter the profession, since it was perceived by the larger society that teachers had a nurturing role. This point of view, which is largely taken for granted today, was not necessarily held by many people prior to the common school movement, when teachers were seen in a more authoritarian and dictatorial light.

Female teachers were significantly discriminated against compared to their male counterparts, a reality that has continued to some extent even into the present. Rarely was a woman made a school superintendent until well into the twentieth century. Salary discrimination based on gender was the norm. In 1880, the beginning salary for a female high school teacher in the United States was $850 a year; a male teacher received $2,000. Just as White male teachers made more money than White female teachers, White teachers made more money than Black teachers. Thus Black female teachers were particularly discriminated against.

Ebb and Flow of Men

During the Civil War, women teachers naturally outnumbered men, sixteen to one, as men went off to war and war-related industries. Since most women taught in elementary schools, these schools were not as disrupted by the war as were the high schools. By 1870, there were 123,000 women and 78,000 men teaching in the United States. Most of the men taught at the secondary level. It was perceived that women were more suited to teach in the primary grades, especially if a school was graded.

In the first survey of teachers, conducted in 1910, it was determined that the majority of teachers were

White women, and most of the women were the daughters of farmers and small businessmen. The female teacher was often one of the few role models of a "working woman" available for many young girls, who often followed their mothers, sisters, or other female relatives into the profession. Teaching was an "acceptable" job for many young women, until they got married. In fact, in St. Louis, Missouri, and other cities, as late as the mid-1940s, a female teacher had to resign if she got married. Teaching also provided economic independence and status to the women who chose not to get married or to be "dependent old maids," living with their relatives.

By 1930 there were five times as many female teachers as male teachers in the United States. As women came to dominate the profession, its status fell in comparison with other professions that were dominated by men, such as law and medicine. During the Great Depression, men were often given preference over women when teaching jobs were being filled, so that the number of male teachers increased to 25 percent of the total number of teachers in the United States. That percentage fell again during World War II, and then picked up again after the war as men were recruited into the profession (the same phenomenon had occurred after World War I). One of reasons given for recruiting men was to give boys, especially adolescent boys, strong role models in the classroom.

Rather than returning to teaching following the war, many men who had been teachers took advantage of the GI Bill. As a result, many married women who had been "allowed" to teach during the war were kept on; the "spinster teachers" were aging, and there simply weren't enough young single women to fill the need. By the end of the 1940s, restrictions on women being married and teaching were dropped across the country. For the first time, middle-class, married women with children began filling the ranks of teachers. By 1960, married women made up 71 percent of the female teaching force. Their presence created a new twist on the disparity between salaries for male versus female teachers: It was felt that since a married woman's salary was a second income for her family, the male teacher should still be paid more money.

Recent History

By the 1980s, one third of the teachers in the United States were men, two thirds women. Perhaps of more importance is the fact that there were almost an equal number of men and women teaching at the high school level; salary equality was at last being fully achieved. As salary levels across professions increased, many talented women dropped out of the profession, bypassing traditional nurturing jobs such as nursing, teaching, and social work for the status and increased income found in the business world and the professions of law and medicine.

Because teaching is a feminized profession, male teachers suffer the lesser status afforded women in American culture. This issue is deeply rooted in historical traditions, one which is only beginning to be overcome through legislation and changes in social attitudes as women continue to achieve greater equality in American society. At some time in the not-too-distant future, it is hoped that the status of teachers—male or female—will increase along with the general status of women in the culture. At that point, the feminization of the teaching profession may remain relevant only as an interesting historical artifact.

Eugene F. Provenzo, Jr.

See also Education, History of; Teachers, Professional Status of

See Visual History Chapter 2, Early Textbooks; Chapter 3, Teachers in the Early and Middle Nineteenth Century

Further Readings

Clifford, G. J. (1989). Man/woman/teacher: Gender, family, and career in American educational history. In D. Warren (Ed.), *American teachers: Histories of a profession at work* (pp. 293–243). New York: Macmillan.

Provenzo, E. F., Jr., & McCloskey, G. N. (1996). *Schoolteachers and schooling: Ethoses in conflict.* Norwood, NJ: Ablex.

Rury, J. L. (1989). Who became teachers? The social characteristics of teachers in American history. In D. Warren (Ed.), *American teachers: Histories of a profession at work* (pp. 9–48). New York: Macmillan.

Sedlak, M. W. (1989). Let us go and buy a school master: Historical perspectives on the hiring of teachers in the United States, 1750–1890. In D. Warren (Ed.), *American teachers: Histories of a profession at work* (pp. 257–290). New York: Macmillan.

FIRST-PERSON ACCOUNTS OF TEACHING

First-person accounts of teaching can be defined as any written recollections of personal teaching experiences left by current or former teachers. The form in which these accounts are made available to the public and the purposes they serve depend primarily on the intent of the authors, the situations in which the accounts were written, and the diligence of those who study the lives of teachers. In considering the role or value of first-person accounts it is helpful to first identify the format or type of writing in which the accounts can be found, as this entry does. That, in turn, will help us discern the authors' intentions in sharing the accounts. Knowing the authors' purposes can then help the reader get the most out of the writing.

Private Correspondence

Many first-person accounts available today were probably not intended to be read by the general public. Instead, they were written in the form of personal journals, diaries, or letters. These types of recollections date as far back as the colonial period in the United States—and further back to ancient Greece and beyond if considering the world arena.

Given the personal and sometimes anonymous nature of the accounts, it can be difficult to determine the original intentions of the authors. They commonly focus on the day-to-day work of the teacher, along with classroom anecdotes detailing encounters with unruly students, a less-than-pleasant work environment, and personal living conditions. Few teachers tried to offer profound insight into the profession or children. The most obvious value of these first-person accounts is the glimpse they provide into the daily life and thinking of the time and place in which they were written and into the personal and emotional lives of the persons who chose teaching.

Formal Autobiography

Many teachers have documented their experiences by writing a narrative deliberately crafted for a public audience. Autobiographical accounts often reflect not only the authors' points of view but broader cultural perspectives as well. Accounts like Edward Eggelston's *The Hoosier Schoolmaster* from 1871 or William Alcott's *Confessions of a Schoolmaster* from 1856 focus on the brave but frustrating efforts of individual frontier schoolteachers to keep reluctant students in school.

A similar theme can be found in autobiographical accounts from the 1980s and early 1990s but with a variation that reflects the criticism of public schools voiced by numerous national reports of the time. *My Posse Don't Do Homework* by LouAnne Johnson and Marva Collins's *Marva Collins' Way* sent the message that brave individual teachers were fighting against the low expectations of apathetic schools. Those accounts, and others of the era, portrayed the teacher as a folk hero who recognizes that students simply need teachers who have high expectations for both the students and themselves.

Autobiographical accounts of teaching were plentiful in the 1960s and 1970s. They, too, represented the struggle of individual teachers against significant odds, but unlike the later accounts, authors such as Herbert Kohl, Vivian Paley, Jonathon Kozol, Robert Kendell, and Sunny Decker were self-deprecating in their portrayals, emphasizing their positions as White outsiders in all-Black schools. Mirroring the social upheaval of the era, the authors emphasized what they had to learn about and from their students, the crippling nature of poverty and discrimination, and the emotional toll exacted on everyone involved.

In every era there were exceptions to these categories that ran counter to the prevailing cultural perceptions and portrayed hope in difficult situations and the promise of empowering students with compassion and student-centered teaching. J. K. Stableton's *Diary of a Western School-master* in 1900 portrayed a great love and respect for the nature and potential of adolescent boys struggling for an education. In 1936, Katherine Camp Mayhew and Anna Camp Mayhew described the experience-based model of education at John Dewey's laboratory school in Chicago. Eliot Wigginton's 1985 *Sometimes a Shining Moment* recounted his efforts to motivate his poor, rural students by having them explore their own cultural heritage. And in the 1970s, '80s, and

'90s, authors like Ira Shor, Paulo Freire, and Peter McLaren wrote of their experiences in using education as a means of empowerment and liberation.

Personal Inquiry or Self-Study

A type or use of first-person accounts that is relatively new to the genre is the writing and study of first-person accounts for the distinct and direct purpose of personal insight and professional development. These accounts are often much shorter than autobiography and more intentionally and narrowly focused than daily diary entries, although they can take the form of a teacher's life history as it shaped his or her teaching and dissertation-length studies of a teacher's practice.

Teacher educators and others who work with teacher professional development are increasingly turning to the type of first-person accounts referred to variously as teacher narratives, autobiography, life history research, teacher lore, and by other such terms. It is believed that writing about and studying their own experiences can help teachers develop a more systematic and critically reflective nature and begin to explore the various family, cultural, professional, and psychological influences that have shaped their teaching and professional identity. Similarly, by reading the stories in other teachers' first-person accounts, future teachers can learn what it means to grow as a profession and to become a teacher. This approach has gained in acceptance as the teacher's work, workplace, and experience have become a legitimate source of knowledge about teaching and learning.

Rick A. Breault

See also Archives and Library Collections on Education; Popular Culture; Teachers, Literary Portrayals of

Further Readings

Brizman, D. P. (2003). *Practice makes practice: A critical study of learning to teach.* Albany: State University of New York Press.
Cohen, R. M., & Scheer, S. (Eds.). (1997). *The work of teachers in America: A social history through stories.* Mahwah, NJ: Lawrence Erlbaum.

Covello, L. (1958). *The heart is the teacher.* New York: McGraw-Hill.

Preskill, S. L. (2001). *Stories of teaching: A foundation for educational renewal.* Upper Saddle River, NJ: Merrill Prentice Hall.

Schubert, W. H., & Ayers, W. C. (1992). *Teacher lore: Learning from our own experience.* New York: Longman.

FOLKLORE

Folklore refers to a dimension of culture comprised of traditional forms—including verbal art, material culture, belief, music, dance, and visual art—expressed by individuals in performance. Though definitions vary according to purpose and use, U.S. folklorist Dan Ben-Amos's 1972 definition of folklore as "artistic communication in small groups" is basic to the discipline as it has developed in the United States since the 1950s.

Folklore is passed from person to person (whether directly or mediated), with artistic communication encompassing both aesthetic and ethical, relational dimensions. Grandparents tell histories to grandchildren that they will not read in textbooks. Aunts teach jump-rope rhymes as well as taunts to nieces. Children exchange jokes and street knowledge. Experienced teachers transmit both time-tested advice and well-honed biases to new colleagues. Parents exhort children about "the way we do things." Community experts share techniques ranging from gardening to grassroots political action. And politicians call forth popular responses by fitting contemporary persons and events into traditional generic forms. All of this involves folklore. This entry looks at general folklore concepts; the ways folklore is used in education, including a historical review; and the contemporary scene.

Definitions

Folklore consists of the concrete, verbal, auditory, kinetic, and behavioral artifacts that can be described as instantiations of any group's culture. People use folklore to connect to their past, but also as resources to accomplish particular goals through performance and communication in present social settings.

For those seeking to apply folklore and folkloristic research to fields of education, particularly salient and prevalent definitions of folklore describe it as "people's knowledge" and "noninstitutional"—though it is recognized that folklore can also be co-opted and used to promote antidemocratic, politically institutionalized goals.

In 1938, the Progressive scholar-activist Benjamin Botkin, who was national folklore editor of the Depression era Federal Writers Project, usefully defined folklore as a body of traditional belief, custom, and expression passed down by word of mouth outside of commercial and academic communications. This definition serves to highlight the expression and authority of folklore as existing independent of both popular and elite dominant culture as it is perpetuated through the mass media and schools.

At the same time, however, folklore can be used and spread through the media and schools in order to bolster the authority of officials and to lend credibility to their claims. The nature of folklore as separate from both popular culture and elite culture, as well as the way folklore has been used in popular and elite versions in order to create a sense of national identity, makes the discipline of folklore a useful complement to the disciplinary approaches more widely used in the study of the social and cultural foundations of education.

Folklore in Education

The work of folklorists in education can be grouped into five approaches, four of which focus on how individuals communicate within, around, and despite dominating cultural institutions, with the fifth focusing on helping students identify the use of folk belief by officials in the dominant culture in order to garner public approval.

One approach has been to study folklore in schools, that is, how students and teachers form folk groups and create culture independent of or despite official culture. A second approach, developed initially as part of a broader response to the misrepresentations of cultural deprivation theory, has been to use folklore of students and their communities as texts within the curriculum. A third approach has been exemplified by the Folk Arts in Education (FAIE) and Folk Arts in Schools (FAIS) programs, which involve both bringing traditional artists into schools as authoritative teachers and training students as competent fieldworkers and researchers. A fourth approach has been analyzing folk genres as critiques of, or alternative models to, institutionalized elite and popular genres.

Finally, the fifth approach involves students in analyzing politicians' and other leaders' rhetoric to identify legends and other expressions of belief presented as truth. This approach problematizes the idea of "folk" as being marginal and highlights the fact that all groups, including those with institutional power, rely on shared beliefs and communicative resources in order to create a sense of shared identity among their members.

Useful Elements of Folkloristic Theory

Folklore's original author is "anonymous," and even if thought to be known, the identity of an individual supposed to have originated a particular form is inconsequential, as folkloristic knowledge is powerful because it is both collectively known and dynamically transformed. Folklore is often performed by specialists within the group: The key is that it always changes and exists in variations, and people learn to use it in variable and changeable ways, in daily interaction as well as in specialized settings. Tradition—usually defined as continuous existence through time or across space—has been important in describing folklore, although in the last fifty years theorists have also emphasized the creativity exercised by individuals in using traditional forms for new purposes as well as the dubious project of "inventing traditions" to justify social entitlements and political projects.

Essential to its nature, folklore has no prototypical, authoritative, or "right" version and cannot be codified. Furthermore, true folklore cannot be reproduced exactly; rather, each reiteration involves re-creation and therefore creative change on the part of the individual producing it. U.S. folklorist Barre Toelken coined the "twin laws" of folklore as *tradition* and

dynamic innovation, with tradition being preexisting, culture-specific, but not static materials, and dynamic innovation being the inevitable and energizing changes resulting in each performance of the tradition by each individual. As a result, all folklore exists in "multiple nonstandard variations."

Consider the game hide-and-seek. The traditional aspect of this piece of folklore is that people hide and are found. The dynamic, nonstandard variation, however, includes much more: Who is "it," or are there multiple "its"? Is the goal to race to a "home" to be "home free," or is the goal to be the last one found? How high does "it" count to allow the others to hide, and what does "it" say when "it" is about to begin searching? Are there boundaries within which hiders must stay? While the game is traditional around the world, the essence of the game resides in the variations, which arise from individual creativity, collective compromise, and adaptation of the basic form to be appropriate for the setting and participants involved.

"Folk culture" stands in contrast to "elite culture" (those behaviors and forms having capital in dominant culture institutions) and to "popular culture" (behaviors learned and forms promulgated through corporations and mass marketing), though culture is fluid and moves between these categories as folk culture is co-opted and commoditized (e.g., graffiti becomes fine art and ingredients in willow bark become aspirin), or popular or elite culture is used in traditional, creative ways (e.g., soft drink cans are recycled into toy airplanes, or high art is spoofed in burlesques).

Emerging in the 1970s, "performance theory" centers attention on how individuals draw on communicative resources (i.e., traditional texts of the community) to perform them in particular social settings for particular purposes. Important analytic questions include which members of the community are recognized as having the authority to "take" texts from their traditional, authoritative settings and to re-create them in different social settings in order to meet their own particular social goals. Key questions relevant to folklore in schools are: Who has the authority, in a given social setting, to decontextualize and recontextualize (i.e., to perform) a given text? Who decides if the performance is legitimate, authoritative, or "good"?

Historical Review

Eighteenth and Nineteenth Century Roots

Though now international in scope, the discipline of folklore has its roots in antiquarian and nationalistic movements of eighteenth-century Europe. As avocational scholars of the privileged classes, in reaction to the rise of Rationalism, joined in romanticizing primitive society across Europe, Johann Gottfried Herder gathered *Volkslieder* (folksongs) as the spiritual voice of *das Volk,* in the hope of codifying "the cultural heart and soul of a nation," and thus elevating the idea of "peoplehood" to the basis for political movements, a philosophy and method that influenced nation builders across Europe as well as to the new United States.

N. F. S. Grundtvig, a nineteenth-century Dane, seems to have been the first to argue explicitly that folklife, as essential to the nation's welfare, should be promoted by teachers in formal schooling. Grundtvig led an educational reform that resulted in the folk high school movement, as well as revitalization of trade schools and adult education including handicraft. At the end of the nineteenth century, the folk arts movement took hold in some elite schools in the United States.

Professionalization and the Progressive Era

At turn of the twentieth century in the United States, Progressive reformers idealized folk culture as a challenge to emerging industrial capitalist society, and following the Arts and Crafts movement begun by William Morris and his followers, held that preindustrial work processes and handicrafts could effect social and cultural change. A cultural nationalism drawing upon work of ballad collectors in the Appalachian region developed, based largely on romanticizing the colonial past and downplaying diversity and the impact of immigration. This move, however, was not uncontested: Though epitomized in such institutions as Henry Ford's new Greenfield Village, it was challenged by a plethora of "Homelands Exhibits" and international festivals highlighting the richness of immigrant culture.

Within the Progressive education movement, proponents of social efficiency worked to divide control of schools from their communities, with reformers attacking this "rural school problem," while at the same time expressing nostalgia for disappearing ways of life. Social efficiency proponents erased individual and community traditions in their desire to standardize, and in this way equalize, educational opportunity. As African Americans and immigrants learned through schooling to be ashamed of their differences, some Progressive reformers began to examine the lack of fit between groups and schools, to question how schools damaged family and community culture.

Such views were actualized in folkloristic projects including Jane Addams's Hull House, where art shows included both elite art borrowed from museums; workers' art documenting their homelands as well as their current predicament; Lucy Sprague Mitchell's work at the Bureau for Educational Experiments (later, Bank Street), taking New York students out into the city to explore the folk culture of their neighborhoods; and Dorothy Howard's and others' work making folklore accessible to schoolteachers.

Cultural Deprivation Theory and the Rise of Folk Arts in Education

From the 1950s through the 1970s, explicit critiques of cultural deprivation theory as well as complementary work in education contributed to a continuing Progressive strain of schooling. As psychologists and sociologists promoted "cultural deprivation theory" as an improvement on biologically based theories explaining why some groups of people tended to be less successful in dominant culture schooling than did others, folklorists argued the flaws of such theory, drawing upon empirical studies of the folklore of marginalized groups, and explaining the dynamic between these noninstitutionalized, marginalized cultures and dominant, school culture.

Also at this time, prototypes to Folk Arts in Education (FAIE) emerged, as scholars promoted including lives of "undistinguished Americans" in curricula as essential to American culture. Officially Folk Artists in the Schools (FAIS) programs were established with funding from the National Endowment for the Arts in 1976, with the purpose of including a wider range of artists than those generally included in the more widely known Artists in Schools programs.

Contemporary Folklore and Education Efforts

Currently, FAIE programs are housed not only in schools, but also in libraries, museums, and community agencies, with the shared aim of humanistic understanding of individuals and social groups, through engaging students in close documentation and analysis of local culture. Folklorists have also recognized the inevitability of the standards movement and have produced comprehensive frameworks for folklore standards and integrated curricula.

Analysis of FAIE publications reveals five prevalent goals. First, FAIE programs help students and teachers learn to value their own and familiar individuals and groups and their vernacular, everyday artistic expressions: Typically, this is described as helping young people see that people can be creative artists outside of dominant culture institutions like museums and concert halls.

Second, this recognition plus the folklorist's outsider perspective helps students see the value and importance of familiar heroes and local events, especially due to many programs' focus on students' families and neighbors in the context of history, politics, and economics. Common activities include visits to local workplaces, including mills and factories, with students prompted to examine how the dominant culture threatens local cultures.

Third, FAIE programs engage teachers and students in critically observing differences between elite and popular culture, and the folk culture of their own communities, thus helping students recognize their own "cultural capital" as equally authoritative to that sponsored by schools and the media.

Fourth, FAIE recenters authority outside of institutions. A central, though usually unstated, purpose of all FAIE curricula is challenging the exclusive legitimacy of official knowledge and thus challenging institutions to include truly heterogeneous authorities, bringing community knowledge into the classroom as authoritative, and community people in as teachers.

Finally, because FAIE projects are based on students' participation in real learning situations outside the classroom, the work is inherently collaborative, connecting students in classrooms with people and organizations in larger community settings.

Folklorists working in education have created rich resources for use in schools; however, since these are often published through museums and government agencies, they are often difficult to find. Thus, folklorists continue to work to build relationships with those working primarily in schools in order to increase the impact of their work. Important resources for locating and obtaining both materials and the theoretical discussions that frame them include the online newsletter of the Folklore and Education Section of the American Folklore Society; the American Folklife Center's online *A Teacher's Guide to Folklife Resources;* and Paddy Bowman's 2006 article, "Standing at the Crossroads of Folklore and Education," which provides an excellent listing of online resources. In addition, C. A. Bowers's work in ecojustice pedagogy provides an excellent framework and rationale for integrating folkloristic studies into social foundations curricula.

Lynne Hamer

See also Cultural Capital; Multicultural Education; Progressive Education

Further Readings

American Folklife Center. (2006). *A teacher's guide to folklife resources for K–12 classrooms.* Retrieved November 29, 2006, from http://www.loc.gov/folklife/teachers

American Folklore Society. (2006). *What is folklore?* Retrieved November 29, 2006, from http://www.afsnet.org/aboutfolklore/aboutFL.cfm

Bauman, R., & Briggs, C. (1990). Poetics and performance as critical perspectives on language and social life. *Annual Review of Anthropology, 19,* 59–88.

Becker, J. (1988). Revealing traditions: The politics of culture and community in America, 1888–1988. In J. Becker & B. Franco (Eds.), *Folk roots, new roots: Folklore in American life* (pp. 19–60). Lexington, MA: Museum of Our National Heritage.

Ben-Amos, D. (1972). Toward a definition of folklore in context. In A. Paredes & R. Bauman (Eds.), *Toward new perspectives in folklore* (pp. 3–15). Austin: University of Texas Press for the American Folklore Society.

Botkin, B. (1938). The folk and the individual: Their creative reciprocity. *The English Journal, 27,* 21–35.

Bowers, C. (2001). How colleges of education package the myth of modernity. In S. Goodlad (Ed.), *The last best hope: A democracy reader* (pp. 207–215). San Francisco: Jossey-Bass.

Bowman, P. (2006). Standing at the crossroads of folklore and education. *Journal of American Folklore, 119*(471), 66–79.

Bronner, S. (2002). *Folk nation: Folklore in the creation of American tradition.* Wilmington, DE: American Visions.

Hamer, L. (1999). Folklore in schools and multicultural education: Toward institutionalizing noninstitutional knowledge. *Journal of American Folklore, 113*(447), 44–69.

Hamer, L. (1999). A folkloristic approach to understanding teachers as storytellers. *International Journal of Qualitative Studies in Education, 12*(4), 363–380.

Haut, J. (1994). How can acting like a fieldworker enrich pluralistic education? In M. Jones (Ed.), *Putting folklore to use* (pp. 45–61). Lexington: University Press of Kentucky.

Howard, D. (1950). Folklore in the schools. *New York Folklore Quarterly, 6*(2), 99–107.

Kirshenblatt-Gimblett, B. (1983). An accessible aesthetic: The role of folk arts and the folk artist in the curriculum. *New York Folklore, 9*(3/4), 9–18.

Rosenberg, J. (2004). Reflections on folklife and education: Is there a unified history of folklore and education? *AFS Folklore and Education Section Newsletter.* Retrieved September 13, 2006, from, http://www.afsnet.org/sections/education/Spring2004

FOREIGN LANGUAGE INSTRUCTION

According to Old Testament accounts, the building of the Tower of Babel was the first instance of multilingualism. If this is indeed the occasion when humans began using more than one language, then this must also be the beginning point for the need for foreign language instruction.

There are three terms used for language instruction. It is important to clarify the differences between bilingual education, second language instruction, and foreign language instruction. *Bilingual education* takes place in schools and requires that children be taught all subjects in two target languages, in order to allow each child to reach equal fluency in the languages. Although bilingual education is currently the focus of educators, it is not a new concept, as subjects other than language were taught in the student's second language as early as the Middle Ages.

Second language instruction occurs when the learner must reach a high degree of fluency in a second language in order to be able to live for an extended period of time and conduct business in a region where that language is spoken. The goal of *foreign language instruction* is to allow basic communication in the target language and usually occurs outside the area where the target language is spoken, where there is neither direct daily contact nor imminent necessity to communicate in that language. Thus, foreign language instruction is mostly classroom based, while classroom-based second language instruction and bilingual education are often supplemented by daily activities and organizations outside the school setting, such as the home, community, and church.

Historical Trends

Throughout the centuries, there have been multiple methods of foreign language instruction, but all methods can be categorized under two headings. Methods are labeled *inductive* where there is no formal grammar instruction and students must figure out the grammar rules as they learn. Methods are labeled *deductive* where language rules are presented before practice and learning of the language takes place.

The popularity of inductive and deductive methodologies has shifted across centuries. The classical era focused on inductive instruction. In the fourth century, St. Augustine encouraged a focus on meaningful content. Medieval methods were generally deductive. With the introduction of grammatical theories by Erasmus and Comenius in the sixteenth and seventeenth centuries, classroom-based instruction, without the availability of access to authentic language situations, revolved primarily around grammar-based approaches to instruction using artificial contexts. Inductive methods were again popular during the Renaissance era, while methods in the eighteenth and nineteenth centuries were mostly deductive. The twentieth century began with an emphasis on deductive methods and ended with a shift to inductive instruction.

Foreign language instruction in the United States has generally followed methods used in other parts of the Western world. In the late eighteenth century, François Gouin introduced the *natural method,* so named because of its emphasis on learning the way a child learns his or her native language from family and environment, making use of mime and demonstration. The *direct method* added scientific rationale such as psychology, phonetics, dictionaries, and structural analysis to the natural method. Its purpose was to immerse students in the language with little to no explanation of grammar. There were many variations of the natural and direct methods: "the dramatization method," "the object method," "the indirect method," "the direct constructive method," "the theme method," "the observation method," "the pictorial method," "the development method," "the conversation method," "the phonic method," "the textbook method," and "the laboratory method."

The first half of the twentieth century saw the introduction of the *grammar translation method* in the United States. Using this method, students translated sentences from their first language to the target language or vice versa. These sentences reflected the particular grammar rule to be learned during that class period, often with no evident contextual purpose. The teacher taught in the student's native language and communication in the target language was rarely practiced. In the 1950s, the *audio lingual method* (ALM) came into vogue. Using this method, students memorized dialogues and practiced substitution drills, all based on a particular grammatical element, often in language laboratories. Decontextualized speaking and listening was common.

During the second half of the twentieth century, the shift continued from a deductive approach to an inductive approach. Perhaps the greatest impetus to this shift came in 1965 when Noam Chomsky presented his theory of transformational-generative grammar. His theory distinguished between the *competence* of a native speaker and the *performance* of a nonnative speaker, thus, differentiating forms of language used by a native speaker from those used by a nonnative speaker. He concluded that language is not merely structures to be learned through habit, but is formed by creative and abstract principles, which are more complex than the mere learning of formulas and structures.

Current Practice

In 1980, Michael Canale and Merrill Swain developed a conceptual framework that formulated a theoretical design for communicative competence. This design breaks linguistic competence into four distinct components: grammatical competence (mastery of grammar, vocabulary, and pronunciation), sociolinguistic competence (mastery of communicative genre such as narration, description, and persuasion), discourse competence (mastery of coherent discourse), and strategic competence (mastery of verbal and nonverbal communication).

This framework was further refined by Lyle Bachman, who divided language competence into two distinct components: organizational competence, which includes the structures of language (i.e., grammar, phonology, semantics) and pragmatic competence, which refers to the ability of the speaker to use organizational structures in contextual or culture-specific situations. Based on this framework, pragmatic competence is considered equal to organizational competence in determining overall language competence.

With the new emphasis on competence versus performance, foreign language instruction in the early twenty-first century has shifted away from a deductive, grammar-based instruction to an inductive, communicative-based approach, which focuses on real-life situations and active language skills (i.e., speaking and listening), as opposed to decontextualized, passive skills (i.e., reading and writing). Formulaic instruction in grammar is reserved for situations where further communication is impossible without formal clarification. Most modern textbooks make use of a variation on communicative-based instruction, and foreign language teachers are encouraged to use grammar-based instruction only when necessary.

Annis N. Shaver

See also Bilingual Education, History of

Further Readings

Bachman, L. F. (1990). *Fundamental considerations in language testing.* Oxford, UK: Oxford University Press.

Canale, M. (1983). From communicative competence to communicative language pedagogy. In J. Richards & R. Richards (Eds.), *Language and communication* (pp. 2–27). London: Longman.

Canale, M., & Swain, M. (1980). Theoretical bases of communicative approaches to second language teaching and testing. *Applied Linguistics, 1,* 1–47.

Chomsky, N. (1965). *Aspects of the theory of syntax.* Cambridge: MIT Press.

Cook, V. (1999). Going beyond the native speaker in language teaching. *TESOL Quarterly, 33*(2), 185–332.

Ellis, R. (1997). *SLA research and language teaching.* Hong Kong: Oxford University Press.

Finegan, E. (1999). *Language: Its structure and use.* New York: Harcourt Brace.

Hadley, A. O. (2001). *Teaching language in context.* Boston: Heinle & Heinle.

Kelly, L. (1976). *Twenty-five centuries of language teaching.* Newbury, MA: Rowley House.

Freedmen's Bureau

During the short-lived Reconstruction period after the Civil War, the task of rebuilding the economic and social infrastructure of the South was assigned to the Bureau of Refugees, Freedmen, and Abandoned Lands. Its official responsibility was to assist former slaves, provide relief to war refugees, and dispose of confiscated Confederate property. Education, however, became an important and perhaps the most successful part of its agenda, as it built thousands of schools including several important historically Black colleges. This entry reviews the historical context of the Freedmen's Bureau, its larger role, and its contributions to education.

After the Civil War

The destruction of crops, farmlands, and infrastructure throughout the South displaced thousands of workers of all races. The war had removed primary wage earners from many homes, increasing the ranks of the poor. Literally thousands of people both Black and White found themselves landless, jobless, and homeless. Whites and Blacks experienced nearly a complete breakdown of everyday life. In the face of mounting need, it became increasingly clear that local resources would not be sufficient to meet the needs of the South. The sources of relief for African Americans were almost nonexistent. Most private aid societies in the South either had little interest in providing assistance to Black persons or simply were unable to do so because resources were so scarce. As the size and intensity of the relief crisis grew, new private aid societies in the North demanded that the federal government create a formal support system for the former slaves. Among the aid societies were the American Missionary Association, the National Freedmen's Relief Association, the American Freedmen's Union, and the Western Freedmen's Aid Commission, which sent clothes, money, school books, and teachers. These groups, however, soon concluded that their meager resources were no match for the enormity of the problem. Rather, a government office seemed necessary to ensure that freedom actually changed the lives of African Americans.

Creation of the Bureau

On March 3, 1865, a bill to create the Bureau of Refugees, Freedmen, and Abandoned Lands was established and signed into law on the same day by President Abraham Lincoln. The most noteworthy characteristic of the Freedmen's Bureau bill was negative: its funding. The Bureau was established as a temporary federal division of the War Department and slated to operate for only one year after the Civil War. The U.S. Congress appropriated no funds to support the Bureau's work, and during its first year of operation, it depended upon donations from benevolent societies and rents collected from tenants working abandoned lands. Once President Andrew Johnson, a White supremacist, restored lands to former land owners, rents declined significantly. Despite these limitations, the Bureau undertook the monumental task of providing welfare services to freed persons and White refugees. It provided food, clothing, and fuel to the destitute, aged, ill, and insane among both White refugees and freedmen; established schools for freedmen; supplied medical services; implemented a workable system of free labor in the South through the supervision of contracts between the freedmen and their employers; managed confiscated or abandoned lands, leasing and selling some of them to freedmen; and attempted to secure for Blacks equal justice before the law.

The Bureau also helped locate jobs, supervised labor contracts to ensure fairness, established hospitals, and worked to protect the civil liberties of Blacks in hostile towns. Each local Bureau agent was expected not only to accomplish these tasks in the post–Civil War environment but also to win the confidence of Blacks and Whites alike in an atmosphere poisoned by centuries of mutual distrust and conflicting interests.

How successful the Bureau was in accomplishing its tasks—land, labor policy, education, and relief—hinged on the ability of individual agents to make their case before Blacks and Whites and to inculcate respect for law. The Bureau lacked the institutional and financial resources to fully effect relief, recovery, and reform, and local differences in culture and conditions meant constantly having to adapt broad Bureau philosophy and interests to very particular conditions. As a result, outcomes across the South were far from uniform. What was uniform was that the Bureau agents were overworked in the field, for there were never enough agents; caseloads were staggering; agents lived and operated alone; and diminishing military support bolstered White opposition.

Educational Role

Given general supervision over the education of freed slaves after its creation in 1865 by the reconstructionist Congress, the Bureau was not given authority to fund and run schools, but it assumed the leadership for this responsibility. The funds needed for its programs were obtained by selling confiscated Confederate lands. The Bureau initiated 4,239 schools, hired 9,307 teachers, and provided instruction for almost one quarter of a million children. The Bureau advocated normal schools to train Black teachers to educate former slaves in elementary schools as early as 1866.

The philosophy of the Bureau stressed the values of obedience to the law, respect for property rights, racial harmony, patience, and moderation. The Bureau also protected Black schools and their personnel from White violence and intimidation. It encouraged the establishment of teacher-training institutions to train Black teachers, and by 1869, a majority of teachers in the Bureau's schools were Black.

The Bureau clearly achieved its greatest success in education. It established or supervised all kinds of schools: day, night, Sunday, and industrial as well as colleges. Many of the nation's best known Black colleges

and universities were founded with aid from the Bureau: Howard University, Hampton Institute, St. Augustine's College, Atlanta University, Fisk University, and Biddle Memorial Institute (now Johnson C. Smith University). When the Bureau's education work stopped in 1879, there were 247, 222 students in 4,239 schools.

These statistics in some ways overestimate the Bureau's success in education. In fact, most schools were in or near towns while many Blacks lived in rural areas; most Black children did not attend school and those who did attended for only a few months; every school was segregated by race, for Whites refused to attend freedmen's schools and the Bureau did not require racial desegregation; and the Bureau could not take credit for the many schools staffed by Blacks and Southern Whites.

Clearly, Black education in the postemancipation South was a joint venture combining the efforts and philosophy of the Bureau, benevolent associations, and Black themselves. Yet to discount the Bureau's achievements is to miss the dynamic of the Bureau's role in Reconstruction. Without the Bureau's resources and resolve, the freed people's education and social opportunity would have been even more sporadic and limited than it was. The Bureau laid a foundation and set a course of social action for others to follow.

Paul E. Green

See also African American Education: From Slave to Free

See Visual History Chapter 7, The Education of African Americans

Further Readings

Kujovich, G. (1992). Equal opportunity in higher education and the Black public college: The era of separate but equal. In *Race, law, and American history, 1700–1990: The African American experience.* New York: Garland.

Marcus, L. R., & Stickney, B. D. (1981). *Race and education: The unending controversy.* Springfield, IL: Charles C Thomas.

Nieman, D. G. (1994). *The Freedmen's Bureau and Black freedom.* New York: Garland.

Weinberg, M. (1983). *The search for quality integrated education: Policy and research on minority students in school and college.* Westport, CT: Greenwood Press.

FREE SCHOOL MOVEMENT

The period of cultural and political upheaval during the 1960s included a passionate critique of schooling expressed in writings such as *Summerhill* (1960) by A. S. Neill, *How Children Fail* (1964) by John Holt, *Death at an Early Age* (1967) by Jonathan Kozol, *The Lives of Children* (1969) by George Dennison, and *Deschooling Society* (1970) by Ivan Illich, among others, and work by social critics like Paul Goodman and Edgar Z. Friedenberg. These critics argued that schools had become authoritarian institutions that repressed individuality, freedom, and the joy of learning, making education sterile and irrelevant both to students' lives and the serious issues affecting society. While some educators sought to introduce progressive reforms (such as "open education") into public schools (as described in Charles Silberman's 1970 *Crisis in the Classroom*), thousands of students, young teachers, and parents withdrew from public education to launch independent alternatives that were commonly known as "free schools."

While the exact number of such schools is difficult to determine, research suggests that between 400 and 800 of them were founded in the decade after 1962. They were small (forty students or fewer), often disorganized, and usually short lived. Yet by the late 1960s participants in these schools identified themselves as a coherent countercultural movement; they published various periodicals (such as *This Magazine Is About Schools* and *The New Schools Exchange Newsletter*), held regional and national conferences, and gave radical educators and students venues for putting their ideals of participatory democracy, opposition to hierarchy and commercialism, personal authenticity, and political activism into practice in intimate community settings.

Free school activists shared a core ideology. They emphasized the child's "natural" or "organic" desire to learn and argued that school structures and routines (such as tests and grades, timed lessons contained by classroom walls, segregation by age) inhibit genuine learning. They believed that personal relationships, emotional expression, and active participation in community were as important to education as academic work. They gave students extensive choice in their learning, such as what to study and when; they generally made class attendance optional. They valued spontaneity and argued that curricula and teaching should be immediately responsive to the lived situation of a given place and time. They saw their schools as refuges from a materialistic, militaristic culture, as seedbeds of the new society that was then being described by the New Left and the counterculture.

Yet there were ideological fissures within the movement as well. Some activists, following Neill, primarily emphasized personal freedom and happiness, while others argued that in a society they considered racist, violent, and corrupt, simple withdrawal from society was morally inadequate and free schoolers needed to address society's suffering directly. In *Free Schools* (1972), Kozol famously referred to the "romantic" free school, serving privileged White families, as being equivalent to "a sandbox for children of the SS Guards at Auschwitz."

The movement declined rapidly after 1972, but approximately twenty to forty such schools have remained intact or have been started in recent years. The more progressive elements of the homeschooling movement (e.g., "unschoolers") retain much of the free school ideology.

Ron Miller

See also Activist Teachers; Homeschooling; Summerhill

Further Readings

Graubard, A. (1974). *Free the children: Radical reform and the free school movement.* New York: Vintage.

Kozol, J. (1972). *Free schools.* Boston: Houghton Mifflin.

Mercogliano, C. (1998). *Making it up as we go along: The story of the Albany Free School.* Portsmouth, NH: Heinemann.

Miller, R. (2002). *Free schools, free people: Education and democracy after the 1960s.* Albany: State University of New York Press.

Silberman, C. E. (1970). *Crisis in the classroom: The remaking of American education.* New York: Random House.

FUNDRAISING IN SCHOOLS

Perhaps more then ever, America's schools need additional funds. Increasingly, primary and secondary schools are faced with demands for accountability with regard to their teaching. They are also adapting curricula to be more in line with the nation's increasing plurality, diverse learning styles, and ever-changing technology. However, traditional school budgets, provided by public funds, are often not able to meet these demands. As a result, public and private schools throughout the nation are starting separate education foundations to raise, handle, and redirect supplemental funds toward these vital tasks. Fundraising can also be seen from the perspective of student giving rather than receiving, through programs that encourage student philanthropy. This entry looks at both phenomena.

Local Education Foundations

Local education foundations are different from parent-teacher associations (PTAs) in the sense that the foundations do not have any oversight responsibility within the school system. Typically these foundations raise about 0.3 percent of their district's budget. Some suggest that the money raised by these foundations is relatively small and therefore these nonprofits should be seen more as public relations tools than fundraisers for the schools that they serve.

While the amount raised by the foundations is small in comparison to the district budgets, its impact is not insignificant. A 1995 longitudinal study found that foundations with an annual fundraising income of less than $10,000 provide mini-grants and scholarships, while those in the $20,000 to $50,000 range provide training, enrichment programs, and other teacher resources. And, those foundations able to raise more that $100,000 in a year often provide support for additional teaching positions.

This further differentiates local education foundations from PTAs. Parent-teacher associations, while often engaged in fundraising, raise considerably less. These small amounts support particular "extras" such as costumes and scenery for plays or extra funding for field trips. As with other nonprofits, education foundations are required to report their activity to the Internal Revenue Service but are not told how to specifically spend what they have raised.

Researchers and critics, such as Faith Crampton and Paul Bauman, are concerned about the potential inequities that could further expand the divide between poorly funded and wealthy districts. However, Ron Zimmer and others at the Rand Corporation believe that the proliferation of foundations has helped close this funding gap. Notably, the number of foundations does not differ significantly across communities of different economic status.

Educational philosophers, such as Emily Cuatto, are worried about the effects and unintended consequences of local education foundations. Stipulating that education is a public good that gives students the necessary skills to be productive members of society, Cuatto suggests that it is the government's responsibility not only to provide education to its citizens but to fully support it. By having education foundations raise supplemental funds, Cuatto believes that local, state, and federal governments are relieved of their responsibility to fully support education, thereby relinquishing their duty to provide this public good.

Youth Empowerment and Philanthropy

Other than fundraising for schools, teaching about philanthropy and primary and secondary student involvement in giving back to society through monetary means and volunteerism increased substantially at the close of the twentieth century. Youth engagement in philanthropy is the focus of many nonprofit organizations and foundations. Between 1988 and 2003, the W. K. Kellogg Foundation gave over $100 million in grants to fund and engage students in social, civic, and community building through volunteerism and philanthropy.

In addition to foundations supplementing district budgets, some nonprofits, such as the Youth Leadership Institute (San Francisco), Michigan Community Foundations' Youth Project, and the Ewing Marion Kauffman Foundation (Kansas City, Missouri), have begun teaching K–12 students about the importance of philanthropy by empowering the students in the grant-writing and -making process.

An estimated 500 foundations across the country are giving secondary school students the opportunity to create requests for proposals (RFPs) and then evaluate them and decide, along with adults, which programs meet their goals and are deserving of funding. By involving youth in this process, these foundations teach students how to incorporate their ideas and needs assessments in making funding allocation decisions and expose the students to the idea of giving, all while helping solve the foundation's pressing issues.

Casting philanthropy wider than just monetary giving, schools are learning from these youth empowerment foundations to include actions of community service and philanthropy in their curricula. Richard Bentley and Luana Nissan have explored how primary school students learn philanthropy and altruistic behavior. Their study found that witnessing an influential adult, such as a parent or guardian, teacher, or a religious or youth organization leader, engage in acts of philanthropy is most effective in passing along the importance of helping others. This teachable moment is intensified when it is coupled with a discussion about the importance of such actions.

Finally, the most effective tool is for the child to participate in giving and serving activities to help reinforce the positive feeling associated with helping others. Research by Laurent Daloz found that providing opportunities for community service helped children learn the importance of philanthropy. According to the U.S. Department of Education, more than half of the high schools in the country require community service

as a condition to graduate, up from 9 percent in 1984. Between 1984 and 1997, student volunteers increased from 900,000 to 6 million—a growth of 686 percent.

Further, according to the Higher Education Research Institute, nearly 83 percent of incoming college students in 2001 indicated they had volunteered prior to graduating high school, up from 66 percent in 1989. In theory, through these new policies of requiring community service and engaging students in opportunities to partake in other civic engagement and service learning projects, schools will produce a more philanthropic generation.

Noah D. Drezner

See also Philanthropy, Educational; School Funding

Further Readings

Bentley, R. J., & Nissan, L. G. (1996). *The roots of giving and serving: a literature review studying how school-age children learn the philanthropic tradition.* Indianapolis: Center on Philanthropy at Indiana University.

Cuatto, E. V. (2003). Not your average PTA: Local education foundations and the problems of allowing private funding for public schools. *Philosophy of Education,* 220–229.

Daloz, L. (1999). *Mentor: Guiding the journey of adult learners.* San Francisco: Jossey-Bass.

Ginsberg, A., & Gasman, M. (2007). *Gender and educational philanthropy: New perspectives on funding, collaboration, and assessment.* New York: Palgrave Macmillian.

McCormick, D. H., Bauer, D. G., & Ferguson, D. E. (2001). *Creating foundations for American schools.* Gaithersburg, MD: Aspen.

G

GALLUP POLLS

In 1935, educator and researcher George Gallup (1901–1984) founded the precursor to the Gallup Organization with his creation of the American Institute of Public Opinion. Although the Gallup Organization serves multiple functions in business, management, and consulting, it is best known for its international reputation as a trusted source for measuring public opinion through its numerous and varied Gallup Polls. In addition to its national and global surveys related to multiple social and political matters, the Gallup Organization has also made significant contributions to the field of education through its annual survey of public attitudes related to public schools in conjunction with Phi Delta Kappa (PDK). This entry looks at the organization and its educational role.

The Gallup Organization

When Dr. Gallup founded the Gallup Organization, he set out with a personal dedication to gathering and reporting the "public will" through independent and objective polling. The Gallup Organization has kept its founder's personal vision in focus. To this day, the Gallup Organization refuses requests for sponsored or paid polls and will not undertake polling that represents any particular agenda or special interest group. Similar to its historic dedication to objectivity and independence, the Gallup Organization also remains firmly committed to discovering public attitudes along a wide array of current issue areas.

"Gallup" became a household name in 1936, when the first Gallup Poll contradicted the most popular pollster of the time to successfully predict that Franklin Delano Roosevelt would win the U.S. presidency. With its genesis as a barometer for predominantly political issues, the Gallup Poll has expanded its focus over the years and now covers a diverse and comprehensive list of topics related to political, social, and economic subjects. The Gallup Organization has also grown beyond its original location in Princeton, New Jersey, and now conducts business from offices across the world. Likewise, the subjects of Gallup's public opinion polls have extended well beyond U.S. borders. The first global polls were conducted in the late 1930s to gather and report public opinion across almost fifty countries prior to the start of World War II.

With the addition of its landmark global quality of life survey in 1976, the Gallup Poll has become an internationally recognized and respected source for public opinion data. Today, the Gallup Poll continues to provide thorough and in-depth examinations of public attitudes across an expansive range of matters such as politics, elections, crime, education, civil liberties, moral and controversial issues, economics, business, the environment, religion, war, personal concerns, and so on. Overall, the Gallup Poll provides a useful service to many different arenas, including, but not limited to, the field of education.

Contributions to Education

For educators, "Gallup Poll" is synonymous with the annual Phi Delta Kappa/Gallup Poll of the Public's Attitudes Toward the Public Schools that began in the late 1960s and was originally envisioned by James Kettering and Edward Brainard of the Kettering Foundation. George Gallup became involved as the first director of this well-known educational public opinion poll in 1969. The PDK/Gallup Poll, published annually in the *Phi Delta Kappan* education journal, collects and reports America's thoughts on a series of contemporary issues in public education. George Gallup was involved in the yearly generation of each PDK/Gallup Poll until his son and cochair of the Gallup Organization took his place upon his death.

Today, a team of coauthors oversees the creation and production of the annual education poll. Although a variety of funders have provided financial support for the poll since its inception in the late 1960s, the Phi Delta Kappa Educational Foundation has been the sole funder of the annual education poll since 2004.

The annual PDK/Gallup Poll was originally intended to reach an audience consisting primarily of educators to inform their understanding and practice. Although the poll certainly continues to meet this original requirement, it has achieved greater significance over the years. Today, the PDK/Gallup Poll is largely seen as a meaningful source of information for educators, policy makers, political leaders, and the general public. Each Gallup Poll, including the annual education poll, is focused on significant and timely issues of the day. Poll readers will find information relevant to contemporary issues in education, as well as lines of questioning intended to track public attitudes through polling trends over time.

Another fundamental aspect of the annual PDK/Gallup Poll that often gets widespread attention in the general press relates to poll respondents' "grades" of the public schools both overall and in their communities. Because public schools are inherently accountable to the public, the annual PDK/Gallup Poll of the Public's Attitudes Toward the Public Schools serves a noteworthy function to the field.

In addition to its contributions to the field of education through the annual Gallup Education Poll, the Gallup Organization also provides consulting and research services to public and private educational organizations through its education branch. Overall, the Gallup Organization provides important services to the field of education and successfully illustrates how an outside organization can inform, support, and influence the field.

Carri Anne Schneider

See also Corporate Involvement in Education

Further Readings

Gallup, A. M. (1999). *The Gallup Poll cumulative index: Public opinion, 1935–1997.* Lanham, MD: SR Books.

Moore, D. W. (1995). *The superpollsters: How they measure and manipulate public opinion in America.* New York: Four Walls Eight Windows.

Mueller, J., Niemi, R., & Smith, T. (Eds.). (1989). *Trends in public opinion: A compendium of survey data.* New York: Greenwood.

Rose, L. C. (2006). A brief history of the Phi Delta Kappa/Gallup Poll. *Phi Delta Kappan, 87*(8), 631–633.

Web Sites

Gallup Organization: http://www.gallup.com
PDK/Gallup Poll Resources:
   http://www.pdkintl.org/kappan/kpollpdf.htm

GANGS IN SCHOOLS

An estimated 26,000 youth gangs with more than 840,500 members exist in the United States. Although the term *gang* may have different meanings in different contexts, for the purposes of this entry, *gang* is defined as a neighborhood group that is identified by others, and whose members recognize themselves, as a distinct group; its members are involved in activities that are illegal or considered inappropriate by neighborhood residents and/or law enforcement groups. Delinquency generally distinguishes gangs from other youth organizations. Youth gangs participate in some illegal activities and regularly violate school policies. This entry describes the scope of gang activity in the United States and then reviews reasons why youth join gangs.

The mid-1990s witnessed a decrease in gang activity in many schools and communities due to the development of federal, state, and local gang task forces. However, there was a dramatic increase in gang activity in 2003–2004, and current trends show a steady increase in youth gang activity in many communities and school districts. This poses a potential threat to the safety of others and a danger to the future of the young people who are drawn into gangs. Schools have become a place of recruitment and sources of territorial wars, or fights among rival gangs over geographic territory. Youth gang activity is anticipated for the foreseeable future.

Some scholarship suggests that urbanization and urbanism are influencing factors on youth gang activity and provide models that stimulate gang activity, even in small towns and rural areas. Gangs have been glamorized within the popular culture. Since the mid-1980s, youth gangs have grown in suburban and rural areas of the nation, increasing by 27 percent in suburban areas and by 29 percent in rural areas between 1998 and 1999. Overall, gang membership across the country increased from 731,500 in 2002 to 800,000 in 2007. Larger cities and suburban areas report more gang membership than smaller cities and rural areas, accounting for 80 percent of gang membership in 2005.

In most cases, gangs consist of members who share some common traits, such as age, gender, socioeconomic status, and race or ethnicity. Although once the domain for adults, gang activity today is viewed primarily as a teenage phenomenon. Juveniles have become the dominant members of gang culture, and their members mature out of the gang before adulthood through a process of gradual disaffiliation. The traditional age range of gang members in most cities is eight to twenty-one years of age. Gangs in local communities are found in high schools, middle schools, and elementary schools.

Gender is also a relevant factor that influences youth gang activity. Youth gangs have always been seen as a mostly male phenomenon. However, females constitute as much as 25 percent of gang membership, and they account for more behaviors that are associated with gangs than commonly thought. They commit acts that are just as violent as those of their male counterparts.

Some research indicates that the greater the socioeconomic deprivation, the more likely gangs will exist. Although youth from culturally, racially, and ethnically diverse backgrounds are more likely to form gangs, the fundamental reason is not their culture, race, or ethnicity, but rather the low socioeconomic status that they often experience in this view. Subsequently, a large percentage of youth from low socioeconomic backgrounds join "drug gangs," which primarily sell and distribute drugs for profit. Many join because participation is a way to change their economic status and provide financial supports in the home.

In contrast to this perspective is research showing that economically affluent youth also belong to gangs. Proponents of this view say that it is a misconception that poor youth are more delinquent than affluent youth. Rather, they say, society is more lenient and forgiving with affluent youth, and therefore, the same behavior perceived to be "gang behavior" among poorer youngsters is appraised differently. They assert that youth gangs are unfairly labeled as the result of socioeconomic deprivation when there are actually other salient factors in the evaluation of delinquency.

Why Youth Join Gangs

There is a misconception that juveniles who join gangs are "bad." Similar reasons why students join school organizations apply to why youth join gangs. Gang affiliation may be the student's way of making friends and gaining a sense of acceptance and worth. Similarly, many youth join gangs to feel like they have a voice and control where they may normally feel out of control and a sense of helplessness. Some youth join gangs to fulfill needs of power and leadership that are seen as otherwise unattainable in society because of their race, ethnicity, and socioeconomic status. When a system denies privilege (e.g., institutional racism that is prevalent in schools), this often results in deprivation of power, privileges, and resources, which may cause many youth to develop their own institutionalized organizations.

Additionally, many youth gangs are a form of family for its members and serve as supports. Some youth join gangs for security and self-protection in response to threatening school and community environments. Acquiring economic gain may serve as a form of incentive for gang affiliation. After all, achieving wealth is an incentive in the case of members in society. Youth who may have difficulty meeting basic financial needs may join drug gangs for employment opportunities to earn money.

In understanding why youth join gangs, we also need to ask what factors are lacking in family, school, and community systems that draw students into a culture, and what is missing in the lives and experience of gang members that draws them to join. Schools have the potential to play a critical role in offering youth alternatives to gang membership.

Satasha L. Green

See also Gender and School Violence; Violence in Schools

See Visual History Chapter 15, Progressive Reform and Schooling

Further Readings

Ball, R. A., & Curry, G. D. (1995). The logic of definition in criminology: Purposes and methods for defining "gangs." *Criminology, 33,* 225–245.

Bilchik, S. (1999). *1997 National Youth Gang Survey.* Washington, DC: Office of Juvenile Justice and Delinquency Prevention.

Cummings, S., & Monti, D. J. (1993). *Gangs: The origins and impact of contemporary youth gangs in the United States.* Albany: State University of New York Press.

Curry, G. D., Ball, R. A., & Fox, R. J. (1994). *Final report: National assessment of law enforcement anti-gang information resources.* Washington, DC: National Institute of Justice.

Lasley, J. R. (1992). Age, social context, and street gang membership: Are "youth" gangs becoming "adult" gangs? *Youth & Society, 23,* 434–451.

Web Sites

Focus Adolescent Services, Gangs:
    http://www.focusas.com/Gangs.html
National School Safety and Security Services:
    http://www.schoolsecurity.org

GARY (INDIANA) MODEL

The Gary, Indiana, public schools, developed by Superintendent William A. Wirt (1874–1938), quickly grew into a famous example of progressive education. Born in eastern Indiana, Wirt attended nearby Bluffton High School, graduated from DePauw University, and returned to Bluffton as school superintendent in 1899. His school innovations, particularly a diversified elementary curriculum, led to his move to Gary in 1907. Founded by U.S. Steel Corporation the previous year, Gary grew quickly and attracted a heterogeneous population, many from eastern and southern Europe.

The Work-Study-Play system, or Platoon School Plan, as it was later known, focused on two central features, but only in the elementary grades. Wirt believed in maximizing school facilities by constant use of all classrooms. He also expanded the curriculum to include manual training (e.g., shops for the boys and cooking for the girls), recreation, nature study, and daily auditorium activities. Organized into two platoons, during the morning, Platoon A students occupied the specialized academic classrooms (math, science, English, history), whereas Platoon B students were in the auditorium, shops, gardens, swimming pools, gym, or playground. They switched during the afternoon. Gary's large schools were unique because they were unit schools, including all grades, K–12. By the late 1920s, about half of the system's 22,000 students were attending such schools, with the remainder in the smaller elementary buildings.

The Work-Study-Play plan attracted national publicity, and by 1929, 202 cities had more than 1000 platoon schools. Although the Gary schools captured the positive spirit of progressive education, they also incorporated some troubling aspects. There was the perception that the inclusion of manual training classes was designed to channel the working classes (the majority of Gary's students) into vocational trades. The schools were also racially segregated. The 2,759 Black children in 1930 mostly attended all-Black elementary schools. The situation worsened as the Black enrollment increased to 6,700 by 1949 (34 percent of the student population), despite the school board's decision in 1946 to promote building integration. By 1960, 97 percent of the 23,055 Black pupils (more than half of the 41,000 students) were in eighteen, mostly Black schools. The trend would continue as the Black population increased and the White population decreased over the following decades.

The Gary schools barely survived the Depression years, when budgets were severely cut. Wirt's death in 1938, and a critical study in 1940, led to the slow process, not completed until the 1960s, of abandoning the platoon system and diversified curriculum, instituting the contained classroom in the elementary grades. The student population had exploded by the 1960s, but soon began to decline. There were 20,000 African American students (and few others) by 2000. Endemic social and economic problems, compounded by mandated state testing and the federal No Child Left Behind Act, put additional stress on the students and their schools.

Ronald D. Cohen

See also Progressive Education

Further Readings

Case, R. D. (1931). *The platoon school in America.* Stanford, CA: Stanford University Press.

Cohen, R. D. (1990). *Children of the mill: Schooling and society in Gary, Indiana, 1906–1960.* Bloomington: Indiana University Press.

Cohen, R. D., & Mohl, R. A. (1979). *The paradox of progressive education: The Gary plan and urban schooling.* Port Washington, NY: Kennikat.

GENDER AND SCHOOL VIOLENCE

Although school violence may refer to any form of violence within schools, including a broad range of bullying, fights, and even murder, more recently, the notion of school violence has become increasingly associated with school shootings. Male gender has been a common factor in the most lethal forms of school violence; thus, scholars and researchers interested in understanding and preventing violence in schools have begun to consider the link between masculinity and violence. Researchers have also noted and searched for answers to account for the seeming increase of girls' violence in the 1990s and early twentieth century. This entry looks at school violence and its relationship to gender.

Increasing Violence

During the mid- to late 1990s, a series of highly publicized school shootings by young suburban White males brought school violence into the national spotlight. The 1997 Heath High School shooting in Paducah, Kentucky, and the 1998 shooting in Jonesboro, Arkansas, both were featured heavily in national news. The shootings were notable particularly because of the young ages of the shooters—fourteen years old in Paducah, and thirteen and fourteen years old in Jonesboro.

The notorious shooting of the late 1990s was the 1999 killing of twelve students and a teacher at Columbine High School in Littleton, Colorado. The murders became the most deadly high school shooting in the history of the United States, thereafter serving as an inevitable reference point for any subsequent discussion of school violence. The Columbine shooting has also served as a reference point for young men fascinated with school violence, including those interested in perpetuating similar crimes. In 2006 alone, at least three different incidents of teenagers specifically mimicking Columbine were reported in North America, including the shooting of more than twenty people at Dawson College in Montreal. In April 2007, the deadliest school shooting in the United States occurred when one gunman killed thirty-two people and wounded twenty-five with two semi-automatic handguns at Virginia Tech University.

In the wake of Columbine, schools enacted stricter policies for violence prevention, including zero-tolerance policies requiring expulsion for any act or threat of violence. Metal detectors and video cameras also became more frequent within schools. While schools attempted to push for student safety, scholars and journalists searched for both causes of and solutions to the violence. In the national media, family problems, lax discipline, video games, violent films and music, access to guns, and bullying have been prominent factors discussed and debated as possible contributing factors to the crimes.

Boys Who Bully

One factor that was common to the shootings, but rarely discussed initially, was the gender of the perpetrators. In almost all of the school shootings of the late 1990s, the shooters were boys. In addition, all of the murder victims were girls in both the Paducah and Jonesboro school shootings. Despite the common factor of male gender among perpetrators, masculinity was not a prominent consideration in the popular media. Some scholars have pointed to a similar trend in studies of bullying, wherein masculinity often has been ignored as a factor in school violence despite the fact that boys are perpetrators in most cases of school bullying. Many school shootings have been related to a perceived failure at masculinity and the desire to establish masculinity through dominance and violence. Bullying is a common factor in boys' concerns at failed manliness, and bullying often has a distinctly homophobic aspect.

Particularly in instances of bullying, boys have seen retaliatory violence as the most effective way to confirm their masculinity. Studies indicate that many violent boys are depressed, yet they often shut themselves off from their feelings, repressing their sadness and turning it outward into rage and aggression. If boys have low self-esteem and buy into traditional notions of masculinity, they may be more at risk. Research shows that boys who adhere to traditional masculinity are more likely to get in trouble at school and become involved in illegal activities. This may be because within the limits of traditional masculinity, fighting back can seem like the only viable choice to a boy.

Hegemonic masculinity celebrates toughness and the capacity for violence more than the ability to express emotions effectively; thus, boys may view aggressive emotions and actions as their only possible outlet for expression. Media images of emotionally expressive and nonviolent men are limited, and instances of male violence are often normalized in media representations of men and in the sports culture that exists nationally and locally. In public schools, an example of this normalization of aggression may be seen in the popularity of high school football.

Aggressive Girls

Although the effects of hegemonic masculinity and sports culture have begun to garner more attention in the post-Columbine era, a parallel trend in the 1990s and early twenty-first century has been an increased

focus on aggressive behavior in girls and young women. In the last decade of the twentieth century, overall arrest rates for girls increased while arrest rates for boys declined. In particular, girls' arrests for assault increased at a rate that was ten times the increase for boys.

Yet some scholars have been skeptical of the notion that girls are becoming more violent, pointing to the decreased arrest rates for more violent crimes and the decreased reports of girls' violence in self-reported data. Some researchers have discussed escalated awareness rather than increased incidence of girls' crime and increasingly severe zero-tolerance policies as explanations for the rising arrest rates of girls.

Robert Pleasants

See also Bullying; Gangs in Schools; Hate Crimes in Schools; Homophobia

Further Readings

Benbenishty, R., & Astor, R. A. (2005). *School violence in context.* Oxford, UK: Oxford University Press.

Chesney-Lind, M. (2004). *Girls and violence: Is the gender gap closing?* [Online]. Harrisburg, PA: National Resource Center on Domestic Violence. Retrieved September 3, 2006, from http://www.vawnet.org/DomesticViolence/Research/VAWnetDocs/AR_GirlsViolence.php

Messerschmidt, J. W. (2000). *Nine lives: Adolescent masculinities, the body, and violence.* Boulder, CO: Westview.

Mills, M. (2001). *Challenging violence in schools: An issue of masculinities.* Buckingham, UK: Open University Press.

Newman, K. S., Fox, C., Roth, W., & Mehta, J. (2004). *Rampage: The social roots of school shootings.* New York: Basic Books.

Talbot, M. (2002, February 24). Girls just want to be mean. *The New York Times Magazine,* pp. 24–65.

GENERAL EDUCATION BOARD (1901–1964)

The General Education Board (GEB) was a philanthropy started by John D. Rockefeller and a small cadre of friends, in large part to remedy the deplorable state of education for southern rural African Americans. The GEB, over its more than six decades of life, supported a wide variety of educational programs and research, both in the United States and abroad. Abraham Flexnor's many educational surveys represent the most famous of these efforts. However, the board's support of African American education, despite representing a small percentage of its overall allocations throughout its history, remains remarkable. Arguably, despite its support of segregation, no other organization, save the NAACP and its success with *Brown v. Board of Education,* has done more to improve African American schooling.

The GEB's support of Black schooling started slowly. Indeed, in concert with the Southern Education Board, an older group that it backed financially for a number of years, the GEB espoused a curious ideology that direct aid to White schools was the best course to improve Black education. The GEB, in its early years, funded the work of rural school supervisors and professors of secondary education, all with a focus on White children and youth. However, its 1910 placement of Jackson Davis as the first State Agent of Negro Education, in Virginia's state department of education, signaled a policy turn toward direct assistance of Black schooling. GEB's efforts over the next half-century would radically alter the educational landscape for Southern African Americans.

GEB support and supervision of the State Agents of Negro Education, fundamentally assistant state superintendents, was foundational to all of its actions in support of Black schooling. To be sure, GEB's monetary support for Southern African American education remained significant throughout its life. However, using its supported State Agents as a regional network of educational policy actors, the GEB impressively reworked the Southern public school systems to include African Americans. Indeed, the GEB significantly moved away from its earlier focus on industrial education; it formulated and implemented policies that brought robust academic work to Black schools.

Beginning in the early 1940s, the GEB began to wind down its philanthropic efforts. Over the next two decades, it divested its funds and organizational obligations to other groups, principally the Southern Education Foundation. The GEB ceased operations in 1964.

Matthew D. Davis

See also African American Education; Phelps Stokes Fund; Philanthropy, Educational; Rosenwald Schools

Further Readings

Anderson, E., & Moss, A. A., Jr. (1999). *Dangerous donations: Northern philanthropy and Southern Black education, 1902–1930.* Columbia: University of Missouri Press.

Davis, M. D. (2005). Behind-the-scenes ally: The GEB, Southern Black high schools, and inter-war curriculum reform. In *Curriculum history 2004.* College Station, TX: Society for the Study of Curriculum History.

Fosdick, R. F. (1962). *Adventure in giving.* New York: Harper & Row.

Watkins, W. H. (2001). *The White architects of Black education: Ideology and power in America, 1865–1954.* New York: Teachers College Press.

GI BILL OF RIGHTS (SERVICEMEN'S READJUSTMENT ACT)

The Servicemen's Readjustment Act of 1944 (P.L. 346, 78th Congress), referred to as the "GI Bill of Rights," offered a variety of supports to returning veterans, including money to pursue higher education and purchase homes. Members of the American Legion had drafted the bill, and President Franklin Roosevelt and many persons in Congress embraced it. The supporters of this legislation wished to demonstrate their gratitude to the 16 million servicemen and servicewomen who were making wartime sacrifices.

However, they also hoped to prevent domestic and economic problems similar to those that had followed World War I. During that earlier war, the departure of young males from the homeland labor force had created employment opportunities for women, African Americans, older citizens, and persons with disabilities. Later, some returning veterans were unable to regain employment. Understandably, they were disgruntled. Those postwar civilian employees who had secured jobs but who were forced to relinquish them were equally disgruntled. President Wilson, who was preoccupied with efforts to persuade Americans to enter the League of Nations, seemed to pay little attention to these problems.

The severity of the postwar problems became evident after racial and labor riots disturbed the summer of 1919. Because of the destruction, bloodshed, and death associated with this period, journalists referred to it as "the red summer." The national insecurity and suffering were accentuated by a flu pandemic that infected one out of every four Americans. The American fatalities from the pandemic were ten times greater than the 115,000 soldiers who had died in World War I battles. The state of the nation deteriorated further during the Great Depression. In 1932, more than 30,000 former servicemen journeyed to Washington and lobbied the federal government for financial help. They requested the early award of the bonuses that they had been promised. The march of this "bonus army" culminated in violent clashes with the police and the militia. The American public was horrified as it read about the burning of the makeshift village in which the marchers had set up camp. Even more dismaying, they viewed reports and photos of veterans who had been beaten and killed.

Wishing to reduce the conditions that could lead to domestic unrest after World War II, the advocates of the GI Bill of Rights ensured that it would help discharged soldiers secure unemployment stipends, medical care, and loans with which to purchase homes or businesses. They also offered financial support for the veterans to attend vocational schools or colleges. Some people had questioned whether this bill's budget could support the services that it promised. Their skepticism was appropriate. Before subsequent GI Bills were enacted in 1952 and 1966, critics underscored the fiscal miscalculations of the early sponsors. For example, the proponents of the original 1944 bill had estimated that several hundred thousand people would take advantage of the educational benefits. However, more than one million veterans used the GI Bill to pay for higher education during the three-year period that followed the war. By 1952, more than two million veterans had drawn stipends to attend colleges or universities. Another six million veterans had used

their stipends for various types of vocational training. Within seven years of the war's conclusion, the total federal expenses for the GI Bill of Rights had amounted to more than $10 billion.

The unprecedented influx of students swelled postwar enrollments at colleges and universities. In response to the surge, college administrators erected classroom buildings, laboratories, and dormitories. To keep costs down, they frequently employed the prefabricated structures that the wartime army had developed. As additional cost-saving measures, they began to offer classes during evenings and summers. They placed special emphasis on classes in engineering, mathematics, technology, and the sciences. These fields, which had risen in importance during World War II, continued to be national priorities during the politically tense postwar years.

College administrators recognized that their student bodies had not only increased but become more diverse. Those students who were using the GI Bill of Rights to attend college included older students, mid-career students, female students, students from the economically lower classes, and students from racial minorities. Although many of the 1.2 million African Americans who had served in the war took advantage of the GI Bill of Rights, most of those who attended college lived in the North rather than the less-prosperous and racially segregated South. Many of these students were the first persons in their families ever to attend an institution of higher education. Their eventual successes changed the prevailing assumptions about the type of students who could benefit from college.

The cost of the GI Bill of Rights greatly exceeded the preliminary estimates of its sponsors. Nonetheless, this legislation was lauded because it enabled the discharged servicemen who attended college to fuel the nation's robust postwar economic progress. By 1950, the nation's gross national product had increased by 50 percent from the level at which it had been a decade earlier. The gross national product increased by more than 100 percent during the subsequent decade. Although multiple conditions contributed to this economic growth, the preparation of university-educated workers was a critical factor. Without the financial support of the GI Bill, significantly fewer workers would have been able to enroll in the universities. After they had graduated, university-educated veterans had a decisive influence on the economy. They had an equally profound impact on culture and politics.

Gerard Giordano

See also Higher Education, History of; Politics of Education

Further Readings

Giordano, G. (2004). *Wartime education: How World War II changed American education.* New York: Peter Lang.

GIFTED EDUCATION, DIVERSITY ISSUES AND

Special educational programs for highly able students are not federally mandated in the United States, so public support for these programs rises and falls over a cycle that historically has peaked every two to three decades. During periods of low support, particularly since the 1970s, criticism of such programs has focused on their alleged elitist nature. Diversity issues have formed the foundation of these critiques, probably because a cursory inspection reveals relatively few students of color participating in programs for the gifted. African American and Latino students, in particular, are underrepresented in gifted education programs in comparison to their presence in the overall school population. In recent years, attention to diversity has broadened to include students from low-socioeconomic-status households and students who are English language learners. These students also are generally underrepresented in gifted education settings, in comparison to their prevalence in the overall school population.

Historical Development

Early research concerning academically advanced learners, such as Lewis Terman's well-known longitudinal study begun in the 1920s, devoted little attention to diversity. By the late 1950s, a small handful of published works considered Black students who had high IQ scores, but this work had little impact. It was not until the late 1960s and early 1970s that diversity issues began to receive widespread attention in gifted education circles.

Beginning in the early 1970s, following the formal implementation of school desegregation, identifying the academically gifted Black student became a primary focus of diversity-related research in gifted education. Scholars of color such as Mary M. Frasier and Alexinia Y. Baldwin played pivotal roles in these efforts. Scholars during the 1970s also began to devote attention to gifted learners among Native American and Latino populations. Here, too, early efforts focused primarily on identification. More recently, such scholarship has broadened to include recruitment and retention of diverse learners in programs for the gifted, as well as studies seeking to develop appropriate curricula for use with gifted learners.

Since the 1990s, gifted identification procedures have gradually moved away from emphasizing a single-score representation of ability such as IQ. Although IQ scores are still widely used, newer operational definitions of giftedness allow additional information to be used for making placement decisions. These definitions may include criteria that address academic achievement and motivation, as well as related characteristics that are less strongly correlated with IQ, such as creativity and leadership ability.

The use of multiple criteria for identification appears to be having the desired outcome of narrowing the discrepancy in gifted program participation across diverse groups of learners. Because gifted identification policies vary widely from one state to the next, state-level data can offer a promising source of information to investigate the effects of policy on equity and diversity in gifted education.

Legal actions have played a prominent role in recent years. Actual or threatened lawsuits, often based in civil rights law, have driven changes in gifted education policy in some states. Other states have developed policies designed to increase diversity as a proactive measure, in advance of any specific legal challenge.

Emerging Directions

Existing trends seem likely to continue. These include devoting greater attention to equitable representation, movement toward a construct of giftedness that permits identification via multiple criteria, and incorporation of issues of student retention in gifted programs and appropriateness of the curriculum and instruction that such programs provide.

Examination of recent publications in gifted education suggests that researchers' conceptualizations of diversity are becoming more nuanced. Although early publications may have lumped together all students living in poverty, or all Asian learners, recent scholarship increasingly has emphasized diversity within these broad categories. Narrower descriptions, such as "of [Asian] Indian descent," are increasingly evident in the literature.

Research designs are becoming more sophisticated as well. Researchers are beginning to apply advanced quantitative methods such as hierarchical linear modeling, and they are increasingly likely to report effect sizes when appropriate. Qualitative and mixed-methods research designs add rich detail to the literature. Such scholarship emphasizes the social context of diversity, including peer factors, the school climate, and family and community characteristics that influence achievement among diverse learners.

Michael S. Matthews

See also Achievement Gap; Educational Equity: Race/Ethnicity; Immigrant Education: Contemporary Issues; Intelligence, Theories of; Tracking and Detracking

Further Readings

Baldwin, A. Y., & Vialle, W. (1999). *The many faces of giftedness: Lifting the masks.* Belmont, CA: Wadsworth.

Boothe, D., & Stanley, J. C. (Eds.). (2004). *In the eyes of the beholder: Critical issues for diversity in gifted education.* Waco, TX: Prufrock.

Castellano, J. A., & Díaz, E. I. (Eds.). (2002). *Reaching new horizons: Gifted and talented education for culturally and linguistically diverse students.* Boston: Allyn & Bacon.

Frasier, M. M. (1997). Multiple criteria: The mandate and the challenge. *Roeper Review, 20,* A4–A6.

GIFTED EDUCATION, HISTORY OF

Gifted education in America has waxed and waned in its presence and prominence over the past two hundred years. The need to identify and make special provisions for gifted students has been counterbalanced by a persistent belief that they need no unusual educational measures. This entry reviews that history.

Early Public Education

During the early years of the American public school system, gifted education programs were notably absent. Through the early 1800s, philosophical and behaviorist theories that one could be molded entirely based on controlled experiences were supported by the democratic ideal that all men are created equal and provided a strong basis upon which gifted education was deemed unwarranted.

Around 1850, scholars began to talk about the gifted or academically talented child. It was then thought that a very thin line separated genius and insanity, and the psychology of the gifted child provided the impetus for further study. Sir Francis Galton performed the first scientific study of giftedness in the late 1800s, ranking subjects based on their percentile intelligence score compared to the general population, thus furnishing the first comprehensive description of the gifted.

In 1861, William Torrey Harris, then Superintendent of Schools in St. Louis, Missouri, established the first acceleration program for gifted students based on the concept of flexible promotions wherein students could be promoted to the next grade level after either a year, semester, quarter, or five-week time period. However, this program did not give any consideration to a gifted child's social needs.

From 1880 to 1900, the first homogeneously grouped gifted programs began. These programs provided advanced academic studies and social interaction between gifted students; however, such programs for the gifted were limited. The general belief among educators was that the gifted child should remain in the heterogeneous classroom, with the teacher making appropriate modifications for the student in the regular curriculum.

Specific Programs Begin

Gifted programs expanded to include special schools for the gifted with accelerated academic programs in the early 1900s. Whether grouped in a special class or school, homogeneous grouping of gifted students was proposed as a major step toward making education of the gifted (and all students) more efficient; this same rationale continues to be used today in justifying homogeneous grouping of gifted students.

During the 1920s, the Binet-Simon intelligence test was first used to study large groups of gifted children. At Stanford University, Lewis M. Terman supervised the modification of the original Binet-Simon test into the Stanford-Binet Intelligence Scale, used the test to identify more than 1,500 gifted children, and performed extensive field studies on these children throughout their lives.

The advent of a quantifiable measuring device for identifying gifted children was crucial to the continuation and refinement of gifted education programs. Gifted education programs in the 1920s were generally enrichment programs where the traditional curriculum was expanded upon in various ways. The influence of William H. Kilpatrick's project method, which was developed during this time period, likely aided in influencing this shift from acceleration to enrichment orientation.

Although a few gifted education programs continued and flourished during the 1930s and 1940s, in general, neither gifted nor mentally retarded programs received widespread attention during this time. A 1931 White House conference report stated that although 1.5 million children with IQs greater than 120 had been identified in the United States, less than 1 percent of those children were enrolled in special classes. Of the students who were enrolled in special classes, the primary method of instruction used was still homogeneous grouping with less emphasis on acceleration than in the early 1900s.

Technology Focus

With the end of World War II and the rise of technological careers in the United States, gifted education gained attention. In 1950, the National Education Association Educational Policies Commission produced a report titled "Education of the Gifted," in which a conservative increase in attention to the needs of and opportunities for gifted children was suggested, but special classes and homogeneous grouping of gifted children was not recommended.

In the early 1950s, the concept of giftedness was expanded to include talented youth. Talent could be expressed artistically and musically, with spatial relationships, mental reasoning, and other facets of intelligence not normally measured in IQ evaluations. Established in 1953, the Talented Youth Project at the Horace Mann-Lincoln Institute of School Experimentation in New York City was one of the first programs to study the various aspects of talented youth.

The gifted education movement came to the forefront of American public schooling with the launching of the Russian rocket *Sputnik* in 1957; better education of the gifted was seen as a means to protect national security. The American government responded to what was viewed as a national educational crisis with the establishment of the National Defense Education Act (NDEA) in 1958. Through NDEA, funding was allocated for counselors to work with gifted children and for educational experiments on gifted children to be performed. In addition to the funding of gifted programs, individual students now were able to receive funding for postsecondary education, particularly in technological areas. The National Merit Scholarship program was begun; the National Science Foundation provided numerous scholarships to students studying science in college; and the Advanced Placement program was established.

In the early 1960s, concentrated study into creativity in education and the creative abilities of students began. E. Paul Torrance's research showed that gifted children in special classes had more confidence in their ability to be creative than did gifted children of comparable ability in regular classes. Torrance's Test of Creativity would later be used to identify children for gifted education programs. The emphasis in gifted teacher education classes at the time was on how to develop powers of creative thinking in gifted students.

Federal Interventions

The civil rights movement and President Johnson's war on poverty in the 1960s shifted the nation's attention to the economically and socially disadvantaged and precipitated efforts to identify gifted students from minority and low socioeconomic populations. The gifted curriculum programs of the 1960s had four categories of curriculum differentiation: (1) acceleration, or the presentation of older age material; (2) enrichment, characterized by extra work and extra resources; (3) sophistication, or learning more from the same curriculum; and (4) novelty, interdisciplinary, or unique classes.

In 1970, "Provisions Related to Gifted and Talented Children" (Section 806) was added to the Elementary and Secondary Education Act Amendments of 1969, enabling federal funds to be used on gifted education. The provisions also directed the U.S. Commissioner of Education to study the extent to which special education provisions are necessary for the gifted and talented, whether federal programs currently established are meeting their needs, and how federal programs could be more effective.

Public Law 94-142's passage in 1975 required that every American child be provided with a "free and appropriate public education." Since then, gifted education has been recognized as a part of special (or exceptional) education. As such, students who display characteristics of giftedness are often referred for psychological evaluation and intelligence testing under the identification procedures used for special education students.

The first Gifted and Talented Children's Education Act in 1978 authorized between $25 million and $50 million to be spent on gifted education programs. Repealed by President Reagan as a part of his platform of "new federalism," gifted education spending policies were returned to the states, where they continue to reside today with states implementing a wide variety of funding formulae for gifted education programs.

The Current Situation

The gifted curriculum programs of the 1970s emphasized mastery of thinking skills underlying productive and creative thinking. The previously described methods of curriculum differentiation were also used throughout the decade and into the 1980s, with novelty and enrichment overshadowing the other methods.

In 1983, the publication of *A Nation at Risk* caused gifted education to receive attention once again because of a perceived threat to the superior status of the United States over other countries. Gifted education programs resumed their emphasis on academic acceleration and sophistication, with renewed attention

to math and science. Although teaching of creative thinking continued, the use of creativity in problem solving was emphasized.

In 1989, President George H. W. Bush and the governors of the United States signed Education 2000, a reform effort to increase the cognitive abilities of American students. In 1993, the U.S. Department of Education released its first study on the gifted in two decades, in which differential education for gifted was favored and greater efforts to identify the gifted and talented from minority groups urged. However, since the enactment of No Child Left Behind under President George W. Bush, students who are underperforming receive the majority of resources, and gifted funding and existence of programs have been reduced significantly, helping to reestablish the previously held belief that education of the gifted is unnecessary.

In those states and districts that continue to provide gifted programs, all of the categories of curriculum differentiation can be found. Not only do gifted education programs and funding vary widely from state to state, but they frequently vary within states as well. Programs are provided in a variety of school settings: part-time pullout programs, full-time gifted education centers, special summer academies, magnet schools, regular schools that provide gifted classes, and even the traditional heterogeneous classroom.

Roxanne Greitz Miller

See also Gifted Education, Policy Issues

Further Readings

Colangelo, N., & Davis, G. A. (2002). *Handbook of gifted education.* Boston: Allyn & Bacon.

Miller, R. G. (1997). *Gifted selection criteria and performance in gifted sixth grade science.* Unpublished doctoral dissertation, Florida International University.

Rickover, H. G. (1959). *Education and freedom.* New York: Dutton.

GIFTED EDUCATION, POLICY ISSUES

Gifted education programs are often the subject of criticism based on claims that they are elitist and educationally unnecessary, consume funding and resources that would be better spent on more needy students, and cater to types of intelligence more readily identified in students from dominant cultural and socioeconomic groups. Because of these criticisms and the limitations of adequate federal and state funding to support all educational programs in a comprehensive manner, gifted education programs often are the targets of budget cuts and/or elimination.

Supporters of gifted education maintain that children who are gifted have an equal and intense need for specialized education programs as children who are underperforming their peers. The numerous studies of gifted underachievers and of the psychological and social benefits experienced by students enrolled in gifted programs provide evidence to counter the claims that the programs are elitist and unnecessary.

With regard to the underrepresentation of students from minority groups and lower socioeconomic backgrounds in gifted education programs, these discrepancies may be attributable to multiple explanations, including test bias; cultural values that may tend to limit learning in certain situations (such as attitudes against competition, sex-role stereotyping, emphasis on family over individual achievement, and disregard for education after high school); parents' lack of knowledge of available programs and of educational rights under law; the unavailability of intelligence tests and proctors in languages other than English; the inability of teachers who do not speak the student's language or hail from the student's cultural background to recognize giftedness in the minority student; or teacher bias.

To aid in raising the numbers of students from underrepresented groups participating in gifted programs, some school districts and states have expanded the qualification criteria by which students are evaluated for eligibility for gifted programs. For example, rather than relying solely on an individual IQ score in the top 3 percent of the population as traditionally required for program eligibility, students may qualify based on achievement test scores, scores on tests of creativity, teacher recommendations, or a combination of these criteria. However, in states that have implemented a two-tier eligibility system (traditional eligibility criteria for majority students and alternative criteria for minority), these efforts have sustained

criticisms as being unfair to majority students who are denied access to gifted programs when they have equal scores to those minority children who gain admittance under alternative criteria, and such systems have been subsequently challenged by parents and/or repealed by the courts.

Roxanne Greitz Miller

See also Gifted Education, Diversity Issues and; Gifted Education, History of

Further Readings

Colangelo, N., & Davis, G. A. (2002). *Handbook of gifted education.* Boston: Allyn & Bacon.
Miller, R. G. (1997). *Gifted selection criteria and performance in sixth grade gifted science.* Unpublished doctoral dissertation, Florida International University.

GIRL SCOUTS OF AMERICA

Most famous for their fundraising cookie sales, the Girl Scouts of America counts 50 million American women as alumnae and boasts a current membership of 2.7 million girls. Nearly 1 million women volunteer as leaders and mentors within the organization. Troop Capitol Hill is an honorary Scout troop comprised of members of the U.S. House of Representatives and U.S. Senate who are former members. Important leaders of this group include Senators Kay Bailey Hutchinson and Barbara Mikulski.

The history of the Girl Scouts mirrors the social, economic, and political progress women have made in America since the beginning of the twentieth century. Inspired by the founder of the Boy Scouts and Girl Guides, Sir Robert Baden-Powell, Juliette "Daisy" Gordon Low (1860–1927) organized the first Girl Scout troop on March 12, 1912, in Savannah, Georgia. In 1915, the organization was formally incorporated. As early as the 1920s, members could earn badges in areas such as Economist and Motorist. Also during this time, troops for Native Americans and Mexican Americans were founded.

The 1930s saw the division of the group into three age divisions: the now widely recognized Brownie group as well as Intermediate and Senior ranks. Also during this time, the first cookie sales took place. During World War II, Girl Scouts volunteered to assist with war efforts on the home front. During the 1950s, the Scouts continued to grow in membership and formed racially integrated troops.

In the 1960s, the Girl Scouts advocated civil rights and passed resolutions banning discrimination. In the 1970s, feminist leader Betty Friedan served on the Girl Scouts' national board of directors, and in 1975, Dr. Gloria Randall Scott became the Girl Scouts' first African American president. The 1980s saw the introduction of the Daisy Scout age rank, which serves girls of kindergarten age. Moving into the present, such badges as Global Awareness, Adventure Sports, Stress Less, and Environmental Health were established to reflect current concerns.

In 2000, the Girl Scouts Research Institute was formed with the goal of producing research and programs focusing on the developmental and social needs of girls. The Girl Scouts have avoided the controversies regarding sexual orientation of its members and leaders that plagued the Boy Scouts organization.

John P. Renaud

See also Mentoring, Youth

Further Readings

Kutler, S. J. (Ed.). (2003). The Girl Scouts. In *Dictionary of American history*. New York: Scribner's.

Schultz, G. D. (1958). *The lady from Savannah: The life of Juliette Low*. New York: Lippincott.

Soto, C. (1987). *The Girl Scouts*. New York: Exeter Books.

GLOBAL AWARENESS EXCHANGE

Global awareness exchange refers to programs and projects that aim to increase understanding and contact among peoples of different countries through the exchange of information, people, and ideas. Global awareness exchanges are based on the philosophy that better understanding among citizens of different countries will promote such altruistic goals as world peace, cultural sensitivity, human rights, and global teamwork. This entry examines types of global awareness

exchange and the benefits and risks associated with such exchanges.

Global awareness exchange activities can take many forms, such as reciprocal exchanges of students, researchers, businesspeople, activists, and others, in which participants from one country travel to the other; internationalized grassroots campaigns on issues pertinent to the global economy, such as workers' rights, fair trade, and immigration; and Internet and videoconferences among peoples from different countries. Common types of programs that focus on or include a component of global awareness exchange are study abroad programs sponsored by an educational institution such as a college or high school; fellowship programs for research and study abroad funded by foundations such as Fulbright; fellowship and exchange programs sponsored by private, altruistic organizations such as the Rotarians; international exchanges of people belonging to a given religious denomination or church; and grassroots advocacy campaigns such as those carried out by the nonprofit "Global Exchange." A global awareness exchange can last from a few days to several months.

Global awareness exchange programs are directly related to the constantly evolving movement to internationalize educational systems and to the growing importance of cross-national contacts in fields such as business, law, education, and medicine. The main benefits of global awareness exchanges are a better understanding and empathy for foreign cultures, increased international contacts, and increased knowledge on how to solve common problems.

Yet the benefits of such exchanges for countries in development are often considered within the context of the risks. Such risks include the "brain drain," whereby educated citizens depart but never return to their country of origin; growing inequality between those with and those without access to the Internet and other technological advances; and the adoption of inapplicable models discovered in a foreign country but impractical or unavailable in the country of origin. Furthermore, yet to be resolved are the ethical implications of spending scarce educational funds on projects and programs focusing on global awareness while millions of people worldwide do not have access to even minimal formal education. Despite these possible risks and ethical dilemmas, however, most governments, educational institutions, activists, and businesspeople worldwide consider global awareness exchange necessary and beneficial.

Moira Murphy

See also Activism and the Social Foundations of Education; Comparative and International Education; Globalization and Education; Internet, Social Impact of

Further Readings

Clifford, B. (2005). *The marketing of rebellion: Insurgents, media, and international activism.* New York: Cambridge University Press.

Enders, J. (2004). Higher education, internationalisation and the nation state: Recent developments and challenges to governance theory. *Higher Education, 47,* 361–382.

Hofstede, G. (1991). *Cultures and organizations: Software of the mind.* New York: McGraw-Hill.

GLOBAL CHILD ADVOCACY

Global child advocacy emphasizes the protection of children's rights, including the right to be treated fairly, to be protected from violence, to have the opportunity to develop fully, and to be free from abuse and exploitation. The violation of rights can adversely affect children's well-being as well as their growth and development. Children are particularly vulnerable to violence, exploitation, and abuse because they lack the social mechanisms or power to protect themselves. In an effort to promote stronger action on behalf of children, alliances of people who share these ideals champion children's causes and collectively work to bring about positive social change. An associated goal is the empowerment of youth to actively participate in decision making and community life as a means to demonstrate respect for their views and their inherent value as human beings. By valuing children's contributions and incorporating their voices into family, cultural, and social life, a protective environment can be fostered that promotes the fundamental rights of children to be treated with dignity and to remain free from harm.

Positive Directions

The Convention on the Rights of the Child is the landmark UN covenant that sets forth principles to support the creation of protective and nurturing environments for children to grow and develop. By mobilizing collaborations between the government, national child service partners, social agencies, individuals within the community, families, and youth, social movements can be fostered that ensure that the special legal protections assigned to young people are safeguarded and upheld with dignity and fairness.

Universal success in meeting goals for children's well-being has remained elusive, but the current conditions of young people are not absolute. Positive change for many young lives has resulted from progress in the education of greater numbers of children, initiatives to protect children from abuse and exploitation, and national commitments to children's issues. Social movements that promote the rights of children and advance humanity have made tremendous strides in the past decade. Continued mobilization of resources for a global movement to prevent the suffering of children is of paramount importance to secure the dignity and worth of children worldwide.

Challenges

Exposure to traumatic experiences has both short-term and long-term consequences in a child's life and can contribute to physical and mental health problems as well as educational impairments. Investments in children's present and future functioning necessitate allocation of resources to address education, physical health, socioemotional well-being, and economic security. Children are injured and killed in armed conflicts and exploited in the commercial sex industry. The goal is not only to reduce child fatalities that stem from abuse, exploitation, disease, conflicts, malnourishment, and other areas of vulnerability, but also to improve the quality of children's lives.

There is now more common acceptance of the critical periods of childhood and of the cumulative effects of missed opportunities for physical, emotional, and educational development. Regardless of age, children need secure and supportive environments where caring adults advocate for their safety and optimal functioning.

Whereas young children require family and community-based supports that enhance the skills of caregivers to build a strong foundation for their development, adolescents require opportunities to help shape their future through active participation. Advocacy initiatives can provide the impetus for accessing the energy and ingenuity of youth who can be partners in improving the future status of their peers. Moreover, global efforts are an asset to children's issues by strengthening international collaboration and the sharing of information that can foster children's investment in the rights of the young.

Awareness of the deficits and gaps in children's opportunities to achieve their optimum capabilities across all realms of functioning highlights strides that have been made and emphasizes continuing areas of vulnerability. These areas in need of attention include public policies and legal actions that perpetuate responses that fail to recognize children's needs and rights. Educators and education are critical to the process of intervention by providing safe and supportive environments where professionals and families have the opportunity to learn about abuses against children and their complex risk factors.

Advocacy Efforts

Global child advocacy highlights global efforts to recognize deficits and facilitate protection of children from threats to their healthy functioning. These initiatives optimize human capabilities and inform us of the conditions that contribute to the social, physical, and emotional development of children and those that deprive children of their chance for success and happiness. Child advocates diligently work toward crafting a framework for action that is integrated across disciplines. Despite divergent perspectives and problems that are addressed, a shared commitment to explore the issues and challenges of children creates a common vision and goal to recognize and promote the rights and well-being of children worldwide.

Global child advocacy seeds ongoing efforts that foster future action for children. These initiatives are needed to not only mobilize the involvement of professionals as advocates, but also foster the inclusion of children and families. These collaborations can help advance a partnership for exploring and developing solutions that support protective and nurturing environments in which children can grow and develop.

Success in promoting children's issues not only advances the future of children but also represents a commitment to safeguarding the dignity and worth of all members of our society. Global child advocacy comprises more than the expression of a value statement. Child advocates voice the concerns and interests of children who may be too young, vulnerable, or marginalized to be heard. They work to create safe and protected environments for children at risk for harm, and for those children who already have suffered adversity, child advocates foster the enhancement of service capacity and delivery, pursue policy changes to create mechanisms that are child-centered, and seek out justice for rights violations. Global child advocacy entails the combination of social will with political forces and the allocation of resources as part of an international response. Tasks include the development of resources that contribute to the emerging knowledge of children's issues, the creation of forums to focus on the progress that is possible and the interventions that are still needed, and the infusion of policies that foster new insights and seed opportunities for greater strides to be realized.

Advocacy for children offers a mechanism to prioritize children's issues and amplify their voice so that no child goes unheard. Who are these children in need of a voice? They are the young who reside in communities throughout the world. Our failure to act to protect and support children exacerbates the suffering and tragedy of each new generation. By directing our passion and commitment to informing others, evolving solutions, and implementing action, we can embrace and safeguard children's right to grow and develop. Even the most disadvantaged and marginalized children can be represented in these efforts, have an opportunity to progress in their development, and have their needs and rights heard. The combination of innovation and expertise can give shape and form to the dreams, vision, and voice of the children around us.

Michael J. Berson and Ilene R. Berson

See also Child Abuse: Issues for Teachers; Child Labor; Gender and School Violence; Human Rights Education; Social Justice, Education for; Social Studies Education; Violence in Schools

Further Readings

Berson, I. R., Berson, M. J., & Cruz, B. C. (Eds.). (2001). *Research in global child advocacy: Cross-cultural perspectives.* Greenwich, CT: Information Age Publishing.

Kugelmass, J. W., & Ritchie, D. J. (Eds.). (2003). *Advocating for children and families in an emerging democracy: The post-Soviet experience in Lithuania.* Greenwich, CT: Information Age Publishing.

Pattnaik, J. (Ed.). (2004). *Childhood in South Asia: A critical look at issues, policies, and programs.* Greenwich, CT: Information Age Publishing.

Web Sites

UNICEF, Convention on the Rights of the Child:
http://www.unicef.org/crc

UNICEF, The State of the World's Children:
http://www.unicef.org/sowc

GLOBALIZATION AND EDUCATION

Globalization involves the integration of economic markets around the world and the increased movement of people, ideas, goods, services, and information across national borders. It has been marked by a rise in the power of corporations vis-à-vis nation-states. The influence of globalization is growing in education spheres as well. For example, the standardization of education under the No Child Left Behind Act is certainly connected to a desire for global competitiveness, particularly in educating citizens to participate in the global economy. So, too, is expanded corporate involvement in schools. This entry provides a brief overview of globalization and then looks more closely at its impact on schools.

This entry first defines globalization and explores its technological, political, cultural, and economic dimensions. It then describes concerns about the downsides of globalization, in particular, how many see it as synonymous with global capitalism, and thus the cause of various forms of social misery, such as a widening gap between the wealthy and poor, ecological destruction, homogenization of cultures, and excessive consumption and greed among

the privileged. Next, it examines the ways in which globalization has led to significant shifts in educational priorities. For example, in the United States, there has been increased competitive standardization of teaching and learning, growing commodification of education, and a move toward seeing schooling as primarily a private good. Finally, the entry considers some ways of harnessing the democratic potential of globalization through creating an expanded notion of global citizenship, using new forms of technology in the service of social change activism, and reinvigorating discussions of democracy and social justice.

Globalization may be the word that best characterizes the twenty-first-century world. It is a term talked about across academic disciplines, in the media, in advertising, and by politicians and world leaders. Yet despite the fact that this word is talked about in so many different contexts, both popular and scholarly, there is no clear and/or agreed-upon definition of globalization. It is an idea that is elusive, complicated, and contentious. People often seem to use the term in contradictory ways depending on their social position, cultural perspective, and level of investment in current political and economic systems. Some herald globalization as the path toward a future of growing prosperity, intercultural cooperation, and technological advancement. For others, it is simply the most current manifestation of the forces of colonialism, imperialism, and capitalist greed, with the inevitable outcome being increased impoverishment and marginalization of many of the world's people, as well as wide-scale environmental and cultural destruction.

The term *globalization* is increasingly used in education spheres as well, though perhaps not as quickly as in other academic disciplines. For example, the standardization of education under the No Child Left Behind Act is certainly connected to a desire for global competitiveness, particularly in educating citizens to participate in the global economy. So, too, is expanded corporate involvement in schools. The fact that so many people are talking about the phenomenon of globalization, and in so many different ways, indicates that important issues are at stake in how people come to understand what many call the defining reality of the contemporary era.

What Is Globalization?

It is difficult to describe concisely the phenomenon of globalization. It is referred to variously as an ideology, a practice, a trend, or simply the best way to characterize the contemporary world. Some of the confusion surrounding globalization is surely due to the fact that the concept is used in so many different places and in multiple ways. Although the word itself is relatively new, the processes to which it refers—especially movements and interactions between cultures, countries, and regions—have been around seemingly forever. John Coatsworth claims that there have been several cycles of globalization, beginning with the period of global exploration in the fifteenth and sixteenth centuries, running through the creation of conquest colonies in the Americas, Africa, and Asia, and leading to more contemporary efforts by major superpowers to develop an international system of trade rules and regulations, and to remove artificial barriers to the spread of free-market capitalism. Although there were surely some noble goals in these initial phases of exploration, there is no doubt that, viewed from this perspective, there are also distinct parallels between globalization and colonialism, as even in its initial phases, globalization involved a desire to obtain wealth and power.

Jan Scholte usefully offers five different conceptual usages of the term *globalization*: internationalization, liberalization, universalization, modernization, and deterritorialization. *Internationalization* simply refers to international relationship, exchange, and interdependency. Often, this is facilitated by *liberalization,* that is, the removal of government barriers in order to create a more fluid and open world economy. Similarly, neoliberalism, or the deregulation of economic markets and the growth of a competitive private sector, is also frequently used in connection to globalization. When people, goods, and ideas are spread throughout the world, a kind of *universalization* takes place, where the same products, beliefs, and world-views become seemingly pervasive everywhere.

What tend to get universalized are the values and social structures of modernity: capitalist economic arrangements, rational forms of understanding, bureaucratic organizational structures, industrial processes, and media forms. Such *modernization* contributes to the destruction of indigenous cultures and the diminishment of self-determination. Finally, globalization involves changes in the integrity of countries, or *deterritorialization,* such that geographic places, distances, and borders no longer solely mark social spaces. As part of these geographic changes, different regions of the world are now much more closely linked, and actions in one part of the world can affect, and be affected by, people in other places both near and far.

In the current climate, the integration of people and places across national borders seems to have happened almost overnight, and in ways faster than most people's ability to comprehend or control it. In part, this is due to technological advances such as the Internet, which have allowed people in one country easy access to others around the world, facilitating the sharing of knowledge, the trading of products, and the diffusion of ideas. Moreover, the economies of countries throughout the world have become increasingly intertwined. More people than ever before have access to means of communication (computers, cell phones, cable systems); they can buy, sell, trade, and otherwise invest money right from their home computers; and through Internet and satellite technology, they can quickly learn what is going on around the world.

Paralleling the various definitions of the term *globalization,* there are multiple arenas in which this idea takes shape: political, technological, cultural, and economic. Politically, it involves the lessening of the strength of nation-states as large corporations, through transnational capitalist processes, dominate spheres of decision making and influence. These transnational corporations tend to have more power than many countries. Arguably, by locating businesses and investing in developing countries, these corporations create economic growth and job opportunities, and contribute to an increased standard of living for many people. Technologically, there is a dramatic increase in electronically mediated forms of communication to the degree that people begin to see the world, and their place in it, differently. Older, industrial-type factories have increasingly been replaced by high-tech, computerized companies.

Culturally, interconnection among citizens throughout the globe is becoming commonplace. One can enter an online discussion group about this topic of globalization and, in real time, talk to people from Albania to Zimbabwe. This increase in global communication can lead to new forms of collaboration, problem solving, and creativity. At the same time, it can also result in the homogenization and Americanization of cultures, as people everywhere come to desire the same consumer products and watch the same mass media news and entertainment.

Although the political, cultural, and technological dimensions of globalization are certainly important, it is the economic dimension of globalization that most advocates and critics address, most particularly, the ways in which globalization has amounted to a seeming celebration of unfettered, free-market capitalism. Here, the integration of the world's people is largely about creating more potential consumers and markets; about greater access by the privileged elite to both human and natural resources throughout the globe. Critics charge that, ultimately, globalization is about greed, profits, and the desire for private gain.

The increased contact among peoples from different cultures can stimulate creativity and innovation, and, concurrently, economic development and productivity. Moreover, global sensitivity can enhance collaborative international efforts for ameliorative social change. For example, social justice activists can now work together more easily to expose, and bring attention to, violations of human rights, and consequently pressure governments to ensure basic protections for their citizens. Although international relationships have existed for hundreds of years, what seems new in this current era is the pace of change and the degree to which the lives and livelihoods of all people in the world are now so closely intertwined, even though people may not be fully aware of the depth of those connections.

The Dark Side of Globalization

Despite the promises of worldwide economic growth and the creation of a more harmonious global community, there are also dark sides to globalization. These are linked to uneven and inequitable relationships between countries and geographic regions, such as between the "developed" and the "developing" world,

and to the uncontrolled growth of free-market capitalism. It sometimes appears that the desire for cross-cultural exchange by wealthy countries is really a desire for economic gain through access to cheap raw materials, low-paid labor, and new export markets.

Capitalists in wealthy countries claim that their activities are a necessary part of the growth process for developing countries, and that the fruits of these efforts trickle down to even the poorest of citizens. The problem is that many people in poorer countries may not see these fruits and may feel that they have been exploited and that the quality of their lives has actually gotten worse. Poor citizens in wealthy countries feel the effects of this system too, as their places of employment are downsized and jobs are sent overseas. Thus, many see globalization as tantamount to capitalism without any barriers, limitations, or protections and fear that what results is a world of growing inequity, of the haves and the have-nots.

In addition to contributing to mounting economic inequities, this expansion of capitalism significantly complicates the democratic promises of public education. Arguably one of the central goals of education in U.S. society is to cultivate the habits and dispositions of democratic citizenship. These include commitments to diversity, equity, cooperation, reflective thinking, social reform, and a concern for the common good. Yet the market-driven imperatives that largely underlie most manifestations of globalization often run counter to these goals.

For many years, scholars in the foundations of education have been troubled by the tenuous relationship between capitalism and democracy. Implicitly and explicitly, they have been arguing against the processes that are currently so much a part of globalization. They have called for schools to nurture democratic habits, teach compassion, and foster equality of opportunity and social responsibility. Similarly, critical pedagogues have called for educators to foreground the social justice issues related to the effects of a capitalist economic structure on the quality of people's lives. In the current context of globalization, rethinking the relationships among education, democracy, and capitalism is increasingly crucial.

In mass movements around the world, people have protested contemporary manifestations of globalization, most notably whenever the World Trade Organization meets. These antiglobalization activists represent a diverse range of concerns. They include labor organizers, environmentalists, human rights workers, students, indigenous peoples, and citizens from developing countries who see their ways of life being irreparably altered when the driving motivation for global interaction seems to be profit. What loosely unites these activists is a shared fear about the consequences of uncontrolled expansion of global capitalism.

Global capitalism and globalization are routinely treated as synonymous in the literature and by critics, as the economic dimension of globalization dominates much of the thought about this phenomenon. Proponents of capitalism claim that the internationalization of this system will raise the standard of living for people throughout the world. The logic is simple. Competition is stimulated by a free-market system in which barriers to trade are eliminated, foreign investment is encouraged, and public goods are privatized. This in turn necessitates more efficient use of resources, creates innovation, enhances productivity, and ultimately lowers prices.

By opening up markets, companies can manufacture products in the most advantageous locations, such as where they are close to natural resources or cheap labor. This makes consumers happy, because they can then buy products more cheaply, and purchase more, which leads to a desire for more, which stimulates growth. The ultimate assumption is that efficiency and competition invariably lead to economic growth, the benefits of which will trickle down to the poorest members of all societies.

There are multiple problems with this logic, however. Primarily, many argue that this system has made the wealthy richer, but it has not had the same effects for the poor, and that the extremes of wealth and poverty have grown rather than shrunk in the era of globalization. This is largely due to the fact that the playing field for economic competition has historically been quite uneven. Given multiple different ways of measuring growth, as well as determining inequality, supporters and critics of globalization argue back and forth about whether free trade has raised the global standard of living. Yet even when some indications of economic growth can be shown to be the result of trade liberalization policies in one country, they are often at the expense of those in other places.

There is also a danger of conflating quality of life simply with economic measures such as the gross domestic product. In other ways, the quality of people's lives is compromised when they are motivated by the quest for personal profit and gain. For example, many Americans consume excessively and wastefully, are burdened by huge debts, and are stressed out and overworked. In response to concerns about the quality of people's lives under a system driven by capitalist motivations, antiglobalization activists maintain that at its most basic level, the problem with globalization is that it is a system that puts profits before people. It encourages competition, greed, exploitation, and a winner-take-all mentality that divides rather than unites citizens of the world. For many, the reality of globalization is simply that it elevates economic gain above all else, including the quality of people's lives. Here, the intimate connection between globalization and global capitalism is a significant cause for concern.

For many critics, one of the biggest problems with capitalism as the guiding international system is that it is amoral. The goal of this system is for money to make money; the bottom line for capitalists is profit. Allan Johnson argues that the system does not require ethical or moral reflection; what matters is not what people produce (e.g., healthy food, affordable housing, health care, drugs, weapons, pollution, slavery), but whether there is a market where they can sell their products for a profit. At the same time, capitalism contributes to the commodification of our lives, as workers who do not own the means of production are forced to sell their labor for wages. Where profit is the bottom line, other dimensions of human relationships are ignored and other social considerations are overshadowed. This is a particular challenge to education for democracy because there are more important considerations in assessing the quality of people's lives than simply how much they can acquire and consume.

Despite the claims that economic globalization makes life better for everyone, the realities and consequences of this movement are well documented by critics: a widening gap between the wealthy and poor, loss of job security as mobile companies race to find the cheapest labor, ecological destruction resulting in part from corporations moving to countries with few environmental protections, sweatshop work conditions in developing nations eager for capital influx, excessive greed and consumption by those driven by a profit motive, homogenization of world cultures, insurmountable debt crises, diminishment of biodiversity, cultivation of dependency where there was once self-sufficiency, massive pollution, threatened national sovereignty, and widespread poverty in the Third World.

Impact on Education

When the measure of worth is profit, and material gain is the criterion by which social growth and progress are judged, it becomes increasingly difficult for educators to argue for schooling as a public good, to decouple individualistic consumption from democratic citizenship, and to work toward a world of peace and harmony as opposed to one of exploitation. Yet just as globalization can mean many different things, the relationship between globalization and education is equally contested. Certainly, expanded international relationships and interconnections can inspire challenges to parochialism and ethnocentrism in schools, especially so students can better work with, and learn from, those who are different from themselves. New modes of technology can lead to novel forms of research, inquiry, and pedagogy. As teachers and students attempt to develop global networks for collaboration and cooperation, the fact that they can communicate more easily with people throughout the world is surely advantageous. In this sense, globalization can be truly democratizing, as expanded access to information and people can result in more equality of opportunity, greater intercultural awareness, and new avenues for social justice activism.

However, just as the neoliberal economic policies of global capitalism tend to be the defining feature of globalization, neoliberal ideology also tends to be the dominant force currently influencing educational reform, eclipsing the potential of more democratic goals. Rather than educational changes that are aimed at helping marginalized citizens become part of a larger global community marked by more just social arrangements, typical reforms are overwhelmingly consistent with a neoliberal, corporate agenda of standardization, competition, and privatization. Corporations have infiltrated schools and policy makers have increasingly sought market solutions (such as vouchers, private schools, and choice programs) for educational problems. Corporate influence over schooling is manifested in more standardized approaches to teaching and learning, and, concurrently, what some may find as excessive testing and competition; the use of supposedly more efficient forms of pedagogy, such as distance learning and online courses; and calls for the privatization of education and a diminishment in the belief that education is a public good.

Beyond such obvious forms as subtle and overt advertising in schools and the use of corporate-constructed curriculum materials, business management ideas encapsulated in such words as *efficiency, accountability, competitiveness, world-class standards, calculability,* and *control* have grown in popularity among educational leaders. The No Child Left Behind Act, one of the most sweeping pieces of educational legislation in recent history, emphasizes mastery of content standards, regular measurement of student performance through frequent testing, and accountability schemes that punish students and teachers in already struggling schools.

Critics argue that schools increasingly teach toward tests; creativity is suppressed in favor of a narrow vision of performance; teaching is increasingly tantamount to transmission; and competition among students, schools, districts, and states is exacerbated and seemingly celebrated. Yet, at the same time, there is the illusion of fairness and equality of opportunity when everyone takes the same tests, and thus a belief that the winners in this system deserve the rewards heaped upon them. The logic behind such a corporate vision of schooling is that education should prepare students to succeed in the global marketplace. The way to do this is to condition them to engage in the competitive behaviors that are supposedly necessary to economic flourishing, in particular, the elevation of individual, self-interested achievement above all else.

The idea that education is fundamentally a means for personal growth and a path to individual gain is especially pervasive on college campuses, where corporate funding streams, student demands, and the prevalence of new technologies have significantly shifted educational priorities. Students increasingly enter higher education with the mindset of consumers. They seek degree programs with guaranteed job placement and think of education instrumentally: as a means to more earning power. They demand greater convenience, flexibility, and immediate relevance, and thus online courses and occupational, as opposed to liberal arts, programs have grown in popularity.

At the same time, colleges operate as big businesses, restructuring programs and priorities to meet the needs of the market. From a business perspective, online classes and programs are popular because of their cost efficiency; if students learn to desire them, even better. They require minimal human resources, yet generate large income streams. So, too, do large, lecture-based classes, also increasingly prevalent on campuses. Learning is commodified when faculty are pressured to seek external funds for their research, often from corporate sources, and marketability is the primary criterion for determining course offerings.

Perhaps the most significant way in which the forces of globalization have influenced education is the trend toward the privatization of schooling. This is not surprising, as the privatization of public goods is a defining political and economic feature of neoliberalism and, concurrently, globalization. To succeed in a globalized world, Thomas Friedman maintains that countries must don a "golden straitjacket." Among other things, this entails making the private sector the central engine for economic growth, shrinking state bureaucracies, privatizing public institutions and industries, and encouraging domestic competition.

As conservative critics have argued that public school systems are top-heavy and cumbersome bureaucracies, and that absent competition, they are not pressured to improve performance, the calls for privatization have gained increasing popularity. The push toward privatization begins with the rhetoric that schools are now failing, despite the existence of evidence that would refute this claim. When people are convinced that schools lack rigor, that students are failing to master even basic skills, and that students in other countries outperform Americans in many measures of academic achievement, it becomes easy to also convince them that the United States needs to drastically overhaul education. Here, the logic of privatization becomes persuasive, especially when it can be linked to abstract democratic ideas such as freedom, choice, and individual rights, as well as to the mythologies that support capitalism, such as meritocracy and social Darwinism.

The practices put into place under the No Child Left Behind Act seem to greatly support the path toward privatization, particularly in the form of vouchers, school choice programs, and the eventual development of even more for-profit schools. This is because the Act mandates that students meet performance standards but does not ensure that they have the necessary resources and support to do so. When schools fail to meet these standards, they must provide options for students to transfer to other schools, although there is no provision that other schools must accept them, nor is there any guarantee that space will be available at these other schools. This mandate thus seems implicitly designed to create a market for alternative educational programs, and thus opens spaces for privatization, especially as the Act allows for failing schools to reconstitute as charter schools and/or to solicit private management firms to run daily operations.

The assumption behind privatization is that the competitive climate of free-market schooling will force all schools to get better. At the same time, a privatized system rewards individual initiative and conceptualizes education as a private good. This echoes the logic of global capitalism in suggesting that competition stimulates growth and innovation, the benefits of which supposedly trickle down to all citizens. Yet a belief in schooling as a public good, critical to the development of more than simply self-centered consumers, is missing from this corporate vision of schooling, and from many of the educational manifestations of globalization. This corporate vision is seen to conflict with the goal of cultivating democratic citizens committed to equity, justice, ethics, compassion, human flourishing, and ultimately, to the common good.

Democratic Visions in an Era of Globalization

The democratic promise of education is significantly complicated in the current phase of globalization. Educators have been asked to narrowly prepare students to participate in the economic market, students have developed an even more instrumental rationality in the face of schooling, and corporate influences have permeated every sphere of academic life. Yet there are forces within the globalization movement itself that can help to challenge these trends and to reassert the importance of critical democratic citizenship, which fundamentally involves responsibility to others and to social betterment. As part of uncovering these forces, Douglas Kellner calls for the development of a critical pedagogy of globalization, or a globalization from below, in which people resist the negative consequences of a free-market-fueled capitalist globalization and use the forces of globalization for more socially just ends. In particular, he argues that the new technologies that are so much a part of globalization can be used in more utopian ways: to circulate information, provide avenues for creative expression, offer a vehicle for the development of collaborative social change strategies, and link networks of resistance. For example, the Internet can allow activists to band together, expose corporate abuses, market socially and environmentally conscious products, and rally citizens to hold corporations accountable for more ethical behavior.

There are a number of ways for educators to respond to the realities of globalization and to use the tools and technology that it has unleashed in order to foster more democratic ends. These include developing an expanded conception of democratic community and global citizenship, encouraging the use of new media and technology in the service of activist work, and responding to the dark sides of globalization with renewed critical discussion on the meaning of democracy and justice in the contemporary era. As globalization has created deep interconnections among people and places around the world, there are glimmerings of a new, potentially more powerful conception of democratic citizenship developing as well. In this vision, global citizens would recognize their interdependence; see their happiness as linked to the happiness of others; and believe it important and valuable to learn to work amid differences and across such artificial boundaries as race, class, religion, ethnicity, and nation.

Living in a globalized world compels people to think more deeply about their responsibilities to others both locally and globally. To be good global citizens, people ought to learn to understand and value cultural diversity, work collaboratively with others both near and far, communicate better with those who don't necessarily share their language or values, and look at the consequences of their choices in much more nuanced ways. All of these represent new priorities for contemporary education as well as important democratic values.

Taking the idea of a global community more seriously could compel students and teachers alike to rethink their responsibilities to others as citizens of the world, not just citizens of a particular geographical location. This would help all people to realize, for example, exploitation anywhere in the world, especially for the sake of the private gains of a few, hurts all of people in the long run.

The technological tools of globalization have certainly provided people the ability to develop a more global outlook in relation to the world's problems. The Internet has created a climate of increasing transparency and enhanced access to information. For example, no longer can human rights abuses in remote regions of the world be hidden from broader public view and critique. Through satellite, television, and Internet technology, barriers to information are more porous than ever. These technological advances offer powerful tools for activists around the world, who can and do use electronically mediated forms of communication to circulate information, galvanize support, organize protests, and pressure corporations and governments to be more socially and ecologically responsible.

Educators could certainly help students use these new forms of technology to express themselves, become active citizens, and take action against the oppressive elements of the world around them. In this sense, increased access to information, along with newly developed avenues for freedom of expression, can contribute to empowering citizens to imagine and create more democratic social, economic, and political relationships.

Ultimately, globalization has both dark sides and spaces for possibility. When conceptualized narrowly as a celebration of the uncontrolled growth of capitalism, the deleterious effects of globalization are most evident. Yet exposing the dark side of globalization can also shed light on new possibilities. That is, the more educators talk about problems, as well as imagine more sustainable alternatives, the more they can help to reinvigorate discussion on matters of democracy, social justice, and civic responsibility. This discussion is central to keeping alive the promise of democracy in the face of increasingly undemocratic international practices and relationships. Arguably, many educators believe that democracy is the ideal form of social life, or at least the best form of living that citizens have yet come up with. This is because it is a way of life that most consciously strives for social justice by aiming for the fulfillment of individuals and the growth of communities, and by balancing individual rights with commitment and responsibility toward others. Free-market-fueled globalization presents a significant challenge to both the idea of democracy, broadly conceived, and educating for democratic citizenship.

Educators need to invest much more energy into understanding the dynamics of globalization, challenging its problematic effects, and harnessing its democratic potential. One place to start is by helping to revive the public discourse around education for democracy by asking and exploring critical questions about the global realities of our contemporary world. What are the ethical and social responsibilities of global citizenship? What are the most socially just economic arrangements? What is the relationship between democracy and capitalism, and can they coexist? What are the conditions that make democracy possible? What protections must be put into place to ensure environmental justice and ecological sustainability? How do, and should, actions in the global sphere reflect the values that should be passed on to children? What constitutes the good life? The current context of globalization, although obviously troubling in many ways, could also provide the impetus educators need to take issues of democracy, justice, and citizenship much more seriously in our public and educational discourse. In this way, educators might begin to harness the democratic potential of living in a truly globally interconnected world.

Kathy Hytten

See also Citizenship Education; Corporate Involvement in Education; Economic Inequality; No Child Left Behind Act; Privatization; Technologies in Education

Further Readings

Aronowitz, S. (2000). *The knowledge factory: Dismantling the corporate university and creating true higher learning.* Boston: Beacon Press.

Bigelow, B., & Peterson, B. (Eds.). (2002). *Rethinking globalization: Teaching for justice in an unjust world.* Milwaukee, WI: Rethinking Schools Press.

Burbules, N. C., & Torres, C. A. (Eds.). (2000). *Globalization and education: Critical perspectives.* New York: Routledge.

Coatsworth, J. H. (2004). Globalization, growth, and welfare in history. In M. M. Suárez-Orozco & D. B. Qin-Hilliard (Eds.), *Globalization: Culture and education in the new millennium* (pp. 38–55). Berkeley: University of California Press.

Friedman, T. (2000). *The Lexus and the olive tree.* New York: Anchor.

Giddens, A. (1990). *The consequences of modernity.* Stanford, CA: Stanford University Press.

Giroux, H. A. (2000). *Impure acts: The practical politics of cultural studies.* New York: Routledge.

Johnson, A. G. (1997). *Privilege, power, and difference.* Boston: McGraw-Hill.

Kellner, D. (2002). Globalization and new social movements: Lessons for critical theory and pedagogy. In N. C. Burbules & C. A. Torres (Eds.), *Globalization and education: Critical perspectives* (pp. 299–321). New York: Routledge.

Schirato, T., & Webb, J. (2003). *Understanding globalization.* London: Sage.

Scholte, J. A. (2000). *Globalization: A critical introduction.* New York: St. Martin's.

Stromquist, N. P. (2002). *Education in a globalized world: The connectivity of economic power, technology, and knowledge.* Lanham, MD: Rowman and Littlefield.

GREAT BOOKS OF THE WESTERN WORLD

In 1952, Encyclopedia Britannica published a fifty-four-volume set titled *Great Books of the Western*

World. The *Great Books* were intended by Dr. Mortimer Adler and Dr. Robert Hutchins to establish a standard curriculum for American schools, but the public response to the first edition was tepid. Sales of the volume set rendered the multimillion-dollar project a financial failure. Nevertheless, a second edition was published in 1990 with few alterations. Many critics deplored it for failing to reflect the changing cultural landscape of the twentieth century.

Hutchins and Adler conceived the project as a means of delimiting and promoting a distinctly Western literary canon. There were 443 works representing seventy-six authors in the first edition, and selection criteria were based on the work's relevance to 102 Great Ideas. Both the selection criteria and the notion of a list of Great Ideas met with immediate controversy. For one thing, a number of celebrated French authors are conspicuously absent: Molière, Racine, Balzac, and Flaubert. No works are represented for several important continental authors, including Friedrich Nietzsche, Søren Kierkegaard, John Calvin, and Martin Luther. Among the missing works of English authors are Christopher Marlowe's *Dr. Faustus,* any poems by John Donne, and John Webster's *Duchess of Malfi.* Four volumes are devoted to Aristotle and Thomas Aquinas without either a rationale or an introduction to their highly specialized use of philosophical terms. The same is true of the six volumes apportioned to scientific works. The lack of explanatory material has given occasion for critics to dismiss the project for lacking relevance to any but the privileged.

The following authors do appear in *Great Books of the Western World*:

First Edition

Homer
Aeschylus
Sophocles
Euripides
Aristophanes
Herodotus
Thucydides
Plato
Aristotle
Hippocrates
Galen
Euclid
Archimedes
Apollonius of Perga
Nicomachus of Gerasa
Lucretius
Epictetus
Marcus Aurelius
Virgil
Plutarch
Tacitus
Ptolemy
Copernicus
Kepler
Plotinus
Augustine

Thomas Aquinas
Dante Alighieri
Geoffrey Chaucer
Nicolò Machiavelli
Thomas Hobbes
François Rabelais
Michel de Montaigne
William Shakespeare
William Gilbert
Galileo Galilei
William Harvey
Miguel de Cervantes
Francis Bacon
René Descartes
Baruch Spinoza
John Milton
Blaise Pascal
Isaac Newton
Christiaan Huygens
John Locke
George Berkeley
David Hume
Jonathan Swift
Laurence Sterne
Henry Fielding

Charles de Secondat, baron
   de Montesquieu
Jean-Jacques Rousseau
Adam Smith
Edward Gibbon
Immanuel Kant
Alexander Hamilton
James Madison
John Jay
John Stuart Mill
James Boswell
Antoine Lavoisier
Jean Baptiste
   Joseph Fourier
Michael Faraday
Georg Wilhelm
   Friedrich Hegel
Johann Wolfgang Von Goethe
Herman Melville
Charles Darwin
Karl Marx
Friedrich Engels
Leo Tolstoy
Fyodor Dostoevsky
William James
Sigmund Freud

Added to the Second Edition

Added to the Original Volumes

John Calvin
Erasmus
Molière
Jean Racine
Voltaire
Denis Diderot
Søren Kierkegaard
Friedrich Nietzsche
Alexis De Tocqueville
Honoré De Balzac
Jane Austen
George Eliot
Charles Dickens
Mark Twain
Henrik Ibsen

Removed From the Original Volumes

Apollonius of Perga
Laurence Sterne
Henry Fielding
Jean Baptiste Joseph Fourier

New Volumes on 20th-Century Material

20th-Century Philosophy and Religion:

William James
Henri Bergson

John Dewey
Alfred North Whitehead
Bertrand Russell
Martin Heidegger
Ludwig Wittgenstein
Karl Barth

20th-Century Natural Science:

Henri Poincaré
Max Planck
Alfred North Whitehead
Albert Einstein
Arthur Eddington
Niels Bohr
Albert Einstein
G. H. Hardy
Werner Heisenberg
Erwin Schrödinger
Theodosius Dobzhansky
C. H. Waddington

20th-Century Social Science (I):

Thorstein Veblen
R.H. Tawney
John Maynard Keynes

20th-Century Social Science (II):

James George Frazer
Max Weber

Johan Huizinga
Claude Lévi-Strauss

20th-Century Imaginative Literature (I):

Henry James
George Bernard Shaw
Joseph Conrad
Anton Chekhov
Luigi Pirandello
Marcel Proust
Willa Cather
Thomas Mann
James Joyce

20th-Century Imaginative Literature (II):

Virginia Woolf
Franz Kafka
D. H. Lawrence
T. S. Eliot
Eugene O'Neill
F. Scott Fitzgerald
William Faulkner
Bertolt Brecht
Ernest Hemingway
George Orwell
Samuel Beckett

Among the most interesting innovations involving the *Great Books* was the creation of a multivolume *Synopticon* written by Adler in which articles on subjects as diverse as "Love," "Politics," and "War" were linked to appropriate sections where these topics were discussed in the *Great Books*.

Perhaps a testament to the enduring attractiveness of the project for some, *Great Books* programs at St. John's College, the University of Chicago, and Biola University continue with steady enrollment numbers.

Shawn Pendley

See also Classical Curriculum; Trivium and Quadrivium

Further Readings

Adler, M. J. (2005). *How to think about the Great Ideas.* Chicago: Open Court.

Adler, M. J., Fadiman, C., & Goetz, P. W., Eds. (1990). *Great Books of the Western World* (2nd ed.) Chicago: Encyclopedia Britannica.

Center for Programs in Contemporary Writing, the University of Pennsylvania. (2006). Dwight MacDonald, "The Book-of-the-Millenium Club." Retrieved from http://www.writing.upenn.edu/~afilreis/50s/macdonald-great-books.html

Hutchins, R. M. (1952). *Great Books of the Western World.* Chicago: Encyclopedia Britannica.

GREAT DEPRESSION

In January 1933, the President of the United States, Herbert Hoover, in remarks to the Conference on the Crisis in Education, made the following statement: "There is no safety for your Republic without the education of our youth. That is the first charge upon all citizens and local governments." One year later, addressing a similarly themed Citizens Conference on the Crisis in Education, the new president, Franklin Delano Roosevelt, offered an equally grave warning: "Although the effects of the present lack of adequate educational opportunities on our national life may not be noticeable today, the time may soon come when dire effects will be apparent." Assessing both the changes and continued problems since he assumed office, Roosevelt repeated this statement in late 1935 when he stated,

> The biggest stride we have made in the past two and half years has been in interesting the American people in their own Government . . . their social problems and their educational problems. . . . The depression hit education in the United States more than anything else. . . . It is hard to bring back the facilities in education as quickly or as easily as it is to raise farm prices or open banks.

These presidential statements demonstrate how the economic crisis of the Great Depression exerted a direct impact on elementary and secondary schooling. Initially in the United States, but quickly around the world, the Depression was felt in schools as businesses and banks failed, tax revenue decreased, and public funding was cut. In 1932, George Strayer, Professor of Educational Administration at Teachers College, Columbia University, described how city and rural schools had been closed, terms shortened, teacher salaries reduced, class sizes increased, major offerings in the curriculum dropped, classroom supplies and materials denied, health services and physical education dropped, standards for entry into teaching dropped, building programs discontinued,

and night programs and continuation schools closed—"in short, the whole program of education is being curtailed, if not indeed placed in jeopardy."

These warnings were echoed by the National Education Association, whose 1931 report urged American citizens "to choose carefully the public enterprises which they support during the crisis with a view to averting the sacrifice of children." The Committee on the Emergency in Education formed by the Progressive Education Association warned that schools in many states "would continue in their downward plunge to educational disaster." Amplifying the pressure educators felt to curtail their services, Ward G. Reeder declared, "The battle lines are drawn; in fact, the conflict has already begun and daily becomes more tense."

Worldwide Impact

Similar processes occurred in other countries, as the economic crisis forced governments to make significant cuts in educational budgets. The Great Depression provides evidence of an early phase of globalization, as economic conditions, such as rising unemployment, bank failures, and decreasing trade, produced social effects, such as community dislocation, decreasing living standards, and loss of confidence, which in turn shaped political responses, such as loss of trust in economic institutions, growing support for political extremes, and demands for public solutions.

The Great Depression thus needs to be understood through this integration of national and international perspectives that illustrate the connections between levels of experience and the complex shaping of collective and individual responses. Educators across the world described the same processes outlined by Strayer: delaying construction or repair of buildings, reducing supplies, restricting course offerings, shortening the school day or curtailing the school year, and especially reducing the money spent on employing teachers. Salary cuts, hiring bans, dismissals, and requiring teachers to work without pay all made sense economically, as teachers' salaries made up the largest single item in most school budgets, but these short-term solutions threatened to have long-term consequences in terms of both student learning and teachers' professional development.

And yet it was precisely the optimistic, progressive, and constructive role assigned to schools in the midst of crisis that makes the relationship between the Depression and education historically significant. How could educators, facing the realities of this economic crisis, assign such great expectations to their schools, the ideas and practices of pedagogy, and the future of this young generation? The economic crisis exerted a direct impact on educational institutions, inspiring educators to seek new approaches to improving, expanding, and valuing public schools. As Roosevelt's 1935 statement suggests, one of the most important legacies of the Depression was to change attitudes toward the government's responsibility to address social and educational problems.

A Positive Outcome

Responding to, and indeed pioneering, this shift in attitudes, many progressive educators looked at the Depression as an opportunity to prove that their ideas and institutions not only could survive the immediate conditions of the crisis, but would, in fact, emerge stronger and more influential than in the past. Experiments with progressive schools in even the most conservative political contexts, the attractions of a system of rationally planned education, the appeals for more government investment in schools and children, visions of teachers' professional autonomy, and innovative pedagogies and practices—all of which flourished in the 1930s—demonstrated how the crisis of education provoked critical but also creative thinking about educational opportunities and possibilities.

These ideals were significant not just in the context of the Depression; they also had a contemporary resonance as legacies of this earlier era when crisis conditions provoked a search for alternatives and the pursuit of new opportunities. It is easy from a later vantage point to dismiss these views as naive, politically opportunistic, or simply misguided, yet at the time, these views represented a broad current in both American and world educational perspectives that assigned a constructive role to the ideals and the institutions of schools.

Schools always have some element of the future embedded in them because of the youth of their constituents, but in the Depression, the schools were assigned even greater significance as the public institutions that could preserve, enhance, and project that hope most effectively into the future. It is this combination of economic conditions, educational ideals, government policies, and institutional practices that make the relationship between education and the Great Depression significant not only as a means to enhance historical understanding, but also as illustrations of the possibilities of schools even in times of economic and political crisis.

E. Thomas Ewing

See also Educational Policy and the American Presidency; Politics of Education; Progressive Education

See Visual History Chapter 24, The Farm Security Administration's Photographs of Schools

Further Readings

Hoover, H. (1933, January 5). Remarks to the Conference on the Crisis in Education.

Mort, P. R. (1933). National support for our public schools. *Progressive Education, 10*(8), 442–443.

Reeder, W. G. (1931). A crisis confronts the schools. *Educational Research Bulletin, 10*, 271–272.

Roosevelt, F. D. (1934, March 27). Letter on public school problems.

Roosevelt, F. D. (1935, December 11). Remarks to the State Superintendents of Education.

Strayer, G. D. (1932). Adequate support of education: The condition of an effective service. *School and Society, 35*, 374–375.

H

HAMPTON MODEL

Founded in 1868 by Samuel Chapman Armstrong, Hampton Institute established the model for education among Southern Blacks. Born in Hawai'i to American missionaries, Armstrong grew up in a family immersed in the islands' religious, social, and educational life. His father had served as the islands' Superintendent of Public Instruction, helping to found the islands' Hilo Boarding and Manual Labor School. In Armstrong's opinion, this type of school would also best meet the needs of Southern Blacks by addressing the problems of emancipation, enfranchisement, and the Christian civilizing of dark-skinned people like the Hawaiians of his youth. This entry examines the Hampton model of industrial education, which was born out of Armstrong's early life experiences and reflected his worldview, his social class, and his values.

Armstrong intended that the Hampton Institute's concentration on industrial education, along with its focus on character building, morality, and religion, would serve as the model to help solve the South's "Negro problem." Freed slaves and their children would be transformed into responsible, self-reliant citizens who were to be trained as efficient laborers for the region's new industries. The school's pedagogy was designed to teach Blacks to concentrate on economic development through agriculture and to reject political power as an avenue to prosperity and equality.

Armstrong expected to spread this view throughout the Black community in the churches and schools. So

his chief aim at Hampton was to train conservative teachers who would socialize or civilize the Black population. The teachers' primary role was to adjust their Black students to a subservient role in Southern society. To that end, Armstrong established a normal school, which offered, in addition to its academic curriculum, manual labor training as a method to building character.

Armstrong established a farm and other industries where the students learned a manual skill while earning money for their school expenses—both with the primary aim of character building through manual labor. Twenty years after its founding, the financially unprofitable manual labor training gave way to technical instruction in certain trades. With Armstrong's death in 1893, the emphasis shifted from head, heart, and hand to hand, heart, and head. This revision of the school's curriculum was instigated by Armstrong's successor Howard Frissell, one of his closest associates and the school's chaplain.

Within two years of Armstrong's death, Frissell began awarding trade certificates, opened a trade school, and developed an entrance examination based on taking a trade. Frissell reported in 1904 that students who put shop work first and their academic work second made greater gains in developing their character and initiative. He became one of America's leading experts on the Hampton model of education with the development of the industrial school as a part of the school curriculum.

Even though the Hampton model gave birth to many other industrial schools, including

Booker T. Washington's famous Tuskegee Institute, it was not widely supported among the intellectuals in the Black community around the turn of the twentieth century. But it was the rigid and narrow-minded determination of Frissell, Northern industrialists, and Southern political leaders to expand across the region that led to the struggle over how to educate Black people and their leaders, not as accommodationists to the Southern political powers but as challengers and equals in determining their way of life. The Hampton model did not make its way into the secondary and college levels of schooling. It did, however, gain support across the region as the primary means of educating Blacks at normal schools and industrial training schools, such as Voorhees Industrial School in South Carolina, the Mount Meigs School in Alabama, and the St. Paul School in Virginia.

Louise Anderson Allen

See also African American Education; Values Education

See Visual History Chapter 7, The Education of African Americans

Further Readings

Anderson, J. D. (1988). *The education of Blacks in the South, 1860–1935*. Chapel Hill: University of North Carolina Press.

Watkins, W. H. (2001). *White architects of Black education: Ideology and power in America, 1865–1955*. New York: Teachers College Press.

Wright, S. J. (1949). The development of the Hampton-Tuskegee pattern of higher education. *Phylon, 10*(4), 334–342.

HATE CRIMES IN SCHOOLS

A number of federal and state laws define particular acts as hate or bias crimes and incidents as a means of protecting select victim groups. General definitions agree that such actions are motivated in whole or in part by the perpetrator's hatred or bias toward the victim's perceived group affiliation. Groups that are recognized under federal law for protection include those targeted for violence on account of race, religion, sexual orientation, and ethnicity. Some states include other victim categories targeted because of physical disability, skin color, creed, ancestry, mental disability, and gender. Hatred or bias is not always manifested in physical harm to individuals but also includes threats, harassment, intimidation, and creation of hostile environments. Sometimes hatred or bias toward individuals and communities is displayed indirectly through arson and destruction, damage, or vandalism of property.

School-age youth and young adults perpetrate a significant proportion of the hate and bias crimes committed in the United States. Sociologists argue whether children are externally motivated to act out their biases by a society that struggles with tolerance and xenophobia. Psychologists argue whether children are inherently mischievous and egocentric but can be taught to modify their behavior and resolve intra- and interpersonal conflict. Social scientific theories notwithstanding, many would agree that educators are well poised to dramatically impact youth development and steer youth toward empathy and acceptance of difference and away from prejudiced attitudes that lead to hatred and violence. Schools recognize that success with students and neighborhood youth cannot be accomplished alone. Parents, families, communities, and law enforcement must do their part to encourage young people to respect all human life in spite of physical, mental, and cultural differences.

The American school system is experiencing major demographic shifts in its student population, going from its predominantly English-speaking European American past to a future that will become dominated by immigrant students from African, Asian, and Latin countries, who will learn English for the first time at school. This reconfiguration may bode well for a more tolerant future American society where hate and bias crimes become indistinguishable from other types of crime. However, the current reality reveals a school system that is not getting high marks when it comes to cross-cultural acceptance and intergroup harmony.

The infamous Columbine high school massacre in Colorado in 1999 was at least in part motivated by racial, gender, and possibly sexual orientation hatred. A year earlier, two boys who claimed that University of Wyoming student Matthew Shepard made sexual advances toward them murdered him. Wyoming state law prevented prosecution of crimes committed on the basis of sexual orientation. In the wake of the September 11, 2001 attacks on New York's World Trade Center, Muslims have become increasingly suspect and victims of hate crime because of their religious affiliation with the alleged perpetrators of the attacks.

Schools do more than educate young people; they also socialize youth for positioning in society. Adolescence and early adulthood are experienced from middle school through college; this represents a time when students wrestle with identity, sexuality, knowledge, beliefs, and ability. Competition to succeed can be fierce and schools are often held responsible for creating equitable, supportive, and safe environments. In a situation with high stakes and little room for failure, students can be particularly vulnerable and succumb to the types of behavior that result in hate crimes. Experimentation with drugs and alcohol is often the catalyst for impulsive and premeditated acts of violence against targeted groups.

Schools that anticipate the possibility of hate and bias criminal activity prepare by establishing rules and policies that spell out the consequences for students who unfairly violate protected individuals and groups. They realize that prevention through training, advertisement, and even the curriculum is the best way to deal with such behavior. High school clubs and athletic teams and college fraternities and sororities that haze students are put on notice that such practices can escalate to the point where outside law enforcement may be brought in to prosecute criminal behavior. If after investigation it is determined that the crime committed was motivated by hate, then the consequences are likely to be harsher, such as more jail time or increased fines.

American schools are indeed challenged to educate an increasingly diverse student body. No one is exactly sure about the best strategy to adopt to ensure that individuals and groups that have not traditionally enjoyed widespread social acceptance are provided safe and supportive learning environments. Some educators advocate multicultural education because it incorporates the significance and contribution of various cultural heritages to student learning and recognizes the value of good human relations in student development. Other educators, while acknowledging the import of such strategies as multicultural education, if it is taken seriously, place more emphasis on the importance of the larger society taking responsibility to work harder toward promoting the rights of historically oppressed, hated, and violated groups.

Jonathan Lightfoot

See also Discrimination and Prejudice; Homophobia; Immigrant Education: Contemporary Issues; Violence in Schools

Further Readings

Anti-Defamation League. (1997). *How to combat bias and hate crimes: An ADL blueprint for action.* Available from http://www.adl.org/blueprint.pdf

Herek, G. M., Cogan, J. C., & Gillis, J. R. (2002). Victim experiences in hate crimes based on sexual orientation. *Journal of Social Issues, 58*(2), 319–339.

Web Sites

FBI Uniform Crime Reporting Program, Hate Crime Statistics 2006: http://www.fbi.gov/ucr/hc2006/abouthc.htm

HAWTHORNE EFFECT

The *Hawthorne effect* is a psychological phenomenon named after a series of research experiments performed by Harvard Business School professor Elton Mayo in the 1920s. The term generally refers to the tendency of test subjects to attempt to please researchers and the resultant positive effect of researchers on subjects' performance. In education, it is believed that teachers who are passionate about what they are teaching and who genuinely care about students as individuals can have a positive impact on student learning. Therefore, a teacher who motivates students and gives them attention will positively affect their learning, and more measurable changes in attitude or behavior will result. While the findings of the original experiments have been deemed flawed, the Hawthorne effect has been an influential idea in educational and business settings.

In 1924, efficiency experts at the Hawthorne, Illinois, plant of the Western Electric Company assumed that better lighting would result in higher worker productivity. Mayo manipulated variables related to working conditions. First, he examined physical and environmental factors such the brightness of lights and humidity, then he tested psychological factors such as breaks and working hours. The findings were that employee production increased no matter which factor was manipulated. Even those workers in the control group were more productive. The conclusion was that employees responded positively to the attention they received from the experimenters, not necessarily to the changes in environmental and psychological factors. Mayo also noted that due to the extra attention from researchers and management, the workers changed how they viewed themselves and their role in the company. No longer isolated individuals, they saw themselves as participating members of the greater group, which elicited feelings of affiliation, competence, and achievement.

In education, the practical implication of the Hawthorne effect is that learning takes place most effectively when the teacher has a high level of interaction with students and remains concerned about students as individuals, valuing their contributions. The Hawthorne effect can operate negatively in classrooms if a teacher is told that one group of students is gifted and another group of students is low achieving. The teacher might treat each group differently and ultimately not set high expectations for the low achievers, while pushing the gifted students harder in the classroom. Because of the prominence that teachers have in the teaching and learning act, Hawthorne-like effects need to be examined to help elucidate and contextualize findings from classroom-based studies.

Researchers have long attempted to control for Hawthorne effects. However, an examination of the literature reveals unsatisfactory descriptions of these effects, with ill-defined intervening variables that might not be intervening at all. It has been suggested that subjects be interviewed after a study to determine if Hawthorne effects are present. Since the mid-1970s, the Hawthorne studies and their purported results have become a topic of debate, with statistical methods and data collection procedures coming into question and

alternate explanations being offered to justify the original results.

Lina Lopez Chiappone

See also Observation Research

Further Readings

Adair, J. G. (1984). The Hawthorne effect: A reconsideration of the methodological artifact. *Journal of Applied Psychology, 69,* 334–435.

Head Start

Head Start and Early Head Start and its program branches are comprehensive child development programs that serve children from birth to age five, pregnant women, and their families. As expressed in the Head Start Act, the purpose of the Head Start program is "to promote school readiness by enhancing the social and cognitive development of low-income children through the provision, to low-income children and their families, of health, educational, nutritional, social, and other services that are determined, based on family needs assessments, to be necessary." The comprehensive nature of the program strives to ensure educational benefits, economic benefits, health benefits, and law enforcement benefits. This entry records the program's history and current implementation.

Program History

Head Start began during the mid-1960s as part of President Lyndon Johnson's "War on Poverty." The Economic Opportunity Act of 1964 authorized programs to help communities meet the needs of preschool-age children in disadvantaged circumstances. At the request of the federal government, a panel of child development experts created a report that became the framework of an eight-week summer program. This program, launched by the Office of Economic Opportunity, was named Project Head Start.

Head Start was and still is a comprehensive effort to help end poverty by providing services to children age three to school-entry age who are from low-income families. These services were intended to meet the emotional, health, nutritional, social, and psychological needs of its participants. In 1969, the Nixon Administration transferred Head Start from the Office of Economic Opportunity to the Office of Child Development in the Department of Health, Education, and Welfare (later the Department of Health and Human Services). The 1994 reauthorization of the Head Start Act established the Early Head Start program for low-income families with infants and toddlers. In total, the Head Start program has enrolled more than 23 million children since it began in 1965.

Today's Efforts

Today Head Start is a well-established program administered by the Head Start Bureau, the Administration on Children, Youth and Families, the Administration for Children and Families, and the Department of Health and Human Services. Programs are locally administered by community-based nonprofit organizations and local education agencies. Head Start grants are awarded by Department of Health and Human Services regional offices, with the exception of American Indian and Migrant Head Start programs, which are administered in Washington, D.C. Today Head Start is the most successful, longest running, national school-readiness program in the United States; it serves children and their families in rural and urban areas in all fifty states, the District of Columbia, Puerto Rico, and the U.S. Territories. This includes American Indians and children in migrant families.

For fiscal year 2005, the $6.8+ billion budget provided services to 906,993 children, 57 percent of whom were four years old or older and 43 percent of whom were three years old or younger, at an average cost of $7,287 per child. More than 12 percent of the Head Start enrollment consisted of children with disabilities. Services for all children were provided by 1,604 different programs scattered across every state. Although paid staff numbers nearly 212,000 people, volunteers account for six times as many individuals working with children in these programs. Children are

eligible to participate in Head Start if they are from low-income families or if their families are eligible for public assistance. The Head Start Act establishes income eligibility for participation in Head Start programs based on the poverty guidelines updated annually in the Federal Register by the U.S. Department of Health and Human Services.

Several subdivisions have been established over the years. Early Head Start serves infants and toddlers birth to age three and promotes healthy prenatal outcomes, promotes healthy family functioning, and enhances the development of infants and toddlers. Head Start itself is designed to foster healthy development in low-income children. Program grantees and delegate agencies deliver a range of services that are responsive and appropriate to each child's and each family's heritage and experience. These services encompass all aspects of a child's development and learning. The Migrant and Seasonal Program provides consistent and high quality services to support healthy child development across the nation. These programs cater to the specific needs of children and families who move across the country with their families to pursue seasonal work in agriculture. The American Indian-Alaska Native Program provides children and families with comprehensive health, educational, nutritional, socialization, and other developmental services that promote school readiness. These services are tailored for preschool children (ages three to five) and infants and toddlers (birth through age three) who are American Indian or Alaska Native and are from impoverished circumstances.

In addition, the program provides services to meet particular needs. Full inclusion of children with disabilities is a required element of the Head Start program. Head Start legislation mandates that at least 10 percent of enrollment is available for children with disabilities. Current prevalence supersedes this requirement. All programs provide the full range of services to children with disabilities and their families.

A primary goal of Head Start is to ensure that all children begin school ready to learn. Educational standards are fully described in national performance standards. Activities are directed toward skill and knowledge domains and domain elements. Indicators of each child's progress are incorporated in the program's annual self-assessment. Head Start also recognizes the vital contributions made by parents and community members to education and development in their children and communities. Both groups are involved in the operation, governance, and evaluation of the program. Recognizing that health is a significant factor in each child's ability to thrive and develop, Head Start provides health screenings and regular health checkups. The program teaches and incorporates good practices in oral health, hygiene, nutrition, personal care, and safety.

Michelle Larocque

See also Early Childhood Education; Economic Inequality

Further Readings

Vinovkis, M. A. (2005). *The birth of Head Start: Preschool education policies in the Kennedy and Johnson administrations*. Chicago: University of Chicago Press.

Web Sites

Head Start Information and Publication Center: http://www.headstartinfo.org
National Head Start Association: http://www.nhsa.org

HEGEMONY

Hegemony refers to one group systematically overpowering and dominating another group, and it can occur economically, ideologically, culturally, and socially by privileging certain values, information, and social norms to the exclusion of others. Theories of hegemony seek to analyze the ability of dominant groups to maintain social and economic privilege through their influence over societal constructs such as the media, advertising, books, and film. Other theories see hegemony as a consequence of current educational practices. These regard the values, knowledge, and social norms stressed in schools as working to advance the desires of the dominant group. The subjugated are left no choice but to accept and assume the dominant ideology. In this way, the dominant group maintains their advantaged status through ideology rather than aggression. This subtle and covert control ensures that domination is sustained through inherent inequity. This entry will discuss the historical foundations of hegemony as well as its current use as a theoretical tool for analyzing sustained social, economic, and educational disparity.

Up to the early 1900s, education was heavily influenced by logical positivism, which held that certain norms were valid simply because they were supported and accepted through authority and reason. In response, Theodor Adorno (1903–1969), Jürgen Habermas (1929–), Max Horkheimer (1895–1973), Herbert Marcuse (1898–1979), and others were drawn to establish the Frankfurt School. Using aspects of Marxism to examine the entrenched social stratification and positivistic approaches to education, Frankfurt School theorists recognized the education system as constructed in such a way as to safeguard the economic and social interests of the elite. The Frankfurt School successfully established a connection between hegemony and educational practice; however, they failed to consider the possibility of individuals actively resisting social and economic subjugation.

Influenced by the Frankfurt School, critical theorists have analyzed the role of hegemony in modern societies to better understand how hegemony and inequality are sustained. Antonio Gramsci viewed capitalism as largely perpetuating hegemony. Embracing communism, Gramsci supported revolution as a means to liberate the subjugated. Henry Giroux utilized a neo-Marxist approach to critically examine the role of hegemony and agreed with the Frankfurt School's social theorists acknowledging the role of education in reproducing class stratification. However, Giroux questioned the inflexibility of social stratification and alleged that students and teachers could actively resist hegemony.

Michael Apple examined the underpinnings of hegemony in modern society and viewed the curricular and organizational choices educators and administrators employ in schools as highly subjective. Apple viewed education as political with schools reproducing societal class stratifications through the set of courses offered to particular students. For Apple, education does not encourage social mobility; rather, it safeguards the existing economic and social hierarchies. Apple critically examined hegemony to enlighten educators as to their uninformed participation in the social reproduction of dominant society's ideology.

Contemporary views of hegemony have moved away from traditional Marxism and incorporate a multifaceted approach. Peter McLaren extends the concept of hegemony to include gender, race, ethnicity, sexual orientation, and class. Using hegemony to understand subjugation, scholars are broadening hegemony's scope by applying emerging critical theories such as critical race theory and critical feminist theory to better understand inequality and oppression.

Melanie C. Brooks

See also Critical Theory; Cultural Capital

Further Readings

Apple, M. (2004). *Ideology and curriculum: 25th anniversary edition.* New York: Routledge.

Aronowitz, S., & Giroux, H. A. (1991). *Postmodern education: Politics, culture, and social criticism.* Minneapolis: University of Minnesota Press.

Bourdieu, P., & Passeron, J. (1977). *Reproduction in education, society and culture.* London: Sage.

Giroux, H. A. (1983). *Theory and resistance in education: A pedagogy for the opposition.* Hadley, MA: Bergin & Garvey.

Giroux, H. A. (1991). *Border crossings: Cultural workers and the politics of education.* New York: Routledge.

Gramsci, A. (1988). *An Antonio Gramsci reader: Selected writings, 1916–1935* (D. Forgacs, Ed.). London: Lawrence & Wishart.

McLaren, P. (1989). *Life in schools: An introduction to critical pedagogy in the foundations of education.* New York: Longman.

HIDDEN AND NULL CURRICULUM

The hidden curriculum is an important concept for those interested in the schools as socializing agents and as agents of cultural reproduction. Closely related to the idea of the hidden curriculum is the concept of the null curriculum, which focuses on what schools *don't* teach.

The hidden and null curricula, as they manifest themselves in various ways in the schools, represent subtle and deeply influential forces in the shaping of attitudes and beliefs. Because they are not immediately evident, as is the case with the formal curriculum, does not mean that they can be disregarded. Both hidden and null curricula are described in this entry.

Unofficial Expectations

The concept of the hidden curriculum was first developed by Phillip Jackson in his 1968 book *Life in Classrooms.* According to Jackson, there are three factors embedded in schools: (1) crowds, (2) praise, and (3) power. The hidden curriculum as defined by Jackson must be mastered by students if they are to successfully make their way through the school system. In the context of Jackson's work, the "unofficial or implicit expectations" are what constitute the hidden curriculum.

Examples of the hidden curriculum as identified by Jackson might include the automatic assumption in schools that males will typically take on leadership positions, the importance of certain sports (football, for example) for character development, and the idea that certain specific social manners and values are normative.

Peter McLaren (1998) expanded on the work of Jackson by identifying the hidden curriculum as "the unintended outcomes of the schooling process." These unintended outcomes are often unrecognized by those who teach in and administer schools. David Sadker and Myra Sadker provide examples of what McLaren is talking about in their analysis about how boys are unconsciously given greater attention than girls in elementary educational settings. As a result, boys and girls are taught that males deserve more attention than females. In addition to being potentially privileged because of the greater attention they receive, boys also end up receiving more instruction.

Another interpretation of the hidden curriculum comes from Stanley Aronowitz and Henry Giroux. Essentially, they argue that there are implicit messages found in the social structures of the schools. Thus, in the period prior to desegregation and to a certain extent in the decades that followed, the unequal funding of White over Black schools in the same communities represented a hidden curriculum—one that suggests that the needs of African American students are not as great as those of their White counterparts.

A final interpretation of the hidden curriculum comes from the work of Bensen Snyder who maintains that while teachers may dictate formal tasks, these may be reinterpreted by students to suit their own needs. As a result, formal curricular needs and objectives may be redefined by students to create an alternative curriculum. Thus a group of high school students might become very active in a drama or music program not so much because they are interested in performing, but because they are interested in being part of a social group associated with the program or activity, or they like to have access to the interesting things found in the theater department.

Missing Information

The null curriculum was first defined by Elliot Eisner in *The Educated Imagination*. According to Eisner, the null curriculum is what we teach by not teaching something. This happens, according to him, at two levels. The first involves the cognitive processes that are stressed or disregarded. An example of this would be when science teaching involves mostly learning specific facts and formulas. This would be in contrast to an approach that emphasized hands-on learning and discovery. The first approach de-emphasizes creativity and independence while the second emphasizes them. Thus, a curriculum that emphasizes rote facts and memorization implicitly teaches or suggests that creativity and independence are not as important or valued by society.

A second dimension of the null curriculum identified by Eisner is the idea that something is taught by not actually including it in the curriculum. This, the exclusion of African Americans or women in American history textbooks prior to the 1960s, is an example of a null curriculum. Likewise, the more recent exclusion of important gay and lesbian leaders or issues in history and literature textbooks represents a similar example of the null curriculum at work.

A similar example to the cases cited above would be the historical preference given to funding men's sports in high schools over women's sports. In such social situations, the social message (i.e., curriculum) being communicated through the null curriculum is clear—men and their activities count more than women and what they do.

Essentially, the null curriculum teaches what is valued and what is not valued by society. As a result, traditional values and power structures are reinforced, and minority opinions and values are often marginalized and given little value or credence.

Eugene F. Provenzo, Jr.

See also Curriculum Theory; Ideology and Schooling

Further Readings

Ahwee, S., et al. (2004). The hidden and null curriculums: An experiment in collective educational biography. *Educational Studies, 35*(1), 25–43.

Aronowitz, S., & Giroux, H. A, (1985). *Education under siege: The conservative, liberal, and radical debate over schooling.* Westport, CT: Bergin & Garvey.

Eisner, E. W. (1985). *The educational imagination: On the design and evaluation of school programs* (2nd ed.). New York: Macmillan.

Jackson, P. W. (1968). *Life in classrooms.* New York: Holt, Reinhart & Winston.

McLaren, P. (1998). *Life in schools: An introduction to critical pedagogy in the foundations of education* (3rd ed.). New York: Longman.

Portelli, J. P. (1993). Exposing the hidden curriculum. *Journal of Curriculum Studies, 25,* 343–358.

Snyder, B. R. (1971). *The hidden curriculum.* New York: Alfred A. Knopf.

HIGHER EDUCATION, HISTORY OF

The history of higher education is one of expanded choice and opportunities for students as well as innovative delivery systems such as the correspondence school, distance learning, and Internet information retrieval. Diversity through the years has expanded as federal court decisions have found it to be a compelling state interest. From higher education enrollment limited to the few to egalitarianism, higher education has become a major influence in U.S. society. With nearly 18 million students and over 631,000 faculty members, higher education continues to reflect the ever-changing needs of society.

Historical Background

Higher education emerged from the works of scribes and theological schools. Ancient scholars, peripatetic teachers, imparted knowledge through lectures. Groups of individuals would follow teachers, often inspired by their worldviews. Priests, scribes, apprentices were teachers and repositories of knowledge. Written works were developed and continually added to with observation and reflection.

Teachers were protected by ruling classes who found cadres of literate people indispensable. Socrates, Plato, and Aristotle taught and recorded philosophical views of the world. Egypt, Greece, and Italy were seats of early teaching and learning. Oratory, dialectic, and rhetoric were much prized in education. These early educational contributions have been passed down to our time. Aristotle's Lyceum and Plato's Academy were early models of higher education.

From the fourth century BCE to the eleventh century CE, tribal conflicts limited educational efforts. In the eleventh and twelfth centuries, education of the clergy in their own schools was encouraged. The Cathedral School of Notre Dame became the University of Paris. With protection from kings and the pope, the University of Paris became an autonomous institution. Guilds or groups of scholars or masters and students provided the corporate structure for an autonomous institution. Such autonomy continues with faculty in charge of curriculum and admissions.

Bologna became a center for the study of law, with student guilds or collegia forming the organizational structure of the university. Renaissance humanism was often not well received by established universities. The Reformation had mixed outcomes and consequences, including rabid sectarianism and a high degree of institutional stagnation. However, both occurred in a period of cultural and intellectual ferment that led to an expansion of higher education.

Origins of Universities

Continental universities provided the model for the universities of Oxford and Cambridge in England. The rites and rituals of Oxford and Cambridge were incorporated in America's universities and colleges. Harvard College, although more of a secondary school than a college, provided education for theologians, teachers, and government leaders.

Harvard was founded in 1636, William and Mary in 1693, Yale in 1701, College of New Jersey (Princeton) in 1746, King's College (Columbia University) in 1754, College of Rhode Island (Brown) in 1765, Queens College (Rutgers) in 1766, and Dartmouth in 1769—all as private religious institutions. The curriculum based on continental universities was the trivium (grammar, rhetoric, and dialectic) and quadrivium (arithmetic, music, geometry, and astronomy).

The Supreme Court in the Dartmouth College case of 1819 ruled that the college's charter was a valid contract. Dartmouth was a private institution not subject to public control. Control, financing, and management of private institutions of higher education became the domain of boards of trustees. The ruling led to an expansion of private higher education and to protecting private institutions from legislative interference.

Early Women's Colleges

Women's colleges were founded in the nineteenth century. Mt. Holyoke Female Seminary was founded in 1837 and Georgia Female College, later Wesleyan College, opened in 1839. They were private schools that provided women access to traditional academic disciplines. Vassar provided a transitional curriculum with a focus on women's conversational skills, feminine arts, and a classical course of study.

Ohio's Oberlin College, founded in 1833, was one of the first coeducational colleges that offered a traditional baccalaureate degree. There was fear that women could become unsexed, lose their charm and gentleness, become unmarriageable, and be subject to nervous breakdowns with too much learning or too strenuous studies. The American Women's Education Association founded in 1852 stimulated the development and expansion of higher education for women.

The curriculum was based on the liberal arts and the classical tradition.

Harvard faculty began to offer courses for women in 1879. Near the turn of the twentieth century, Harvard Annex became Radcliffe College for women. Early women's colleges often offered courses for teaching, an early career choice for women. To meet the growing demand for teachers, Normal Schools were created often becoming state teachers' colleges. As the demand for professional schools grew, state teachers' colleges became state universities offering an expanded curriculum.

Political activism of the suffragists led to the Nineteenth Amendment to the U.S. Constitution providing women voting rights in 1920. Bryn Mawr organized a summer school for working women in 1921. Women's participation in higher education continued to grow.

An Expansion

The Northwest Ordinance of 1787 authorized two full townships in each new state to be reserved for a university. The Northwest Ordinance of 1785, which set aside land for the support of schools within a township, and the 1787 act became precedents for land grants to the states for public schools and universities. The demand for expanded education curricula led to the Morrill Act in 1862, which provided for Land Grant Colleges for agriculture, the trades, and education.

The Fourteenth Amendment to the Constitution in 1868 gave Blacks American citizenship. Black colleges developed in the South through the efforts of Booker T. Washington, who received an honorary doctorate from Harvard. The Tuskegee Normal and Industrial School was a model for Black education. The Morrill Act of 1890 required the states to make public education available to African Americans. Seventeen Southern states had separate land-grant colleges for African Americans. Eventually every state had a land-grant college.

In 1828 Yale professors found that what is ultimately worth knowing in college were the liberalizing, liberating liberal arts. In 1945, the Harvard faculty in General Education for a Free Society provided a framework for meeting the common needs of an undergraduate education.

John Hopkins University opened in 1876, providing an impetus for the development of graduate programs based on a German research model. Daniel Coit Gilman, a Yale graduate, was the first president of Johns Hopkins. At Johns Hopkins, faculty and students were required to do research and to seek new knowledge through scientific investigation. This provided a model for research universities.

There were periodic efforts to develop common standards for college admission, and in 1892, the National Education Association appointed a Committee of Ten including Harvard President Charles Eliot to make recommendations about common high school curricula. The result was the Carnegie Unit, which provided for standard units of credit for high school subjects and college admissions.

In 1869, Harvard president Charles Eliot broke with tradition and led the development of electives in higher education. The elective system provided opportunities for professors to pursue their professional interests and for students to be able to choose their courses for career interests. Academic departments were formed around these interests and universities offered an expanded curriculum based on student and professor interests.

Postwar Change

With the GI Bill of 1944 (the Servicemen's Readjustment Act), thousands of returning veterans enrolled in higher education. The GI Bill proved a success. Fears of flooding universities with unqualified, unprepared students disappeared as returning veterans proved to be good students and contributors to their communities. Legislation for war veterans has been extended through the years.

President Harry Truman formed the Commission on Education in 1947. The commission recommended expanding higher education through the junior or community college level. Currently many community colleges are moving to four-year degree institutions or becoming satellites of university systems.

American higher education reflects the Zeitgeist or spirit of the times in which it exists. Jeffersonian democracy focused on meritocracy, while Jacksonian democracy stressed egalitarianism. As the nation grew, colleges reflected a spirit of progressivism. State universities during the 1900s were expected to perform a service function. Dealing with state problems and issues became an important goal of university missions. The University of Wisconsin developed the idea of using the institution's formidable resources to deal with public problems, needs, and issues. Higher education theorists continue to debate the role of professional schools versus liberal arts colleges.

Current Directions

Technology

With technological advances, students and faculty are accessing library and resource information through the Internet. Computer access to information continues to expand as more knowledge bases are on the World Wide Web. With the Internet era, traditional universities and colleges compete with new online distance-learning programs offered by nontraditional universities like University of Phoenix. Students are able to complete courses and degrees anywhere through online networks.

In response, colleges and universities have expanded their distance-learning undergraduate and graduate degree programs. With more information accessed through the Internet, higher education institutions place greater emphasis on ready access to computers in libraries, and the traditional card catalogue has been replaced. The Library of Congress and a growing library of the classics and academic knowledge provide speed as well as accuracy in accessing information. With increasing focus on collaborative research, faculty can network with each other through the Internet. Flash cards or jump drives make it easy to carry information anywhere.

Equity and Access

Economic and social justice advocates seek greater opportunities for minorities and people of color. *Brown v. Board of Education of Topeka, Kansas* (1954) led to the integration of higher education institutions. Equity in and access to higher education institutions continue to be expanded through political activism. With an expanded multicultural population, special efforts are made to provide remedial training in basic subjects including English for English language learners, low-income students, and students at risk.

In *Bakke v. Regents of the University of California* (1976), the Supreme Court ruled that the state has an interest in diversity that may be served by consideration of race and ethnicity in admissions. Several decades later, in two 2003 Michigan cases, *Gratz v. Bolinger* and *Grutter v. Bolinger,* the high court again upheld the importance of diversity as a compelling state interest in higher education. Recruiting minorities, women, and people of color as students and faculty is a major goal of national accrediting agencies. Universities have minority recruiting offices to increase minority student enrollment.

Student retention in higher education is a major concern, and efforts are made to provide support services to retain students, particularly in the freshman years. William Bowen, president of Princeton, and Derek Bok, president of Harvard, conducted a research study to determine the long-term consequences of considering race in college admissions. Their conclusion was that with mentoring and support, minority students could perform well in higher education and make major contributions in their chosen careers and in their communities. Diversity was found to enrich the college environment for both learners and teachers.

Funding

A continuing concern in higher education is adequate funding for institutions. University presidents and boards of trustees face the problem of economic cycles that affect their enrollment as well as their ability to recruit highly skilled faculty, update facilities, and expand Internet access throughout the campuses. Private universities' tuition costs require special efforts to recruit, retain, and provide scholarships to maintain diverse student bodies. Since the early days at Harvard, special efforts have been made to recruit low-income, at-risk students. That effort continues.

State university and college systems continue to compete in state legislatures for adequate funding for faculty and staff salaries and for recruiting low-income, at-risk students. Tuition increases can meet only a part of the higher education budget. State legislative and private funding is essential for quality education.

Academic freedom is vital in a free society, and university officials and boards of trustees work to assure academic freedom when confronted with internal or external ideological conflicts.

Productivity

In research universities, faculty members are expected to keep up their academic productivity through peer-reviewed publication, grant acquisition, and recognition in their professional fields. To assure such productivity, senior faculty are often subject to five-year peer review. If they fall short, efforts are made to provide support, encouragement, and mentoring to increase productivity. University investment in the professorate continues to expand as inflation requires more fundraising. Retaining top quality professors is essential in attracting the best students, and in universities' promotion efforts.

Lifelong Learning

Most universities have programs for lifelong learning. These can be through correspondence, weekend sessions, distance-learning programs or lectures and seminars. With increased longevity, senior citizens are provided with a variety of programs, courses, and lectures for interest areas. Adult education programs have expanded through the years.

Federal Involvement

In recent years, federal legislation has provided increased civil rights protection for women, minorities, and disabled students. The National Defense Education Act of 1958 provided funds for science, math, and modern foreign language education, as well as other subjects. The Civil Rights Act of 1964, Title VII, prohibits discrimination based on race, color, sex, or national origin. The Higher Education Act of 1965 and 1998 amendments provided for grants and contracts to identify qualified individuals from disadvantaged backgrounds to prepare them and provide support for their higher-education programs. In addition, the act provides for motivating and preparing students for doctoral programs.

First-generation American college students are given financial support and mentoring support. Talent Search is an effort to identify qualified students for postsecondary education. Upward Bound programs provide a variety of assistance for low-income, underrepresented, disadvantaged students in higher education. A variety of federal support programs have been developed for special needs students in higher education. Title IX of the Educational Amendments of 1972 bans sex discrimination in educational institutions that receive federal aid. Universities provide athletic opportunities and assure equal employment opportunities for women.

Then and Now

From the early religious and private colonial colleges to the elite colleges, higher education established its ability to adjust to historical influences and currents. The scholasticism of continental universities evolved into the traditional classical curriculum based on the trivium and quadrivium. Students and faculty gained more choice for their interest areas with expansion of the elective system. The Renaissance and Reformation eventually led to secularism in higher education.

State colleges and universities have offered service curricula to meet the needs of government, corporations, and individuals, for assistance with policy making, business development, and those with special needs. Prestige and public relations have been important student recruiters. State flagship universities have worked to achieve research status through faculty recruiting, fundraising, and scholarships to attract top-performing students. In general, the challenge for higher education in the future will be to address issues involving greater equity and opportunity, as well as the challenges posed by an increasingly technologically oriented and global culture.

James J. Van Patten

See also Academic Freedom; Affirmative Action; Corporate Involvement in Education; Educational Policy and the American Presidency

See Visual History Chapter 7, The Education of African Americans

Further Readings

Bowen, W. G., & Bok, D. (2000). *The shape of the river: Long term consequences of considering race in college and university admissions.* Princeton, NJ: Princeton University Press.

Eby, F. (1940). *The history and philosophy of education ancient and medieval.* New York: Prentice Hall.

Hofstadter, R., & Smith, W. (1961). *American higher education.* Chicago: University of Chicago Press.

Lucas, C. (1994). *American higher education.* New York: St. Martin's.

Rudolph, F. (1965). *The American university.* New York: Vintage Books.

Veblen, T. (1954). *The higher learning in America.* Stanford, CA: Academic Reprints.

HIGHLANDER FOLK SCHOOL

Myles Horton (1905–1990) and Don West (1906–1992) founded the Highlander Folk School in Grundy County, Tennessee, at the height of the Great Depression in 1932. Now operating as the Highlander Research and Education Center, its goals continue the traditions of its founders: providing education and fighting against economic injustice, poverty, and prejudice. Through educational programs and related services, Highlander tries to provide grassroots leaders with the tools to create broad-based movements for social change. This entry looks at its history and contributions.

The early years of Highlander focused on the progressive labor movement. During these years, the school created its first education programs for workers. The aim of Highlander's education programs was to empower workers and solidify the labor movement. As a means to achieve this goal, Highlander sought to train all poor laborers regardless of their race or ethnicity. Highlander became one of the first educational organizations in the South to integrate. By the late 1930s, it was regularly holding integrated meetings and educational workshops, although the first fully integrated workshop was not held until 1942.

Highlander's commitment to desegregation began its second phase of social activity: the civil rights movement. The political landscape during the early 1940s was not ready for and fought against Highlander's agenda of economic, political, and social equity. Prior to the civil rights movement, Highlander held integrated leadership workshops and educational programs that were attended by figures such as Rosa Parks and Martin Luther King, Jr., who were then largely unknown outside of their communities. In an attempt to thwart Highlander's growing contribution to the fight for equity, its opponents started using propaganda to tarnish its image, associating it with Communism.

Despite a smear campaign, however, Highlander's resolve did not waiver. The epitome of this resolve was Highlander's work with Esau Jenkins and the formation of "citizenship schools." Citizenship schools began in the Sea Islands in South Carolina and led to the campaign to register African Americans to vote. The success of the citizenship schools was a catalyst for the civil rights movement, and Highlander was once again in the middle of mobilizing people for social and economic justice.

The opposition to Highlander from segregationists continued, however, and the state of Tennessee succeeded in shutting down the school. However, the leaders of the school had obtained a new charter for the Highlander Research and Education Center, and Highlander relocated to Knoxville, Tennessee. It remained there until 1971, when it moved to its current location in New Market, Tennessee, twenty miles east of Knoxville.

As the civil rights movement began to define its own leadership, Highlander turned its attention back to its original interest, helping the people of Appalachia. During the 1970s and 1980s, Highlander focused its efforts on environmental and quality of life issues confronted by the region. While maintaining its fight for environmental, social, and economic justice, Highlander in the 1990s increasingly turned its attention to the needs of immigrants—mostly laborers from Mexico and Central America—in the South by helping them politically organize and by providing an organization through which they could connect with different people and address their problems and needs.

The Highlander Research and Education Center has contributed to the social foundations of education on two primary levels: philosophically and practically. At the philosophical level, Highlander has demonstrated how education can be a catalyst for social change through collective civic action regardless of race, creed, or social class. At the core of this belief is the notion that people have the answers to the problems that they face. Through communication and the exchange of ideas, people are able to find solutions to the problems with which they are confronted. Highlander has also been an example of and exercise in democratic and socially responsible education that empowers the people. Highlander's efforts in the field of social justice provide an exemplar of the possibilities of critical thought, action, and execution.

Benjamin Thomas Lester

See also Adult Education and Literacy; Social Justice, Education for

Further Readings

Adams, F., & Horton, M. (1975). *Unearthing seeds of fire: The idea of Highlander.* Winston-Salem, NC: J. F. Blair.

Horton, M., & Freire, P. (1990). *We make the road by walking: Conversations on education and social change.* Philadelphia: Temple University Press.

Horton, M., Kohl, J., & Kohl, H. (1990). *The long haul: An autobiography.* New York: Doubleday.

Jacobs, D. (Ed.). (2003). The *Myles Horton reader: Education for social cha*nge. Knoxville: University of Tennessee Press.

Web Sites

Highlander Research and Education Center: http://www.highlandercenter.org

HIGH-STAKES TESTING

High-stakes tests are examinations used to make critical decisions about examinees and those who work with the examinees. The hallmark of a high-stakes test is that the results are associated with consequences for those connected to the assessment, such as graduates of professional programs, students in public schools, and teachers and administrators in public schools. High-stakes tests contribute to making decisions about examinees and institutions in many societies, including the United States, Germany, Japan, and Singapore. The consequences of such tests include benefits and detriments. Professional organizations offer guidance in the implementation of high-stakes testing programs that, if followed, should result in fewer of the negative consequences currently associated with high-stakes tests. This entry describes high-stakes tests, their consequences, and strategies for ensuring their fairness and contribution to quality education.

How Tests Work

Examples of high-stakes tests include examinations for high school graduation, college credit (e.g., Advanced Placement or International Baccalaureate), college admissions (e.g., SAT; ACT; Graduate Record Examination, or GRE; and licensure such as the U. S. Medical Licensing Examination). In public schools, high-stakes tests have been used by policy makers to hold students and educators accountable for student outcomes. At the postsecondary level, admissions offices use test results to predict which applicants will most likely be successful at their institution. In addition, examinations have been used to award college credit for coursework completed in high school. In the case of licensure examinations, the purpose of the tests is to assure the public of the qualifications of aspiring professionals.

The interpretation of high-stakes test scores might be norm or criterion referenced. Norm-referenced interpretations are based on the comparison of an examinee's score with scores of other examinees. The ACT, SAT, and GRE are all examples of high-stakes tests that provide norm-referenced interpretations. For example, an examinee's score of eighty-eighth percentile on the GRE indicates that her raw score (i.e., number of test items correct) was higher than the scores of 88 percent of the other examinees. In contrast, criterion-referenced tests in state testing programs use a student's item-correct score to classify his performance as basic, proficient, or advanced. Such criterion-referenced interpretations do not provide information about the student's performance as compared to other examinees.

In terms of response format, some high-stakes tests use only a multiple-choice format, whereas others use multiple-choice and constructed-response items. For example, some states administer end-of-course examinations that contribute to a student's final course grade. In some instances these examinations use only the multiple-choice format. The GRE, however, incorporates both multiple-choice items and an analytic writing component.

The Stakes

The federal No Child Left Behind legislation (NCLB, Public Law 107-110) provides an example of public policy that requires high-stakes testing. NCLB requires states to test all students in Grades 3–8 annually in (a) reading or language arts and (b) mathematics. In addition, testing is required in science at one grade level in the grade spans of 3–5, 6–9, 10–12. Also, NCLB requires states to test high school students in one grade level annually. The state tests must describe two levels of high achievement (proficient and advanced) to gauge student mastery of the state content standards and a level of basic achievement to gauge the progress of lower achieving students toward attaining higher achievement levels.

Test results are disaggregated and reported by ethnicity, poverty level, disability, and English language learners (ELLs). The target is for all students to be at the proficient or higher level in reading or language arts and mathematics by the 2013–2014 school year. Schools that do not meet adequate yearly progress (AYP) targets are required to develop school improvement plans and the school district must provide students and parents with public school choice. Schools that do not meet AYP for several years potentially face such sanctions as restructuring, dismissal of staff, and external oversight.

The types of stakes associated with a high-stakes testing program vary across constituencies. To continue the school example, in some states, schools with high test scores receive financial awards or public recognition. The stakes are raised in terms of public awareness when states publish school report cards that contain test scores and ratings (A to F, Excellent to Unsatisfactory) based on the school's test scores. Stakes for schools, and for neighborhoods, increase when realtors provide families with a school's test scores to sell a house.

The stakes for educators include the award of bonuses or pay increases for teachers if test scores are high. In low-performing schools, possible sanctions for teachers include denial of tenure, dismissal, reassignment, and withholding of salary increases. Administrators in low-performing schools may be dismissed or receive a salary reduction, whereas in high-performing schools, an administrator may receive a bonus.

In the case of students, high-stakes tests have been used to determine grade-level promotion. Tests are used to track students in classes based on their achievement levels. Tests inform decisions about the qualification of students for special education services (e.g., gifted, learning disability). Scores on high-stakes tests determine whether students meet high-school graduation requirements and whether students receive diplomas of distinction. At the end of secondary school, students complete examinations that are used to make college admission decisions and some students receive scholarships based on the test scores. In concluding their postsecondary education, aspiring professionals, such as students in medicine, law, and teaching, must pass a licensure examination.

Consequences

High-stakes tests are associated with both beneficial and detrimental consequences. For example, the establishment and publication of content standards associated with state-level tests allow teachers and students to understand the important content that students must know and be able to do. Information from the tests can be used to identify problem areas in instruction and to plan changes. However, high-stakes tests typically cannot be used for diagnostic purposes because too few test items assess a specific content area for reliable reporting, and the scores typically are reported in the summer.

Another benefit is associated with the NCLB Act and its requirement that schools report students' test results by socioeconomic level, disabilities, ELLs, and race/ethnicity. Such disaggregated reporting of students' test results allows educators to examine whether *all* students are learning key content knowledge. Disaggregation allows monitoring of achievement gaps between examinees in, for example, high and low socioeconomic groups, and reduction of any achievement gap.

Harmful consequences associated with high-stakes testing include educators' narrowing of the curriculum. One instance of narrowing the curriculum occurs when teachers focus instruction on those subject areas tested, such as reading and mathematics, and attend less to subjects not tested, such as history or art. Another form of narrowing of the curriculum is illustrated by the minimum competency tests of the 1980s. To prepare students for these tests of basic skills, teachers narrowed instruction in terms of depth in order to focus on basics. Thus, at the expense of student mastery of more complex skills, teachers narrowed their instruction to address minimal competencies. Also, narrowing occurs when learning activities are aligned with the test format. For example, teachers use commercial test-preparation materials in their instruction, replacing problem-based learning activities.

A consequence of the narrowing of the curriculum is that test scores may no longer accurately represent student learning. Scores on a test are indicators of student performance in the broader content domain from which the test items were sampled. The usefulness of test information depends on the degree to which the scores on a specific test represent what students can do in the broader content domain of interest. Scores on a high-stakes test become inflated as when teaching is based on the content of a specific test because the scores no longer reflect students' understanding of the broader content domain.

Although high-stakes tests provide information for improving instruction, in some instances, educators narrowly target student groups for intervention. Such a consequence can be seen when a school decides to focus efforts on students with borderline scores on a high-stakes test and dedicates less resources to high- or low-performing student groups.

High-stakes testing policies have focused attention on student groups that may have been ignored in the past; however, the negative consequences of high-stakes testing may disproportionately affect these same groups. African American and Hispanic students have high failure rates on graduation examinations. In addition, states that have scholarship programs to support students in their undergraduate studies have test-score requirements that impede minority students from qualifying for the scholarship.

Conditions for High-Stakes Testing

The increasing use of high-stakes tests as instruments of policy has led to publication of position statements by the American Educational Research Association and the American Evaluation Association, both national organizations of professionals who conduct research and evaluation in education. The position statements indicate that high-stakes testing programs in education should meet certain conditions. Included in the conditions are the following:

- Decisions about students should be based on multiple, high-quality measures, not a single test. Critical decisions about grade-level promotion or high school graduation require that students have multiple opportunities to demonstrate their proficiency. In addition, if evidence indicates that the score from a test does not reflect a student's actual proficiency, then alternate methods for assessing the student's proficiency level are required.
- Validity studies should examine the accuracy of test-score interpretations when using labels of "basic," "proficient," or "advanced" to indicate students' proficiency or "passing" to describe examinees' performance.
- Students must be provided the opportunity to learn the content and cognitive skills that are tested prior to implementation of high-stakes policies. This requires evidence that the content has been integrated into both the curriculum and instruction prior to its use in a high-stakes context.
- Rules designating which students are to be tested and which may be exempted from testing must be established and enforced if test results for schools or districts are to be compared or results compared over time.
- Appropriate test accommodations should be made for ELL students and students with disabilities. Appropriate accommodations will assure the scores of ELL students and disabled students represent the intended construct, such as social studies or

mathematics achievement, and not characteristics external to the construct, such as text reading level.

- Students who fail a high-stakes test should be provided remediation in the knowledge and skills of the broad content domain that the test represents.

- Each use of a high-stakes test must be validated. For example, a test used for making decisions about individual students would also require a study of the use of the test for making decisions about teachers or administrators.

- The reliability of scores should be sufficient for each use. For example, the reliability of school means might be sufficient for making decisions about overall student performance; however, the reliability of subgroup means (e.g., for ethnic, socioeconomic groups) might be insufficient for making school improvement decisions.

- The consequences of a high-stakes test should be evaluated and findings communicated to policy makers, educators, and the public.

- Tests should align with the whole curriculum, not the portion that is easiest to assess.

Robert L. Johnson

See also Achievement Tests

Further Readings

American Educational Research Association (AERA). (2000). AERA position statements: High stakes testing in PreK–12 education. Retrieved August 19, 2006, from http://www.aera.net/policyandprograms/?id=378

American Evaluation Association. (2002). American Evaluation Association position statement on high stakes testing in PreK–12 education. Retrieved August 19, 2006, from http://www.eval.org/hst3.htm

Amrein, A., & Berliner, D. (2002). High stakes testing, uncertainty, and student learning. *Educational Policy Analysis Archives, 10*(18). Retrieved August 22, 2006, from http://epaa.asu.edu/epaa/v10n18

Heubert, J., & Hauser, R. (1999). *High stakes testing for tracking, promotion, and graduation.* Washington, DC: National Academy Press.

Horn, C. (2003). High-stakes testing and students: Stopping or perpetuating a cycle of failure? *Theory Into Practice, 42*(1), 30–41.

Linn, R. (2005). *Fixing the NCLB accountability system: CRESST Policy Brief 8.* Available from http://www.cse.ucla.edu/products/newsletters/policybrief8.pdf

No Child Left Behind of 2001, Pub. L. No. 107–110. Available from http://www.ed.gov/policy/elsec/leg/esea02/index.html

Shepard, L. (2002). The hazards of high-stakes testing. *Issues in Science and Technology, 19*(2), 53–58.

Sloane, F., & Kelly, A. (2003). Issues in high-stakes testing programs. *Theory Into Practice, 42*(1), 12–17.

WestEd. (2000). *The high stakes of high-stakes testing* [Policy brief]. Available from http://www.wested.org/cs/we/view/rs/181

HISPANIC EDUCATION

There has been a radical rise over the last twenty-five years in the number of people that self-identify as "Hispanic" on the U.S. Census and other official forms. Between 1980 and 2005 the Hispanic population nearly tripled, increasing from 14.6 million to 41.9 million. In 2005, Hispanics made up 14.5 percent of the total U.S. population, and the latest projections are that Hispanics will be 24.4 percent of the population in 2050. From meat-packing plants in Nebraska to poultry plants in north Georgia, from central Washington to central Iowa, a new human landscape is being formed in places where Spanish was not heard and salsa was not sold. Public schools set in that landscape are profoundly affected by their new Hispanic students.

At the start, it should be noted that language, culture, and history determine how we categorize and name groups of people. *Hispanic* connotes someone from a Spanish-speaking background (usually, from a former Spanish colony), while *Latino* commonly refers to a person from Latin America and does not necessarily exclude indigenous or non-Spanish-speaking people. To be inclusive of divergent viewpoints about these words, *Hispanic/Latino* will serve as a general adjective here, and *Hispanic* will be used when an official government term is required.

Background of Hispanic/Latino People

Some Hispanics/Latinos, although certainly not a majority, are not immigrants. *Hispanos* in New Mexico, and many Hispanics living near the Mexican border in southern Texas, New Mexico, Arizona, and California, are ancient residents of the land their families settled long before the U.S. became a nation.

Most Hispanics/Latinos, however, have immigrated to the United States in the last three decades. Although nearly half of all Hispanics/Latinos live in just two states—California and Texas—recent patterns show the greatest percentage increases in states without a history of major immigration, such as North Carolina, Arkansas, Kansas, and Nevada.

Prior educational experiences for each immigrant generation vary. Immigrants come from different nations, and the sociohistorical context of their native country affects how they respond to schooling. The major national origins of Hispanics in 2005 were 64.0 percent Mexican (constituting 9.3 percent of the entire U.S. population), 15.2 percent Caribbean (9.0 percent Puerto Rican, 3.5 percent Cuban, and 2.7 percent Dominican), 7.4 percent Central American (3 percent from El Salvador), 5.5 percent South American (1.7 percent from Colombia), and about 8 percent from elsewhere.

Hispanics in the United States are predominantly in the lower economic groups. In 2004, 29 percent of all Hispanic children (and nearly 50 percent of children in single-mother families) lived below the poverty line. The per capita income for Hispanics was $12,111, which was only 56 percent of the $21,587 per capita income for Whites. Almost 60 percent of Hispanic fourth graders were in public schools in which more than half of the students were eligible for free and reduced-price lunch.

The Spanish language is a primary social factor. According to 2005 data, in three states (Texas, California, and New Mexico), nearly 30 percent of the entire population age five or older speaks Spanish at home; in the United States as a whole, that figure is 12 percent. It is also true that in half of the states, Spanish is spoken at home by less than 5 percent of the people. Only 14 percent of Hispanics speak English poorly or not at all.

The world's most populous Spanish-speaking country, Mexico, shares a porous 2,000-mile border with the United States, which results in a contentious social situation for Hispanics/Latinos. Since 1990, movements to eliminate bilingual education, make English the official state and national language, and report all undocumented workers exposed a political fault line among Hispanics/Latinos, and between ethnic groups.

The parents of many immigrant children in public schools are afraid of being deported and are aware of prejudice against them, even as they struggle to adapt to a new society. Hispanics/Latinos who have lived here for generations, often in low-income enclaves, also have to deal with cultural stereotypes.

Educational Issues

It is important that educators know where immigrant families and students originate and what pressures to acculturate (or not) they face once they arrive. For example, immigrant children from an urban area such as Mexico City have had educational experiences quite different from those of children from an isolated rural community in the southern Mexican state of Chiapas. Ethnic background and social class also matter: Indigenous people from Guatemala, Mestizos from Nicaragua, and Europeans from Argentina may approach language and schooling differently.

Immigrants also enter different communities. Going to school in a large, relatively homogeneous Hispanic neighborhood (e.g., in New York's Spanish Harlem or Chicago's Pilsen) is a different matter than attending school in a more heterogeneous and less Hispanic area (e.g., in metro Atlanta or rural Alabama). And there remain many thousands of migrant students whose schooling histories are frequently fragmented and poorly documented.

Three educational conditions of Hispanics/Latinos are highlighted here: School segregation, school achievement, and school attainment. Residential segregation has resulted in school segregation (or "resegregation," according to some analyses). Nearly two thirds (65 percent) of all Hispanic students live in big cities. In the ten largest public school districts in this country, four of every ten students are Hispanic. In 2003, nearly one third of Hispanic students attended schools that had greater than 75 percent Hispanic enrollment, and more than half attended schools that were over 50 percent Hispanic.

Standardized test scores from the National Assessment of Educational Progress (NAEP) in reading, mathematics, and science in 1999 offer a mixed view of Hispanic students' school achievement. Hispanic students' scores have improved over the last several decades in all three areas, but the gap between them and White students did not narrow, and their scores still are significantly lower than those of White students.

Another fundamental measure of success for Hispanics or any other group of children is the level of school attainment and the rate of school attrition (the dropout rate). In 2003, the proportion of Hispanic/Latino eighteen- to twenty-four-year-olds who had a high school diploma or the equivalent was 64 percent, compared to 84 percent of Blacks and 92 percent of Whites. Hispanic/Latino students had a dropout rate of 23.5 percent, while the rate was 10.9 percent for Blacks and 6.3 percent for Whites.

Important Initiatives

Given the complex economic, linguistic, political, and educational contexts of life for Hispanics/Latinos, how can educators help to lower the dropout rate and raise student achievement? What do educators need to know and do?

Language Learning

At every level—classroom, school, district, state, and nation—language is both a pedagogical and a policy issue. Prior to several influential court decisions, schools could essentially offer little or no accommodation for nonnative English speakers; now, laws require that schools provide services to new English learners. Given that mandate, however, there are numerous possible arrangements for Hispanic children to learn English—and their school subjects.

When nonnative speakers of English begin their schooling, "transitional" language programs move them as quickly as possible into English-only classes. In most cases, Spanish speakers take a class each day in English for Speakers of Other Languages (ESOL). One major problem with such classes is that there is no unified ESOL curriculum in many states and school districts, and there is a great divergence in the availability of pedagogical resources. On a positive note, most states now require that prospective teachers—in some states, all teachers—take courses in how to teach children who are new English learners.

Bilingual education programs teach students in their native language and in English. "Weak" bilingual programs push students as quickly as possible into fully mainstreamed classrooms. "Strong" programs focus on the maintenance of students' native language, along with learning English. One approach to bringing bilingual education into the regular classroom is through "sheltered instruction," where students in subjects such as social studies learn the content through a combination of Spanish and English.

Dual-language immersion programs are an "enrichment" version of bilingual education, where all students in a school learn English and a second language (in the case of heavily Hispanic/Latino schools, it would be Spanish). Strong bilingual and dual immersion programs see language not as a "barrier," but as a resource that can benefit all students and the school.

Curriculum and Instruction

In terms of curriculum, one major issue is whether to augment traditional textbooks with material that may be more meaningful to Hispanic/Latino students. Some educators are dubious about the value of a special "month" for different ethnic groups and are working to incorporate multicultural perspectives throughout the curriculum. Some would introduce elements of Hispanic/Latino cultures in content areas such as mathematics and science, and not only in language arts and social studies, as is most common.

There is also debate over how to assess new Hispanic/Latino students who are nonnative speakers of English. Some schools have opted for initial testing in Spanish, to determine students' literacy and mathematics skills in their first language. Schools also set policies (or accept practices) about grading, classroom-based testing, and standardized testing at the end of each year. The issue is how to assess students' learning meaningfully, and not make judgments about academic ability based on someone's English-language capability.

School Experience

Numerous ethnographic accounts paint a nuanced portrait of Hispanic/Latino students' lives in various corners of our country, from urban Boston to rural Georgia to the Mexican border. One goal of these books is to examine Hispanic students' school engagement and disengagement. With high dropout rates for Hispanic/Latino students and the need to increase their academic achievement, it is vital to document how these students can become more engaged in school life.

Hispanic/Latino students sometimes lack the requisite social and academic networks in school. Students need positive peers and a sense of belonging; they need to develop a "school identity." Students create this sort of identity when they find a niche in academic and extracurricular programs. There is solid evidence that girls are more likely than boys to engage in academics and to establish positive peer networks, so educators may need to examine motivational strategies for boys and girls.

Connecting Families, Schools, and Communities

Collective values are important in Hispanic/Latino families, and work is strongly emphasized. To be *bién educado,* "well educated," is a matter of knowing how to act for the collective good, and not just of amassing a certain number of years in school. Still, it is apparent from the ethnographic studies and other research that Hispanic/Latino students and parents aspire to advance educationally—at least toward a high school diploma and often higher. However, certain national groups express expectations far below their aspirations. Because of parents' limited educational advancement or success (Hispanic/Latino parents' education levels are still far below those of White and African American parents), and many families' disconnection with school, students may not place priority on excelling at schoolwork and attaining good grades, the building blocks of school success.

Developing parental involvement can prove difficult, for many reasons. Immigrant Hispanic/Latino parents usually come to the United States with a cultural background of respecting and not questioning teachers. They may fear deportation and, particularly for recent immigrant women, limited English skills may make them reticent to attend school functions. In spite of these obstacles, there are many stirring examples of how to get families and the community deeply involved in school life.

Charting a Course

Enhancing the education of Hispanic/Latino students depends on the quality of teaching, which turns on teachers' openness to learning. Because of how teachers are assigned (the most recent graduates of teacher preparation programs usually are placed in the most difficult school environments) and the shortage of teachers in certain inner-city areas and in growing school districts, there can be problems with teachers teaching out of their fields or lacking sufficient prior educational interaction with students from diverse ethnic groups. Changes in placement policies and mentoring practices can mitigate these "qualification" problems, but the "quality" of actual instruction depends on how teachers communicate with and engage Hispanic/Latino students and family members in classroom and school life. All such changes require improved teacher preparation and ongoing professional development.

Hispanic/Latino children and adolescents have a strong cultural foundation on which to build academic engagement. They tend to be fluently bilingual, live in tightly bound family systems, respect adult authority, and maintain a strong work ethic. Any course of action that is intended to improve how they are educated should begin from a stance of respect for students' academic and social strengths; be carried out as part of a whole-school collaboration that increases students' access to rich, multilingual learning; and end up with deeper connections to teachers and school programs.

H. James McLaughlin

See also Bilingual Education, History of; Cultural Pluralism; Educational Equity: Race/Ethnicity; Immigrant Education: Contemporary Issues; Migrant Education

Further Readings

Carger, C. L. (1996). *Of borders and dreams: A Mexican-American experience of urban education.* New York: Teachers College Press.

Delgado-Gaitán, C. (2001). *The power of community: Mobilizing for family and schooling.* Lanham, MD: Rowman & Littlefield.

Flores-González, N. (2002). *School kids/street kids: Identity development in Latino students.* New York: Teachers College Press.

García, E. (2001). *Hispanic education in the United States.* Lanham, MD: Rowman & Littlefield.

Gibson, M. A., Gándara, P., & Koyama, J. P. (Eds.). (2004). *School connections: U.S. Mexican youth, peers, and school achievement.* New York: Teachers College Press.

Montero-Sieburth, M., & Villaruel, F. A. (Eds.). (2000). *Making invisible Latino adolescents visible.* New York: Falmer.

Pugach, M. C. (1998). *On the border of opportunity: Education, community, and language at the U.S.-Mexico line.* Mahwah, NJ: Lawrence Erlbaum.

Stanton-Salazar, R. D. (2001). *Manufacturing hope and despair: The school and kin support networks of U.S.-Mexican youth.* New York: Teachers College Press.

Valdés, G. (1996). *Con respeto: Bridging the distances between culturally diverse families and schools.* New York: Teachers College Press.

HISTORICALLY BLACK CATHOLIC SCHOOLS

With the emancipation of the slaves in 1865, Roman Catholic bishops expressed in the Second Plenary (1866) and Third Plenary councils (1884) that bishops and their parishes should make every effort to establish churches, schools, orphanages, and homes for immigrants, Blacks, and the poor. The few Catholic schools that served Black children were operated by Black Catholic men and women (Josephite Fathers, Fathers of the Holy Ghost, Fathers of the Divine Word, African Mission Fathers, Capuchin Franciscan, Franciscan Sisters, Mission Helpers, Servants of the Sacred Heart, Sister Servants of the Holy Ghost, Oblate Sisters, Sisters of the Holy Family).

Prior to 1954, a quiet but firm desegregation of Catholic parishes and schools marked the migration of Blacks from the South to inner cities and communities in the Northeast, Midwest, and West. After 1954 and throughout the civil rights movement of the 1960s, the Catholic Church required in its theological teachings and schools respect for the individual, thereby embracing the education of Black students and its community. White flight between 1960s and 1980s placed many parishes and schools, once supported by immigrant communities and students, in dire financial condition. Today, historically Catholic African American schools continue as viable and important alternatives to public schooling. But African American Catholic education is challenged by poor neighborhoods and rapid demographic shifts. The traditional mission of Catholic elementary and secondary schools and the thirty-two historically African American Catholic high schools is being tested as parochial schools (Lutheran, Episcopal, and Methodist), also educate large numbers of racial and ethnic students.

Paul E. Green

See also African American Education

See Visual History Chapter 6, Catholic Schools and the Separation of Church and State

Further Readings

Irvine, J. J., & Foster, M. (1996). *Growing up African American in Catholic schools.* New York: Teachers College Press.

HISTORICALLY BLACK COLLEGES AND UNIVERSITIES

The historically Black colleges and universities (HBCUs) are unique American higher education institutions. These institutions often began as elementary and secondary schools and overcame significant barriers associated with racism and discrimination. Since their founding, primarily in the late nineteenth century, they have evolved into centers of leadership development for African Americans, and have produced over 90 percent of the African American college graduates during the past 100 years, although today many African Americans attend other universities. This entry provides a basic description and brief history of historically Black schools, and looks ahead to the future of these institutions.

Basic Facts

Historically Black colleges and universities are defined as institutions established specifically for the education of African Americans. Black colleges reflect the tension between the aspirations of the African Americans for equality and economic and social justice and the second-class citizenship of African Americans in American society.

HBCU's represent 105 colleges and universities, down from a peak of 117. Thirty-eight are private, mostly religious. Many still have affiliations with their founding religious organizations. The remaining Black universities and colleges are public institutions that are located in the South, with the exception of Central State University in Ohio and Cheney State and Lincoln universities in Pennsylvania.

While they account for only 3 percent of all colleges and universities in the United States, HBCUs produce approximately 23 percent of all bachelor's degrees earned by African Americans, 13 percent of all master's degrees, and 20 percent of all first professional degrees. Three quarters of all African American Ph.D.s in the United States did their undergraduate work at historically Black colleges and universities. Early in the twentieth century, the Black militant and scholar W. E. B. Du Bois described how Black colleges inculcated their students with a sense of racial pride and instilled in them the confidence to fight against the injustices of the American social order.

Historical Context

Higher education for African Americans was limited prior to the Civil War. There were only twenty-eight African Americans recorded as receiving a college degree up to that time. Most opportunities for higher education for African Americans were limited to the New England and Middle Atlantic states, and were highly restricted. Oberlin College in Ohio and Berea College in Kentucky were among the few colleges open to African Americans.

Cheney State University (1837) and Lincoln University (1854) in Pennsylvania and Wilburforce College (1856) in Ohio are generally considered the first colleges established for African Americans. The American Colonization Society, which was concerned with sending African Americans back to Africa, and various Protestant religious denominations were the two major groups supporting the establishment of Black colleges during this period.

Reconstruction

The end of the Civil War and the emancipation of the slaves brought to Black education a new hope, with visions of opportunity and equality in fulfilling the dreams of the freed people. The reasons for these dreams were the Thirteenth Amendment to the Constitution, abolishment of slavery; the Fourteenth Amendment, equal access; and the Fifteenth Amendment, the right to vote.

Three separate and distinct philanthropic groups shaped and established Black colleges. They were the African American benevolent societies headed up by Black churches and led by the Baptists and African Methodist Episcopal denominations, the Northern White benevolent and denominational societies, and a group of philanthropists consisting of leaders of large corporations and wealthy individuals. Each had its own agenda.

The New England Missionaries included the Methodist, Baptist, Presbyterian, and the Congregationalist religious denominations. They responded immediately by establishing schools, colleges, and normal (teacher training) schools. These groups established forty colleges and seventeen public colleges between 1865 and 1890.

The Congregationalists (the American Missionary Association, or AMA) established seven Black private colleges and thirteen "normal" (teacher training) schools by 1890. These schools began as colleges in name only, but the title signified their eventual purpose. Each included at its inception elementary and preparatory schools, since there were no high schools or academies for African Americans. Atlanta, Fisk, Howard, and Leland universities were able to begin college divisions by 1872.

The curriculum of these Black, private colleges was and still is largely classical, including foreign languages, mathematics, science, and philosophy. The missionary philanthropists felt that a classical education was the best means for African Americans to achieve racial equality. Thus, education, according to missionary societies, was to prepare a college-bred African American leadership that would uplift their race. The imprint of belief education, as well as a sense of purpose, morality, and order of those religious groups from the North has had a lasting effect on the climate of the Black college.

The Negro philanthropies also established a number of Black colleges. Some of the most notable ones were Allen, Morris, and Benedict (South Carolina). The Negro philanthropies' main goals were to increase the literacy of African Americans; continue the struggle for equality and social justice; and to promote ethical, moral behavior, and racial uplift, along with training for economic improvement.

The industrial philanthropists were concerned with where African Americans fit socially and economically in the "new" South. Corporate leaders of large industries established foundations such as the Peabody and the Phelps Stokes foundations. These leaders changed the nature of the education of African Americans. The type of education that these foundations promoted was called industrial education or training. Its purpose was actually more to maintain distinct social classes than to provide occupational training. African Americans were trained for fields that corresponded with their low-status class.

The philosophy of these foundations was a combination of Christian missionary and capitalism, with the intention of insuring that African Americans remained in low-caste status. By 1890 these industrial/corporate foundations had eclipsed the religion-based missionaries in ideology and the funding of Black colleges.

The Jim Crow Era

By 1877 the White Southern state governments were reestablished by the Compromise of 1876, beginning one of the darkest periods for African Americans. They lost political representation and their right to vote, and the equality of opportunity was abrogated.

The *Plessy v. Ferguson* (1898) Supreme Court case codified the blatant apartheid racial system between the races with the so-called separate but equal status of Blacks and Whites. A highly discriminatory dual public higher education system was established, one for Whites and one for Blacks. The discrimination against Black public colleges and schools was so blatant that the corporate/industrial foundations, such as the Slater and Rosenwald foundations, had to intervene

with funds to build schools for Blacks and pressure Southern state legislatures to increase funding for Black education.

State legislatures began to establish Black public colleges to train teachers by the end of the nineteenth century in order to meet the needs of the burgeoning African American population. By 1915, thirty-four public colleges were established. The Rosenwald, General Board, Phelp-Stokes, and Slater funds (corporate/industrialist-based foundations), established numerous normal (i.e., teacher training) schools and supported state and private colleges and universities during that period.

The industrial education model was the method of African American education preferred by the industrial foundations and Southern governments during that period. It was developed by Chapman Armstrong and incorporated into his Hampton Institute. Booker T. Washington, a former slave and protégée of Armstrong, expanded the model through his institution, the Tuskegee Institute in Alabama.

The famous Booker T. Washington and W. E. B. Du Bois debates centered on the choice between classical education (equality) and industrial education (political accommodation) in the context of the political status of African Americans in the United States. These philosophies were proxies for the political debate on the place of African Americans in American society.

Despite numerous barriers to higher education, such as isolation and the lack of funds and recognition by the greater society, the Black private and public colleges began to evolve into unique and viable institutions for African Americans. The schools became centers of leadership development. They were able to nurture and instill in the students confidence and a commitment to community service and racial uplift.

In the late nineteenth and early twentieth centuries, Black public colleges were able to expand and improve somewhat the quality of education for their students through the assistance of the federal government and philanthropic groups such as the Slater and Rosenwald foundations.

The Morrill Act, in particular, helped improve Black public higher education. The first Morrill Act was enacted in 1862 to help states establish public colleges and universities to teach agriculture, military tactics, and the mechanical arts; these were known as land-grant universities and colleges. The second Morrill Act was most important for Black education. It corrected the discriminatory policies of Southern states against African Americans when the land-grant institutions were established. African Americans were denied entrance into these institutions. The law forced the Southern states that had land-grant institutions, to establish a Black land-grant institution too. Sixteen were established throughout the South. This act allowed these colleges to provide scientifically oriented agricultural and mechanical arts programs.

Brown v. Board of Education

There were over 100 HBCUs by 1954, when the U.S. Supreme Court ruled through the *Brown v. Board of Education* case that the separate but equal laws upheld in the *Plessy v. Ferguson* case were unconstitutional, thus ending legal apartheid in the United States. This edict did not immediately shift the African American student population from Black colleges and universities, but it established the legal basis for the eventual desegregation of all-White, higher education institutions. Black colleges and universities continued to enroll over 90 percent of the African American college-going population.

The Civil Rights Movement

By 1967 there were 111 historically Black colleges and universities. The civil rights movement ushered in a positive change of attitude in American society toward African Americans. Congress passed the Civil Rights Act of 1964, which put teeth into the enforcement of the *Brown v. Board of Education* decision along with implementation of affirmative action in the workplace. The Higher Education Amendments of the Civil Rights Act helped shape these changes of attitude and privilege of White Americans. Predominantly White universities were required to open their doors to African Americans. They responded by providing African American students with scholarships, special admissions, and academic support programs. However, these changes challenged the continued existence of Black colleges and universities. African American students could now choose between the two systems.

As a result of these events, there was a dramatic shift in the late 1970s in which African Americans began attending predominantly White colleges and universities. Over 70 percent of African Americans now attend predominantly White universities. As a result, a number of Black colleges have closed, and many are in financial jeopardy of closing.

The civil rights movement period also saw court challenges by the historical Black public universities over the blatant inequality of the dual educational system in the South. By 1967, these institutions were serving the majority of African American college and university students. Yet, their facilities were not up to standards. These challenges exposed the Black public universities to the possibility of being eliminated. They were governed by White majority legislatures that were still hostile to Black education. Most needed millions of dollars to replace or rehabilitate the campus facilities. In the *United States v. Fordice* Supreme Court case (against the Mississippi state higher education system), Mississippi was ordered to upgrade the Black institutions in the areas of academic programs and facilities, and to do away with the dual higher education system. The 1973 case of *Adams v. Richardson* affected the border and Southern states that maintained a dual university system. These states agreed to improve their Black public universities, and the Black schools were allowed to maintain their special mission.

Looking to the Future

Many critics point to the autocratic governance of a number of HBCUs, their mismanagement, and the low graduation rates. Some of the major present-day challenges for HBCUs are the lack of sufficient endowment to ensure scholarships, the inability to attract excellent staff and improve facilities, and the fact that a number of schools have been placed on probation by accreditation agencies. Numerous Black colleges have increased their endowments by establishing institutional advancement offices; cultivating donors and graduates; and obtaining help from the federal government, foundations, and organizations such as the United Negro College Fund.

Beginning with President Ronald Reagan, presidents have issued executive orders to recognize and enhance federal support of HBCUs. Congress has provided funds to enhance HBCUs through the Black College University Act (1986). HBCUs will continue to serve as institutions to train African Americans for leadership, for citizenship, and to be agents for the equality of opportunities for the African American community. In doing so, they fulfill an important function in American higher education.

John William Long

See also African American Education; Higher Education, History of

See Visual History Chapter 7, The Education of African Americans; Chapter 13, Exhibit of American Negroes: *Exposition Universelle de 1900*

Further Readings

Adams v. Richardson, 351 f. 2D 36 (D.C., 1973).

Adams v. Bennett, 675 F. Supp. 668 (D.D.C., 1987).

Anderson, J. D. (1988). *The education of Blacks in the South, 1860–1935*. Chapel Hill: University of North Carolina

Bowles, F., & DeCosta, F. D. (1971). *Between two worlds*. New York McGraw-Hill.

Brown v. Board of Education, 347 U.S. 483 (1954).

Du Bois, W. E. B. (1910). *College-bred Negro American*. Atlanta, GA: Atlanta University.

Hale, F. W., Jr. (Ed.). (2006). *How Black colleges empower Black students: Lessons for higher education.* Sterling, VA: Stylus.

United States v. Fordice, 958 U.S. (1992).

Watkins, W. H. (2001). *The White architects of Black education: Ideology and power in America, 1865–1954.* New York: Teachers College Press.

Willie, C. V., & Edmunds, R. R. (Eds.). (1978). *Black colleges in America.* New York: Teachers College.

HISTORY OF EDUCATION SOCIETY

The History of Education Society grew from the intellectual ferment and institutional transformations in the field of the history of education. Although some work in this area had been done in the late nineteenth century, Ellwood P. Cubberley and Paul Monroe formalized history of education as an academic subject with their institutional, proselytizing style during the first half of the twentieth century. As a service course for prospective classroom teachers, history of education extolled the institutional evolution of the public school system and portrayed it as an inevitable outcome of consensus forged by a democratic society.

This field of study first assumed institutional form in 1948, when the History of Education Section appeared under the auspices of the National Society for College Teachers of Education, with the *History of Education Journal* (*HEJ*) serving as its official organ and Claude Eggertson as editor. A stormy debate erupted in the 1950s over the intellectual mission of educational history—utilitarian versus scholarly—virtually paralyzing that organization. In 1957, the Ford Foundation's Fund for the Advancement of Education formed the Committee on the Role of Education in American History in order to move *educational* history closer to *academic* history, a scholarly approach rather than an institutional narrative, a broad history of education instead of a narrow history of public schools.

The History of Education Society, an independent organization, replaced the Section in 1960. This represented more than simple institutional displacement; it symbolized the field's emergence as a legitimate area of research. The *History of Education Quarterly,* the society's "scholarly journal," replaced *HEJ* the following year. The journal was based at the University of Pittsburgh, with Ryland W. Crary as its first editor. The *Quarterly* reflected the intellectual undercurrents of the society as it moved to New York University, Indiana University, Slippery Rock University, and the University of Illinois, with Henry J. Perkinson, Paul H. Mattingly, James McLachlan, B. Edward McClellan, William J. Reese, Richard J. Altenbaugh, and James D. Anderson serving as editors at various times.

Another significant scholarly metamorphosis occurred during the 1970s. Revisionist historians introduced the concept of conflict and challenged education historians to reevaluate the role of public schooling in democratic America, generally dismissing it as a source of political, social, and economic liberation and intellectual and personal growth. Debates over the revisionist view dominated the society's annual meetings and the pages of its journal. By the late twentieth century, the field had expanded its scope, analysis, and research methods, revealing a mature and vibrant subject. It transcended the mere history of schooling by emphasizing the educational functions of other cultural institutions, like the family, religion, and media, among others.

The society began a long-term affiliation with the International Conference for the Study of the History of Education in 1988. Incorporated in 1994 as a nonprofit organization, the society holds its annual meetings in different regions of North America, often sponsored with local associations like the Midwest History of Education Society, Southern History of Education Society, and Canadian History of Education Society. The History of Education Society offers a variety of prizes that recognize noteworthy, scholarly contributions.

Richard J. Altenbaugh

See also Educational Research, History of

Further Readings

Altenbaugh, R. J. (Ed.). (1999). *Historical dictionary of American education.* Westport, CT: Greenwood Press.

Cohen, S. (1976). The history of the history of American education, 1900–1976. *Harvard Educational Review, 46,* 298–330.

Mulhern, J. (1961). Perspectives. *History of Education Quarterly, 1,* 1–3.

HISTORY STANDARDS, NATIONAL

In 1994 the National Center for History in the Schools (NCHS) released the "National Standards for History," a 250-page document outlining methods and content for teaching U.S. and world history in elementary and secondary schools. The NCHS spent over two years developing the standards, which include recommendations from thirty-five national education organizations. This entry describes what led up to the report and summarizes its recommendations as well as criticisms and revisions of the standards.

Origins

The National Standards for History was developed from the National Education Goals adopted by President George H. W. Bush and the National Governors' Association in 1990. His successor, President Bill Clinton, signed that report into law in 1994 as the GOALS 2000, Educate America Act. GOALS 2000 was the culmination of an education reform agenda announced by President Bush in 1991, which called for national standards in the subjects of English, mathematics, science, history, and geography. The education reform agenda enjoyed broad support from both politicians and the American public.

The National History Standards Project began in 1992 with funding provided by the National Endowment for the Humanities, led by Lynne Cheney, and the U.S. Department of Education, led by Secretary of Education Lamar Alexander. The project's goal was to develop an understanding of the purpose of history education in the school curriculum, successful methods for history instruction, the specific historical knowledge students should acquire, and the thought processes students should learn. The thirty-member National Council for History Standards, consisting of leaders from organizations like the American Historical Association and the National Council for Social Studies, worked with the participants of the National Assessment of Education Progress in United States History to ensure that the new National Standards for History were aligned with that organization's work.

Standards

The National Standards for History is a curriculum guide for students in elementary and secondary school. The standards are divided into ten historical eras beginning with the migration of Asian peoples to North America and ending with the modern United States. For each era, between two and four standards describe the themes, content, and methodologies that students should master at each grade level. The specific details of assignments, activities, and content are left to individual instructors or school systems to determine.

One of the goals of the National Standards for History was to create a history curriculum that was focused not on rote learning of dates, facts, and names, but on ideas and issues in each historical era. The leaders of the NCHS also strove to make the standards as inclusive as possible, working to ensure that the roles of women and minorities in U.S. history received a more equal footing with the traditional figures that dominate the teaching of U.S. history, such as George Washington and James Madison.

In addition to defining the historical content students should master, the standards also address the types of historical thinking that students should master by the end of high school. The standards categorize historical thinking skills into five areas: Chronological Thinking, Historical Comprehension, Historical Analysis and Interpretation, Historical Research Capabilities, and Historical Issues—Analysis and Decision-Making. The Thinking Standards are presented to assist teachers in developing lesson plans that teach not only historical content, but also the skills to understand and use that content.

Criticism and Response

The National Standards for History met fierce criticism from both politicians and educators when they were released in 1994, particularly from former National Endowment for the Humanities head Cheney. Much of the political criticism reflected the so-called "culture wars" between conservative and liberal political figures during the 1990s and focused on the standards' expanded attention to women and minorities. Criticism from educators included complaints that the standards focused too much on small details and not enough on larger events or themes. Some educators were also concerned by the appearance of presentism, the practice of making judgments of past events or cultures based on the values or morals of the present time, as in the case of elementary school students declaring that Christopher Columbus committed genocide.

Cheney led the criticism of the National Standards for History by arguing that the standards were an example of political correctness and focused on the negative aspects of American and European history. As examples, Cheney claimed that the standards mention McCarthyism nineteen times while ignoring heroes like Ulysses S. Grant, who is included only once. Cheney also argued that the standards did not treat the failures of non-European cultures with the same rigor applied to the failures of the United States and European nations, stating that the standards discuss the

advanced nature of Aztec civilization while ignoring issues like the Aztec practice of human sacrifice.

Other critics include William J. Bennetta, a fellow of the California Academy of Sciences, who wrote that the National Standards for History ignored the role of technology and science in the development of the United States by ignoring the contributions of individuals like the Wright brothers, Thomas Edison, and Albert Einstein while focusing on figures like Booker T. Washington, who were not of the same importance.

In response to the criticism the standards received, they were revised in 1996 to accommodate recommendations of two panels organized by the Council for Basic Education, funded by the Pew Charitable Trusts and the John D. and Catherine T. MacArthur Foundation. After reviewing the standards, the council concluded that most of the criticisms of the standards were a result of the teaching examples included in the standards, not the standards themselves.

Christopher J. Levesque

See also American Education, Themes in the History of; Citizenship Education; Democracy and Education; Ideology and Schooling; Multiculturalism, Philosophical Implications; No Child Left Behind Act; Politics of Education; Social Studies Education; Standards

Further Readings

Bennetta, W. J. (1994). *Phony "standards" and fake "history."* Retrieved August 20, 2006, from http://www.textbookleague.org/55ucla.htm

H-Net. (1994). *National standards for history discussion on h-net lists.* Retrieved August 20, 2006, from http://www.hnet.org/percent7eteach/threads/standard.html

Nash, G. B., Crabtree, C., & Dunn, R. E. (2000). *History on trial: Culture wars and the teaching of the past.* New York: Random House.

National Center for History Standards. (1996). *National standards for history.* Retrieved August 20, 2006, from http://nchs.ucla.edu/standards/toc.html

HIV/AIDS

The human immunodeficiency virus (HIV) and acquired immunodeficiency syndrome (AIDS) is a global crisis and a leading development obstacle for many nations. There is no known cure for HIV and the cost and availability of antiretroviral therapy (ART) make treatment very expensive. The disease has affected millions of individuals and devastated several national economies and societies. Education has become an important component in efforts to stem the spread of this disease. This entry provides an overview of the epidemic and examines educational initiatives and their impact.

The Epidemic

HIV was first identified in 1981, but epidemiologists have tracked blood samples containing the HIV back to the 1950s. Several scholars designate the Great Lakes region of East Africa as the HIV epicenter, though others have argued that the epicenter also includes portions of Central Africa. An accurate number of people infected with and who have died from the disease is difficult to measure. Many individuals were pronounced dead as a result of one of several opportunistic infections, or by other names such as "slim" disease in Uganda.

In the late 1980s and early 1990s, the rate of disease reached epidemic levels in several global regions and, except in a few countries, continues to escalate. The *2007 AIDS Epidemic Update* by UNAIDS and the World Health Organization (WHO) estimates that there are between 30.6 and 36.1 million people infected with HIV around the world. The disease has created millions of AIDS orphans. With no respect to race, gender, or social class, the disease has wreaked havoc in many nations. High-risk population groups include youth, young adults, and migrant workers, who make up significant portions of the labor supply's most productive members.

Although HIV is a worldwide pandemic, there are vast disparities among geographic regions in the number of people living with HIV (PLHIV). Sub-Saharan Africa and the South and Southeast Asian regions account for 83 percent of the world's total infection rates. Sub-Saharan Africa, with about 11 percent of the total world population, accounts for 76 percent of the total female infections and roughly 87 percent of all infected children. Oceania, with .5 percent of

the world's population, represents roughly .2 percent of infection and deaths from HIV. Sub-Saharan Africa is thus overrepresented in terms of adults, children, and women infected with HIV and in the total number of deaths from AIDS. The high rates of infection and the resulting fear have led many to blame and discriminate against those who are infected with or affected by HIV/AIDS.

Because of its transmission and effects on the body, HIV and AIDS have predominantly been labeled a health-only issue. But this approach to the disease is too narrow. As early as 1987, WHO proposed a multisectoral approach to addressing HIV/AIDS. The multisectoral response has been promoted by UNAIDS and other major multi- and bilateral development agencies and has been adapted from successful multisectoral models such as those of Uganda, Senegal, and the United States. Governments and the international community have stressed inclusion, participation, and cooperation with nongovernmental organizations, community-based organizations, faith-based organizations, and the private sector to increase the effectiveness, outreach, and reduce duplicate efforts by multiple actors in the HIV response. This multisectoral strategy brings together community members, health care providers, religious leaders, government agencies, the business community, and school personnel and administrators in a comprehensive response to HIV and AIDS under one umbrella plan directed by the government and a coordinating council of stakeholders. Government commitment, multisectoral collaboration between government sectors, political stability, and a democratic society are all precursors for an effective HIV/AIDS education campaign. Well-formulated and context-relevant national HIV/AIDS strategic frameworks and policy statements are essential documents that provide coordination underpinnings to a successful multisectoral response.

Educational Initiatives

The education sector is an essential component of the multisectoral approach in countries that have reduced their HIV-seroprevalence rates. Education attainment is a potential predictor to poverty reduction and the overall health within a country. Further, some studies show a negative relationship between education and seroprevalence rates. Education is considered an essential means to influence knowledge and create behavior changes in youth. Formal education interventions include strategies based on abstinence, being faithful within a relationship, and condom use (i.e., the ABCs of HIV prevention); inclusion of HIV/AIDS in the curriculum; and school-supported programs such as peer-education groups, school clubs, dramatizations, and in-service training for teachers and administrators.

While schools are positioned as ideal settings for successful behavioral communication change (BCC), schools are not always the best avenue for disseminating life skills. Depending on the curricular requirements, administrative support, and teacher knowledge, schools can be limited in what is offered by means of HIV/AIDS prevention, treatment, and stigma. If teachers lack sufficient training regarding the disease, it is doubtful that they will be willing or able to share the necessary life-saving skills for successful HIV/AIDS-prevention education. Therefore, other, nonformal education avenues must also be taken to achieve successful HIV/AIDS-education dissemination to the target student population. Parents, family and community members, peer groups, the mass media, voluntary counseling and testing services, literacy programs, and cultural performances (such as dramas that focus on the disease) are successful, nonformal, education media through which HIV/AIDS-prevention messages can occur.

AIDS stigma is a leading impediment to AIDS education efforts, which in turn creates a major obstacle to effective prevention, treatment, and care of the disease. AIDS stigma is a social construct that can take on many different forms, causing victims to be rejected, isolated, blamed, or ashamed. Education efforts can help curb the negative and vicious cycle that inevitably results from AIDS stigma and help prevent children from dropping out of school, unnecessary marginalization, and increased suffering. In an effort to stem stigma and increase accurate knowledge about prevention and transmission, it is necessary that government leaders, school administrators, and teachers address AIDS stigma in schools.

Research on Education's Impact

Education and HIV/AIDS exist in a cyclical relationship, influencing and being influenced by the other. Education impacts an individual's knowledge, behavior, and attitudes toward the disease. Recent studies have shown an education effect on HIV infection rates, with better educated individuals having lower infection rates, more knowledge about HIV and AIDS, and greater acceptance of PLHIV. Inversely, HIV infection negatively impacts both the teaching workforce and student attendance. HIV infection and AIDS among teachers and administrators increases absenteeism from illness, reduces productivity, and eventually depletes the teaching workforce and knowledge base in several countries faster than it can be replaced. HIV also impacts student learning, as students with infected family members are required to drop out of school to care for ill family members, take employment to compensate for lost income from ill caregivers, or care for younger siblings. In the face of escalating adversity, education is perhaps the most essential means for prevention of HIV and AIDS and ultimately overcoming the global pandemic.

W. James Jacob and John M. Collins

See also Sex Education

Further Readings

de Walque, D. (2004). *How does the impact of an HIV/AIDS information campaign vary with educational attainment? Evidence from rural Uganda (WPS 3289)*. Washington, DC: The World Bank.

Gao, F., Bailes, E., Robertson, D. L., Chen, Y., Rodenburg, C. M., Michael, S. F., et al. (1999). Origin of HIV-1 in the chimpanzee Pan troglodytes troglodytes. *Nature, 397,* 436–441.

Holsinger, D. B., & Jacob, W. J. (Eds.). (2008). *Inequality in education: Comparative and international perspectives.* Dordrecht, The Netherlands: Springer.

Jacob, W. J., Morisky, D. E., Nsubuga, Y. K., & Hite, S. J. (2006). Evaluation of HIV/AIDS education programs in Uganda. In D. E. Morisky, W. J. Jacob, Y. K. Nsubuga, & S. J. Hite (Eds.), *Overcoming AIDS: Lessons learned from Uganda* (pp. 63–83). Greenwich, CT: Information Age.

Jacob, W. J., Shaw, S. A., Morisky, D. E., Hite, S. J., & Nsubuga, Y. K. (2007). HIV/AIDS education: What African youth say is effective. *Families in Society, 88*(1), 1–11.

Joint United Nations Project on HIV/AIDS, & World Health Organization. (2007). *2007 AIDS epidemic update.* Geneva: Author.

Nsubuga, Y. K., & Jacob, W. J. (2006). Fighting stigma and discrimination as a strategy for HIV/AIDS prevention and control. In D. E. Morisky, W. J. Jacob, Y. K. Nsubuga, & S. J. Hite (Eds.), *Overcoming AIDS: Lessons learned from Uganda* (pp. 15–42). Greenwich, CT: Information Age.

Nsubuga, Y. K., & Jacob, W. J. (2006). A multisectoral strategy for overcoming AIDS in Uganda. In D. E. Morisky, W. J. Jacob, Y. K. Nsubuga, & S. J. Hite (Eds.), *Overcoming AIDS: Lessons learned from Uganda* (pp. 43–59). Greenwich, CT: Information Age.

Serwadda, D., et al. (1985). Slim disease: A new disease in Uganda and its association with HTLV-III infection. *Lancet, 2*(8460), 849–852.

United Nations Population Fund. (2006). *UNFPA state of the world population 2006: A passage to hope—women and international migration.* New York: Author.

HOLISTIC EDUCATION

Though the principles, perspectives, and frameworks of *holistic education* can be traced far back in recorded history to early philosophical and religious teachings, the contemporary use of the term is rather new. Definitions, methods, philosophies, and descriptions of holistic education have varied somewhat among educators and scholars as it has been viewed from different perspectives, but it is basically concerned with educating the whole person—body, mind, and soul—to develop his or her fullest potential. This entry looks at the field's historical background and the principles behind its practice.

Background

The terms *holism* and *holistic* were coined by Jan Smuts from the Greek words *holus,* which means "whole," and *holon,* which means "entity." Smuts saw holism as a process of creative evolution in which the tendency of nature is to form wholes that are greater than the sum of their parts. He developed a philosophy of holism early in the twentieth century that viewed reality as organic and evolutionary, including both its material and spiritual aspects. These ideas, which were published in his most important book, *Holism and Evolution,* in 1926, have recently become more accepted, though holistic educators do not generally regard Smuts as an important influence.

The historical philosophical and psychological figures who are considered to have more directly influenced the field of holistic education often include Jean-Jacques Rousseau, Ralph Waldo Emerson, Johann Heinrich Pestalozzi, Friedrich Froebel, Maria Montessori, Rudolf Steiner, Carl Jung, Jiddu Krishnamurti, Alfred North Whitehead, and Abraham Maslow. A more recent list of influences on holistic education might include the following individuals: Carl Rogers, Marilyn Ferguson, Fritjof Capra, Joseph Chilton Pearce, David Bohm, Douglas Sloan, Ken Wilber, P. Parker Palmer, and Theodore Roszak. Although none of these individuals identified themselves as holistic educators or would be identified as leaders of holistic education, their ideas and writings have been an influence on the field. John Miller and Ron Miller are current writers who identify with holistic education and are considered leading figures in the field.

From the list of influences above it can be seen that holistic education has some relation to and can to some extent be identified with, but not limited to, traditions of romanticism, transcendentalism, humanism, systems theory, and integralism.

Philosophic Principles

Holistic education has developed largely as a reaction to what its proponents view as the mechanistic, reductionistic, and materialistic conceptions that have come to dominate popular thinking and education in the last century. As they see it, the result of these paradigms has been a fragmented and limited approach to human development and education that has led to a focus on developing physical, behavioral, and intellectual capacities for economic and material benefits while ignoring or discounting social, emotional, psychological, moral, creative, aesthetic, and spiritual natures and capacities. Holistic education has emerged out of a need to address this imbalance and the growing disillusionment in some circles with what are viewed as dysfunctional approaches to further individual and collective human interests and potentialities. As holistic education challenges the dominant worldview and practice in education, it has been marginalized, and its influence in educational, scientific, and political areas limited.

Holistic educators believe that the body, mind, and soul are integral aspects of human nature that should be considered in treating the whole person, and that holistic education is a more defensible, practical, and effective approach to developing well-balanced and healthy people who can be valued contributors to society according to their potentialities and the opportunities available to them. Until all aspects of the human being and the environment are properly treated in education, these educators believe individuals and humanity will suffer from a lack of balance and the denial of part of their reality.

Holistic education views all aspects of life as interconnected, interrelated, and interdependent. As such, it is ecological and global, encouraging an understanding and appreciation of multiple contexts and connections. Proponents hold that when people disconnect or dissociate from reality, and especially from parts of themselves, they are limiting development. Besides considering the whole person—physically, mentally, and spiritually—holistic educators see a need to recognize that people affect their environment and their environment affects them.

Holistic educators are especially concerned with the failure of modern education to consider the emotional, social, and spiritual natures of students. It seeks to develop the full potential of the person in a humanistic fashion that recognizes and honors each individual's unique talents and capacities. Holistic education sees active positive engagement in relationships with the world and others as one of the most powerful means of authentic education. It believes in the innate goodness of people and that they will develop into happy, healthy, and well-balanced individuals given the right conditions.

Education then is primarily a drawing out or unfolding of the individual's potentialities, not a dispensing of information or instilling of learning. To do this requires the educators to be well developed themselves and to be sensitive, knowledgeable, and creative in helping their students realize their true natures. Holistic education encourages individual and collective responsibility in an ongoing quest for greater realization, fulfillment, meaning, understanding, and

connection. Proponents find traditional education harmful in that it fragments and compartmentalizes knowledge and learning into subjects and discrete unconnected units, encourages competition over compassion and cooperation, and is subject and teacher centered rather than spirit and learner centered. Holistic education sees the whole as greater than the sum of its parts and that the whole-system approach requires moving from the limitations of a rationalistic, linear, and simple approach to a more intuitive, nonlinear, and complex view. It connects and makes a relationship among linearity and intuition; body, mind, and spirit; the individual and the collective; and the many and varied forms of knowing and knowledge. As a result, individuals educated holistically attain a degree of autonomy and authenticity that allows them to be progressive agents in advancing their own and others' development and welfare.

Rodney H. Clarken

See also Waldorf Education

Further Readings

Forbes, S. H. (2003). *Holistic education: An analysis of its ideas and nature.* Brandon, VT: Foundation for Educational Renewal.

Miller, J. P. (1993). *The holistic curriculum.* Toronto, ON, Canada: OISE Press.

Miller, R. (1992). *What are schools for? Holistic education in American culture* (2nd ed.). Brandon, VT: Holistic Education Press.

HOLMES GROUP

Initially comprised of primarily deans of education from universities across the United States, and chaired by Dr. Judith E. Lanier (then Dean of the College of Education at Michigan State University), the Holmes Group convened in 1983 in response to charges that in order to effectively impact the educational landscape, leaders in higher education needed to become more involved in reform efforts, especially in the area of teacher education. From an initial goal of establishing updated and higher standards for teacher education, the Holmes Group grew to include over a hundred research universities and broadened its focus to encompass an ambitious reform agenda impacting both teacher education and the teaching profession.

In focusing attention on teacher education reform, the Holmes Group established five framing goals aimed at producing teachers better prepared to effectively teach in the "real world" of contemporary classrooms. They argued for making the education of teachers more intellectually rigorous and for establishing entrance requirements to the profession. In addition, the Holmes Group recognized the essential need for connecting more effectively and collegially with schools. By encouraging teacher educators from the universities to work more closely in school settings and by inviting K–12 teachers to be more integrally involved in the preparation of preservice teachers, the Holmes Group envisioned a "simultaneous renewal" effect occurring, thus enhancing the preparation of preservice teachers while also improving schools as places where teachers work and learn.

This emphasis on collaboration between universities and public schools broke with much previous interaction between these entities that tended to be top-down models in which university professors dispensed the results of their research and prescribed best practices to teachers, often without recognizing constraints and obstacles faced in the constantly changing contexts of contemporary classrooms. The Holmes Group's model also recognized and validated the importance and role of teacher-practitioner knowledge in informing and supporting the preparation of preservice teachers. From this model came the concept the Holmes Group is perhaps most recognized for, the development of new institutions called Professional Developments Schools (PDS).

In 1996, the Holmes Group commissioned a study chaired by Dr. Michael Fullan, an acknowledged authority on organizational change, to evaluate the group's accomplishments and to identify progress made toward its goals. This study indicated that effecting the systemic reform of education in the United States could not be achieved by any one reform effort. Consequently, the Holmes Group broadened its base from universities and schools to include formalized partnerships with seven other organizations representing professional educators. Thus, the Holmes Group became the Holmes Partnership. Although the name changed, the goals for the new partnership remained the same—improving teacher education and the teaching profession.

Cathy J. Siebert

See also Educational Reform; Teacher Preparation

Further Readings

Holmes Group. (1986). *Tomorrow's teachers.* East Lansing, MI: Author.

Holmes Group. (1990). *Tomorrow's schools: Principles for the design of professional development schools.* East Lansing, MI: Author.

Holmes Group. (1995). *Tomorrow's schools of education.* East Lansing, MI: Author.

Web Sites

Holmes Partnership: http://www.holmespartnership.org

National Association of Professional Development Schools: http://napds.missouri.edu

HOLOCAUST EDUCATION

The Holocaust, led by Germany's Adolf Hitler, was the systematic slaughter (1941–1945) of 11 million people, including 6 million Jews ($1^1/_2$ million of whom were children) and 5 million others, including homosexuals, disabled people, Roma (Gypsies), Jehovah's Witnesses, and political prisoners. This entry briefly summarizes the facts of the Holocaust and discusses how it has been treated in schools.

Historical Background

As the Nazi war machine rolled across Europe during World War II, Jews and others in each successively conquered country were identified, registered, removed from their homes and held in ghettos, rounded up, and shipped in cattle cars without proper food, water, or sanitation to more than one hundred forced labor, concentration, and extermination camps. They were held in inhuman conditions, starved, tortured, and disease ridden. Many died from these conditions; others (particularly the elderly and children whose labor would have no value to the German state) were immediately sent to gas chambers. Hitler wanted nothing less than to eradicate the Jews, to render them an extinct race. He very nearly succeeded; one in ten Jewish children in Europe survived his murderous rampage.

In the sixty years since the end of the World War II, it has become clear that Hitler redefined the meaning of genocide through his efficient use of technology. In Bosnia, Chechnya, Rwanda, and the Sudan, to name but a few locations, genocide has proceeded with little outside intervention. Moreover, in spite of the world's horror at what Hitler wrought, a revitalized, more virulent strain of anti-Semitism (often conflated with anti-Zionism and criticism of the state of Israel) has gathered momentum in Europe, the Middle East, and North America, particularly in the aftermath of September 11, 2001.

This has taken place despite efforts to provide education about the Holocaust. Because some have viewed the Holocaust primarily as a Jewish issue rather than a human one, Holocaust education has rarely been central to public school curricula. History textbooks may devote only a page or two to what some argue was the defining event of the last century; many teachers, hesitant to approach this difficult history, choose to ignore it entirely. A recent poll of 4,000 people in Britain revealed that half of them had never heard of the Holocaust.

Educational Approach

Guided by John Dewey's vision, contemporary education is often reluctant to examine the darker side of human history and behavior. Nel Noddings notes that American curriculum veers away from treating anything that suggests grief. Against this, theorist Marla Morris posits the model of a "dystopic" curriculum that would admit the presence of the Holocaust and the darker, more realistic view of human nature that entails. This is uncertain ground for teachers whose own pedagogical training may have provided little experience with engaging complex moral dilemmas.

Holocaust education has generally not been included in the antiracist curriculum developed and implemented in the last twenty years. Where *race* is construed narrowly as determined only by skin color, anti-Semitism is not included. Prevailing opinion prior to 9/11 was that antipathy to the Jews was a thing of the past, that the world would "never again" target them for violence. As a result of this, some assert that anti-Semitism is the least explored "ism" in a politically correct world. Textbooks used in the schools of the Arab Middle East make no mention of the Holocaust; many North American Muslims have never heard of this event. Holocaust scholar Alvin Rosenfeld maintains that where there has been good Holocaust education, anti-Semitism cannot logically follow.

The two pivotal points of cultural reference for the existence of the Holocaust are the extermination camp at Auschwitz and Anne Frank's *Diary of a Young Girl,* the journal of a fourteen-year-old Jewish girl in hiding from the Nazis. Anne's *Diary* has sold 31 million copies in 67 languages. Across the boundaries of culture, gender, and time, students continue to recognize Anne's name, know that she wrote a diary, and want to read it. As such, this text may provide a worthwhile entry point for approaching the complex topic of the Holocaust across a variety of classroom subject areas and grade levels. Anne's struggle to believe that people were fundamentally "good at heart" reflects her moral choice to embrace goodness while understanding the potential for evil residing within each human being.

An abundance of testimony and excellent curricula have been developed to aid teachers in teaching about the Holocaust; much of this is easily accessible through the Internet. George Santayana warned that those who fail to remember their own history are doomed to repeat it. Thus, Holocaust education has a critical role to play in mainstream human rights education.

Lesley Shore

See also Discrimination and Prejudice; Eugenics; Human Rights Education; Peace Education

Further Readings

Blair, J. (Producer). (1995). *Anne Frank remembered.* [Video]. Culver City, CA: Sony Pictures.

Frank, A. (1989). *The diary of Anne Frank: The critical edition* (prepared by The Netherlands State Institute for War

Documentation; D. Barnouw & G. Van Der Stroom, Eds.; A. J. Pomerans & B. M. Mooyart-Doubleday, Trans.). New York: Doubleday. (Original work published 1947)

Freedom Writers, with E. Gruwell. (1999). *The freedom writers diary: How a teacher and 150 teens used writing to change themselves and the world around them.* New York: Broadway Books.

Miller, J. (1990). *One by one by one: Facing the Holocaust.* New York: Simon & Schuster.

Morris, M. (2001). *Curriculum and the Holocaust: Competing sites of memory and representation.* Mahwah, NJ: Lawrence Erlbaum.

Oliner, S. P., & Oliner, P. M (1988). *The altruistic personality: Rescuers of Jews in Nazi Europe.* New York: Free Press.

Rosenfeld, A. H. (1991). Popularization and memory: The case of Anne Frank. In P. Hayes (Ed.), *Lessons and legacies: The meaning of the Holocaust in a changing world* (pp. 243–278). Evanston, IL: Northwestern University Press.

Strom. M. S. (1994). *Facing history and ourselves: Holocaust and human behavior.* Brookline, MA: Facing History and Ourselves.

Web Sites

Anne Frank Museum, Amsterdam: http://www.annefrank.com
Facing History and Ourselves: http://www.facinghistory.org

Homeless Children and Adolescents, Education of

Families with children, as well as unaccompanied children, comprise a large percentage of those who are considered homeless in the United States. The changing face of the homeless has shifted from an unemployed adult without a family to working families who simply cannot afford to pay for housing on their incomes. These families keep up with their housing payments as long as they can, but when unexpected financial hardships arise (loss of job, unforeseen medical costs, car accidents, and so on) and the family cannot make their housing payment, the result is loss of housing.

Homeless children have consistently displayed academic and emotional problems, as well as poor social skills. In addition to these factors, homeless children are disproportionately at risk for health problems and often suffer from malnutrition. This entry briefly describes how homelessness affects all aspects of a child's life and then looks at some educational approaches that may help homeless children.

Impact of Homelessness

Homeless children seldom receive the routine medical examinations that are recommended for all children, thus they receive little to no preventive medical care. The result is that homeless children are often in poor health and are often chronically ill, both of which adversely affect their development. Families are often denied access to shelters if a family member is ill, and this leads to periods of time spent sleeping outdoors, often in inclement weather. More than children who are not homeless, homeless children are affected by common childhood illnesses such as respiratory infections, ear infections, skin disease, common colds and flus, and diarrhea. Hunger and malnutrition are other factors that adversely affect homeless children's health.

In addition to physical health, homelessness also adversely affects children's development and often leads to psychological and behavioral problems. Homeless children's lives can be described as chaotic. Living in a shelter, on the street, or in an automobile is not conducive to getting a good night's sleep. Homeless children often suffer from sleep disorders and/or sleep deprivation, which can often be linked to short attention spans, distractibility, and an inability to see a task through from start to finish. Behavioral and psychological problems that homeless children are disproportionately affected by, include but are in no way limited to, the following: short attention span; aggression; separation anxiety; poor social interactions; delays in gross, motor, speech, and language development; high levels of stress; and depression. These health, developmental, behavioral, and psychological dynamics make it no surprise that homeless children are also typically behind their peers academically.

Schools for the Homeless

To meet the myriad needs of homeless children, individuals and groups have founded schools that educate solely homeless children. One such example is the

Thomas J. Pappas Education Center in Phoenix, Arizona. The school, founded in 1990, serves a large number of students in kindergarten through eighth grade. The Pappas School is founded on the principle that homeless children face extreme amounts of humiliation and stress in traditional public schools, and removing these feelings will foster academic achievement, as well as psychological, emotional, and behavioral development. The school is designed to give homeless children the kind of stability that housed children have in traditional public schools. This stability is believed to foster homeless children's abilities to make and maintain friendships, which is believed to directly affect a student's ability to thrive in other areas of their lives.

Upon enrolling in the Pappas School, each student is met by a counselor, nurse, outreach worker, and Welcoming Center coordinator to assess the individual child's needs. After assessments are made, and the student's needs are identified, a member from the team designs an individualized learning plan. This plan includes how to deal with academic, emotional, behavioral, and psychological needs. The school also attends to additional needs; for example, the clothing room distributes clothing, food, and toiletries.

The school's academic structure is quite different than that in traditional public schools. Reading, writing, and mathematics are the core subjects at the Pappas School. Children are grouped, by their abilities, into MALTs (multi-age learning teams). Students progress as their abilities, and not their age, dictates. Students are classified by, but not grouped by, their grade level. Classrooms are also structured under the premise that behavior problems will be the norm, not the exception. Students' behavioral problems are dealt with in a positive, problem-solving manner, and not a punitive manner.

While the Pappas School provides an example of an entire school that is designed to serve homeless children, a majority of schools consisting exclusively of homeless children are one-room schools that are located within a shelter. Children of all ages and abilities are all in one classroom, where the teachers are usually not required to follow standards and curricula dictated by the states to traditional public schools. The basic premise of schools that exclusively serve

children who are homeless is that these children have a great deal of stress and uncertainty in their lives, and schools should be designed to meet all of their needs (with the exception of housing) on site. There should be no need to access outside community resources to meet a child's needs when the school can do it all in one place. This is in direct opposition to the prevailing ideas of how traditional public schools can meet the needs of homeless children.

Other Educational Approaches

One dominant model that public schools employ to meet the needs of homeless children is often called the communities of learning model. The model is founded on the principle that schools know how to best educate children, but homeless children need more support than is typically given to the average student in order to succeed academically. They also recognize that the other factors (behavorial, psychological, emotional, etc.) that children must cope with will have a dramatic effect on their ability to learn. Therefore, communities of learning incorporate family support, adult education opportunities, the expertise of social service providers, and the expertise of school employees to best meet homeless students' needs.

In this model, schools work with shelters and other service providers to forge a partnership that results in a collaborative effort that best meets homeless students' needs. There are tutoring programs: adult education programs that also provide transportation and day care; and supportive services such as counseling, behavior therapy, and so on that are offered in locations which are convenient to children and their parents. An important piece of the program is the adult education component because parents who value education are more likely to promote the values of education to their children. Many schools do not possess the desire or the ability to institute a community-of-care model. This does not, however, mean that these schools are not doing anything to better serve homeless youth.

A common practice in schools that are actively attempting to better serve their homeless students is to have their staff go through intensive training on the issues surrounding homelessness. It is important for all staff who come in direct contact with students to receive training, and the training should in no way be limited to teachers and administrators. Secretaries, bus drivers, and other support staff are often the first contact a student has with a school employee. Unfortunately, these individuals seldom receive the kind of training that is necessary to sensitize them to the needs of homeless children. This training is necessary because these employees often set the tone for the type of experience a student will have.

In addition to educating the school community, many programs reach out to the larger community to educate the general public on the issues of homelessness, how children are affected, what can be done, and so on. The common elements of public schools' efforts to best meet the needs of homeless children are as follows: collaboration with outside service providers, transportation and child care assistance, teacher and staff training, availability of tutoring, adult education opportunities, focusing on the relationship between the curriculum and the children's daily life experiences, and flexibility.

While not all elements of a child's life can directly be affected by their schooling, schools are an integral piece in the comprehensive approach that is needed to make substantial gains in a child's chances to flourish as an adult. It should not be assumed that the school should be solely responsible for implementing programs that can have a positive influence on the lives of homeless children. Schools, working in conjunction with parents, social service providers, and other community resources, should all come together to realize the dramatic effects they can have on homeless children.

Joshua Diem

See also Economic Inequality

Further Readings

Burt, M., Aron, L., Douglas, T., Valente, J., Lee, E., & Ewen, B. (1999). *Homelessness programs and the people they serve: Findings of the national survey of homeless assistance providers and clients.* Washington, DC: Urban Institute.

Gewirtzman, R., & Fodor, I. (1987). The homeless child at school: From welfare hotel to classroom. *Child Welfare,* 237–245.

Huesel, K. (1995). *Homeless children: Their perspective.* New York: Garland.

Kusmer, K. (2002). *Down and out, on the road: The homeless in American history.* New York: Oxford University Press.

Reed-Victor, E., & Pelco, L. (1999). Helping homeless students build resilience. *Journal for a Just & Caring Education, 5*(1), 51–72.

Stronge, J. H. (1992). *Educating homeless children and adolescents: Evaluating policy and practice.* Newbury Park, CA: Sage.

United States Conference of Mayors—Sodexho, Inc. (2005). *Hunger and homelessness survey: A status report on hunger and homelessness in America's cities.* Available from http://www.usmayors.org/hungersurvey/2005/HH2005FINAL.pdf

Urban Institute. (2000). *A new look at homelessness in America.* Washington, DC: Author.

Woods, C. (1997). Pappas School: A response to homeless students. *Clearing House, 70*(6), 302–304.

Web Sites

National Association for the Education of Homeless Children and Youth (NAEHCY): http://www.naehcy.org

National Coalition for the Homeless: http://www.nationalhomeless.org

HOMESCHOOLING

Homeschooling is in some ways the newest and most radical form of private education in the United States—and is, from another perspective, the oldest and most basic approach, as children have always learned from their families. Homeschooling is in some ways the ultimate type of privatization, as it is typically privately funded, privately provided, and (almost fully) privately regulated by parents in the home. About 1.35 million children in the country are being formally and officially educated by their parents or guardians at home—after a titanic struggle between 1975 and 1999 to legalize the effort, as homeschooling was once deemed a violation of "compulsory education" policies in all fifty states. This entry traces the history of that struggle, the pros and cons of the practice, and how it is typically implemented.

The Right to Homeschool

Groups like the National Home School Legal Defense Association have fought in court and in legislatures to assure parents the right to homeschool; now all fifty states recognize the prerogatives of the family as the primary educator. However, universal *public* education stands as the central principle of most modern societies, with laws requiring that children attend schools from ages about six to eighteen. Homeschooling only became a sticky judicial and policy issue because of these state compulsory education requirements. While some states require parents to report to local school superintendents on their children's homeschooling progress, all now allow parents to ignore compulsory education and teach their children themselves at home.

Although parents initially wanted to extricate their children from the hands of the state, some families are now turning back to the public schools to help their children. Families are requesting access to after-school activities at their local public schools (e.g., sports, games, club activities), admission to classes/courses that parents feel unqualified to teach (such as physics, calculus, or the German language), or special services such as speech pathology, counseling, and testing-diagnostic services. While homeschooling parents once fought legally and politically to escape the control of the public schools, some are now pushing the system to admit their children to activities and services that the children may need.

Parents and their advocates such as the National Legal Defense Association have (a) created a strong political base in the United States; (b) built a fast-reacting lobbying mechanism that unites a range of families and interest groups around issues of concern to these parents; and (c) increasingly placed homeschooling in the public eye, such as when homeschooled children have won the National Spelling Bee. Leaders of the homeschooling movement understand the importance of the war of words and ideas, and have done well in entering the spotlight and the hearts of Americans.

Pros and Cons

Interest in homeschooling differs by family, but some patterns do emerge. The majority of homeschoolers, about 60 percent, are Christian families who may find the values and behaviors in public schools intolerable. Sex education, absence of prayer and Bible study, and

the lack of lessons grounded in Scripture, for example, may make these parents uncomfortable.

Other examples of homeschoolers include parents whose children are in need of special attention (as with gifted, special needs, psychologically troubled children) and who want to handle these problems or concerns themselves at home. Thus, while some parents come to homeschooling for religious or philosophical reasons, other families mainly consider the homeschooling option after the traditional schools have failed to meet the needs of their children.

Many parents worry that public schools are physically dangerous environments; that is, they are seen as filled with drugs, violence, and other physical dangers to the very lives of their children. With the development of Internet technology and printed curricular materials, parents can now buy or download lessons and activities that help them keep current with the latest teaching methods and materials. And homeschooling networks may make up for the isolation, as students and their parents can use the Internet to get assistance with questions and problems, and to connect to one another in a worldwide education network and social community.

Four arguments are often heard when people defend public schools and attack homeschooling. First, critics argue that homeschooling removes children from the wider community—isolating them from important social experiences of schooling. Second, parents who homeschool are not usually trained, licensed educators; thus some critics believe that these families cannot teach their children to high enough standards. Third, homeschooling also diverts interest and in some cases funds from public schools, since many state and local funding formulas are based on Average Daily Attendance (ADA). And fourth, homeschooling is seen as a selfish effort to remove children from the mainstream—and thus their parents from supporting public schools—for example, when bond issues, budgets, and programs are up for public scrutiny and votes.

In important ways, homeschooling is a peek into the future, as Americans take control of their lives and work to overcome the influences of large institutions. While public education in the United States is a major institution based on key familial values, so too is homeschooling an active national return to rugged individualism. Research seems to show that home-schooled children do as well as public school students on tests and are just as likely to go on to college. So the end result of homeschooling is in keeping with the overall purposes and products of K–12 education in the United States.

Bruce S. Cooper

See also Privatization; School Choice

Further Readings

Apple, M. W. (2005). Away with all teachers: The cultural politics of homeschooling. In B. S. Cooper (Ed.), *Homeschooling in full view: A reader* (pp. 75–95). Greenwich, CT: Information Age.

Belfield, C. R., & Levin, H. M. (2005). *Privatizing educational choice: Consequences for parents, schools, and public policy*. Boulder, CO: Paradigm.

Princiotta, D., & Bielick, S. (2006). *Homeschooling in the United States: 2003* (NCES 2006–042). Washington, DC: U.S. Department of Education, National Center for Education Statistics.

Ray, B. D. (2000). Homeschooling for individuals' gain and society's common good. *Peabody Journal of Education, 75*(1 & 2), 272–293.

Somerville, S. W. (2005). Legal rights for homeschool families. In B. S. Cooper (Ed.), *Homeschooling in full view: A reader* (pp. 135–149). Greenwich, CT: Information Age.

Sutton, J., & Galloway, R. (2000). College success of students from three high school settings. *Journal of Research and Development in Education, 33*(3), 137–146.

HOMEWORK

Homework has been a controversial issue in American education for over 100 years, and the arguments have changed little over time. Proponents of homework believe that it promotes increased learning, better study habits, and improved home-school communication. Opponents argue that it deprives children of time to spend on other worthwhile pursuits (including play), usurps parents' rights to plan their children's time after school, increases the achievement gap between higher and lower socioeconomic classes, harms children's health, and fails to produce academic benefits.

Parents have generally favored moderate amounts of homework, but educators' support for homework has been somewhat cyclical. In the nineteenth century, when pedagogy was based on drill, memorization, and recitation, homework was necessary if students were going to be able to recite memorized lessons in class. Students probably found it boring, repetitive, and exhausting, but there was little organized opposition to it.

Organized criticism of homework began in the 1890s. Physicians cited the health dangers of homework, such as curvature of the spine, stress, and eye strain, as reasons to abolish homework. Then in 1897, Dr. Joseph Mayer Rice reported that spelling practice at home did not even lead to better spelling.

Attacks on homework increased during the progressive education movement of the early twentieth century. Progressive educators favored meaningful learning through experience, so old-fashioned homework based on memorization was incompatible with their pedagogy and philosophy. Moreover, they believed that teaching should be based on scientific principles known only to trained teachers, so parents attempting to help their children with homework would only confuse them. Antihomework activists succeeded in making their position educational dogma in 1941, when the *Encyclopedia of Educational Research* published an article that stated that "research evidence is none too favorable to homework."

Since the progressive era, favorable opinions toward homework have been more common during campaigns for academic excellence. Homework came back into favor during the Cold War era of the 1950s and 1960s, when more rigor in education was seen as essential to national defense. After increasing in the early 1960s, homework decreased during the Vietnam era, when attention shifted to social issues. After the publication of the report *A Nation at Risk* in 1983, support for homework reemerged as part of the back-to-basics movement meant to preserve the economic position of the United States. Educators, parents, and policy makers all generally favored homework during the 1980s and 1990s. There is still substantial support for homework, and the amount of time students spend on homework has increased slightly in recent years.

There are still concerns about homework, however. Research shows that homework is more likely to be associated with achievement gains as students get older, but recently students in the primary grades are the ones most likely to receive extra homework. Inequities in resources at home for the completion of homework may increase the achievement gap between wealthier and poorer students. According to Etta Kralovec and John Buell, homework-induced stress even causes some students to drop out of school. The ramifications of assigning homework may be far less, or far greater, than a teacher expects.

Pamela P. Hufnagel

See also *Nation at Risk, A; Progressive Education; Sputnik*

Further Readings

Cooper, H., Robinson, J., & Patall, E. (2006). Does homework improve academic achievement? A synthesis of research, 1987–2003. *Review of Educational Research, 76*, 1–62.

Gill, B., & Schlossman, S. (2004). Villain or savior? The American discourse on homework, 1850–2003. *Theory Into Practice, 43*, 174–181.

HOMOPHOBIA

Homophobia, defined as an irrational fear of, aversion to, or discrimination against homosexuals, continues to be a rampant problem in North American schools. Homophobia derives from heterosexist ideology, that is, the belief that heterosexuality is inherently superior to, and justifiably dominant over, nonheterosexuality in its various forms. Heterosexism manifests in two main forms: cultural heterosexism, the stigmatization, denial, or denigration of nonheterosexuality in cultural institutions; and psychological heterosexism, a person's internalization of this worldview, which erupts into homophobia. The world of schooling, which requires attendance and is charged with teaching, nurturing, developing minds and bodies, has frequently proven to be fertile ground for perpetuating both sorts of heterosexism. Manifestations of heterosexism are woven throughout curricula, and homophobic attitudes commonly erupt into verbal and physical harassment/violence among school peers, often with teachers and administrators doing little to interrupt it.

Most first-grade children already have ideas about what it means to be gay, even though much of what they have learned may well be incorrect, born of fear and prejudice rather than factual information. Derogatory epithets surface among peers during primary education and become routine in high school, where homophobia often ripens into verbal and physical abuse. Schools are in a position to correct children's misinformation early on, but this unenviable position as a fierce battleground for this divisive issue prompts many teachers and administrators to avoid such conflicts by conflating gay and lesbian identity with "talk about sex," labeling both "age inappropriate." Much peer harassment goes uncorrected by teachers who are afraid to address students directly on issues of sexual identity, not because of teachers' animus against lesbian, gay, bisexual, transgender, and questioning (henceforth LGBTQ) people, but because they feel ineffective dealing with such issues.

While pressures of coming into sexual identity are difficult for all adolescents, LGBTQ teens face particular struggles. Fearing being labeled lesbian or gay, or facing those feelings in oneself, inhibits development of close relationships with members of the same sex in *all* youth, not just gay and lesbian teens. However, LGBTQ teenagers are especially preoccupied with their social discomfort, often encountering difficulty concentrating in class, shunning classroom participation, shying away from extracurricular activities, and dropping out of school. With few traditional support structures to lean on for help, LGBTQ youth often perceive themselves to be stranded in an environment that shuns their very existence.

These negative sentiments damage the self-esteem of LGBTQ adolescents and increase the likelihood of self-destructive behavior. Thus, LGBTQ youth are one of the nation's highest risk groups. Many LGBTQ teens fend off accusations of being lesbian or gay by engaging in premature heterosexual involvement, leading to high percentages of teen pregnancy and sexually transmitted disease. Further, LGBTQ youth are not only more likely than their heterosexual peers to use drugs and drink alcohol to excess, but studies on youth suicide consistently find that they are two to six times more likely to attempt suicide than other youth.

The situation in schools is dire for LGBTQ teens, but they are not alone in suffering the consequences of heterosexist manifestations in schools. Curricula on the family are standard fare in most elementary schools. Yet, most progressive approaches to diverse family constellations still do not embrace discussions of families with same-sex parents despite the fact that 6 to 14 million children in the United States are reared by at least one gay or lesbian parent and that as many as one family in four includes a lesbian or gay member. The educational system's function as a heteronormative community creates confusing scenarios for children torn between love for their families and the need for acceptance by peers and teachers.

Further, while lesbians and gay men are growing more visible in many walks of North American life, teachers who come out in school still risk harassment, dismissal, and physical violence. Thirty-nine states have no employment protection for lesbian and gay teachers, so coming out is both financially and psychically risky. Regardless of merit, vast numbers of dedicated LGB teachers do not feel physically safe in school because of their sexual identity.

Heterosexism has not been without challenge in schools. The National Education Association (NEA) adopted their Code of Ethics in 1975, which specifically states that educators shall not exclude, deny benefits, or grant advantages to students because of sexual orientation. Online organizations educate citizens about how to promote educational policies and reforms that can foster the health and well-being of lesbian and gay students. Chapters of PFLAG (Parents and Friends of Lesbians and Gays) in some school districts provide support, education, and advocacy for sexually diverse students, teachers, and families. GLSEN (Gay, Lesbian and Straight Educational Network) has also developed a presence in many communities by providing assistance in setting up gay-straight alliances in schools, providing educational materials, and lobbying legislative bodies.

That said, conservative Christian groups, like Focus on the Family and the Eagle Forum, continue to expend enormous amounts of time and financial resources fighting the efforts of the National Education Association and lesbian-gay advocacy groups. With growing numbers of gay-straight student alliances now in existence, many of these opposition groups have shifted their focus to the curriculum, hoping to prohibit any discussion of LGBTQ issues, even in sex education classrooms.

Teachers, counselors, administrators, and teacher educators, who so frequently have deemed questions of sexual diversity to be outside their purview, undoubtedly will be called upon to take a stand in the battle to create environments that are both physically and psychically safe from the often-disastrous effects of homophobia in schools.

Susan Birden

See also Lesbian, Gay, Bisexual, and Transgendered Students: Advocacy Groups for; Lesbian, Gay, Bisexual, and Transgendered Students and Teachers: Rights of; Sexuality, Gender, and Education

Further Readings

Birden, S. (2005). *Rethinking sexual identity in education.* Lanham, MD: Rowman & Littlefield.

Letts, W. J., IV, & Sears, J. T. (Eds.). (1999). *Queering elementary education: Advancing the dialogue about sexualities and schooling.* Lanham, MD: Rowman & Littlefield.

Sears, J. T., & W. L. Williams (Eds.). (1997). *Overcoming heterosexism and homophobia: Strategies that work.* New York: Columbia University Press.

HORACE MANN SCHOOL (NEW YORK CITY)

Established in 1887 by Nicholas Murray Butler in New York City, the Horace Mann School captured two late-nineteenth-century trends in secondary schooling: the country day school, which combined the rigor of boarding schools with outdoor physical exercise; and the progressive school, which aimed to counter the sterility of public schools. As president of the Industrial Education Association, which trained underprivileged girls in domestic skills, Butler spearheaded an effort to expand the curriculum to include academic subjects as well, but he also wanted to train teachers specifically for this unique curriculum. He changed the school's name to the New York College for the Training of Teachers and also founded the Model School, as part of Teachers College, where students could observe and practice teaching methods; soon after, the school was renamed the Horace Mann School.

Shortly after Teachers College and Columbia University became affiliated in 1897, the Horace Mann School moved to the Morningside Heights area of New York City, where it remained until 1914. In that year, the Boys' School moved to the school's present location at 246th Street in the Bronx. In addition, it moved away from the original philosophy of Teachers College; its mission was to prepare boys for college or business life through a full schedule of courses, extracurricular activities, and athletics. The Girls' School stayed at Morningside Heights until 1940 when it merged with the Lincoln School, which took on a more experimental approach to teaching. In 1946, the Horace Mann-Lincoln School closed.

The remaining Horace Mann School was able to separate financially from Teachers College and become an independent day school for boys, with an official charter granted in 1951. Through a series of mergers with other schools, including the New York School for Nursery Years and Barnard School, Horace Mann reestablished coeducation and took on its present organization. Since the early 1970s, boys and girls have been educated together in the school's four divisions: Nursery (three-year-olds to kindergarten age), Lower (kindergarten to fifth grade), Middle (sixth to eighth grade), and Upper (ninth to twelfth grade).

Today, the Horace Mann School has three campuses: in Manhattan; Riverdale (Bronx); and Washington, Connecticut.

The liberal arts are emphasized in its curriculum, which centers on five "core values," including the "life of the mind," which encourages analytical thinking early on; "mature behavior," in which students are expected to illustrate age-appropriate behavior; "mutual respect," which fosters respect for diversity; "a secure and healthful environment," which secures a climate free from sexual harassment, racism, or other behaviors that hinder the learning process; and "a balance between individual achievement and a caring community," which helps students to look beyond themselves. In addition to its rigorous academics (twenty advanced placement courses and eight foreign languages), the Horace Mann School also boasts a national reputation for extensive extracurricular activities (including an award-winning weekly student newspaper), more than 220 faculty members (many of whom hold advanced degrees), and a diverse student body.

Mary K. Clingerman

See also Teachers College, Columbia University

See Visual History Chapter 10, Kindergartens

Further Readings

McCardell, R. A. (Ed.). (1962). *The Country Day School: History, curriculum, philosophy of Horace Mann School.* Dobbs Ferry, NY: Oceana.

Web Sites

Horace Mann School: http://www.horacemann.org

HUMAN RIGHTS EDUCATION

Education is considered a basic human right. Human rights education, however, is the dissemination of knowledge about people's rights and responsibilities individually and collectively in relation to their society (locally, nationally, and internationally). In 1924, the League of Nations endorsed the first Declaration of the Rights of the Child. The United Nations Charter (1945) also laid much of the groundwork for the Convention by urging nations to promote and encourage respect for human rights and fundamental freedoms for all. Yet, it was not until 1989 that the United Nations adopted the Convention on the Rights of the Child. All but two countries have ratified this Convention (United States and Somalia). The principles are overwhelmingly supported by governments, their implementation less so.

Greater attention has been paid to the development of human rights education, particularly since the United Nations General Assembly recommended and put forth the United Nations Decade for Human Rights Education from 1995 to 2004. During this decade, the hope was to develop a plan of action at local, national, and international levels for the dissemination and promotion of human rights. Eight key target areas were identified, among them three related to education: (1) integration of human rights standards into educational curricula; (2) introduction of human rights standards into literacy education; and (3) promotion of nonformal and mass human rights education programs.

Curricular development in human rights education has focused largely on teaching the basic principles of fundamental human rights as outlined in the Charter of the United Nations Universal Declaration of Human Rights. The ideals of fostering tolerance and respect for oneself and others are at the fore of these rights. The goal is for individuals to understand and exercise their fundamental rights, as recognized at local and international levels; where human rights are not protected at the regional level, efforts to secure those individual rights should be a matter of international humanitarian law.

The United Nations' goal is to have human rights education permeate all levels of schooling and all levels of the community. Human rights education is often taught as a specific discipline, for example, as citizenship education, but it can also be part of all the disciplines, thus developing an inherent ethos embedded in the educational program. These principles underpin human rights education; the implementation and emphasis of human rights education widely diverge in different local and national contexts.

Dianne Gereluk

See also Citizenship Education; Rights of Students; Social Justice, Education for

Further Readings

Archard, D. (2004). *Children, rights and childhood.* London: Routledge.

Hart, S., et al. (2001). (Eds.). *Children's rights in education.* London: Jessica Kingsley.

United Nations. (1999). *The right to human rights education.* New York: Office of the United Nations High Commissioner for Human Rights.